The Meaning And Explanation Of The Glorious Qur'an (Vol 2)

Second Edition

The Meaning And Explanation Of The Glorious Qur'an (Vol 2)

Second Edition

With
Arabic Script, Transliteration, Meaning, Maududi's & Ibn Kathir's Introductions and Ibn Kathir's Abridged Explanation (Tafsir)

Chapter 3: Al-i-'Imran (The Family Of 'Imran), Verses 93-200
Chapter 4: An-Nisaa (The Women), Verses 1-176
Chapter 5: Al-Ma'ida (The Table Spread), Verses 1-82

Muhammad Saed Abdul-Rahman
BSc, DipHE

MSA Publication Limited

ISBN for volume 2 paperback 978-1-86179-644-8
ISBN for volume 2 hardback 978-1-86179-645-5
ISBN for volume 2 pdf eBook 978-1-86179-646-2

British Library Cataloguing in Publication Data. A Catalogue record for this book is available from the British Library

Designed, Typeset and produced by:
MSA Publication Limited, 4 Bello Close, Herne Hill,
London SE24 9BW
United Kingdom

Cover design: Houriyah Abdul-Rahman

TABLE OF CONTENTS

PRELUDE

Opening Serman

Indeed, all praise is due to Allah. We praise Him and seek His help and forgiveness. We seek refuge with Allah from our soul's evil and our wrong doings. He whom Allah guides, no one can misguide; and he whom He misguides, no one can guide

I bear witness that there is no (true) god except Allah – alone without a partner, and I bear witness that Muhammad (peace and blessings of Allah be upon him) is His 'abd (servant) and messenger.

يَٰٓأَيُّهَا ٱلَّذِينَ ءَامَنُوا۟ ٱتَّقُوا۟ ٱللَّهَ حَقَّ تُقَاتِهِۦ وَلَا تَمُوتُنَّ إِلَّا وَأَنتُم مُّسْلِمُونَ ﴿١٠٢﴾

O you who believe! Fear Allâh (by doing all that He has ordered and by abstaining from all that He has forbidden) as He should be feared. (Obey Him, be thankful to Him, and remember Him always), and die not except in a state of Islâm (as Muslims (with complete submission to Allâh)).

يَٰٓأَيُّهَا ٱلنَّاسُ ٱتَّقُوا۟ رَبَّكُمُ ٱلَّذِى خَلَقَكُم مِّن نَّفْسٍ وَٰحِدَةٍ وَخَلَقَ مِنْهَا زَوْجَهَا وَبَثَّ
مِنْهُمَا رِجَالًا كَثِيرًا وَنِسَآءً ۚ وَٱتَّقُوا۟ ٱللَّهَ ٱلَّذِى تَسَآءَلُونَ بِهِۦ وَٱلْأَرْحَامَ ۚ إِنَّ ٱللَّهَ كَانَ
عَلَيْكُمْ رَقِيبًا ﴿١﴾

O mankind! Be dutiful to your Lord, Who created you from a single person (Adam), and from him (Adam) He created his wife (Hawwâ (Eve)) and from them both He created many men and women; and fear Allâh through Whom you demand (your mutual rights), and (do not cut the relations of) the wombs (kinship). Surely, Allâh is Ever an All-Watcher over you.

يُصْلِحْ لَكُمْ أَعْمَٰلَكُمْ وَيَغْفِرْ لَكُمْ ذُنُوبَكُمْ ۗ وَمَن يُطِعِ ٱللَّهَ وَرَسُولَهُۥ فَقَدْ فَازَ فَوْزًا
عَظِيمًا ﴿٧١﴾

He will direct you to do righteous good deeds and will forgive you your sins. And whosoever obeys Allâh and His Messenger (peace be upon him), he has indeed achieved a great achievement (i.e. he will be saved from the Hell-fire and will be admitted to Paradise).

Indeed, the best speech is Allah's Book and the best guidance is Muhammad's () guidance. The worst affairs (of religion) are those innovated (by people), for every such innovation is an act of misguidance leading to the Fire

Our Mission

Our mission is to gather in one place, for the English-speaking public, all relevant information needed to make the Qur'an more understandable and easier to study. This book tries to do this by providing the following:

1. The Arabic Text for those who are able to read Arabic
2. Transliteration of the Arabic text for those who are unable to read the Arabic script. This will give them a sample of the sound of the Qur'an, which they could not otherwise comprehend from reading the English meaning.
3. The meaning of the qur'an (translated by Dr. Muhammad Taqi-ud-Din Al-Hilali, Ph.D. and Dr. Muhammad Muhsin Khan)
4. Background introductions by two famous Islamic scholars, Maududi and Ibn Kathir
5. Explanation (abridged Tafsir) by Ibn Kathir (translated by Safi-ur-Rahman al-Mubarakpuri)

We hope that by doing this an ordinary English-speaker will be able to pick up a copy of this book and study and comprehend The Glorious Qur'an in a way that is acceptable to the understanding of the Rightly-guided Muslim Ummah (Community).

Biography of Hafiz Ibn Kathir (701 H - 774 H)

By the Honored Shaykh `Abdul-Qadir Al-Arna'ut, may Allah protect him.

He is the respected Imam, Abu Al-Fida', `Imad Ad-Din Isma il bin 'Umar bin Kathir Al-Qurashi Al-Busrawi - Busraian in origin; Dimashqi in training, learning and residence.

Ibn Kathir was born in the city of Busra in 701 H. His father was the Friday speaker of the village, but he died while Ibn Kathir was only four years old. Ibn Kathir's brother, Shaykh Abdul-Wahhab, reared him and taught him until he moved to Damascus in 706 H., when he was five years old.

Ibn Kathir's Teachers

Ibn Kathir studied Fiqh - Islamic jurisprudence - with Burhan Ad-Din, Ibrahim bin `Abdur-Rahman Al-Fizari, known as Ibn Al-Firkah (who died in 729 H). Ibn Kathir heard Hadiths from `Isa bin Al-Mutim, Ahmad bin Abi Talib, (Ibn Ash-Shahnah) (who died in 730 H), Ibn Al-Hajjar, (who died in 730 H), and the Hadith narrator of Ash-Sham (modern day Syria and surrounding areas); Baha Ad-Din Al-Qasim bin Muzaffar bin `Asakir (who died in 723 H), and Ibn Ash-Shirdzi, Ishaq bin Yahya Al-Ammuddi, also known as `Afif Ad-Din, the Zahiriyyah Shaykh who died in 725 H, and Muhammad bin Zarrad. He remained with Jamal Ad-Din, Yusuf bin Az-Zaki AlMizzi who died in 724 H, he benefited from his knowledge and also married his daughter. He also read with Shaykh Al-Islam, Taqi Ad-Din Ahmad bin `Abdul-Halim bin `Abdus-Salam bin Taymiyyah who died in 728 H. He also read with the Imam Hafiz and historian Shams Ad-Din, Muhammad bin Ahmad bin Uthman bin Qaymaz Adh-Dhahabi, who died in 748 H. Also, Abu Musa Al-Qarafai, Abu Al-Fath Ad-Dabbusi and 'Ali bin `Umar As-Suwani and others who gave him permission to transmit the knowledge he learned with them in Egypt.

In his book, Al-Mu jam Al-Mukhtas, Al-Hafiz Adh-Dhaliabi wrote that Ibn Kathir was, "The Imam, scholar of jurisprudence, skillful scholar of Hadith, renowned Fagih and scholar of Tafsir who wrote several beneficial books."

Further, in Ad-Durar Al-Kdminah, Al-Hafiz Ibn Hajar AlAsqalani said, "Ibn Kathir worked on the subject of the Hadith in the areas of texts and chains of narrators. He had a good memory, his books became popular during his lifetime, and people benefited from them after his death."

Also, the renowned historian Abu Al-Mahasin, Jamal Ad-Din Yusuf bin Sayf Ad-Din (Ibn Taghri Bardi), said in his book, AlManhal As-Safi, "He is the Shaykh, the Imam, the great scholar `Imad Ad-Din Abu Al-Fida'. He learned extensively and was very active in collecting knowledge and writing. He was excellent in the areas of Fiqh, Tafsfr and Hadith. He collected knowledge, authored (books), taught, narrated Hadith and wrote. He had immense knowledge in the fields of Hadith, Tafsir, Fiqh, the Arabic language, and so forth. He gave Fatawa (religious verdicts) and taught until he died, may Allah grant him mercy. He was known for his precision and vast knowledge, and as a scholar of history, Hadith and Tafsir."

Ibn Kathir's Students

Ibn Hajji was one of Ibn Kathir's students, and he described Ibn Kathir: "He had the best memory of the Hadith texts. He also had the most knowledge concerning the narrators and authenticity, his contemporaries and teachers admitted to these qualities. Every time I met him I gained some benefit from him."

Also, Ibn Al-`Imad Al-Hanbali said in his book, Shadhardt Adh-Dhahab, "He is the renowned Hafiz `Imad Ad-Din, whose memory was excellent, whose forgetfulness was miniscule, whose understanding was adequate, and who had good knowledge in the Arabic language." Also, Ibn Habib said about Ibn Kathir, "He heard knowledge and collected it and wrote various books. He brought comfort to the ears with his Fatwas and narrated Hadith and brought benefit to other people. The papers that contained his Fatwas were transmitted to the various (Islamic) provinces. Further, he was known for his precision and encompassing knowledge."

Ibn Kathir's Books

1 - One of the greatest books that Ibn Kathir wrote was his Tafsir of the Noble Qur'an, which is one of the best Tafsir that rely on narrations [of Ahadith, the Tafsir of the Companions, etc.]. The Tafsir by Ibn Kathir was printed many times and several scholars have summarized it.

2- The History Collection known as Al-Biddyah, which was printed in 14 volumes under the name Al-Bidayah wanNihdyah, and contained the stories of the Prophets and previous nations, the Prophet's Seerah (life story) and Islamic history until his time. He also added a book Al-Fitan, about the Signs of the Last Hour.

3- At-Takmil ft Ma`rifat Ath-Thiqat wa Ad-Du'afa wal Majdhil which Ibn Kathir collected from the books of his two Shaykhs Al-Mizzi and Adh-Dhahabi; Al-Kdmal and Mizan Al-Ftiddl. He added several benefits regarding the subject of Al-Jarh and AtT'adil.

4- Al-Hadi was-Sunan ft Ahadith Al-Masdnfd was-Sunan which is also known by, Jami` Al-Masdnfd. In this book, Ibn Kathir collected the narrations of Imams Ahmad bin Hanbal, Al-Bazzar, Abu Ya`la Al-Mawsili, Ibn Abi Shaybah and from the six collections of Hadith: the Two Sahihs [Al-Bukhari and Muslim] and the Four Sunan [Abu Dawud, At-Tirmidhi, AnNasa and Ibn Majah]. Ibn Kathir divided this book according to areas of Fiqh.

5-Tabaqat Ash-Shaf iyah which also contains the virtues of Imam Ash-Shafi.

6- Ibn Kathir wrote references for the Ahadith of Adillat AtTanbfh, from the Shafi school of Fiqh.

7- Ibn Kathir began an explanation of Sahih Al-Bukhari, but he did not finish it.

8- He started writing a large volume on the Ahkam (Laws), but finished only up to the Hajj rituals.

9- He summarized Al-Bayhaqi's 'Al-Madkhal. Many of these books were not printed.

10- He summarized `Ulum Al-Hadith, by Abu `Amr bin AsSalah and called it Mukhtasar `Ulum Al-Hadith. Shaykh Ahmad Shakir, the Egyptian Muhaddith, printed this book along with his commentary on it and called it Al-Ba'th Al-Hathfth fi Sharh Mukhtasar `Ulum Al-Hadith.

11- As-Sfrah An-Nabawiyyah, which is contained in his book Al-Biddyah, and both of these books are in print.

12- A research on Jihad called Al-Ijtihad ft Talabi Al-Jihad, which was printed several times.

Ibn Kathir's Death

Al-Hafiz Ibn Hajar Al-Asgalani said, "Ibn Kathir lost his sight just before his life ended. He died in Damascus in 774 H." May Allah grant mercy upon Ibn Kathir and make him among the residents of His Paradise.

Biography of Abul Ala Maududi (1903 – 1979)

Abul Ala was born on Rajab 3, 1321 AH (September 25, 1903 AD) in Aurangabad, a well-known town in the former princely state of Hyderabad (Deccan), presently Maharashtra, India. Born in a respectable family, his ancestry on the paternal side is traced back to the Holy Prophet Muhammad (peace and blessing of Allah be upon him)

Maududi's forefathers had moved to the Subcontinent from Chisht towards the end of the 9th century of the Islamic calendar (15th century of the Christian calendar). The first one to arrive was Maududi's namesake, Abul Ala Maududi (d. 935 AH).Maududi's father, Ahmad Hasan, born in 1855 AD, a lawyer by profession, was a highly religious and devout person. Abul Ala was the youngest of his three sons.

Educational & Intellectual Growth:

After acquiring early education at home, Abul Ala was admitted in Madrasah Furqaniyah, a high school which attempted to combine the modern Western with the traditional Islamic education. After successfully completing his secondary education, young Abul Ala was at the stage of undergraduate studies at Darul Uloom, Hyderabad, when his formal education was disrupted by the illness and eventual death of his father. This did not deter Maududi from continuing his studies though these had to be outside of the regular educational institutions. By the early 1920s, Abul Ala knew enough Arabic, Persian and English, besides his mother-tongue, Urdu, to study the subjects of his interest independently. Thus, most of what he learned was self-acquired though for short spells of time he also received systematic instruction and guidance from some competent scholars. Thus, Maududi's intellectual growth was largely a result of his own effort and the stimulation he received from his teachers.

Moreover, his uprightness, his profound regard for propriety and righteousness largely reflect the religious piety of his parents and their concern for his proper moral upbringing.

Involvement in Journalism:

After the interruption of his formal education, Maududi turned to journalism in order to make his living. In 1918, he was already contributing to a leading Urdu newspaper, and in 1920, at the age of 17, he was appointed editor of Taj, which was being published from Jabalpore, a city in the province now called Madhya Pradesh, India. Late in 1920, Maududi came to Delhi and first assumed the editorship of the newspaper Muslim (1921-23), and later of al-Jam'iyat (1925-28), both of which were the organs of the Jam'iyat-i 'Ulama-i Hind, an organisation of Muslim religious scholars. Under his editorship, al-Jam'iyat became the leading newspaper of the Muslims of India.

Interest in Politics:

Around the year 1920, Maududi also began to take some interest in politics. He participated in the Khilafat Movement, and became associated with the Tahrik-e Hijrat, which was a movement in opposition to the British rule over India and urged the Muslims of that country to migrate en masse to Afghanistan. However, he fell foul of the leadership of the movement because of his insistence that the aims and strategy of the movement should be realistic and well-planned. Maududi withdrew more and more into academic and journalistic pursuits.

First Book:

During 1920-28, Maulana Maududi also translated four different books, one from Arabic and the rest from English. He also made his mark on the academic life of the Subcontinent by writing his first major book, al-Jihad fi al-Islam. This is a masterly treatise on the Islamic law of war and peace. It was first serialised in al-Jam'iyat in 1927 and was formally published in 1930. It was highly acclaimed both by the famous poet-philosopher Muhammad Iqbal (d. 1938) and Maulana Muhammad Ali Jauhar (d. 1931), the famous leader of the Khilafat Movement. Though written during his '20s, it is one of his major and most highly regarded works.

Research & Writings:

After his resignation from al-Jam'iyat in 1928, Maududi moved to Hyderabad and devoted himself to research and writing. It was in this connection that he took up the editorship of the monthly Tarjuman al-Qur'an in 1933, which since then has been the main vehicle for the dissemination of Maududi's ideas. He proved to be a highly prolific writer, turning out several scores of pages every month. Initially, he concentrated on the exposition of ideas, values and basic principles of Islam. He paid special attention to the questions arising out of the conflict between the Islamic and the contemporary Western whorl. He also attempted to discuss some of the major problems of the modern age and sought to present Islamic solutions to those problems. He also developed a new methodology to study those problems in the context of the experience of the West and the Muslim world, judging them on the theoretical criterion of their intrinsic soundness and viability and conformity with the teachings of the Qur'an and the Sunnah. His writings revealed his erudition and scholarship, a deep perception of the significance of the teachings of the Qur'an and the Sunnah and a critical awareness of the mainstream of Western thought and history. All this brought a freshness to Muslim approach to these problems and lent a wider appeal to his message.

In the mid '30s, Maududi started writing on major political and cultural issues confronting the Muslims of India at that time and tried to examine them from the Islamic perspective rather than merely from the viewpoint of short-term political and economic interests. He relentlessly criticised the newfangled ideologies which had begun to cast a spell over the minds and hearts of his brethren-in-faith and attempted to show the hollowness of those ideologies. In this connection, the idea of nationalism received concerted attention from Maududi when he forcefully explained its dangerous potentialities as well as its incompatibility with the teachings of Islam. Maududi also emphasised that nationalism in the context of India meant the utter destruction of the separate identity of Muslims. In the meantime, an invitation from the philosopher-poet Allama Muhammad Iqbal persuaded him to leave Hyderabad and settle down at a place in the Eastern part of Punjab, in the district of Pathankot. Maududi established what was essentially an academic and research centre called Darul-Islam where, in collaboration with Allama Iqbal, he planned to train competent scholars in Islamics to produce works of outstanding quality on Islam, and above all, to carry out the reconstruction of Islamic Thought.

Founding the Party:

Around the year 1940, Maududi developed ideas regarding the founding of a more comprehensive and ambitious movement and this led him to launch a new organisation under the name of the Jamaat-e-Islami. Maududi was elected Jamaat's first Ameer and remained so till 1972 when he withdrew from the responsibility for reasons of health.

Struggle & Persecution:

After migrating to Pakistan in August 1947, Maududi concentrated his efforts on establishing a truly Islamic state and society in the country. Consistent with this objective, he wrote profusely to explain the different aspects of the Islamic way of life, especially the socio-political aspects. This concern for the implementation of the Islamic way of life led Maududi to criticise and oppose the policies pursued by the successive governments of Pakistan and to blame those in power for failing to transform Pakistan into a truly Islamic state. The rulers reacted with severe reprisal measures. Maududi was often arrested and had to face long spells in prison.

During these years of struggle and persecution, Maududi impressed all, including his critics and opponents, by the firmness and tenacity of his will and other outstanding qualities. In 1953, when he was sentenced to death by the martial law authorities on the charge of writing a seditious pamphlet on the Qadyani problem, he resolutely turned down the opportunity to file a petition for mercy. He cheerfully expressed his preference for death to seeking clemency from those who wanted, altogether unjustly, to hang him for upholding the right. With unshakeable faith that life and death lie solely in the hands of Allah, he told his son as well as his colleagues: "If the time of my death has come, no one can keep me from it; and if it has not come, they cannot send me to the gallows even if they hang themselves upside down in trying to do so." His family also declined to make any appeal for mercy. His firmness astonished the government which was forced, under strong public pressure both from within and without, to commute the death sentence to life imprisonment and then to cancel it.

Intellectual Contribution:

Maulana Maududi has written over 120 books and pamphlets and made over a 1000 speeches and press statements of which about 700 are available on record.

Maududi's pen was simultaneously prolific, forceful and versatile. The range of subjects he covered is unusually wide. Disciplines such as Tafsir, Hadith, law, philosophy and history, all have received the due share of his attention. He discussed a wide variety of problems (political, economic, cultural, social, theological etc.) and attempted to state how the teachings of Islam were related to those problems. Maududi has not delved into the technical world of the specialist, but has expounded the essentials of the Islamic approach in most of the fields of learning and inquiry. His main contribution, however, has been in the fields of the Qur'anic exegesis (Tafsir), ethics, social studies and the problems facing the movement of Islamic revival. His greatest work is his monumental tafsir in Urdu of the Qur'an, Tafhim al-Qur'an, a work he took 30 years to complete. Its chief characteristic lies in presenting the meaning and message of the Qur'an in a language and style that penetrates the hearts and minds of the men and women of today and shows the relevance of the Qur'an to their everyday problems, both on the individual and societal planes. He translated the Qur'an in direct and forceful modern Urdu idiom. His translation is much more readable and eloquent than ordinary literal translations of the Qur'an. He presented the Qur'an as a book of guidance for human life and as a guide-book for the movement to implement and enforce that guidance in human life. He attempted to explain the verses of the Qur'an in the context of its total message. This tafsir has made a far-reaching impact on contemporary Islamic thinking in the Subcontinent, and through its translations, even abroad.

The influence of Maulana Maududi is not confined to those associated with the Jamaat-e-Islami. His influence transcends the boundaries of parties and organisations. Maududi is very much like a father-figure for Muslims all over the world. As a scholar and writer, he is the most widely read Muslim writer of our time. His books have been translated into most of the major languages of the world C Arabic, English, Turkish, Persian, Hindi, French, German, Swahili, Tamil, Bengali, etc. C and are now increasingly becoming available in many more of the Asian, African and European languages.

Travels & Journeys Abroad:

The several journeys which Maududi undertook during the years 1956-74 enabled Muslims in many parts of the world to become acquainted with him personally and appreciate many of his qualities. At the same time, these journeys were educative for Maududi himself as well as they provided to him the opportunity to gain a great deal of first-hand knowledge of the facts of life and to get acquainted with a large number of persons in different parts of the world. During these numerous tours, he lectured in Cairo, Damascus, Amman, Makkah, Madinah, Jeddah, Kuwait, Rabat, Istanbul, London, New York, Toronto and at a host of international centres. During these years, he also participated in some 10 international conferences. He also made a study tour of Saudi Arabia, Jordan (including Jerusalem), Syria and Egypt in 1959-60 in order to study the geographical aspects of the places mentioned in the Qur'an. He was also invited to serve on the Advisory Committee which prepared the scheme for the establishment of the Islamic University of Madinah and was on its Academic Council ever since the inception of the University in 1962.

He was also a member of the Foundation Committee of the Rabitah al-Alam al-Islami, Makkah, and of the Academy of Research on Islamic Law, Madinah. In short, he was a tower of inspiration for Muslims the world over and influenced the climate and pattern of thought of Muslims, as the Himalayas or the Alps influence the climate in Asia or Europe without themselves moving about.

His Last Days:

In April 1979, Maududi's long-time kidney ailment worsened and by then he also had heart problems. He went to the United States for treatment and was hospitalised in Buffalo, New York, where his second son worked as a physician. Even at Buffalo, his time was intellectually productive. He spent many hours reviewing Western works on the life of the Prophet and meeting with Muslim leaders, their followers and well-wishers.

Following a few surgical operations, he died on September 22, 1979 at the age of 76. His funeral was held in Buffalo, but he was buried in an unmarked grave at his residence (Ichra) in Lahore after a very large funeral procession through the city.

May Allah bless him with His mercy for his efforts and reward him amply for the good that he has rendered for the nation of Islam (Ummah).

PREFACE

2nd Edition

The first edition of this book contained many formatting and typing errors. In this new edition,we have corrected all the errors found in the first edition. We have also re-arranged the structure of the book and added the full Arabic Text of the thirty Parts of the Qur'an. The reader is now able to read not only the meaning, the transliteration and the tafsir (explanation) of the Glorious Qur'an but also the full Arabic text as well.

The Glorious Qur'an Juz' 4 (Part 4): Chapter (Surah) 3: Al-I-'Imran (The Family of Imran) 093 To Chapter (Surah) 4: An-Nisaa (The Women) 023

PART 4 FULL ARABIC TEXT

Chapter (Surah) 3: Al-i-'Imran 093-200

۞ كُلُّ ٱلطَّعَامِ كَانَ حِلًّا لِّبَنِىٓ إِسْرَٰٓءِيلَ إِلَّا مَا حَرَّمَ إِسْرَٰٓءِيلُ عَلَىٰ نَفْسِهِۦ مِن قَبْلِ
أَن تُنَزَّلَ ٱلتَّوْرَىٰةُ ۗ قُلْ فَأْتُوا۟ بِٱلتَّوْرَىٰةِ فَٱتْلُوهَآ إِن كُنتُمْ صَٰدِقِينَ ﴿٩٣﴾ فَمَنِ ٱفْتَرَىٰ
عَلَى ٱللَّهِ ٱلْكَذِبَ مِنۢ بَعْدِ ذَٰلِكَ فَأُو۟لَٰٓئِكَ هُمُ ٱلظَّٰلِمُونَ ﴿٩٤﴾ قُلْ صَدَقَ ٱللَّهُ ۗ فَٱتَّبِعُوا۟
مِلَّةَ إِبْرَٰهِيمَ حَنِيفًا وَمَا كَانَ مِنَ ٱلْمُشْرِكِينَ ﴿٩٥﴾ إِنَّ أَوَّلَ بَيْتٍ وُضِعَ لِلنَّاسِ لَلَّذِى بِبَكَّةَ
مُبَارَكًا وَهُدًى لِّلْعَٰلَمِينَ ﴿٩٦﴾ فِيهِ ءَايَٰتٌۢ بَيِّنَٰتٌ مَّقَامُ إِبْرَٰهِيمَ ۖ وَمَن دَخَلَهُۥ كَانَ ءَامِنًا ۗ
وَلِلَّهِ عَلَى ٱلنَّاسِ حِجُّ ٱلْبَيْتِ مَنِ ٱسْتَطَاعَ إِلَيْهِ سَبِيلًا ۚ وَمَن كَفَرَ فَإِنَّ ٱللَّهَ غَنِىٌّ عَنِ
ٱلْعَٰلَمِينَ ﴿٩٧﴾ قُلْ يَٰٓأَهْلَ ٱلْكِتَٰبِ لِمَ تَكْفُرُونَ بِـَٔايَٰتِ ٱللَّهِ وَٱللَّهُ شَهِيدٌ عَلَىٰ مَا
تَعْمَلُونَ ﴿٩٨﴾ قُلْ يَٰٓأَهْلَ ٱلْكِتَٰبِ لِمَ تَصُدُّونَ عَن سَبِيلِ ٱللَّهِ مَنْ ءَامَنَ تَبْغُونَهَا عِوَجًا
وَأَنتُمْ شُهَدَآءُ ۗ وَمَا ٱللَّهُ بِغَٰفِلٍ عَمَّا تَعْمَلُونَ ﴿٩٩﴾ يَٰٓأَيُّهَا ٱلَّذِينَ ءَامَنُوٓا۟ إِن تُطِيعُوا۟ فَرِيقًا
مِّنَ ٱلَّذِينَ أُوتُوا۟ ٱلْكِتَٰبَ يَرُدُّوكُم بَعْدَ إِيمَٰنِكُمْ كَٰفِرِينَ ﴿١٠٠﴾ وَكَيْفَ تَكْفُرُونَ وَأَنتُمْ تُتْلَىٰ
عَلَيْكُمْ ءَايَٰتُ ٱللَّهِ وَفِيكُمْ رَسُولُهُۥ ۗ وَمَن يَعْتَصِم بِٱللَّهِ فَقَدْ هُدِىَ إِلَىٰ
صِرَٰطٍ مُّسْتَقِيمٍ ﴿١٠١﴾ يَٰٓأَيُّهَا ٱلَّذِينَ ءَامَنُوا۟ ٱتَّقُوا۟ ٱللَّهَ حَقَّ تُقَاتِهِۦ وَلَا تَمُوتُنَّ إِلَّا وَأَنتُم

مُّسۡلِمُونَ ﴿١٠٢﴾ وَٱعۡتَصِمُواْ بِحَبۡلِ ٱللَّهِ جَمِيعٗا وَلَا تَفَرَّقُواْۚ وَٱذۡكُرُواْ نِعۡمَتَ ٱللَّهِ عَلَيۡكُمۡ إِذۡ

كُنتُمۡ أَعۡدَآءٗ فَأَلَّفَ بَيۡنَ قُلُوبِكُمۡ فَأَصۡبَحۡتُم بِنِعۡمَتِهِۦٓ إِخۡوَٰنٗا وَكُنتُمۡ عَلَىٰ شَفَا حُفۡرَةٖ مِّنَ

ٱلنَّارِ فَأَنقَذَكُم مِّنۡهَاۗ كَذَٰلِكَ يُبَيِّنُ ٱللَّهُ لَكُمۡ ءَايَٰتِهِۦ لَعَلَّكُمۡ تَهۡتَدُونَ ﴿١٠٣﴾ وَلۡتَكُن مِّنكُمۡ

أُمَّةٞ يَدۡعُونَ إِلَى ٱلۡخَيۡرِ وَيَأۡمُرُونَ بِٱلۡمَعۡرُوفِ وَيَنۡهَوۡنَ عَنِ ٱلۡمُنكَرِۚ وَأُوْلَٰٓئِكَ هُمُ

ٱلۡمُفۡلِحُونَ ﴿١٠٤﴾ وَلَا تَكُونُواْ كَٱلَّذِينَ تَفَرَّقُواْ وَٱخۡتَلَفُواْ مِنۢ بَعۡدِ مَا جَآءَهُمُ ٱلۡبَيِّنَٰتُۚ

وَأُوْلَٰٓئِكَ لَهُمۡ عَذَابٌ عَظِيمٞ ﴿١٠٥﴾ يَوۡمَ تَبۡيَضُّ وُجُوهٞ وَتَسۡوَدُّ وُجُوهٞۚ فَأَمَّا ٱلَّذِينَ ٱسۡوَدَّتۡ

وُجُوهُهُمۡ أَكَفَرۡتُم بَعۡدَ إِيمَٰنِكُمۡ فَذُوقُواْ ٱلۡعَذَابَ بِمَا كُنتُمۡ تَكۡفُرُونَ ﴿١٠٦﴾ وَأَمَّا ٱلَّذِينَ

ٱبۡيَضَّتۡ وُجُوهُهُمۡ فَفِي رَحۡمَةِ ٱللَّهِ هُمۡ فِيهَا خَٰلِدُونَ ﴿١٠٧﴾ تِلۡكَ ءَايَٰتُ ٱللَّهِ نَتۡلُوهَا عَلَيۡكَ

بِٱلۡحَقِّۗ وَمَا ٱللَّهُ يُرِيدُ ظُلۡمٗا لِّلۡعَٰلَمِينَ ﴿١٠٨﴾ وَلِلَّهِ مَا فِي ٱلسَّمَٰوَٰتِ وَمَا فِي ٱلۡأَرۡضِۚ وَإِلَى ٱللَّهِ

تُرۡجَعُ ٱلۡأُمُورُ ﴿١٠٩﴾ كُنتُمۡ خَيۡرَ أُمَّةٍ أُخۡرِجَتۡ لِلنَّاسِ تَأۡمُرُونَ بِٱلۡمَعۡرُوفِ وَتَنۡهَوۡنَ عَنِ

ٱلۡمُنكَرِ وَتُؤۡمِنُونَ بِٱللَّهِۗ وَلَوۡ ءَامَنَ أَهۡلُ ٱلۡكِتَٰبِ لَكَانَ خَيۡرٗا لَّهُمۚ مِّنۡهُمُ

ٱلۡمُؤۡمِنُونَ وَأَكۡثَرُهُمُ ٱلۡفَٰسِقُونَ ﴿١١٠﴾ لَن يَضُرُّوكُمۡ إِلَّآ أَذٗىۖ وَإِن يُقَٰتِلُوكُمۡ

يُوَلُّوكُمُ ٱلۡأَدۡبَارَ ثُمَّ لَا يُنصَرُونَ ﴿١١١﴾ ضُرِبَتۡ عَلَيۡهِمُ ٱلذِّلَّةُ أَيۡنَ مَا ثُقِفُوٓاْ إِلَّا بِحَبۡلٖ مِّنَ

ٱللَّهِ وَحَبۡلٖ مِّنَ ٱلنَّاسِ وَبَآءُو بِغَضَبٖ مِّنَ ٱللَّهِ وَضُرِبَتۡ عَلَيۡهِمُ ٱلۡمَسۡكَنَةُۚ ذَٰلِكَ بِأَنَّهُمۡ

كَانُواْ يَكۡفُرُونَ بِـَٔايَٰتِ ٱللَّهِ وَيَقۡتُلُونَ ٱلۡأَنۢبِيَآءَ بِغَيۡرِ حَقّٖۚ ذَٰلِكَ بِمَا عَصَواْ

وَّكَانُواْ يَعۡتَدُونَ ﴿١١٢﴾ ۞ لَيۡسُواْ سَوَآءٗۗ مِّنۡ أَهۡلِ ٱلۡكِتَٰبِ أُمَّةٞ قَآئِمَةٞ يَتۡلُونَ ءَايَٰتِ ٱللَّهِ

ءَانَآءَ ٱلَّيۡلِ وَهُمۡ يَسۡجُدُونَ ﴿١١٣﴾ يُؤۡمِنُونَ بِٱللَّهِ وَٱلۡيَوۡمِ ٱلۡأٓخِرِ وَيَأۡمُرُونَ بِٱلۡمَعۡرُوفِ

وَيَنْهَوْنَ عَنِ ٱلْمُنكَرِ وَيُسَـٰرِعُونَ فِى ٱلْخَيْرَٰتِ وَأُو۟لَـٰٓئِكَ مِنَ ٱلصَّـٰلِحِينَ ﴿١١٤﴾ وَمَا
يَفْعَلُوا۟ مِنْ خَيْرٍ فَلَن يُكْفَرُوهُ ۗ وَٱللَّهُ عَلِيمٌۢ بِٱلْمُتَّقِينَ ﴿١١٥﴾ إِنَّ ٱلَّذِينَ كَفَرُوا۟ لَن
تُغْنِىَ عَنْهُمْ أَمْوَٰلُهُمْ وَلَآ أَوْلَـٰدُهُم مِّنَ ٱللَّهِ شَيْـًٔا ۖ وَأُو۟لَـٰٓئِكَ أَصْحَـٰبُ ٱلنَّارِ ۚ هُمْ فِيهَا
خَـٰلِدُونَ ﴿١١٦﴾ مَثَلُ مَا يُنفِقُونَ فِى هَـٰذِهِ ٱلْحَيَوٰةِ ٱلدُّنْيَا كَمَثَلِ رِيحٍ فِيهَا صِرٌّ أَصَابَتْ
حَرْثَ قَوْمٍ ظَلَمُوٓا۟ أَنفُسَهُمْ فَأَهْلَكَتْهُ ۚ وَمَا ظَلَمَهُمُ ٱللَّهُ وَلَـٰكِنْ أَنفُسَهُمْ يَظْلِمُونَ ﴿١١٧﴾
يَـٰٓأَيُّهَا ٱلَّذِينَ ءَامَنُوا۟ لَا تَتَّخِذُوا۟ بِطَانَةً مِّن دُونِكُمْ لَا يَأْلُونَكُمْ خَبَالًا وَدُّوا۟ مَا عَنِتُّمْ قَدْ
بَدَتِ ٱلْبَغْضَآءُ مِنْ أَفْوَٰهِهِمْ وَمَا تُخْفِى صُدُورُهُمْ أَكْبَرُ ۚ قَدْ بَيَّنَّا لَكُمُ ٱلْـَٔايَـٰتِ ۖ إِن كُنتُمْ
تَعْقِلُونَ ﴿١١٨﴾ هَـٰٓأَنتُمْ أُو۟لَآءِ تُحِبُّونَهُمْ وَلَا يُحِبُّونَكُمْ وَتُؤْمِنُونَ بِٱلْكِتَـٰبِ كُلِّهِۦ وَإِذَا لَقُوكُمْ
قَالُوٓا۟ ءَامَنَّا وَإِذَا خَلَوْا۟ عَضُّوا۟ عَلَيْكُمُ ٱلْأَنَامِلَ مِنَ ٱلْغَيْظِ ۚ قُلْ مُوتُوا۟ بِغَيْظِكُمْ ۗ إِنَّ ٱللَّهَ
عَلِيمٌۢ بِذَاتِ ٱلصُّدُورِ ﴿١١٩﴾ إِن تَمْسَسْكُمْ حَسَنَةٌ تَسُؤْهُمْ وَإِن تُصِبْكُمْ سَيِّئَةٌ يَفْرَحُوا۟ بِهَا ۖ
وَإِن تَصْبِرُوا۟ وَتَتَّقُوا۟ لَا يَضُرُّكُمْ كَيْدُهُمْ شَيْـًٔا ۗ إِنَّ ٱللَّهَ بِمَا يَعْمَلُونَ مُحِيطٌ ﴿١٢٠﴾ وَإِذْ
غَدَوْتَ مِنْ أَهْلِكَ تُبَوِّئُ ٱلْمُؤْمِنِينَ مَقَـٰعِدَ لِلْقِتَالِ ۗ وَٱللَّهُ سَمِيعٌ عَلِيمٌ ﴿١٢١﴾ إِذْ هَمَّت
طَّآئِفَتَانِ مِنكُمْ أَن تَفْشَلَا وَٱللَّهُ وَلِيُّهُمَا ۗ وَعَلَى ٱللَّهِ فَلْيَتَوَكَّلِ ٱلْمُؤْمِنُونَ ﴿١٢٢﴾ وَلَقَدْ
نَصَرَكُمُ ٱللَّهُ بِبَدْرٍ وَأَنتُمْ أَذِلَّةٌ ۖ فَٱتَّقُوا۟ ٱللَّهَ لَعَلَّكُمْ تَشْكُرُونَ ﴿١٢٣﴾ إِذْ تَقُولُ لِلْمُؤْمِنِينَ
أَلَن يَكْفِيَكُمْ أَن يُمِدَّكُمْ رَبُّكُم بِثَلَـٰثَةِ ءَالَـٰفٍ مِّنَ ٱلْمَلَـٰٓئِكَةِ مُنزَلِينَ ﴿١٢٤﴾ بَلَىٰٓ ۚ إِن تَصْبِرُوا۟
وَتَتَّقُوا۟ وَيَأْتُوكُم مِّن فَوْرِهِمْ هَـٰذَا يُمْدِدْكُمْ رَبُّكُم بِخَمْسَةِ ءَالَـٰفٍ مِّنَ
ٱلْمَلَـٰٓئِكَةِ مُسَوِّمِينَ ﴿١٢٥﴾ وَمَا جَعَلَهُ ٱللَّهُ إِلَّا بُشْرَىٰ لَكُمْ وَلِتَطْمَئِنَّ قُلُوبُكُم بِهِۦ ۗ وَمَا

ٱلنَّصۡرُ إِلَّا مِنۡ عِندِ ٱللَّهِ ٱلۡعَزِيزِ ٱلۡحَكِيمِ ﴿١٢٦﴾ لِيَقۡطَعَ طَرَفٗا مِّنَ ٱلَّذِينَ كَفَرُوٓاْ أَوۡ يَكۡبِتَهُمۡ
فَيَنقَلِبُواْ خَآئِبِينَ ﴿١٢٧﴾ لَيۡسَ لَكَ مِنَ ٱلۡأَمۡرِ شَيۡءٌ أَوۡ يَتُوبَ عَلَيۡهِمۡ أَوۡ يُعَذِّبَهُمۡ فَإِنَّهُمۡ
ظَٰلِمُونَ ﴿١٢٨﴾ وَلِلَّهِ مَا فِي ٱلسَّمَٰوَٰتِ وَمَا فِي ٱلۡأَرۡضِۚ يَغۡفِرُ لِمَن يَشَآءُ وَيُعَذِّبُ مَن
يَشَآءُۚ وَٱللَّهُ غَفُورٞ رَّحِيمٞ ﴿١٢٩﴾ يَٰٓأَيُّهَا ٱلَّذِينَ ءَامَنُواْ لَا تَأۡكُلُواْ ٱلرِّبَوٰٓاْ أَضۡعَٰفٗا
مُّضَٰعَفَةٗۖ وَٱتَّقُواْ ٱللَّهَ لَعَلَّكُمۡ تُفۡلِحُونَ ﴿١٣٠﴾ وَٱتَّقُواْ ٱلنَّارَ ٱلَّتِيٓ أُعِدَّتۡ لِلۡكَٰفِرِينَ ﴿١٣١﴾
وَأَطِيعُواْ ٱللَّهَ وَٱلرَّسُولَ لَعَلَّكُمۡ تُرۡحَمُونَ ﴿١٣٢﴾ ۞ وَسَارِعُوٓاْ إِلَىٰ مَغۡفِرَةٖ مِّن رَّبِّكُمۡ
وَجَنَّةٍ عَرۡضُهَا ٱلسَّمَٰوَٰتُ وَٱلۡأَرۡضُ أُعِدَّتۡ لِلۡمُتَّقِينَ ﴿١٣٣﴾ ٱلَّذِينَ يُنفِقُونَ فِي ٱلسَّرَّآءِ
وَٱلضَّرَّآءِ وَٱلۡكَٰظِمِينَ ٱلۡغَيۡظَ وَٱلۡعَافِينَ عَنِ ٱلنَّاسِۗ وَٱللَّهُ يُحِبُّ ٱلۡمُحۡسِنِينَ ﴿١٣٤﴾
وَٱلَّذِينَ إِذَا فَعَلُواْ فَٰحِشَةً أَوۡ ظَلَمُوٓاْ أَنفُسَهُمۡ ذَكَرُواْ ٱللَّهَ فَٱسۡتَغۡفَرُواْ لِذُنُوبِهِمۡ وَمَن
يَغۡفِرُ ٱلذُّنُوبَ إِلَّا ٱللَّهُ وَلَمۡ يُصِرُّواْ عَلَىٰ مَا فَعَلُواْ وَهُمۡ يَعۡلَمُونَ ﴿١٣٥﴾ أُوْلَٰٓئِكَ
جَزَآؤُهُم مَّغۡفِرَةٞ مِّن رَّبِّهِمۡ وَجَنَّٰتٞ تَجۡرِي مِن تَحۡتِهَا ٱلۡأَنۡهَٰرُ خَٰلِدِينَ فِيهَاۚ وَنِعۡمَ أَجۡرُ
ٱلۡعَٰمِلِينَ ﴿١٣٦﴾ قَدۡ خَلَتۡ مِن قَبۡلِكُمۡ سُنَنٞ فَسِيرُواْ فِي ٱلۡأَرۡضِ فَٱنظُرُواْ كَيۡفَ كَانَ عَٰقِبَةُ
ٱلۡمُكَذِّبِينَ ﴿١٣٧﴾ هَٰذَا بَيَانٞ لِّلنَّاسِ وَهُدٗى وَمَوۡعِظَةٞ لِّلۡمُتَّقِينَ ﴿١٣٨﴾ وَلَا تَهِنُواْ وَلَا
تَحۡزَنُواْ وَأَنتُمُ ٱلۡأَعۡلَوۡنَ إِن كُنتُم مُّؤۡمِنِينَ ﴿١٣٩﴾ إِن يَمۡسَسۡكُمۡ قَرۡحٞ فَقَدۡ مَسَّ ٱلۡقَوۡمَ قَرۡحٞ
مِّثۡلُهُۥۚ وَتِلۡكَ ٱلۡأَيَّامُ نُدَاوِلُهَا بَيۡنَ ٱلنَّاسِ وَلِيَعۡلَمَ ٱللَّهُ ٱلَّذِينَ ءَامَنُواْ وَيَتَّخِذَ مِنكُمۡ
شُهَدَآءَۗ وَٱللَّهُ لَا يُحِبُّ ٱلظَّٰلِمِينَ ﴿١٤٠﴾ وَلِيُمَحِّصَ ٱللَّهُ ٱلَّذِينَ ءَامَنُواْ وَيَمۡحَقَ
ٱلۡكَٰفِرِينَ ﴿١٤١﴾ أَمۡ حَسِبۡتُمۡ أَن تَدۡخُلُواْ ٱلۡجَنَّةَ وَلَمَّا يَعۡلَمِ ٱللَّهُ ٱلَّذِينَ جَٰهَدُواْ مِنكُمۡ

وَيَعْلَمَ ٱلصَّٰبِرِينَ ﴿١٤٢﴾ وَلَقَدْ كُنتُمْ تَمَنَّوْنَ ٱلْمَوْتَ مِن قَبْلِ أَن تَلْقَوْهُ فَقَدْ رَأَيْتُمُوهُ وَأَنتُمْ
تَنظُرُونَ ﴿١٤٣﴾ وَمَا مُحَمَّدٌ إِلَّا رَسُولٌ قَدْ خَلَتْ مِن قَبْلِهِ ٱلرُّسُلُ ۚ أَفَإِي۟ن مَّاتَ أَوْ قُتِلَ
ٱنقَلَبْتُمْ عَلَىٰٓ أَعْقَٰبِكُمْ ۚ وَمَن يَنقَلِبْ عَلَىٰ عَقِبَيْهِ فَلَن يَضُرَّ ٱللَّهَ شَيْـًٔا ۗ وَسَيَجْزِى ٱللَّهُ
ٱلشَّٰكِرِينَ ﴿١٤٤﴾ وَمَا كَانَ لِنَفْسٍ أَن تَمُوتَ إِلَّا بِإِذْنِ ٱللَّهِ كِتَٰبًا مُّؤَجَّلًا ۗ وَمَن يُرِدْ
ثَوَابَ ٱلدُّنْيَا نُؤْتِهِۦ مِنْهَا وَمَن يُرِدْ ثَوَابَ ٱلْءَاخِرَةِ نُؤْتِهِۦ مِنْهَا ۚ وَسَنَجْزِى ٱلشَّٰكِرِينَ ﴿١٤٥﴾
وَكَأَيِّن مِّن نَّبِىٍّ قَٰتَلَ مَعَهُۥ رِبِّيُّونَ كَثِيرٌ فَمَا وَهَنُوا۟ لِمَآ أَصَابَهُمْ فِى سَبِيلِ ٱللَّهِ وَمَا ضَعُفُوا۟
وَمَا ٱسْتَكَانُوا۟ ۗ وَٱللَّهُ يُحِبُّ ٱلصَّٰبِرِينَ ﴿١٤٦﴾ وَمَا كَانَ قَوْلَهُمْ إِلَّآ أَن قَالُوا۟ رَبَّنَا ٱغْفِرْ لَنَا
ذُنُوبَنَا وَإِسْرَافَنَا فِىٓ أَمْرِنَا وَثَبِّتْ أَقْدَامَنَا وَٱنصُرْنَا عَلَى ٱلْقَوْمِ ٱلْكَٰفِرِينَ ﴿١٤٧﴾ فَـَٔاتَىٰهُمُ
ٱللَّهُ ثَوَابَ ٱلدُّنْيَا وَحُسْنَ ثَوَابِ ٱلْءَاخِرَةِ ۗ وَٱللَّهُ يُحِبُّ ٱلْمُحْسِنِينَ ﴿١٤٨﴾ يَٰٓأَيُّهَا ٱلَّذِينَ
ءَامَنُوٓا۟ إِن تُطِيعُوا۟ ٱلَّذِينَ كَفَرُوا۟ يَرُدُّوكُمْ عَلَىٰٓ أَعْقَٰبِكُمْ فَتَنقَلِبُوا۟ خَٰسِرِينَ ﴿١٤٩﴾ بَلِ
ٱللَّهُ مَوْلَىٰكُمْ ۖ وَهُوَ خَيْرُ ٱلنَّٰصِرِينَ ﴿١٥٠﴾ سَنُلْقِى فِى قُلُوبِ ٱلَّذِينَ كَفَرُوا۟ ٱلرُّعْبَ بِمَآ
أَشْرَكُوا۟ بِٱللَّهِ مَا لَمْ يُنَزِّلْ بِهِۦ سُلْطَٰنًا ۖ وَمَأْوَىٰهُمُ ٱلنَّارُ ۚ وَبِئْسَ مَثْوَى ٱلظَّٰلِمِينَ ﴿١٥١﴾
وَلَقَدْ صَدَقَكُمُ ٱللَّهُ وَعْدَهُۥٓ إِذْ تَحُسُّونَهُم بِإِذْنِهِۦ ۖ حَتَّىٰٓ إِذَا فَشِلْتُمْ وَتَنَٰزَعْتُمْ فِى
ٱلْأَمْرِ وَعَصَيْتُم مِّنۢ بَعْدِ مَآ أَرَىٰكُم مَّا تُحِبُّونَ ۚ مِنكُم مَّن يُرِيدُ ٱلدُّنْيَا وَمِنكُم
مَّن يُرِيدُ ٱلْءَاخِرَةَ ۚ ثُمَّ صَرَفَكُمْ عَنْهُمْ لِيَبْتَلِيَكُمْ ۖ وَلَقَدْ عَفَا عَنكُمْ ۗ وَٱللَّهُ ذُو فَضْلٍ
عَلَى ٱلْمُؤْمِنِينَ ﴿١٥٢﴾ ۞ إِذْ تُصْعِدُونَ وَلَا تَلْوُۥنَ عَلَىٰٓ أَحَدٍ وَٱلرَّسُولُ يَدْعُوكُمْ
فِىٓ أُخْرَىٰكُمْ فَأَثَٰبَكُمْ غَمًّۢا بِغَمٍّ لِّكَيْلَا تَحْزَنُوا۟ عَلَىٰ مَا فَاتَكُمْ وَلَا مَآ أَصَٰبَكُمْ ۗ

وَٱللَّهُ خَبِيرُۢ بِمَا تَعۡمَلُونَ ﴿١٥٣﴾ ثُمَّ أَنزَلَ عَلَيۡكُم مِّنۢ بَعۡدِ ٱلۡغَمِّ أَمَنَةً نُّعَاسًا يَغۡشَىٰ طَآئِفَةً
مِّنكُمۡۖ وَطَآئِفَةٌ قَدۡ أَهَمَّتۡهُمۡ أَنفُسُهُمۡ يَظُنُّونَ بِٱللَّهِ غَيۡرَ ٱلۡحَقِّ ظَنَّ ٱلۡجَٰهِلِيَّةِۖ
يَقُولُونَ هَل لَّنَا مِنَ ٱلۡأَمۡرِ مِن شَيۡءٍۗ قُلۡ إِنَّ ٱلۡأَمۡرَ كُلَّهُۥ لِلَّهِۗ يُخۡفُونَ فِيٓ أَنفُسِهِم مَّا لَا
يُبۡدُونَ لَكَۖ يَقُولُونَ لَوۡ كَانَ لَنَا مِنَ ٱلۡأَمۡرِ شَيۡءٌ مَّا قُتِلۡنَا هَٰهُنَاۗ قُل لَّوۡ كُنتُمۡ فِي بُيُوتِكُمۡ
لَبَرَزَ ٱلَّذِينَ كُتِبَ عَلَيۡهِمُ ٱلۡقَتۡلُ إِلَىٰ مَضَاجِعِهِمۡۖ وَلِيَبۡتَلِيَ ٱللَّهُ مَا فِي صُدُورِكُمۡ
وَلِيُمَحِّصَ مَا فِي قُلُوبِكُمۡۗ وَٱللَّهُ عَلِيمُۢ بِذَاتِ ٱلصُّدُورِ ﴿١٥٤﴾ إِنَّ ٱلَّذِينَ تَوَلَّوۡاْ مِنكُمۡ يَوۡمَ
ٱلۡتَقَى ٱلۡجَمۡعَانِ إِنَّمَا ٱسۡتَزَلَّهُمُ ٱلشَّيۡطَٰنُ بِبَعۡضِ مَا كَسَبُواْۖ وَلَقَدۡ عَفَا ٱللَّهُ عَنۡهُمۡۗ إِنَّ
ٱللَّهَ غَفُورٌ حَلِيمٞ ﴿١٥٥﴾ يَٰٓأَيُّهَا ٱلَّذِينَ ءَامَنُواْ لَا تَكُونُواْ كَٱلَّذِينَ كَفَرُواْ وَقَالُواْ لِإِخۡوَٰنِهِمۡ إِذَا
ضَرَبُواْ فِي ٱلۡأَرۡضِ أَوۡ كَانُواْ غُزّٗى لَّوۡ كَانُواْ عِندَنَا مَا مَاتُواْ وَمَا قُتِلُواْ لِيَجۡعَلَ ٱللَّهُ ذَٰلِكَ
حَسۡرَةٗ فِي قُلُوبِهِمۡۗ وَٱللَّهُ يُحۡيِۦ وَيُمِيتُۗ وَٱللَّهُ بِمَا تَعۡمَلُونَ بَصِيرٞ ﴿١٥٦﴾ وَلَئِن قُتِلۡتُمۡ فِي سَبِيلِ
ٱللَّهِ أَوۡ مُتُّمۡ لَمَغۡفِرَةٞ مِّنَ ٱللَّهِ وَرَحۡمَةٌ خَيۡرٞ مِّمَّا يَجۡمَعُونَ ﴿١٥٧﴾ وَلَئِن مُّتُّمۡ أَوۡ قُتِلۡتُمۡ لَإِلَى
ٱللَّهِ تُحۡشَرُونَ ﴿١٥٨﴾ فَبِمَا رَحۡمَةٖ مِّنَ ٱللَّهِ لِنتَ لَهُمۡۖ وَلَوۡ كُنتَ فَظًّا غَلِيظَ ٱلۡقَلۡبِ لَٱنفَضُّواْ
مِنۡ حَوۡلِكَۖ فَٱعۡفُ عَنۡهُمۡ وَٱسۡتَغۡفِرۡ لَهُمۡ وَشَاوِرۡهُمۡ فِي ٱلۡأَمۡرِۖ فَإِذَا عَزَمۡتَ فَتَوَكَّلۡ عَلَى
ٱللَّهِۚ إِنَّ ٱللَّهَ يُحِبُّ ٱلۡمُتَوَكِّلِينَ ﴿١٥٩﴾ إِن يَنصُرۡكُمُ ٱللَّهُ فَلَا غَالِبَ لَكُمۡۖ وَإِن يَخۡذُلۡكُمۡ فَمَن
ذَا ٱلَّذِي يَنصُرُكُم مِّنۢ بَعۡدِهِۦۗ وَعَلَى ٱللَّهِ فَلۡيَتَوَكَّلِ ٱلۡمُؤۡمِنُونَ ﴿١٦٠﴾ وَمَا كَانَ لِنَبِيٍّ أَن يَغُلَّۚ
وَمَن يَغۡلُلۡ يَأۡتِ بِمَا غَلَّ يَوۡمَ ٱلۡقِيَٰمَةِۚ ثُمَّ تُوَفَّىٰ كُلُّ نَفۡسٖ مَّا كَسَبَتۡ وَهُمۡ لَا
يُظۡلَمُونَ ﴿١٦١﴾ أَفَمَنِ ٱتَّبَعَ رِضۡوَٰنَ ٱللَّهِ كَمَنۢ بَآءَ بِسَخَطٖ مِّنَ ٱللَّهِ وَمَأۡوَىٰهُ جَهَنَّمُۚ وَبِئۡسَ

ٱلْمَصِيرُ ﴿١٦٢﴾ هُمْ دَرَجَـٰتٌ عِندَ ٱللَّهِ ۗ وَٱللَّهُ بَصِيرٌۢ بِمَا يَعْمَلُونَ ﴿١٦٣﴾ لَقَدْ مَنَّ ٱللَّهُ عَلَى
ٱلْمُؤْمِنِينَ إِذْ بَعَثَ فِيهِمْ رَسُولًا مِّنْ أَنفُسِهِمْ يَتْلُوا۟ عَلَيْهِمْ ءَايَـٰتِهِۦ وَيُزَكِّيهِمْ وَيُعَلِّمُهُمُ
ٱلْكِتَـٰبَ وَٱلْحِكْمَةَ وَإِن كَانُوا۟ مِن قَبْلُ لَفِى ضَلَـٰلٍ مُّبِينٍ ﴿١٦٤﴾ أَوَلَمَّآ أَصَـٰبَتْكُم مُّصِيبَةٌ
قَدْ أَصَبْتُم مِّثْلَيْهَا قُلْتُمْ أَنَّىٰ هَـٰذَا ۖ قُلْ هُوَ مِنْ عِندِ أَنفُسِكُمْ ۗ إِنَّ ٱللَّهَ عَلَىٰ كُلِّ شَىْءٍ
قَدِيرٌ ﴿١٦٥﴾ وَمَآ أَصَـٰبَكُمْ يَوْمَ ٱلْتَقَى ٱلْجَمْعَانِ فَبِإِذْنِ ٱللَّهِ وَلِيَعْلَمَ ٱلْمُؤْمِنِينَ ﴿١٦٦﴾ وَلِيَعْلَمَ
ٱلَّذِينَ نَافَقُوا۟ ۚ وَقِيلَ لَهُمْ تَعَالَوْا۟ قَـٰتِلُوا۟ فِى سَبِيلِ ٱللَّهِ أَوِ ٱدْفَعُوا۟ ۖ قَالُوا۟ لَوْ نَعْلَمُ قِتَالًا
لَّٱتَّبَعْنَـٰكُمْ ۗ هُمْ لِلْكُفْرِ يَوْمَئِذٍ أَقْرَبُ مِنْهُمْ لِلْإِيمَـٰنِ ۚ يَقُولُونَ بِأَفْوَٰهِهِم مَّا لَيْسَ فِى
قُلُوبِهِمْ ۗ وَٱللَّهُ أَعْلَمُ بِمَا يَكْتُمُونَ ﴿١٦٧﴾ ٱلَّذِينَ قَالُوا۟ لِإِخْوَٰنِهِمْ وَقَعَدُوا۟ لَوْ أَطَاعُونَا مَا قُتِلُوا۟ ۗ
قُلْ فَٱدْرَءُوا۟ عَنْ أَنفُسِكُمُ ٱلْمَوْتَ إِن كُنتُمْ صَـٰدِقِينَ ﴿١٦٨﴾ وَلَا تَحْسَبَنَّ ٱلَّذِينَ قُتِلُوا۟ فِى
سَبِيلِ ٱللَّهِ أَمْوَٰتًۢا ۚ بَلْ أَحْيَآءٌ عِندَ رَبِّهِمْ يُرْزَقُونَ ﴿١٦٩﴾ فَرِحِينَ بِمَآ ءَاتَىٰهُمُ ٱللَّهُ مِن
فَضْلِهِۦ وَيَسْتَبْشِرُونَ بِٱلَّذِينَ لَمْ يَلْحَقُوا۟ بِهِم مِّنْ خَلْفِهِمْ أَلَّا خَوْفٌ عَلَيْهِمْ وَلَا هُمْ
يَحْزَنُونَ ﴿١٧٠﴾ ۞ يَسْتَبْشِرُونَ بِنِعْمَةٍ مِّنَ ٱللَّهِ وَفَضْلٍ وَأَنَّ ٱللَّهَ لَا يُضِيعُ
أَجْرَ ٱلْمُؤْمِنِينَ ﴿١٧١﴾ ٱلَّذِينَ ٱسْتَجَابُوا۟ لِلَّهِ وَٱلرَّسُولِ مِنۢ بَعْدِ مَآ أَصَابَهُمُ ٱلْقَرْحُ ۚ لِلَّذِينَ
أَحْسَنُوا۟ مِنْهُمْ وَٱتَّقَوْا۟ أَجْرٌ عَظِيمٌ ﴿١٧٢﴾ ٱلَّذِينَ قَالَ لَهُمُ ٱلنَّاسُ إِنَّ ٱلنَّاسَ قَدْ جَمَعُوا۟ لَكُمْ
فَٱخْشَوْهُمْ فَزَادَهُمْ إِيمَـٰنًا وَقَالُوا۟ حَسْبُنَا ٱللَّهُ وَنِعْمَ ٱلْوَكِيلُ ﴿١٧٣﴾ فَٱنقَلَبُوا۟ بِنِعْمَةٍ مِّنَ
ٱللَّهِ وَفَضْلٍ لَّمْ يَمْسَسْهُمْ سُوٓءٌ وَٱتَّبَعُوا۟ رِضْوَٰنَ ٱللَّهِ ۗ وَٱللَّهُ ذُو فَضْلٍ عَظِيمٍ ﴿١٧٤﴾ إِنَّمَا
ذَٰلِكُمُ ٱلشَّيْطَـٰنُ يُخَوِّفُ أَوْلِيَآءَهُۥ فَلَا تَخَافُوهُمْ وَخَافُونِ إِن كُنتُم مُّؤْمِنِينَ ﴿١٧٥﴾ وَلَا

يَحۡزُنكَ ٱلَّذِينَ يُسَٰرِعُونَ فِي ٱلۡكُفۡرِۚ إِنَّهُمۡ لَن يَضُرُّواْ ٱللَّهَ شَيۡـٔٗاۗ يُرِيدُ ٱللَّهُ أَلَّا يَجۡعَلَ لَهُمۡ
حَظّٗا فِي ٱلۡأٓخِرَةِۖ وَلَهُمۡ عَذَابٌ عَظِيمٌ ﴿١٧٦﴾ إِنَّ ٱلَّذِينَ ٱشۡتَرَوُاْ ٱلۡكُفۡرَ بِٱلۡإِيمَٰنِ لَن يَضُرُّواْ
ٱللَّهَ شَيۡـٔٗا وَلَهُمۡ عَذَابٌ أَلِيمٞ ﴿١٧٧﴾ وَلَا يَحۡسَبَنَّ ٱلَّذِينَ كَفَرُوٓاْ أَنَّمَا نُمۡلِي لَهُمۡ خَيۡرٞ لِّأَنفُسِهِمۡۚ
إِنَّمَا نُمۡلِي لَهُمۡ لِيَزۡدَادُوٓاْ إِثۡمٗاۚ وَلَهُمۡ عَذَابٞ مُّهِينٞ ﴿١٧٨﴾ مَّا كَانَ ٱللَّهُ لِيَذَرَ ٱلۡمُؤۡمِنِينَ عَلَىٰ
مَآ أَنتُمۡ عَلَيۡهِ حَتَّىٰ يَمِيزَ ٱلۡخَبِيثَ مِنَ ٱلطَّيِّبِۗ وَمَا كَانَ ٱللَّهُ لِيُطۡلِعَكُمۡ عَلَى ٱلۡغَيۡبِ وَلَٰكِنَّ
ٱللَّهَ يَجۡتَبِي مِن رُّسُلِهِۦ مَن يَشَآءُۖ فَـَٔامِنُواْ بِٱللَّهِ وَرُسُلِهِۦۚ وَإِن تُؤۡمِنُواْ وَتَتَّقُواْ فَلَكُمۡ أَجۡرٌ
عَظِيمٞ ﴿١٧٩﴾ وَلَا يَحۡسَبَنَّ ٱلَّذِينَ يَبۡخَلُونَ بِمَآ ءَاتَىٰهُمُ ٱللَّهُ مِن فَضۡلِهِۦ هُوَ خَيۡرٗا لَّهُمۖ بَلۡ
هُوَ شَرّٞ لَّهُمۡۖ سَيُطَوَّقُونَ مَا بَخِلُواْ بِهِۦ يَوۡمَ ٱلۡقِيَٰمَةِۗ وَلِلَّهِ مِيرَٰثُ ٱلسَّمَٰوَٰتِ وَٱلۡأَرۡضِۗ وَٱللَّهُ
بِمَا تَعۡمَلُونَ خَبِيرٞ ﴿١٨٠﴾ لَّقَدۡ سَمِعَ ٱللَّهُ قَوۡلَ ٱلَّذِينَ قَالُوٓاْ إِنَّ ٱللَّهَ فَقِيرٞ وَنَحۡنُ أَغۡنِيَآءُۘ
سَنَكۡتُبُ مَا قَالُواْ وَقَتۡلَهُمُ ٱلۡأَنۢبِيَآءَ بِغَيۡرِ حَقّٖ وَنَقُولُ ذُوقُواْ عَذَابَ ٱلۡحَرِيقِ ﴿١٨١﴾ ذَٰلِكَ
بِمَا قَدَّمَتۡ أَيۡدِيكُمۡ وَأَنَّ ٱللَّهَ لَيۡسَ بِظَلَّامٖ لِّلۡعَبِيدِ ﴿١٨٢﴾ ٱلَّذِينَ قَالُوٓاْ إِنَّ ٱللَّهَ عَهِدَ
إِلَيۡنَآ أَلَّا نُؤۡمِنَ لِرَسُولٍ حَتَّىٰ يَأۡتِيَنَا بِقُرۡبَانٖ تَأۡكُلُهُ ٱلنَّارُۗ قُلۡ قَدۡ جَآءَكُمۡ رُسُلٞ مِّن
قَبۡلِي بِٱلۡبَيِّنَٰتِ وَبِٱلَّذِي قُلۡتُمۡ فَلِمَ قَتَلۡتُمُوهُمۡ إِن كُنتُمۡ صَٰدِقِينَ ﴿١٨٣﴾ فَإِن كَذَّبُوكَ
فَقَدۡ كُذِّبَ رُسُلٞ مِّن قَبۡلِكَ جَآءُو بِٱلۡبَيِّنَٰتِ وَٱلزُّبُرِ وَٱلۡكِتَٰبِ ٱلۡمُنِيرِ ﴿١٨٤﴾ كُلُّ نَفۡسٖ
ذَآئِقَةُ ٱلۡمَوۡتِۗ وَإِنَّمَا تُوَفَّوۡنَ أُجُورَكُمۡ يَوۡمَ ٱلۡقِيَٰمَةِۖ فَمَن زُحۡزِحَ عَنِ ٱلنَّارِ وَأُدۡخِلَ
ٱلۡجَنَّةَ فَقَدۡ فَازَۗ وَمَا ٱلۡحَيَوٰةُ ٱلدُّنۡيَآ إِلَّا مَتَٰعُ ٱلۡغُرُورِ ﴿١٨٥﴾ ۞ لَتُبۡلَوُنَّ فِيٓ أَمۡوَٰلِكُمۡ
وَأَنفُسِكُمۡ وَلَتَسۡمَعُنَّ مِنَ ٱلَّذِينَ أُوتُواْ ٱلۡكِتَٰبَ مِن قَبۡلِكُمۡ وَمِنَ ٱلَّذِينَ أَشۡرَكُوٓاْ

أَذًى كَثِيرًا ۚ وَإِن تَصْبِرُوا۟ وَتَتَّقُوا۟ فَإِنَّ ذَٰلِكَ مِنْ عَزْمِ ٱلْأُمُورِ ﴿١٨٦﴾ وَإِذْ أَخَذَ ٱللَّهُ مِيثَٰقَ
ٱلَّذِينَ أُوتُوا۟ ٱلْكِتَٰبَ لَتُبَيِّنُنَّهُۥ لِلنَّاسِ وَلَا تَكْتُمُونَهُۥ فَنَبَذُوهُ وَرَآءَ ظُهُورِهِمْ وَٱشْتَرَوْا۟ بِهِۦ
ثَمَنًا قَلِيلًا ۖ فَبِئْسَ مَا يَشْتَرُونَ ﴿١٨٧﴾ لَا تَحْسَبَنَّ ٱلَّذِينَ يَفْرَحُونَ بِمَآ أَتَوا۟ وَّيُحِبُّونَ أَن
يُحْمَدُوا۟ بِمَا لَمْ يَفْعَلُوا۟ فَلَا تَحْسَبَنَّهُم بِمَفَازَةٍ مِّنَ ٱلْعَذَابِ ۖ وَلَهُمْ عَذَابٌ أَلِيمٌ ﴿١٨٨﴾ وَلِلَّهِ
مُلْكُ ٱلسَّمَٰوَٰتِ وَٱلْأَرْضِ ۗ وَٱللَّهُ عَلَىٰ كُلِّ شَىْءٍ قَدِيرٌ ﴿١٨٩﴾ إِنَّ فِى خَلْقِ ٱلسَّمَٰوَٰتِ
وَٱلْأَرْضِ وَٱخْتِلَٰفِ ٱلَّيْلِ وَٱلنَّهَارِ لَءَايَٰتٍ لِّأُو۟لِى ٱلْأَلْبَٰبِ ﴿١٩٠﴾ ٱلَّذِينَ يَذْكُرُونَ ٱللَّهَ قِيَٰمًا
وَقُعُودًا وَعَلَىٰ جُنُوبِهِمْ وَيَتَفَكَّرُونَ فِى خَلْقِ ٱلسَّمَٰوَٰتِ وَٱلْأَرْضِ رَبَّنَا مَا خَلَقْتَ هَٰذَا
بَٰطِلًا سُبْحَٰنَكَ فَقِنَا عَذَابَ ٱلنَّارِ ﴿١٩١﴾ رَبَّنَآ إِنَّكَ مَن تُدْخِلِ ٱلنَّارَ فَقَدْ أَخْزَيْتَهُۥ ۖ وَمَا
لِلظَّٰلِمِينَ مِنْ أَنصَارٍ ﴿١٩٢﴾ رَّبَّنَآ إِنَّنَا سَمِعْنَا مُنَادِيًا يُنَادِى لِلْإِيمَٰنِ أَنْ ءَامِنُوا۟ بِرَبِّكُمْ
فَـَٔامَنَّا ۚ رَبَّنَا فَٱغْفِرْ لَنَا ذُنُوبَنَا وَكَفِّرْ عَنَّا سَيِّـَٔاتِنَا وَتَوَفَّنَا مَعَ ٱلْأَبْرَارِ ﴿١٩٣﴾ رَبَّنَا وَءَاتِنَا
مَا وَعَدتَّنَا عَلَىٰ رُسُلِكَ وَلَا تُخْزِنَا يَوْمَ ٱلْقِيَٰمَةِ ۗ إِنَّكَ لَا تُخْلِفُ ٱلْمِيعَادَ ﴿١٩٤﴾ فَٱسْتَجَابَ
لَهُمْ رَبُّهُمْ أَنِّى لَآ أُضِيعُ عَمَلَ عَٰمِلٍ مِّنكُم مِّن ذَكَرٍ أَوْ أُنثَىٰ ۖ بَعْضُكُم مِّنۢ بَعْضٍ ۖ فَٱلَّذِينَ
هَاجَرُوا۟ وَأُخْرِجُوا۟ مِن دِيَٰرِهِمْ وَأُوذُوا۟ فِى سَبِيلِى وَقَٰتَلُوا۟ وَقُتِلُوا۟ لَأُكَفِّرَنَّ عَنْهُمْ سَيِّـَٔاتِهِمْ
وَلَأُدْخِلَنَّهُمْ جَنَّٰتٍ تَجْرِى مِن تَحْتِهَا ٱلْأَنْهَٰرُ ثَوَابًا مِّنْ عِندِ ٱللَّهِ ۗ وَٱللَّهُ عِندَهُۥ حُسْنُ
ٱلثَّوَابِ ﴿١٩٥﴾ لَا يَغُرَّنَّكَ تَقَلُّبُ ٱلَّذِينَ كَفَرُوا۟ فِى ٱلْبِلَٰدِ ﴿١٩٦﴾ مَتَٰعٌ قَلِيلٌ ثُمَّ مَأْوَىٰهُمْ جَهَنَّمُ
ۚ وَبِئْسَ ٱلْمِهَادُ ﴿١٩٧﴾ لَٰكِنِ ٱلَّذِينَ ٱتَّقَوْا۟ رَبَّهُمْ لَهُمْ جَنَّٰتٌ تَجْرِى مِن تَحْتِهَا ٱلْأَنْهَٰرُ
خَٰلِدِينَ فِيهَا نُزُلًا مِّنْ عِندِ ٱللَّهِ ۗ وَمَا عِندَ ٱللَّهِ خَيْرٌ لِّلْأَبْرَارِ ﴿١٩٨﴾ وَإِنَّ مِنْ أَهْلِ

ٱلۡكِتَٰبِ لَمَن يُؤۡمِنُ بِٱللَّهِ وَمَآ أُنزِلَ إِلَيۡكُمۡ وَمَآ أُنزِلَ إِلَيۡهِمۡ خَٰشِعِينَ لِلَّهِ لَا يَشۡتَرُونَ
بِـَٔايَٰتِ ٱللَّهِ ثَمَنٗا قَلِيلًاۗ أُوْلَٰٓئِكَ لَهُمۡ أَجۡرُهُمۡ عِندَ رَبِّهِمۡۗ إِنَّ ٱللَّهَ
سَرِيعُ ٱلۡحِسَابِ ﴿١٩٩﴾ يَٰٓأَيُّهَا ٱلَّذِينَ ءَامَنُواْ ٱصۡبِرُواْ وَصَابِرُواْ وَرَابِطُواْ وَٱتَّقُواْ ٱللَّهَ
لَعَلَّكُمۡ تُفۡلِحُونَ ﴿٢٠٠﴾

Chapter (Surah) 4: An-Nisaa 001-023

بِسۡمِ ٱللَّهِ ٱلرَّحۡمَٰنِ ٱلرَّحِيمِ

يَٰٓأَيُّهَا ٱلنَّاسُ ٱتَّقُواْ رَبَّكُمُ ٱلَّذِي خَلَقَكُم مِّن نَّفۡسٖ وَٰحِدَةٖ وَخَلَقَ مِنۡهَا زَوۡجَهَا وَبَثَّ
مِنۡهُمَا رِجَالٗا كَثِيرٗا وَنِسَآءٗۚ وَٱتَّقُواْ ٱللَّهَ ٱلَّذِي تَسَآءَلُونَ بِهِۦ وَٱلۡأَرۡحَامَۚ إِنَّ ٱللَّهَ كَانَ
عَلَيۡكُمۡ رَقِيبٗا ﴿١﴾ وَءَاتُواْ ٱلۡيَتَٰمَىٰٓ أَمۡوَٰلَهُمۡۖ وَلَا تَتَبَدَّلُواْ ٱلۡخَبِيثَ بِٱلطَّيِّبِۖ وَلَا تَأۡكُلُوٓاْ
أَمۡوَٰلَهُمۡ إِلَىٰٓ أَمۡوَٰلِكُمۡۚ إِنَّهُۥ كَانَ حُوبٗا كَبِيرٗا ﴿٢﴾ وَإِنۡ خِفۡتُمۡ أَلَّا تُقۡسِطُواْ فِي ٱلۡيَتَٰمَىٰ
فَٱنكِحُواْ مَا طَابَ لَكُم مِّنَ ٱلنِّسَآءِ مَثۡنَىٰ وَثُلَٰثَ وَرُبَٰعَۖ فَإِنۡ خِفۡتُمۡ أَلَّا تَعۡدِلُواْ فَوَٰحِدَةً
أَوۡ مَا مَلَكَتۡ أَيۡمَٰنُكُمۡۚ ذَٰلِكَ أَدۡنَىٰٓ أَلَّا تَعُولُواْ ﴿٣﴾ وَءَاتُواْ ٱلنِّسَآءَ صَدُقَٰتِهِنَّ نِحۡلَةٗۚ فَإِن
طِبۡنَ لَكُمۡ عَن شَيۡءٖ مِّنۡهُ نَفۡسٗا فَكُلُوهُ هَنِيٓـٔٗا مَّرِيٓـٔٗا ﴿٤﴾ وَلَا تُؤۡتُواْ ٱلسُّفَهَآءَ أَمۡوَٰلَكُمُ ٱلَّتِي
جَعَلَ ٱللَّهُ لَكُمۡ قِيَٰمٗا وَٱرۡزُقُوهُمۡ فِيهَا وَٱكۡسُوهُمۡ وَقُولُواْ لَهُمۡ قَوۡلٗا مَّعۡرُوفٗا ﴿٥﴾ وَٱبۡتَلُواْ
ٱلۡيَتَٰمَىٰ حَتَّىٰٓ إِذَا بَلَغُواْ ٱلنِّكَاحَ فَإِنۡ ءَانَسۡتُم مِّنۡهُمۡ رُشۡدٗا فَٱدۡفَعُوٓاْ إِلَيۡهِمۡ أَمۡوَٰلَهُمۡۖ وَلَا
تَأۡكُلُوهَآ إِسۡرَافٗا وَبِدَارًا أَن يَكۡبَرُواْۚ وَمَن كَانَ غَنِيّٗا فَلۡيَسۡتَعۡفِفۡۖ وَمَن كَانَ فَقِيرٗا فَلۡيَأۡكُلۡ
بِٱلۡمَعۡرُوفِۚ فَإِذَا دَفَعۡتُمۡ إِلَيۡهِمۡ أَمۡوَٰلَهُمۡ فَأَشۡهِدُواْ عَلَيۡهِمۡۚ وَكَفَىٰ بِٱللَّهِ حَسِيبٗا ﴿٦﴾ لِّلرِّجَالِ
نَصِيبٞ مِّمَّا تَرَكَ ٱلۡوَٰلِدَانِ وَٱلۡأَقۡرَبُونَ وَلِلنِّسَآءِ نَصِيبٞ مِّمَّا تَرَكَ ٱلۡوَٰلِدَانِ وَٱلۡأَقۡرَبُونَ
مِمَّا قَلَّ مِنۡهُ أَوۡ كَثُرَۚ نَصِيبٗا مَّفۡرُوضٗا ﴿٧﴾ وَإِذَا حَضَرَ ٱلۡقِسۡمَةَ أُوْلُواْ ٱلۡقُرۡبَىٰ وَٱلۡيَتَٰمَىٰ
وَٱلۡمَسَٰكِينُ فَٱرۡزُقُوهُم مِّنۡهُ وَقُولُواْ لَهُمۡ قَوۡلٗا مَّعۡرُوفٗا ﴿٨﴾ وَلۡيَخۡشَ ٱلَّذِينَ لَوۡ تَرَكُواْ

مِنْ خَلْفِهِمْ ذُرِّيَّةً ضِعَٰفًا خَافُوا۟ عَلَيْهِمْ فَلْيَتَّقُوا۟ ٱللَّهَ وَلْيَقُولُوا۟ قَوْلًا سَدِيدًا ﴿٩﴾ إِنَّ
ٱلَّذِينَ يَأْكُلُونَ أَمْوَٰلَ ٱلْيَتَٰمَىٰ ظُلْمًا إِنَّمَا يَأْكُلُونَ فِى بُطُونِهِمْ نَارًا ۖ وَسَيَصْلَوْنَ
سَعِيرًا ﴿١٠﴾ يُوصِيكُمُ ٱللَّهُ فِىٓ أَوْلَٰدِكُمْ ۖ لِلذَّكَرِ مِثْلُ حَظِّ ٱلْأُنثَيَيْنِ ۚ فَإِن كُنَّ نِسَآءً فَوْقَ
ٱثْنَتَيْنِ فَلَهُنَّ ثُلُثَا مَا تَرَكَ ۖ وَإِن كَانَتْ وَٰحِدَةً فَلَهَا ٱلنِّصْفُ ۚ وَلِأَبَوَيْهِ لِكُلِّ وَٰحِدٍ مِّنْهُمَا
ٱلسُّدُسُ مِمَّا تَرَكَ إِن كَانَ لَهُۥ وَلَدٌ ۚ فَإِن لَّمْ يَكُن لَّهُۥ وَلَدٌ وَوَرِثَهُۥٓ أَبَوَاهُ فَلِأُمِّهِ ٱلثُّلُثُ ۚ
فَإِن كَانَ لَهُۥٓ إِخْوَةٌ فَلِأُمِّهِ ٱلسُّدُسُ ۚ مِنۢ بَعْدِ وَصِيَّةٍ يُوصِى بِهَآ أَوْ دَيْنٍ ۗ ءَابَآؤُكُمْ وَأَبْنَآؤُكُمْ
لَا تَدْرُونَ أَيُّهُمْ أَقْرَبُ لَكُمْ نَفْعًا ۚ فَرِيضَةً مِّنَ ٱللَّهِ ۗ إِنَّ ٱللَّهَ كَانَ عَلِيمًا حَكِيمًا ﴿١١﴾
۞ وَلَكُمْ نِصْفُ مَا تَرَكَ أَزْوَٰجُكُمْ إِن لَّمْ يَكُن لَّهُنَّ وَلَدٌ ۚ فَإِن كَانَ لَهُنَّ وَلَدٌ
فَلَكُمُ ٱلرُّبُعُ مِمَّا تَرَكْنَ ۚ مِنۢ بَعْدِ وَصِيَّةٍ يُوصِينَ بِهَآ أَوْ دَيْنٍ ۚ وَلَهُنَّ ٱلرُّبُعُ
مِمَّا تَرَكْتُمْ إِن لَّمْ يَكُن لَّكُمْ وَلَدٌ ۚ فَإِن كَانَ لَكُمْ وَلَدٌ فَلَهُنَّ ٱلثُّمُنُ مِمَّا تَرَكْتُم ۚ
مِّنۢ بَعْدِ وَصِيَّةٍ تُوصُونَ بِهَآ أَوْ دَيْنٍ ۗ وَإِن كَانَ رَجُلٌ يُورَثُ كَلَٰلَةً أَوِ ٱمْرَأَةٌ وَلَهُۥٓ
أَخٌ أَوْ أُخْتٌ فَلِكُلِّ وَٰحِدٍ مِّنْهُمَا ٱلسُّدُسُ ۚ فَإِن كَانُوٓا۟ أَكْثَرَ مِن ذَٰلِكَ فَهُمْ شُرَكَآءُ
فِى ٱلثُّلُثِ ۚ مِنۢ بَعْدِ وَصِيَّةٍ يُوصَىٰ بِهَآ أَوْ دَيْنٍ غَيْرَ مُضَآرٍّ ۚ وَصِيَّةً مِّنَ ٱللَّهِ ۗ وَٱللَّهُ عَلِيمٌ
حَلِيمٌ ﴿١٢﴾ تِلْكَ حُدُودُ ٱللَّهِ ۚ وَمَن يُطِعِ ٱللَّهَ وَرَسُولَهُۥ يُدْخِلْهُ جَنَّٰتٍ تَجْرِى مِن
تَحْتِهَا ٱلْأَنْهَٰرُ خَٰلِدِينَ فِيهَا ۚ وَذَٰلِكَ ٱلْفَوْزُ ٱلْعَظِيمُ ﴿١٣﴾ وَمَن يَعْصِ ٱللَّهَ
وَرَسُولَهُۥ وَيَتَعَدَّ حُدُودَهُۥ يُدْخِلْهُ نَارًا خَٰلِدًا فِيهَا وَلَهُۥ عَذَابٌ مُّهِينٌ ﴿١٤﴾ وَٱلَّٰتِى
يَأْتِينَ ٱلْفَٰحِشَةَ مِن نِّسَآئِكُمْ فَٱسْتَشْهِدُوا۟ عَلَيْهِنَّ أَرْبَعَةً مِّنكُمْ ۖ فَإِن شَهِدُوا۟
فَأَمْسِكُوهُنَّ فِى ٱلْبُيُوتِ حَتَّىٰ يَتَوَفَّىٰهُنَّ ٱلْمَوْتُ أَوْ يَجْعَلَ ٱللَّهُ لَهُنَّ سَبِيلًا ﴿١٥﴾ وَٱلَّذَانِ
يَأْتِيَٰنِهَا مِنكُمْ فَـَٔاذُوهُمَا ۖ فَإِن تَابَا وَأَصْلَحَا فَأَعْرِضُوا۟ عَنْهُمَآ ۗ إِنَّ ٱللَّهَ كَانَ
تَوَّابًا رَّحِيمًا ﴿١٦﴾ إِنَّمَا ٱلتَّوْبَةُ عَلَى ٱللَّهِ لِلَّذِينَ يَعْمَلُونَ ٱلسُّوٓءَ بِجَهَٰلَةٍ ثُمَّ يَتُوبُونَ
مِن قَرِيبٍ فَأُو۟لَٰٓئِكَ يَتُوبُ ٱللَّهُ عَلَيْهِمْ ۗ وَكَانَ ٱللَّهُ عَلِيمًا حَكِيمًا ﴿١٧﴾ وَلَيْسَتِ ٱلتَّوْبَةُ
لِلَّذِينَ يَعْمَلُونَ ٱلسَّيِّـَٔاتِ حَتَّىٰٓ إِذَا حَضَرَ أَحَدَهُمُ ٱلْمَوْتُ قَالَ إِنِّى تُبْتُ ٱلْـَٰٔنَ وَلَا

ٱلَّذِينَ يَمُوتُونَ وَهُمْ كُفَّارٌ ۚ أُو۟لَٰٓئِكَ أَعْتَدْنَا لَهُمْ عَذَابًا أَلِيمًا ﴿١٨﴾ يَٰٓأَيُّهَا ٱلَّذِينَ
ءَامَنُوا۟ لَا يَحِلُّ لَكُمْ أَن تَرِثُوا۟ ٱلنِّسَآءَ كَرْهًا ۖ وَلَا تَعْضُلُوهُنَّ لِتَذْهَبُوا۟ بِبَعْضِ مَآ
ءَاتَيْتُمُوهُنَّ إِلَّآ أَن يَأْتِينَ بِفَٰحِشَةٍ مُّبَيِّنَةٍ ۚ وَعَاشِرُوهُنَّ بِٱلْمَعْرُوفِ ۚ فَإِن كَرِهْتُمُوهُنَّ
فَعَسَىٰٓ أَن تَكْرَهُوا۟ شَيْـًٔا وَيَجْعَلَ ٱللَّهُ فِيهِ خَيْرًا كَثِيرًا ﴿١٩﴾ وَإِنْ أَرَدتُّمُ ٱسْتِبْدَالَ زَوْجٍ
مَّكَانَ زَوْجٍ وَءَاتَيْتُمْ إِحْدَىٰهُنَّ قِنطَارًا فَلَا تَأْخُذُوا۟ مِنْهُ شَيْـًٔا ۚ أَتَأْخُذُونَهُۥ بُهْتَٰنًا
وَإِثْمًا مُّبِينًا ﴿٢٠﴾ وَكَيْفَ تَأْخُذُونَهُۥ وَقَدْ أَفْضَىٰ بَعْضُكُمْ إِلَىٰ بَعْضٍ وَأَخَذْنَ
مِنكُم مِّيثَٰقًا غَلِيظًا ﴿٢١﴾ وَلَا تَنكِحُوا۟ مَا نَكَحَ ءَابَآؤُكُم مِّنَ ٱلنِّسَآءِ إِلَّا مَا قَدْ
سَلَفَ ۚ إِنَّهُۥ كَانَ فَٰحِشَةً وَمَقْتًا وَسَآءَ سَبِيلًا ﴿٢٢﴾ حُرِّمَتْ عَلَيْكُمْ أُمَّهَٰتُكُمْ
وَبَنَاتُكُمْ وَأَخَوَٰتُكُمْ وَعَمَّٰتُكُمْ وَخَٰلَٰتُكُمْ وَبَنَاتُ ٱلْأَخِ وَبَنَاتُ ٱلْأُخْتِ وَأُمَّهَٰتُكُمُ
ٱلَّٰتِىٓ أَرْضَعْنَكُمْ وَأَخَوَٰتُكُم مِّنَ ٱلرَّضَٰعَةِ وَأُمَّهَٰتُ نِسَآئِكُمْ وَرَبَٰٓئِبُكُمُ ٱلَّٰتِى فِى
حُجُورِكُم مِّن نِّسَآئِكُمُ ٱلَّٰتِى دَخَلْتُم بِهِنَّ فَإِن لَّمْ تَكُونُوا۟ دَخَلْتُم بِهِنَّ فَلَا جُنَاحَ
عَلَيْكُمْ وَحَلَٰٓئِلُ أَبْنَآئِكُمُ ٱلَّذِينَ مِنْ أَصْلَٰبِكُمْ وَأَن تَجْمَعُوا۟ بَيْنَ ٱلْأُخْتَيْنِ إِلَّا
مَا قَدْ سَلَفَ ۗ إِنَّ ٱللَّهَ كَانَ غَفُورًا رَّحِيمًا ﴿٢٣﴾

INTRODUCTION TO CHAPTER (SURAH) 3: AL-I-'IMRAN (THE FAMILY OF IMRAN)

Maududi's Introduction

Name

This Surah takes its name from v. 33. Al-i-Imran, like the names of many other surahs, is merely a name to distinguish it from other surahs and does not imply that the family of Imran has been discussed in it.

The Period of Revelation

This Surah consists of four discourses The first discourses :-

The first discourse (vv. 1-32) was probably revealed soon after the Battle of Badr.

The second discourse (vv. 33-63) was revealed in 9 A. H. on the occasion of the visit of the deputation from the Christians of Najran.

The third discourse (vv. 64-120) appears to have been revealed immediately after the first one.

The fourth discourse (vv. 121-200) was revealed after the Battle of Uhd.

Subject

Though these discourses were revealed at different periods and on different occasions, they are so inter-linked and so inter-connected iii regard to their aim, object and central theme that they make together one continuous whole. This Surah has been especially addressed to two groups-the people of the Book (the Jews and the Christians) and the followers of Muhammad (Allah's peace be upon him).

The message has been extended to the Jews and the Christians in continuation of the invitation in Al-Baqarah, in which they have been admonished for their erroneous beliefs and evil morals and advised to accept, as a remedy, the Truth of the Quran. They have been told here that Muhammad (Allah's peace be, upon him) taught the same right way of life that had been preached by their own Prophets; that it alone was the Right Way, the way of Allah; hence any deviation from it will be wrong even according to their own Scriptures.

The second group, the Muslims, who had been declared to be the best Community in Al-Baqarah and appointed torch-bearers of the Truth and entrusted with the responsibility of reforming the world, have been given additional instructions in continuation of those given in the preceding Surah. The Muslims have been warned to learn a lesson from the religious and moral degeneration of the former communities and to refrain from treading in their footsteps. Instructions have also been given about the reformative work they had to perform. Besides this, they have been taught how to deal with the people of the Book and the hypocrites who were putting different kinds of hindrances in the way of Allah. Above all, they have been warned to guard against those weaknesses which had come to the surface in the Battle Uhd.

Background

The following is the background of the Surah:

1. The Believers had met with all sorts of trials and hardships about which they had been forewarned in Al- Baqarah. Though they had come out victorious in the Battle of Badr, they were not out of danger yet. Their victory had aroused the enmity of all those powers in Arabia which were opposed to the Islamic Movement. Signs of threatening storms had begun to appear on all sides and the Muslims were in a perpetual state of fear and anxiety. It looked as if the whole Arabian world around the tiny state of Al- Madinah -- which was no more than a village state at that time -- was bent upon blotting out its very existence. This state of war was also adversely affecting its economy, which had already been badly disturbed by the influx of the Muslim refugees from Makkah.

2. Then there was the disturbing problem of the Jewish clans who lived in the suburbs of Al-Madinah. They were discarding the treaties of alliance they had made with the Holy Prophet after his migration from Makkah. So much so that on the occasion of the Battle of Badr, these people of the Book sympathized with the evil aims of the idolaters, in spite of the fact that their fundamental articles of the Faith -- Oneness of Allah, Prophethood, Life-after- death -- were

the same as those of the Muslims. After the Battle of Badr, they openly began to incite the Quraish and other Arab clans to wreak their vengeance on the Muslims. Thus those Jewish clans set aside their centuries-old friendly and neighborly relations with the people of Al-Madinah. At last when their mischievous actions and breaches of treaties became unbearable, the Holy Prophet attacked the Bani- Qainu-qa'a, the most mischievous of all the other Jewish clans who had conspired with the hypocrites of Al-Madinah and the idolatrous Arab clans to encircle the Believers on all sides. The magnitude of the peril might be judged from the fact that even the life of the Holy Prophet himself was always in danger. Therefore his Companions slept in their armors during that period and kept watch at night to guard against any sudden attack, and whenever the Holy Prophet happened to be out of sight even for a short while, they would at once set out in search of him.

3. This incitement by the Jews added fuel to the fire which was burning in the hearts of the Quraish and they began to make preparations to avenge the defeat they had suffered at Bad. A year after this an army of 3,000 strong marched out of Makkah to invade Al-Madinah and a battle took place at the foot of Mount Uhd. The Holy Prophet came out of Al-Madinah with one thousand men to meet the enemy. While they were marching to the battle-field, three hundred hypocrites deserted the army and returned to Al-Madinah, but there still remained a small band of hypocrites among the seven hundred who accompanied the Holy Prophet. They played their part and did their worst to create mischief and chaos in the ranks of the Believers during the Battle. This was the first clear indication of the fact that within the fold of the Muslim Community there was quite a large number of saboteurs who were always ready to conspire with the external enemies to harm their own brethren.

4. Though the devices of the hypocrites had played a great part in the set-back at Uhd, the weaknesses of the Muslims themselves contributed no less to it. And it was but natural that the Muslims should show signs of moral weakness for they were a new community which had only recently been formed on a new ideology and had not as yet got a thorough moral training. Naturally in this second hard test of their physical and moral strength, some weaknesses came to the surface. That is why a detailed review of the Battle of Uhd was needed to warn the Muslims of their shortcomings and to issue instructions for their reform. It should also be noted that this review of the Battle is quite different from the reviews that are usually made by generals on similar occasions.

Subject: Guidance

This Surah is the sequel to, Al-Baqarah and the invitation therein is continued to the people of the Book. In Al- Baqarah the Jews were pointedly invited to accept the Guidance and in this Surah the Christians have particularly been admonished to give up their erroneous beliefs and accept the Guidance of the Quran. At the same time, the Muslims have been instructed to nourish the virtues that may enable them to carry out their obligations and spread the Divine Guidance.

Topics and their Interconnection

In these introductory verses, the fundamental truths about Allah, Revelation and Life-after-death have been reiterated to serve as fitting preliminaries, leading to the main topics discussed in the Surah. **1 - 32**

This discourse is particularly addressed to the Christians and invites them to accept Islam. It clears Jesus and his mother not only from the stigma maliciously set upon them by the Jews, but also refutes the erroneous Christian creed of the Divinity of Jesus which had been formulated because of his miraculous birth. For this purpose the instances of John the Baptist to a barren woman and an extremely aged man and that of Adam without father and mother have been cited to show that there is nothing in the birth of Jesus without a father to entitle him to Divinity. **33 - 65**

In these verses the people of the Book, the Jews, have been invited to give up their sinister ways and accept the divine Guidance. At the same time the Muslims have been warned to be on their guard against their malicious intentions, erroneous ways and absurd objections. **66 - 101**

The Muslims have been instructed to learn lessons from the history of the people of the Book and also to guard themselves against their machinations, and to prepare and train themselves to establish virtue and eradicate evil. **102 - 120**

In this portion, a review of the Battle of Uhd has been mad to teach and reassure the Muslims that the machinations of their enemies could do them no harm, if they would practise restraint and fortitude and have fear of Allah. It has been pointed out that the set-back they had suffered was due to the lack of some moral qualities and the existence of some evils. Since the main cause of the defeat was the greed of the archers, guarding the pass, the taking of interest has been prohibited to eradicate this evil. **121 - 175**

The main theme of the verses **109 - 120** has been resumed to reassure and encourage the Muslims against the dangerous plots of their enemies. **175 - 189**

This is the conclusion of the Surah and is not directly connected with the verses immediately preceding it but with the theme of the Surah as a whole. **190 - 200**

Ibn Kathir's Introduction

Surah Al `Imran was revealed in Al-Madinah, as evident by the fact that the first eighty-three Ayat in it relate to the delegation from Najran that arrived in Al-Madinah on the ninth year of Hijrah (632 CE). We will elaborate on this subject when we explain the Ayah about the Mubahalah (3:61) in this Surah, Allah willing. We should also state that we mentioned the virtues of Surah Al `Imran along with the virtues of Surat Al-Baqarah in the beginning of the Tafsir of Surat Al-Baqarah

CHAPTER (SURAH) 3: AL-I-'IMRAN (THE FAMILY OF 'IMRAN), VERSES 093-200

Surah: 3 Ayah: 93, Ayah: 94 & Ayah: 95

﴿ ۞ كُلُّ ٱلطَّعَامِ كَانَ حِلًّا لِّبَنِىٓ إِسْرَٰٓءِيلَ إِلَّا مَا حَرَّمَ إِسْرَٰٓءِيلُ عَلَىٰ نَفْسِهِۦ مِن قَبْلِ أَن
تُنَزَّلَ ٱلتَّوْرَىٰةُ ۗ قُلْ فَأْتُوا۟ بِٱلتَّوْرَىٰةِ فَٱتْلُوهَآ إِن كُنتُمْ صَـٰدِقِينَ ﴿٩٣﴾ ﴾

93. All food was lawful to the Children of Israel, except what Israel made unlawful for himself before the Taurât (Torah) was revealed. Say (O Muhammad (peace be upon him)) "Bring here the Taurât (Torah) and recite it, if you are truthful."

﴿ فَمَنِ ٱفْتَرَىٰ عَلَى ٱللَّهِ ٱلْكَذِبَ مِنۢ بَعْدِ ذَٰلِكَ فَأُو۟لَـٰٓئِكَ هُمُ ٱلظَّـٰلِمُونَ ﴿٩٤﴾ ﴾

94. Then after that, whosoever shall invent a lie against Allâh, ... such shall indeed be the Zâlimûn (disbelievers).

﴿ قُلْ صَدَقَ ٱللَّهُ ۗ فَٱتَّبِعُوا۟ مِلَّةَ إِبْرَٰهِيمَ حَنِيفًا وَمَا كَانَ مِنَ ٱلْمُشْرِكِينَ ﴿٩٥﴾ ﴾

95. Say (O Muhammad (peace be upon him)) "Allâh has spoken the truth; follow the religion of Ibrâhim (Abraham) Hanifa (Islâmic Monotheism, i.e. he used to worship Allâh Alone), and he was not of Al-Mushrikûn." (See V.2:105)

Transliteration

93. Kullu alttaAAami kana hillan libanee isra-eela illa ma harrama isra-eelu AAala nafsihi min qabli an tunazzala alttawratu qul fa/too bialttawrati faotlooha in kuntum sadiqeena 94. Famani iftara AAala Allahi alkathiba min baAAdi thalika faola-ika humu althalimoona 95. Qul sadaqa Allahu faittabiAAoo millata ibraheema haneefan wama kana mina almushrikeena

Tafsir Ibn Kathir

The Questions that the Jews Asked Our Prophet

Imam Ahmad recorded that Ibn `Abbas said, "A group of Jews came to Allah's Prophet and said, `Talk to us about some things we will ask you and which only a Prophet would know.' He said, `Ask me about whatever you wish. However, give your pledge to Allah, similar to the pledge that Ya`qub took from his children, that if I tell you something and you recognize its truth, you will follow me in Islam.' They said, `Agreed.' The Prophet said, `Ask me about whatever you wish.' They said, `Tell us about four matters: 1. What kinds of food did Isra'il prohibit for himself 2. What about the sexual discharge of the woman and the man, and what role does each play in producing male or female offspring 3. Tell us about the condition of the unlettered Prophet during sleep, 4. And who is his Wali (supporter) among the angels' The Prophet took their covenant that they will follow him if he answers these questions, and they agreed. He said, `I ask you by He Who sent down the Tawrah to Musa, do you not know that Isra'il once became very ill When his illness was prolonged, he vowed to Allah that if He cures His illness, he would prohibit the best types of drink and food for himself. Was not the best food to him camel meat and the best drink camel milk' They said, `Yes, by Allah.' The Messenger said, `O Allah, be Witness against them.' The Prophet then said, `I ask you by Allah, other than Whom there is no deity (worthy of worship), Who sent down the Tawrah to

Musa, do you not know that man's discharge is thick and white and woman's is yellow and thin If any of these fluids becomes dominant, the offspring will take its sex and resemblance by Allah's leave. Hence, if the man's is more than the woman's, the child will be male, by Allah's leave. If the woman's discharge is more than the man's, then the child will be female, by Allah's leave.' They said, `Yes.' He said, `O Allah, be Witness against them.' He then said, `I ask you by He Who sent down the Tawrah to Musa, do you not know that the eyes of this unlettered Prophet sleep, but his heart does not sleep' They said, `Yes, by Allah!' He said, `O Allah, be Witness.' They said, `Tell us now about your Wali among the angels, for this is when we either follow or shun you.' He said, `My Wali (who brings down the revelation from Allah) is Jibril, and Allah never sent a Prophet, but Jibril is his Wali.' They said, `We then shun you. Had you a Wali other than Jibril, we would have followed you.' On that, Allah, the Exalted revealed,

(Say: "Whoever is an enemy to Jibril...") (2:97)."

Allah's statement,

(before the Tawrah was revealed) (3:93), means, Isra'il forbade that for himself before the Tawrah was revealed. There are two objectives behind revealing this segment of the Ayah. First, he forbade himself the most delightful things for Allah's sake. This practice was allowed during his period of Law, and is, thus, suitable that it is mentioned after Allah's statement,

(By no means shall you attain Al-Birr, unless you spend of that which you love) (3: 92).

What we are allowed in our Law is to spend in Allah's obedience from what we like and covet (but not to prohibit what Allah has allowed). Allah said in other Ayat;

(And gives his wealth, in spite of love for it,) (2:177), and;

(And they give food, in spite of their love for it,) (76:8).

The second reason is that after Allah refuted the false Christian beliefs and allegations about `Isa and his mother. Allah started refuting the Jews here, may Allah curse them, by stating that the abrogation of the Law, that they denied occurs, already occurred in their Law. For instance, Allah has stated in their Book, the Tawrah, that when Nuh departed from the ark, Allah allowed him to eat the meat of all types of animals. Afterwards, Isra'il forbade the meat and milk of camels for himself, and his children imitated this practice after him. The Tawrah later on prohibited this type of food, and added several more types of prohibitions. Allah allowed Adam to marry his daughters to his sons, and this practice was later forbidden. The Law of Ibrahim allowed the man to take female servants as companions along with his wife, as Ibrahim did when he took Hajar, while he was married to Sarah. Later on, the Tawrah prohibited this practice. It was previously allowed to take two sisters as wives at the same time, as Ya`qub married two sisters at the same time. Later on, this practice was prohibited in the Tawrah. All these examples are in the Tawrah and constitute a Naskh (abrogation) of the Law. Therefore, let the Jews consider what Allah legislated for `Isa and if such legislation falls under the category of abrogation or not. Why do they not then follow `Isa in this regard Rather, the Jews defied and rebelled against `Isa and against the correct religion that Allah sent Muhammad with.

This is why Allah said,

(All food was lawful to the Children of Israel, except what Isra'il made unlawful for himself before the Tawrah was revealed) (3:93) meaning, before the Tawrah was revealed, all types of foods were allowed, except what Isra'il prohibited for himself. Allah then said,

(Say: "Bring here the Tawrah and recite it, if you are truthful."),

for the Tawrah affirms what we are stating here. Allah said next,

(Then after that, whosoever shall invent a lie against Allah, then these it is that are the wrongdoers.) (3:94), in reference to those who lie about Allah and claim that He made the Sabbath and the Tawrah eternal. They are those who claim that Allah did not send another Prophet calling to Allah with the proofs and evidences, although evidence indicates that abrogation, as we have described, occurred before in the Tawrah,

(then these it is that are the wrongdoers.)

Allah then said,

(Say, "Allah has spoken the truth;") (3:95) meaning, O Muhammad, say that Allah has said the truth in what He conveyed and legislated in the Qur'an,

(follow the religion of Ibrahim the Hanif, and he was not of the idolators.") (3:95).

Therefore, follow the religion of Ibrahim that Allah legislated in the Qur'an. Indeed, this is the truth, there is no doubt in it, and the perfect way, and no Prophet has brought a more complete, clear, plain and perfect way than he did. Allah said in other Ayat,

(Say: "Truly, my Lord has guided me to a straight path, a right religion, the religion of Ibrahim, the Hanif, and he was not of the idolators.") (6:161)

and,

(Then, We have sent the revelation to you (saying): "Follow the religion of Ibrahim, the Hanif, and he was not of the idolaters.) (16:123).

Surah: 3 Ayah: 96 & Ayah: 97

﴿إِنَّ أَوَّلَ بَيْتٍ وُضِعَ لِلنَّاسِ لَلَّذِى بِبَكَّةَ مُبَارَكًا وَهُدًى لِّلْعَـٰلَمِينَ ﴿٩٦﴾﴾

96. Verily, the first House (of worship) appointed for mankind was that at Bakkah (Makkah), full of blessing, and a guidance for Al-'Alamîn (the mankind and jinn).

﴿فِيهِ ءَايَـٰتٌۢ بَيِّنَـٰتٌ مَّقَامُ إِبْرَٰهِيمَ ۖ وَمَن دَخَلَهُۥ كَانَ ءَامِنًا ۗ وَلِلَّهِ عَلَى ٱلنَّاسِ حِجُّ ٱلْبَيْتِ مَنِ
ٱسْتَطَاعَ إِلَيْهِ سَبِيلًا ۚ وَمَن كَفَرَ فَإِنَّ ٱللَّهَ غَنِىٌّ عَنِ ٱلْعَـٰلَمِينَ ﴿٩٧﴾﴾

97. In it are manifest signs (for example), the Maqâm (place) of Ibrâhim (Abraham); whosoever enters it, he attains security. And Hajj (pilgrimage to Makkah) to the House (Ka'bah) is a duty that mankind owes to Allâh, those who can afford the expenses (for one's conveyance, provision and residence); and whoever disbelieves (i.e. denies Hajj (pilgrimage to Makkah), then he is a disbeliever of Allâh), then Allâh stands not in need of any of the 'Alamîn (mankind, jinn and all that exists).

Transliteration

96. Inna awwala baytin wudiAAa lilnnasi lallathee bibakkata mubarakan wahudan lilAAalameena 97. Feehi ayatun bayyinatun maqamu ibraheema waman dakhalahu kana aminan walillahi AAala alnnasi hijju albayti mani istataAAa ilayhi sabeelan waman kafara fa-inna Allaha ghaniyyun AAani alAAalameena

Tafsir Ibn Kathir

The Ka`bah is the First House of Worship

Allah said,

(Verily, the first House appointed for mankind) for all people, for their acts of worship and religious rituals. They go around the House (in Tawaf), pray in its vicinity and remain in its area in I`tikaf.

(was that at Bakkah,) meaning, the Ka`bah that was built by Ibrahim Al-Khalil, whose religion the Jews and Christians claim they follow. However, they do not perform Hajj to the house that Ibrahim built by Allah's command, and to which he invited the people to perform Hajj. Allah said next, i

(full of blessing), sanctified,

(and a guidance for Al-`Alamin.)

Imam Ahmad recorded that Abu Dharr said; "I said, `O Allah's Messenger! Which Masjid was the first to be built on the surface of the earth' He said, `Al-Masjid Al-Haram (in Makkah).' I said, `Which was built next' He replied `Al-Masjid Al-Aqsa (in Jerusalem).' I said, `What was the period of time between building the two' He said, `Forty years.' He added,

«ثُمَّ حَيْثُ أَدْرَكْتَ الصَّلَاةَ فَصَلِّ، فَكُلُّهَا مَسْجِد»

(Wherever (you may be, and) the prayer becomes due, perform the prayer there, for the whole earth was made a Masjid.)" Al-Bukhari and Muslim also collected this Hadith.

The Names of Makkah, Such As `Bakkah

Allah said,

(was that at Bakkah), where Bakkah is one of the names of Makkah. Bakkah means, `it brings Buka' (crying, weeping) to the tyrants and arrogant, meaning they cry and become humble in its vicinity. It was also said that Makkah was called Bakkah because people do Buka next to it, meaning they gather around it. There are many names for Makkah, such as Bakkah, Al-Bayt Al-`Atiq (the Ancient House), Al-Bayt Al-Haram (the Sacred House), Al-Balad Al-Amin (the City of Safety) and Al-Ma'mun (Security). Makkah's names include Umm Rahm (Mother of Mercy), Umm Al-Qura (Mother of the Towns), Salah, (as well as others).

The Station of Ibrahim

Allah's statement,

(In it are manifest signs) (3:97), means, clear signs that Ibrahim built the Ka`bah and that Allah has honored and blessed it. Allah then said,

(the Maqam (station) of Ibrahim) When the building (the Ka`bah) was raised, Ibrahim stood on; the Maqam so that he could raise the walls higher, while his son Isma`il was handing the stones to him. We should mention that the Maqam used to be situated right next to the House. Later, and during his reign, `Umar bin Al-Khattab moved the Maqam farther to the east, so that those who go around the House in Tawaf are able to perform it easily, without disturbing those who pray next to the Maqam after finishing their Tawaf. Allah commanded us to pray next to the Maqam;

(And take you (people) the Maqam (station) of Ibrahim as a place of prayer) (2:125).

We mentioned the Hadiths about this subject before, and all the thanks are due to Allah. Al-`Awfi said that, Ibn `Abbas commented on Allah's statement,

(In it are manifest signs, the Maqam of Ibrahim;)

"Such as the Maqam and Al-Mash`ar (Al-Haram)." Mujahid said, "The impression of Ibrahim's feet remains on the Maqam as a clear sign." It was reported that `Umar bin `Abdul-`Aziz, Al-Hasan, Qatadah, As-Suddi, Muqatil bin Hayyan and others said similarly.

Al-Haram, the Sacred Area, is a Safe Area

Allah said,

(whosoever enters it, he attains security,) (3:97) meaning, the Haram of Makkah is a safe refuge for those in a state of fear. There in its vicinity, they will be safe, just as was the case during the time of Jahiliyyah. Al-Hasan Al-Basri said, "(During the time of Jahiliyyah) a man would commit murder, then wear a piece of wool around his neck and enter the Haram. And even when the son of the murdered person would meet him, he would not make a move against him, until he left the sanctuary." Allah said,

(Have they not seen that We have made (Makkah) a secure sanctuary, while men are being snatched away from all around them) (29:67), and,

(So let them worship (Allah) the Lord of this House (the Ka`bah). (He) Who has fed them against hunger, and has made them safe from fear) (106:3-4).

It is not allowed for anyone to hunt in the Haram or to drive game out of its den to be hunted, or cut the trees in its vicinity, or pick its grass, as the Hadiths of the Prophet and the statements of the Companions testify. The Two Sahihs recorded (this being the wording of Muslim) that Ibn `Abbas said, "On the day of the conquest of Makkah, the Messenger of Allah said,

«لَا هِجْرَةَ، وَلَـــكِنْ جِهَادٌ وَنِيَّـــةٌ، وَإِذَا اسْتُنْفِرْتُمْ فَانْفِرُوا»

(There is no more Hijrah (migration to Makkah), only Jihad and good intention. If you were mobilized, then march forth.)

He also said on the day of the conquest of Makkah,

«إِنَّ هَذَا الْبَلَدَ حَرَّمَهُ اللهُ يَوْمَ خَلَقَ السَّموات وَالْأَرْضَ، فَهُوَ حَرَامٌ بِحُرْمَةِ اللهِ إِلى يَوْمِ الْقِيَامَةِ، وَإِنَّهُ لَمْ يَحِلَّ الْقِتَالُ فِيهِ لِأَحَدٍ قَبْلِي، وَلَمْ يَحِلَّ لِي إِلَّا فِي سَاعَةٍ مِنْ نَهَارٍ، فَهُوَ حَرَامٌ بِحُرْمَةِ اللهِ إِلَى يَوْمِ الْقِيَامَةِ، لَا يُعْضَدُ شَوْكُهُ، وَلَا يُنَفَّرُ صَيْدُهُ، وَلَا يَلْتَقِطُ لُقَطَتَهَا إِلَّا مَنْ عَرَّفَهَا، وَلَا يُخْتَلَى خَلَاهَا»

(Beware! Allah made this town (Makkah) a sanctuary when He created the heavens and earth, and it is sacred by Allah's decree until the Day of Resurrection. Fighting in Makkah was not permitted for anyone before me, and it was made legal for me for only a few hours or so on that day. No doubt it is at this moment a sanctuary by Allah's decree until the Day of Resurrection. It is not allowed to uproot its thorny shrubs, hunt its game, pick up its lost objects, except by announcing it, or to uproot its trees.)

Al-`Abbas said, `Except the lemon grass, O Allah's Messenger, as they use it in their houses and graves.' The Prophet said:

«إِلَّا الْإِذْخِرِ»

(Except lemongrass)."

The Two Sahihs also recorded that Abu Shurayh Al-`Adawi said that he said to `Amr bin Sa`id while he was sending the troops to Makkah (to fight `Abdullah bin Az-Zubayr), "O Commander! Allow me to tell you what Allah's Messenger said on the day following the conquest of Makkah. My ears heard it and my heart memorized it thoroughly, and I saw the Prophet with my own eyes when he, after glorifying and praising Allah, said,

«إِنَّ مَكَّةَ حَرَّمَهَا اللهُ، وَلَمْ يُحَرِّمْهَا النَّاسُ، فَلَا يَحِلُّ لِامْرِى يُؤْمِنُ بِاللهِ وَالْيَوْمِ الْآخِرِ أَنْ يَسْفِكَ بِهَا دَمًا، وَلَا يَعْضِدَ بِهَا شَجَرَةً، فَإِنْ أَحَدٌ تَرَخَّصَ بِقِتَالِ رَسُولِ اللهصلى الله عليه وسلّم فِيهَا فَقُولُوا لَهُ: إِنَّ اللهَ أَذِنَ لِرَسُولِهِ وَلَمْ يَأْذَنْ لَكُمْ، وَإِنَّمَا أَذِنَ لِي فِيهَا سَاعَةً مِنْ نَهَارٍ، وَقَدْ عَادَتْ حُرْمَتُهَا الْيَوْمَ كَحُرْمَتِهَا بِالْأَمْسِ فَلْيُبَلِّغِ الشَّاهِدُ الْغَائِب»

(Allah, not the people, made Makkah a sanctuary. Therefore, anybody who has belief in Allah and the Last Day, should neither shed blood in it nor cut down its trees. If anybody argues that fighting in it is permissible on the basis that Allah's Messenger fought in Makkah, say to him, `Allah allowed His Messenger and did not allow you.' Allah allowed me only for a few hours on that day (of the conquest), and today its sanctity is as valid as it was before. So, those who are present, should inform those who are absent of this fact.)."

Abu Shurayh was asked, "What did `Amr reply" He said that `Amr said, "O Abu Shurayh! I know better than you in this respect; Makkah does not give protection to a sinner, a murderer or a thief."

Jabir bin `Abdullah said, "I heard the Messenger of Allah saying,

«لَا يَحِلُّ لِأَحَدِكُمْ أَنْ يَحْمِلَ بِمَكَّةَ السِّلَاحِ»

(None of you is allowed to carry a weapon in Makkah.) Muslim recorded this Hadith.

`Abdullah bin `Adi bin Al-Hamra' Az-Zuhri said that he heard the Messenger of Allah say while standing at Al-Hazwarah in the marketplace of Makkah,

«وَاللهِ إِنَّكِ لَخَيْرُ أَرْضِ اللهِ، وَأَحَبُّ أَرْضِ اللهِ إِلَى اللهِ، وَلَوْلَا أَنِّي أُخْرِجْتُ مِنْكِ مَا خَرَجْت»

(By Allah! You are the best of Allah's land and the most beloved land to Allah. Had it not been for the fact that I was driven out of you, I would not have left you.)

Imam Ahmad collected this Hadith and this is his wording. At-Tirmidhi, An-Nasa'i and Ibn Majah also collected it. At-Tirmidhi said, "Hasan Sahih."

The Necessity of Performing Hajj

Allah said,

(And Hajj to the House is a duty that mankind owes to Allah, for those who are able to undertake the journey) (3:97).

This Ayah established the obligation of performing Hajj. There are many Hadiths that mention it as one of the pillars and fundamentals of Islam, and this is agreed upon by the Muslims. According to texts and the consensus of the scholars, it is only obligatory for the adult Muslim to perform it once during his lifetime. Imam Ahmad recorded that Abu Hurayrah said that the Messenger of Allah once gave a speech in which he said,

«أَيُّهَا النَّاسُ قَدْ فُرِضَ عَلَيْكُمُ الْحَجُّ فَحُجُّوا»

(O people! Hajj has been enjoined on you, therefore, perform Hajj.)

A man asked, "Is it every year, O Allah's Messenger" The Prophet remained silent until the man repeated the question three times and he then said,

«لَوْ قُلْتُ: نَعَمْ لَوَجَبَتْ وَلَمَا اسْتَطَعْتُم»

(Had I said yes, it would have become an obligation and you would not have been able to fulfill it.) He said next,

«ذَرُونِي مَا تَرَكْتُكُمْ فَإِنَّمَا هَلَكَ مَنْ كَانَ قَبْلَكُمْ بِكَثْرَةِ سُؤَالِهِمْ وَاخْتِلَافِهِمْ عَلَى أَنْبِيَائِهِمْ، وَإِذَا أَمَرْتُكُمْ بِشَيْءٍ فَأْتُوا مِنْهُ مَا اسْتَطَعْتُمْ، وَإِذَا نَهَيْتُكُمْ عَنْ شَيْءٍ فَدَعُوه»

(Leave me as I leave you, those before you were destroyed because of their many questions and disputing with their Prophets. If I command you with something, perform it as much as you can. If I forbid something for you, then refrain from it.) Muslim recorded similarly.

Meaning of `Afford' in the Ayah

There are several categories of "the ability to under take the journey". There is the physical ability of the person himself and the ability that is related to other things as mentioned in the books of jurisprudence. Abu `Isa At-Tirmidhi recorded that Ibn `Umar said, "A man stood up and asked the Messenger of Allah , `O Messenger of Allah! Who is the pilgrim' He said, `He who has untidy hair and clothes.' Another man asked, `Which Hajj is better, O Messenger of Allah' He said, `The noisy (with supplication to Allah) and bloody (with sacrifice).' Another man asked, `What is the ability to undertake the journey, O Messenger of Allah' He said, `Having provision and a means of transportation."' This is the narration that Ibn Majah collected. Al-Hakim narrated that Anas said that the Messenger of Allah was asked about Allah's statement,

(for those who are able to undertake the journey;) (3:97) "What does `able to undertake the journey' mean" The Prophet answered, "Having sufficient provision and a means of transportation." Al-Hakim stated that this Hadith's chain of narration is authentic, following the guidelines of Muslim in his Sahih, but the Two Sahihs did not collect it. Ahmad recorded that Ibn `Abbas said that the Messenger of Allah said,

«مَنْ أَرَادَ الْحَجَّ فَلْيَتَعَجَّل»

(Whoever intends to perform Hajj, let him rush to perform it.) Abu Dawud also collected this Hadith.

The One who Denies the Necessity of Hajj Becomes a Disbeliever

Allah said,

(...and whoever disbelieves, then Allah stands not in need of any of the `Alamin) (3:97).

Ibn `Abbas, Mujahid and several others commented on this Ayah, "Whoever denies the necessity of Hajj becomes disbeliever, and Allah is far Richer than to need him." Al-Hafiz Abu Bakr Al-Isma`ili recorded that `Umar bin Al-Khattab said, "Whoever can afford Hajj but did not perform it, there is no difference in his case if he dies while Jew or Christian." This has an authentic chain of narration leading to `Umar.

Surah: 3 Ayah: 98 & Ayah: 99

﴿ قُلْ يَـٰٓأَهْلَ ٱلْكِتَـٰبِ لِمَ تَكْفُرُونَ بِـَٔايَـٰتِ ٱللَّهِ وَٱللَّهُ شَهِيدٌ عَلَىٰ مَا تَعْمَلُونَ ﴿٩٨﴾ ﴾

98. Say: "O people of the Scripture (Jews and Christians)! Why do you reject the Ayât of Allâh (proofs, evidences, verses, lessons, signs, revelations, etc.) while Allâh is Witness to what you do?"

﴿ قُلْ يَـٰٓأَهْلَ ٱلْكِتَـٰبِ لِمَ تَصُدُّونَ عَن سَبِيلِ ٱللَّهِ مَنْ ءَامَنَ تَبْغُونَهَا عِوَجًا وَأَنتُمْ شُهَدَآءُ ۗ وَمَا ٱللَّهُ بِغَـٰفِلٍ عَمَّا تَعْمَلُونَ ﴿٩٩﴾ ﴾

99. Say: "O people of the Scripture (Jews and Christians)! Why do you stop those who have believed, from the Path of Allâh, seeking to make it seem crooked, while you (yourselves) are witnesses (to Muhammad (peace be upon him) as a Messenger of Allâh and Islâm (Allâh's Religion, i.e. to worship none but Him Alone)) And Allâh is not unaware of what you do."

Transliteration

98. Qul ya ahla alkitabi lima takfuroona bi-ayati Allahi waAllahu shaheedun AAala ma taAAmaloona 99. Qul ya ahla alkitabi lima tasuddoona AAan sabeeli Allahi man amana tabghoonaha AAiwajan waantum shuhadao wama Allahu bighafilin AAamma taAAmaloona

Tafsir Ibn Kathir

Chastising the People of the Book for Their Disbelief and Blocking the Path of Allah

In this Ayah Allah criticizes the disbelieving People of the Book for refusing the truth, rejecting Allah's Ayat and hindering those who seek to believe from His path, although they know that what the Messenger was sent with is the truth from Allah. They learned this from the previous Prophets and honorable Messengers, may Allah's peace and blessings be on them all. They all brought the glad tidings and the good news of the coming of the unlettered, Arab, Hashimi Prophet from Makkah, the master of the Children of Adam, the Final Prophet and the Messenger of the Lord of heavens and earth. Allah has warned the People of the Book against this behavior, stating that He is Witness over what they do, indicating their defiance of the knowledge conveyed to them by the Prophets. They rejected, denied and refused the very Messenger whom they were ordered to convey the glad tidings about his coming. Allah states that He is never unaware of what they do, and He will hold them responsible for their actions,

(The Day whereon neither wealth nor sons will avail) (26:88).

Surah: 3 Ayah: 100 & Ayah: 101

﴿ يَـٰٓأَيُّهَا ٱلَّذِينَ ءَامَنُوٓا۟ إِن تُطِيعُوا۟ فَرِيقًا مِّنَ ٱلَّذِينَ أُوتُوا۟ ٱلْكِتَـٰبَ يَرُدُّوكُم بَعْدَ إِيمَـٰنِكُمْ كَـٰفِرِينَ ﴿١٠٠﴾ ﴾

100. O you who believe! If you obey a group of those who were given the Scripture (Jews and Christians), they would (indeed) render you disbelievers after you have believed!

﴿ وَكَيْفَ تَكْفُرُونَ وَأَنتُمْ تُتْلَىٰ عَلَيْكُمْ ءَايَـٰتُ ٱللَّهِ وَفِيكُمْ رَسُولُهُۥ ۗ وَمَن يَعْتَصِم بِٱللَّهِ فَقَدْ هُدِىَ إِلَىٰ صِرَٰطٍ مُّسْتَقِيمٍ ﴿١٠١﴾ ﴾

101. And how would you disbelieve, while unto you are recited the Verses of Allâh, and among you is His Messenger (Muhammad (peace be upon him)) And whoever holds firmly to Allâh, (i.e. follows Islâm - Allâh's Religion, and obeys all that Allâh has ordered, practically), then he is indeed guided to the Right Path.

Transliteration

100. Ya ayyuha allatheena amanoo in tuteeAAoo fareeqan mina allatheena ootoo alkitabu yaruddookum baAAda eemanikum kafireena 101. Wakayfa takfuroona waantum tutla AAalaykum ayatu Allahi wafeekum rasooluhu waman yaAAtasim biAllahi faqad hudiya ila siratin mustaqeemin

Tafsir Ibn Kathir

Warning Muslims Against Imitating People of the Scriptures

Allah warns His believing servants against obeying the People of the Book, who envy the believers for the favor that Allah gave them by sending His Messenger . Similarly, Allah said,

(Many of the People of the Scripture (Jews and Christians) wish that they could turn you away as disbelievers after you have believed, out of their own envy) (2:109).

In this Ayah (3:100), Allah said,

(If you obey a group of those who were given the Scripture (Jews and Christians), they would (indeed) render you disbelievers after you have believed!), then said,

(And how would you disbelieve, while unto you are recited the verses of Allah, and among you is His Messenger), meaning, disbelief is far from touching you, since the Ayat of Allah are being sent down on His Messenger day and night, and he recites and conveys them to you. Similarly, Allah said,

(And what is the matter with you that you believe not in Allah! While the Messenger invites you to believe in your Lord; and He has indeed taken your covenant, if you are real believers) (57:8). A Hadith states that one day, the Prophet said to his Companions,

«أَيُّ الْمُؤْمِنِينَ أَعْجَبُ إِلَيْكُمْ إِيمَانًا؟»

("Who among the faithful believers do you consider has the most amazing faith" They said, "The angels." He said,

«وَكَيْفَ لَا يُؤْمِنُونَ وَهُمْ عِنْدَ رَبِّهِم»

"Why would they not believe, since they are with their Lord" They mentioned the Prophets, and the Prophet said,

«وَكَيْفَ لَا يُؤْمِنُونَ وَالْوَحْيُ يَنْزِلُ عَلَيْهِمْ؟»

"Why would they not believe while the revelation is sent down to them" They said, "Then, we are." He said,

«وَكَيْفَ لَا تُؤْمِنُونَ وَأَنَا بَيْنَ أَظْهُرِكُمْ؟»

"Why would not you believe when I am among you" They asked, "Who has the most amazing faith" The Prophet said,

«قَوْمٌ يَجِيئُونَ مِنْ بَعْدِكُمْ يَجِدُونَ صُحُفًا يُؤْمِنُونَ بِمَا فِيهَا»

"A people who will come after you and who will find only books that they will believe in.")

Allah said next,

(And whoever depends upon Allah, then he is indeed guided to the right path) (3:101) for trusting and relying on Allah are the basis of achieving the right guidance and staying away from the path of wickedness. They also represent the tool to acquiring guidance and truth and achieving the righteous aims.

Surah: 3 Ayah: 102 & Ayah: 103

﴿يَٰٓأَيُّهَا ٱلَّذِينَ ءَامَنُوا۟ ٱتَّقُوا۟ ٱللَّهَ حَقَّ تُقَاتِهِۦ وَلَا تَمُوتُنَّ إِلَّا وَأَنتُم مُّسْلِمُونَ ١٠٢﴾

102. O you who believe! Fear Allâh (by doing all that He has ordered and by abstaining from all that He has forbidden) as He should be feared. (Obey Him, be thankful to Him, and remember Him always), and die not except in a state of Islâm (as Muslims (with complete submission to Allâh)).

﴿وَٱعْتَصِمُوا۟ بِحَبْلِ ٱللَّهِ جَمِيعًا وَلَا تَفَرَّقُوا۟ ۚ وَٱذْكُرُوا۟ نِعْمَتَ ٱللَّهِ عَلَيْكُمْ إِذْ كُنتُمْ أَعْدَآءً
فَأَلَّفَ بَيْنَ قُلُوبِكُمْ فَأَصْبَحْتُم بِنِعْمَتِهِۦٓ إِخْوَٰنًا وَكُنتُمْ عَلَىٰ شَفَا حُفْرَةٍ مِّنَ ٱلنَّارِ فَأَنقَذَكُم
مِّنْهَا ۗ كَذَٰلِكَ يُبَيِّنُ ٱللَّهُ لَكُمْ ءَايَٰتِهِۦ لَعَلَّكُمْ تَهْتَدُونَ ١٠٣﴾

103. And hold fast, all of you together, to the Rope of Allâh (i.e. this Qur'ân), and be not divided among yourselves, and remember Allâh's Favor on you, for you were enemies one to another but He joined your hearts together, so that, by His Grace, you became brethren (in Islâmic Faith), and you were on the brink of a pit of Fire, and He saved you from it. Thus Allâh makes His Ayât (proofs, evidences, verses, lessons, signs, revelations, etc.,) clear to you, that you may be guided.

Transliteration

102. Ya ayyuha allatheena amanoo ittaqoo Allaha haqqa tuqatihi wala tamootunna illa waantum muslimoona 103. WaiAAtasimoo bihabli Allahi jameeAAan wala tafarraqoo waothkuroo niAAmata Allahi AAalaykum ith kuntum aAAdaan faallafa bayna quloobikum faasbahtum biniAAmatihi ikhwanan wakuntum AAala shafa hufratin mina alnnari faanqathakum minha kathalika yubayyinu Allahu lakum ayatihi laAAallakum tahtadoona

Tafsir Ibn Kathir

Meaning of Taqwa of Allah

Ibn Abi Hatim recorded that `Abdullah bin Mas`ud commented on the Ayah,

(Have Taqwa of Allah as is His due,)

"That He is obeyed and not defied, remembered and not forgotten and appreciated and not unappreciated." This has an authentic chain of narration to `Abdullah bin Mas`ud. Al-Hakim collected this Hadith in his Mustadrak, from Ibn Mas`ud, who related it to the Prophet . Al-Hakim said, "It is authentic according to the criteria of the Two Shaykhs (Al-Bukhari and Muslim), and they did not record it." This is what he said, but it appears that it is only a statement of `Abdullah bin Mas`ud, and Allah knows best. It was also reported that Anas said, "The servant will not have Taqwa of Allah as is His due until he keeps his tongue idle." Allah's statement,

(and die not except as (true) Muslims) (3:102), means, preserve your Islam while you are well and safe, so that you die as a Muslim. The Most Generous Allah has made it His decision that whatever state one lives in, that is what he dies upon and is resurrected upon. We seek refuge from dying on other than Islam.

Imam Ahmad recorded that Mujahid said, "The people were circling around the Sacred House when Ibn `Abbas was sitting, holding a bent-handled walking stick. Ibn `Abbas said, The Messenger of Allah (recited),

(Have Taqwa of Allah as is His due, die not except as (true) Muslims.) (3:102), (then he said;)

«وَلَوْ أَنَّ قَطْرَةً مِنَ الزَّقُّومِ قُطِرَتْ لَأَمَرَّتْ عَلى أَهْلِ الْأَرْضِ عِيشَتَهُمْ، فَكَيْفَ بِمَنْ لَيْسَ لَهُ طَعَامٌ إِلَّا الزَّقُّومُ؟»

(Verily, if a drop of Zaqqum (a tree in Hell) falls, it will spoil life for the people of earth. What about those whose food is only from Zaqqum)"

This was recorded by At-Tirmidhi, An-Nasa'i, Ibn Majah, Ibn Hibban in his Sahih and Al-Hakim his Mustadrak. At-Tirmidhi said, "Hasan Sahih'" while Al-Hakim said; "It meets the conditions of the Two Sahihs and they did not record it."

Imam Ahmad recorded that Jabir said that three nights before the Messenger of Allah died he heard him saying;

«لَا يَمُوتَنَّ أَحَدُكُمْ إِلَّا وَهُوَ يُحْسِنُ الظَّنَّ بِاللهِ عَزَّ وَجَلَّ»

(None of you should die except while having sincere trust in Allah, the Exalted and Most Honorable.) Muslim also recorded it. The Two Sahihs record that Abu Hurayrah said that the Messenger of Allah said,

«يَقُولُ اللهُ: أَنَا عِنْدَ ظَنِّ عَبْدِي بِي»

(Allah said, "I am as My servant thinks of Me.")

The Necessity of Holding to the Path of Allah and the Community of the Believers

Allah said next,

(And hold fast, all of you together, to the Rope of Allah, and be not divided among yourselves.) It was said that,

(to the Rope of Allah) refers to Allah's covenant, just as Allah said in the following Ayah,

(Indignity is put over them wherever they may be, except when under a covenant (of protection) from Allah, and from men;) (3:112), in reference to pledges and peace treaties.

Allah's statement

(and be not divided among yourselves), orders sticking to the community of the believers and forbids division. There are several Hadiths that require adhering to the Jama\`ah (congregation of believers) and prohibit division. Muslim recorded that Abu Hurayrah said that the Messenger of Allah said,

«إِنَّ اللهَ يَرْضَى لَكُمْ ثَلَاثًا، وَيَسْخَطُ لَكُمْ ثَلَاثًا: يَرْضَى لَكُمْ أَنْ تَعْبُدُوهُ وَلَا تُشْرِكُوا بِهِ شَيْئًا، وَأَنْ تَعْتَصِمُوا بِحَبْلِ اللهِ جَمِيعًا وَلَا تَفَرَّقُوا،وَأَنْ تَنَاصَحُوا مَنْ وَلَّاهُ اللهُ أَمْرَكُمْ. وَيَسْخَطُ لَكُمْ ثَلَاثًا: قِيلَ وَقَالَ، وَكَثْرَةَ السُّؤَالِ، وَإِضَاعَةَ الْمَالِ»

(It pleases Allah for you to acquire three qualities and displeases Him that you acquire three characteristics. It pleases Him that you worship Him Alone and not associate anything or anyone with Him in worship, that you hold on to the Rope of Allah altogether and do not divide, and that you advise whoever Allah appoints as your Leader. The three that displease Him are that you say, \`It was said,' and, \`So-and-so said,' asking many unnecessary questions and wasting money.)

Allah said,

(and remember Allah's favor on you, for you were enemies one to another but He joined your hearts together, so that, by His grace, you became brethren) (3:103).

This was revealed about the Aws and Khazraj. During the time of Jahiliyyah, the Aws and Khazraj were at war and had great hatred, enmity and ill feelings towards each other, causing long conflicts and battles to occur between them. When Allah brought Islam, those among them who embraced it became brothers who loved each other by Allah's grace, having good ties for Allah's sake and helping each other in righteousness and piety. Allah said,

(He it is Who has supported you with His Help and with the believers. And He has united their hearts. If you had spent all that is in the earth, you could not have united their hearts, but

Allah has united them)(8:62,63), until the end of the Ayah. Before Islam, their disbelief had them standing at the edge of a pit of the Fire, but Allah saved them from it and delivered them to faith. The Messenger of Allah reminded the Ansar (from both Aws and Khazraj) of this bounty when he was dividing the war booty of Hunayn. During that time, some Ansar did not like the way the booty was divided, since they did not get what the others did, although that was what Allah directed His Prophet to do. The Messenger of Allah gave them a speech, in which he said,

«يَا مَعْشَرَ الْأَنْصَارِ أَلَمْ أَجِدْكُمْ ضُلَّالًا فَهَدَاكُمُ اللهُ بِي، وَكُنْتُمْ مُتَفَرِّقِينَ فَأَلَّفَكُمُ اللهُ بِي، وَعَالَةً فَأَغْنَاكُمُ اللهُ بِي؟»

(O Ansar! Did I not find you misguided and Allah directed you to guidance because of me Were you not divided beforehand and Allah united you around me Were you not poor and Allah enriched you because of me)

Whenever the Prophet asked them a question, they would answer, "Indeed, Allah and His Messenger have granted us bounty."

Surah: 3 Ayah: 104, Ayah: 105, Ayah: 106, Ayah: 107, Ayah: 108 & Ayah: 109

﴿ وَلْتَكُن مِّنكُمْ أُمَّةٌ يَدْعُونَ إِلَى ٱلْخَيْرِ وَيَأْمُرُونَ بِٱلْمَعْرُوفِ وَيَنْهَوْنَ عَنِ ٱلْمُنكَرِ ۚ وَأُو۟لَٰٓئِكَ هُمُ ٱلْمُفْلِحُونَ ﴿١٠٤﴾ ﴾

104. Let there arise out of you a group of people inviting to all that is good (Islâm), enjoining Al-Ma'rûf (i.e. Islâmic Monotheism and all that Islâm orders one to do) and forbidding Al-Munkar (polytheism and disbelief and all that Islâm has forbidden). And it is they who are the successful.

﴿ وَلَا تَكُونُوا۟ كَٱلَّذِينَ تَفَرَّقُوا۟ وَٱخْتَلَفُوا۟ مِنۢ بَعْدِ مَا جَآءَهُمُ ٱلْبَيِّنَٰتُ ۚ وَأُو۟لَٰٓئِكَ لَهُمْ عَذَابٌ عَظِيمٌ ﴿١٠٥﴾ ﴾

105. And be not as those who divided and differed among themselves after the clear proofs had come to them. It is they for whom there is an awful torment.

﴿ يَوْمَ تَبْيَضُّ وُجُوهٌ وَتَسْوَدُّ وُجُوهٌ ۚ فَأَمَّا ٱلَّذِينَ ٱسْوَدَّتْ وُجُوهُهُمْ أَكَفَرْتُم بَعْدَ إِيمَٰنِكُمْ فَذُوقُوا۟ ٱلْعَذَابَ بِمَا كُنتُمْ تَكْفُرُونَ ﴿١٠٦﴾ ﴾

106. On the Day (i.e. the Day of Resurrection) when some faces will become white and some faces will become black; as for those whose faces will become black (to them will be said): "Did you reject Faith after accepting it? Then taste the torment (in Hell) for rejecting Faith."

﴿وَأَمَّا ٱلَّذِينَ ٱبْيَضَّتْ وُجُوهُهُمْ فَفِى رَحْمَةِ ٱللَّهِ هُمْ فِيهَا خَـٰلِدُونَ ﴿١٠٧﴾﴾

107. And for those whose faces will become white, they will be in Allâh's Mercy (Paradise), therein they shall dwell forever.

﴿تِلْكَ ءَايَـٰتُ ٱللَّهِ نَتْلُوهَا عَلَيْكَ بِٱلْحَقِّ ۗ وَمَا ٱللَّهُ يُرِيدُ ظُلْمًا لِّلْعَـٰلَمِينَ ﴿١٠٨﴾﴾

108. These are the Verses of Allâh: We recite them to you (O Muhammad (peace be upon him)) in truth, and Allâh wills no injustice to the 'Alâmîn (mankind, jinn and all that exists).

﴿وَلِلَّهِ مَا فِى ٱلسَّمَـٰوَٰتِ وَمَا فِى ٱلْأَرْضِ ۚ وَإِلَى ٱللَّهِ تُرْجَعُ ٱلْأُمُورُ ﴿١٠٩﴾﴾

109. And to Allâh belongs all that is in the heavens and all that is in the earth. And all matters go back (for decision) to Allâh.

Transliteration

104. Waltakun minkum ommatun yadAAoona ila alkhayri waya/muroona bialmaAAroofi wayanhawna AAani almunkari waola-ika humu almuflihoona 105. Wala takoonoo kaallatheena tafarraqoo waikhtalafoo min baAAdi ma jaahumu albayyinatu waolaika lahum AAathabun AAatheemun 106. Yawma tabyaddu wujoohun wataswaddu wujoohun faamma allatheena iswaddat wujoohuhum akafartum baAAda eemanikum fathooqoo alAAathaba bima kuntum takfuroona 107. Waamma allatheena ibyaddat wujoohuhum fafee rahmati Allahi hum feeha khalidoona 108. Tilka ayatu Allahi natlooha AAalayka bialhaqqi wama Allahu yureedu thulman lilAAalameena 109. Walillahi ma fee alssamawati wama fee al-ardi wa-ila Allahi turjaAAu al-omooru

Tafsir Ibn Kathir

The Command to Establish the Invitation to Allah

Allah said,

(Let there arise out of you a group of people)

that calls to righteousness, enjoins all that is good and forbids evil in the manner Allah commanded,

(And it is they who are the successful.)

Ad-Dahhak said, "They are a special group of the Companions and a special group of those after them, that is those who perform Jihad and the scholars."

The objective of this Ayah is that there should be a segment of this Muslim Ummah fulfilling this task, even though it is also an obligation on every member of this Ummah, each according to his ability. Muslim recorded that Abu Hurayrah said that the Messenger of Allah said,

«مَنْ رَأَى مِنْكُمْ مُنْكَرًا فَلْيُغَيِّرْهُ بِيَدِهِ، فَإِنْ لَمْ يَسْتَطِعْ فَبِلِسَانِهِ، فَإِنْ لَمْ يَسْتَطِعْ فَبِقَلْبِهِ، وَذلِكَ أَضْعَفُ الْإِيمَانِ»

(Whoever among you witnesses an evil, let him change it with his hand. If he is unable, then let him change it with his tongue. If he is unable, then let him change it with his heart, and this is the weakest faith.) In another narration, The Prophet said,

«وَلَيْسَ وَرَاءَ ذَلِكَ مِنَ الْإِيمَانِ حَبَّةُ خَرْدَلٍ»

(There is no faith beyond that, not even the weight of a mustard seed.)

Imam Ahmad recorded that Hudhayfah bin Al-Yaman said that the Prophet said,

«وَالَّذِي نَفْسِي بِيَدِهِ، لَتَأْمُرُنَّ بِالْمَعْرُوفِ، وَلَتَنْهَوُنَّ عَنِ الْمُنْكَرِ، أَوْ لَيُوشِكَنَّ اللهُ أَنْ يَبْعَثَ عَلَيْكُمْ عِقَابًا مِنْ عِنْدِهِ، ثُمَّ لَتَدْعُنَّــــــهُ فَلَا يَسْتَجِيبَ لَكُم»

(By He in Whose Hand is my soul! You will enjoin righteousness and forbid evil, or Allah shall send down a punishment from Him to you. Then, you will supplicate to Him, but He will not accept your supplication.)

At-Tirmidhi also collected this Hadith and said, "Hasan". There are many other Hadiths and Ayat on this subject, which will be explained later.

The Prohibition of Division

Allah said,

(And be not as those who divided and differed among themselves after the clear proofs had come to them) (3:105).

In this Ayah, Allah forbids this Ummah from imitating the division and discord of the nations that came before them. These nations also abandoned enjoining righteousness and forbidding evil, although they had proof of its necessity.

Imam Ahmad recorded that Abu `Amir `Abdullah bin Luhay said, "We performed Hajj with Mu`awiyah bin Abi Sufyan. When we arrived at Makkah, he stood up after praying Zuhr and said, `The Messenger of Allah said,

«إِنَّ أَهْلَ الْكِتَابَيْنِ افْتَرَقُوا فِي دِينِهِمْ عَلَى ثِنْتَيْنِ وَسَبْعِينَ مِلَّةً، وَإِنَّ هذِهِ الْأُمَّةَ سَتَفْتَرِقُ عَلَى ثَلَاثٍ وَسَبْعِينَ مِلَّةً يَعْنِي الْأَهْوَاءَ كُلُّهَا فِي النَّارِ إِلَّا وَاحِدَةً وَهِيَ

الْجَمَاعَةُ وَإِنَّهُ سَيَخْرُجُ فِي أُمَّتِي أَقْوَامٌ تَجَارَى بِهِمْ تِلْكَ الْأَهْوَاءُ كَمَا يَتَجَارَى الْكَلَبُ بِصَاحِبِه، لَا يَبْقَى مِنْهُ عِرْقٌ وَلَا مَفْصِلٌ إِلَّا دَخَلَه»

(The People of the Two Scriptures divided into seventy-two sects. This Ummah will divide into seventy-three sects, all in the Fire except one, that is, the Jama`ah. Some of my Ummah will be guided by desire, like one who is infected by rabies; no vein or joint will be saved from these desires.)

(Mu`awiyah said next:) By Allah, O Arabs! If you do not adhere to what came to you from your Prophet then other people are even more prone not to adhere to it. " Similar was recorded by Abu Dawud from Ahmad bin Hanbal and Muhammad bin Yahya.

The Benefits of Brotherly Ties and Unity and the Consequence of Division on the Day of the Gathering

Allah said next,

(On the Day when some faces will become white and some faces will become black;) (3:106) on the Day of Resurrection. This is when the faces of followers of the Sunnah and the Jama`ah will radiate with whiteness, and the faces of followers of Bid`ah (innovation) and division will be darkened, as has been reported from Ibn `Abbas. Allah said,

(As for those whose faces will become black (to them will be said): "Did you reject faith after accepting it")

Al-Hasan Al-Basri said, "They are the hypocrites."

(Then taste the torment (in Hell) for rejecting faith,) and this description befits every disbeliever.

(And for those whose faces will become white, they will be in Allah's mercy (Paradise), therein they shall dwell forever.) in Paradise, where they will reside for eternity and shall never desire to be removed. Abu `Isa At-Tirmidhi recorded that Abu Ghalib said, "Abu Umamah saw heads (of the Khawarij sect) hanging on the streets of Damascus. He commented, `The Dogs of the Fire and the worst dead people under the cover of the sky. The best dead men are those whom these have killed.' He then recited,

(On the Day (i.e. the Day of Resurrection) when some faces will become white and some faces will become black;) until the end of the Ayah. I said to Abu Umamah, `Did you hear this from the Messenger of Allah' He said, `If I only heard it from the Messenger of Allah once, twice, thrice, four times, or seven times, I would not have narrated it to you.' " At-Tirmidhi said, "This Hadith is Hasan." Ibn Majah and Ahmad recorded similarly.

Allah said,

(These are the Ayat of Allah. We recite them to you) meaning, `These are the verses of Allah, His proofs and signs that We reveal to you, O Muhammad,'

(in truth) making known the true reality of this world and the Hereafter.

(and Allah wills no injustice to the `Alamin.) for He never treats them with injustice. Rather, He is the Just Ruler Who is able to do everything and has knowledge of everything. Therefore, He does not need to treat any of His creatures with injustice, and this is why He said next,

(and to Allah belongs all that is in the heavens and all that is in the Earth.),

they are all His servants and His property,

(And all matters go back to Allah,) for His is the decision concerning the affairs of this life and the Hereafter, and His is the Supreme Authority in this life and the Hereafter.

Surah: 3 Ayah: 110, Ayah: 111 & Ayah: 112

﴿ كُنتُمْ خَيْرَ أُمَّةٍ أُخْرِجَتْ لِلنَّاسِ تَأْمُرُونَ بِٱلْمَعْرُوفِ وَتَنْهَوْنَ عَنِ ٱلْمُنكَرِ وَتُؤْمِنُونَ
بِٱللَّهِ ۗ وَلَوْ ءَامَنَ أَهْلُ ٱلْكِتَٰبِ لَكَانَ خَيْرًا لَّهُم ۚ مِّنْهُمُ ٱلْمُؤْمِنُونَ وَأَكْثَرُهُمُ
ٱلْفَٰسِقُونَ ﴿١١٠﴾ ﴾

110. You (true believers in Islâmic Monotheism, and real followers of Prophet Muhammad (peace be upon him) and his Sunnah) are the best of peoples ever raised up for mankind; you enjoin Al-Ma'rûf (i.e. Islâmic Monotheism and all that Islâm has ordained) and forbid Al-Munkar (polytheism, disbelief and all that Islâm has forbidden), and you believe in Allâh. And had the people of the Scripture (Jews and Christians) believed, it would have been better for them; among them are some who have faith, but most of them are Al-Fâsiqûn (disobedient to Allâh - and rebellious against Allâh's Command).

﴿ لَن يَضُرُّوكُمْ إِلَّآ أَذًى ۖ وَإِن يُقَٰتِلُوكُمْ يُوَلُّوكُمُ ٱلْأَدْبَارَ ثُمَّ لَا يُنصَرُونَ ﴿١١١﴾ ﴾

111. They will do you no harm, barring a trifling annoyance; and if they fight against you, they will show you their backs, and they will not be helped.

﴿ ضُرِبَتْ عَلَيْهِمُ ٱلذِّلَّةُ أَيْنَ مَا ثُقِفُوٓا۟ إِلَّا بِحَبْلٍ مِّنَ ٱللَّهِ وَحَبْلٍ مِّنَ ٱلنَّاسِ وَبَآءُو بِغَضَبٍ مِّنَ
ٱللَّهِ وَضُرِبَتْ عَلَيْهِمُ ٱلْمَسْكَنَةُ ۚ ذَٰلِكَ بِأَنَّهُمْ كَانُوا۟ يَكْفُرُونَ بِـَٔايَٰتِ ٱللَّهِ وَيَقْتُلُونَ ٱلْأَنۢبِيَآءَ
بِغَيْرِ حَقٍّ ۚ ذَٰلِكَ بِمَا عَصَوا۟ وَّكَانُوا۟ يَعْتَدُونَ ﴿١١٢﴾ ﴾

112. Indignity is put over them wherever they may be, except when under a covenant (of protection) from Allâh, and from men; they have drawn on themselves the Wrath of Allâh, and destruction is put over them. This is because they disbelieved in the Ayât (proofs, evidences, verses, lessons, signs, revelations, etc.) of Allâh and killed the Prophets without right. This is because they disobeyed (Allâh) and used to transgress beyond bounds (in Allâh's disobedience, crimes and sins).

Transliteration

110. Kuntum khayra ommatin okhrijat lilnnasi ta/muroona bialmaAAroofi watanhawna AAani almunkari watu/minoona biAllahi walaw amana ahlu alkitabi lakana khayran lahum minhumu almu/minoona waaktharuhumu alfasiqoona 111. Lan yadurrookum illa athan wa-in yuqatilookum yuwallookumu al-adbara thumma la yunsaroona 112. Duribat AAalayhimu

alththillatu ayna ma thuqifoo illa bihablin mina Allahi wahablin mina alnnasi wabaoo bighadabin mina Allahi waduribat AAalayhimu almaskanatu thalika bi-annahum kanoo yakfuroona bi-ayati Allahi wayaqtuloona al-anbiyaa bighayri haqqin thalika bima AAasaw wakanoo yaAAtadoona

Tafsir Ibn Kathir

Virtues of the Ummah of Muhammad (peace and blessings of Allah be upon him) - the Best Nation Ever

Allah states that the Ummah of Muhammad is the best nation ever,

(You are the best of peoples ever raised up for mankind) (3:110).

Al-Bukhari recorded that Abu Hurayrah commented on this Ayah, "(You, Muslims, are) the best nation of people for the people, you bring them tied in chains on their necks (capture them in war) and they later embrace Islam." Similar was said by Ibn `Abbas, Mujahid, `Atiyah Al-`Awfi, `Ikrimah, `Ata' and Ar-Rabi` bin Anas that,

(You are the best of peoples ever raised up for mankind;) means, the best of peoples for the people.

The meaning of the Ayah is that the Ummah of Muhammad is the most righteous and beneficial nation for mankind. Hence Allah's description of them,

(you enjoin Al-Ma`ruf and forbid Al-Munkar and believe in Allah) (3:110).

Ahmad, At-Tirmidhi, Ibn Majah, and Al-Hakim recorded that Hakim bin Mu`awiyah bin Haydah narrated that his father said that the Messenger of Allah said,

«أَنْتُمْ تُوَفُّون سَبْعِينَ أُمَّةً، أَنْتُمْ خَيْرُهَا، وَأَنْتُمْ أَكْرَمُ عَلَى اللهِ عَزَّ وَجَلّ»

(You are the final of seventy nations, you are the best and most honored among them to Allah.)

This is a well-known Hadith about which At-Tirmidhi said, "Hasan", and which is also narrated from Mu`adh bin Jabal and Abu Sa`id. The Ummah of Muhammad achieved this virtue because of its Prophet, Muhammad, peace be upon him, the most regarded of Allah's creation and the most honored Messenger with Allah. Allah sent Muhammad with the perfect and complete Law that was never given to any Prophet or Messenger before him. In Muhammad's Law, few deeds take the place of the many deeds that other nations performed. For instance, Imam Ahmad recorded that `Ali bin Abi Talib said, "The Messenger of Allah said,

«أُعْطِيتُ مَا لَمْ يُعْطَ أَحَدٌ مِنَ الْأَنْبِيَاء»

(I was given what no other Prophet before me was given.)

We said, `O Messenger of Allah! What is it' He said,

«نُصِرْتُ بِالرُّعْبِ، وَأُعْطِيتُ مَفَاتِيحَ الْأَرْضِ، وَسُمِّيتُ أَحْمَدَ، وَجُعِلَ التُّرَابُ لِي طَهُورًا، وَجُعِلَتْ أُمَّتِي خَيْرَ الْأُمَمِ»

(I was given victory by fear, I was given the keys of the earth, I was called Ahmad, the earth was made a clean place for me (to pray and perform Tayammum with it) and my Ummah was made the best Ummah.)."

The chain of narration for this Hadith is Hasan. There are several Hadiths that we should mention here.

The Two Sahihs recorded that Az-Zuhri said that, Sa`id bin Al-Musayyib said that Abu Hurayrah narrated to him, "I heard the Messenger of Allah saying,

«يَدْخُلُ الْجَنَّـــــةَ مِنْ أُمَّتِي زُمْرَةٌ وَهُمْ سَبْعُونَ أَلْفًا، تُضِيءُ وُجُوهُهُمْ إِضَاءَةَ الْقَمَرِ لَيْلَةَ الْبَدْرِ»

(A group of seventy thousand from my Ummah will enter Paradise, while their faces are radiating, just like the moon when it is full.'`Ukkashah bin Mihsan Al-Asadi stood up, saying, `O Messenger of Allah! Supplicate to Allah that I am one of them.' The Messenger of Allah said,

«اللَّهُمَّ اجْعَلْهُ مِنْهُم»

`O Allah! Make him one of them.' A man from the Ansar also stood and said, `O Messenger of Allah! Supplicate to Allah that I am one of them.' The Messenger said,

«سَبقَكَ بِهَا عُكَّاشَة»

`Ukkashah has beaten you to it.')

Another Hadith that Establishes the Virtues of the Ummah of Muhammad in this Life and the Hereafter.

Imam Ahmad recorded that Jabir said, "I heard the Messenger of Allah saying,

«إِنِّي لَأَرْجُو أَنْ يَكُونَ مَنْ يَتَّبِعُنِي مِنْ أُمَّتِي يَوْمَ الْقِيَامَةِ رُبُعَ الْجَنَّـــــةِ»

(`I hope that those who follow me will be one-fourth of the residents of Paradise on the Day of Resurrection.' We said, `Allahu Akbar'. He then said,

«أَرْجُو أَنْ يَكُونُوا ثُلُثَ النَّاس»

`I hope that they will be one-third of the people.' We said, `Allahu Akbar'. He then said,

«أَرْجُو أَنْ تَكُونُوا الشَّطْر»

`I hope that you will be one-half.')"

Imam Ahmad recorded the same Hadith with another chain of narration, and this Hadith meets the criteria of Muslim in his Sahih. In the Two Sahihs, it is recorded that `Abdullah bin Mas`ud said, "The Messenger of Allah said to us,

«أَمَا تَرْضَوْنَ أَنْ تَكُونُوا رُبُعَ أَهْلِ الْجَنَّـــةِ؟»

(Does it please you that you will be one-fourth of the people of Paradise)

We said, `Allahu Akbar!' He added,

«أَمَا تَرْضَوْنَ أَنْ تَكُونُوا ثُلُثَ أَهْلِ الْجَنَّـــةِ؟»

(Does it please you that you will be one-third of the people of Paradise) We said, `Allahu Akbar!' He said,

«إِنِّي لَأَرْجُو أَنْ تَكُونُوا شَطْرَ أَهْلِ الْجَنَّـــةِ؟»

(I hope that you will be half of the people of Paradise.)" Another Hadith

Imam Ahmad recorded that Buraydah said that the Prophet said,

«أَهْلُ الْجَنَّةِ عِشْرُونَ وَمِائَةُ صَفَ، هذِهِ الْأُمَّةُ مِنْ ذلِكَ ثَمَانُونَ صَفًّا»

(The people of Paradise are one hundred and twenty rows, this Ummah takes up eighty of them.)

Imam Ahmad also collected this Hadith through another chain of narration. At-Tirmidhi and Ibn Majah also collected this Hadith, and At-Tirmidhi said, `This Hadith is Hasan. `Abdur-Razzaq recorded that Abu Hurayrah said that, the Prophet said,

«نَحْنُ الْآخِرُونَ الْأَوَّلُونَ يَوْمَ الْقِيَامَةِ، نَحْنُ أَوَّلُ النَّاسِ دُخُولًا الْجَنَّـــةَ، بَيْدَ أَنَّهُمْ أُوتُوا الْكِتَابَ مِنْ قَبْلِنَا وَأُوتِينَاهُ مِنْ بَعْدِهِمْ، فَهَدَانَا اللهُ لِمَا اخْتَلَفُوا فِيهِ مِنَ الْحَقِّ، فَهَذَا الْيَوْمُ الَّذِي اخْتَلَفُوا فِيهِ، النَّاسُ لَنَا فِيهِ تَبَعٌ، غَدًا لِلْيَهُودِ، وَلِلنَّصَارَى بَعْدَ غَد»

(We (Muslims) are the last to come, but the foremost on the Day of Resurrection, and the first people to enter Paradise, although the former nations were given the Scriptures before us and we after them. Allah gave us the guidance of truth that they have been disputing about. This (Friday) is the Day that they have been disputing about, and all the other people are behind us in this matter: the Jews' (day of congregation is) tomorrow (Saturday) and the Christians' is the day after tomorrow (Sunday).)

Al-Bukhari and Muslim collected this Hadith. Muslim recorded Abu Hurayrah saying that the Messenger of Allah said,

«نَحْنُ الْآخِرُونَ الْأَوَّلُونَ يَوْمَ الْقِيَامَةِ، نَحْنُ أَوَّلُ مَنْ يَدْخُلُ الْجَنَّــــــــة»

(We (Muslims) are the last (to come), but (will be) the foremost on the Day of Resurrection, and will be the first people to enter Paradise...) until the end of the Hadith.

These and other Hadiths conform to the meaning of the Ayah,

(You are the best of peoples ever raised up for mankind; you enjoin Al-Ma`ruf (all that Islam has ordained) and forbid Al-Munkar (all that Islam has forbidden), and you believe in Allah).

Therefore, whoever among this Ummah acquires these qualities, will have a share in this praise. Qatadah said, "We were told that `Umar bin Al-Khattab recited this Ayah (3:110) during a Hajj that he performed, when he saw that the people were rushing. He then said, `Whoever likes to be among this (praised) Ummah, let him fulfill the condition that Allah set in this Ayah.'" Ibn Jarir recorded this. Those from this Ummah who do not acquire these qualities will be just like the People of the Scriptures whom Allah criticized, when He said,

(They did not forbid one another from the Munkar which they committed...) (5:79).

This is the reason why, after Allah praised the Muslim Ummah with the qualities that He mentioned, He criticized the People of the Scriptures and chastised them, saying,

(And had the People of the Scripture (Jews and Christians) believed) (3:110),

in what was sent down to Muhammad ,

(it would have been better for them; among them are some who have faith, but most of them are Fasiqun (rebellious).)

Therefore only a few of them believe in Allah and in what was sent down to you and to them. The majority of them follow deviation, disbelief, sin and rebellion.

The Good News that Muslims will Dominate the People of the Book

While delivering the good news to His believing servants that victory and dominance will be theirs against the disbelieving, atheistic People of the Scriptures, Allah then said,

(They will do you no harm, barring a trifling annoyance; and if they fight against you, they will show you their backs, and they will not be helped.) (3:111)

This is what occurred, for at the battle of Khaybar, Allah brought humiliation and disgrace to the Jews. Before that, the Jews in Al-Madinah, the tribes of Qaynuqa`, Nadir and Qurayzah, were also humiliated by Allah. Such was the case with the Christians in the area of Ash-Sham later on, when the Companions defeated them in many battles and took over the leadership of Ash-Sham forever. There shall always be a group of Muslims in Ash-Sham area until `Isa, son of Maryam, descends while they are like this (on the truth, apparent and victorious). `Isa will at that time rule according to the Law of Muhammad , break the cross, kill the swine, banish the Jizyah and only accept Islam from the people.

Allah said next,

(Indignity is put over them wherever they may be, except when under a covenant (of protection) from Allah, and a covenant from men;) meaning, Allah has placed humiliation and disgrace on them wherever they may be, and they will never be safe,

(except when under a covenant from Allah,) under the Dhimmah (covenant of protection) from Allah that requires them to pay the Jizyah (tax, to Muslims,) and makes them subservient to Islamic Law.

(and a covenant from men;) meaning, covenant from men, such as pledges of protection and safety offered to them by Muslim men and women, and even a slave, according to one of the sayings of the scholars. Ibn `Abbas said that,

(except when under a covenant from Allah, and a covenant from men;) refers to a covenant of protection from Allah and a pledge of safety from people. Similar was said by Mujahid, `Ikrimah, `Ata', Ad-Dahhak, Al-Hasan, Qatadah, As-Suddi and Ar-Rabi` bin Anas. Allah's statement,

(they have drawn on themselves the wrath of Allah,) means, they earned Allah's anger, which they deserved,

(and destitution is put over them), meaning they deserve it by decree and legislatively.

Allah said next,

(This is because they disbelieved in the Ayat of Allah and killed the Prophets without right.) meaning, what drove them to this was their arrogance, transgression and envy, earning them humiliation, degradation and disgrace throughout this life and the Hereafter. Allah said,

(This is because they disobeyed and used to transgress (the limits set by Allah).) meaning, what lured them to disbelieve in Allah's Ayat and kill His Messengers, is the fact that they often disobeyed Allah's commands, committed His prohibitions and transgressed His set limits. We seek refuge from this behavior, and Allah Alone is sought for each and every type of help.

Surah: 3 Ayah: 113, Ayah: 114, Ayah: 115, Ayah: 116 & Ayah: 117

﴿ ۞ لَيْسُوا۟ سَوَآءً ۗ مِّنْ أَهْلِ ٱلْكِتَـٰبِ أُمَّةٌ قَآئِمَةٌ يَتْلُونَ ءَايَـٰتِ ٱللَّهِ ءَانَآءَ ٱلَّيْلِ وَهُمْ يَسْجُدُونَ ﴿١١٣﴾ ﴾

113. Not all of them are alike; a party of the people of the Scripture stand for the right, they recite the Verses of Allâh during the hours of the night, prostrating themselves in prayer.

﴿ يُؤْمِنُونَ بِٱللَّهِ وَٱلْيَوْمِ ٱلْـَٔاخِرِ وَيَأْمُرُونَ بِٱلْمَعْرُوفِ وَيَنْهَوْنَ عَنِ ٱلْمُنكَرِ
وَيُسَـٰرِعُونَ فِى ٱلْخَيْرَٰتِ وَأُو۟لَـٰٓئِكَ مِنَ ٱلصَّـٰلِحِينَ ١١٤ ﴾

114. They believe in Allâh and the Last Day; they enjoin Al-Ma'rûf (Islâmic Monotheism, and following Prophet Muhammad (peace be upon him)) and forbid Al-Munkar (polytheism, disbelief and opposing Prophet Muhammad (peace be upon him)) and they hasten in (all) good works; and they are among the righteous.

﴿ وَمَا يَفْعَلُوا۟ مِنْ خَيْرٍ فَلَن يُكْفَرُوهُ ۗ وَٱللَّهُ عَلِيمٌۢ بِٱلْمُتَّقِينَ ١١٥ ﴾

115. And whatever good they do, nothing will be rejected of them; for Allâh knows well those who are Al-Muttaqûn (the pious - see V.2:2).

﴿ إِنَّ ٱلَّذِينَ كَفَرُوا۟ لَن تُغْنِىَ عَنْهُمْ أَمْوَٰلُهُمْ وَلَآ أَوْلَـٰدُهُم مِّنَ ٱللَّهِ شَيْـًٔا ۖ وَأُو۟لَـٰٓئِكَ
أَصْحَـٰبُ ٱلنَّارِ ۚ هُمْ فِيهَا خَـٰلِدُونَ ١١٦ ﴾

116. Surely, those who reject Faith (disbelieve in Muhammad (peace be upon him) as being Allâh's Prophet and in all that which he has brought from Allâh), neither their properties, nor their offspring will avail them aught against Allâh. They are the dwellers of the Fire, therein they will abide. (Tafsir At-Tabarî).

﴿ مَثَلُ مَا يُنفِقُونَ فِى هَـٰذِهِ ٱلْحَيَوٰةِ ٱلدُّنْيَا كَمَثَلِ رِيحٍ فِيهَا صِرٌّ أَصَابَتْ حَرْثَ قَوْمٍ
ظَلَمُوٓا۟ أَنفُسَهُمْ فَأَهْلَكَتْهُ ۚ وَمَا ظَلَمَهُمُ ٱللَّهُ وَلَـٰكِنْ أَنفُسَهُمْ يَظْلِمُونَ ١١٧ ﴾

117. The likeness of what they spend in this world is the likeness of a wind which is extremely cold; it struck the harvest of a people who did wrong against themselves and destroyed it, (i.e. the good deed of a person is only accepted if he is a monotheist and believes in all the Prophets of Allâh, including the Christ (peace be upon him) and Muhammad (peace be upon him)) Allâh wronged them not, but they wronged themselves.

Transliteration

113. Laysoo sawaan min ahli alkitabi ommatun qa-imatun yatloona ayati Allahi anaa allayli wahum yasjudoona 114. Yu/minoona biAllahi waalyawmi al-akhiri waya/muroona bialmaAAroofi wayanhawna AAani almunkari wayusariAAoona fee alkhayrati waola-ika mina alssaliheena 115. Wama yafAAaloo min khayrin falan yukfaroohu waAllahu AAaleemun bialmuttaqeena 116. Inna allatheena kafaroo lan tughniya AAanhum amwaluhum wala awladuhum mina Allahi shayan waola-ika as-habu alnnari hum feeha khalidoona 117. Mathalu ma yunfiqoona fee hathihi alhayati alddunya kamathali reehin feeha sirrun asabat hartha qawmin thalamoo anfusahum faahlakat-hu wama thalamahumu Allahu walakin anfusahum yathlimoona

Tafsir Ibn Kathir

Virtues of the People of the Scriptures Who Embrace Islam

Muhammad bin Ishaq and others, including Al-`Awfi who reported it from Ibn `Abbas, said; "These Ayat were revealed about the clergy of the People of the Scriptures who embraced the faith. For instance, there is `Abdullah bin Salam, Asad bin `Ubayd, Tha`labah bin Sa`yah, Usayd bin Sa`yah, and so forth. This Ayah means that those among the People of the Book whom Allah rebuked earlier are not at all the same as those among them who embraced Islam. Hence Allah's statement,

(Not all of them are alike) (3:113)."

Therefore, these two types of people are not equal, and indeed, there are believers and also criminals among the People of the Book, just as Allah said,

(a party of the People of the Scripture stand for the right) for they implement the Book of Allah, adhere to His Law and follow His Prophet Muhammad . Therefore, this type is on the straight path,

(they recite the verses of Allah during the hours of the night, prostrating themselves in prayer.)

They often stand in prayer at night for Tahajjud, and recite the Qur'an in their prayer,

(They believe in Allah and the Last Day; they enjoin Al-Ma`ruf and forbid Al-Munkar; and they hasten in (all) good works; and they are among the righteous) (3: 114).

This is the same type of people mentioned at the end of the Surah;

(And there are, certainly, among the People of the Scripture (Jews and Christians), those who believe in Allah and in that which has been revealed to you, and in that which has been revealed to them, humbling themselves before Allah.) (3:199).

Allah said here,

(And whatever good they do, nothing will be rejected of them;) (3:115) meaning, their good deeds will not be lost with Allah. Rather, He will award them the best rewards,

(for Allah knows well the Muttaqin (the pious).) for no deed performed by any person ever escapes His knowledge, nor is any reward for those who do good deeds ever lost with Him. Allah mentions the disbelieving polytheists:

(neither their properties nor their offspring will avail them against Allah) (3:116). meaning, nothing can avert Allah's torment and punishment from striking them,

(They are the dwellers of the Fire, therein they will abide.)

The Parable of What the Disbelievers Spend in This Life

Allah gave a parable for what the disbelievers spend in this life, as Mujahid, Al-Hasan and As-Suddi said.

(The likeness of what they spend in this world is the likeness of a wind of Sir;) a frigid wind, as Ibn `Abbas, `Ikrimah, Sa`id bin Jubayr, Al-Hasan, Qatadah, Ad-Dahhak, Ar-Rabi` bin Anas and others have said. `Ata' said that Sir, means, `cold and snow.' Ibn `Abbas and Mujahid are also reported to have said that Sir means, `fire'. This latter meaning does not contradict the meanings we mentioned above, because extreme cold weather, especially when accompanied by snow, burns plants and produce, and has the same effect fire has on such growth.

(It struck the harvest of a people who did wrong against themselves and destroyed it) (3:117), by burning. This Ayah mentions a calamity that strikes produce that is ready to harvest, destroying it by burning and depriving its owner of it when he needs it the most. Such is the case with the disbelievers, for Allah destroys the rewards for their good deeds in this life, just as He destroyed the produce of the sinner because of his sins. Both types did not build their work on firm foundations,

(And Allah wronged them not, but they wronged themselves.)

Surah: 3 Ayah: 118, Ayah: 119 & Ayah: 120

﴿ يَٰٓأَيُّهَا ٱلَّذِينَ ءَامَنُواْ لَا تَتَّخِذُواْ بِطَانَةً مِّن دُونِكُمۡ لَا يَأۡلُونَكُمۡ خَبَالٗا وَدُّواْ مَا عَنِتُّمۡ قَدۡ
بَدَتِ ٱلۡبَغۡضَآءُ مِنۡ أَفۡوَٰهِهِمۡ وَمَا تُخۡفِي صُدُورُهُمۡ أَكۡبَرُۚ قَدۡ بَيَّنَّا لَكُمُ ٱلۡأٓيَٰتِۖ إِن كُنتُمۡ
تَعۡقِلُونَ ١١٨ ﴾

118. O you who believe! Take not as (your) Bitânah (advisors, consultants, protectors, helpers, friends) those outside your religion (pagans, Jews, Christians, and hypocrites) since they will not fail to do their best to corrupt you. They desire to harm you severely. Hatred has already appeared from their mouths, but what their breasts conceal is far worse. Indeed We have made plain to you the Ayât (proofs, evidences, verses) if you understand.

﴿ هَٰٓأَنتُمۡ أُوْلَآءِ تُحِبُّونَهُمۡ وَلَا يُحِبُّونَكُمۡ وَتُؤۡمِنُونَ بِٱلۡكِتَٰبِ كُلِّهِۦ وَإِذَا لَقُوكُمۡ قَالُوٓاْ ءَامَنَّا
وَإِذَا خَلَوۡاْ عَضُّواْ عَلَيۡكُمُ ٱلۡأَنَامِلَ مِنَ ٱلۡغَيۡظِۚ قُلۡ مُوتُواْ بِغَيۡظِكُمۡۗ إِنَّ ٱللَّهَ عَلِيمُۢ بِذَاتِ
ٱلصُّدُورِ ١١٩ ﴾

119. Lo! You are the ones who love them but they love you not, and you believe in all the Scriptures (i.e. you believe in the Taurât (Torah) and the Injeel (Gospel), while they disbelieve in your Book, the Qur'ân). And when they meet you, they say, "We believe". But when they are alone, they bite the tips of their fingers at you in rage. Say: "Perish in your rage. Certainly, Allâh knows what is in the breasts (all the secrets)."

﴿ إِن تَمۡسَسۡكُمۡ حَسَنَةٞ تَسُؤۡهُمۡ وَإِن تُصِبۡكُمۡ سَيِّئَةٞ يَفۡرَحُواْ بِهَاۖ وَإِن تَصۡبِرُواْ وَتَتَّقُواْ لَا
يَضُرُّكُمۡ كَيۡدُهُمۡ شَيۡـًٔاۗ إِنَّ ٱللَّهَ بِمَا يَعۡمَلُونَ مُحِيطٞ ١٢٠ ﴾

120. If a good befalls you, it grieves them, but if some evil overtakes you, they rejoice at it. But if you remain patient and become Al-Muttaqûn (the pious - see V.2:2), not the least harm will their cunning do to you. Surely, Allâh surrounds all that they do.

Transliteration

118. Ya ayyuha allatheena amanoo la tattakhithoo bitanatan min doonikum la ya/loonakum khabalan waddoo ma AAanittum qad badati albaghdao min afwahihim wama tukhfee sudooruhum akbaru qad bayyanna lakumu al-ayati in kuntum taAAqiloona 119. Ha antum ola-i tuhibboonahum wala yuhibboonakum watu/minoona bialkitabi kullihi wa-itha laqookum qaloo amanna wa-itha khalaw AAaddoo AAalaykumu al-anamila mina alghaythi qul mootoo

bighaythikum inna Allaha AAaleemun bithati alssudoori 120. In tamsaskum hasanatun tasu/hum wa-in tusibkum sayyi-atun yafrahoo biha wa-in tasbiroo watattaqoo la yadurrukum kayduhum shay-an inna Allaha bima yaAAmaloona muheetun

Tafsir Ibn Kathir

The Prohibition of Taking Advisors From Among the Disbelievers

Allah forbids His believing servants from taking the hypocrites as advisors, so that the hypocrites do not have the opportunity to expose the secrets of the believers and their plans against their enemies. The hypocrites try their very best to confuse, oppose and harm the believers any way they can, and by using any wicked, evil means at their disposal. They wish the very worst and difficult conditions for the believers. Allah said,

(Take not as (your) Bitanah those other than your own) (3:118), in reference to taking followers of other religions as consultants and advisors, for advisors of a certain person have access to his most secret affairs. Al-Bukhari and An-Nasa'i recorded that, Abu Sa`id said that the Messenger of Allah said,

«مَا بَعَثَ اللهُ مِنْ نَبِيَ وَلَا اسْتَخْلَفَ مِنْ خَلِيفَةٍ إِلَّا كَانَتْ لَهُ بِطَانَتَانِ: بِطَانَةٌ تَأْمُرُهُ بِالْخَيْرِ وَتَحُضُّهُ عَلَيْهِ، وَبِطَانَةٌ تَأْمُرُهُ بِالسُّوءِ وَتَحُضُّهُ عَلَيْهِ، وَالْمَعْصُومُ مَنْ عَصَمَ اللهُ»

(Allah has not sent any Prophet nor was there any Khalifah but they have two types of advisors, one that commands him with righteousness and advises it, and another that commands him with evil and advises him with it. Only those whom Allah gives immunity are immune.)

Ibn Abi Hatim reported that Ibn Abi Ad-Dahqanah said, "`Umar bin Al-Khattab was told, `There is young man here from the people of Hirah (in Iraq, who were Christians) who is a proficient scribe. Why do you not appoint him as a scribe' `Umar said, `I would then be taking advisors from among the disbelievers.'" This Ayah and the story about `Umar testify to the fact that Muslims are not allowed to use Ahl Adh-Dhimmah to be scribes in matters that affect the affairs of Muslims and expose their secrets, for they might convey these secrets to combatant disbelievers. This is why Allah said,

(since they will not fail to do their best to corrupt you. They desire to harm you severely.)

Allah then said,

(Hatred has already appeared from their mouths, but what their breasts conceal is far worse.) meaning, enmity appears on their faces and in what they sometimes utter, as well as, the enmity they have against Islam and its people in their hearts. Since this fact is apparent to every person who has sound comprehension, therefore,

(Indeed We have made plain to you the Ayat if you understand.)

Allah said next,

(O! You are the ones who love them but they love you not), meaning, O believers! You like the hypocrites because you think they are believers, for they pretend to be so, but they do not like you publicly or secretly.

(And you believe in all the Scriptures) meaning, you have no doubt in any part of Allah's Book, while the hypocrites have deep doubts, confusion and reservations about it.

Muhammad bin Ishaq reported that Ibn `Abbas said that,

(and you believe in all the Scriptures,) means, you believe in your Book, their Book, and the previous Books, while the hypocrites disbelieve in your Book, and this is why they deserve that you dislike them instead of them disliking you. Ibn Jarir collected this statement.

(And when they meet you, they say, "We believe." But when they are alone, they bite their Anamil at you in rage.)

The word Anamil, means the tips of the fingers, as Qatadah stated. This is the behavior of the hypocrites who pretend to be believers and kind when they are with the believers, all the while concealing the opposite in their hearts in every respect. This is the exact situation that Allah describes,

(But when they are alone, they bite their Anamil at you in rage) and rage is extreme anger and fury. Allah said to them,

(Say: "Perish in your rage. Certainly, Allah knows what is in the breasts (all the secrets).") for no matter how much you envy the believers and feel rage towards them, know that Allah shall perfect His favor on His believing servants, complete His religion, raise high His Word and give dominance to His religion. Therefore, O hypocrites, die in rage,

(Allah knows what is in the breasts.)

Allah has perfect knowledge of what you conceal in your hearts and chests and in the rage, envy and hatred you have against the believers. Allah will punish you for all this in this life, and they will have the good that you dislike for them. In the Hereafter, you will suffer severe torment in the Fire where you will remain for eternity.

Thereafter, Allah said,

(If a good befalls you, it grieves them, but if some evil overtakes you, they rejoice at it) (3:120). This only emphasizes the severity of the enmity that the hypocrites feel against the believers. If the believers enjoy fertile years, victories, support and their numbers and following increase, the hypocrites become displeased. When the Muslims suffer a drought or their enemies gain the upper hand against them, by Allah's decree, just as occurred during the battle of Uhud, the hypocrites become pleased. Allah said to His believing servants,

(But if you remain patient and have Taqwa, not the least harm will their cunning do to you.)

Allah directs the believers to safety from the wickedness of evil people and the plots of the sinners, by recommending them to revert to patience and by having fear of Allah and trusting Him. Allah encompasses the enemies of the believers, all the while the believers have no power or strength except from Him. Whatever Allah wills, occurs, and whatever He does not will, does not occur. Nothing happens in His Kingdom except with His decision and according to His decrees. Verily, whoever relies on Allah, Allah shall suffice for him.

Allah then mentions the story of Uhud, the defeat that He tested the believers with, His distinguishing the believers from the hypocrites and their patience.

Surah: 3 Ayah: 121, Ayah: 122 & Ayah: 123

﴿وَإِذْ غَدَوْتَ مِنْ أَهْلِكَ تُبَوِّئُ ٱلْمُؤْمِنِينَ مَقَٰعِدَ لِلْقِتَالِ ۗ وَٱللَّهُ سَمِيعٌ عَلِيمٌ ﴿١٢١﴾﴾

121. And (remember) when you (Muhammad (peace be upon him)) left your household in the morning to post the believers at their stations for the battle (of Uhud). And Allâh is All-Hearer, All-Knower.

﴿إِذْ هَمَّت طَّآئِفَتَانِ مِنكُمْ أَن تَفْشَلَا وَٱللَّهُ وَلِيُّهُمَا ۗ وَعَلَى ٱللَّهِ فَلْيَتَوَكَّلِ ٱلْمُؤْمِنُونَ ﴿١٢٢﴾﴾

122. When two parties from among you were about to lose heart, but Allâh was their Walî (Supporter and Protector). And in Allâh should the believers put their trust.

﴿وَلَقَدْ نَصَرَكُمُ ٱللَّهُ بِبَدْرٍ وَأَنتُمْ أَذِلَّةٌ ۖ فَٱتَّقُوا۟ ٱللَّهَ لَعَلَّكُمْ تَشْكُرُونَ ﴿١٢٣﴾﴾

123. And Allâh has already made you victorious at Badr, when you were a weak little force. So fear Allâh much that you may be grateful.

Transliteration

121. Wa-ith ghadawta min ahlika tubawwi-o almu/mineena maqaAAida lilqitali waAllahu sameeAAun AAaleemun 122. Ith hammat ta-ifatani minkum an tafshala waAllahu waliyyuhuma waAAala Allahi falyatawakkali almu/minoona 123. Walaqad nasarakumu Allahu bibadrin waantum athillatun faittaqoo Allaha laAAallakum tashkuroona

Tafsir Ibn Kathir

The Battle of Uhud

According to the majority of scholars, these Ayat are describing the battle of Uhud, as Ibn `Abbas, Al-Hasan, Qatadah, As-Suddi and others said. The battle of Uhud occurred on a Saturday, in the month of Shawwal on the third year of Hijrah. `Ikrimah said that Uhud occurred in the middle of the month of Shawwal, and Allah knows best.

The Reason Behind the Battle of Uhud

The idolators suffered many casualties among their noble men at the battle of Badr. The caravan that Abu Sufyan led (before Badr) returned safely to Makkah, prompting the remaining Makkan leaders and the children of those who were killed at Badr to demand from Abu Sufyan to, "Spend this money on fighting Muhammad!" Consequently, they spent the money from the caravan on warfare expenses and mobilized their forces including the Ahabish tribes (tribes living around the city). They gathered three thousand soldiers and marched until they camped near Uhud facing Al-Madinah. The Messenger of Allah led the Friday prayer and when he finished with it, he performed the funeral prayer for a man from Bani An-Najjar called Malik bin `Amr. The Prophet then asked the Muslims for advice, if they should march to meet the disbelievers, or fortify themselves in Al-Madinah. `Abdullah bin Ubayy (the chief hypocrite) advised that they should remain in Al-Madinah, saying that if the disbelievers lay siege to Al-

Madinah, the siege would be greatly disadvantageous to them. He added that if they decide to attack Al-Madinah, its men would face off with them, while women and children could throw rocks at them from above their heads; and if they decide to return to Makkah, they would return with failure. However, some companions who did not attend the battle of Badr advised that the Muslims should go out to Uhud to meet the disbelievers.

The Messenger of Allah went to his home, put on his shield and came out. The companions were weary then and said to each other, "Did we compel the Messenger of Allah to go out" They said, "O Messenger of Allah! If you wish, we will remain in Al-Madinah. " The Messenger of Allah said,

«مَا يَنْبَغِي لِنَبِيَ إِذَا لَبِسَ لَأْمَتَهُ أَنْ يَرْجِعَ حَتَّى يَحْكُمَ اللهُ لَه»

(It is not for a Prophet to wear his shield for war then lay down his arms before Allah decides in his favor.)

The Messenger of Allah marched with a thousand of his Companions. When they reached the Shawt area, `Abdullah bin Ubayy went back to Al-Madinah with a third of the army, claiming he was angry the Prophet did not listen to his advice. He and his supporters said, "If we knew that you would fight today, we would have accompanied you. However, we do not think that you will fight today." The Messenger of Allah marched until he reached the hillside in the area of Uhud, where they camped in the valley with Mount Uhud behind them. The Messenger of Allah said,

«لَا يُقَاتِلَنَّ أَحَدٌ حَتَّى نَأْمُرَهُ بِالْقِتَال»

(No one starts fighting until I issue the command to fight.)

The Messenger prepared his forces for battle, and his army was seven hundred men. He appointed `Abdullah bin Jubayr, from Bani `Amr bin `Awf, to lead the archers who were fifty men. The Prophet said to them,

«انْضَحُوا الْخَيْلَ عَنَّا، وَلَا نُؤْتَيَنَّ مِنْ قِبَلِكُمْ، وَالْزَمُوا مَكَانَكُمْ، إِنْ كَانَتِ النَّوْبَةُ لَنَا أَوْ عَلَيْنَا، وَإِنْ رَأَيْتُمُونَا تَخْطَفُنَا الطَّيْرُ فَلَا تَبْرَحُوا مَكَانَكُم»

(Keep the horsemen away from us, and be aware that we might be attacked from your direction. If victory was for or against us, remain in your positions. And even if you see us being picked up by birds, do not abandon your positions.)

The Prophet wore two protective shields and gave the flag to Mus`ab bin `Umayr of Bani `Abd Ad-Dar. The Prophet also allowed some young men to participate in fighting, but not others, whom he allowed to participate in the battle of Al-Khandaq two years later. The Quraysh mobilized their forces of three thousand men with two hundred horsemen on each flank. They appointed Khalid bin Al-Walid to lead the right side of the horsemen and `Ikrimah Ibn Abi Jahl on the left side. They also gave their grand flag to the tribe of Bani `Abd Ad-Dar. Allah willing, we will mention the details of this battle later on, if Allah wills. Allah said here,

(And (remember) when you left your household in the morning to post the believers at their stations for the battle) (3:121), designating them to various positions, dividing the army to the left and right sides and placing them wherever you command them.

(And Allah is All-Hearer, All-Knower), He hears what you say and knows what you conceal in your hearts. Allah said next,

(When two parties from among you were about to lose heart,) (3:122).

Al-Bukhari recorded that Jabir bin `Abdullah said, "The Ayah,

(When two parties from among you were about to lose heart) was revealed about us, (the two Muslim tribes of) Bani Harithah and Bani Salamah. I (or we) would not be pleased if it was not revealed, because Allah said in it,

(but Allah was their Wali (Supporter and Protector)) (3:122)."

Muslim recorded this Hadith from Sufyan bin `Uyaynah.

Reminding the Believers of Their Victory at Badr

Allah said,

(And Allah has already made you victorious at Badr,)(3:123) meaning, during the battle of Badr, which occurred on a Friday, the seventeenth of Ramadan, in the second year of Hijrah.

The day of Badr is known as Yawm Al-Furqan (the Day of the Clarification), by which Allah gave victory and dominance to Islam and its people and disgraced and destroyed Shirk, even though the Muslims were few. The Muslims numbered three hundred and thirteen men, with two horses and seventy camels. The rest were foot soldiers without enough supplies for the battle. The enemy army consisted of nine hundred to a thousand men, having enough shields and supplies, battle-ready horses and even various adornments.

However, Allah gave victory to His Messenger , supported His revelation, and illuminated success on the faces of the Prophet and his following. Allah also brought disgrace to Shayatan and his army. This is why Allah reminded His believing servants and pious party of this favor,

(And Allah has already made you victorious at Badr, when you were a weak little force), cwhen you were few then. This Ayah reminds them that victory is only from Allah, not because of a large army and adequate supplies. This is why Allah said in another Ayah,

(. .and on the day of Hunayn (battle) when you rejoiced at your great number, but it availed you naught) (9:25), until,

(And Allah is Oft-Forgiving, Most Merciful) (9:27).

Badr is an area between Makkah and Al-Madinah and is known by the well that bears its name, which in turn was so named after Badr bin An-Narayn, the person who dug the well.

(So have Taqwa of Allah that you may be grateful.) (3:123), means, fulfill the obligations of His obedience.

Surah: 3 Ayah: 124, Ayah: 125, Ayah: 126, Ayah: 127, Ayah: 128 & Ayah: 129

﴿إِذۡ تَقُولُ لِلۡمُؤۡمِنِينَ أَلَن يَكۡفِيَكُمۡ أَن يُمِدَّكُمۡ رَبُّكُم بِثَلَٰثَةِ ءَالَٰفٖ مِّنَ ٱلۡمَلَٰٓئِكَةِ
مُنزَلِينَ ١٢٤﴾

124. (Remember) when you (Muhammad (peace be upon him)) said to the believers, "Is it not enough for you that your Lord (Allâh) should help you with three thousand angels sent down?"

﴿بَلَىٰٓۚ إِن تَصۡبِرُواْ وَتَتَّقُواْ وَيَأۡتُوكُم مِّن فَوۡرِهِمۡ هَٰذَا يُمۡدِدۡكُمۡ رَبُّكُم بِخَمۡسَةِ ءَالَٰفٖ مِّنَ
ٱلۡمَلَٰٓئِكَةِ مُسَوِّمِينَ ١٢٥﴾

125. "Yes, if you hold on to patience and piety, and the enemy comes rushing at you; your Lord will help you with five thousand angels having marks (of distinction)."

﴿وَمَا جَعَلَهُ ٱللَّهُ إِلَّا بُشۡرَىٰ لَكُمۡ وَلِتَطۡمَئِنَّ قُلُوبُكُم بِهِۦۗ وَمَا ٱلنَّصۡرُ إِلَّا مِنۡ عِندِ ٱللَّهِ ٱلۡعَزِيزِ
ٱلۡحَكِيمِ ١٢٦﴾

126. Allâh made it not but as a message of good news for you and as an assurance to your hearts. And there is no victory except from Allâh, the All-Mighty, the All-Wise.

﴿لِيَقۡطَعَ طَرَفٗا مِّنَ ٱلَّذِينَ كَفَرُوٓاْ أَوۡ يَكۡبِتَهُمۡ فَيَنقَلِبُواْ خَآئِبِينَ ١٢٧﴾

127. That He might cut off a part of those who disbelieve, or expose them to infamy, so that they retire frustrated.

﴿لَيۡسَ لَكَ مِنَ ٱلۡأَمۡرِ شَيۡءٌ أَوۡ يَتُوبَ عَلَيۡهِمۡ أَوۡ يُعَذِّبَهُمۡ فَإِنَّهُمۡ ظَٰلِمُونَ ١٢٨﴾

128. Not for you (O Muhammad (peace be upon him) but for Allâh) is the decision; whether He turns in mercy to (pardons) them or punishes them; verily, they are the Zâlimûn (polytheists, disobedients, and wrong-doers).

﴿وَلِلَّهِ مَا فِي ٱلسَّمَٰوَٰتِ وَمَا فِي ٱلۡأَرۡضِۚ يَغۡفِرُ لِمَن يَشَآءُ وَيُعَذِّبُ مَن يَشَآءُۚ وَٱللَّهُ غَفُورٞ
رَّحِيمٞ ١٢٩﴾

129. And to Allâh belongs all that is in the heavens and all that is in the earth. He forgives whom He wills, and punishes whom He wills. And Allâh is Oft-Forgiving, Most Merciful.

Transliteration

124. Ith taqoolu lilmu/mineena alan yakfiyakum an yumiddakum rabbukum bithalathati alafin mina almala-ikati munzaleena 125. Bala in tasbiroo watattaqoo waya/tookum min fawrihim hatha yumdidkum rabbukum bikhamsati alafin mina almala-ikati musawwimeena 126. Wama jaAAalahu Allahu illa bushra lakum walitatma-inna quloobukum bihi wama alnnasru illa min AAindi Allahi alAAazeezi alhakeemi 127. LiyaqtaAAa tarafan mina allatheena kafaroo aw

yakbitahum fayanqaliboo kha-ibeena 128. Laysa laka mina al-amri shay-on aw yatooba AAalayhim aw yuAAaththibahum fa-innahum thalimoona 129. Walillahi ma fee alssamawati wama fee al-ardi yaghfiru liman yashao wayuAAaththibu man yashao waAllahu ghafoorun raheemun

Tafsir Ibn Kathir

The Support of the Angels

The scholars of Tafsir differ over whether the promise contained in these Ayat referred to the battle of Badr or Uhud. The First View

There are two opinions about this, one of them saying that Allah's statement,

((Remember) when you said to the believers) (3:124), is related to His statement,

(And Allah has already made you victorious at Badr) (3:123).

This was reported from Al-Hasan Al-Basri, `Amr Ash-Sha`bi, Ar-Rabi` bin Anas and several others, Ibn Jarir also agreed with this opinion. `Abbad bin Mansur said that Al-Hasan said that Allah's statement,

((Remember) when you said to the believers, "Is it not enough for you that your Lord should help you with three thousand angels") (3:124), is about the battle of Badr; Ibn Abi Hatim also recorded this statement.

Ibn Abi Hatim then reported that `Amr Ash-Sha`bi said, "On the day of Badr, the Muslims received information that Kurz bin Jabir (a prominent tribe chief) was aiding the idolators, and this news was hard on them, so Allah revealed;

("Is it not enough for you that your Lord (Allah) should help you with three thousand angels sent down"), until,

(having marks (of distinction)) (3:124,125).

The news of the defeat of the idolators (at Badr) reached Kurz and he did not reinforce them, and thus, Allah did not reinforce the Muslims with the five (thousands of angels)."

As for Ar-Rabi` bin Anas, he said, "Allah supported the Muslims with one thousand (angels), then the number reached three thousand, then five thousand." If one asks, according to this opinion, how can we combine between this Ayah and Allah's statement about Badr,

((Remember) when you sought help of your Lord and He answered you (saying): "I will help you with a thousand angels, each behind the other (following one another) in succession.") (8:9), until,

(Verily! Allah is All-Mighty, All-Wise) We say that the one thousand mentioned here does not contradict the three thousand mentioned in the above Ayah (3:124). The word "in succession" means they follow each other and thus indicates that thousands more will follow them. The two Ayat above (8:9 and 3:124) are similar in meaning and it appears that they both were about the battle of Badr, because the angels did fight in the battle of Badr, as the evidence indicates. Allah knows best. Allah's statement,

(But if you hold on to patience and have Taqwa,) (3:125) means, if you observe patience while fighting the enemy, all the while fearing Me and obeying My command. Al-Hasan, Qatadah, Ar-Rabi` and As-Suddi said that Allah's statement,

(and they will come rushing) means, they (angels) will rush to you instantaneously. Al-`Awfi said that Ibn `Abbas said that the Ayah means, "All at once". It is also said that it means, before their anger subsides (against the disbelievers). The Second View

The second opinion stipulates that the promise mentioned here (concerning the angels participating in battle) is related to Allah's statement,

(And (remember) when you left your household in the morning to post the believers at their stations for the battle) of Uhud. However, we should add, the angels did not come to the aid of Muslims at Uhud, because Allah made it conditional,

(But if you hold on to patience and have Taqwa) (3: 125).

The Muslims were not patient at Uhud. Rather, they ran away and, consequently, did not receive the support of even one angel.

Allah's statement,

(your Lord will help you with five thousand angels having marks), of distinction.

Abu Ishaq As-Subay`i said; from Harithah bin Mudarrib said that `Ali bin Abi Talib said, "The angels were distinguished by wearing white wool at Badr." The angels also had special markings distinguishing their horses.

Allah said,

(Allah made it not but as a message of good news for you and as an assurance to your hearts) (3:126).

This Ayah means, "Allah sent down angels and told you about their descent to encourage you and to comfort and reassure your hearts. You should know that victory only comes from Allah and that if He willed, He would have defeated your enemy without you having to fight them." For instance, Allah said after commanding the believers to fight,

(But if it had been Allah's will, He Himself could certainly have punished them (without you). But (He lets you fight) in order to test some of you with others. But those who are killed in the way of Allah, He will never let their deeds be lost. He will guide them and set right their state. And admit them to Paradise which He has made known to them) (47:4-6).

This is why Allah said here,

(Allah made it not but as a message of good news for you and as an assurance to your hearts. And there is no victory except from Allah, the All-Mighty, the All-Wise) (3:126).

This Ayah means, "Allah is the Almighty Whose power can never be undermined, and He has the perfect wisdom in His decrees and in all His decisions." Allah said,

(That He might cut off a part of those who disbelieve,) (3:127) meaning, out of His wisdom, He commands you to perform Jihad and to fight.

Allah then mentions the various consequences of performing Jihad against the disbelievers. For instance, Allah said,

(That He might cut off a part...) meaning, to cause a part of a nation to perish,

(of those who disbelieve, or expose them to infamy,) by disgracing them and forcing them to return with only their rage, having failed in their aim to harm you. This is why Allah said next,

(or expose them to infamy, so that they retire) to go back to their land,

(frustrated) without achieving their aims.

Allah then mentions a statement that testifies that the decision in this life and the Hereafter is for Him Alone without partners,

(Not for you is the decision) (3:128)

meaning, "The matter is all in My Hand." Allah also said,

(your duty is only to convey (the Message) and on Us is the reckoning.) (13:40), and,

(Not upon you is their guidance, but Allah guides whom He wills.) (2:272), and,

(Verily, you guide not whom you like, but Allah guides whom He wills) (28: 56).

Muhammad bin Ishaq said that Allah's statement,

(Not for you is the decision;), means, "No part of the decision regarding My servants is yours, except what I command you." Allah then mentions the rest of the consequences of Jihad,

(whether He pardons them) concerning the acts of disbelief that they commit, thus delivering them from misguidance to the guidance.

(or punishes them;) in this life and the Hereafter because of their disbelief and errors,

(verily, they are the wrongdoers), and thus, they deserve such a fate.

Al-Bukhari recorded that, Salim bin `Abdullah said that his father said that he heard the Messenger of Allah saying -- when he raised his head from bowing in the second unit of the Fajr prayer -- "O Allah! Curse so-and-so," after saying; Sami` Allahu Liman Hamidah, Rabbana wa lakal-Hamd. Thereafter, Allah revealed this Ayah,

(Not for you is the decision;) This was also recorded by An-Nasa'i. Imam Ahmad recorded that Salim bin `Abdullah said that his father said that he heard the Messenger of Allah saying,

«اللَّهُمَّ الْعَنْ فُلَانًا، اللَّهُمَّ الْعَنِ الْحَارِثَ بْنَ هِشَامٍ، اللَّهُمَّ الْعَنْ سُهَيْلَ بْنَ عَمْرٍو، اللَّهُمَّ الْعَنْ صَفْوَانَ بْنَ أُمَيَّةَ»

(O Allah! Curse so-and-so. O Allah! Curse Al-Harith bin Hisham. O Allah! Curse Suhayl bin `Amr. O Allah! Curse Safwan bin Umayyah.)

Thereafter, this Ayah was revealed;

(Not for you is the decision; whether He turns in mercy to (pardon) them or punishes them; verily, they are the wrongdoers) (3:128).

All these persons were pardoned (after they embraced Islam later on).

Al-Bukhari recorded that Abu Hurayrah said that when Allah's Messenger would supplicate against or for someone, he would do so when he was finished bowing and saying; Sami` Allahu Liman Hamidah, Rabbana wa lakal-Hamd. He would then say, (the Qunut)

«اللَّهُمَّ أَنْجِ الْوَلِيدَ بْنَ الْوَلِيدِ، وَسَلَمَةَ بْنَ هِشَامٍ وَعَيَّاشَ بْنَ أَبِي رَبِيعَةَ، وَالْمُسْتَضْعَفِينَ مِنَ الْمُؤْمِنِينَ، اللَّهُمَّ اشْدُدْ وَطْأَتَكَ عَلى مُضَرَ، وَاجْعَلْهَا عَلَيْهِمْ سِنِينَ كَسِنِي يُوسُف»

(O Allah! Save Al-Walid bin Al-Walid, Salamah bin Hisham, `Ayyash bin Abi Rabi`ah and the weak and the helpless people among the faithful believers. O Allah! Be hard on the tribe of Mudar and let them suffer from years of famine like that of the time of Yusuf.)

He would say this supplication aloud. He sometimes would supplicate during the Dawn prayer, "O Allah! Curse so-and-so (persons)," mentioning some Arab tribes. Thereafter, Allah revealed,

(Not for you is the decision.)

Al-Bukhari recorded that Hamid and Thabit said that, Anas bin Malik said that the Prophet was injured during the battle of Uhud and said,

«كَيْفَ يُفْلِحُ قَوْمٌ شَجُّوا نَبِيَّهُمْ؟»

(How can a people achieve success after having injured their Prophet)

Thereafter,

(Not for you is the decision,) was revealed.

Imam Ahmad recorded that Anas said that, the Prophet's front tooth was broken during the battle of Uhud and he also sustained injuries on his forehead until blood dripped on his face. The Prophet said,

«كَيْفَ يُفْلِحُ قَوْمٌ فَعَلُوا هذَا بِنَبِيِّهِمْ، وَهُوَ يَدْعُوهُمْ إِلى رَبِّهِمْ عَزَّ وَجَلَّ؟»

(How can a people achieve success after having done this to their Prophet who is calling them to their Lord, the Exalted and Most Honored) Allah revealed,

(Not for you is the decision; whether He turns in mercy to (pardons) them or punishes them; verily, they are the wrongdoers.) Muslim also collected this Hadith.

Allah then said,

(And to Allah belongs all that is in the heavens and all that is in the Earth.) (3:129), everything is indeed the property of Allah and all are servants in His Hand.

(He forgives whom He wills, and punishes whom He wills.) for His is the decision and none can resist His decision. Allah is never asked about what He does, while they will be asked,

(and Allah is Oft-Forgiving, Most Merciful.)

Surah: 3 Ayah: 130, Ayah: 131, Ayah: 132, Ayah: 133, Ayah: 134, Ayah: 135 & Ayah: 136

﴿ يَٰٓأَيُّهَا ٱلَّذِينَ ءَامَنُواْ لَا تَأۡكُلُواْ ٱلرِّبَوٰٓاْ أَضۡعَٰفٗا مُّضَٰعَفَةٗۖ وَٱتَّقُواْ ٱللَّهَ لَعَلَّكُمۡ
تُفۡلِحُونَ ١٣٠ ﴾

130. O you who believe! Eat not Ribâ (usury) doubled and multiplied, but fear Allâh that you may be successful.

﴿ وَٱتَّقُواْ ٱلنَّارَ ٱلَّتِيٓ أُعِدَّتۡ لِلۡكَٰفِرِينَ ١٣١ ﴾

131. And fear the Fire, which is prepared for the disbelievers.

﴿ وَأَطِيعُواْ ٱللَّهَ وَٱلرَّسُولَ لَعَلَّكُمۡ تُرۡحَمُونَ ١٣٢ ﴾

132. And obey Allâh and the Messenger (Muhammad (peace be upon him)) that you may obtain mercy.

﴿ ۞ وَسَارِعُوٓاْ إِلَىٰ مَغۡفِرَةٖ مِّن رَّبِّكُمۡ وَجَنَّةٍ عَرۡضُهَا ٱلسَّمَٰوَٰتُ وَٱلۡأَرۡضُ أُعِدَّتۡ
لِلۡمُتَّقِينَ ١٣٣ ﴾

133. And march forth in the way (which leads to) forgiveness from your Lord, and for Paradise as wide as the heavens and the earth, prepared for Al-Muttaqûn (the pious - see V.2:2).

﴿ ٱلَّذِينَ يُنفِقُونَ فِي ٱلسَّرَّآءِ وَٱلضَّرَّآءِ وَٱلۡكَٰظِمِينَ ٱلۡغَيۡظَ وَٱلۡعَافِينَ عَنِ ٱلنَّاسِۗ وَٱللَّهُ
يُحِبُّ ٱلۡمُحۡسِنِينَ ١٣٤ ﴾

134. Those who spend (in Allâh's Cause) in prosperity and in adversity, who repress anger, and who pardon men; verily, Allâh loves Al-Muhsinûn (the good-doers).

﴿ وَٱلَّذِينَ إِذَا فَعَلُواْ فَٰحِشَةً أَوۡ ظَلَمُوٓاْ أَنفُسَهُمۡ ذَكَرُواْ ٱللَّهَ فَٱسۡتَغۡفَرُواْ لِذُنُوبِهِمۡ وَمَن
يَغۡفِرُ ٱلذُّنُوبَ إِلَّا ٱللَّهُ وَلَمۡ يُصِرُّواْ عَلَىٰ مَا فَعَلُواْ وَهُمۡ يَعۡلَمُونَ ١٣٥ ﴾

135. And those who, when they have committed Fahishah (illegal sexual intercourse) or wronged themselves with evil, remember Allâh and ask forgiveness for their sins; - and none can forgive sins but Allâh - And do not persist in what (wrong) they have done, while they know.

﴿ أُوْلَـٰٓئِكَ جَزَآؤُهُم مَّغْفِرَةٌ مِّن رَّبِّهِمْ وَجَنَّـٰتٌ تَجْرِى مِن تَحْتِهَا ٱلْأَنْهَـٰرُ خَـٰلِدِينَ فِيهَا ۚ وَنِعْمَ أَجْرُ ٱلْعَـٰمِلِينَ ﴿١٣٦﴾ ﴾

136. For such, the reward is Forgiveness from their Lord, and Gardens with rivers flowing underneath (Paradise), wherein they shall abide forever. How excellent is this reward for the doers (who do righteous deeds according to Allâh's Orders).

Transliteration

130. Ya ayyuha allatheena amanoo la ta/kuloo alrriba adAAafan mudaAAafatan waittaqoo Allaha laAAallakum tuflihoona 131. Waittaqoo alnnara allatee oAAiddat lilkafireena 132. WaateeAAoo Allaha waalrrasoola laAAallakum turhamoona 133. WasariAAoo ila maghfiratin min rabbikum wajannatin AAarduha alssamawatu waal-ardu oAAiddat lilmuttaqeena 134. Allatheena yunfiqoona fee alssarra-i waalddarra-i waalkathimeena alghaytha waalAAafeena AAani alnnasi waAllahu yuhibbu almuhsineena 135. Waallatheena itha faAAaloo fahishatan aw thalamoo anfusahum thakaroo Allaha faistaghfaroo lithunoobihim waman yaghfiru alththunooba illa Allahu walam yusirroo AAala ma faAAaloo wahum yaAAlamoona 136. Ola-ika jazaohum maghfiratun min rabbihim wajannatun tajree min tahtiha al-anharu khalideena feeha waniAAma ajru alAAamileena

Tafsir Ibn Kathir

Interest (Riba) is Prohibited

Allah prohibits His believing servants from dealing in Riba and from requiring interest on their capital, just as they used to do during the time of Jahiliyyah. For instance, when the time to pay a loan comes, the creditor would say to the debtor, "Either pay now, or the loan will incur interest." If the debtor asks for deferment of the loan, the creditor would require interest and this would occur year after year until the little capital becomes multiplied many times. Allah also commands His servants to have Taqwa of Him so that they may achieve success in this life and the Hereafter. Allah also threatens them with the Fire and warns them against it, saying,

(And fear the Fire, which is prepared for the disbelievers. And obey Allah and the Messenger that you may obtain mercy.) (3:131,132).

The Encouragment to Do Good for which Paradise is the Result

Allah encourages His servants to perform righteous deeds and to rush to accomplish the acts of obedience. Allah said,

(And march forth in the way (which leads to) forgiveness from your Lord, and for Paradise as wide as the heavens and the earth, prepared for the Muttaqin (the pious)) (3:133).

Just as the Fire was prepared for the disbelievers. It was reported that the meaning of Allah's statement, (as wide as the heavens and the earth) draws the attention to the spaciousness of Paradise. For instance, Allah said in another Ayah, while describing the couches of Paradise,

(lined with silk brocade) (55:54), so what about their outer covering It was also said that Paradise is as wide as its length, because it is a dome under the Throne. The width and length of a dome or a circle are the same in distance. This is supported by what is found in the Sahih;

«إِذَا سَأَلْتُمُ اللهَ الْجَنَّـــةَ فَاسْأَلُوهُ الْفِرْدَوْسَ، فَإِنَّهُ أَعْلَى الْجَنَّـــةِ، وَأَوْسَطُ الْجَنَّةِ، وَمِنْهُ تَفَجَّرُ أَنْهَارُ الْجَنَّةِ، وَسَقْفُهَا عَرْشُ الرَّحْمَنِ»

(When you ask Allah for Paradise, ask Him for Al-Firdaws which is the highest and best part of Paradise. From it originate the rivers of Paradise, and above it is the Throne of the Most Beneficent (Allah).)

This Ayah (3:133 above) is similar to Allah's statement in Surat Al-Hadid,

(Race with one another in hastening towards forgiveness from your Lord (Allah), and Paradise the width whereof is as the width of the heaven and the Earth) (57:21).

Al-Bazzar recorded that Abu Hurayrah said that a man came to the Messenger of Allah and asked him, about Allah's statement,

(Paradise as wide as the heavens and the Earth) (3:133); "Where is the Fire then" The Prophet said,

«أَرَأَيْتَ اللَّيْلَ إِذَا جَاءَ لَبِسَ كُلَّ شَيْءٍ، فَأَيْنَ النَّهَارُ؟»

(When the night comes, it overtakes everything, so where is the day) The man said, "Where Allah wants it to be." The Prophet said,

«وَكَذلِكَ النَّارُ تَكُونُ حَيْثُ شَاءَ اللهُ عَزَّ وَجَلَ»

(Similarly, the Fire is where Allah wants it to be.) This Hadith has two possible meanings. First, when we do not see the night during the day, this does not mean that the night is not somewhere else, even though we cannot see it. Such is the case with Hell-fire, for it is where Allah wants it to be. The second meaning is that when the day overcomes this part of the world, the night overtakes the other part. Such is the case with Paradise, for it is in the utmost heights above the heavens and under the Throne. The width of Paradise is, as Allah stated,

(whereof is as the width of the heaven and the Earth) (57:21).

The Fire, on the other hand, is in the lowest of lows. Therefore, Paradise being as wide as the heavens and Earth does not contradict the fact that the Fire exists wherever Allah wills it to be.

Allah said, while describing the people of Paradise,

(Those who spend (in Allah's cause) in prosperity and in adversity) (3:134), in hard times and easy times, while active (or enthusiastic) and otherwise, healthy or ill, and in all conditions, just as Allah said in another Ayah,

(Those who spend their wealth (in Allah's cause) by night and day, in secret and in public) (2:274) These believers are never distracted from obeying Allah, spending on what pleases Him, being kind to His servants and their relatives, and other acts of righteousness. Allah said,

(who repress anger, and who pardon men;) (3:134) for when they are angry, they control their anger and do act upon it. Rather, they even forgive those who hurt them. Imam Ahmad recorded that Abu Hurayrah said that the Prophet said,

«لَيْسَ الشَّدِيدُ بِالصُّرَعَةِ، وَلكِنَّ الشَّدِيدَ الَّذِي يَمْلِكُ نَفْسَهُ عِنْدَ الْغَضَبِ»

(The strong person is not he who is able to physically overcome people. The strong person is he who overcomes his rage when he is angry.)

This Hadith is also recorded in the Two Sahihs. Imam Ahmad recorded that Ibn `Abbas said that the Messenger of Allah said,

«مَنْ أَنْظَرَ مُعْسِرًا أَوْ وَضَعَ لَهُ، وَقَاهُ اللهُ مِنْ فَيْحِ جَهَنَّمَ، أَلَا إِنَّ عَمَلَ الْجَنَّــةِ حَزْنٌ بِرَبْوَةٍ ثَلَاثًا أَلَا إِنَّ عَمَلَ النَّارِ سَهْلٌ بِسَهْوَةٍ. وَالسَّعِيدُ مَنْ وُقِيَ الْفِتَنَ، وَمَا مِنْ جَرْعَةٍ أَحَبُّ إِلَى اللهِ مِنْ جَرْعَةِ غَيْظٍ يَكْظِمُهَا عَبْدٌ، مَا كَظَمَهَا عَبْدٌ للهِ إِلَّا مَلَأَ جَوْفَهُ إِيمَانًا»

(He who gives time to a debtor or forgives him, then Allah will save him from the heat of Jahannam (Hell-fire). Behold! The deeds of Paradise are difficult to reach, for they are on top of a hill, while the deeds of the Fire are easy to find in the lowlands. The happy person is he who is saved from the tests. Verily, there is no dose of anything better to Allah than a dose of rage that the servant controls, and whenever the servant of Allah controls it, he will be internally filled with faith.)

This Hadith was recorded by Imam Ahmad, its chain of narration is good, it does not contain any disparraged narrators, and the meaning is good.

Imam Ahmad recorded that Sahl bin Mu`adh bin Anas said that his father said that the Messenger of Allah said,

«مَنْ كَظَمَ غَيْظًا وَهُوَ قَادِرٌ عَلى أَنْ يُنْفِذَهُ دَعَاهُ اللهُ عَلى رُؤُوسِ الْخَلَائِقِ حَتَّى يُخَيِّرَهُ مِنْ أَيِّ الْحُورِ شَاء»

(Whoever controlled rage while able to act upon it, then Allah will call him while all creation is a witness, until He gives him the choice of any of the Huris (fair females with wide, lovely eyes - as mates for the pious) he wishes.)

Abu Dawud, At-Tirmidhi and Ibn Majah collected this Hadith, which At-Tirmidhi said was "Hasan Gharib".

Ibn Marduwyah recorded that Ibn `Umar said that the Messenger of Allah said,

«مَا تَجَرَّعَ عَبْدٌ مِنْ جَرْعَةٍ أَفْضَلَ أَجْرًا مِنْ جَرْعَةِ غَيْظٍ كَظَمَهَا ابْتِغَاءَ وَجْهِ اللهِ»

(There is not a dose of anything that the servant takes which is better than a dose of control of rage that he feels, when he does it seeking Allah's Face.) Ibn Jarir and Ibn Majah also collected this Hadith.

Allah said,

(who repress anger) meaning, they do not satisfy their rage upon people. Rather, they refrain from harming them and await their rewards with Allah, the Exalted and Most Honored. Allah then said,

(and who pardon men;) They forgive those who treat them with injustice. Therefore, they do not hold any ill feelings about anyone in their hearts, and this is the most excellent conduct in this regard. This is why Allah said,

(verily, Allah loves the Muhsinin (the good-doers)).

This good conduct is a type of Ihsan (excellence in the religion). There is a Hadith that reads,

«ثَلَاثٌ أُقْسِمُ عَلَيْهِنَّ: مَا نَقَصَ مَالٌ مِنْ صَدَقَةٍ، وَمَا زَادَ اللهُ عَبْدًا بِعَفْوٍ إِلَّا عِزًّا، وَمَنْ تَوَاضَعَ للهِ رَفَعَهُ اللهُ»

(I swear regarding three matters: no charity shall ever decrease the wealth; whenever one forgives people, then Allah will magnify his honor; and he who is humble for Allah, then Allah will raise his rank.)

Allah said,

(And those who, when they have committed Fahishah or wronged themselves with evil, remember Allah and ask forgiveness for their sins) (3:135).

Therefore, if they commit an error they follow it with repentance and ask forgiveness. Imam Ahmad recorded that Abu Hurayrah said that the Prophet said,

«إِنَّ رَجُلًا أَذْنَبَ ذَنْبًا فَقَالَ: رَبِّ إِنِّي أَذْنَبْتُ ذَنْبًا فَاغْفِرْهُ، فَقَالَ اللهُ عَزَّ وَجَلَّ: عَبْدِي عَمِلَ ذَنْبًا فَعَلِمَ أَنَّ لَهُ رَبًّا يَغْفِرُ الذَّنْبَ وَيَأْخُذُ بِهِ، قَدْ غَفَرْتُ لِعَبْدِي، ثُمَّ عَمِلَ ذَنْبًا آخرَ فَقَالَ: رَبِّ إِنِّي عَمِلْتُ ذَنْبًا فَاغْفِرْهُ، فَقَالَ تَبَارَكَ وَتَعَالَى: عَلِمَ عَبْدِي أَنَّ لَهُ رَبًّا يَغْفِرُ الذَّنْبَ وَيَأْخُذُ بِهِ،قَدْ غَفَرْتُ لِعَبْدِي، ثُمَّ عَمِلَ ذَنْبًا آخرَ فَقَالَ: رَبِّ إِنِّي عَمِلْتُ ذَنْبًا فَاغْفِرْهُ لِي، فَقَالَ اللهُ عَزَّ وَجَلَّ: عَلِمَ عَبْدِي أَنَّ لَهُ رَبًّا يَغْفِرُ الذَّنْبَ وَيَأْخُذُ بِهِ، قَدْ غَفَرْتُ لِعَبْدِي، ثُمَّ عَمِلَ ذَنْبًا آخرَ فَقَالَ: رَبِّ إِنِّي عَمِلْتُ ذَنْبًا فَاغْفِرْهُ لِي، فَقَالَ اللهُ عَزَّ وَجَلَّ: عَلِمَ عَبْدِي أَنَّ لَهُ رَبًّا يَغْفِرُ الذَّنْبَ وَيَأْخُذُ بِهِ، أُشْهِدُكُمْ أَنِّي قَدْ غَفَرْتُ لِعَبْدِي فَلْيَعْمَلْ مَا شَاء»

(A man once committed an error and said, `O Lord! I committed an error, so forgive me.' Allah said, `My servant committed an error and knew that he has a Lord Who forgives or punishes for the error. I have forgiven My servant.' The man committed another error and said, `O Lord! I committed an error, so forgive me.' Allah said, `My servant knew that he has a Lord Who forgives or punishes for the sin. I have forgiven My servant.' The man committed another error and said, `O Lord! I committed an error, so forgive me.' Allah said, `My servant knew that he has a Lord Who forgives or punishes for the error. I have forgiven my servant.' He then committed another error and said, `O Lord! I committed an error, so forgive me.' Allah said, `My servant knew that he has a Lord Who forgives or punishes for the error. Bear witness that I have forgiven My servant, so let him do whatever he likes.') A similar narration was collected in the Sahih.

`Abdur-Razzaq recorded that Anas bin Malik said, "I was told that when the Ayah,

(And those who, when they have committed Fahishah or wronged themselves with evil, remember Allah and ask forgiveness for their sins,) was revealed, Iblis (Shayatan) cried." Allah's statement,

(and none can forgive sins but Allah), means that none except Allah forgives sins. tAllah said,

(And do not persist in what (wrong) they have done, while they know), for they repent from their error, return to Allah before death, do not insist on error, and if they err again, they repent from it. Allah said here,

(while they know) Mujahid and `Abdullah bin `Ubayd bin `Umayr commented, "Whoever repents, then Allah will forgive him." Similarly, Allah said,

(Know they not that Allah accepts repentance from His servants) (9:104), and,

(And whoever does evil or wrongs himself but afterwards seeks Allah's forgiveness, he will find Allah Oft-Forgiving, Most Merciful.) (4: 110) and there are several examples similar to this Ayah.

Next, Allah said after this description,

(For such, the reward is forgiveness from their Lord) (3:136), as a reward for these qualities,

(forgiveness from their Lord, and Gardens with rivers flowing underneath (Paradise)) carrying all kinds of drinks,

(wherein they shall abide forever) and ever,

(How excellent is this reward for the doers) Allah praises Paradise in this part of the Ayah.

Surah: 3 Ayah: 137, Ayah: 138, Ayah: 139, Ayah: 140, Ayah: 141, Ayah: 142 & Ayah: 143

﴿ قَدْ خَلَتْ مِن قَبْلِكُمْ سُنَنٌ فَسِيرُوا۟ فِى ٱلْأَرْضِ فَٱنظُرُوا۟ كَيْفَ كَانَ عَـٰقِبَةُ
ٱلْمُكَذِّبِينَ ﴿١٣٧﴾ ﴾

137. Many similar ways (and mishaps of life) were faced by nations (believers and disbelievers) that have passed away before you (as you have faced in the battle of Uhud), so travel through the earth, and see what was the end of those who disbelieved (in the Oneness of Allâh, and disobeyed Him and His Messengers).

﴿ هَـٰذَا بَيَانٌ لِّلنَّاسِ وَهُدًى وَمَوْعِظَةٌ لِّلْمُتَّقِينَ ﴿١٣٨﴾ ﴾

138. This (the Qur'ân) is a plain statement for mankind, a guidance and instruction to those who are Al-Muttaqûn (the pious - see V.2:2).

﴿ وَلَا تَهِنُوا۟ وَلَا تَحْزَنُوا۟ وَأَنتُمُ ٱلْأَعْلَوْنَ إِن كُنتُم مُّؤْمِنِينَ ﴿١٣٩﴾ ﴾

139. So do not become weak (against your enemy), nor be sad, and you will be superior (in victory) if you are indeed (true) believers.

﴿ إِن يَمْسَسْكُمْ قَرْحٌ فَقَدْ مَسَّ ٱلْقَوْمَ قَرْحٌ مِّثْلُهُۥ ۚ وَتِلْكَ ٱلْأَيَّامُ نُدَاوِلُهَا بَيْنَ ٱلنَّاسِ
وَلِيَعْلَمَ ٱللَّهُ ٱلَّذِينَ ءَامَنُوا۟ وَيَتَّخِذَ مِنكُمْ شُهَدَآءَ ۗ وَٱللَّهُ لَا يُحِبُّ ٱلظَّـٰلِمِينَ ﴿١٤٠﴾ ﴾

140. If a wound (and killing) has touched you, be sure a similar wound (and killing) has touched the others. And so are the days (good and not so good), We give to men by turns, that Allâh may test those who believe, and that He may take martyrs from among you. And Allâh likes not the Zâlimûn (polytheists and wrong-doers).

﴿ وَلِيُمَحِّصَ ٱللَّهُ ٱلَّذِينَ ءَامَنُوا۟ وَيَمْحَقَ ٱلْكَـٰفِرِينَ ﴿١٤١﴾ ﴾

141. And that Allâh may test (or purify) the believers (from sins) and destroy the disbelievers.

﴿ أَمْ حَسِبْتُمْ أَن تَدْخُلُوا۟ ٱلْجَنَّةَ وَلَمَّا يَعْلَمِ ٱللَّهُ ٱلَّذِينَ جَٰهَدُوا۟ مِنكُمْ وَيَعْلَمَ ٱلصَّٰبِرِينَ ﴿١٤٢﴾ ﴾

142. Do you think that you will enter Paradise before Allâh tests those of you who fought (in His Cause) and (also) tests those who are As-Sâbirin (the patient)?

﴿ وَلَقَدْ كُنتُمْ تَمَنَّوْنَ ٱلْمَوْتَ مِن قَبْلِ أَن تَلْقَوْهُ فَقَدْ رَأَيْتُمُوهُ وَأَنتُمْ تَنظُرُونَ ﴿١٤٣﴾ ﴾

143. You did indeed wish for death (Ash-Shahâdah - martyrdom) before you met it. Now you have seen it openly with your own eyes.

Transliteration

137. Qad khalat min qablikum sunanun faseeroo fee al-ardi faonthuroo kayfa kana AAaqibatu almukaththibeena 138. Hatha bayanun lilnnasi wahudan wamawAAithatun lilmuttaqeena 139. Wala tahinoo wala tahzanoo waantumu al-aAAlawna in kuntum mu/mineena 140. In yamsaskum qarhun faqad massa alqawma qarhun mithluhu watilka al-ayyamu nudawiluha bayna alnnasi waliyaAAlama Allahu allatheena amanoo wayattakhitha minkum shuhadaa waAllahu la yuhibbu alththalimeena 141. Waliyumahhisa Allahu allatheena amanoo wayamhaqa alkafireena 142. Am hasibtum an tadkhuloo aljannata walamma yaAAlami Allahu allatheena jahadoo minkum wayaAAlama alssabireena 143. Walaqad kuntum tamannawna almawta min qabli an talqawhu faqad raaytumoohu waantum tanthuroona

Tafsir Ibn Kathir

The Wisdom Behind the Losses Muslims Suffered During Uhud

Allah states to His believing servants who suffered losses in the battle of Uhud, including seventy dead,

(Many similar ways (and mishaps of life) were faced before you), for the previous nations who followed their Prophets before you, they too suffered losses. However, the good end was theirs, and the ultimate defeat was for the disbelievers. This is why Allah said,

(so travel through the earth, and see what was the end of those who denied). Allah said next,

(This is a plain statement for mankind), meaning, the Qur'an explains the true reality of things and narrates how the previous nations suffered by the hands of their enemies.

(And a guidance and instruction) for the Qur'an contains the news of the past, and,

(guidance) for your hearts,

(and instruction for the Muttaqin) to discourage committing the prohibited and forbidden matters. Allah comforts the believers by saying,

(So do not become weak), because of what you suffered,

(nor be sad, and you will be triumphant if you are indeed believers), for surely, the ultimate victory and triumph will be yours, O believers.

(If a wound has touched you, be sure a similar wound has touched the others) (3:140).

Therefore, the Ayah says, if you suffered injuries and some of you were killed, then your enemies also suffered injuries and fatalities.

(And so are the days, that We give to men by turns) , and at times -- out of wisdom -- We allow the enemy to overcome you, although the final good end will be yours.

(and that Allah may know (test) those who believe,) meaning, "So that We find out who would be patient while fighting the enemies," according to Ibn `Abbas.

(and that He may take martyrs from among you) those who would be killed in Allah's cause and gladly offer their lives seeking His pleasure.

(And Allah likes not the wrongdoers. And that Allah may test those who believe) (3:140,141), by forgiving them their sins if they have any. Otherwise, Allah will raise their grades according to the losses they suffered. Allah's statement,

(and destroy the disbelievers), for it is their conduct that if they gain the upper hand, they transgress and commit aggression. However, this conduct only leads to ultimate destruction, extermination, perishing and dying out.

Allah then said,

(Do you think that you will enter Paradise before Allah knows (tests) those of you who will perform Jihad and (also) knows (tests) those who are the patient) (3:142).

The Ayah asks, do you think that you will enter Paradise without being tested with warfare and hardships Allah said in Surat Al-Baqarah,

(Or think you that you will enter Paradise without such (trials) as came to those who passed away before you They were afflicted with severe poverty and ailments and were so shaken. ..) (2:214). Allah said,

(Alif Lam Mim. Do people think that they will be left alone because they say: "We believe," and will not be tested) (29:1,2), This is why He said here,

(Do you think that you will enter Paradise before Allah knows (tests) those of you who will perform Jihad and (also) knows (tests) those who are the patient) (3:142) meaning, you will not earn Paradise until you are tested and thus Allah knows who among you are the ones who struggle and fight in His cause and are patient in the face of the enemy. Allah said,

(You did indeed wish for death (martyrdom) before you met it. Now you have seen it openly with your own eyes) (3:143).

The Ayah proclaims, O believers! Before today, you wished that you could meet the enemy and were eager to fight them. What you wished has occurred, so fight them and be patient.

In the Two Sahihs it is recorded that the Messenger of Allah said,

«لَا تَتَمَنَّوْا لِقَاءَ الْعَدُوِّ، وَسَلُوا اللهَ الْعَافِيَةَ، فَإِذَا لَقِيتُمُوهُمْ فَاصْبِرُوا، وَاعْلَمُوا أَنَّ الْجَنَّـــةَ تَحْتَ ظِلَالِ السُّيُوفِ»

(Do not wish to encounter the enemy, and ask Allah for your well-being. However, if you do encounter them, then observe patience and know that Paradise is under the shade of swords.)

This is why Allah said here,

(Now you have seen it): death, you saw it when the swords appeared, the blades were sharpened, the spears crisscrossed and men stood in lines for battle. This part of the Ayah contains a figure of speech that mentions imagining what can be felt but not seen.

Surah: 3 Ayah: 144, Ayah: 145, Ayah: 146, Ayah: 147 & Ayah: 148

﴿ وَمَا مُحَمَّدٌ إِلَّا رَسُولٌ قَدْ خَلَتْ مِن قَبْلِهِ ٱلرُّسُلُ ۚ أَفَإِيْن مَّاتَ أَوْ قُتِلَ ٱنقَلَبْتُمْ عَلَىٰٓ أَعْقَٰبِكُمْ ۚ وَمَن يَنقَلِبْ عَلَىٰ عَقِبَيْهِ فَلَن يَضُرَّ ٱللَّهَ شَيْـًٔا ۗ وَسَيَجْزِى ٱللَّهُ ٱلشَّٰكِرِينَ ١٤٤ ﴾

144. Muhammad (peace be upon him) is no more than a Messenger, and indeed (many) Messengers have passed away before him. If he dies or is killed, will you then turn back on your heels (as disbelievers)? And he who turns back on his heels, not the least harm will he do to Allâh; and Allâh will give reward to those who are grateful.

﴿ وَمَا كَانَ لِنَفْسٍ أَن تَمُوتَ إِلَّا بِإِذْنِ ٱللَّهِ كِتَٰبًا مُّؤَجَّلًا ۗ وَمَن يُرِدْ ثَوَابَ ٱلدُّنْيَا نُؤْتِهِۦ مِنْهَا وَمَن يُرِدْ ثَوَابَ ٱلْءَاخِرَةِ نُؤْتِهِۦ مِنْهَا ۚ وَسَنَجْزِى ٱلشَّٰكِرِينَ ١٤٥ ﴾

145. And no person can ever die except by Allâh's Leave and at an appointed term. And whoever desires a reward in (this) world, We shall give him of it; and whoever desires a reward in the Hereafter, We shall give him thereof. And We shall reward the grateful.

﴿ وَكَأَيِّن مِّن نَّبِىٍّ قَٰتَلَ مَعَهُۥ رِبِّيُّونَ كَثِيرٌ فَمَا وَهَنُوا۟ لِمَآ أَصَابَهُمْ فِى سَبِيلِ ٱللَّهِ وَمَا ضَعُفُوا۟ وَمَا ٱسْتَكَانُوا۟ ۗ وَٱللَّهُ يُحِبُّ ٱلصَّٰبِرِينَ ١٤٦ ﴾

146. And many a Prophet (i.e. many from amongst the Prophets) fought (in Allâh's Cause) and along with him (fought) large bands of religious learned men. But they never lost heart for that which did befall them in Allâh's Way, nor did they weaken nor degrade themselves. And Allâh loves As-Sâbirin (the patient).

﴿ وَمَا كَانَ قَوْلَهُمْ إِلَّآ أَن قَالُوا۟ رَبَّنَا ٱغْفِرْ لَنَا ذُنُوبَنَا وَإِسْرَافَنَا فِىٓ أَمْرِنَا وَثَبِّتْ أَقْدَامَنَا وَٱنصُرْنَا عَلَى ٱلْقَوْمِ ٱلْكَٰفِرِينَ ١٤٧ ﴾

147. And they said nothing but: "Our Lord! Forgive us our sins and our transgressions (in keeping our duties to You), establish our feet firmly, and give us victory over the disbelieving folk."

﴿ فَـَٔاتَىٰهُمُ ٱللَّهُ ثَوَابَ ٱلدُّنْيَا وَحُسْنَ ثَوَابِ ٱلْءَاخِرَةِ ۗ وَٱللَّهُ يُحِبُّ ٱلْمُحْسِنِينَ ١٤٨ ﴾

148. So Allâh gave them the reward of this world, and the excellent reward of the Hereafter. And Allâh loves Al-Muhsinûn (the good-doers).

Transliteration

144. Wama muhammadun illa rasoolun qad khalat min qablihi alrrusulu afa-in mata aw qutila inqalabtum AAala aAAqabikum waman yanqalib AAala AAaqibayhi falan yadurra Allaha shay-an wasayajzee Allahu alshshakireena 145. Wama kana linafsin an tamoota illa bi-ithni Allahi kitaban mu-ajjalan waman yurid thawaba alddunya nu/tihi minha waman yurid thawaba al-akhirati nu/tihi minha wasanajzee alshshakireena 146. Wakaayyin min nabiyyin qatala maAAahu ribbiyyoona katheerun fama wahanoo lima asabahum fee sabeeli Allahi wama daAAufoo wama istakanoo waAllahu yuhibbu alssabireena 147. Wama kana qawlahum illa an qaloo rabbana ighfir lana thunoobana wa-israfana fee amrina wathabbit aqdamana waonsurna AAala alqawmi alkafireena 148. Faatahumu Allahu thawaba alddunya wahusna thawabi al-akhirati waAllahu yuhibbu almuhsineena

Tafsir Ibn Kathir

The Rumor that the Prophet was Killed at Uhud

When Muslims suffered defeat in battle at Uhud and some of them were killed, Shaytan shouted, "Muhammad has been killed." Ibn Qami'ah went back to the idolators and claimed, "I have killed Muhammad." Some Muslims believed this rumor and thought that the Messenger of Allah had been killed, claiming that this could happen, for Allah narrated that this occurred to many Prophets before. Therefore, the Muslims' resolve was weakened and they did not actively participate in battle. This is why Allah sent down to His Messenger His statement,

(Muhammad is no more than a Messenger, and indeed Messengers have passed away before him.) he is to deliver Allah's Message and may be killed in the process, just as what happened to many Prophets before. Ibn Abi Najih said that his father said that a man from the Muhajirin passed by an Ansari man who was bleeding (during Uhud) and said to him, "O fellow! Did you know that Muhammad was killed" The Ansari man said, "Even if Muhammad was killed, he has indeed conveyed the Message. Therefore, defend your religion." The Ayah,

(Muhammad is no more than a Messenger, and indeed (many) Messengers have passed away before him), was revealed. This story was collected by Al-Hafiz Abu Bakr Al-Bayhaqi in Dala'il An-Nubuwwah.

Allah said next, while chastising those who became weak,

(If he dies or is killed, will you then turn back on your heels), become disbelievers,

(And he who turns back on his heels, not the least harm will he do to Allah; and Allah will give reward to those who are grateful), those who obeyed Allah, defended His religion and followed His Messenger whether he was alive or dead. The Sahih, Musnad and Sunan collections gathered various chains of narration stating that Abu Bakr recited this Ayah when the Messenger of Allah died. Al-Bukhari recorded that `A'ishah said that Abu Bakr came riding his horse from his dwelling in As-Sunh. He dismounted, entered the Masjid and did not speak to anyone until he came to her (in her room) and went directly to the Prophet, who was covered with a marked blanket. Abu Bakr uncovered his face, knelt down and kissed him, then started weeping and proclaimed, "My father and my mother be sacrificed for you! Allah will not combine two deaths on you. You have died the death, which was written for you."

Ibn `Abbas narrated that Abu Bakr then came out, while `Umar was addressing the people, and Abu Bakr told him to sit down but `Umar refused, and the people attended to Abu Bakr and left `Umar. Abu Bakr said, "To proceed; whoever among you worshipped Muhammad, then Muhammad is dead, but whoever worshipped Allah, Allah is alive and will never die. Allah said,

(Muhammad is no more than a Messenger and indeed (many) Messengers have passed away before him. If he dies or is killed, will you then turn back on your heels And he who turns back on his heels, not the least harm will he do to Allah; and Allah will reward the grateful.)"

The narrator added, "By Allah, it was as if the people never knew that Allah had revealed this verse before until Abu Bakr recited it, and then whoever heard it, started reciting it." Sa`id bin Al-Musayyib said that `Umar said, "By Allah! When I heard Abu Bakr recite this Ayah, my feet could not hold me, and I fell to the ground."

Allah said,

(And no person can ever die except by Allah's leave and at an appointed term.) (3:145) meaning, no one dies except by Allah's decision, after he has finished the term that Allah has destined for him. This is why Allah said,

(at an appointed term) which is similar to His statements,

(And no aged man is granted a length of life nor is a part cut off from his life, but it is in a Book) (35:11), and,

(He it is Who has created you from clay, and then has decreed a (stated) term (for you to die). And there is with Him another determined term (for you to be resurrected)) (6:2).

This Ayah (3:145) encourages cowards to participate in battle; for doing so, or avoiding battle neither decreases, nor increases the life term. Ibn Abi Hatim narrated that, Habib bin Suhban said that a Muslim man, Hujr bin `Adi, said in a battle, "What prevents you from crossing this river (the Euphrates) to the enemy

(And no person can ever die except by Allah's leave and at an appointed term)" He then crossed the river riding his horse, and when he did, the Muslims followed him. When the enemy saw them, they started shouting, "Diwan (Persian; crazy)," and they ran away.

Allah said next,

(And whoever desires a reward in the world, We shall give him of it; and whoever desires a reward in the Hereafter, We shall give him thereof).

Therefore, the Ayah proclaims, whoever works for the sake of this life, will only earn what Allah decides he will earn. However, he will not have a share in the Hereafter. Whoever works for the sake of the Hereafter, Allah will give him a share in the Hereafter, along with what He decides for him in this life. In similar statements, Allah said,

(Whosoever desires (by his deeds) the reward of the Hereafter, We give him increase in his reward, and whosoever desires the reward of this world (by his deeds), We give him thereof (what is decreed for him), and he has no portion in the Hereafter.) (42:20), and,

(Whoever desires the quick-passing (transitory enjoyment of this world), We readily grant him what We will for whom We like. Then, afterwards, We have appointed for him Hell; he will burn therein disgraced and despised. And whoever desires the Hereafter and strives for it, with the necessary effort due for it while he is a believer, then such are the ones whose striving shall be appreciated) (17:18-19).

In this Ayah (3:145), Allah said,

(And We shall reward the grateful.) meaning, We shall award them with Our favor and mercy in this life and the Hereafter, according to the degree of their appreciation (of Allah) and their good deeds.

Allah then comforts the believers because of what they suffered in Uhud,

(And many a Prophet fought and along with him many Ribbiyyun.)

It was said that this Ayah means that many Prophets and their companions were killed in earlier times, as is the view chosen by Ibn Jarir. It was also said that the Ayah means that many Prophets witnessed their companions' death before their eyes. However, Ibn Ishaq mentioned another explanation in his Sirah, saying that this Ayah means, "Many a Prophet was killed, and he had many companions whose resolve did not weaken after their Prophet died, and they did not become feeble in the face of the enemy. What they suffered in Jihad in Allah's cause and for the sake of their religion did not make them lose heart. This is patience,

(and Allah loves the patient.)" As-Suhayli agreed with this explanation and defended it vigorously. This view is supported by Allah saying;

(And along with him many Ribbiyyun).

In his book about the battles, Al-Amawi mentioned only this explanation for the Ayah. Sufyan Ath-Thawri reported that, Ibn Mas`ud said that,

(many Ribbiyyun) means, thousands. Ibn `Abbas, Mujahid, Sa`id bin Jubayr, `Ikrimah, Al-Hasan, Qatadah, As-Suddi, Ar-Rabi` and `Ata' Al-Khurasani said that the word Ribbiyyun means, `large bands'. `Abdur-Razzaq narrated that Ma`mmar said that Al-Hasan said that,

(many Ribbiyyun) means, many scholars. He also said that it means patient and pious scholars.

(But they never lost heart for that which befell them in Allah's way, nor did they weaken nor degrade themselves.)

Qatadah and Ar-Rabi` bin Anas said that,

(nor did they weaken), means, after their Prophet was killed.

(nor degrade themselves), by reverting from the true guidance and religion. Rather, they fought on the path that Allah's Prophet fought on until they met Allah. Ibn `Abbas said that,

(nor degrade themselves) means, nor became humiliated, while As-Suddi and Ibn Zayd said that it means, they did not give in to the enemy.

(And Allah loves the patient. And they said nothing but: "Our Lord! Forgive us our sins and our transgressions, establish our feet firmly, and give us victory over the disbelieving folk.") (3:146-147), and this was the statement that they kept repeating. Therefore,

(So Allah gave them the reward of this world) victory, triumph and the good end,

(and the excellent reward of the Hereafter) added to the gains in this life,

(And Allah loves the good-doers).

Surah: 3 Ayah: 149, Ayah: 150, Ayah: 151, Ayah: 152 & Ayah: 153

﴿ يَٰٓأَيُّهَا ٱلَّذِينَ ءَامَنُوٓاْ إِن تُطِيعُواْ ٱلَّذِينَ كَفَرُواْ يَرُدُّوكُمْ عَلَىٰٓ أَعْقَٰبِكُمْ فَتَنقَلِبُواْ
خَٰسِرِينَ ﴿١٤٩﴾ ﴾

149. O you who believe! If you obey those who disbelieve, they will send you back on your heels, and you will turn back (from Faith) as losers.

﴿ بَلِ ٱللَّهُ مَوْلَىٰكُمْ ۖ وَهُوَ خَيْرُ ٱلنَّٰصِرِينَ ﴿١٥٠﴾ ﴾

150. Nay, Allâh is your Maulâ (Patron, Lord, Helper, Protector), and He is the Best of helpers.

﴿ سَنُلْقِى فِى قُلُوبِ ٱلَّذِينَ كَفَرُواْ ٱلرُّعْبَ بِمَآ أَشْرَكُواْ بِٱللَّهِ مَا لَمْ يُنَزِّلْ بِهِۦ سُلْطَٰنًا ۖ
وَمَأْوَىٰهُمُ ٱلنَّارُ ۚ وَبِئْسَ مَثْوَى ٱلظَّٰلِمِينَ ﴿١٥١﴾ ﴾

151. We shall cast terror into the hearts of those who disbelieve, because they joined others in worship with Allâh, for which He had sent no authority; their abode will be the Fire and how evil is the abode of the Zâlimûn (polytheists and wrong-doers).

﴿ وَلَقَدْ صَدَقَكُمُ ٱللَّهُ وَعْدَهُۥٓ إِذْ تَحُسُّونَهُم بِإِذْنِهِۦ ۖ حَتَّىٰٓ إِذَا فَشِلْتُمْ وَتَنَٰزَعْتُمْ فِى
ٱلْأَمْرِ وَعَصَيْتُم مِّنۢ بَعْدِ مَآ أَرَىٰكُم مَّا تُحِبُّونَ ۚ مِنكُم مَّن يُرِيدُ ٱلدُّنْيَا وَمِنكُم مَّن
يُرِيدُ ٱلْءَاخِرَةَ ۚ ثُمَّ صَرَفَكُمْ عَنْهُمْ لِيَبْتَلِيَكُمْ ۖ وَلَقَدْ عَفَا عَنكُمْ ۗ وَٱللَّهُ ذُو فَضْلٍ عَلَى
ٱلْمُؤْمِنِينَ ﴿١٥٢﴾ ﴾

152. And Allâh did indeed fulfil His Promise to you when you were killing them (your enemy) with His Permission; until (the moment) you lost your courage and fell to disputing about the order, and disobeyed after He showed you (of the booty) which you love. Among you are some that desire this world and some that desire the Hereafter. Then He made you flee from them (your enemy), that He might test you. But surely, He forgave you, and Allâh is Most Gracious to the believers.

﴿ ۞ إِذْ تُصْعِدُونَ وَلَا تَلْوُۥنَ عَلَىٰٓ أَحَدٍ وَٱلرَّسُولُ يَدْعُوكُمْ فِىٓ أُخْرَىٰكُمْ
فَأَثَٰبَكُمْ غَمًّۢا بِغَمٍّ لِّكَيْلَا تَحْزَنُواْ عَلَىٰ مَا فَاتَكُمْ وَلَا مَآ أَصَٰبَكُمْ ۗ وَٱللَّهُ خَبِيرٌۢ بِمَا
تَعْمَلُونَ ﴿١٥٣﴾ ﴾

153. (And remember) when you ran away (dreadfully) without even casting a side glance at anyone, and the Messenger (Muhammad (peace be upon him)) was in your rear calling you back. There did Allâh give you one distress after another by way of requital to teach you not to grieve for that which had escaped you, nor for that which had befallen you. And Allâh is Well-Aware of all that you do.

Transliteration

149. Ya ayyuha allatheena amanoo in tuteeAAoo allatheena kafaroo yaruddookum AAala aAAqabikum fatanqaliboo khasireena 150. Bali Allahu mawlakum wahuwa khayru alnnasireena 151. Sanulqee fee quloobi allatheena kafaroo alrruAAba bima ashrakoo biAllahi ma lam yunazzil bihi sultanan wama/wahumu alnnaru wabi/sa mathwa alththalimeena 152. Walaqad sadaqakumu Allahu waAAdahu ith tahussoonahum bi-ithnihi hatta itha fashiltum watanazaAAtum fee al-amri waAAasaytum min baAAdi ma arakum ma tuhibboona minkum man yureedu alddunya waminkum man yureedu al-akhirata thumma sarafakum AAanhum liyabtaliyakum walaqad AAafa AAankum waAllahu thoo fadlin AAala almu/mineena 153. Ith tusAAidoona wala talwoona AAala ahadin waalrrasoolu yadAAookum fee okhrakum faathabakum ghamman bighammin likay la tahzanoo AAala ma fatakum wala ma asabakum waAllahu khabeerun bima taAAmaloona

Tafsir Ibn Kathir

The Prohibition of Obeying the Disbelievers; the Cause of Defeat at Uhud

Allah warns His believing servants against obeying the disbelievers and hypocrites, because such obedience leads to utter destruction in this life and the Hereafter. This is why Allah said,

(If you obey those who disbelieve, they will send you back on your heels, and you will turn back (from faith) as losers) (3:149).

Allah also commands the believers to obey Him, take Him as their protector, seek His aid and trust in Him. Allah said,

(Nay, Allah is your protector, and He is the best of helpers).

Allah next conveys the good news that He will put fear of the Muslims, and feelings of subordination to the Muslims in the hearts of their disbelieving enemies, because of their Kufr and Shirk. And Allah has prepared torment and punishment for them in the Hereafter. Allah said,

(We shall cast terror into the hearts of those who disbelieve, because they joined others in worship with Allah, for which He sent no authority; their abode will be the Fire and how evil is the abode of the wrongdoers). In addition, the Two Sahihs recorded that Jabir bin `Abdullah said that the Messenger of Allah said,

«أُعْطِيتُ خَمْسًا لَمْ يُعْطَهُنَّ أَحَدٌ مِنَ الْأَنْبِيَاءِ قَبْلِي: نُصِرْتُ بِالرُّعْبِ مَسِيرَةَ شَهْرٍ، وَجُعِلَتْ لِيَ الْأَرْضُ مَسْجِدًا وَطَهُورًا، وَأُحِلَّتْ لِيَ الْغَنَائِمُ، وَأُعْطِيتُ الشَّفَاعَةَ، وَكَانَ النَّبِيُّ يُبْعَثُ إِلَى قَوْمِهِ خَاصَّةً وَبُعِثْتُ إِلَى النَّاسِ عَامَّةً»

(I was given five things that no other Prophet before me was given. I was aided with fear the distance of one month, the earth was made a Masjid and clean place for me, I was allowed war booty, I was given the Intercession, and Prophets used to be sent to their people, but I was sent to all mankind particularly.)

Allah said,

(And Allah did indeed fulfill His promise to you) (3:152),

in the beginning of the day of Uhud,

(when you were killing them), slaying your enemies,

(with His permission), for He allowed you to do that against them,

(until when you Fashiltum). Ibn Jurayj said that Ibn `Abbas said that Fashiltum means, `lost courage'.

(and fell to disputing about the order, and disobeyed) such as the mistake made by the archers,

(after He showed you what you love), that is, victory over the disbelievers,

(Among you are some that desire this world) referring to those who sought to collect the booty when they saw the enemy being defeated,

(and some that desire the Hereafter. Then He made you flee from them, that He might test you).

This Ayah means, Allah gave them the upper hand to try and test you, O believers,

(but surely, He forgave you),

He forgave the error you committed, because, and Allah knows best, the idolators were many and well supplied, while Muslims had few men and few supplies.

Al-Bukhari recorded that Al-Bara' said, "We met the idolators on that day (Uhud) and the Prophet appointed `Abdullah bin Jubayr as the commander of the archers. He instructed them, `Retain your position, and if you see that we have defeated them, do not abandon your positions. If you see that they defeated us, do not rush to help us.' The disbelievers gave flight when we met them, and we saw their women fleeing up the mountain while lifting up their clothes revealing their anklets and their legs. So, the companions (of `Abdullah bin Jubayr) said, `The booty, the booty!' `Abdullah bin Jubayr said, `Allah's Messenger commanded me not to allow you to abandon your position.' They refused to listen, and when they left their position, Muslims were defeated and seventy of them were killed. Abu Sufyan shouted, `Is Muhammad present among these people' The Prophet said, `Do not answer him.' Then he asked, `Is the son of Abu Quhafah (Abu Bakr) present among these people' The Prophet said, `Do not answer him.' He asked again, `Is the son of Al-Khattab (`Umar) present among these people As for these (men), they have been killed, for had they been alive, they would have answered me.' `Umar could not control himself and said (to Abu Sufyan), `You lie, O enemy of Allah! The cause of your misery is still present.' Abu Sufyan said, `O Hubal, be high!' On that the Prophet said (to his Companions), `Answer him back.' They said, `What shall we say'

He said, `Say, Allah is Higher and more Sublime.' Abu Sufyan said, `We have the (idol) Al-`Uzza, and you have no `Uzza.' The Prophet said, `Answer him back.' They asked, `What shall we say' He said, `Say, Allah is our protector and you have no protector.' Abu Sufyan said, `Our victory today is vengeance for yours in the battle of Badr, and in war (the victory) is always undecided and is shared in turns by the belligerents. You will find some of your killed men mutilated, but I did not urge my men to do so, yet I do not feel sorry for their deed.'" Only Al-Bukhari collected this Hadith using this chain of narration. cMuhammad bin Ishaq said that, `Abdullah bin Az-Zubayr narrated that Az-Zubayr bin Al-`Awwam said, "By Allah! I saw the female servants and female companions of Hind (Abu Sufyan's wife) when they uncovered their legs and gave flight. At that time, there was no big or small effort separating us from capturing them. However, the archers went down the mount when the enemy gave flight from the battlefield, seeking to collect the booty. They uncovered our back lines to the horsemen of the disbelievers, who took the chance and attacked us from behind. Then a person shouted, `Muhammad has been killed.' So we pulled back, and the disbelievers followed us, after we had killed those who carried their flag, and none of them dared to come close the flag, until then.'" Muhammad bin Ishaq said next, "The flag of the disbelievers was left on the ground until `Amrah bint `Alqamah Al-Harithiyyah picked it up and gave it to the Quraysh who held it."

Allah said,

(Then He made you flee from them, that He might test you) (3:152).

Al-Bukhari recorded that Anas bin Malik said, "My uncle Anas bin An-Nadr was absent from the battle of Badr. He said, `I was absent from the first battle the Prophet fought (against the pagans). (By Allah) if Allah gives me a chance to fight along with the Messenger of Allah, then Allah will see how (bravely) I will fight.' On the day of Uhud when the Muslims turned their backs and fled, he said, `O Allah! I apologize to You for what these (meaning the Muslims) have done, and I denounce what these pagans have done.' Then he advanced lifting his sword, and when Sa`d bin Mu`adh met him, he said to him, `O Sa`d bin Mu`adh! Where are you! Paradise! I am smelling its aroma coming from before (Mount) Uhud,' and he went forth, fought and was killed. We found more than eighty stab wounds, sword blows or arrow holes on his body, which was mutilated so badly that none except his sister could recognize him, and she could only do so by his fingers or by a mole." This is the narration reported by Al-Bukhari, Muslim also collected a similar narration from Thabit from Anas.

The Defeat that the Muslims Suffered During the Battle of Uhud

Allah said,

((And remember) when you (Tus`iduna) ran away dreadfully without casting even a side glance at anyone), and Allah made the disbelievers leave you after you went up the mount, escaping your enemy. Al-Hasan and Qatadah said that, Tus`iduna, means, `go up the mountain'.

(without even casting a side glance at anyone) meaning, you did not glance at anyone else due to shock, fear and fright.

(and the Messenger was in your rear calling you back), for you left him behind you, while he was calling you to stop fleeing from the enemy and to return and fight.

As-Suddi said, "When the disbelievers attacked Muslim lines during the battle of Uhud and defeated them, some Muslims ran away to Al-Madinah, while some of them went up Mount Uhud, to a rock and stood on it. On that, the Messenger of Allah kept heralding, `Come to me, O servants of Allah! Come to me, O servants of Allah!' Allah mentioned that the Muslims went up the Mount and that the Prophet called them to come back, and said,

((And remember) when you ran away without even casting a side glance at anyone, and the Messenger was in your rear calling you back)." Similar was said by Ibn `Abbas, Qatadah, Ar-Rabi` and Ibn Zayd.

The Ansar and Muhajirin Defended the Messenger

Al-Bukhari recorded that Qays bin Abi Hazim said, "I saw Talhah's hand, it was paralyzed, because he shielded the Prophet with it." meaning on the day of Uhud. It is recorded in the Two Sahihs that Abu `Uthman An-Nahdi said, "On that day (Uhud) during which the Prophet fought, only Talhah bin `Ubaydullah and Sa`d remained with the Prophet."

Sa`id bin Al-Musayyib said, "I heard Sa`d bin Abi Waqqas saying, `The Messenger of Allah gave me arrows from his quiver on the day of Uhud and said, `Shoot, may I sacrifice my father and mother for you.''' Al-Bukhari also collected this Hadith. The Two Sahihs recorded that Sa`d bin Abi Waqqas said, "On the day of Uhud, I saw two men wearing white clothes, one to the right of the Prophet and one to his left, who were defending the Prophet fiercely. I have never seen these men before or after that day." Meaning angels Jibril and Mika'il, peace be upon them.

Abu Al-Aswad said that, `Urwah bin Az-Zubayr said, "Ubayy bin Khalaf of Bani Jumah swore in Makkah that he would kill the Messenger of Allah . When the Messenger was told of his vow, he said, `Rather, I shall kill him, Allah willing.' On the day of Uhud, Ubayy came while wearing iron shields and proclaiming, `May I not be saved, if Muhammad is saved.' He then headed to the direction of the Messenger of Allah intending to kill him, but Mus`ab bin `Umayr, from Bani Abd Ad-Dar, intercepted him and shielded the Prophet with his body, and Mus`ab bin `Umayr was killed. The Messenger of Allah saw Ubayy's neck exposed between the shields and helmet, stabbed him with his spear, and Ubayy fell from his horse to the ground. However, no blood spilled from his wound. His people came and carried him away while he was moaning like an ox. They said to him, `Why are you so anxious, it is only a flesh wound' Ubayy mentioned to them the Prophet's vow, `Rather, I shall kill Ubayy', then commented, `By He in Whose Hand is my soul! If what hit me hits the people of Dhul-Majaz (a popular pre-Islamic marketplace), they would all have perished.' He then died and went to the Fire,

(So, away with the dwellers of the blazing Fire!) (67:11)."

This was collected by Musa bin `Uqbah from Az-Zuhri from Sa`id bin Al-Musayyib.

It is recorded in the Two Sahih that when he was asked about the injuries the Messenger sustained (in Uhud), Sahl bin Sa`d said, "The face of Allah's Messenger was injured, his front tooth was broken and his helmet was smashed on his head. Therefore, Fatimah, the daughter of Allah's Messenger washed off the blood while `Ali was pouring water on her hand. When Fatimah saw that the bleeding increased more by the water, she took a mat, burnt it, and placed the ashes in the wound of the Prophet and the blood stopped oozing out." Allah said next,

(There did Allah give you one distress after another) (3:153),

He gave you grief over your grief. Ibn `Abbas said, `The first grief was because of the defeat, especially when it was rumored that Muhammad was killed. The second grief was when the idolators went up the mount and The Messenger of Allah said, `O Allah! It is not for them to rise above us.'"

`Abdur-Rahman bin `Awf said, "The first distress was because of the defeat and the second when a rumor started that Muhammad was killed, which to them, was worse than defeat." Ibn Marduwyah recorded both of these. Mujahid and Qatadah said, "The first distress was when they heard that Muhammad was killed and the second when they suffered casualties and injury." It has also been reported that Qatadah and Ar-Rabi` bin Anas said that it was the opposite (order). As-Suddi said that the first distress was because of the victory and booty that they missed and the second because of the enemy rising above them (on the mount). Allah said,

(by way of requital to teach you not to grieve for that which had escaped you), for that you missed the booty and triumph over your enemy.

(nor for what struck you), of injury and fatalities, as Ibn `Abbas, `Abdur-Rahman bin `Awf, Al-Hasan, Qatadah and As-Suddi stated. Allah said next,

(And Allah is Well-Aware of all that you do.) all praise is due to Him, and thanks, there is no deity worthy of worship except Him, the Most High, Most Honored.

Surah: 3 Ayah: 154 & Ayah: 155

﴿ ثُمَّ أَنزَلَ عَلَيْكُم مِّنۢ بَعْدِ ٱلْغَمِّ أَمَنَةً نُّعَاسًا يَغْشَىٰ طَآئِفَةً مِّنكُمْ ۖ وَطَآئِفَةٌ قَدْ
أَهَمَّتْهُمْ أَنفُسُهُمْ يَظُنُّونَ بِٱللَّهِ غَيْرَ ٱلْحَقِّ ظَنَّ ٱلْجَٰهِلِيَّةِ ۖ يَقُولُونَ هَل لَّنَا مِنَ
ٱلْأَمْرِ مِن شَىْءٍ ۗ قُلْ إِنَّ ٱلْأَمْرَ كُلَّهُۥ لِلَّهِ ۗ يُخْفُونَ فِىٓ أَنفُسِهِم مَّا لَا يُبْدُونَ لَكَ ۖ
يَقُولُونَ لَوْ كَانَ لَنَا مِنَ ٱلْأَمْرِ شَىْءٌ مَّا قُتِلْنَا هَٰهُنَا ۗ قُل لَّوْ كُنتُمْ فِى بُيُوتِكُمْ لَبَرَزَ ٱلَّذِينَ
كُتِبَ عَلَيْهِمُ ٱلْقَتْلُ إِلَىٰ مَضَاجِعِهِمْ ۖ وَلِيَبْتَلِىَ ٱللَّهُ مَا فِى صُدُورِكُمْ وَلِيُمَحِّصَ مَا فِى
قُلُوبِكُمْ ۗ وَٱللَّهُ عَلِيمٌۢ بِذَاتِ ٱلصُّدُورِ ﴿١٥٤﴾

154. Then after the distress, He sent down security for you. Slumber overtook a party of you, while another party was thinking about themselves (as how to save their own selves, ignoring the others and the Prophet (peace be upon him)) and thought wrongly of Allâh - the thought of ignorance. They said, "Have we any part in the affair?" Say you (O Muhammad (peace be upon him)) "Indeed the affair belongs wholly to Allâh." They hide within themselves what they dare not reveal to you, saying: "If we had anything to do with the affair, none of us would have been killed here." Say: "Even if you had remained in your homes, those for whom death was decreed would certainly have gone forth to the place of their death," but that Allâh might test what is in your breasts; and to purify that which was in your hearts (sins), and Allâh is All-Knower of what is in (your) breasts.

﴿ إِنَّ ٱلَّذِينَ تَوَلَّوْا۟ مِنكُمْ يَوْمَ ٱلْتَقَى ٱلْجَمْعَانِ إِنَّمَا ٱسْتَزَلَّهُمُ ٱلشَّيْطَـٰنُ بِبَعْضِ مَا كَسَبُوا۟ ۖ
وَلَقَدْ عَفَا ٱللَّهُ عَنْهُمْ ۗ إِنَّ ٱللَّهَ غَفُورٌ حَلِيمٌ ﴿١٥٥﴾ ﴾

155. Those of you who turned back on the day the two hosts met (i.e. the battle of Uhud), it was Shaitân (Satan) who caused them to backslide (run away from the battlefield) because of some (sins) they had earned. But Allâh, indeed, has forgiven them. Surely, Allâh is Oft-Forgiving, Most Forbearing.

Transliteration

154. Thumma anzala AAalaykum min baAAdi alghammi amanatan nuAAasan yaghsha ta-ifatan minkum wata-ifatun qad ahammat-hum anfusuhum yathunnoona biAllahi ghayra alhaqqi thanna aljahiliyyati yaqooloona hal lana mina al-amri min shay-in qul inna al-amra kullahu lillahi yukhfoona fee anfusihim ma la yubdoona laka yaqooloona law kana lana mina al-amri shay-on ma qutilna hahuna qul law kuntum fee buyootikum labaraza allatheena kutiba AAalayhimu alqatlu ila madajiAAihim waliyabtaliya Allahu ma fee sudoorikum waliyumahhisa ma fee quloobikum waAllahu AAaleemun bithati alssudoori 155. Inna allatheena tawallaw minkum yawma iltaqa aljamAAani innama istazallahumu alshshaytanu bibaAAdi ma kasaboo walaqad AAafa Allahu AAanhum inna Allaha ghafoorun haleemun

Tafsir Ibn Kathir

Slumber Overcame the Believers; the Fear that the Hypocrites Suffered

Allah reminds His servants of His favor when He sent down on them tranquillity and slumber that overcame them while they were carrying their weapons and feeling distress and grief. In this case, slumber is a favor and carries meanings of calmness and safety. For instance, Allah said in Surat Al-Anfal about the battle of Badr,

((Remember) when He covered you with a slumber as a security from Him) (8:11).

Al-Bukhari recorded that Anas said that, Abu Talhah said, "I was among those who were overcome by slumber during the battle of Uhud. My sword fell from my hand several times and I would pick it up, then it would fall and I would pick it up again." Al-Bukhari collected this Hadith in the stories of the battles without a chain of narration, and in the book of Tafsir with a chain of narrators. At-Tirmidhi, An-Nasa'i and Al-Hakim recorded from Anas that Abu Talhah said, "On the day of Uhud, I raised my head and looked around and found that everyone's head was nodding from slumber." This is the wording of At-Tirmidhi, who said, "Hasan Sahih". An-Nasa'i also recorded this Hadith from Anas who said that Abu Talhah said, "I was among those who were overcome by slumber."

The second group mentioned in the Ayah were the hypocrites who only thought about themselves, for they are the most cowardly people and those least likely to support the truth,

(and thought wrongly of Allah - the thought of ignorance) (3:154), for they are liars and people who have doubts and evil thoughts about Allah, the Exalted and Most Honored. Allah said,

(Then after the distress, He sent down security for you. Slumber overtook a party of you), the people of faith, certainty, firmness and reliance (on Allah) who are certain that Allah shall give victory to His Messenger and fulfill his objective.

(While another party was thinking about themselves), and they were not overcome by slumber because of their worry, fright and fear,

(and thought wrongly of Allah --- the thought of ignorance).

Similarly, Allah said in another statement,

(Nay, but you thought that the Messenger and the believers would never return to their families) (48:12).

This group thought that the idolators achieved ultimate victory, when their forces took the upper hand in battle, and that Islam and its people would perish. This is typical of people of doubt and hesitation, in the event of a hardship, they fall into such evil thoughts. Allah then described them that,

(they said) in this situation,

("Have we any part in the affair") Allah replied,

(Say: "Indeed the affair belongs wholly to Allah." They hide within themselves what they dare not reveal to you.) wAllah exposed their secrets, that is,

(saying: "If we had anything to do with the affair, none of us would have been killed here.") although they tried to conceal this thought from the Messenger of Allah .

Ibn Ishaq recorded that `Abdullah bin Az-Zubayr said that Az-Zubayr said, "I was with the Messenger of Allah when fear intensified and Allah sent sleep to us (during the battle of Uhud). At that time, every man among us (except the hypocrites) was nodding off. By Allah! As if in a dream, I heard the words of Mu`attib bin Qushayr, `If we had anything to do with the affair, none of us would have been killed here.' I memorized these words of his, which Allah mentioned later on,

(saying: "If we had anything to do with the affair, none of us would have been killed here.)"

Ibn Abi Hatim collected this Hadith.

Allah the Exalted said,

(Say: "Even if you had remained in your homes, those for whom death was decreed would certainly have gone forth to the place of their death,") meaning, this is Allah's appointed destiny and a decision that will certainly come to pass, and there is no escaping it. Allah's statement,

(that Allah might test what is in your breasts; and to purify that which was in your hearts,) means, so that He tests you with whatever befell you, to distinguish good from evil and the deeds and statements of the believers from those of the hypocrites,

(and Allah is All-Knower of what is in the breasts), and what the hearts conceal.

Some of the Believers Give Flight on the Day of Uhud

Allah then said, (Those of you who turned back on the day the two hosts met, Shaytan only caused them to err because of some of what they had earned) (3:155), because of some of their previous errors. Indeed, some of the Salaf said, "The reward of the good deed includes being directed to another good deed that follows it, while the retribution of sin includes committing another sin that follows it." Allah then said,

(but Allah, indeed, has forgiven them), their giving flight,

(surely, Allah is Oft-Forgiving, Most Forbearing)

He forgives sins, pardons and exonerates His creatures. Imam Ahmad recorded that Shaqiq said, " `Abdur-Rahman bin `Awf met Al-Walid bin `Uqbah, who said to him, `Why did you desert `Uthman, the Leader of the Faithful' `Abdur-Rahman said, `Tell him that I did not run away during Uhud, remain behind during Badr, nor abandon the Sunnah of `Umar.' Al-Walid told `Uthman what `Abdur-Rahman said. `Uthman replied, `As for his statement, `I did not run away during Uhud,' how can he blame me for an error that Allah has already forgiven. Allah said,

(Those of you who turned back on the day the two hosts met, Shaytan only caused them to err because of some of what they had earned. But Allah, indeed, has forgiven them).

As for his statement that I remained behind from participating in Badr, I was nursing Ruqayyah, the daughter of the Messenger of Allah , until she passed away. The Messenger of Allah gave me a share in the booty of Badr, and whoever gets a share in the booty from the Messenger of Allah will have participated in battle. As for his statement that I abandoned the Sunnah of `Umar, neither I nor he are able to endure it. Go and convey this answer to him.'"

Surah: 3 Ayah: 156, Ayah: 157 & Ayah: 158

﴿ يَـٰٓأَيُّهَا ٱلَّذِينَ ءَامَنُوا۟ لَا تَكُونُوا۟ كَٱلَّذِينَ كَفَرُوا۟ وَقَالُوا۟ لِإِخْوَٰنِهِمْ إِذَا ضَرَبُوا۟ فِى ٱلْأَرْضِ أَوْ
كَانُوا۟ غُزًّى لَّوْ كَانُوا۟ عِندَنَا مَا مَاتُوا۟ وَمَا قُتِلُوا۟ لِيَجْعَلَ ٱللَّهُ ذَٰلِكَ حَسْرَةً فِى قُلُوبِهِمْ ۗ وَٱللَّهُ
يُحْىِۦ وَيُمِيتُ ۗ وَٱللَّهُ بِمَا تَعْمَلُونَ بَصِيرٌ ﴿١٥٦﴾ ﴾

156. O you who believe! Be not like those who disbelieve (hypocrites) and who say to their brethren when they travel through the earth or go out to fight: "If they had stayed with us, they would not have died or been killed," so that Allâh may make it a cause of regret in their hearts. It is Allâh that gives life and causes death. And Allâh is All-Seer of what you do.

﴿ وَلَئِن قُتِلْتُمْ فِى سَبِيلِ ٱللَّهِ أَوْ مُتُّمْ لَمَغْفِرَةٌ مِّنَ ٱللَّهِ وَرَحْمَةٌ خَيْرٌ مِّمَّا يَجْمَعُونَ ﴿١٥٧﴾ ﴾

157. And if you are killed or die in the Way of Allâh, forgiveness and mercy from Allâh are far better than all that they amass (of worldly wealths).

﴿ وَلَئِن مُّتُّمْ أَوْ قُتِلْتُمْ لَإِلَى ٱللَّهِ تُحْشَرُونَ ﴿١٥٨﴾ ﴾

158. And whether you die, or are killed, verily, unto Allâh you shall be gathered.

Transliteration

156. Ya ayyuha allatheena amanoo la takoonoo kaallatheena kafaroo waqaloo li-ikhwanihim itha daraboo fee al-ardi aw kanoo ghuzzan law kanoo AAindana ma matoo wama qutiloo liyajAAala Allahu thalika hasratan fee quloobihim waAllahu yuhyee wayumeetu waAllahu bima taAAmaloona baseerun 157. Wala-in qutiltum fee sabeeli Allahi aw muttum lamaghfiratun mina Allahi warahmatun khayrun mimma yajmaAAoona 158. Wala-in muttum aw qutiltum la-ila Allahi tuhsharoona

Tafsir Ibn Kathir

Prohibiting the Ideas of the Disbeleivers about Death and Predestination

Allah forbids His believing servants from the disbelievers' false creed, seen in their statement about those who died in battle and during travel; "Had they abandoned these trips, they would not have met their demise." Allah said,

(O you who believe! Be not like those who disbelieve (hypocrites) and who say to their brethren), about their dead brethren,

(when they travel through the earth) for the purpose of trading and otherwise,

(or go out to fight), participating in battles,

("If they had stayed with us,") in our area,

("they would not have died or been killed,") they would not have died while traveling or been killed in battle. Allah's statement,

(so that Allah may make it a cause of regret in their hearts.) means, Allah creates this evil thought in their hearts so that their sadness and the grief they feel for their loss would increase. Allah refuted them by saying,

(It is Allah that gives life and causes death.) for the creation is under Allah's power, and the decision is His Alone. No one lives or dies except by Allah's leave, and no one's life is increased or decreased except by His decree.

(And Allah is All-Seer of what you do,) for His knowledge and vision encompasses all His creation and none of their affairs ever escapes Him. Allah's statement,

(And if you are killed or die in the way of Allah, forgiveness and mercy from Allah are far better than all that they amass.) (3:157), indicating that death and martyrdom in Allah's cause are a means of earning Allah's mercy, forgiveness and pleasure. This, indeed, is better than remaining in this life with its short lived delights. Furthermore, whoever dies or is killed will return to Allah, the Exalted and Most Honored, and He will reward him if he has done good deeds, or will punish him for his evil deeds. Allah said,

(And whether you die or are killed, verily, unto Allah you shall be gathered.) (3:158).

Surah: 3 Ayah: 159, Ayah: 160, Ayah: 161, Ayah: 162, Ayah: 163 & Ayah: 164

﴿ فَبِمَا رَحْمَةٍ مِّنَ ٱللَّهِ لِنتَ لَهُمْ ۖ وَلَوْ كُنتَ فَظًّا غَلِيظَ ٱلْقَلْبِ لَٱنفَضُّوا۟ مِنْ حَوْلِكَ ۖ
فَٱعْفُ عَنْهُمْ وَٱسْتَغْفِرْ لَهُمْ وَشَاوِرْهُمْ فِى ٱلْأَمْرِ ۖ فَإِذَا عَزَمْتَ فَتَوَكَّلْ عَلَى ٱللَّهِ ۚ إِنَّ ٱللَّهَ يُحِبُّ
ٱلْمُتَوَكِّلِينَ ﴿١٥٩﴾ ﴾

159. And by the Mercy of Allâh, you dealt with them gently. And had you been severe and harsh-hearted, they would have broken away from about you; so pass over (their faults), and ask (Allâh's) Forgiveness for them; and consult them in the affairs. Then when you have taken a decision, put your trust in Allâh, certainly, Allâh loves those who put their trust (in Him).

﴿ إِن يَنصُرْكُمُ ٱللَّهُ فَلَا غَالِبَ لَكُمْ ۖ وَإِن يَخْذُلْكُمْ فَمَن ذَا ٱلَّذِى يَنصُرُكُم مِّنۢ بَعْدِهِۦ ۗ
وَعَلَى ٱللَّهِ فَلْيَتَوَكَّلِ ٱلْمُؤْمِنُونَ ﴿١٦٠﴾ ﴾

160. If Allâh helps you, none can overcome you; and if He forsakes you, who is there after Him that can help you? And in Allâh (Alone) let believers put their trust.

﴿ وَمَا كَانَ لِنَبِىٍّ أَن يَغُلَّ ۚ وَمَن يَغْلُلْ يَأْتِ بِمَا غَلَّ يَوْمَ ٱلْقِيَٰمَةِ ۚ ثُمَّ تُوَفَّىٰ كُلُّ
نَفْسٍ مَّا كَسَبَتْ وَهُمْ لَا يُظْلَمُونَ ﴿١٦١﴾ ﴾

161. It is not for any Prophet to take illegally a part of booty (Ghulul), and whosoever deceives his companions as regards the booty, he shall bring forth on the Day of Resurrection that which he took (illegally). Then every person shall be paid in full what he has earned, and they shall not be dealt with unjustly.

﴿ أَفَمَنِ ٱتَّبَعَ رِضْوَٰنَ ٱللَّهِ كَمَنۢ بَآءَ بِسَخَطٍ مِّنَ ٱللَّهِ وَمَأْوَىٰهُ جَهَنَّمُ ۚ وَبِئْسَ ٱلْمَصِيرُ ﴿١٦٢﴾ ﴾

162. Is then one who follows (seeks) the good Pleasure of Allâh (by not taking illegally a part of the booty) like the one who draws on himself the Wrath of Allâh (by taking a part of the booty illegally - Ghulul)? - his abode is Hell, and worst, indeed is that destination!

﴿ هُمْ دَرَجَٰتٌ عِندَ ٱللَّهِ ۗ وَٱللَّهُ بَصِيرٌۢ بِمَا يَعْمَلُونَ ﴿١٦٣﴾ ﴾

163. They are in varying grades with Allâh, and Allâh is All-Seer of what they do.

﴿ لَقَدْ مَنَّ ٱللَّهُ عَلَى ٱلْمُؤْمِنِينَ إِذْ بَعَثَ فِيهِمْ رَسُولًا مِّنْ أَنفُسِهِمْ يَتْلُوا۟ عَلَيْهِمْ ءَايَٰتِهِۦ
وَيُزَكِّيهِمْ وَيُعَلِّمُهُمُ ٱلْكِتَٰبَ وَٱلْحِكْمَةَ وَإِن كَانُوا۟ مِن قَبْلُ لَفِى ضَلَٰلٍ مُّبِينٍ ﴿١٦٤﴾ ﴾

164. Indeed Allâh conferred a great favor on the believers when He sent among them a Messenger (Muhammad (peace be upon him)) from among themselves, reciting unto them His Verses (the Qur'ân), and purifying them (from sins by their following him), and instructing them (in) the Book (the Qur'ân) and Al-Hikmah (the wisdom and the Sunnah

of the Prophet (peace be upon him) (i.e. his legal ways, statements, acts of worship)) while before that they had been in manifest error.

Transliteration

159. Fabima rahmatin mina Allahi linta lahum walaw kunta faththan ghaleetha alqalbi lainfaddoo min hawlika faoAAfu AAanhum waistaghfir lahum washawirhum fee al-amri fa-itha AAazamta fatawakkal AAala Allahi inna Allaha yuhibbu almutawakkileena 160. In yansurkumu Allahu fala ghaliba lakum wa-in yakhthulkum faman tha allathee yansurukum min baAAdihi waAAala Allahi falyatawakkali almu/minoona 161. Wama kana linabiyyin an yaghulla waman yaghlul ya/ti bima ghalla yawma alqiyamati thumma tuwaffa kullu nafsin ma kasabat wahum la yuthlamoona 162. Afamani ittabaAAa ridwana Allahi kaman baa bisakhatin mina Allahi wama/wahu jahannamu wabi/sa almaseeru 163. Hum darajatun AAinda Allahi waAllahu baseerun bima yaAAmaloona 164. Laqad manna Allahu AAala almu/mineena ith baAAatha feehim rasoolan min anfusihim yatloo AAalayhim ayatihi wayuzakkeehim wayuAAallimuhumu alkitaba waalhikmata wa-in kanoo min qablu lafee dalalin mubeenin

Tafsir Ibn Kathir

Among the Qualities of Our Prophet Muhammad are Mercy and Kindness

Allah addresses His Messenger and reminds him and the believers of the favor that He has made his heart and words soft for his Ummah, those who follow his command and refrain from what he prohibits.

(And by the mercy of Allah, you dealt with them gently) (3:159). meaning, who would have made you this kind, if it was not Allah's mercy for you and them. Qatadah said that,

(And by the mercy of Allah, you dealt with them gently) means, "With Allah's mercy you became this kind." Al-Hasan Al-Basri said that this, indeed, is the description of the behavior that Allah sent Muhammad with. This Ayah is similar to Allah's statement,

(Verily, there has come unto you a Messenger from among yourselves. It grieves him that you should receive any injury or difficulty. He is anxious over you (to be rightly guided, to repent to Allah); for the believers (he is) full of pity, kind, and merciful) (9:128). Allah said next,

(And had you been severe and harsh-hearted, they would have broken away from about you;)

The severe person is he who utters harsh words, and,

(harsh-hearted) is the person whose heart is hard. Had this been the Prophet's behavior, "They would have scattered from around you. However, Allah gathered them and made you kind and soft with them, so that their hearts congregate around you." `Abdullah bin `Amr said that he read the description of the Messenger of Allah in previous Books, "He is not severe, harsh, obscene in the marketplace or dealing evil for evil. Rather, he forgives and pardons."

The Order for Consultation and to Abide by it

Allah said,

(So pardon them, and ask (Allah's) forgiveness for them; and consult them in the affairs.)

The Messenger of Allah used to ask his Companions for advice about various matters, to comfort their hearts, and so they actively implement the decision they reach. For instance, before the battle of Badr, the Prophet asked his Companions for if Muslims should intercept the caravan (led by Abu Sufyan). They said, "O Messenger of Allah! If you wish to cross the sea, we would follow you in it, and if you march forth to Barkul-Ghimad we would march with you. We would never say what the Children of Israel said to Musa, `So go, you and your Lord, and fight you two, we are sitting right here.' Rather, we say march forth and we shall march forth with you; and before you, and to your right and left shall we fight." The Prophet also asked them for their opinion about where they should set up camp at Badr. Al-Mundhir bin `Amr suggested to camp close to the enemy, for he wished to acquire martyrdom.

Concerning the battle of Uhud, the Messenger asked the Companions if they should fortify themselves in Al-Madinah or go out to meet the enemy, and the majority of them requested that they go out to meet the enemy, and he did. He also took their advice on the day of Khandaq (the Trench) about conducting a peace treaty with some of the tribes of Al-Ahzab (the Confederates), in return for giving them one-third of the fruits of Al-Madinah. However, Sa`d bin `Ubadah and Sa`d bin Mu`adh rejected this offer and the Prophet went ahead with their advice. The Prophet also asked them if they should attack the idolators on the Day of Hudaybiyyah, and Abu Bakr disagreed, saying, "We did not come here to fight anyone. Rather, we came to perform `Umrah." The Prophet agreed.

On the day of Ifk, (i.e. the false accusation), the Messenger of Allah said to them, "O Muslims! Give me your advice about some men who falsely accused my wife (`A'ishah). By Allah! I never knew of any evil to come from my wife. And they accused whom They accused he from whom I only knew righteous conduct, by Allah!" The Prophet asked `Ali and Usamah about divorcing `A'ishah. In summary, the Prophet used to take his Companions' advice for battles and other important events.

Ibn Majah recorded that Abu Hurayrah said that the Prophet said;

«الْمُسْتَشَارُ مُؤْتَمَنٌ»

(The one whom advice is sought from is to be entrusted) tThis was recorded by Abu Dawud, At-Tirmidhi, and An-Nasa'i who graded it Hasan.

Trust in Allah After Taking the Dec

Allah's statement,

(Then when you have taken a decision, put your trust in Allah,) means, if you conduct the required consultation and you then make a decision, trust in Allah over your decision,

(certainly, Allah loves those who put their trust (in Him)).

Allah's statement,

(If Allah helps you, none can overcome you; and if He forsakes you, who is there after Him that can help you And in Allah (Alone) let believers put their trust), is similar to His statement that we mentioned earlier,

(And there is no victory except from Allah the Almighty, the All-Wise) (3:126).

Allah next commands the believers to trust in Him,

(And in Allah (Alone) let believers put their trust).

Treachery with the Spoils of War was not a Trait of the Prophet

Allah said,

(It is not for any Prophet to illegally take a part of the booty,)

Ibn `Abbas, Mujahid and Al-Hasan said that the Ayah means, "It is not for a Prophet to breach the trust." Ibn Jarir recorded that, Ibn `Abbas said that, this Ayah,

(It is not for any Prophet to illegally take a part of the booty,) was revealed in connection with a red robe that was missing from the spoils of war of Badr. Some people said that the Messenger of Allah might have taken it. When this rumor circulated, Allah sent down,

(It is not for any Prophet to illegally take a part of the booty, and whosoever is deceitful with the booty, he shall bring forth on the Day of Resurrection that which he took.)

This was also recorded by Abu Dawud and At-Tirmidhi, who said "Hasan Gharib". This Ayah exonerates the Messenger of Allah of all types of deceit and treachery, be it returning what was entrusted with him, dividing the spoils of war, etc.

Allah then said,

(and whosoever is deceitful with the booty, he shall bring forth on the Day of Resurrection that which he took. Then every person shall be paid in full what he has earned, and they shall not be dealt with unjustly.)

This Ayah contains a stern warning and threat against Ghulul (stealing from the booty), and there are also Hadiths, that prohibit such practice. Imam Ahmad recorded that Abu Malik Al-Ashja`i said that the Prophet said,

«أَعْظَمُ الْغُلُولِ عِنْدَ اللهِ ذِرَاعٌ مِنَ الْأَرْضِ، تَجِدُون الرَّجُلَيْنِ جَارَيْنِ فِي الْأَرْضِ أو فِي الدَّارِ فَيَقْطَعُ أَحَدُهُمَا مِنْ حَظِّ صَاحِبِه ذِرَاعًا، فَإِذَا اقْتَطَعَهُ، طُوِّقَهُ مِنْ سَبْعِ أَرَضِينَ إِلى يَوْمِ الْقِيَامَةِ»

(The worst Ghulul (i.e. stealing) with Allah is a yard of land, that is, when you find two neighbors in a land or home and one of them illegally acquires a yard of his neighbor's land. When he does, he will be tied with it from the seven earths until the Day of Resurrection.)

Imam Ahmad recorded that Abu Humayd As-Sa`idi said, "The Prophet appointed a man from the tribe of Al-Azd, called Ibn Al-Lutbiyyah, to collect the Zakah. When he returned he said, `This (portion) is for you and this has been given to me as a gift.' The Prophet stood on the Minbar and said,

«مَا بَالُ الْعَامِلِ نَبْعَثُهُ فَيَجِي فَيَقُولُ: هَذَا لَكُمْ، وَهَذَا أُهْدِيَ لِي، أَفَلَا جَلَسَ فِي بَيْتِ
أَبِيهِ وَأُمِّهِ فَيَنْظُرُ أَيُهْدَى إِلَيْهِ أَمْ لَا؟ وَالَّذِي نَفْسُ مُحَمَّدٍ بِيَدِهِ، لَا يَأْتِي أَحَدٌ مِنْكُمْ
مِنْهَا بِشَيْءٍ إِلَّا جَاءَ بِهِ يَوْمَ الْقِيَامَةِ عَلَى رَقَبَتِهِ، إِنْ كَانَ بَعِيرًا لَهُ رُغَاءٌ، أَوْ بَقَرَةٌ لَهَا
خُوَارٌ، أَوْ شَاةٌ تَيْعَرُ»

(What is the matter with a man whom we appoint to collect Zakah, when he returns he said, `This is for you and this has been given to me as a gift.' Why hadn't he stayed in his father's or mother's house to see whether he would be given presents or not By Him in Whose Hand my life is, whoever takes anything from the resources of the Zakah (unlawfully), he will carry it on his neck on the Day of Resurrection; if it be a camel, it will be grunting; if a cow, it will be mooing; and if a sheep, it will be bleating. The Prophet then raised his hands till we saw the whiteness of his armpits, and he said thrice,

«اللَّهُمَّ هَلْ بَلَّغْتُ»

`O Allah! Haven't I conveyed Your Message.')"

Hisham bin `Urwah added that Abu Humayd said, "I have seen him with my eyes and heard him with my ears, and ask Zayd bin Thabit." This is recorded in the Two Sahihs .

In the book of Ahkam of his Sunan, Abu `Isa At-Tirmidhi recorded that Mu`adh bin Jabal said, "The Messenger of Allah sent me to Yemen, but when I started on the journey, he sent for me to come back and said,

«أَتَدْرِي لِمَ بَعَثْتُ إِلَيْكَ؟ لَا تُصِيبَنَّ شَيْئًا بِغَيْرِ إِذْنِي، فَإِنَّهُ غُلُولٌ»

(Do you know why I summoned you back Do not take anything without my permission, for if you do, it will be Ghulul.)

(and whosoever deceives his companions over the booty, he shall bring forth on the Day of Resurrection that which he took).

(This is why I summoned you, so now go and fulfill your mission.)" At-Tirmidhi said, "This Hadith is Hasan Gharib."

In addition, Imam Ahmad recorded that Abu Hurayrah said, "The Prophet got up among us and mentioned Ghulul and emphasized its magnitude. He then said,

«لَا أُلْفِيَنَّ أَحَدَكُمْ يَجِيءُ يَوْمَ الْقِيَامَةِ عَلَى رَقَبَتِهِ بَعِيرٌ لَهُ رُغَاءٌ، فَيَقُولُ: يَا رَسُولَ اللهِ
أَغِثْنِي، فَأَقُولُ: لَا أَمْلِكُ لَكَ مِنَ اللهِ شَيْئًا، قَدْ أَبْلَغْتُكَ، لَا أُلْفِيَنَّ أَحَدَكُمْ يَجِيءُ يَوْمَ

الْقِيَامَةِ عَلى رَقَبَتِهِ فَرَسٌ لَهَا حَمْحَمَةٌ، فَيقُولُ: يَا رَسُولَ اللهِ أَغِثْنِي، فَأَقُولُ: لَا أَمْلِكُ لَكَ مِنَ اللهِ شَيْئًا، قَدْ أَبْلَغْتُكَ، لَا أُلْفِيَنَّ أَحَدَكُمْ يَجِي يَوْمَ الْقِيَامَةِ عَلى رَقَبَتِهِ رِقَاعٌ تَخْفِقُ فَيَقُولُ: يَا رَسُولَ اللهِ أَغِثْنِي، فَأَقُولُ: لَا أَمْلِكُ لَكَ مِنَ اللهِ شَيْئًا، قَدْ أَبْلَغْتُكَ، لَا أُلْفِيَنَّ أَحَدَكُمْ يَجِي يَوْمَ الْقِيَامَةِ عَلى رَقَبَتِهِ صَامِتٌ، فَيقُولُ: يَا رَسُولَ اللهِ أَغِثْنِي، فَأَقُولُ: لَا أَمْلِكُ لَكَ مِنَ اللهِ شَيْئًا، قَدْ أَبْلَغْتُك»

(I will not like to see anyone among you on the Day of Resurrection, carrying a grunting camel over his neck. Such a man will say, 'O Allah's Messenger! Intercede on my behalf,' and I will say, 'I can't intercede for you with Allah, for I have conveyed (Allah's Message) to you.' I will not like to see any of you coming on the Day of Resurrection while carrying a neighing horse over his neck. Such a man will be saying, `O Allah's Messenger! Intercede on my behalf,' and I will reply, 'I can't intercede for you with Allah, for I have conveyed (Allah's Message) to you.' I will not like to see any of you coming on the Day of Resurrection while carrying clothes that will be fluttering, and the man will say, 'O Allah's Messenger! Intercede (with Allah) for me, ' and I will say, 'I can't help you with Allah, for I have conveyed (Allah's Message) to you.' I will not like to see any of you coming on the Day of Resurrection while carrying gold and silver on his neck. This person will say, 'O Allah's Messenger! Intercede (with Allah) for me.' And I will say, 'I can't help you with Allah, for I have conveyed (Allah's Message) to you.')" This Hadith was recorded in the Two Sahihs .

Imam Ahmad recorded that `Umar bin Al-Khattab said, "During the day (battle) of Khaybar, several Companions of the Messenger of Allah came to him and said, `So-and-so died as a martyr, so-and-so died as a martyr.' When they mentioned a certain man that died as a martyr, the Messenger of Allah said,

«كَلَّا إِنِّي رَأَيْتُهُ فِي النَّارِ فِي بُرْدَةٍ غَلَّهَا أَوْ عَبَاءَةٍ »

(No. I have seen him in the Fire because of a robe that he stole (from the booty).)

The Messenger of Allah then said,

«يَا ابْنَ الْخَطَّابِ، اذْهَبْ فَنَادِ فِي النَّاسِ: إِنَّهُ لَا يَدْخُلُ الْجَنَّةَ إِلَّا الْمُؤْمِنُون»

(O Ibn Al-Khattab! Go and announce to the people that only the faithful shall enter Paradise.)

So I went out and proclaimed that none except the faithful shall enter Paradise." This was recorded by Muslim and At-Tirmidhi, who said "Hasan Sahih".

The Honest and Dishonest are Not Similar

Allah said,

(Is then one who follows (seeks) the pleasure of Allah like the one who draws on himself the wrath of Allah His abode is Hell, and worse indeed is that destination!) (3:162),

This refers to those seeking what pleases Allah by obeying His legislation, thus earning His pleasure and tremendous rewards, while being saved from His severe torment. This type of person is not similar to one who earns Allah's anger, has no means of escaping it and who will reside in Jahannam on the Day of Resurrection, and what an evil destination it is.

There are many similar statements in the Qur'an, such as,

(Shall he then who knows that what has been revealed unto you (O Muhammad) from your Lord is the truth be like him who is blind) (13:19), and,

(Is he whom We have promised an excellent promise (Paradise) which he will find true, like him whom We have made to enjoy the luxuries of the life of (this) world) (28:61).

Allah then said,

(They are in varying grades with Allah,) (3:163) meaning, the people of righteousness and the people of evil are in grades, as Al-Hasan Al-Basri and Muhammad bin Ishaq said. Abu `Ubaydah and Al-Kisa'i said that this Ayah refers to degrees, meaning there are various degrees and dwellings in Paradise, as well as, various degrees and dwellings in the Fire. In another Ayah, Allah said,

(For all there will be degrees (or ranks) according to what they did) (6:132). Next, Allah said,

(and Allah is All-Seer of what they do), and He will compensate or punish them, and will never rid them of a good deed, or increase their evil deeds. Rather, each will be treated according to his deeds.

The Magnificent Blessing in the Advent of Our Prophet Muhammad

Allah the Most High said:

(Indeed Allah conferred a great favor on the believers when He sent among them a Messenger from among themselves,)

Meaning, from their own kind, so that it is possible for them to speak with him, ask him questions, associate with him, and benefit from him. Just as Allah said:

(And among His signs is that he created for them mates, that they may find rest in.)

Meaning; of their own kind. And Allah said;

(Say: "I am only a man like you. It has been revealed to me that your God is One God") (18:110).

(And We never sent before you any of the Messengers but verily, they ate food and walked in the markets) (25:20).

(And We sent not before you any but men unto whom We revealed, from among the people of townships) (12:109), and,

(O you assembly of Jinn and mankind! "Did not there come to you Messengers from among you...") (6:130).

Allah's favor is perfected when His Messenger to the people is from their own kind, so that they are able to talk to him and inquire about the meanings of Allah's Word. This is why Allah said, (reciting unto them His verses) (3:164), the Qur'an,

(and purifying them), commanding them to do righteous works and forbidding them from committing evil. This is how their hearts will be purified and cleansed of the sin and evil that used to fill them when they were disbelievers and ignorant.

(and instructing them (in) the Book and the Hikmah,) the Qur'an and the Sunnah,

(while before that they had been), before sending this Prophet, Muhammad ,

(in manifest error.) indulging in plain and unequivocal error and ignorance that are clear to everyone.

Surah: 3 Ayah: 165, Ayah: 166, Ayah: 167 & Ayah: 168

﴿أَوَلَمَّآ أَصَـٰبَتْكُم مُّصِيبَةٌ قَدْ أَصَبْتُم مِّثْلَيْهَا قُلْتُمْ أَنَّىٰ هَـٰذَا ۖ قُلْ هُوَ مِنْ عِندِ أَنفُسِكُمْ ۗ إِنَّ
ٱللَّهَ عَلَىٰ كُلِّ شَىْءٍ قَدِيرٌ ﴿١٦٥﴾﴾

165. (What is the matter with you?) When a single disaster smites you, although you smote (your enemies) with one twice as great, you say: "From where does this come to us?" Say (to them), "It is from yourselves (because of your evil deeds)." And Allâh has power over all things.

﴿وَمَآ أَصَـٰبَكُمْ يَوْمَ ٱلْتَقَى ٱلْجَمْعَانِ فَبِإِذْنِ ٱللَّهِ وَلِيَعْلَمَ ٱلْمُؤْمِنِينَ ﴿١٦٦﴾﴾

166. And what you suffered (of the disaster) on the day (of the battle of Uhud when) the two armies met, was by the leave of Allâh, in order that He might test the believers.

﴿وَلِيَعْلَمَ ٱلَّذِينَ نَافَقُوا۟ ۚ وَقِيلَ لَهُمْ تَعَالَوْا۟ قَـٰتِلُوا۟ فِى سَبِيلِ ٱللَّهِ أَوِ ٱدْفَعُوا۟ ۖ قَالُوا۟ لَوْ نَعْلَمُ قِتَالًا
لَّٱتَّبَعْنَـٰكُمْ ۗ هُمْ لِلْكُفْرِ يَوْمَئِذٍ أَقْرَبُ مِنْهُمْ لِلْإِيمَـٰنِ ۚ يَقُولُونَ بِأَفْوَٰهِهِم مَّا لَيْسَ فِى
قُلُوبِهِمْ ۗ وَٱللَّهُ أَعْلَمُ بِمَا يَكْتُمُونَ ﴿١٦٧﴾﴾

167. And that He might test the hypocrites, it was said to them: "Come, fight in the Way of Allâh or (at least) defend yourselves." They said: "Had we known that fighting will take place, we would certainly have followed you." They were that day, nearer to disbelief than to Faith, saying with their mouths what was not in their hearts. And Allâh has full knowledge of what they conceal.

﴿ٱلَّذِينَ قَالُوا۟ لِإِخْوَٰنِهِمْ وَقَعَدُوا۟ لَوْ أَطَاعُونَا مَا قُتِلُوا۟ ۗ قُلْ فَٱدْرَءُوا۟ عَنْ أَنفُسِكُمُ ٱلْمَوْتَ
إِن كُنتُمْ صَـٰدِقِينَ ﴿١٦٨﴾﴾

168. (They are) the ones who said about their killed brethren while they themselves sat (at home): "If only they had listened to us, they would not have been killed." Say: "Avert death from your own selves, if you speak the truth."

Transliteration

165. Awa lamma asabatkum museebatun qad asabtum mithlayha qultum anna hatha qul huwa min AAindi anfusikum inna Allaha AAala kulli shay-in qadeerun 166. Wama asabakum yawma iltaqa aljamAAani fabi-ithni Allahi waliyaAAlama almu/mineena 167. WaliyaAAlama allatheena nafaqoo waqeela lahum taAAalaw qatiloo fee sabeeli Allahi awi idfaAAoo qaloo law naAAlamu qitalan laittabaAAnakum hum lilkufri yawma-ithin aqrabu minhum lileemani yaqooloona bi-afwahihim ma laysa fee quloobihim waAllahu aAAlamu bima yaktumoona 168. Allatheena qaloo li-ikhwanihim waqaAAadoo law ataAAoona ma qutiloo qul faidraoo AAan anfusikumu almawta in kuntum sadiqeena

Tafsir Ibn Kathir

The Reason and Wisdom Behind the Defeat at Uhud

Allah said,

(When a single disaster smites you), in reference to when the Muslims suffered seventy fatalities during the battle of Uhud,

(although you smote (your enemies) with one twice as great,) during Badr, when the Muslims killed seventy Mushriks and captured seventy others,

(you say: "From where does this come to us") why did this defeat happen to us

(Say, "It is from yourselves.") Ibn Abi Hatim recorded that `Umar bin Al-Khattab said, "When Uhud occurred, a year after Badr, Muslims were punished for taking ransom from the disbelievers at Badr (in return for releasing the Mushriks whom they captured in that battle). Thus, they suffered the loss of seventy fatalities and the Companions of the Messenger of Allah gave flight and abandoned him. The Messenger suffered a broken tooth, the helmet was smashed on his head and blood flowed onto his face. Allah then revealed,

(When a single disaster smites you, although you smote (your enemies) with one twice as great, you say: "From where does this come to us" Say, "It is from yourselves".), because you took the ransom." Furthermore, Muhammad bin Ishaq, Ibn Jurayj, Ar-Rabi` bin Anas and As-Suddi said that the Ayah,

(Say, "It is from yourselves.") means, because you, the archers, disobeyed the Messenger's command to not abandon your positions.

(And Allah has power over all things.) and He does what He wills and decides what He wills, and there is none who can resist His decision.

Allah then said,

(And what you suffered on the day the two armies met, was by the leave of Allah), for when you ran away from your enemy, who killed many of you and injured many others, all this occurred by Allah's will and decree out of His perfect wisdom, (in order that He might test the believers.) who were patient, firm and were not shaken,

(And that He might test the hypocrites, it was said to them: "Come, fight in the way of Allah or defend yourselves." They said: "Had we known that fighting will take place, we would certainly have followed you.") (3:167),

This refers to the Companions of `Abdullah bin Ubayy bin Salul who went back (to Al-Madinah) with him before the battle. Some believers followed them and encouraged them to come back and fight, saying,

(or defend), so that the number of Muslims increases, as Ibn `Abbas, `Ikrimah, Sa`id bin Jubayr, Ad-Dahhak, Abu Salih, Al-Hasan and As-Suddi stated. Al-Hasan bin Salih said that this part of the Ayah means, help by supplicating for us, while others said it means, man the posts. However, they refused, saying,

("Had we known that fighting will take place, we would certainly have followed you.") meaning, according to Mujahid, if we knew that you would fight today, we would join you, but we think you will not fight. Allah said,

(They were that day, nearer to disbelief than to faith,)

This Ayah indicates that a person passes through various stages, sometimes being closer to Kufr and sometimes closer to faith, as evident by,

(They were that day, nearer to disbelief than to faith,)

Allah then said,

(saying with their mouths what was not in their hearts.) for they utter what they do not truly believe in, such as,

("Had we known that fighting will take place, we would certainly have followed you.")

They knew that there was an army of idolators that came from a far land raging against the Muslims, to avenge their noble men whom the Muslims killed in Badr. These idolators came in larger numbers than the Muslims, so it was clear that a battle will certainly occur. Allah said;

(And Allah has full knowledge of what they conceal.)

((They are) the ones who said about their killed brethren while they themselves sat (at home): "If only they had listened to us, they would not have been killed.") had they listened to our advice and not gone out, they would not have met their demise. Allah said,

(Say: "Avert death from your own selves, if you speak the truth.") meaning, if staying at home saves one from being killed or from death, then you should not die. However death will come to you even if you were hiding in fortified castles. Therefore, fend death off of yourselves, if you are right.

Mujahid said that Jabir bin `Abdullah said, "This Ayah (3:168) was revealed about `Abdullah bin Ubayy bin Salul (the chief hypocrite)."

Surah: 3 Ayah: 169, Ayah: 170, Ayah: 171, Ayah: 172, Ayah: 173, Ayah: 174 & Ayah: 175

﴿وَلَا تَحْسَبَنَّ ٱلَّذِينَ قُتِلُوا۟ فِى سَبِيلِ ٱللَّهِ أَمْوَٰتًۢا ۚ بَلْ أَحْيَآءٌ عِندَ رَبِّهِمْ يُرْزَقُونَ ﴿١٦٩﴾﴾

169. Think not of those who are killed in the Way of Allâh as dead. Nay, they are alive, with their Lord, and they have provision.

﴿فَرِحِينَ بِمَآ ءَاتَىٰهُمُ ٱللَّهُ مِن فَضْلِهِۦ وَيَسْتَبْشِرُونَ بِٱلَّذِينَ لَمْ يَلْحَقُوا۟ بِهِم مِّنْ خَلْفِهِمْ أَلَّا خَوْفٌ عَلَيْهِمْ وَلَا هُمْ يَحْزَنُونَ ﴿١٧٠﴾﴾

170. They rejoice in what Allâh has bestowed upon them of His Bounty and rejoice for the sake of those who have not yet joined them, but are left behind (not yet martyred) that on them no fear shall come, nor shall they grieve.

﴿۞ يَسْتَبْشِرُونَ بِنِعْمَةٍ مِّنَ ٱللَّهِ وَفَضْلٍ وَأَنَّ ٱللَّهَ لَا يُضِيعُ أَجْرَ ٱلْمُؤْمِنِينَ ﴿١٧١﴾﴾

171. They rejoice in a Grace and a Bounty from Allâh, and that Allâh will not waste the reward of the believers.

﴿ٱلَّذِينَ ٱسْتَجَابُوا۟ لِلَّهِ وَٱلرَّسُولِ مِنۢ بَعْدِ مَآ أَصَابَهُمُ ٱلْقَرْحُ ۚ لِلَّذِينَ أَحْسَنُوا۟ مِنْهُمْ وَٱتَّقَوْا۟ أَجْرٌ عَظِيمٌ ﴿١٧٢﴾﴾

172. Those who answered (the Call of) Allâh and the Messenger (Muhammad (peace be upon him)) after being wounded; for those of them who did good deeds and feared Allâh, there is a great reward.

﴿ٱلَّذِينَ قَالَ لَهُمُ ٱلنَّاسُ إِنَّ ٱلنَّاسَ قَدْ جَمَعُوا۟ لَكُمْ فَٱخْشَوْهُمْ فَزَادَهُمْ إِيمَـٰنًا وَقَالُوا۟ حَسْبُنَا ٱللَّهُ وَنِعْمَ ٱلْوَكِيلُ ﴿١٧٣﴾﴾

173. Those (i.e. believers) unto whom the people (hypocrites) said, "Verily, the people (pagans) have gathered against you (a great army), therefore, fear them." But it (only) increased them in Faith, and they said: "Allâh (Alone) is Sufficient for us, and He is the Best Disposer of affairs (for us)."

﴿فَٱنقَلَبُوا۟ بِنِعْمَةٍ مِّنَ ٱللَّهِ وَفَضْلٍ لَّمْ يَمْسَسْهُمْ سُوٓءٌ وَٱتَّبَعُوا۟ رِضْوَٰنَ ٱللَّهِ ۗ وَٱللَّهُ ذُو فَضْلٍ عَظِيمٍ ﴿١٧٤﴾﴾

174. So they returned with Grace and Bounty from Allâh. No harm touched them; and they followed the good Pleasure of Allâh. And Allâh is the Owner of Great Bounty.

﴿إِنَّمَا ذَٰلِكُمُ ٱلشَّيْطَـٰنُ يُخَوِّفُ أَوْلِيَآءَهُۥ فَلَا تَخَافُوهُمْ وَخَافُونِ إِن كُنتُم مُّؤْمِنِينَ ﴿١٧٥﴾﴾

175. It is only Shaitân (Satan) that suggests to you the fear of his Auliyâ' (supporters and friends (polytheists, disbelievers in the Oneness of Allâh and in His Messenger,

Muhammad (peace be upon him))) so fear them not, but fear Me, if you are (true) believers.

Transliteration

169. Wala tahsabanna allatheena qutiloo fee sabeeli Allahi amwatan bal ahyaon AAinda rabbihim yurzaqoona 170. Fariheena bima atahumu Allahu min fadlihi wayastabshiroona biallatheena lam yalhaqoo bihim min khalfihim alla khawfun AAalayhim wala hum yahzanoona 171. Yastabshiroona biniAAmatin mina Allahi wafadlin waanna Allaha la yudeeAAu ajra almu/mineena 172. Allatheena istajaboo lillahi waalrrasooli min baAAdi ma asabahumu alqarhu lillatheena ahsanoo minhum waittaqaw ajrun AAatheemun 173. Allatheena qala lahumu alnnasu inna alnnasa qad jamaAAoo lakum faikhshawhum fazadahum eemanan waqaloo hasbuna Allahu waniAAma alwakeelu 174. Fainqalaboo biniAAmatin mina Allahi wafadlin lam yamsas-hum soo-on waittabaAAoo ridwana Allahi waAllahu thoo fadlin AAatheemin 175. Innama thalikumu alshshaytanu yukhawwifu awliyaahu fala takhafoohum wakhafooni in kuntum mu/mineena

Tafsir Ibn Kathir

Virtues of the Martyrs

Allah states that even though the martyrs were killed in this life, their souls are alive and receiving provisions in the Dwelling of Everlasting Life. In his Sahih, Muslim recorded that Masruq said, "We asked `Abdullah about this Ayah,

(Think not of those as dead who are killed in the way of Allah. Nay, they are alive, with their Lord, and they have provision.)

He said, `We asked the Messenger of Allah the same question and he said,

«أَرْوَاحُهُمْ فِي جَوْفِ طَيْرٍ خُضْرٍ، لَهَا قَنَادِيلُ مُعَلَّقَةٌ بِالْعَرْشِ، تَسْرَحُ مِنَ الْجَنَّةِ حَيْثُ شَاءَتْ، ثُمَّ تَأْوِي إِلَى تِلْكَ الْقَنَادِيلِ، فَاطَّلَعَ إِلَيْهِمْ رَبُّهُمُ اطِّلَاعَةً فَقَالَ: هَلْ تَشْتَهُونَ شَيْئًا؟ فَقَالُوا: أَيَّ شَيْءٍ نَشْتَهِي وَنَحْنُ نَسْرَحُ مِنَ الْجَنَّةِ حَيْثُ شِئْنَا؟ فَفَعَلَ ذَلِكَ بِهِمْ ثَلَاثَ مَرَّاتٍ، فَلَمَّا رَأَوْا أَنَّهُمْ لَنْ يُتْرَكُوا مِنْ أَنْ يُسْأَلُوا، قَالُوا: يَا رَبِّ نُرِيدُ أَنْ تَرُدَّ أَرْوَاحَنَا فِي أَجْسَادِنَا حَتَّى نُقْتَلَ فِي سَبِيلِكَ مَرَّةً أُخْرَى، فَلَمَّا رَأَى أَنْ لَيْسَ لَهُمْ حَاجَةٌ، تُرِكُوا»

(Their souls are inside green birds that have lamps, which are hanging below the Throne (of Allah), and they wander about in Paradise wherever they wish. Then they return to those lamps. Allah looks at them and says, `Do you wish for anything' They say, `What more could we wish for, while we go wherever we wish in Paradise' Allah asked them this question thrice, and when they realize that He will keep asking them until they give an answer, they say, `O Lord! We wish that our souls be returned to our bodies so that we are killed in Your cause again.' Allah knew that they did not have any other wish, so they were left.)'" There are several other similar narrations from Anas and Abu Sa`id.

Imam Ahmad recorded that Anas said that the Messenger of Allah said,

«مَا مِنْ نَفْسٍ تَمُوتُ، لَهَا عِنْدَ اللهِ خَيْرٌ، يَسُرُّهَا أَنْ تَرْجِعَ إِلَى الدُّنْيَا، إِلَّا الشَّهِيدُ، فَإِنَّهُ يَسُرُّهُ أَنْ يَرْجِعَ إِلَى الدُّنْيَا فَيُقْتَلَ مَرَّةً أُخْرَى، لِمَا يَرَى مِنْ فَضْلِ الشَّهَادَةِ»

(No soul that has a good standing with Allah and dies would wish to go back to the life of this world, except for the martyr. He would like to be returned to this life so that he could be martyred again, for he tastes the honor achieved from martyrdom.) Muslim collected this Hadith

In addition, Imam Ahmad recorded that, Ibn `Abbas said that the Messenger of Allah said,

«لَمَّا أُصِيبَ إِخْوَانُكُمْ بِأُحُدٍ، جَعَلَ اللهُ أَرْوَاحَهُمْ فِي أَجْوَافِ طَيْرٍ خُضْرٍ، تَرِدُ أَنْهَارَ الْجَنَّـــةِ، وَتَأْكُلُ مِنْ ثِمَارِهَا، وَتَأْوِي إِلَى قَنَادِيلَ مِنْ ذَهَبٍ فِي ظِلِّ الْعَرْشِ، فَلَمَّا وَجَدُوا طِيبَ مَشْرَبِهِمْ وَمَأْكَلِهِمْ، وَحُسْنَ مُتَقَلَّبِهِمْ قَالُوا: يَا لَيْتَ إِخْوَانَنَا يَعْلَمُونَ مَا صَنَعَ اللهُ لَنَا، لِئَلَّا يَزْهَدُوا فِي الْجِهَادِ، وَلَا يَنْكُلُوا عَنِ الْحَرْبِ، فَقَالَ اللهُ عَزَّ وَجَلَّ: أَنَا أُبَلِّغُهُمْ عَنْكُم»

(When your brothers were killed in Uhud, Allah placed their souls inside green birds that tend to the rivers of Paradise and eat from its fruits. They then return to golden lamps hanging in the shade of the Throne. When they tasted the delight of their food, drink and dwelling, they said, `We wish that our brothers knew what Allah gave us so that they will not abandon Jihad or warfare.' Allah said, `I will convey the news for you.') Allah revealed these and the following Ayat,

(Think not of those as dead who are killed in the way of Allah. Nay, they are alive, with their Lord, and they have provision.)

Qatadah, Ar-Rabi` and Ad-Dahhak said that these Ayat were revealed about the martyrs of Uhud.

Abu Bakr Ibn Marduwyah recorded that Jabir bin `Abdullah said, "The Messenger of Allah looked at me one day and said, `O Jabir! Why do I see you sad' I said, `O Messenger of Allah! My father was martyred and left behind debts and children.' He said,

«أَلَا أُخْبِرُكَ؟ مَا كَلَّمَ اللهُ أَحَدًا قَطُّ إِلَّا مِنْ وَرَاءِ حِجَابٍ، وَإِنَّه كَلَّمَ أَبَاكَ كِفَاحًا»

(Should I tell you that Allah never spoke to anyone except from behind a veil However, He spoke to your father directly. He said,

«قَالَ: سَلْنِي أُعْطِكَ. قَالَ: أَسْأَلُكَ أَنْ أُرَدَّ إِلَى الدُّنْيَا فَأُقْتَلَ فِيكَ ثَانِيَةً، فَقَالَ الرَّبُّ عَزَّ وَجَلَّ: إِنَّهُ قَدْ سَبَقَ مِنِّي الْقَوْلُ: إِنَّهُمْ إِلَيْهَا لَا يَرْجِعُونَ. قَالَ: أَيْ رَبِّ فَأَبْلِغْ مَنْ وَرَائِي»

`Ask Me and I will give you.' He said, `I ask that I am returned to life so that I am killed in Your cause again.' The Lord, Exalted He be, said, `I have spoken the word that they shall not be returned back to it (this life). ' He said, `O Lord! Then convey the news to those I left behind.') Allah revealed,

(Think not of those as dead who are killed in the way of Allah...)"

Imam Ahmad recorded that Ibn `Abbas said that the Messenger of Allah said,

«الشُّهَدَاءُ عَلى بَارِقِ نَهْرٍ بِبَابِ الْجَنَّــةِ، فِي قُبَّةٍ خَضْرَاءَ، يَخْرُجُ عَلَيْهِمْ رِزْقُهُمْ مِنَ الْجَنَّــةِ بُكْرَةً وَعَشِيًّا»

(The martyrs convene at the shore of a river close to the door of Paradise, in a green tent, where their provisions are brought to them from Paradise day and night.)

Ahmad and Ibn Jarir collected this Hadith, which has a good chain of narration. It appears that the martyrs are of different types, some of them wander in Paradise, and some remain close to this river by the door of Paradise. It is also possible that the river is where all the souls of the martyrs convene and where they are provided with their provision day and night, and Allah knows best. Imam Ahmad narrated a Hadith that contains good news for every believer that his soul will be wandering in Paradise, as well, eating from its fruits, enjoying its delights and happiness and tasting the honor that Allah has prepared in it for him. This Hadith has a unique, authentic chain of narration that includes three of the Four Imams. Imam Ahmad narrated this Hadith from Muhammad bin Idris Ash-Shafi`i who narrated it from Malik bin Anas Al-Asbuhi, from Az-Zuhri, from `Abdur-Rahman bin Ka`b bin Malik that his father said that the Messenger of Allah said,

«نَسَمَةُ الْمُؤْمِنِ طَائِرٌ يَعْلُقُ فِي شَجَرِ الْجَنَّــةِ حَتَّى يَرْجِعَهُ اللهُ إِلى جَسَدِهِ يَوْمَ يَبْعَثُه»

(The soul of the believer becomes a bird that feeds on the trees of Paradise, until Allah sends him back to his body when He resurrects him.)

This Hadith states that the souls of the believers are in the shape of a bird in Paradise. As for the souls of martyrs, they are inside green birds, like the stars to the rest of the believing souls. We ask Allah the Most Generous that He makes us firm on the faith.

Allah's statement,

(They rejoice in what Allah has bestowed upon them) indicates that the martyrs who were killed in Allah's cause are alive with Allah, delighted because of the bounty and happiness they are enjoying. They are also awaiting their brethren, who will die in Allah's cause after them, for they will be meeting them soon. These martyrs do not have fear about the future or sorrow for what they left behind. We ask Allah to grant us Paradise. The Two Sahihs record from Anas, the story of the seventy Ansar Companions who were murdered at Bir Ma`unah in one night. In this Hadith, Anas reported that the Prophet used to supplicate to Allah in Qunut in prayer against those who killed them. Anas said, "A part of the Qur'an was revealed about them, but was later abrogated, `Convey to our people that we met Allah and He was pleased with us and made us pleased.'"

Allah said next,

(They rejoice in a grace and a bounty from Allah, and that Allah will not waste the reward of the believers) (3:171).

Muhammad bin Ishaq commented, "They were delighted and pleased because of Allah's promise that was fulfilled for them, and for the tremendous rewards they earned." `Abdur-Rahman bin Zayd bin Aslam said, "This Ayah encompasses all the believers, martyrs and otherwise. Rarely does Allah mention a bounty and a reward that He granted to the Prophets, without following that with what He has granted the believers after them."

The Battle of Hamra' Al-Asad

Allah said,

(Those who answered (the Call of) Allah and the Messenger after being wounded) (3:172).

This occurred on the day of Hamra' Al-Asad. After the idolators defeated the Muslims (at Uhud), they started on their way back home, but soon they were concerned because they did not finish off the Muslims in Al-Madinah, so they set out to make that battle the final one. When the Messenger of Allah got news of this, he commanded the Muslims to march to meet the disbelievers, to bring fear to their hearts and to demonstrate that the Muslims still had strength to fight. The Prophet only allowed those who were present during Uhud to accompany him, except for Jabir bin `Abdullah Al-Ansari, as we will mention. The Muslims mobilized, even though they were still suffering from their injuries, in obedience to Allah and His Messenger .

Ibn Abi Hatim recorded that `Ikrimah said, "When the idolators returned (towards Makkah) after Uhud, they said, `You neither killed Muhammad nor collected female captives. Woe to you for what you did. Let us go back.' When the Messenger of Allah heard this news, he mobilized the Muslim forces, and they marched until they reached Hamra Al-Asad. The idolators said, `Rather, we will meet next year', and the Messenger of Allah went back (to Al-Madinah), and this was considered a Ghazwah (battle). Allah sent down,

(Those who answered (the Call of) Allah and the Messenger after being wounded; for those of them who did good deeds and feared Allah, there is a great reward.)

Al-Bukhari recorded that `A'ishah said to `Urwah about the Ayah;

(Those who answered (the Call of) Allah and the Messenger)

"My nephew! Your fathers Az-Zubayr and Abu Bakr were among them. After the Prophet suffered the calamity at Uhud and the idolators went back, he feared that the idolators might try to come back and he said, `Who would follow them' Seventy men, including Az-Zubayr and Abu Bakr, volunteered." This was recorded by Al-Bukhari alone.

As for Allah's statement,

(Those unto whom the people said, "Verily, the people have gathered against you, therefore, fear them." But it (only) increased them in faith) (3:173), it means, those who threatened the people, saying that the disbelievers have amassed against them, in order to instill fear in them, but this did not worry them, rather, they trusted in Allah and sought His help,

(and they said: "Allah is Sufficient for us, and He is the Best Disposer of affairs.")

Al-Bukhari recorded that Ibn `Abbas said,

("Allah Alone is Sufficient for us and He is the Best Disposer of affairs for us.")

"Ibrahim said it when he was thrown in fire. Muhammad said it when the people said, `Verily, the people have gathered against you, therefore, fear them.' But it only increased them in faith, and they said, `Allah is Sufficient for us and He is the Best Disposer of affairs for us.'" Abu Bakr Ibn Marduwyah recorded that Anas bin Malik said that the Prophet was told on the day of Uhud, "Verily, the people have gathered against you, therefore, fear them." Thereafter, Allah sent down this Ayah (3:173).

This is why Allah said,

(So they returned with grace and bounty from Allah. No harm touched them;) for when they relied on Allah, Allah took care of their worries, He confounded the plots of their enemies, and the Muslims returned to their land,

(with grace and bounty from Allah. No harm touched them;) safe from the wicked plots of their enemies,

(and they followed the pleasure of Allah. And Allah is the Owner of great bounty.)

Al-Bayhaqi recorded that Ibn `Abbas said about Allah's statement,

(So they returned with grace and bounty from Allah,) "The `Grace' was that they were saved. The `Bounty' was that a caravan passed by, and those days were (Hajj) season days. Thus the Messenger of Allah bought and sold and made a profit, which he divided between his Companions."

Allah then said,

(It is only Shaytan that suggests to you the fear of his friends,) (3:175) meaning, Shaytan threatens you with his friends and tries to pretend they are powerful and fearsome. Allah said next,

(so fear them not, but fear Me, if you are indeed believers.) meaning, "If Shaytan brings these thoughts to you, then depend on Me and seek refuge with Me. Indeed, I shall suffice you and make you prevail over them." Similarly, Allah said,

(Is not Allah Sufficient for His servant Yet they try to frighten you with those besides Him!) (39: 36), until,

(Say: "Sufficient for me is Allah; in Him those who trust must put their trust.") (39:38). Allah said,

(So fight you against the friends of Shaytan; ever feeble indeed is the plot of Shaytan.) (4:76) and

(They are the party of Shaytan. Verily, it is the party of Shaytan that will be the losers!) (58:19),

(Allah has decreed: "Verily, it is I and My Messengers who shall be the victorious." Verily, Allah is All-Powerful, All-Mighty.) (58:21) and

(Verily, Allah will help those who help His (cause).) (22:40) and

(O you who believe! If you help (in the cause of) Allah, He will help you) (47:7), and,

(Verily, We will indeed make victorious Our Messengers and those who believe, in this world's life and on the Day when the witnesses will stand forth. The Day when their excuses will be of no profit to wrongdoers. Theirs will be the curse, and theirs will be the evil abode.) (40:51,52)

Surah: 3 Ayah: 176, Ayah: 177, Ayah: 178, Ayah: 179 & Ayah: 180

﴿ وَلَا يَحْزُنكَ ٱلَّذِينَ يُسَـٰرِعُونَ فِى ٱلْكُفْرِ ۚ إِنَّهُمْ لَن يَضُرُّوا۟ ٱللَّهَ شَيْـًٔا ۗ يُرِيدُ ٱللَّهُ أَلَّا يَجْعَلَ لَهُمْ
حَظًّا فِى ٱلْـَٔاخِرَةِ ۖ وَلَهُمْ عَذَابٌ عَظِيمٌ ﴿١٧٦﴾ ﴾

176. And let not those grieve you (O Muhammad (peace be upon him)) who rush with haste to disbelieve; verily, not the least harm will they do to Allâh. It is Allâh's Will to give them no portion in the Hereafter. For them there is a great torment.

﴿ إِنَّ ٱلَّذِينَ ٱشْتَرَوُا۟ ٱلْكُفْرَ بِٱلْإِيمَـٰنِ لَن يَضُرُّوا۟ ٱللَّهَ شَيْـًٔا وَلَهُمْ عَذَابٌ أَلِيمٌ ﴿١٧٧﴾ ﴾

177. Verily, those who purchase disbelief at the price of Faith, not the least harm will they do to Allâh. For them, there is a painful torment.

﴿ وَلَا يَحْسَبَنَّ ٱلَّذِينَ كَفَرُوٓا۟ أَنَّمَا نُمْلِى لَهُمْ خَيْرٌ لِّأَنفُسِهِمْ ۚ إِنَّمَا نُمْلِى لَهُمْ لِيَزْدَادُوٓا۟ إِثْمًا ۚ
وَلَهُمْ عَذَابٌ مُّهِينٌ ﴿١٧٨﴾ ﴾

178. And let not the disbelievers think that Our postponing of their punishment is good for them. We postpone the punishment only so that they may increase in sinfulness. And for them is a disgracing torment.

﴿ مَّا كَانَ ٱللَّهُ لِيَذَرَ ٱلْمُؤْمِنِينَ عَلَىٰ مَآ أَنتُمْ عَلَيْهِ حَتَّىٰ يَمِيزَ ٱلْخَبِيثَ مِنَ ٱلطَّيِّبِ ۗ وَمَا كَانَ
ٱللَّهُ لِيُطْلِعَكُمْ عَلَى ٱلْغَيْبِ وَلَٰكِنَّ ٱللَّهَ يَجْتَبِى مِن رُّسُلِهِۦ مَن يَشَآءُ ۖ فَـَٔامِنُوا۟ بِٱللَّهِ وَرُسُلِهِۦ ۚ
وَإِن تُؤْمِنُوا۟ وَتَتَّقُوا۟ فَلَكُمْ أَجْرٌ عَظِيمٌ ﴿١٧٩﴾ ﴾

179. Allâh will not leave the believers in the state in which you are now, until He distinguishes the wicked from the good. Nor will Allâh disclose to you the secrets of the Ghaib (unseen), but Allâh chooses of His Messengers whom He wills. So believe in Allâh and His Messengers. And if you believe and fear Allâh, then for you there is a great reward.

﴿ وَلَا يَحْسَبَنَّ ٱلَّذِينَ يَبْخَلُونَ بِمَآ ءَاتَىٰهُمُ ٱللَّهُ مِن فَضْلِهِۦ هُوَ خَيْرًا لَّهُم ۖ بَلْ هُوَ شَرٌّ لَّهُمْ ۖ
سَيُطَوَّقُونَ مَا بَخِلُوا۟ بِهِۦ يَوْمَ ٱلْقِيَٰمَةِ ۗ وَلِلَّهِ مِيرَٰثُ ٱلسَّمَٰوَٰتِ وَٱلْأَرْضِ ۗ وَٱللَّهُ بِمَا تَعْمَلُونَ
خَبِيرٌ ﴿١٨٠﴾ ﴾

180. And let not those who covetously withhold of that which Allâh has bestowed on them of His Bounty (Wealth) think that it is good for them (and so they do not pay the obligatory Zakât). Nay, it will be worse for them; the things which they covetously withheld shall be tied to their necks like a collar on the Day of Resurrection. And to Allâh belongs the heritage of the heavens and the earth; and Allâh is Well-Acquainted with all that you do.

Transliteration

176. Wala yahzunka allatheena yusariAAoona fee alkufri innahum lan yadurroo Allaha shay-an yureedu Allahu alla yajAAala lahum haththan fee al-akhirati walahum AAathabun AAatheemun 177. Inna allatheena ishtarawoo alkufra bial-eemani lan yadurroo Allaha shay-an walahum AAathabun aleemun 178. Wala yahsabanna allatheena kafaroo annama numlee lahum khayrun li-anfusihim innama numlee lahum liyazdadoo ithman walahum AAathabun muheenun 179. Ma kana Allahu liyathara almu/mineena AAala ma antum AAalayhi hatta yameeza alkhabeetha mina alttayyibi wama kana Allahu liyutliAAakum AAala alghaybi walakinna Allaha yajtabee min rusulihi man yashao faaminoo biAllahi warusulihi wa-in tu/minoo watattaqoo falakum ajrun AAatheemun 180. Wala yahsabanna allatheena yabkhaloona bima atahummu Allahu min fadlihi huwa khayran lahum bal huwa sharrun lahum sayutawwaqoona ma bakhiloo bihi yawma alqiyamati walillahi meerathu alssamawati waal-ardi waAllahu bima taAAmaloona khabeerun

Tafsir Ibn Kathir

Comforting the Messenger of Allah

Allah said to His Prophet,

(And let not those grieve you who rush with haste to disbelieve) (3:176).

Because the Prophet was eager for people's benefit, he would become sad when the disbelievers would resort to defiance, rebellion and stubbornness. Allah said, `Do not be saddened by this behavior,'

(verily, not the least harm will they do to Allah. It is Allah's will to give them no portion in the Hereafter.) for He decided with His power and wisdom that they shall not acquire any share in the Hereafter,

(For them there is a great torment.)

Allah said about the disbelievers,

(Verily, those who purchase disbelief at the price of faith,) by exchanging disbelief for faith,

(not the least harm will they do to Allah.) Rather, they will only harm themselves,

(For them, there is a painful torment.)

Allah said next,

(And let not the disbelievers think that Our postponing their punishment is good for them. We postpone the punishment only so that they may increase in sinfulness. And for them is a disgraceful torment) (3:178).

This statement is similar to Allah's other statements,

(Do they think that because We have given them abundant wealth and children, (that) We hasten unto them with good things. Nay, but they perceive not.) (23:55,56) and

(Then leave Me Alone with such as belie this Qur'an. We shall punish them gradually from directions they perceive not.) (68:44), and,

(And let not their wealth or their children amaze you. Allah's plan is to punish them with these things in this world, and that their souls shall depart (die) while they are disbelievers) (9:85).

Allah then said,

(Allah will not leave the believers in the state in which you are now, until He distinguishes the wicked from the good.) (3:179), meaning, He allows a calamity to happen, and during this calamity His friend becomes known and His enemy exposed, the patient believer recognized and the sinful hypocrite revealed. This Ayah refers to Uhud, since Allah tested the believers in that battle, thus making known the faith, endurance, patience, firmness and obedience to Allah and His Messenger that the believers had. Allah exposed the hypocrites in their defiance, reverting from Jihad, and the treachery they committed against Allah and His Messenger . This is why Allah said,

(Allah will not leave the believers in the state in which you are now, until He distinguishes the wicked from the good.)

Mujahid commented, "He distinguished between them during the day of Uhud." Qatadah said, "He distinguished between them in Jihad and Hijrah." Allah said next,

(Nor will Allah disclose to you the secrets of the Unseen.) meaning, you do not have access to Allah's knowledge of His creation so that you can distinguish between the believer and the hypocrite, except by the signs of each type that Allah uncovers. Allah's statement,

(but Allah chooses of His Messengers whom He wills.) is similar to another Ayah,

((He Alone is) the All-Knower of the Unseen, and He reveals to none His Unseen. Except to a Messenger (from mankind) whom He has chosen, and then He makes a band of watching guards (angels) to march before him and behind him.) (72:26,27). Allah then said,

(So believe in Allah and His Messengers.) Obey Allah and His Messenger and adhere to the law that he legislated for you,

(and if you believe and fear Allah, then for you there is a great reward.)

The Censure of Selfishness, and Warning Against it

Allah said,

(And let not those who are stingy with that which Allah has bestowed on them of His bounty (wealth) think that it is good for them. Nay, it will be worse for them.) (3:180)

Therefore, the Ayah says that the miser should not think that collecting money will benefit him. Rather, it will harm him in his religion and worldly affairs. Allah mentions the money that the miser collected on the Day of Resurrection,

(the things that they stingy with shall be tied to their necks like a collar on the Day of Resurrection.)

Al-Bukhari recorded that Abu Hurayrah said that the Messenger of Allah said,

«مَنْ آتَاهُ اللهُ مَالًا فَلَمْ يُؤَدِّ زَكَاتَهُ، مُثِّلَ لَهُ شُجَاعًا أَقْرَعَ، لَهُ زَبِيبَتَانِ، يُطَوَّقُهُ يَوْمَ الْقِيَامَةِ، يَأْخُذُ بِلِهْزِمَتَيْهِ يَعْنِي بِشِدْقَيْهِ يَقُولُ: أَنَا مَالُكَ، أَنَا كَنْزُكَ»

(Whoever Allah makes wealthy and he does not pay the Zakah due on his wealth, then (on the Day of Resurrection) his wealth will be made in the likeness of a bald-headed poisonous male snake with two black spots over the eyes. The snake will encircle his neck and bite his cheeks and proclaim, `I am your wealth, I am your treasure.')

The Prophet then recited the Ayah,

[وَلاَ يَحْسَبَنَّ الَّذِينَ يَبْخَلُونَ بِمَآ ءَاتَـــهُمُ اللَّهُ مِن فَضْلِهِ هُوَ خَيْراً لَّهُمْ بَلْ هُوَ شَرٌّ لَّهُمْ]

(And let not those who are stingy with that which Allah has bestowed on them of His bounty think that it is good for them. Nay, it will be worse for them), until the end. Al-Bukhari, but not

Muslim, collected this Hadith using this chain of narration, Ibn Hibban also collected it in his Sahih.

Imam Ahmad recorded that `Abdullah said that the Prophet said,

«مَا مِنْ عَبْدٍ لَا يُؤَدِّي زَكَاةَ مَالِهِ إِلَّا جُعِلَ لَهُ شُجَاعٌ أَقْرَعُ يَتْبَعُهُ، يَفِرُّ مِنْهُ وَهُوَ يَتْبَعُهُ، فَيَقُولُ: أَنَا كَنْزُكَ»

(Every person who does not pay the Zakah due on his wealth, will have his money made into the shape of a bald-headed, poisonous male snake who will follow him. The person will run away from the snake, who will follow him and proclaim, `I am your treasure.')

`Abdullah then recited the Ayah in Allah's Book that testifies to this fact,

[سَيُطَوَّقُونَ مَا بَخِلُواْ بِهِ يَوْمَ الْقِيَـمَةِ]

(the things that they were stingy with shall be tied to their necks like a collar on the Day of Resurrection.)

This was recorded by At-Tirmidhi, An-Nasa'i, and Ibn Majah, and At-Tirmidhi said, "Hasan Sahih."

Allah's statement,

(And to Allah belongs the inheritance of the heavens and the Earth), means,

(and spend of that whereof He has made you trustees) (57: 7). Therefore, since all affairs are under Allah's control, then spend from your money so it will benefit you on the Day of Return,

(and Allah is Well-Acquainted with all that you do.) with your intentions and what your hearts conceal.

Surah: 3 Ayah: 181, Ayah: 182, Ayah: 183 & Ayah: 184

﴿ لَّقَدْ سَمِعَ ٱللَّهُ قَوْلَ ٱلَّذِينَ قَالُوٓاْ إِنَّ ٱللَّهَ فَقِيرٌ وَنَحْنُ أَغْنِيَآءُ ۘ سَنَكْتُبُ مَا قَالُواْ وَقَتْلَهُمُ ٱلْأَنۢبِيَآءَ بِغَيْرِ حَقٍّ وَنَقُولُ ذُوقُواْ عَذَابَ ٱلْحَرِيقِ ﴿١٨١﴾ ﴾

181. Indeed, Allâh has heard the statement of those (Jews) who say: "Truly, Allâh is poor and we are rich!" We shall record what they have said and their killing of the Prophets unjustly, and We shall say: "Taste you the torment of the burning (Fire)."

﴿ ذَٰلِكَ بِمَا قَدَّمَتْ أَيْدِيكُمْ وَأَنَّ ٱللَّهَ لَيْسَ بِظَلَّامٍ لِّلْعَبِيدِ ﴿١٨٢﴾ ﴾

182. This is because of that (evil) which your hands have sent before you. And certainly, Allâh is never unjust to (His) slaves.

﴿ ٱلَّذِينَ قَالُوٓا۟ إِنَّ ٱللَّهَ عَهِدَ إِلَيْنَآ أَلَّا نُؤْمِنَ لِرَسُولٍ حَتَّىٰ يَأْتِيَنَا بِقُرْبَانٍ تَأْكُلُهُ
ٱلنَّارُ ۗ قُلْ قَدْ جَآءَكُمْ رُسُلٌ مِّن قَبْلِى بِٱلْبَيِّنَٰتِ وَبِٱلَّذِى قُلْتُمْ فَلِمَ قَتَلْتُمُوهُمْ إِن
كُنتُمْ صَٰدِقِينَ ﴿١٨٣﴾ ﴾

183. Those (Jews) who said: "Verily, Allâh has taken our promise not to believe in any Messenger unless he brings to us an offering which the fire (from heaven) shall devour." Say: "Verily, there came to you Messengers before me, with clear signs and even with what you speak of; why then did you kill them, if you are truthful?"

﴿ فَإِن كَذَّبُوكَ فَقَدْ كُذِّبَ رُسُلٌ مِّن قَبْلِكَ جَآءُو بِٱلْبَيِّنَٰتِ وَٱلزُّبُرِ وَٱلْكِتَٰبِ
ٱلْمُنِيرِ ﴿١٨٤﴾ ﴾

184. Then if they reject you (O Muhammad (peace be upon him)) so were Messengers rejected before you, who came with Al-Baiyinât (clear signs, proofs, evidences) and the Scripture and the Book of Enlightenment.

Transliteration

181. Laqad samiAAa Allahu qawla allatheena qaloo inna Allaha faqeerun wanahnu aghniyaon sanaktubu ma qaloo waqatlahumu al-anbiyaa bighayri haqqin wanaqoolu thooqoo AAathaba alhareeqi 182. Thalika bima qaddamat aydeekum waanna Allaha laysa bithallamin lilAAabeedin 183. Allatheena qaloo inna Allaha AAahida ilayna alla nu/mina lirasoolin hatta ya/tiyana biqurbanin ta/kuluhu alnnaru qul qad jaakum rusulun min qablee bialbayyinati wabiallathee qultum falima qataltumoohum in kutum sadiqeena 184. Fa-in kaththabooka faqad kuththiba rusulun min qablika jaoo bialbayyinati waalzzuburi waalkitabi almuneeri

Tafsir Ibn Kathir

Allah Warns the Idolators

Sa`id bin Jubayr said that Ibn `Abbas said, "When Allah's statement,

(Who is he that will lend to Allah a goodly loan so that He may multiply it to him many times) (2:245) was revealed, the Jews said, `O Muhammad! Has your Lord become poor so that He asks His servants to give Him a loan' Allah sent down,

(Indeed, Allah has heard the statement of those (Jews) who say: "Truly, Allah is poor and we are rich!") (3:181)."

This Hadith was collected by Ibn Marduwyah and Ibn Abi Hatim.

Allah's statement,

(We shall record what they have said) contains a threat and a warning that Allah followed with His statement,

(and their killing of the Prophets unjustly,)

This is what they say about Allah and this is how they treat His Messengers. Allah will punish them for these deeds in the worst manner,

(and We shall say: "Taste you the torment of the burning (Fire)." This is because of that which your hands have sent before you. And certainly, Allah is never unjust to (His) servants.)

They will be addressed like this as a way of chastising, criticism, disgrace and humiliation.

Allah said,

(Those (Jews) who said: "Verily, Allah has taken our promise not to believe in any Messenger unless he brings to us an offering which the fire (from heaven) shall devour.")

Allah refuted their claim that in their Books, Allah took a covenant from them to only believe in the Messenger whose miracles include fire coming down from the sky that consumes the charity offered by a member of the Messenger's nation, as Ibn `Abbas and Al-Hasan stated. Allah replied,

(Say: "Verily, there came to you Messengers before me, with Al-Bayinat...") with proofs and evidence,

(and even with what you speak of) a fire that consumes the accepted charity, as you asked,

(why then did you kill them) Why did you meet these Prophets with denial, defiance, stubbornness and even murder,

(if you are truthful), if you follow the truth and obey the Messengers.

Allah then comforts His Prophet Muhammad ,

(Then if they reject you, so were Messengers rejected before you, who came with Al-Baiyyinat and the Scripture, and the Book of Enlightenment.) meaning, do not be sad because they deny you, for you have an example in the Messengers who came before you. These Messengers were rejected although they brought clear proofs, plain evidence and unequivocal signs,

(and the Zubur), the divinely revealed Books that were sent down to the Messengers,

(and the Book of Enlightenment) meaning the clarification and best explanation.

Surah: 3 Ayah: 185 & Ayah: 186

﴿ كُلُّ نَفْسٍ ذَآئِقَةُ ٱلْمَوْتِ ۗ وَإِنَّمَا تُوَفَّوْنَ أُجُورَكُمْ يَوْمَ ٱلْقِيَـٰمَةِ ۖ فَمَن زُحْزِحَ عَنِ
ٱلنَّارِ وَأُدْخِلَ ٱلْجَنَّةَ فَقَدْ فَازَ ۗ وَمَا ٱلْحَيَوٰةُ ٱلدُّنْيَآ إِلَّا مَتَـٰعُ ٱلْغُرُورِ ﴿١٨٥﴾ ﴾

185. Everyone shall taste death. And only on the Day of Resurrection shall you be paid your wages in full. And whoever is removed away from the Fire and admitted to Paradise, he indeed is successful. The life of this world is only the enjoyment of deception (a deceiving thing).

﴿ ۞ لَتُبْلَوُنَّ فِىٓ أَمْوَٰلِكُمْ وَأَنفُسِكُمْ وَلَتَسْمَعُنَّ مِنَ ٱلَّذِينَ أُوتُوا۟ ٱلْكِتَٰبَ مِن
قَبْلِكُمْ وَمِنَ ٱلَّذِينَ أَشْرَكُوٓا۟ أَذًى كَثِيرًا ۚ وَإِن تَصْبِرُوا۟ وَتَتَّقُوا۟ فَإِنَّ ذَٰلِكَ مِنْ عَزْمِ
ٱلْأُمُورِ ﴿١٨٦﴾ ﴾

186. You shall certainly be tried and tested in your wealth and properties and in your personal selves, and you shall certainly hear much that will grieve you from those who received the Scripture before you (Jews and Christians) and from those who ascribe partners to Allâh; but if you persevere patiently, and become Al-Muttaqûn (the pious - see V.2:2) then verily, that will be a determining factor in all affairs (and that is from the great matters which you must hold on with all your efforts).

Transliteration

185. Kullu nafsin tha-iqatu almawti wa-innama tuwaffawna ojoorakum yawma alqiyamati faman zuhziha AAani alnnari waodkhila aljannata faqad faza wama alhayatu alddunya illa mataAAu alghuroori 186. Latublawunna fee amwalikum waanfusikum walatasmaAAunna mina allatheena ootoo alkitabu min qablikum wamina allatheena ashrakoo athan katheeran wa-in tasbiroo watattaqoo fa-inna Thalika min AAazmi al-omoori

Tafsir Ibn Kathir

Every Soul Shall Taste Death

Allah issues a general and encompassing statement that every living soul shall taste death. In another statement, Allah said,

(Whatsoever is on it (the earth) will perish. And the Face of your Lord full of majesty and honor will remain forever) (55:26,27).

Therefore, Allah Alone is the Ever-Living Who never dies, while the Jinn, mankind and angels, including those who carry Allah's Throne, shall die. The Irresistible One and Only, will alone remain for ever and ever, remaining Last, as He was the First. This Ayah comforts all creation, since every soul that exists on the earth shall die. When the term of this life comes to an end and the sons of Adam no longer have any new generations, and thus this world ends, Allah will command that the Day of Resurrection commence. Allah will then recompense the creation for their deeds, whether minor or major, many or few, big or small. Surely, Allah will not deal unjustly with anyone, even the weight of an atom, and this is why He said,

(And only on the Day of Resurrection shall you be paid your wages in full) (3:185).

Who Shall Gain Ultimate Victory

Allah said,

(And whoever is moved away from the Fire and admitted to Paradise, he indeed is successful.) meaning, whoever is kept away from the Fire, saved from it and entered into Paradise, will have achieved the ultimate success.

Ibn Abi Hatim recorded that Abu Hurayrah said that the Messenger of Allah said,

«مَوْضِعُ سَوْطٍ فِي الْجَنَّةِ خَيْرٌ مِنَ الدُّنْيَا وَمَا فِيهَا، اقْرَأُوا إِنْ شِئْتُمْ »

(A place in Paradise as small as that which is occupied by a whip is better than the world and whatever is on its surface. Read if you will),

[فَمَن زُحْزِحَ عَنِ النَّارِ وَأُدْخِلَ الْجَنَّةَ فَقَدْ فَازَ]

(And whoever is removed away from the Fire and admitted to Paradise, he indeed is successful). This was collected in the Two Sahihs, but using another chain of narration and without the addition (the Ayah.) Abu Hatim Ibn Hibban recorded it in his Sahih without the addition as did Al-Hakim in his Mustadrak.

Allah said,

(The life of this world is only the enjoyment of deception.) belittling the value of this life and degrading its importance. This life is short, little and finite, just as Allah said,

(Nay, you prefer the life of this world. Although the Hereafter is better and more lasting.) (87:16,17), and,

(And whatever you have been given is an enjoyment of the life of (this) world and its adornment, and that (Hereafter) which is with Allah is better and will remain forever) (28:60). A Hadith states,

«وَاللهِ مَا الدُّنْيَا فِي الْآخِرَةِ إِلَّا كَمَا يَغْمِسُ أَحَدُكُمْ أُصْبُعَهُ فِي الْيَمِّ، فَلْيَنْظُرْ بِمَ تَرْجِعُ إِلَيْه»

(By Allah! This life, compared to the Hereafter, is just as insignificant as when one of you dips his finger in the sea; let him contemplate what his finger will come back with.)

Qatadah commented on Allah's statement,

(The life of this world is only the enjoyment of deception.) "Life is a delight. By Allah, other than Whom there is no deity, it will soon fade away from its people. Therefore, take obedience to Allah from this delight, if you can. Verily, there is no power except from Allah."

The Believer is Tested and Hears Grieving Statements from the Enemy

Allah said,

(You shall certainly be tried and tested in your wealth and properties and in yourselves), just as He said in another Ayah,

(And certainly, We shall test you with something of fear, hunger, loss of wealth, lives and fruits) (2:155).

Therefore, the believer shall be tested, in his wealth, himself, his offspring and family. The believer shall be tested according to the degree of his faith, and when his faith is stronger, the test is larger.

(and you shall certainly hear much that will grieve you from those who received the Scripture before you (Jews and Christians) and from those who ascribe partners to Allah) (3:186).

Allah said to the believers upon their arrival at Al-Madinah, before Badr, while comforting them against the harm they suffered from the People of the Scriptures and the polytheists;

(but if you persevere patiently, and have Taqwa, then verily, that will be a determining factor in all affairs.)

Therefore, Allah commanded the believers to be forgiving, patient and forbearing until He brought His awaited aid.

Al-Bukhari recorded that Usamah bin Zayd said that Allah's Messenger rode a donkey with a saddle covered by a velvet sheet and let Usamah ride behind him (on the donkey). The Prophet wanted to visit Sa`d bin `Ubadah in Bani Al-Harith bin Al-Khazraj, and this occurred before the battle of Badr. The Prophet passed by a gathering in which `Abdullah bin Ubayy bin Salul was sitting, before `Abdullah bin Ubayy became Muslim. That gathering was made up of various Muslims as well as Mushriks, who worshipped the idols, and some Jews. `Abdullah bin Rawahah was sitting in that gathering. When the Prophet reached `Abdullah bin Ubayy, the donkey caused some sand to fall on the group. Then, `Abdullah bin Ubayy covered his nose with his robe and said, `Do not fill us with sand.' The Messenger of Allah greeted the gathering with Salam, called them to Allah and recited some of the Qur'an to them. `Abdullah bin Ubayy said, `O fellow! No other speech is better than what you said, if it was true! However, do not bother us in our gatherings. Go back to your place and whoever came to you, narrate your stories to him.' `Abdullah bin Rawahah said, `Rather, O Messenger of Allah! Attend our gatherings for we like that.' The Muslims, Mushriks and Jews then cursed each other, and they almost fought with each other. The Prophet tried to calm them down, until they finally settled. The Prophet rode his donkey and went to Sa`d bin `Ubadah, saying, `O Sa`d! Have you heard what Abu Hubbab said (meaning `Abdullah bin Ubayy) He said such and such things. ' Sa`d said, `O Messenger of Allah! Forgive and pardon him. By Allah, Who sent down the Book to you, Allah brought us the truth that you came with at a time when the people of this city almost appointed him king. When Allah changed all that with the truth that He gave you, he choked on it, and this is the reason behind the behavior you saw from him.' The Messenger of Allah forgave him. Indeed, the Messenger of Allah and his Companions used to forgive the Mushriks and the People of the Scriptures, just as Allah commanded them, and they used to tolerate the harm that they suffered. Allah said,

(and you shall certainly hear much that will grieve you from those who received the Scripture before you (Jews and Christians) and from those who ascribe partners to Allah;) (3:186), and,

(Many of the People of the Scripture (Jews and Christians) wish that they could turn you away as disbelievers after you have believed, out of envy from their own selves, even after the truth has become manifest unto them. But forgive and overlook, till Allah brings His command) (2:109).

The Prophet used to implement the pardon that Allah commanded him until He gave His command (to fight the disbelievers). When the Messenger fought at Badr, and Allah killed, by his hand, the leaders of the disbelievers from Quraysh, `Abdullah bin Ubayy bin Salul and the Mushriks and idol worshippers who were with him said, `This matter has prevailed,' and they gave their pledge to the Prophet and became Muslims."

Therefore, every person who stands for truth, enjoins righteousness and forbids evil, will be harmed in some manner. In such cases, there is no cure better than being patient in Allah's cause, trusting in Him and returning to Him.

Surah: 3 Ayah: 187, Ayah: 188 & Ayah: 189

﴿وَإِذۡ أَخَذَ ٱللَّهُ مِيثَٰقَ ٱلَّذِينَ أُوتُواْ ٱلۡكِتَٰبَ لَتُبَيِّنُنَّهُۥ لِلنَّاسِ وَلَا تَكۡتُمُونَهُۥ فَنَبَذُوهُ وَرَآءَ
ظُهُورِهِمۡ وَٱشۡتَرَوۡاْ بِهِۦ ثَمَنٗا قَلِيلٗاۖ فَبِئۡسَ مَا يَشۡتَرُونَ ١٨٧﴾

187. (And remember) when Allâh took a covenant from those who were given the Scripture (Jews and Christians) to make it (the news of the coming of Prophet Muhammad (peace be upon him) and the religious knowledge) known and clear to mankind, and not to hide it, but they threw it away behind their backs, and purchased with it some miserable gain! And indeed worst is that which they bought.

﴿لَا تَحۡسَبَنَّ ٱلَّذِينَ يَفۡرَحُونَ بِمَآ أَتَواْ وَّيُحِبُّونَ أَن يُحۡمَدُواْ بِمَا لَمۡ يَفۡعَلُواْ فَلَا تَحۡسَبَنَّهُم
بِمَفَازَةٖ مِّنَ ٱلۡعَذَابِۖ وَلَهُمۡ عَذَابٌ أَلِيمٞ ١٨٨﴾

188. Think not that those who rejoice in what they have done (or brought about), and love to be praised for what they have not done,- think not you that they are rescued from the torment, and for them is a painful torment.

﴿وَلِلَّهِ مُلۡكُ ٱلسَّمَٰوَٰتِ وَٱلۡأَرۡضِۗ وَٱللَّهُ عَلَىٰ كُلِّ شَيۡءٖ قَدِيرٌ ١٨٩﴾

189. And to Allâh belongs the dominion of the heavens and the earth, and Allâh has power over all things.

Transliteration

187. Wa-ith akhatha Allahu meethaqa allatheena ootoo alkitaba latubayyinunnahu lilnnasi wala taktumoonahu fanabathoohu waraa thuhoorihim waishtaraw bihi thamanan qaleelan fabi/sa ma yashtaroona 188. La tahsabanna allatheena yafrahoona bima ataw wayuhibboona an yuhmadoo bima lam yafAAaloo fala tahsabannahum bimafazatin mina alAAathabi walahum AAathabun aleemun 189. Walillahi mulku alssamawati waal-ardi waAllahu AAala kulli shay-in qadeerun

Tafsir Ibn Kathir

Chastising the People of the Scriptures for Breaking the Covenant and Hiding the Truth

In this Ayah, Allah chastises the People of the Scriptures, from whom Allah took the covenant by the words of their Prophets, that they would believe in Muhammad and describe him to the people, so that they would recognize and follow him when Allah sent him. However, they hid this truth and preferred the the small amounts and the material gains instead of the rewards of this life and the Hereafter that they were promised. This is a losing deal and a failing trade, indeed.

These Ayat also contain a warning for the scholars not to imitate their behavior, so that they do not suffer the same fate and become like them. Therefore, the scholars are required to spread the beneficial knowledge that they have, encouraging the various righteous good deeds. They are also warned against hiding any part of their knowledge. A Hadith states that the Prophet said,

«مَنْ سُئِلَ عَنْ عِلْمٍ فَكَتَمَهُ، أُلْجِمَ يَوْمَ الْقِيَامَةِ بِلِجَامٍ مِنْ نَار»

(Whoever was asked about knowledge that he knew but did not disclose it, will be tied with a bridle made of fire on the Day of Resurrection.)

Chastising Those Who Love to be Praised for What They Have not Done

Allah's statement,

(Think not that those who rejoice in what they have done, and love to be praised for what they have not done), refers to those who show off, rejoice in what they do and claim to do what they have not done. The Two Sahihs recorded that the Prophet said,

«مَنِ ادَّعَى دَعْوَةً كَاذِبَةً لِيَتَكَثَّرَ بِهَا، لَمْ يَزِدْهُ اللهُ إِلَّا قِلَّة»

(Whoever issues a false claim to acquire some type of gain, then Allah will only grant him decrease.)

The Sahih also recorded;

«الْمُتَشَبِّعُ بِمَا لَمْ يُعْطَ، كَلَابِسِ ثَوْبَيْ زُور»

(He who claims to do what he has not done, is just like a person who wears two robes made of falsehood.)

Imam Ahmad recorded that Marwan told his guard Rafi` to go to Ibn `Abbas and proclaim to him, "If every person among us who rejoices with what he has done and loves to be praised for what he has not done will be tormented, we all will be tormented." Ibn `Abbas said, "This Ayah was revealed about the People of the Scriptures." He then recited the Ayah,

((And remember) when Allah took a covenant from those who were given the Scripture (Jews and Christians) to make it (the truth) known and clear to mankind, and not to hide it, but they threw it away behind their backs, and purchased with it some miserable gain! And indeed worst is that which they bought.) then the Ayah,

(Think not that those who rejoice in what they have done, and love to be praised for what they have not done)

Ibn `Abbas said, "The Prophet asked them about something, and they hid its knowledge, giving him an incorrect answer. They parted after showing off and rejoicing in front of him because they answered him, so they pretended, and they were delighted that they hid the correct news about what he had asked them." This was recorded by Al-Bukhari, Muslim, At-Tirmidhi and An-Nasa'i.

Al-Bukhari recorded that Abu Sa`id Al-Khudri said, "During the time of the Messenger of Allah , when the Messenger would go to battle, some hypocrite men would remain behind and rejoice because they did not accompany the Prophet in battle. When the Messenger would come back, they would ask him to excuse them swearing to having some excuse, and wanting to be praised for that which they did not do. So Allah revealed,

(Think not that those who rejoice in what they have done, and love to be praised for what they have not done),"

to the end of the Ayah." And Muslim recorded similarly.

Allah said;

(think not that they are rescued from the torment,) Do not think that they will be saved from punishment, rather it will certainly strike them. So Allah said;

(and for them is a painful torment.) Allah then said,

(And to Allah belongs the dominion of the heavens and the earth, and Allah has power over all things.) He is the Owner of everything, able to do all things and nothing escapes His might. Therefore, fear Him, never defy Him and beware of His anger and revenge. He is the Most Great, none is greater than Him, and the Most Able, none is more able than He is.

Surah: 3 Ayah: 190, Ayah: 191, Ayah: 192, Ayah: 193 & Ayah: 194

﴿إِنَّ فِى خَلْقِ ٱلسَّمَـٰوَٰتِ وَٱلْأَرْضِ وَٱخْتِلَـٰفِ ٱلَّيْلِ وَٱلنَّهَارِ لَـَٔايَـٰتٍ لِّأُو۟لِى ٱلْأَلْبَـٰبِ ١٩٠﴾

190. Verily! In the creation of the heavens and the earth, and in the alternation of night and day, there are indeed signs for men of understanding.

﴿ٱلَّذِينَ يَذْكُرُونَ ٱللَّهَ قِيَـٰمًا وَقُعُودًا وَعَلَىٰ جُنُوبِهِمْ وَيَتَفَكَّرُونَ فِى خَلْقِ ٱلسَّمَـٰوَٰتِ
وَٱلْأَرْضِ رَبَّنَا مَا خَلَقْتَ هَـٰذَا بَـٰطِلًا سُبْحَـٰنَكَ فَقِنَا عَذَابَ ٱلنَّارِ ١٩١﴾

191. Those who remember Allâh (always, and in prayers) standing, sitting, and lying down on their sides, and think deeply about the creation of the heavens and the earth, (saying): "Our Lord! You have not created (all) this without purpose, glory to You! (Exalted are You above all that they associate with You as partners). Give us salvation from the torment of the Fire.

﴿رَبَّنَآ إِنَّكَ مَن تُدْخِلِ ٱلنَّارَ فَقَدْ أَخْزَيْتَهُۥ ۖ وَمَا لِلظَّـٰلِمِينَ مِنْ أَنصَارٍ ١٩٢﴾

192. "Our Lord! Verily, whom You admit to the Fire, indeed, You have disgraced him; and never will the Zâlimûn (polytheists and wrong-doers) find any helpers.

﴿ رَّبَّنَآ إِنَّنَا سَمِعۡنَا مُنَادِيٗا يُنَادِي لِلۡإِيمَٰنِ أَنۡ ءَامِنُواْ بِرَبِّكُمۡ فَـَٔامَنَّاۚ رَبَّنَا فَٱغۡفِرۡ لَنَا ذُنُوبَنَا
وَكَفِّرۡ عَنَّا سَيِّـَٔاتِنَا وَتَوَفَّنَا مَعَ ٱلۡأَبۡرَارِ ١٩٣ ﴾

193. "Our Lord! Verily, we have heard the call of one (Muhammad (peace be upon him)) calling to Faith: 'Believe in your Lord,' and we have believed. Our Lord! Forgive us our sins and expiate from us our evil deeds, and make us die (in the state of righteousness) along with Al-Abrâr (the believers of Islâmic Monotheism, the pious and righteous).

﴿ رَبَّنَا وَءَاتِنَا مَا وَعَدتَّنَا عَلَىٰ رُسُلِكَ وَلَا تُخۡزِنَا يَوۡمَ ٱلۡقِيَٰمَةِۗ إِنَّكَ لَا تُخۡلِفُ ٱلۡمِيعَادَ ١٩٤ ﴾

194. "Our Lord! Grant us what You promised unto us through Your Messengers and disgrace us not on the Day of Resurrection, for You never break (Your) Promise."

Transliteration

190. Inna fee khalqi alssamawati waal-ardi waikhtilafi allayli waalnnahari laayatin li-olee al-albabi 191. Allatheena yathkuroona Allaha qiyaman waquAAoodan waAAala junoobihim wayatafakkaroona fee khalqi alssamawati waal-ardi rabbana ma khalaqta hatha batilan subhanaka faqina AAathaba alnnari 192. Rabbana innaka man tudkhili alnnara faqad akhzaytahu wama lilththalimeena min ansarin 193. Rabbana innana samiAAna munadiyan yunadee lil-eemani an aminoo birabbikum faamanna rabbana faighfir lana thunoobana wakaffir AAanna sayyi-atina watawaffana maAAa al-abrari 194. Rabbana waatina ma waAAadtana AAala rusulika wala tukhzina yawma alqiyamati innaka la tukhlifu almeeAAada

Tafsir Ibn Kathir

The Proofs of Tawhid for People of Understanding, their Characteristics, Speech, and Supplications

Allah said,

(Verily, in the creation of the heavens and the Earth,) (3:190), referring to the sky in its height and spaciousness, the earth in its expanse and density, the tremendous features they have of rotating planets, seas, mountains, deserts, trees, plants, fruits, animals, metals and various beneficial colors, scents, tastes and elements.

(And in the alternation of night and day), as one follows and takes from the length of the other. For instance, at times one of them becomes longer than the other, shorter than the other at times and equal to the other at other times, and the same is repeated again and again, and all this occurs by the decision of the Almighty, Most Wise. This is why Allah said,

(there are indeed signs for men of understanding), referring to the intelligent and sound minds that contemplate about the true reality of things, unlike the deaf and mute who do not have sound comprehension. Allah said about the latter type,

(And how many a sign in the heavens and the earth they pass by, while they are averse therefrom. And most of them believe not in Allah except that they attribute partners unto Him) (12:105,106).

Allah then describes those who have good minds,

(Those who remember Allah standing, sitting, and lying down on their sides) (3:191).

Al-Bukhari recorded that `Imran bin Husayn said that, the Messenger of Allah said,

«صَلِّ قَائِمًا، فَإِنْ لَمْ تَسْتَطِعْ فَقَاعِدًا، فَإِنْ لَمْ تَسْتَطِعْ فَعَلَى جَنْب»

(Pray while standing, and if you can't, pray while sitting, and if you cannot do even that, then pray lying on your side.) These people remember Allah in all situations, in their heart and speech,

(and think deeply about the creation of the heavens and the Earth), contemplating about signs in the sky and earth that testify to the might, ability, knowledge, wisdom, will and mercy of the Creator. Allah criticizes those who do not contemplate about His creation, which testifies to His existence, Attributes, Shari`ah, His decree and Ayat. Allah said,

(And how many a sign in the heavens and the Earth they pass by, while they are averse therefrom. And most of them believe not in Allah except that they attribute partners unto Him) (12:105,106).

Allah also praises His believing servants,

(Those who remember Allah standing, sitting, and lying down on their sides, and think deeply about the creation of the heavens and the earth), supplicating;

("Our Lord! You have not created this without purpose,")

You did not create all this in jest and play. Rather, You created it in truth, so that You recompense those who do evil in kind, and reward those who do righteous deeds with what is better.

The faithful believers praise Allah and deny that He does anything in jest and without purpose, saying,

("glory to You,"), for You would never create anything without purpose,

("Give us salvation from the torment of the Fire."), meaning, "O You Who created the creation in truth and justice, Who is far from any shortcomings, or doing things without purpose or with jest, save us from the torment of the Fire with Your power and strength. Direct us to perform the deeds that make You pleased with us. Guide us to righteous work from which You admit us into the delightful Paradise, and save us from Your painful torment."

They next supplicate,

("Our Lord! Verily, whom You admit to the Fire, indeed, You have disgraced him;), by humiliating and disgracing him before all people on the Day of Gathering,

("and never will the wrongdoers find any helpers."), on the Day of Judgment, who would save them from You. Therefore, there is no escaping whatever fate You decided for them.

("Our Lord! Verily, we have heard the call of one calling to faith,"), a caller who calls to faith, referring to the Messenger of Allah ,

(`Believe in your Lord,' and we have believed), accepted his call and followed him.

("Our Lord! Forgive us our sins"), on account of our faith and obeying Your Prophet

("Forgive us our sins"), and cover them,

("and expiate from us our evil deeds"), between us and You, in private,

("and make us die along with Al-Abrar."), join us with the righteous people.

("Our Lord! Grant us what You promised unto us through Your Messengers") for our faith in Your Messengers, or, and this explanation is better; grant us what You promised us by the words of Your Messengers,

("and disgrace us not on the Day of Resurrection,"), before all creation,

("for You never break (Your) Promise."), for surely, the promise that You conveyed to Your Messengers, which includes us being resurrected before You, shall certainly come to pass.

It was the Prophet's tradition to recite the ten Ayat at the end of (Surah) Al `Imran when he woke up at night for (voluntary) prayer. Al-Bukhari recorded that Ibn `Abbas said, "I slept one night at the house of my aunt, Maymunah. The Messenger of Allah spoke with his wife for a while and then went to sleep. When it was the third part of the night, he stood up, looked at the sky and recited,

(Verily, in the creation of the heavens and the earth, and in the alternation of night and day, there are indeed signs for men of understanding) (3:190).

The Prophet then stood up, performed ablution, used Siwak (to clean his teeth) and prayed eleven units of prayer. When Bilal said the Adhan, the Prophet prayed two units of prayer, went out (to the Masjid) and led the people in the Dawn prayer." This was also collected by Muslim.

Ibn Marduwyah recorded that `Ata' said, "I, Ibn `Umar and `Ubayd bin `Umayr went to `A'ishah and entered her room, and there was a screen between us and her. She said, `O `Ubayd! What prevents you from visiting us' He said, `What the poet said, `Visit every once in a while, and you will be loved more.' Ibn `Umar said, `Tell us about the most unusual thing you witnessed from the Messenger of Allah .' She cried and said, `All his matters were amazing. On night, he came close to me until his skin touched my skin and said, `Let me worship my Lord.' I said, `By Allah I love your being close to me. I also love that you worship your Lord.' He used the water-skin and performed ablution, but did not use too much water. He then stood up in prayer and cried until his beard became wet. He prostrated and cried until he made the ground wet. He then laid down on his side and cried. When Bilal came to alert the Prophet for the Dawn prayer, he said, `O Messenger of Allah! What makes you cry, while Allah has forgiven you your previous and latter sins' He said,

«وَيْحَكَ يَا بِلَالُ، وَمَا يَمْنَعُنِي أَنْ أَبْكِيَ، وَقَدْ أُنْزِلَ عَلَيَّ فِي هذِهِ اللَّيْلَة»

(O Bilal! What prevents me from crying, when this night, this Ayah was revealed to me,)

(Verily, in the creation of the heavens and the earth, and in the alternation of night and day, there are indeed signs for men of understanding.)

(Woe to he who recites it but does not contemplate it.)."

Surah: 3 Ayah: 195

﴿ فَٱسْتَجَابَ لَهُمْ رَبُّهُمْ أَنِّى لَآ أُضِيعُ عَمَلَ عَـٰمِلٍ مِّنكُم مِّن ذَكَرٍ أَوْ أُنثَىٰ ۖ بَعْضُكُم مِّنۢ
بَعْضٍ ۖ فَٱلَّذِينَ هَاجَرُوا۟ وَأُخْرِجُوا۟ مِن دِيَـٰرِهِمْ وَأُوذُوا۟ فِى سَبِيلِى وَقَـٰتَلُوا۟ وَقُتِلُوا۟ لَأُكَفِّرَنَّ
عَنْهُمْ سَيِّـَٔاتِهِمْ وَلَأُدْخِلَنَّهُمْ جَنَّـٰتٍ تَجْرِى مِن تَحْتِهَا ٱلْأَنْهَـٰرُ ثَوَابًا مِّنْ عِندِ ٱللَّهِ ۗ وَٱللَّهُ عِندَهُۥ
حُسْنُ ٱلثَّوَابِ ﴿١٩٥﴾ ﴾

195. So their Lord accepted of them (their supplication and answered them), "Never will I allow to be lost the work of any of you, be he male or female. You are (members) one of another, so those who emigrated and were driven out from their homes, and suffered harm in My Cause, and who fought, and were killed (in My Cause), verily, I will exoiate from them their evil deeds and admit them into Gardens under which rivers flow (in Paradise); a reward from Allâh, and with Allâh is the best of rewards."

Transliteration

195. Faistajaba lahum rabbuhum annee la odeeAAu AAamala AAamilin minkum min thakarin aw ontha baAAdukum min baAAdin faallatheena hajaroo waokhrijoo min diyarihim waoothoo fee sabeelee waqataloo waqutiloo laokaffiranna AAanhum sayyi-atihim walaodkhilannahum jannatin tajree min tahtiha al-anharu thawaban min AAindi Allahi waAllahu AAindahu husnu alththawabi

Tafsir Ibn Kathir

Allah Accepts the Supplication of Men of Understanding

Allah said,

(So their Lord accepted of them), answered their invocation. Sa`id bin Mansur recorded that Salamah, a man from the family of Umm Salamah said, "Umm Salamah said, `O Messenger of Allah! Allah does not mention women in connection with Hijrah (Migration).' Allah sent down the Ayah,

(So their Lord accepted of them (their supplication and answered them), "Never will I allow to be lost the work of any of you, be he male or female.)

The Ansar say that Umm Salamah was the first woman to migrate to them." Al-Hakim collected this Hadith in his Mustadrak, and said, "It is Sahih according to the criteria of Al-Bukhari but they (Al-Bukhari and Muslim) did not collect it".

Allah's statement,

("Never will I allow to be lost the work of any of you, be he male or female,) explains the type of answer Allah gave them, stating that no deed of any person is ever lost with Him. Rather, He will completely reward each person for his or her good deeds. Allah's statement,

(You are (members) one of another) means, you are all equal in relation to gaining My reward. Therefore,

(those who emigrated), by leaving the land of Shirk and migrating to the land of faith, leaving behind their loved ones, brethren, friends and neighbors,

(and were driven out from their homes), when the Mushriks tormented them and forced them to migrate,

(and suffered harm in My cause), for their only wrong, to the people, was that they believed in Allah Alone. In similar Ayat, Allah said,

(and have driven out the Messenger and yourselves because you believe in Allah your Lord!) (60:1), and,

(And they had no fault except that they believed in Allah, the Almighty, Worthy of all praise!) (85:8) . Allah's statement,

(and who fought and were killed (in My cause),) (3:195) refers to the highest rank there is, that one fights in the cause of Allah and dies in the process, with his face covered in dust and blood. It is recorded in the Sahih that a man said,

('O Messenger of Allah! If I was killed in Allah's cause, observing patience, awaiting Allah's reward, attacking, not retreating, would Allah forgive my sins' The Prophet said,

«نَعَم»

`Yes.' The Prophet then asked the man,

«كَيْفَ قُلْتَ؟»

`What did you ask' When the man repeated the question, the Prophet said,

«نَعَمْ، إِلَّا الدَّيْنَ، قَالَهُ لِي جِبْرِيلُ آنِفًا»

`Yes, except for the debt, for Jibril conveyed this to me right now'.)

This is why Allah said here,

(verily, I will expiate from them their evil deeds and admit them into Gardens under which rivers flow), within Paradise, where there are rivers of various drinks: milk, honey, wine and fresh water. There is what no eye has ever seen, no ear has ever heard and no heart has ever imagined (of delights in Paradise). Allah's statement, (a reward from Allah) testifies to His might, for the Mighty and Most Great only gives tremendous rewards. Allah's statement,

(and with Allah is the best of rewards.") for those who perform good deeds.

Surah: 3 Ayah: 196, Ayah: 197 & Ayah: 198

﴿ لَا يَغُرَّنَّكَ تَقَلُّبُ ٱلَّذِينَ كَفَرُوا۟ فِى ٱلْبِلَٰدِ ١٩٦ ﴾

196. Let not the free disposal (and affluence) of the disbelievers throughout the land deceive you.

﴿ مَتَٰعٌ قَلِيلٌ ثُمَّ مَأْوَىٰهُمْ جَهَنَّمُ ۚ وَبِئْسَ ٱلْمِهَادُ ١٩٧ ﴾

197. A brief enjoyment; then, their ultimate abode is Hell; and worst indeed is that place for rest.

﴿ لَٰكِنِ ٱلَّذِينَ ٱتَّقَوْا۟ رَبَّهُمْ لَهُمْ جَنَّٰتٌ تَجْرِى مِن تَحْتِهَا ٱلْأَنْهَٰرُ خَٰلِدِينَ فِيهَا نُزُلًا مِّنْ
عِندِ ٱللَّهِ ۗ وَمَا عِندَ ٱللَّهِ خَيْرٌ لِّلْأَبْرَارِ ١٩٨ ﴾

198. But, for those who fear their Lord, are Gardens under which rivers flow (in Paradise); therein are they to dwell (for ever), an entertainment from Allâh; and that which is with Allâh is the Best for Al-Abrâr (the believers of Islâmic Monotheism, the pious and righteous).

Transliteration

196. La yaghurrannaka taqallubu allatheena kafaroo fee albiladi 197. MataAAun qaleelun thumma ma/wahum jahannamu wabi/sa almihadu 198. Lakini allatheena ittaqaw rabbahum lahum jannatun tajree min tahtiha al-anharu khalideena feeha nuzulan min AAindi Allahi wama AAinda Allahi khayrun lil-abrari

Tafsir Ibn Kathir

Warning Against Being Deceived by This Life; the Rewards of the Righteous Believers

Allah said, do not look at the disbelievers, who are enjoying various delights and joys. Soon, they will loose all this and be tied to their evil works, for verily, we are only giving them time, which deceives them, when all they have is,

(A brief enjoyment; then their ultimate abode is Hell; and worst indeed is that place for rest.)

This Ayah is similar to several other Ayat, such as,

(None disputes in the Ayat of Allah but those who disbelieve. So, let not their ability of going about here and there through the land deceive you!) (40:4),

(Verily, those who invent a lie against Allah, will never be successful. (A brief) enjoyment in this world! and then unto Us will be their return, then We shall make them taste the severest torment because they used to disbelieve.) (10:69,70),

(We let them enjoy for a little while, then in the end We shall oblige them to (enter) a great torment.) (31:24),

(So, give a respite to the disbelievers; deal gently with them for a while.) (86:17), and,

(Is he whom We have promised an excellent promise (Paradise) which he will find true -- like him whom We have made to enjoy the luxuries of the life of (this) world, then on the Day of Resurrection, he will be among those brought up (to be punished in the Hell-fire)) (28:61).

After Allah mentioned the condition of the disbelievers in this life and their destination to the Fire, He said,

(But, for those who have Taqwa of their Lord, are Gardens under which rivers flow (in Paradise); therein are they to dwell, an entertainment from Allah,) (3:198), for certainly,

(and that which is with Allah is the best for Al-Abrar.)

Ibn Jarir recorded that Abu Ad-Darda' used to say, "Death is better for every believer. Death is better for every disbeliever, and those who do not believe me should read Allah's statements,

(and that which is with Allah is the best for Al-Abrar), and,

(And let not the disbelievers think that Our postponing of their punishment is good for them. We postpone the punishment only so that they may increase in sinfulness. And for them is a disgraceful torment.) (3:178)."

Surah: 3 Ayah: 199 & Ayah: 200

﴿ وَإِنَّ مِنۡ أَهۡلِ ٱلۡكِتَٰبِ لَمَن يُؤۡمِنُ بِٱللَّهِ وَمَآ أُنزِلَ إِلَيۡكُمۡ وَمَآ أُنزِلَ إِلَيۡهِمۡ خَٰشِعِينَ لِلَّهِ لَا
يَشۡتَرُونَ بِـَٔايَٰتِ ٱللَّهِ ثَمَنٗا قَلِيلًاۚ أُوْلَٰٓئِكَ لَهُمۡ أَجۡرُهُمۡ عِندَ رَبِّهِمۡۗ إِنَّ ٱللَّهَ سَرِيعُ
ٱلۡحِسَابِ ١٩٩ ﴾

199. And there are, certainly, among the people of the Scripture (Jews and Christians), those who believe in Allâh and in that which has been revealed to you, and in that which has been revealed to them, humbling themselves before Allâh. They do not sell the Verses of Allâh for a little price, for them is a reward with their Lord. Surely, Allâh is Swift in account.

﴿ يَٰٓأَيُّهَا ٱلَّذِينَ ءَامَنُواْ ٱصۡبِرُواْ وَصَابِرُواْ وَرَابِطُواْ وَٱتَّقُواْ ٱللَّهَ لَعَلَّكُمۡ تُفۡلِحُونَ ٢٠٠ ﴾

200. O you who believe! Endure and be more patient (than your enemy), and guard your territory by stationing army units permanently at the places from where the enemy can attack you, and fear Allâh, so that you may be successful.

Transliteration

199. Wa-inna min ahli alkitabi laman yu/minu biAllahi wama onzila ilaykum wama onzila ilayhim khashiAAeena lillahi la yashtaroona bi-ayati Allahi thamanan qaleelan ola-ika lahum ajruhum AAinda rabbihim inna Allaha sareeAAu alhisabi 200. Ya ayyuha allatheena amanoo isbiroo wasabiroo warabitoo waittaqoo Allaha laAAallakum tuflihoona

Tafsir Ibn Kathir

The Condition of Some of the People of the Scriptures and their Rewards

Allah states that some of the People of the Book truly believe in Him and in what was sent down to Muhammad , along with believing in the previously revealed Books, and they are obedient to Him and humble themselves before Allah.

(They do not sell the verses of Allah for a small price) (3:199), for they do not hide what they know of the glad tidings about the description of Muhammad , his Prophethood, and the description of his Ummah. Indeed, these are the best people among the People of the Book, whether they were Jews or Christians. Allah said in Surat Al-Qasas,

(Those to whom We gave the Scripture before it, they believe in it (the Qur'an). And when it is recited to them, they say: "We believe in it. Verily, it is the truth from our Lord. Indeed even before it we were Muslims. These will be given their reward twice over, because they are patient,) (28:52-54). Allah said,

(Those to whom We gave the Book, recite it (follow it) as it should be recited (i.e. followed), they are the ones who believe therein.) (2:121),

(And of the people of Musa there is a community who lead with truth and establish justice therewith.) (7:159),

(Not all of them are alike; a party of the people of the Scripture stand for the right, they recite the verses of Allah during the hours of the night, prostrating themselves in prayer.) (3:113), and,

(Say: "Believe in it (the Qur'an) or do not believe (in it). Verily, those who were given knowledge before it, when it is recited to them, fall down on their faces in humble prostration." And they say: "Glory be to our Lord! Truly, the promise of our Lord must be fulfillled." And they fall down on their faces weeping and it increases their humility.) (17:107-109).

These qualities exist in some of the Jews, but only a few of them. For instance, less than ten Jewish rabbis embraced the Islamic faith, such as `Abdullah bin Salam. Many among the Christians, on the other hand, embraced the Islamic faith. Allah said,

(Verily, you will find the strongest among men in enmity to the believers the Jews and those who commit Shirk, and you will find the nearest in love to the believers those who say: "We are Christians.") (5:82), until,

(So because of what they said, Allah rewarded them Gardens under which rivers flow (in Paradise), they will abide therein forever) (5:85). In this Ayah,

Allah said,

(for them is a reward with their Lord) (3:199).

When Ja`far bin Abi Talib recited Surah Maryam (chapter 19) to An-Najashi, King of Ethiopia, in the presence of Christian priests and patriarchs, he and they cried until their beards became wet from crying. The Two Sahihs record that when An-Najashi died, the Prophet conveyed the news to his Companions and said,

«إِنَّ أَخًا لَكُمْ بِالْحَبَشَةِ قَدْ مَاتَ، فَصَلُّوا عَلَيْه»

(A brother of yours from Ethiopia has passed, come to offer the funeral prayer.) He went out with the Companions to the Musalla lined them up in rows, and after that led the prayer.

Ibn Abi Najih narrated that Mujahid said that,

(And there are, certainly, among the People of the Scripture), refers to those among them who embraced Islam. `Abbad bin Mansur said that he asked Al-Hasan Al-Basri about Allah's statement,

(And there are, certainly, among the People of the Scripture, those who believe in Allah).

Al-Hasan said, "They are the People of the Book, before Muhammad was sent, who believed in Muhammad and recognized Islam. Allah gave them a double reward, for the faith that they had before Muhammad , and for believing in Muhammad (after he was sent as Prophet)." Ibn Abi Hatim recorded both of these statements. The Two Sahihs record that Abu Musa said that the Messenger of Allah said,

«ثَلَاثَةٌ يُؤْتَوْنَ أَجْرَهُمْ مَرَّتَيْن»

(Three persons will acquire a double reward.)

He mentioned among them,

«وَرَجُلٌ مِنْ أَهْلِ الْكِتَابِ آمَنَ بِنَبِيِّهِ وَآمَنَ بِي»

(A person from among the People of the Book who believed in his Prophet and in me.)

Allah's statement,

(They do not sell the verses of Allah for a small price), means, they do not hide the knowledge that they have, as the cursed ones among them have done. Rather, they share the knowledge without a price, and this is why Allah said,

(for them is a reward with their Lord. surely, Allah is Swift in account.)

Mujahid commented on the verse,

((Surely, Allah is) swift in account), "He is swift in reckoning," as Ibn Abi Hatim and others have recorded from him.

The Command for Patience and Ribat

Allah said,

(O you who believe! Endure and be more patient, and Rabitu) (3:200).

Al-Hasan Al-Basri said, "The believers are commanded to be patient in the religion that Allah chose for them, Islam. They are not allowed to abandon it in times of comfort or hardship, ease or calamity, until they die as Muslims. They are also commanded to endure against their enemies, those who hid the truth about their religion." Similar explanation given by several other scholars among the Salaf.

As for Murabatah, it is to endure in acts of worship and perseverence. It also means to await prayer after prayer, as Ibn `Abbas, Sahl bin Hanif and Muhammad bin Ka`b Al-Qurazi stated. Ibn Abi Hatim collected a Hadith that was also collected by Muslim and An-Nasa'i from Abu Hurayrah that the Prophet said,

«أَلَا أُخْبِرُكُمْ بِمَا يَمْحُو اللهُ بِهِ الْخَطَايَا، وَيَرْفَعُ بِهِ الدَّرَجَاتِ؟ إِسْبَاغُ الْوُضُوءِ عَلَى الْمَكَارِهِ، وَكَثْرَةُ الْخُطَا إِلَى الْمَسَاجِدِ، وَانْتِظَارُ الصَّلَاةِ بَعْدَ الصَّلَاةِ، فَذلِكُمُ الرِّبَاطُ، فَذلِكُمُ الرِّبَاطُ، فَذلِكُمُ الرِّبَاطُ»

(Should I tell you about actions with which Allah forgives sins and raises the grade Performing perfect ablution in unfavorable conditions, the many steps one takes to the Masajid, and awaiting prayer after the prayer, for this is the Ribat, this is the Ribat, this is the Ribat.)

They also say that the Murabatah in the above Ayah refers to battles against the enemy, and manning Muslim outposts to protect them from enemy incursions inside Muslim territory. There are several Hadiths that encourage Murabatah and mention its rewards. Al-Bukhari recorded that Sahl bin Sa`d As-Sa`idi said that the Messenger of Allah said,

«رِبَاطُ يَوْمٍ فِي سَبِيلِ اللهِ خَيْرٌ مِنَ الدُّنْيَا وَمَا عَلَيْهَا»

(A Day of Ribat in the cause of Allah is better than this life and all that is in it.)

Muslim recorded that Salman Al-Farisi said that the Messenger of Allah said,

«رِبَاطُ يَوْمٍ وَلَيْلَةٍ خَيْرٌ مِنْ صِيَامِ شَهْرٍ وَقِيَامِهِ، وَإِنْ مَاتَ جَرَى عَلَيْهِ عَمَلُهُ الَّذِي كَانَ يَعْمَلُهُ، وَأُجْرِيَ عَلَيْهِ رِزْقُهُ، وَأَمِنَ الْفَتَّانَ»

(Ribat for a day and a night is better than fasting the days of a month and its Qiyam (voluntary prayer at night). If one dies in Ribat, his regular righteous deeds that he used to perform will keep being added to his account, and he will receive his provision, and will be saved from the trials of the grave.)

Imam Ahmad recorded that Fadalah bin `Ubayd said that he heard the Messenger of Allah saying,

«كُلُّ مَيِّتٍ يُخْتَمُ عَلى عَمَلِهِ إِلَّا الَّذِي مَاتَ مُرَابِطًا فِي سَبِيلِ اللهِ،فَإِنَّهُ يَنْمِي لَهُ عَمَلُهُ إِلى يَوْمِ الْقِيَامَةِ، وَيَأْمَنُ فِتْنَةَ الْقَبْرِ»

(Every dead person will have his record of deeds sealed, except for whoever dies while in Ribat in the cause of Allah, for his work will keep increasing until the Day of Resurrection, and he will be safe from the trial of the grave.)

This is the same narration collected by Abu Dawud and At-Tirmidhi, who said, "Hasan Sahih". Ibn Hibban also collected this Hadith in his Sahih. fAt-Tirmidhi recorded that Ibn `Abbas said that he heard the Messenger of Allah saying,

«عَيْنَانِ لَا تَمَسُّهُمَا النَّارُ: عَيْنٌ بَكَتْ مِنْ خَشْيَةِ اللهِ، وَعَيْنٌ بَاتَتْ تَحْرُسُ فِي سَبِيلِ اللهِ»

(Two eyes shall not be touched by the Fire: an eye that cried for fear from Allah and an eye that spent the night guarding in Allah's cause.)

Al-Bukhari recorded in his Sahih that Abu Hurayrah said that the Messenger of Allah said,

«تَعِسَ عَبْدُالدِّينَارِ وَعَبْدُالدِّرْهَمِ وَعَبْدُالْخَمِيصَةِ، إِنْ أُعْطِيَ رَضِيَ، وَإِنْ لَمْ يُعْطَ سَخِطَ، تَعِسَ وَانْتَكَسَ، وَإِذَا شِيكَ فَلَا انْتَقَشَ، طُوبَى لِعَبْدٍ آخِذٍ بِعِنَانِ فَرَسِهِ فِي سَبِيلِ اللهِ، أَشْعَثَ رَأْسُهُ، مُغْبَرَّةٍ قَدَمَاهُ، إِنْ كَانَ فِي الْحِرَاسَةِ كَانَ فِي الْحِرَاسَةِ، وَإِنْ كَانَ فِي السَّاقَةِ كَانَ فِي السَّاقَةِ، إِنِ اسْتَأْذَنَ لَمْ يُؤْذَنْ لَهُ، وَإِنْ شَفَعَ لَمْ يُشَفَّعْ»

(Let the servant of the Dinar, the servant of the Dirham and the servant of the Khamisah (of clothes) perish, as he is pleased if these things are given to him, and if not, he is displeased. Let such a person perish and be humiliated, and if he is pierced with a thorn, let him not find anyone to take it out for him. Paradise is for him who holds the reins of his horse, striving in Allah's cause, with his hair unkempt and feet covered with dust: if he is appointed to the vanguard, he is perfectly satisfied with his post of guarding, and if he is appointed in the rearguard, he accepts his post with satisfaction; if he asks for permission he is not permitted, and if he intercedes, his intercession is not accepted.)

Ibn Jarir recorded that Zayd bin Aslam said, "Abu `Ubaydah wrote to `Umar bin Al-Khattab and mentioned to him that the Romans were mobilizing their forces. `Umar wrote back, `Allah will soon turn whatever hardship a believing servant suffers, to ease, and no hardship shall ever overcome two types of ease. Allah says in His Book,

(O you who believe! Endure and be more patient, and Rabitu, and have Taqwa of Allah, so that you may be successful)' (3:200)."

Al-Hafiz Ibn `Asakir mentioned in the biography of `Abdullah bin Al-Mubarak, that Muhammad bin Ibrahim bin Abi Sakinah said, "While in the area of Tarsus, `Abdullah bin Al-Mubarak dictated this poem to me when I was greeting him goodbye. He sent the poem with me to Al-Fudayl bin `Iyad in the year one hundred and seventy, `O he who worships in the vicinity of the Two Holy Masjids! If you but see us, you will realize that you are only jesting in worship. He who brings wetness to his cheek with his tears, should know that our necks are being wet by our blood. He who tires his horses without purpose, know that our horses are getting tired in battle. Scent of perfume is yours, while our scent is the glimmer of spears and the stench of dust (in battle). We were narrated about in the speech of our Prophet, an authentic statement that never lies. That the dust that erupts by Allah's horses and which fills the nostrils of a man shall never be combined with the smoke of a raging Fire. This, the Book of Allah speaks among us that the martyr is not dead, and the truth in Allah's Book cannot be denied.' I met Al-Fudayl Ibn `Iyad in the Sacred Masjid and gave him the letter. When he read it, his eyes became tearful and he said, `Abu `Abdur-Rahman (`Abdullah bin Al-Mubarak) has said the truth and offered sincere advice to me.' He then asked me, `Do you write the Hadith' I said, `Yes.' He said, `Write this Hadith as reward for delivering the letter of Abu `Abdur-Rahman to me. He then dictated, `Mansur bin Al-Mu`tamir narrated to us that Abu Salih narrated from Abu Hurayrah that a man asked, `O Messenger of Allah! Teach me a good deed that will earn me the reward of the Mujahidin in Allah's cause.' The Prophet said,

«هَلْ تَسْتَطِيعُ أَنْ تُصَلِّيَ فَلَا تَفْتُرَ،وَتَصُومَ فَلَا تُفْطِرَ؟»

(Are you able to pray continuously and fast without breaking the fast) The man said, `O Messenger of Allah! I cannot bear it.' The Prophet said,

«فَوَالَّذِي نَفْسِي بِيَدِهِ لَوْ طُوِّقْتَ ذلِكَ مَا بَلَغْتَ الْمُجَاهِدِينَ فِي سَبِيلِ اللهِ، أَوَ مَا عَلِمْتَ أَنَّ فَرَسَ الْمُجَاهِدِ لَيَسْتَنُّ فِي طِوَلِهِ، فَيُكْتَبُ لَهُ بِذلِكَ الْحَسَنَات»

(By He in Whose Hand is my soul! Even if you were able to do it, you will not achieve the grade of the Mujahidin in Allah's cause. Did you not know that the horse of the Mujahid earns rewards for him as long as it lives.)

Allah said next,

(and have Taqwa of Allah), concerning all your affairs and situations. For instance, the Prophet said to Mu`adh when he sent him to Yemen,

«اتَّقِ اللهَ حَيْثُمَا كُنْتَ، وَأَتْبِعِ السَّيِّئَـــــةَ الْحَسَنَةَ تَمْحُهَا، وَخَالِقِ النَّاسَ بِخُلُقٍ حَسَنٍ»

(Have Taqwa of Allah wherever you may be, follow the evil deed with a good deed and it will erase it, and deal with people in a good manner.)

Allah said next,

(so that you may be successful.), in this life and the Hereafter. Ibn Jarir recorded that Muhammad bin Ka`b Al-Qurazi said that, Allah's statement,

(and have Taqwa of Allah, so that you may be successful.) means, "Fear Me concerning what is between you and Me, so that you may acquire success when you meet Me tomorrow."

The Tafsir of Surah Al `Imran ends here, all praise is due to Allah, and we ask Him that we die while on the path of the Qur'an and Sunnah, Amin.

INTRODUCTION TO CHAPTER (SURAH) 4: AN-NISAA (THE WOMEN)

Maududi's Introduction

Period of Revelation

This Surah comprises several discourses which were revealed on different occasions during the period ranging probably between the end of A. H. 3 and the end of A. H. 4 or the beginning of A. H. 5. Although it is difficult to determine the exact dates of their revelations, yet it is possible to assign to them a fairly correct period with the help of the Commandments and the events mentioned therein and the Traditions concerning them. A few instances are given below by way of illustration :

1. We know that the instructions about the division of inheritance of the martyrs and for the safeguard of the rights of the orphans were sent down after the Battle of Uhd in which 70 Muslims were killed. Then naturally the question of the division of the inheritance of the martyrs and the safeguard of the rights of their orphans arose in many families at Al-Madinah. From this we conclude that vv. 1 -28 were revealed on that occasion.

2. We learn from the Traditions that the Commandment about salat during war time was given on the occasion of Zat-ur-Riqa'a, an expedition which took place in A. H. 4. From this we conclude that the discourse containing v. 102 was revealed on that occasion.

3. The last warning (v. 47) to the Jews was given before the Banu Nadir were exiled from Al- Madinah in Rabi'-ulAwwal, A. H. 4. From this it may safely be concluded that the discourse containing v. 47 must have been revealed some time before that date.

4. The permission about ***tayammum*** (the performance of ablutions with pure dust, in case no water be available) was given during the Bani-al-Mustaliq expedition, which took place in A. H. 5.. Therefore the probable period of the revelation of the discourse containing v. 43 was A. H. 5.

Topics and Their Background

Let us now consider the social and historical considerations of the period in order to understand the Surah. All the discourses in this Surah deal with three main problems which confronted the Holy Prophet at the time. First of all, he was engaged in bringing about an all round development of the Islamic Community that had been formed at the time of his migration to Al-Madinah. For this purpose he was introducing new moral, cultural, social, economic and political ways in place of the old ones of the pre-Islamic period. The second thing that occupied his attention and efforts was the bitter struggle that was going on with the

mushrik Arabs, the Jewish clans and the hypocrites who were opposing tooth and nail his mission of reform. Above all he had to propagate Islam in the face of the bitter opposition of these powers of evil with a view to capturing more and more minds and hearts.

Accordingly, detailed instructions have been given for the consolidation and strengthening of the Islamic Community in continuation of those given in Al-Baqarah. Principles for the smooth running of family life have been laid down and ways of settling family disputes have been taught. Rules have been prescribed for marriage and rights of wife and husband have been apportioned fairly and equitably. The status of women in the society has been determined and the declaration of the rights of orphans has been made laws and regulations have been laid down for the division of inheritance, and instructions have been given to reform economic affairs. The foundation of the penal code has been laid down drinking has been prohibited, and instructions have been given for cleanliness and purity. The Muslims have been taught the kind of relations good men should have with their Allah and fellow men. Instructions have been given for the maintenance of discipline in the Muslim Community.

The moral and religious condition of the people of the Book has been reviewed to teach lessons to the Muslims and to forewarn them to refrain from following in their footsteps. The conduct of the hypocrites has been criticized and the distinctive features of hypocrisy and true faith have been clearly marked off to enable the Muslims to distinguish between the two.

In order to cope with the aftermath of the Battle of Uhd, Inspiring discourses were sent down to urge the Muslims to face the enemy bravely, for the defeat in the Battle had so emboldened the ***mushrik*** Arab clans and the neighboring Jews and the hypocrites at home that they were threatening the Muslims on all sides. At this critical juncture, Allah filled the Muslims with courage and gave them such instructions as were needed during that period of war clouds. In order to counteract the fearful rumors that were being spread by the hypocrites and the Muslims of weak faith, they were asked to make a thorough enquiry into them and to inform the responsible people about them. Then they were experiencing some difficulties in offering their salat during the expeditions to some places where no water was available for performing their ablutions, etc. In such cases they were allowed to cleanse themselves with pure earth and to shorten the salat or to offer the "Salat of Fear", when they were faced with danger. Instructions were also given for the solution of the puzzling problem of those Muslims who were scattered among the unbelieving Arab clans and were often involved in war. They were asked to migrate to Al-Madinah, the abode of Islam.

This Surah also deals with the case of Bani Nadir who were showing a hostile and menacing attitude, in spite of the peace treaties they had made with the Muslims. They were openly siding with the enemies of Islam and hatching plots against the Holy Prophet and the Muslim Community even at AIMadinah itself. They were taken to task for their inimical behavior and given a final warning to change their attitude, and were at last exiled from Al-Madinah on account of their misconduct.

The problem of the hypocrites, who had become very troublesome at that time, was involving the Believers in difficulties-- Therefore they were divided into different categories to enable the Muslims to deal with them appropriately.

Clear instructions were also given regarding the attitude they should adopt towards the nonbelligerent clans. The most important thing needed at that time was to prepare the Muslims for the bitter struggle with the opponents of Islam. For this purpose greatest importance was attached to their character building, for it was obvious that the small Muslim

Community could only come out successful, nay, survive, if the Muslims possessed high moral character. They were, therefore, enjoined to adopt the highest moral qualities and were severely criticized whenever any moral weakness was detected in them.

Though this Surah mainly deals with the moral and social reforms, yet due attention has been paid to propagation of Islam. On the one hand, the superiority of the Islamic morality and culture has been established over that of the Jews, Christians and mushriks; on the other hand, their wrong religious conceptions, their wrong morality and their evil acts have been criticized to prepare the ground for inviting them to the way of the Truth.

Subject: Consolidation of the Islamic Community

The main object of this Surah is to teach the Muslims the ways that unite a people and make them firm and strong. Introductions for the stability of family, which is the nucleus of community have been given. Then they have been urged to prepare themselves for defence. Side by side with these, they have been taught the importance of the propagation of Islam. Above all, the importance of the highest moral character in the scheme of consolidation of the Community has been impressed.

Topics and their Interconnection

Just, fair and equitable laws and regulations for the smooth running of family life have been laid down for the husband and wife. Detailed instructions have been given for the division of inheritance and due regard has been paid to the rights of orphans. 1 - 35

In order to inculcate the right spirit for the observance of rules and regulations, the Muslims have been enjoined to show generosity to all around them and to be free from meanness, selfishness, stinginess of mind, because this is essential for the consolidation of the Communities and helpful for the propagation of Islam. 36 - 42

The ways of the purification of mind and body for the offering of Salat have been taught because it plays the most important part in every scheme of moral and social reform. 43

After moral preparation, instructions for defence have been given. First of all, the Muslims have been warned to be on their guard against the cunning machinations and vile practices of the local Jews who were hostile to the New Movement. This caution was necessary for removing some possible misunderstanding that might have arisen on account of the pre-Islamic alliance between the people of Al-Madinah and the Jews. 44 - 57

Then they have been enjoined to place their trusts and offices of trust in the custody of honest and qualified persons, and to do what is just and right, and to obey Allah and His Messenger and those among themselves entrusted with the conduct of their affairs and to turn to Allah and His Messenger for the settlement of their disputes. As such an attitude and behaviour alone can ensure consolidation, they have been strongly warned that any deviation from this path will lead to their disintegration. 58 - 72

After this pre-requisite, they have been exhorted to make preparation for defence and to fight bravely for the cause of Islam, without showing any kind of cowardice or weakness. They have also been warned to be on their guard against hypocrites. A line of demarcation has been drawn to distinguish the intentional shirkers from the helpless devotees. 73 - 100

Here again instructions have been given for the offering of Salat during military campaigns and actual fighting. This is to impress the importance of Salat even at the time of fear and danger. 101 - 103

Before proceeding on to the next topic, the Muslims have been exhorted to persevere in their fight without showing any kind of weakness. 104

In order to make the Islamic Community firm and strong for defence, the Muslims have been enjoined to observe the highest standard of justice. The Muslims are required to deal out strict justice even in case of the enemy, with whom they might be involved in war. They should also settle disputes between husband and wife with justice. In order to ensure this, they should keep their beliefs and deeds absolutely free from every kind of impurity and should become the standard bearers of justice. 105 - 135

Resuming the theme of defence, the Muslims have been warned to be on their guard against their enemies. They have been admonished to take necessary precautions against the machinations of the hypocrites and the unbelievers and the people of the Book. As belief in Allah, and Revelation and Life-after-death is the only safeguard against every kind of enemy, they should sincerely believe in and follow His Messenger, Muhammad (Allah's peace be upon him). 136 - 175

Though this verse also deals with the family laws contained in verses 1 - 35, it has been added as a supplement at the end of this Surah because it was revealed long after An-Nisa was being recited as a complete Surah. 17

Ibn Kathir's Introduction

Virtues of Surat An-Nisa, A Madinan Surah

Al-`Awfi reported that Ibn `Abbas said that Surat An-Nisa' was revealed in Al-Madinah. Ibn Marduwyah recorded similar statements from `Abdullah bin Az-Zubayr and Zayd bin Thabit. In his Mustadrak, Al-Hakim recorded that `Abdullah bin Mas`ud said, "There are five Ayat in Surat An-Nisa' that I would prefer to the life of this world and all that is in it,

(Surely, Allah wrongs not even the weight of an atom,) (4:40),

(If you avoid the great sins which you are forbidden to do) (4:31),

(Verily, Allah forgives not that partners should be set up with Him (in worship), but He forgives except that (anything else) to whom He wills) (4:48),

(If they (hypocrites), when they had been unjust to themselves, had come to you) (4:64), and,

(And whoever does evil or wrongs himself, but afterwards seeks Allah's forgiveness, he will find Allah Oft-Forgiving, Most Merciful) (4:110)." Al-Hakim recorded that Ibn `Abbas said, "Ask me about Surat An-Nisa', for I learned the Qur'an when I was still young." Al-Hakim said, "This Hadith is Sahih according to the criteria of the Two Sahihs, and they did not collect it."

CHAPTER (SURAH) 4: AN-NISAA (THE WOMEN), VERSES 001-023

﴿ بِسْمِ ٱللَّهِ ٱلرَّحْمَـٰنِ ٱلرَّحِيمِ ۝١ ﴾

In the Name of Allâh, the Most Gracious, the Most Merciful.

Surah: 4 Ayah: 1

﴿ يَـٰٓأَيُّهَا ٱلنَّاسُ ٱتَّقُوا۟ رَبَّكُمُ ٱلَّذِى خَلَقَكُم مِّن نَّفْسٍ وَٰحِدَةٍ وَخَلَقَ مِنْهَا زَوْجَهَا وَبَثَّ مِنْهُمَا رِجَالًا كَثِيرًا وَنِسَآءً ۚ وَٱتَّقُوا۟ ٱللَّهَ ٱلَّذِى تَسَآءَلُونَ بِهِۦ وَٱلْأَرْحَامَ ۚ إِنَّ ٱللَّهَ كَانَ عَلَيْكُمْ رَقِيبًا ۝١ ﴾

1. O mankind! Be dutiful to your Lord, Who created you from a single person (Adam), and from him (Adam) He created his wife (Hawwâ (Eve)) and from them both He created many men and women; and fear Allâh through Whom you demand (your mutual rights), and (do not cut the relations of) the wombs (kinship). Surely, Allâh is Ever an All-Watcher over you.

Transliteration

1. Ya ayyuha alnnasu ittaqoo rabbakumu allathee khalaqakum min nafsin wahidatin wakhalaqa minha zawjaha wabaththa minhuma rijalan katheeran wanisaan waittaqoo Allaha allathee tasaaloona bihi waal-arhama inna Allaha kana AAalaykum raqeeban

Tafsir Ibn Kathir

The Command to have Taqwa, a Reminder about Creation, and Being Kind to Relatives

Allah commands His creatures to have Taqwa of Him by worshipping Him Alone without partners. He also reminds to them of His ability, in that He created them all from a single person, Adam, peace be unto him.

(And from him He created his wife) Hawwa' (Eve), who was created from Adam's left rib, from his back while he was sleeping. When Adam woke up and saw Hawwa', he liked her and had affection for her, and she felt the same toward him. An authentic Hadith states,

«إِنَّ الْمَرْأَةَ خُلِقَتْ مِنْ ضِلَعٍ، وَإِنَّ أَعْوَجَ شَيْءٍ فِي الضِّلَعِ أَعْلَاهُ، فَإِنْ ذَهَبْتَ تُقِيمُهُ كَسَرْتَهُ، وَإِنِ اسْتَمْتَعْتَ بِهَا اسْتَمْتَعْتَ بِهَا وَفِيهَا عِوَجٌ»

(Woman was created from a rib. Verily, the most curved portion of the rib is its upper part, so, if you should try to straighten it, you will break it, but if you leave it as it is, it will remain crooked.) Allah's statement,

(And from them both He created many men and women;) means, Allah created from Adam and Hawwa' many men and women and distributed them throughout the world in various shapes, characteristics, colors and languages. In the end, their gathering and return will be to Allah. Allah then said,

(And have Taqwa of Allah through Whom you demand your mutual (rights) and revere the wombs), protect yourself from Allah by your acts of obedience to Him. Allah's statement,

(through Whom you demand your mutual (rights)), is in reference to when some people say, "I ask you by Allah, and then by the relation of the Rahim (the womb, i.e. my relationship to you)", according to Ibrahim, Mujahid and Al-Hasan. Ad-Dahhak said; "Fear Allah Whom you invoke when you conduct transactions and contracts." "And revere the womb by not cutting the relations of the womb, but keep and honor them, as Ibn `Abbas, `Ikrimah, Mujahid, Al-Hasan, Ad-Dahhak, Ar-Rabi`, and others have stated. Allah's statement,

(Surely, Allah is always watching over you.) means, He watches all your deeds and sees your every circumstance. In another Ayah, Allah said;

(And Allah is Witness over all things.) (58:6). An authentic Hadith states,

«اعْبُدِاللهَ كَأَنَّكَ تَرَاهُ، فَإِنْ لَمْ تَكُنْ تَرَاهُ،فَإِنَّهُ يَرَاكَ»

(Worship Allah as if you see Him, for even though you cannot see Him, He sees you.) This part of the Ayah encourages having a sense of certainty that Allah is always watching, in a complete and perfect manner. Allah mentioned that He has created mankind from a single father and a single mother, so that they feel compassion for each other and are kind to the weaker among them. In his Sahih, Muslim recorded that Jarir bin `Abdullah Al-Bajali said that a delegation from Mudar came to the Messenger of Allah , and he saw their state, wearing striped woolen clothes due to poverty. After the Zuhr prayer, the Messenger of Allah stood up and gave a speech in which he recited,

(O mankind! Have Taqwa of your Lord, Who created you from a single person,) until the end of the Ayah. He also recited,

(O you who believe! Have Taqwa of Allah. And let every person look to what he has sent forth for the tomorrow) (59:18). He also encouraged them to give charity, saying,

«تَصَدَّقَ رَجُلٌ مِنْ دِينَارِهِ، مِنْ دِرْهَمِهِ، مِنْ صَاعِ بُرِّهِ، مِنْ صَاعِ تَمْرِهِ»

(A man gave Sadaqah from his Dinar, from his Dirham, from his Sa` of wheat, from his Sa` of dates) until the end of the Hadith. This narration was also collected by Ahmad and the Sunan compilers from Ibn Mas`ud.

Surah: 4 Ayah: 2, Ayah: 3 & Ayah: 4

﴿وَءَاتُوا۟ ٱلْيَتَـٰمَىٰٓ أَمْوَٰلَهُمْ ۖ وَلَا تَتَبَدَّلُوا۟ ٱلْخَبِيثَ بِٱلطَّيِّبِ ۖ وَلَا تَأْكُلُوٓا۟ أَمْوَٰلَهُمْ إِلَىٰٓ أَمْوَٰلِكُمْ ۚ إِنَّهُۥ كَانَ حُوبًا كَبِيرًا ﴿٢﴾﴾

2. And give unto orphans their property and do not exchange (your) bad things for (their) good ones; and devour not their substance (by adding it) to your substance. Surely, this is a great sin.

﴿ وَإِنۡ خِفۡتُمۡ أَلَّا تُقۡسِطُواْ فِي ٱلۡيَتَٰمَىٰ فَٱنكِحُواْ مَا طَابَ لَكُم مِّنَ ٱلنِّسَآءِ مَثۡنَىٰ وَثُلَٰثَ
وَرُبَٰعَۖ فَإِنۡ خِفۡتُمۡ أَلَّا تَعۡدِلُواْ فَوَٰحِدَةً أَوۡ مَا مَلَكَتۡ أَيۡمَٰنُكُمۡۚ ذَٰلِكَ أَدۡنَىٰٓ أَلَّا تَعُولُواْ ٣ ﴾

3. And if you fear that you shall not be able to deal justly with the orphan-girls then marry (other) women of your choice, two or three, or four; but if you fear that you shall not be able to deal justly (with them), then only one or (the slaves) that your right hands possess. That is nearer to prevent you from doing injustice.

﴿ وَءَاتُواْ ٱلنِّسَآءَ صَدُقَٰتِهِنَّ نِحۡلَةٗۚ فَإِن طِبۡنَ لَكُمۡ عَن شَيۡءٖ مِّنۡهُ نَفۡسٗا فَكُلُوهُ هَنِيٓـٔٗا
مَّرِيٓـٔٗا ٤ ﴾

4. And give to the women (whom you marry) their Mahr (obligatory bridal money given by the husband to his wife at the time of marriage) with a good heart; but if they, of their own good pleasure, remit any part of it to you, take it, and enjoy it without fear of any harm (as Allâh has made it lawful).

Transliteration

2. Waatoo alyatama amwalahum wala tatabaddaloo alkhabeetha bialttayyibi wala ta/kuloo amwalahum ila amwalikum innahu kana hooban kabeeran 3. Wa-in khiftum alla tuqsitoo fee alyatama fainkihoo ma taba lakum mina alnnisa-i mathna wathulatha warubaAAa fa-in khiftum alla taAAdiloo fawahidatan aw ma malakat aymanukum Thalika adna alla taAAooloo 4. Waatoo alnnisaa saduqatihinna nihlatan fa-in tibna lakum AAan shay-in minhu nafsan fakuloohu hanee-an maree-an

Tafsir Ibn Kathir

Protecting the Property of the Orphans

Allah commands that the property of the orphans be surrendered to them in full when they reach the age of adolescence, and He forbids using or confiscating any part of it. So He said;

(and do not exchange (your) bad things for (their) good ones;) Sa`id bin Al-Musayyib and Az-Zuhri commented, "Do not substitute a weak animal of yours for a fat animal (of the orphans)." Ibrahim An-Nakha`i and Ad-Dahhak commented, "Do not give something of bad quality for something of good quality." As-Suddi said, "One of them (caretakers of orphans) would take a fat sheep from the orphan's property and put in its place, a weak sheep of his, saying, `A sheep for a sheep.' He would also take a good Dirham and exchange it for a fake Dirham, saying, `A Dirham for a Dirham.'" Allah's statement,

(and devour not their substance to your substance.) means, do not mix them together so that you eat up both, as Mujahid, Sa`id bin Jubayr, Muqatil bin Hayyan, As-Suddi and Sufyan bin Hassin stated. Allah said,

(Surely, this is a great sin.), a major and substantial sin, according to Ibn `Abbas. This was also reported from Mujahid, `Ikrimah, Sa`id bin Jubayr, Al-Hasan, Ibn Sirin, Qatadah, Muqatil bin Hayyan, Ad-Dahhak, Abu Malik, Zayd bin Aslam and Abu Sinan. The meaning above is: adding their property to your property is a grave sin and a major mistake, so avoid it.

The Prohibition of Marrying Female Orphans Without Giving a Dowry

Allah said,

(And if you fear that you shall not be able to deal justly with the orphan girls, then marry (other) women of your choice, two) Allah commands, when one of you is the caretaker of a female orphan and he fears that he might not give her a dowry that is suitable for women of her status, he should marry other women, who are plenty as Allah has not restricted him. Al-Bukhari recorded that `A'ishah said, "A man was taking care of a female orphan and he married her, although he did not desire to marry her. That girl's money was mixed with his, and he was keeping her portion from her. Afterwards, this Ayah was revealed about his case;

(If you fear that you shall not be able to deal justly)" Al-Bukhari recorded that `Urwah bin Az-Zubayr said that he asked `A'ishah about the meaning of the statement of Allah,

(If you fear that you shall not be able to deal justly with the orphan girls.) She said, "O my nephew! This is about the orphan girl who lives with her guardian and shares his property. Her wealth and beauty may tempt him to marry her without giving her an adequate dowry which might have been given by another suitor. So, such guardians were forbidden to marry such orphan girls unless they treated them justly and gave them the most suitable dowry; otherwise they were ordered to marry woman besides them." `A'ishah further said, "After that verse, the people again asked the Messenger of Allah (about marriage with orphan girls), so Allah revealed the Ayah,

(They ask your instruction concerning the women..) (4:127)." She said, "Allah's statement in this Ayah,

(yet whom you desire to marry) (4:127) refers to the guardian who does not desire to marry an orphan girl under his supervision because she is neither wealthy nor beautiful. The guardians were forbidden to marry their orphan girls possessing property and beauty without being just to them, as they generally refrain from marrying them (when they are neither beautiful nor wealthy)."

The Permission to Marry Four Women

Allah's statement,

(two or three, or four), means, marry as many women as you like, other than the orphan girls, two, three or four. We should mention that Allah's statement in another Ayah,

(Who made the angels messengers with wings, - two or three or four) (35:1), does not mean that other angels do not have more than four wings, as there are proofs that some angels do have more wings. Yet, men are prohibited from marrying more than four wives, as the Ayah decrees, since the Ayah specifies what men are allowed of wives, as Ibn `Abbas and the majority of scholars stated. If it were allowed for them to have more than four wives, the Ayah would have mentioned it. Imam Ahmad recorded that Salim said that his father said that Ghilan bin Salamah Ath-Thaqafi had ten wives when he became Muslim, and the Prophet said to him, "Choose any four of them (and divorce the rest)." During the reign of `Umar, Ghilan divorced his remaining wives and divided his money between his children. When `Umar heard news of this, he said to Ghilan, "I think that the devil has conveyed to your heart the news of your imminent death, from what the devil hears during his eavesdropping. It may as well be that you will not remain alive but for a little longer. By Allah! You will take back your wives and your money, or I will take possession of this all and will order that your grave be stoned as is the case with the grave of Abu Righal (from Thamud, who was saved from their fate because he was in the Sacred Area. But, when he left it, he was tormented like they were)." Ash-Shafi`i, At-Tirmidhi, Ibn Majah, Ad-Daraqutni and Al-Bayhaqi collected this Hadith up to the Prophet's statement, "Choose any four of them." Only Ahmad collected the full version of this Hadith. Therefore, had it been allowed for men to marry more than four women at the same time, the Prophet would have allowed Ghilan to keep more than four of his wives since they all embraced Islam with him. When the Prophet commanded him to keep just four of them and divorce the rest, this indicated that men are not allowed to keep more than four wives at a time under any circumstances. If this is the case concerning those who already had more than four wives upon embracing Islam, then this ruling applies even more so to marrying more than four.

Marrying Only One Wife When One Fears He Might not Do Justice to His Wives

Allah's statement,

(But if you fear that you will not be able to deal justly (with them), then only one or what your right hands possess.) The Ayah commands, if you fear that you will not be able to do justice between your wives by marrying more than one, then marry only one wife, or satisfy yourself with only female captives, for it is not obligatory to treat them equally, rather it is recommended. So if one does so, that is good, and if not, there is no harm on him. In another Ayah, Allah said,

(You will never be able to do perfect justice between wives even if it is your ardent desire) (4:129). Allah said,

(That is nearer to prevent you from Ta`ulu), meaning, from doing injustice. Ibn Abi Hatim, Ibn Marduwyah and Abu Hatim Ibn Hibban, in his Sahih, recorded that `A'ishah said that, the Prophet said that the Ayah,

(That is nearer to prevent you from Ta`ulu), means, from doing injustice. However, Ibn Abi Hatim said that his father said that this Hadith to the Prophet is a mistake, for it should be attributed to `A'ishah not the Prophet . Ibn Abi Hatim reported from Ibn `Abbas, `A'ishah, Mujahid, `Ikrimah, Al-Hasan, Abu Malik, Abu Razin, An-Nakha`i, Ash-Sha`bi, Ad-Dahhak, `Ata' Al-Khurasani, Qatadah, As-Suddi and Muqatil bin Hayyan that Ta`ulu means to deviate (from justice).

Giving the Dowry is Obligatory

`Ali bin Abi Talhah reported Ibn `Abbas saying, Nihlah, in Allah's statement,

(And give to the women (whom you marry) their Saduqat Nihlah) refers to the dowry. Muhammad bin Ishaq narrated from Az-Zuhri that `Urwah said that `A'ishah said that `Nihlah' means `obligatory'. Muqatil, Qatadah and Ibn Jurayj said, `Nihlah' means `obligatory' Ibn Jurayj added: `specified.' Ibn Zayd said, "In Arabic, Nihlah, refers to what is necessary. So Allah is commanding: Do not marry unless you give your wife something that is her right. No person after the Prophet is allowed to marry a woman except with the required dowry, nor by giving false promises about the dowry (intended)." Therefore, the man is required to pay a dowry to his wife with a good heart, just as he gives a gift with a good heart. If the wife gives him part or all of that dowry with a good heart, her husband is allowed to take it, as it is lawful for him in this case. This is why Allah said afterwards,

(But if they, of their own pleasure, remit any part of it to you, take it, and enjoy it without fear of any harm.)

Surah: 4 Ayah: 5 & Ayah: 6

﴿وَلَا تُؤْتُوا۟ ٱلسُّفَهَآءَ أَمْوَٰلَكُمُ ٱلَّتِى جَعَلَ ٱللَّهُ لَكُمْ قِيَـٰمًا وَٱرْزُقُوهُمْ فِيهَا وَٱكْسُوهُمْ وَقُولُوا۟
لَهُمْ قَوْلًا مَّعْرُوفًا ﴿٥﴾﴾

5. And give not unto the foolish your property which Allâh has made a means of support for you, but feed and clothe them therewith, and speak to them words of kindness and justice.

﴿وَٱبْتَلُوا۟ ٱلْيَتَـٰمَىٰ حَتَّىٰٓ إِذَا بَلَغُوا۟ ٱلنِّكَاحَ فَإِنْ ءَانَسْتُم مِّنْهُمْ رُشْدًا فَٱدْفَعُوٓا۟ إِلَيْهِمْ أَمْوَٰلَهُمْ ۖ
وَلَا تَأْكُلُوهَآ إِسْرَافًا وَبِدَارًا أَن يَكْبَرُوا۟ ۚ وَمَن كَانَ غَنِيًّا فَلْيَسْتَعْفِفْ ۖ وَمَن كَانَ فَقِيرًا فَلْيَأْكُلْ
بِٱلْمَعْرُوفِ ۚ فَإِذَا دَفَعْتُمْ إِلَيْهِمْ أَمْوَٰلَهُمْ فَأَشْهِدُوا۟ عَلَيْهِمْ ۚ وَكَفَىٰ بِٱللَّهِ حَسِيبًا ﴿٦﴾﴾

6. And try orphans (as regards their intelligence) until they reach the age of marriage; if then you find sound judgement in them, release their property to them, but consume it not wastefully, and hastily fearing that they should grow up, and whoever (amongst guardians) is rich, he should take no wages, but if he is poor, let him have for himself what is just and reasonable (according to his labor). And when you release their property to them, take witness in their presence; and Allâh is All-Sufficient in taking account.

Transliteration

5. Wala tu/too alssufahaa amwalakumu allatee jaAAala Allahu lakum qiyaman waorzuqoohum feeha waoksoohum waqooloo lahum qawlan maAAroofan 6. Waibtaloo alyatama hatta itha balaghoo alnnikaha fa-in anastum minhum rushdan faidfaAAoo ilayhim amwalahum wala ta/kulooha israfan wabidaran an yakbaroo waman kana ghaniyyan falyastaAAfif waman kana faqeeran falya/kul bialmaAAroofi fa-itha dafaAAtum ilayhim amwalahum faashhidoo AAalayhim wakafa biAllahi haseeban

Tafsir Ibn Kathir

Holding the Property of the Unwise in Escrow

Allah prohibited giving the unwise the freedom to do as they wish with wealth, which Allah has made as a means of support for people. This ruling sometimes applies because of being young, as young people are incapable of making wise decisions. It also applies in cases of insanity, erratic behavior and having a weak intellect or religious practice. It applies in cases of bankruptcy, when the debtors ask that the property of a bankrupt person is put in escrow, when his debts cannot be paid off with his money. Ad-Dahhak reported that Ibn `Abbas said that Allah's statement,

(And give not unto the unwise your property) refers to children and women. Similar was also said by Ibn Mas`ud, Al-Hakam bin `Uyaynah, Al-Hasan and Ad-Dahhak: "Women and boys." Sa`id bin Jubayr said that `the unwise' refers to the orphans. Mujahid, `Ikrimah and Qatadah said; "They are women."

Spending on the Unwise with Fairness

Allah said,

(but feed and clothe them therewith, and speak to them words of kindness and justice.) `Ali bin Abi Talhah said that Ibn `Abbas commented, "Do not give your wealth, what Allah has made you responsible for and made a means of sustenance to you, to your wife or children. Rather, hold on to your money, take care of it, and be the one who spends on them for clothes, food and provision." Mujahid said that the Ayah,

(and speak to them words of kindness and justice.) refers to kindness and keeping good relations. This honorable Ayah commands kind treatment, in deed, with family and those under one's care. One should spend on them for clothes and provisions, and be good to them, such as saying good words to them.

Giving Back the Property of the Orphans When They Reach Adulthood

Allah said,

(And test orphans) meaning, test their intelligence, as Ibn `Abbas, Mujahid, Al-Hasan, As-Suddi and Muqatil bin Hayyan stated.

(until they reach the age of marriage), the age of puberty, according to Mujahid. The age of puberty according to the majority of scholars comes when the child has a wet dream. In his Sunan, Abu Dawud recorded that `Ali said, "I memorized these words from the Messenger of Allah ,

«لَا يُتْمَ بَعْدَ احْتِلَامٍ، وَلَا صُمَاتَ يَوْمٍ إِلَى اللَّيْلِ»

(There is no orphan after the age of puberty nor vowing to be silent throughout the day to the night.) In another Hadith, `A'ishah and other Companions said that the Prophet said,

«رُفِعَ الْقَلَمُ عَنْ ثَلَاثَةٍ، عَنِ الصَّبِيِّ حَتَّى يَحْتَلِمَ، وَعَنِ النَّائِمِ حَتَّى يَسْتَيْقِظَ، وَعَنِ الْمَجْنُونِ حَتَّى يُفِيقَ»

(The pen does not record the deeds of three persons: the child until the age of puberty, the sleeping person until waking up, and the senile until sane.) Or, the age of fifteen is considered the age of adolescence. In the Two Sahihs, it is recorded that Ibn `Umar said, "I was presented in front of the Prophet on the eve of the battle of Uhud, while I was fourteen years of age, and he did not allow me to take part in that battle. But I was presented in front of him on the eve of the battle of Al-Khandaq (The Trench) when I was fifteen years old, and he allowed me (to join that battle)." `Umar bin `Abdul-`Aziz commented when this Hadith reached him, "This is the difference between a child and an adult." There is a difference of opinion over whether pubic hair is considered a sign of adulthood, and the correct opinion is that it is. The Sunnah supports this view, according to a Hadith collected by Imam Ahmad from `Atiyah Al-Qurazi who said, We were presented to the Prophet on the day of Qurizah, whoever had pubic hair was killed, whoever did not was left free to go, I was one of those who did not, so I was left free." The Four Sunan compilers also recorded similar to it. At-Tirmidhi said, "Hasan Sahih." Allah's statement,

(if then you find sound judgment in them, release their property to them,) Sa`id bin Jubayr said that this portion of the Ayah means, when you find them to be good in the religion and wise with their money. Similar was reported from Ibn `Abbas, Al-Hasan Al-Basri and others among the Imams. The scholars of Fiqh stated that when the child becomes good in the religion and wise concerning with money, then the money that his caretaker was keeping for him should be surrendered to him.

Poor Caretakers are Allowed to Wisely Spend from the Money of the Orphan Under Their Care, to Compensate for Their Work

Allah said,

(But consume it not wastefully and hastily, fearing that they should grow up.) Allah commands that the money of the orphan should not be spent unnecessarily,

(Wastefully and hastily) for fear they might grow up. Allah also commands,

(And whoever among guardians is rich, he should take no wages,) Hence, the guardian who is rich and does not need the orphan's money, should not take any of it as wages.

(but if he is poor, let him have for himself what is just and reasonable.) Ibn Abi Hatim recorded that `A'ishah said, "This Ayah,

(And whoever among guardians is rich, he should take no wages, but if he is poor, let him have for himself what is just and reasonable.) was revealed about the guardian of the orphan and pertains to whatever work he does for the orphan's estate. " Al-Bukhari also collected this Hadith. Imam Ahmad recorded that `Amr bin Shu`ayb said that his father said that his father told him that a man asked the Messenger of Allah , "I do not have money, but I have an orphan under my care." The Messenger said,

«كُلْ مِنْ مَالِ يَتِيمِكَ غَيْرَ مُسْرِفٍ وَلَا مُبَذِّرٍ وَلَا مُتَأَثِّلٍ مَالًا، وَمِنْ غَيْرِ أَنْ تَقِيَ مَالَكَ أَوْ قَالَ تَفْدِيَ مَالَكَ بِمَالِه»

(Eat from your orphan's wealth without extravagance or wastefulness, or mixing it, and without saving your money by spending his.)" Allah said,

(And when you release their property to them.) after they become adults, and you see that they are wise, then,

(take a witness in their presence;) Allah commands the guardians of orphans to surrender the property of the orphans who become consenting adults, in the presence of witnesses, so that none of them denies the fact that he received his money. Allah said next, (and Allah is All-Sufficient in taking account.) meaning, Allah is sufficient as Witness, Reckoner and Watcher over their work for orphans, and when they surrender their money to them, whether their property was complete and whole, or deficient and less. Indeed, Allah knows all of that. In his Sahih, Muslim recorded that the Messenger of Allah said,

«يَا أَبَا ذَرٍّ إِنِّي أَرَاكَ ضَعِيفًا، وَإِنِّي أُحِبُّ لَكَ مَا أُحِبُّ لِنَفْسِي، لَا تَأَمَّرَنَّ عَلَى اثْنَيْنِ، وَلَا تَلِيَنَّ مَالَ يَتِيمٍ»

(O Abu Dharr! Verily, you are weak, and I love for you what I love for myself. Do not become a leader of two nor assume guardianship of an orphan's property.)

Surah: 4 Ayah: 7, Ayah: 8, Ayah: 9 & Ayah: 10

﴿ لِّلرِّجَالِ نَصِيبٌ مِّمَّا تَرَكَ ٱلْوَٰلِدَانِ وَٱلْأَقْرَبُونَ وَلِلنِّسَآءِ نَصِيبٌ مِّمَّا تَرَكَ ٱلْوَٰلِدَانِ وَٱلْأَقْرَبُونَ مِمَّا قَلَّ مِنْهُ أَوْ كَثُرَ نَصِيبًا مَّفْرُوضًا ﴿٧﴾ ﴾

7. There is a share for men and a share for women from what is left by parents and those nearest related, whether the property be small or large - a legal share.

﴿ وَإِذَا حَضَرَ ٱلْقِسْمَةَ أُو۟لُوا۟ ٱلْقُرْبَىٰ وَٱلْيَتَـٰمَىٰ وَٱلْمَسَـٰكِينُ فَٱرْزُقُوهُم مِّنْهُ وَقُولُوا۟ لَهُمْ قَوْلًا مَّعْرُوفًا ﴿٨﴾ ﴾

8. And when the relatives and the orphans and Al-Masâkin (the poor) are present at the time of division, give them out of the property, and speak to them words of kindness and justice.

﴿ وَلْيَخْشَ ٱلَّذِينَ لَوْ تَرَكُوا۟ مِنْ خَلْفِهِمْ ذُرِّيَّةً ضِعَـٰفًا خَافُوا۟ عَلَيْهِمْ فَلْيَتَّقُوا۟ ٱللَّهَ وَلْيَقُولُوا۟ قَوْلًا سَدِيدًا ﴿٩﴾ ﴾

9. And let those (executors and guardians) have the same fear in their minds as they would have for their own, if they had left weak offspring behind. So let them fear Allâh and speak right words.

﴿ إِنَّ ٱلَّذِينَ يَأْكُلُونَ أَمْوَٰلَ ٱلْيَتَـٰمَىٰ ظُلْمًا إِنَّمَا يَأْكُلُونَ فِى بُطُونِهِمْ نَارًا ۖ وَسَيَصْلَوْنَ سَعِيرًا ﴿١٠﴾ ﴾

10. Verily, those who unjustly eat up the property of orphans, they eat up only fire into their bellies, and they will be burnt in the blazing Fire!

Transliteration

7. Lilrrijali naseebun mimma taraka alwalidani waal-aqraboona walilnnisa-i naseebun mimma taraka alwalidani waal-aqraboona mimma qalla minhu aw kathura naseeban mafroodan 8. Wa-

itha hadara alqismata oloo alqurba waalyatama waalmasakeenu faorzuqoohum minhu waqooloo lahum qawlan maAAroofan 9. Walyakhsha allatheena law tarakoo min khalfihim thurriyyatan diAAafan khafoo AAalayhim falyattaqoo Allaha walyaqooloo qawlan sadeedan 10. Inna allatheena ya/kuloona amwala alyatama thulman innama ya/kuloona fee butoonihim naran wasayaslawna saAAeeran

Tafsir Ibn Kathir

The Necessity of Surrendering the Inheritance According to the Portions that Allah Ordained

Sa`id bin Jubayr and Qatadah said, "The idolators used to give adult men a share of inheritance and deprive women and children of it. Allah revealed;

(There is a share for men from what is left by parents and those nearest in relation)." Therefore, everyone is equal in Allah's decision to inherit, even though their shares vary according to the degree of their relationship to the deceased, whether being a relative, spouse, etc. Ibn Marduwyah reported that Jabir said, "Umm Kujjah came to the Messenger of Allah and said to him, `O Messenger of Allah! I have two daughters whose father died, and they do not own anything.' So Allah revealed;

(There is a share for men from what is left by parents and those nearest in relation.)" We will mention this Hadith when explaining the two Ayat about inheritance. Allah knows best. Allah said,

(are present at the time of division,) those who do not have a share in the inheritance,

(and the orphans and the poor), are also present upon dividing the inheritance, give them a share of the inheritance. Al-Bukhari recorded that Ibn `Abbas said that the Ayah,

(And when the relatives and the orphans and the poor are present at the time of division), was not abrogated. Ibn Jarir recorded that Ibn `Abbas said that this Ayah still applies and should be implemented. Ath-Thawri said that Ibn Abi Najih narrated from Mujahid that implementing this Ayah, "Is required from those who have anything to inherit, paid from whatever portions their hearts are satisfied with giving away." Similar explanation was reported from Ibn Mas`ud, Abu Musa, `Abdur-Rahman bin Abi Bakr, Abu Al-`Aliyah, Ash-Sha`bi and Al-Hasan. Ibn Sirin, Sa`id bin Jubayr, Makhul, Ibrahim An-Nakha`i, `Ata' bin Abi Rabah, Az-Zuhri and Yahya bin Ya`mar said this payment is obligatory. Others say that this refers to the bequeathal at the time of death. And others say that it was abrogated. Al-`Awfi reported that Ibn `Abbas said that this Ayah,

(And when are present at the time of division), refers to divisions of inheritance. So, when poor relatives, who are ineligible for inheritance, orphans, and the poor attend the division of the inheritance, which is sometimes substantial, their hearts will feel eager to have a share, seeing each eligible person assuming his share; while they are desperate, yet are not given anything. Allah the Most Kind, Most Compassionate, commands that they should have a share in the inheritance as an act of kindness, charity, compassion and mercy for them.

Observing Fairness in the Will

Allah said, (And let those have the same fear in their minds as they would have for their own, if they had left behind...) `Ali bin Abi Talhah reported that Ibn `Abbas said that this part of the Ayah, "Refers to a man who is near death and he dictates a will and testament that harms some of the rightful inheritors. Allah commands whoever hears such will to fear Allah, and direct the dying man to do what is right and to be fair, being as eager to protect the inheritors of the dying man as he would be with his own." Similar was reported from Mujahid and several others. The Two Sahihs record that when the Messenger of Allah visited Sa`d bin Abi Waqqas during an illness he suffered from, Sa`d said to the Messenger, "O Messenger of Allah! I am wealthy and have no inheritors except a daughter. Should I give two-thirds of my property in charity" He said, "No." Sa`d asked, "Half" He said, "No." Sa`d said, "One-third" The Prophet said;

«الثُّلُثُ، وَالثُّلُثُ كَثِير»

(One-third, and even one-third is too much.) The Messenger of Allah then said,

«إِنَّكَ أَنْ تَذَرَ وَرَثَتَكَ أَغْنِيَاءَ خَيْرٌ مِنْ أَنْ تَذَرَهُمْ عَالَةً يَتَكَفَّفُونَ النَّاس»

(You'd better leave your inheritors wealthy rather than leaving them poor, begging from others.)

A Stern Warning Against Those Who Use Up the Orphan's Wealth

It was also said that the Ayah

(consume it not wastefully and hastily, fearing that they should grow up,) means, let them have Taqwa of Allah when taking care of the orphan's wealth, as Ibn Jarir recorded from Al-`Awfi who reported this explanation from Ibn `Abbas. This is a sound opinion that is supported by the warning that follows against consuming the orphan's wealth unjustly. In this case, the meaning becomes: Just as you would want your offspring to be treated fairly after you, then treat other people's offspring fairly when you are given the responsibility of caring for them. Allah proclaims that those who unjustly consume the wealth of orphans, will be eating fire into their stomach, this is why Allah said,

(Verily, those who unjustly eat up the property of orphans, they eat up only a fire into their bellies, and they will be burnt in the blazing Fire!) meaning, when you consume the orphan's wealth without a right, then you are only consuming fire, which will kindle in your stomach on the Day of Resurrection. It is recorded in the Two Sahihs that Abu Hurayrah said that the Messenger of Allah said,

«اجْتَنِبُوا السَّبْعَ الْمُوبِقَات»

(Avoid the seven great destructive sins.) The people asked, "O Allah's Messenger! What are they" He said,

«الشِّرْكُ بِاللهِ، وَالسِّحْرُ، وَقَتْلُ النَّفْسِ الَّتِي حَرَّمَ اللهُ إِلَّا بِالْحَقِّ، وَأَكْلُ الرِّبَا، وَأَكْلُ مَالِ الْيَتِيمِ، وَالتَّوَلِّي يَوْمَ الزَّحْفِ، وَقَذْفُ الْمُحْصَنَاتِ الْمُؤْمِنَاتِ الْغَافِلَات»

(To join others in worship along with Allah, magic, to kill the life which Allah has forbidden except for a just cause, to consume interest, to consume an orphan's property, to turn your back to the enemy and flee from the battlefield at the time of fighting, and to accuse chaste women who never even think of anything harmful to their chastity being good believers.)

Surah: 4 Ayah: 11

﴿ يُوصِيكُمُ ٱللَّهُ فِىٓ أَوْلَـٰدِكُمْ ۖ لِلذَّكَرِ مِثْلُ حَظِّ ٱلْأُنثَيَيْنِ ۚ فَإِن كُنَّ نِسَآءً فَوْقَ ٱثْنَتَيْنِ فَلَهُنَّ
ثُلُثَا مَا تَرَكَ ۖ وَإِن كَانَتْ وَٰحِدَةً فَلَهَا ٱلنِّصْفُ ۚ وَلِأَبَوَيْهِ لِكُلِّ وَٰحِدٍ مِّنْهُمَا ٱلسُّدُسُ مِمَّا
تَرَكَ إِن كَانَ لَهُۥ وَلَدٌ ۚ فَإِن لَّمْ يَكُن لَّهُۥ وَلَدٌ وَوَرِثَهُۥٓ أَبَوَاهُ فَلِأُمِّهِ ٱلثُّلُثُ ۚ فَإِن كَانَ لَهُۥٓ إِخْوَةٌ
فَلِأُمِّهِ ٱلسُّدُسُ ۚ مِنۢ بَعْدِ وَصِيَّةٍ يُوصِى بِهَآ أَوْ دَيْنٍ ۗ ءَابَآؤُكُمْ وَأَبْنَآؤُكُمْ لَا تَدْرُونَ أَيُّهُمْ
أَقْرَبُ لَكُمْ نَفْعًا ۚ فَرِيضَةً مِّنَ ٱللَّهِ ۗ إِنَّ ٱللَّهَ كَانَ عَلِيمًا حَكِيمًا ﴿١١﴾

11. Allâh commands you as regards your children's (inheritance): to the male, a portion equal to that of two females; if (there are) only daughters, two or more, their share is two-thirds of the inheritance; if only one, her share is half. For parents, a sixth share of inheritance to each if the deceased left children; if no children, and the parents are the (only) heirs, the mother has a third; if the deceased left brothers or (sisters), the mother has a sixth. (The distribution in all cases is) after the payment of legacies he may have bequeathed or debts. You know not which of them, whether your parents or your children, are nearest to you in benefit; (these fixed shares) are ordained by Allâh. And Allâh is Ever All-Knower, All-Wise.

Transliteration

11. Yooseekumu Allahu fee awladikum liliththakari mithlu haththi alonthayayni fa-in kunna nisaan fawqa ithnatayni falahunna thulutha ma taraka wa-in kanat wahidatan falaha alnnisfu wali-abawayhi likulli wahidin minhuma alssudusu mimma taraka in kana lahu waladun fa-in lam yakun lahu waladun wawarithahu abawahu fali-ommihi alththuluthu fa-in kana lahu ikhwatun fali-ommihi alssudusu min baAAdi wasiyyatin yoosee biha aw daynin abaokum waabnaokum la tadroona ayyuhum aqrabu lakum nafAAan fareedatan mina Allahi inna Allaha kana AAaleeman hakeeman

Tafsir Ibn Kathir

Learning the Various Shares of the Inheritance is Encouraged

This, the following, and the last honorable Ayah in this Surah contain the knowledge of Al-Fara'id, inheritance. The knowledge of Al-Fara'id is derived from these three Ayat and from the Hadiths on this subject which explain them. Learning this knowledge is encouraged, especially the specific things mentioned in the Ayat. Ibn `Uyaynah said; "Knowledge of Al-Fara'id was called half of knowledge, because it effects all people."

The Reason Behind Revealing Ayah 4:11

Explaining this Ayah, Al-Bukhari recorded that Jabir bin `Abdullah said, "Allah's Messenger came visiting me on foot with Abu Bakr at Banu Salamah's (dwellings), and the Prophet found me unconscious. He asked for some water, performed ablution with it, then poured it on me, and I regained consciousness. I said, `What do you command me to do with my money, O Allah's Messenger' this Ayah was later revealed,

(Allah commands you for your children's (inheritance); to the male, a portion equal to that of two females)." This is how it was recorded by Muslim and An-Nasa'i. The remainder of the Six compilers also collected this Hadith. Another Hadith from Jabir concerning the reason behind revealing Ayah 4:11 Ahmad recorded from Jabir that he said, "The wife of Sa`d bin Ar-Rabi` came to Allah's Messenger and said to him, `O Allah's Messenger! These are the two daughters of Sa`d bin Ar-Rabi`, who was killed as a martyr at Uhud. Their uncle took their money and did not leave anything for them. They will not be married unless they have money.' The Messenger said, `Allah will decide on this matter.' The Ayah about the inheritance was later revealed and the Messenger of Allah sent word to their uncle commanding him,

«أَعْطِ ابْنَتَيْ سَعْدٍ الثُّلُثَيْنِ، وَأُمَّهُمَا الثُّمُنَ، وَمَا بَقِيَ فَهُوَ لَك»

(Give two-thirds (of Sa`d's money) to Sa`d's two daughters and one eighth for their mother, and whatever is left is yours.)" Abu Dawud, At-Tirmidhi, and Ibn Majah collected this Hadith. It is apparent, however, that the first Hadith from Jabir was about the case of the last Ayah in the Surah (4:176, rather than 4:11), for at the time this incident occurred, Jabir had sisters and did not have daughters, parents or offspring to inherit from him. Yet, we mentioned the Hadith here just as Al-Bukhari did.

Males Get Two Times the Share of Females for Inheritance

Allah said,

(Allah commands you for your children's (inheritance): to the male, a portion equal to that of two females;) Allah commands: observe justice with your children. The people of Jahiliyyah used to give the males, but not the females, a share in the inheritance. Therefore, Allah commands that both males and females take a share in the inheritance, although the portion of the males is twice as much as that of the females. There is a distinction because men need money to spend on their dependants, commercial transactions, work and fulfillling their obligations. Consequently, men get twice the portion of the inheritance that females get. Allah's statement,

(Allah commands you for your children's (inheritance): to the male, a portion equal to that of two females;) testifies to the fact that Allah is more merciful with children than their own parents are with them, since He commands the parents to be just and fair with their own children. An authentic Hadith stated that a captured woman was looking for her child and when she found him, she held him, gave him her breast and nursed him. The Messenger of Allah said to his Companions,

«أَتُرَوْنَ هذِهِ طَارِحَةً وَلَدَهَا فِي النَّارِ وَهِيَ تَقْدِرُ عَلى ذَلِك»

؟ (Do you think that this woman would willingly throw her child in the fire) They said, "No, O Messenger of Allah." He said,

«فَوَاللهِ للهُ أَرْحَمُ بِعِبَادِهِ مِنْ هذِهِ بِوَلَدِهَا»

(By Allah! Allah is more merciful with His servants than this woman is with her own child.) Al-Bukhari recorded that Ibn `Abbas said, "The custom (in old days) was that the property of the deceased would be inherited by his offspring; as for the parents (of the deceased), they would inherit by the will of the deceased. Then Allah cancelled whatever He willed from that custom and ordained that the male get twice the amount inherited by the female, and for each parent a sixth (of the whole legacy), for the wife an eighth or a fourth, and for the husband a half or a fourth."

The Share of the Females When They Are the Only Eligible Heirs

Allah said,

(if only daughters, two or more, their share is two-thirds of the inheritance;) We should mention here that some people said the Ayah only means two daughters, and that `more' is redundant, which is not true. Nothing in the Qur'an is useless or redundant. Had the Ayah been talking about only two women, it would have said, "The share of both of them is two-thirds." As for the daughters, two or more, the ruling that they get two-thirds was derived from this Ayah, stating that the two sisters get two-thirds. We also mentioned the Hadith in which the Prophet commanded that two-thirds be the share of the two daughters of Sa`d bin Ar-Rabi`. So this is proven in the Book and the Sunnah.

(if only one, her share is half.) If there are two daughters, then there are texts to prove they share a half. Therefore, two-thirds is the share of the two daughters or sisters, and Allah knows best.

Share of the Parents in the Inheritance

Allah said,

(For parents, a sixth share of inheritance to each) There are several forms of the share that the parents get in the inheritance. 1. If the deceased left behind children, the parents get a sixth each. When the deceased had only one daughter, she gets half of the inheritance and the parents each one sixth, and another sixth is given to the father. 2. When the parents are the only inheritors, the mother gets one-third while the father gets the remaining two-thirds. In this case, the father's share will be twice the mother's share. If the deceased had a surviving spouse, the spouse gets half, in the case of a husband, or a fourth in the case of a surviving wife. In both cases, the mother of the deceased gets one-third of the remaining inheritance. This is because the remaining portion of the inheritance is treated just as the entire legacy in regard to the parents' share. Allah has given the mother one-half of what the father gets. Therefore, the mother gets a third of the remaining inheritance while the father gets two-thirds. 3. If the deceased left behind surviving brothers and sisters, whether half brothers, half sisters or from the same father and mother, their presence does not cause reduction in the father's share. Yet, their presence reduces the share of the mother to one-sixth instead of one-third, and the father gets the rest, when there are no other heirs. Ibn Abi Hatim recorded that Qatadah commented on the Ayah,

(If the deceased left brothers or (sisters), the mother has a sixth.) "Their presence will reduce the share of the mother, but they will not inherit. If there is only one surviving brother, the mother's share will remain one-third, but her share will be reduced if there is more than one surviving brother. The people of knowledge attribute this reduction in the mother's share from one-third (to one-sixth) to the fact that the father is the one who helps the brothers (and sisters) of the deceased get married, spending from his own money for this purpose. The mother does not spend from her money for this purpose." This is a sound opinion.

First the Debts are Paid Off, then the Will, then the Fixed Inheritance

Allah said,

((The distribution in all cases is) after the payment of legacies he may have bequeathed or debts.) The scholars of the Salaf and the Khalaf agree that paying debts comes before fulfilling the will, and this is apparent to those who read the Ayah carefully. Allah said next,

(You know not which of them, whether your parents or your children, are nearest to you in benefit.) This Ayah means: We have appointed a share to the parents and children, contrary to the practice of Jahiliyyah and the early Islamic era, when the inheritance would go to the children, and parents get a share only if they were named in the will, as Ibn `Abbas stated. Allah abrogated this practice and appointed a fixed share for the children and for the parents. One may derive benefit in this life or for the Hereafter from his parents, the likes of which he could not get from his children. The opposite of this could also be true. Allah said,

(You know not which of them, whether your parents or your children, are nearest to you in benefit,): since benefit could come from one or the other of these relatives, We appointed a fixed share of inheritance for each. Allah knows best. Allah said,

(ordained by Allah), meaning: These appointed shares of inheritance that We mentioned and which give some inheritors a bigger share than others, is a commandment from Allah that He has decided and ordained,

(And Allah is Ever All-Knower, All-Wise.), Who places everything in its rightful place and gives each his rightful share.

Surah: 4 Ayah: 12

۞ وَلَكُمْ نِصْفُ مَا تَرَكَ أَزْوَاجُكُمْ إِن لَّمْ يَكُن لَّهُنَّ وَلَدٌ ۚ فَإِن كَانَ لَهُنَّ وَلَدٌ
فَلَكُمُ الرُّبُعُ مِمَّا تَرَكْنَ ۚ مِن بَعْدِ وَصِيَّةٍ يُوصِينَ بِهَا أَوْ دَيْنٍ ۚ وَلَهُنَّ الرُّبُعُ مِمَّا
تَرَكْتُمْ إِن لَّمْ يَكُن لَّكُمْ وَلَدٌ ۚ فَإِن كَانَ لَكُمْ وَلَدٌ فَلَهُنَّ الثُّمُنُ مِمَّا تَرَكْتُم ۚ مِّن بَعْدِ
وَصِيَّةٍ تُوصُونَ بِهَا أَوْ دَيْنٍ ۗ وَإِن كَانَ رَجُلٌ يُورَثُ كَلَالَةً أَوِ امْرَأَةٌ وَلَهُ أَخٌ أَوْ أُخْتٌ
فَلِكُلِّ وَاحِدٍ مِّنْهُمَا السُّدُسُ ۚ فَإِن كَانُوا أَكْثَرَ مِن ذَٰلِكَ فَهُمْ شُرَكَاءُ فِي الثُّلُثِ ۚ مِن
بَعْدِ وَصِيَّةٍ يُوصَىٰ بِهَا أَوْ دَيْنٍ غَيْرَ مُضَارٍّ ۚ وَصِيَّةً مِّنَ اللَّهِ ۗ وَاللَّهُ عَلِيمٌ حَلِيمٌ ﴿١٢﴾

12. In that which your wives leave, your share is a half if they have no child; but if they leave a child, you get a fourth of that which they leave after payment of legacies that they may have bequeathed or debts. In that which you leave, their (your wives) share is a fourth if you leave no child; but if you leave a child, they get an eighth of that which you leave after payment of legacies that you may have bequeathed or debts. If the man or woman whose inheritance is in question has left neither ascendants nor descendants, but has left a brother or a sister, each one of the two gets a sixth; but if more than two, they share in

a third, after payment of legacies he (or she) may have bequeathed or debts, so that no loss is caused (to anyone). This is a Commandment from Allâh; and Allâh is Ever All-Knowing, Most-Forbearing.

Transliteration

12. Walakum nisfu ma taraka azwajukum in lam yakun lahunna waladun fa-in kana lahunna waladun falakumu alrrubuAAu mimma tarakna min baAAdi wasiyyatin yooseena biha aw daynin walahunna alrrubuAAu mimma taraktum in lam yakun lakum waladun fa-in kana lakum waladun falahunna alththumunu mimma taraktum min baAAdi wasiyyatin toosoona biha aw daynin wa-in kana rajulun yoorathu kalalatan awi imraatun walahu akhun aw okhtun falikulli wahidin minhuma alssudusu fa-in kanoo akthara min thalika fahum shurakao fee alththuluthi min baAAdi wasiyyatin yoosa biha aw daynin ghayra mudarrin wasiyyatan mina Allahi waAllahu AAaleemun haleemun

Tafsir Ibn Kathir

Share of the Spouses in the Inheritance

Allah says to the husband, you get half of what your wife leaves behind if she dies and did not have a child. If she had a child, you get one-fourth of what she leaves behind, after payment of legacies that she may have bequeathed, or her debts. We mentioned before that payment of debts comes before fulfilling the will, and then comes the will, then the inheritance, and there is a consensus on this matter among the scholars. And the rule applies to the grandchildren as well as the children, even if they are great-grandchildren (or even further in generation) Allah then said,

(In that which you leave, their (your wives) share is a fourth) and if there is more than one wife, they all share in the fourth, or one-eighth that the wife gets. Earlier, we explained Allah's statement,

(After payment of legacies)

The Meaning of Kalalah

Allah said,

(If the man or woman whose inheritance is in question was left in Kalalah.) Kalalah is a derivative of Iklil; the crown that surrounds the head. The meaning of Kalalah in this Ayah is that the person's heirs come from other than the first degree of relative. Ash-Sha`bi reported that when Abu Bakr As-Siddiq was asked about the meaning of Kalalah, he said, "I will say my own opinion about it, and if it is correct, then this correctness is from Allah. However, if my opinion is wrong, it will be my error and because of the evil efforts of Shaytan, and Allah and His Messenger have nothing to do with it. Kalalah refers to the man who has neither descendants nor ascendants." When `Umar became the Khalifah, he said, "I hesitate to contradict an opinion of Abu Bakr." This was recorded by Ibn Jarir and others. In his Tafsir, Ibn Abi Hatim recorded that Ibn `Abbas said, "I was among the last persons to see `Umar bin Al-Khattab, and he said to me, `What you said was the correct opinion.' I asked, `What did I say' He said, `That Kalalah refers to the person who has no child or parents.'" This is also the opinion of `Ali bin Abi Talib, Ibn Mas`ud, Ibn `Abbas, Zayd bin Thabit, Ash-Sha`bi, An-Nakha`i, Al-Hasan Al-Basri, Qatadah, Jabir bin Zayd and Al-Hakam . This is also the view of the people of Al-Madinah, Kufah, Basrah, the Seven Fuqaha', the Four Imams and the majority of scholars of the past and present, causing some scholars to declare that there is a consensus on this opinion.

The Ruling Concerning Children of the Mother From Other Than the Deceased's Father

Allah said,

(But has left a brother or a sister), meaning, from his mother's side, as some of the Salaf stated, including Sa`d bin Abi Waqqas. Qatadah reported that this is the view of Abu Bakr As-Siddiq.

(Each one of the two gets a sixth; but if more than two, they share in a third.) There is a difference between the half brothers from the mother's side and the rest of the heirs. First, they get a share in the inheritance on account of their mother. Second, the males and females among them get the same share. Third, they only have a share in the inheritance when the deceased's estate is inherited in Kalalah, for they do not have a share if the deceased has a surviving father, grandfather, child or grandchild. Fourth, they do not have more than a third, no matter how numerous they were. aAllah's statement,

(After payment of legacies he (or she) may have bequeathed or debts, so that no loss is caused (to anyone).) means, let the will and testament be fair and free of any type of harm, without depriving some rightful heirs from all, or part of their share, or adding to the fixed portion that Allah or dained for some heirs. Indeed, whoever does this, will have disputed with Allah concerning His decision and division. An authentic Hadith states,

«إِنَّ اللهَ قَدْ أَعْطَى كُلَّ ذِي حَقَ حَقَّهُ فَلَا وَصِيَّةَ لِوَارِث»

(Allah has given each his fixed due right. Therefore, there is no will for a rightful inheritor.)

Surah: 4 Ayah: 13 & Ayah: 14

﴿ تِلْكَ حُدُودُ ٱللَّهِ ۚ وَمَن يُطِعِ ٱللَّهَ وَرَسُولَهُۥ يُدْخِلْهُ جَنَّٰتٍ تَجْرِى مِن تَحْتِهَا ٱلْأَنْهَٰرُ خَٰلِدِينَ فِيهَا ۚ وَذَٰلِكَ ٱلْفَوْزُ ٱلْعَظِيمُ ﴿١٣﴾ ﴾

13. These are the limits (set by) Allâh (or ordainments as regards laws of inheritance), and whosoever obeys Allâh and His Messenger (Muhammad (peace be upon him)) will be admitted to Gardens under which rivers flow (in Paradise), to abide therein, and that will be the great success.

﴿ وَمَن يَعْصِ ٱللَّهَ وَرَسُولَهُۥ وَيَتَعَدَّ حُدُودَهُۥ يُدْخِلْهُ نَارًا خَٰلِدًا فِيهَا وَلَهُۥ عَذَابٌ مُّهِينٌ ﴿١٤﴾ ﴾

14. And whosoever disobeys Allâh and His Messenger (Muhammad (peace be upon him)) and transgresses His limits, He will cast him into the Fire, to abide therein; and he shall have a disgraceful torment.

Transliteration

13. Tilka hudoodu Allahi waman yutiAAi Allaha warasoolahu yudkhilhu jannatin tajree min tahtiha alanharu khalideena feeha wathalika alfawzu alAAatheemu 14. Waman yaAAsi Allaha warasoolahu wayataAAadda hudoodahu yudkhilhu naran khalidan feeha walahu AAathabun muheenun

Tafsir Ibn Kathir

Warning Against Transgressing the Limits for Inheritance

Meaning, the Fara'id are Allah's set limits. This includes what Allah has alloted for the heirs, according to the degree of relation they have to the deceased, and their degree of dependency on him. Therefore, do not transgress or violate them. So Allah said;

(And whosoever obeys Allah and His Messenger,) regarding the inheritance, and does not add or decrease any of these fixed shares by use of tricks and plots. Rather, he gives each his appointed share as Allah commanded, ordained and decided,

(Will be admitted to Gardens under which rivers flow (in Paradise), to abide therein, and is the great success. And whosoever disobeys Allah and His Messenger, and transgresses His (set) limits, He will cast him into the Fire, to abide therein; and he shall have a disgraceful torment.) This is because he changed what Allah has ordained and disputed with His judgment. Indeed, this is the behavior of those who do not agree with what Allah has decided and divided, and this is why Allah punishes them with humiliation in the eternal, painful torment. Imam Ahmad recorded that Abu Hurayrah said that, the Messenger of Allah said,

«إِنَّ الرَّجُلَ لَيَعْمَلُ بِعَمَلِ أَهْلِ الْخَيْرِ سَبْعِينَ سَنَةً، فَإِذَا أَوْصَى حَافَ فِي وَصِيَّتِهِ، فَيُخْتَمُ لَهُ بِشَرِّ عَمَلِهِ، فَيَدْخُلُ النَّارَ، وَإِنَّ الرَّجُلَ لَيَعْمَلُ بِعَمَلِ أَهْلِ الشَّرِّ سَبْعِينَ سَنَةً، فَيَعْدِلُ فِي وَصِيَّتِهِ فَيُخْتَمُ لَهُ بِخَيْرِ عَمَلِهِ فَيَدْخُلُ الْجَنَّةَ»

(A man might perform the actions of righteous people for seventy years, but when it is time to compile his will, he commits injustice. So his final work will be his worst, and he thus enters the Fire. A man might perform the deeds of evil people for seventy years, yet he is fair in his will. So his final work will be his best, and he thus enters Paradise.) Abu Hurayrah said, "Read, if you will,

(These are the limits (set by) Allah) until,

(a disgraceful torment.)." In the chapter on injustice in the will, Abu Dawud recorded in his Sunan that Abu Hurayrah said that the Messenger of Allah said,

«إِنَّ الرَّجُلَ لَيَعْمَلُ أَوِ الْمَرْأَةَ بِطَاعَةِ اللهِ سِتِّينَ سَنَةً، ثُمَّ يَحْضُرُهُمَا الْمَوْتُ، فَيُضَارَّانِ فِي الْوَصِيَّـــةِ، فَتَجِبُ لَهُمَا النَّارُ»

(A man or a woman might perform actions in obedience to Allah for sixty years. Yet, when they are near death, they leave an unfair will and thus acquire the Fire.) Abu Hurayrah then recited the Ayah,

(After payment of legacies he (or she) may have bequeathed or debts, so that no loss is caused), until,

(and that is the great success.) This was also recorded by At-Tirmidhi and Ibn Majah, and At-Tirmidhi said, "Hasan Gharib".

Surah: 4 Ayah: 15 & Ayah: 16

﴿ وَٱلَّٰتِي يَأۡتِينَ ٱلۡفَٰحِشَةَ مِن نِّسَآئِكُمۡ فَٱسۡتَشۡهِدُواْ عَلَيۡهِنَّ أَرۡبَعَةٗ مِّنكُمۡۖ فَإِن
شَهِدُواْ فَأَمۡسِكُوهُنَّ فِي ٱلۡبُيُوتِ حَتَّىٰ يَتَوَفَّىٰهُنَّ ٱلۡمَوۡتُ أَوۡ يَجۡعَلَ ٱللَّهُ لَهُنَّ سَبِيلٗا ١٥ ﴾

15. And those of your women who commit illegal sexual intercourse, take the evidence of four witnesses from amongst you against them; and if they testify, confine them (i.e. women) to houses until death comes to them or Allâh ordains for them some (other) way.

﴿ وَٱلَّذَانِ يَأۡتِيَٰنِهَا مِنكُمۡ فَـَٔاذُوهُمَاۖ فَإِن تَابَا وَأَصۡلَحَا فَأَعۡرِضُواْ عَنۡهُمَآۗ إِنَّ ٱللَّهَ كَانَ
تَوَّابٗا رَّحِيمًا ١٦ ﴾

16. And the two persons (man and woman) among you who commit illegal sexual intercourse, hurt them both. And if they repent (promise Allâh that they will never repeat, i.e. commit illegal sexual intercourse and other similar sins) and do righteous good deeds, leave them alone. Surely, Allâh is Ever All-Forgiving (the One Who accepts repentance), (and He is) Most Merciful.

Transliteration

15. Waallatee ya/teena alfahishata min nisa-ikum faistashhidoo AAalayhinna arbaAAatan minkum fain shahidoo faamsikoohunna fee albuyooti hatta yatawaffahunna almawtu aw yajAAala Allahu lahunna sabeelan 16. Waallathani ya/tiyaniha minkum faathoohuma fa-in taba waaslaha faaAAridoo AAanhuma inna Allaha kana tawwaban raheeman

Tafsir Ibn Kathir

The Adulteress is Confined in her House; A Command Later Abrogated

At the begining of Islam, the ruling was that if a woman commits adultery as stipulated by sufficient proof, she was confined to her home, without leave, until she died. Allah said,

(And those of your women who commit illegal sexual intercourse, take the evidence of four witnesses from among you against them; and if they testify, confine them (i.e. women) to houses until death comes to them or Allah ordains for them some (other) way.) `Some other way' mentioned here is the abrogation of this ruling that came later. Ibn `Abbas said, "The early ruling was confinement, until Allah sent down Surat An-Nur (chapter 24) which abrogated that ruling with the ruling of flogging (for fornication) or stoning to death (for adultery)." Similar was reported from `Ikrimah, Sa`id bin Jubayr, Al-Hasan, `Ata' Al-Khurasani, Abu Salih, Qatadah, Zayd bin Aslam and Ad-Dahhak, and this is a matter that is agreed upon. Imam Ahmad recorded that `Ubadah bin As-Samit said, "When the revelation descended upon the Messenger of Allah , it would affect him and his face would show signs of strain. One day, Allah sent down a revelation to him, and when the Messenger was relieved of its strain, he said,

«خُذُوا عَنِّي، قَدْ جَعَلَ اللهُ لَهُنَّ سَبِيلًا، الثَّيِّبُ بِالثَّيِّبِ، وَالْبِكْرُ بِالْبِكْرِ، الثَّـــيِّبُ جَلْدُ مِائةٍ، وَرَجْمٌ بِالْحِجَارَةِ، وَالْبِكْرُ جَلْدُ مِائَةٍ ثُمَّ نَفْيُ سَنَة»

(Take from me: Allah has made some other way for them. The married with the married, the unmarried with the unmarried. The married gets a hundred lashes and stoning to death, while the unmarried gets a hundred lashes then banishment for a year.)" Muslim and the collectors of the Sunan recorded that `Ubadah bin As-Samit said that the Prophet said,

«خُذُوا عَنِّي خُذُوا عَنِّي، قَدْ جَعَلَ اللهُ لَهُنَّ سَبِيلًا، الْبِكْرُ بِالْبِكْرِ جَلْدُ مِائَةٍ وَتَغْرِيبُ عَامٍ، وَالثَّيِّبُ بِالثَّيِّبِ جَلْدُ مِائةٍ وَالرَّجْم»

(Take from me, take from me. Allah has made some other way for them: the (unmarried) gets a hundred lashes and banishment for one year, while the (married) gets a hundred lashes and stoning to death.) At-Tirmidhi said, "Hasan Sahih". Allah said,

(And the two persons among you who commit illegal sexual intercourse, punish them both.) Ibn `Abbas and Sa`id bin Jubayr said that this punishment includes cursing, shaming them and beating them with sandals. This was the ruling until Allah abrogated it with flogging or stoning, as we stated. Mujahid said, "It was revealed about the case of two men who do it." As if he was referring to the actions of the people of Lut, and Allah knows best. The collectors of Sunan recorded that Ibn `Abbas said that the Messenger of Allah said,

«مَنْ رَأَيْتُمُوهُ يَعْمَلُ عَمَلَ قَوْمِ لُوطٍ، فَاقْتُلُوا الْفَاعِلَ وَالْمَفْعُولَ بِه»

(Whoever you catch committing the act of the people of Lut (homosexuality), then kill both parties to the act.) Allah said,

(And if they repent and do righteous good deeds), by refraining from that evil act, and thereafter their actions become righteous,

(leave them alone), do not verbally abuse them after that, since he who truly repents is just like he who has no sin,

(Surely, Allah is Ever the One Who accepts repentance, Most Merciful.) The following is recorded in the Two Sahihs:

«إِذَا زَنَتْ أَمَةُ أَحَدِكُمْ، فَلْيَجْلِدْهَا الْحَدَّ، وَلَا يُثَرِّبْ عَلَيْهَا»

(When the slave-girl of one of you commits illegal sexual intercouse, let him flog her and not chastise her afterwards.) because the lashes she receives erase the sin that she has committed.

Surah: 4 Ayah: 17 & Ayah: 18

﴿ إِنَّمَا ٱلتَّوْبَةُ عَلَى ٱللَّهِ لِلَّذِينَ يَعْمَلُونَ ٱلسُّوٓءَ بِجَهَٰلَةٍ ثُمَّ يَتُوبُونَ مِن قَرِيبٍ فَأُو۟لَٰٓئِكَ يَتُوبُ ٱللَّهُ عَلَيْهِمْ ۗ وَكَانَ ٱللَّهُ عَلِيمًا حَكِيمًا ﴿١٧﴾ ﴾

17. Allâh accepts only the repentance of those who do evil in ignorance and foolishness and repent soon afterwards; it is they whom Allâh will forgive and Allâh is Ever All-Knower, All-Wise.

﴿ وَلَيْسَتِ ٱلتَّوْبَةُ لِلَّذِينَ يَعْمَلُونَ ٱلسَّيِّـَٔاتِ حَتَّىٰٓ إِذَا حَضَرَ أَحَدَهُمُ ٱلْمَوْتُ قَالَ إِنِّى تُبْتُ ٱلْـَٰٔنَ وَلَا ٱلَّذِينَ يَمُوتُونَ وَهُمْ كُفَّارٌ ۚ أُو۟لَٰٓئِكَ أَعْتَدْنَا لَهُمْ عَذَابًا أَلِيمًا ﴿١٨﴾ ﴾

18. And of no effect is the repentance of those who continue to do evil deeds until death faces one of them and he says: "Now I repent;" nor of those who die while they are disbelievers. For them We have prepared a painful torment.

Transliteration

17. Innama alttawbatu AAala Allahi lillatheena yaAAmaloona alssoo-a bijahalatin thumma yatooboona min qareebin faola-ika yatoobu Allahu AAalayhim wakana Allahu AAaleeman hakeeman 18. Walaysati alttawbatu lillatheena yaAAmaloona alssayyi-ati hatta itha hadara ahadahumu almawtu qala innee tubtu al-ana wala allatheena yamootoona wahum kuffarun ola-ika aAAtadna lahum AAathaban aleeman

Tafsir Ibn Kathir

Repentance is Accepted Until one Faces death

Allah states that He accepts repentance of the servant who commits an error in ignorance and then repents, even just before he sees the angel who captures the soul, before his soul reaches his throat. Mujahid and others said, "Every person who disobeys Allah by mistake, or intentionally is ignorant, until he refrains from the sin." Qatadah said that Abu Al-`Aliyah narrated that the Companions of the Messenger of Allah used to say, "Every sin that the servant commits, he commits out of ignorance." `Abdur-Razzaq narrated that, Ma`mar said that Qatadah said that, the Companions of the Messenger of Allah agreed that every sin that is committed by intention or otherwise, is committed in ignorance." Ibn Jurayj said, "Abdullah bin Kathir narrated to me that Mujahid said, `Every person who disobeys Allah (even willfully), is ignorant while committing the act of disobedience.'" Ibn Jurayj said, "`Ata' bin Abi Rabah told me something similar." Abu Salih said that Ibn `Abbas commented, "It is because of one's ignorance that he commits the error." `Ali bin Abi Talhah reported that Ibn `Abbas said about the Ayah, (and repent soon (afterwards)), "Until just before he (or she) looks at the angel of death." Ad-Dahhak said, "Every thing before death is `soon (afterwards).'" Al-Hasan Al-Basri said about the Ayah,

(and repent soon afterwards), "Just before his last breath leaves his throat." `Ikrimah said, "All of this life is `soon (afterwards).'" Imam Ahmad recorded that Ibn `Umar said that the Messenger said,

«إِنَّ اللهَ يَقْبَلُ تَوْبَةَ الْعَبْدِمَالَمْ يُغَرْغِرِ»

(Allah accepts the repentance of the servant as long as the soul does not reach the throat.) This Hadith was also collected by At-Tirmidhi and Ibn Majah, and At-Tirmidhi said, "Hasan Gharib". By mistake, Ibn Majah mentioned that this Hadith was narrated through `Abdullah bin `Amr. However, what is correct is that `Abdullah bin `Umar bin Al-Khattab was the narrator. Allah said,

(It is they to whom Allah will forgive and Allah is Ever All-Knower, All-Wise.) Surely, when hope in continued living diminishes, the angel of death comes forth and the soul reaches the throat, approaches the chest and arrives at the state where it is being gradually pulled out, then there is no accepted repentance, nor a way out of that certain end. Hence Allah's statements,

(And of no effect is the repentance of those who continue to do evil deeds until death faces one of them and he says: "Now I repent,") and,

(So when they saw Our punishment, they said: "We believe in Allah Alone...") (40:84) Allah decided that repentance shall not be accepted from the people of the earth when the sun rises from the west, as Allah said,

(The day that some of the signs of your Lord do come, no good will it do to a person to believe then, if he believed not before, nor earned good through his faith.) (6:158). Allah said,

(nor of those who die while they are disbelievers.) Consequently, when the disbeliever dies while still a disbeliever and polytheist, his sorrow and repentance shall not avail him. If he were to ransom himself, even with the earth's fill of gold, it will not be accepted from him. Ibn `Abbas, Abu Al-`Aliyah and Ar-Rabi` bin Anas said that the Ayah:

(nor of those who die while they are disbelievers), was revealed about the people of Shirk. Imam Ahmad recorded that Usamah bin Salman said that Abu Dharr said that the Messenger of Allah said,

«إِنَّ اللهَ يَقْبَلُ تَوْبَةَ عَبْدِهِ أَوْ يَغْفِرُ لِعَبْدِهِ مَالَمْ يَقَعِ الْحِجَابِ»

(Allah accepts the repentance of His servant, or forgives His servant, as long as the veil does not drop.) They asked, "And what does the drop of the veil mean " He said,

«أَنْ تَخْرُجَ النَّفْسُ وَهِيَ مُشْرِكَة»

(When the soul is removed while one is a polythiest.) Allah then said,

(For them We have prepared a painful torment), torment that is severe, eternal and enormous.

Surah: 4 Ayah: 19, Ayah: 20, Ayah: 21 & Ayah: 22

﴿ يَٰٓأَيُّهَا ٱلَّذِينَ ءَامَنُوا۟ لَا يَحِلُّ لَكُمْ أَن تَرِثُوا۟ ٱلنِّسَآءَ كَرْهًا ۖ وَلَا تَعْضُلُوهُنَّ لِتَذْهَبُوا۟ بِبَعْضِ
مَآ ءَاتَيْتُمُوهُنَّ إِلَّآ أَن يَأْتِينَ بِفَٰحِشَةٍ مُّبَيِّنَةٍ ۚ وَعَاشِرُوهُنَّ بِٱلْمَعْرُوفِ ۚ فَإِن كَرِهْتُمُوهُنَّ
فَعَسَىٰٓ أَن تَكْرَهُوا۟ شَيْـًٔا وَيَجْعَلَ ٱللَّهُ فِيهِ خَيْرًا كَثِيرًا ﴿١٩﴾ ﴾

19. O you who believe! You are forbidden to inherit women against their will; and you should not treat them with harshness, that you may take away part of the Mahr you have given them, unless they commit open illegal sexual intercourse; And live with them honorably. If you dislike them, it may be that you dislike a thing and Allâh brings through it a great deal of good.

﴿ وَإِنْ أَرَدتُّمُ ٱسْتِبْدَالَ زَوْجٍ مَّكَانَ زَوْجٍ وَءَاتَيْتُمْ إِحْدَىٰهُنَّ قِنطَارًا فَلَا تَأْخُذُوا۟ مِنْهُ
شَيْـًٔا ۚ أَتَأْخُذُونَهُۥ بُهْتَٰنًا وَإِثْمًا مُّبِينًا ﴿٢٠﴾ ﴾

20. But if you intend to replace a wife by another and you have given one of them a Qintar (of gold i.e. a great amount) as Mahr, take not the least bit of it back; would you take it wrongfully without a right and (with) a manifest sin?

﴿ وَكَيْفَ تَأْخُذُونَهُۥ وَقَدْ أَفْضَىٰ بَعْضُكُمْ إِلَىٰ بَعْضٍ وَأَخَذْنَ مِنكُم مِّيثَٰقًا
غَلِيظًا ﴿٢١﴾ ﴾

21. And how could you take it (back) while you have gone in unto each other, and they have taken from you a firm and strong covenant?

﴿ وَلَا تَنكِحُوا۟ مَا نَكَحَ ءَابَآؤُكُم مِّنَ ٱلنِّسَآءِ إِلَّا مَا قَدْ سَلَفَ ۚ إِنَّهُۥ كَانَ فَٰحِشَةً
وَمَقْتًا وَسَآءَ سَبِيلًا ﴿٢٢﴾ ﴾

22. And marry not women whom your fathers married, except what has already passed; indeed it was shameful and most hateful, and an evil way.

Transliteration

19. Ya ayyuha allatheena amanoo la yahillu lakum an tarithoo alnnisaa karhan wala taAAduloohunna litathhaboo bibaAAdi ma ataytumoohunna illa an ya/teena bifahishatin mubayyinatin waAAashiroohunna bialmaAAroofi fa-in karihtumoohunna faAAasa an takrahoo shay-an wayajAAala Allahu feehi khayran katheeran 20. Wa-in aradtumu istibdala zawjin makana zawjin waataytum ihdahunna qintaran fala ta/khuthoo minhu shay-an ata/khuthoonahu buhtanan wa-ithman mubeenan 21. Wakayfa ta/khuthoonahu waqad afda baAAdukum ila baAAdin waakhathna minkum meethaqan ghaleethan 22. Wala tankihoo ma

nakaha abaokum mina alnnisa-i illa ma qad salafa innahu kana fahishatan wamaqtan wasaa sabeelan

Tafsir Ibn Kathir

Meaning of `Inheriting Women Against Their Will

Al-Bukhari recorded that Ibn `Abbas said about the Ayah,

(O you who believe! You are not permitted to inherit women against their will,) "Before, the practice was that when a man dies, his male relatives used to have the right to do whatever they wanted with his wife. If one of them wants, he would marry her, give her in marriage, or prevent her from marriage, for they had more right to her than her own family. Thereafter, this Ayah was revealed about this practice,

(O you who believe! You are not permitted to inherit women against their will)."

Women Should not Be Treated with Harshness

Allah said,

(nor to prevent them from marriage, in order to take part of what you have given them,) Allah commands: Do not treat the woman harshly so that she gives back all or part of the dowry that she was given, or forfeits one of her rights by means of coercion and oppression. Allah's statement,

(unless they commit open Fahishah.) Ibn Mas`ud, Ibn `Abbas, Sa`id bin Al-Musayyib, Ash-Sha`bi, Al-Hasan Al-Basri, Muhammad bin Sirin, Sa`id bin Jubayr, Mujahid, `Ikrimah, `Ata' Al-Khurasani, Ad-Dahhak, Abu Qilabah, Abu Salih, As-Suddi, Zayd bin Aslam and Sa`id bin Abi Hilal said that this refers to illicit sex. Meaning that if the wife commits adultery, you are allowed to take back the dowry you gave her. You are also allowed to annoy her, until she gives back the dowry in return for a Khula`." In Surat Al-Baqarah, Allah said,

(And it is not lawful for you (men) to take back (from your wives) any of what you have given them, except when both parties fear that they would be unable to keep the limits ordained by Allah) (2:229). Ibn `Abbas, `Ikrimah and Ad-Dahhak said that Fahishah refers to disobedience and defiance. Ibn Jarir chose the view that it is general, encompasses all these meanings, adultery, disobedience, defiance, rudeness, and so forth. Meaning that he is allowed to annoy his wife when she does any of these acts until she forfeits all or part of her rights and he then separates from her, and this (view) is good, and Allah knows best.

Live With Women Honorably

Allah said,

(And live with them honorably), by saying kind words to them, treating them kindly and making your appearance appealing for them, as much as you can, just as you like the same from them. Allah said in another Ayah,

(And they have rights similar over them to what is reasonable) (2:228). The Messenger of Allah said,

«خَيْرُكُمْ خَيْرُكُمْ لِأَهْلِهِ، وَأَنَا خَيْرُكُمْ لِأَهْلِي»

(The best among you is he who is the best with his family. Verily, I am the best one among you with my family.) It was the practice of the Messenger of Allah to be kind, cheerful, playful with his wives, compassionate, spending on them and laughing with them. The Messenger used to race with `A'ishah, the Mother of the Faithful, as a means of kindness to her. `A'ishah said, "The Messenger of Allah raced with me and I won the race. This occurred before I gained weight, and afterwards I raced with him again, and he won that race. He said,

«هذِهِ بِتِلْكَ»

(This (victory) is for that (victory).)" When the Prophet was at the home of one of his wives, sometimes all of his wives would meet there and eat together, and they would then go back to their homes. He and his wife would sleep in the same bed, he would remove his upper garment, sleeping in only his lower garment. The Prophet used to talk to the wife whose night it was, after praying `Isha' and before he went to sleep. Allah said,

(Indeed in the Messenger of Allah you have a good example to follow) (33:21). Allah said,

(If you dislike them, it may be that you dislike a thing and Allah brings through it a great deal of good.) Allah says that your patience, which is demonstrated by keeping wives whom you dislike, carries good rewards for you in this life and the Hereafter. Ibn `Abbas commented on this Ayah, "That the husband may feel compassion towards his wife and Allah gives him a child with her, and this child carries tremendous goodness." An authentic Hadith states,

«لَا يَفْرَكْ مُؤْمِنٌ مُؤْمِنَةً، إِنْ سَخِطَ مِنْهَا خُلُقًا، رَضِيَ مِنْهَا آخَرَ»

(No believing man should hate his believing wife. If he dislikes a part of her conduct, he would surely like another.)

The Prohibition of Taking Back the Dowry

Allah said,

(But if you intend to replace a wife by another and you have given one of them a Qintar, take not the least bit of it back; would you take it wrongfully without a right and (with) a manifest sin) The Ayah commands: When one of you wants to divorce a wife and marry another one, he must not take any portion of the dowry he gave to the first wife, even if it were a Qintar of money. We mentioned the meaning of Qintar in the Tafsir of Surah Al `Imran. This Ayah is clear in its indication that the dowry could be substantial. `Umar bin Al-Khattab used to discourage giving a large dowry, but later on changed his view. Imam Ahmad recorded that Abu Al-`Ajfa' As-Sulami said that he heard `Umar bin Al-Khattab saying, "Do not exaggerate with the dowry of women, had this practice been an honor in this world or a part of Taqwa, then the Prophet would have had more right to practice it than you. The Messenger of Allah never gave any of his wives, nor did any of his daughters receive a dowry more than twelve Uwqiyah. A man used to pay a substantial dowry and thus conceal enmity towards his wife!" Ahmad and the collectors of Sunan collected this Hadith through various chains of narration, and At-Tirmidhi said, "Hasan Sahih". Al-Hafiz Abu Ya`la recorded that Masruq said, "`Umar bin

Al-Khattab stood up on the Minbar of the Messenger of Allah and said, `O people! Why do you exaggerate concerning the dowry given to women The Messenger of Allah and his Companions used to pay up to four hundred Dirhams for a dowry, or less than that. Had paying more for a dowry been a part of Taqwa or an honor, you would not have led them in this practice. Therefore, I do not want to hear about a man who pays more than four hundred Dirhams for a dowry.' He then went down the Minbar, but a woman from Quraysh said to him, `O Leader of the Faithful! You prohibited people from paying more than four hundred Dirhams in a dowry for women' He said, `Yes.' She said, `Have you not heard what Allah sent down in the Qur'an' He said, `Which part of it' She said, `Have you not heard Allah's statement,

(And you have given one of them a Qintar)' He said, `O Allah! Forgive me...' He then went back and stood up on the Minbar saying, `I had prohibited you from paying more than four hundred Dirhams in a dowry for women. So, let everyone pay what he likes from his money.'" The chain of narration for this Hadith is strong.

(And how could you take it (back) while you have gone in unto each other) how can you take back the dowry from the woman with whom you had sexual relations and she had sexual relations with you Ibn `Abbas, Mujahid, As-Suddi and several others said that this means sexual intercourse. The Two Sahihs record that the Messenger of Allah said three times to the spouses who said the Mula`anah;

«اللهُ يَعْلَمُ أَنَّ أَحَدَكُمَا كَاذِبٌ، فَهَلْ مِنْكُمَا تَائِبٌ؟»

(Allah knows that one of you is a liar, so would any of you repent) The man said, "O Messenger of Allah! My money," referring to the dowry that he gave his wife. The Messenger said,

«لَا مَالَ لَكَ، إِنْ كُنْتَ صَدَقْتَ عَلَيْهَا فَهُوَ بِمَا اسْتَحْلَلْتَ مِنْ فَرْجِهَا، وَإِنْ كُنْتَ كَذَبْتَ عَلَيْهَا فَهُوَ أَبْعَدُ لَكَ مِنْهَا»

(You have no money. If you are the one who said the truth, the dowry is in return for the right to have sexual intercourse with her. If you are the one who uttered the lie, then this money is even farther from your reach.) Similarly Allah said;

(And how could you take it (back) while you have gone in unto each other and they have taken from you a firm and strong covenant) (Be kind with women, for you have taken them by Allah's covenant and earned the right to have sexual relations with them by Allah's Word.)

Marrying the Wife of the Father is Prohibited

Allah said,

(And marry not women whom your fathers married,) Allah prohibits marrying the women whom the father married, in honor and respect to the fathers, not allowing their children to have sexual relations with their wives after they die. A woman becomes ineligible for the son of her husband as soon as the marriage contract is conducted, and there is a consensus on this ruling. Ibn Jarir recorded that Ibn `Abbas said, "During the time of Jahiliyyah, the people used to prohibit what Allah prohibits (concerning marriage), except marrying the stepmother and taking two sisters as rival wives. Allah sent down,

(And marry not women whom your fathers married,) and,

(and two sisters in wedlock at the same time) (4:23)." Similar was reported from `Ata' and Qatadah. Therefore, the practice that the Ayah mentions is prohibited for this Ummah, being disgraced as an awful sin, r

(Indeed it was shameful and Maqtan, and an evil way.) Allah said in other Ayat,

(Come not near to Al-Fawahish (shameful acts) whether committed openly or secretly) (6:151), and,

(And come not near to unlawful sex. Verily, it is a Fahishah and an evil way.) (17:32) In this Ayah (4:22), Allah added,

(and Maqtan), meaning, offensive. It is a sin itself and causes the son to hate his father after he marries his wife. It is usual that whoever marries a woman dislikes those who married her before him. This is one reason why the Mothers of the Faithful were not allowed for anyone in marriage after the Messenger . They are indeed the Mothers of the Faithful since they married the Messenger , who is like the father to the believers. Rather, the Prophet's right is far greater than the right of a father, and his love comes before each person loving himself, may Allah's peace and blessings be on him. `Ata' bin Abi Rabah said that the Ayah,

(and Maqtan), means, Allah will hate him,

(and an evil way), for those who take this way. Therefore, those who commit this practice will have committed an act of reversion from the religion and deserve capital punishment and confiscation of their property, which will be given to the Muslim Treasury. Imam Ahmad and the collectors of Sunan recorded that Al-Bara' bin `Azib said that his uncle Abu Burdah was sent by the Messenger of Allah to a man who married his stepmother to execute him and confiscate his money.

Surah: 4 Ayah: 23

﴿ حُرِّمَتْ عَلَيْكُمْ أُمَّهَٰتُكُمْ وَبَنَاتُكُمْ وَأَخَوَٰتُكُمْ وَعَمَّٰتُكُمْ وَخَٰلَٰتُكُمْ وَبَنَاتُ ٱلْأَخِ
وَبَنَاتُ ٱلْأُخْتِ وَأُمَّهَٰتُكُمُ ٱلَّٰتِىٓ أَرْضَعْنَكُمْ وَأَخَوَٰتُكُم مِّنَ ٱلرَّضَٰعَةِ وَأُمَّهَٰتُ
نِسَآئِكُمْ وَرَبَٰٓئِبُكُمُ ٱلَّٰتِى فِى حُجُورِكُم مِّن نِّسَآئِكُمُ ٱلَّٰتِى دَخَلْتُم بِهِنَّ فَإِن لَّمْ تَكُونُوا۟
دَخَلْتُم بِهِنَّ فَلَا جُنَاحَ عَلَيْكُمْ وَحَلَٰٓئِلُ أَبْنَآئِكُمُ ٱلَّذِينَ مِنْ أَصْلَٰبِكُمْ وَأَن
تَجْمَعُوا۟ بَيْنَ ٱلْأُخْتَيْنِ إِلَّا مَا قَدْ سَلَفَ ۗ إِنَّ ٱللَّهَ كَانَ غَفُورًا رَّحِيمًا ﴿٢٣﴾

23. Forbidden to you (for marriage) are: your mothers, your daughters, your sisters, your father's sisters, your mother's sisters, your brother's daughters, your sister's daughters, your foster mother who gave you suck, your foster milk suckling sisters, your wives' mothers, your step daughters under your guardianship, born of your wives to whom you have gone in - but there is no sin on you if you have not gone in them (to marry their

daughters), - the wives of your sons who (spring) from your own loins, and two sisters in wedlock at the same time, except for what has already passed; verily, Allâh is Oft-Forgiving, Most Merciful.

Transliteration

23. Hurrimat AAalaykum ommahatukum wabanatukum waakhawatukum waAAammatukum wakhalatukum wabanatu al-akhi wabanatu al-okhti waommahatukumu allatee ardaAAnakum waakhawatukum mina alrradaAAati waommahatu nisa-ikum waraba-ibukumu allatee fee hujoorikum min nisa-ikumu allatee dakhaltum bihinna fa-in lam takoonoo dakhaltum bihinna fala junaha AAalaykum wahala-ilu abna-ikumu allatheena min aslabikum waan tajmaAAoo bayna al-okhtayni illa ma qad salafa inna Allaha kana ghafooran raheeman

Tafsir Ibn Kathir

Degrees of Women Never Eligible for One to Marry

This honorable Ayah is the Ayah that establishes the degrees of women relatives who are never eligible for one to marry, because of blood relations, relations established by suckling or marriage. Ibn Abi Hatim recorded that Ibn `Abbas said, "(Allah said) I have prohibited for you seven types of relatives by blood and seven by marriage." Ibn `Abbas then recited the Ayah,

(Forbidden to you (for marriage) are: your mothers, your daughters, your sisters...) At-Tabari recorded that Ibn `Abbas said, "Seven degrees of blood relation and seven degrees of marriage relation are prohibited (for marriage)." He then recited the Ayah,

(Forbidden to you (for marriage) are: your mothers, your daughters, your sisters, your father's sisters, your mother's sisters, your brother's daughters, your sister's daughters) and these are the types prohibited by blood relation." Allah's statement,

(Your foster mothers who suckled you, your foster milk suckling sisters) means, just as your mother who bore you is prohibited for you in marriage, so is your mother from suckling prohibited for you. Al-Bukhari and Muslim recorded that `A'ishah, the Mother of the Faithful, said that the Messenger of Allah said,

«إِنَّ الرَّضَاعَةَ تُحَرِّمُ مَا تُحَرِّمُ الْوِلَادَةُ»

(Suckling prohibits what birth prohibits.) In another narration reported by Muslim,

«يَحْرُمُ مِنَ الرَّضَاعَةِ مَا يَحْرُمُ مِنَ النَّسَب»

(Suckling establishes prohibited degrees just as blood does.)

`Suckling' that Establishes Prohibition for Marriage

Less than five incidents of suckling will not establish prohibition for marriage. In his Sahih, Muslim recorded that `A'ishah said, "Among the parts of the Qur'an that were revealed, is the statement, `Ten incidents of suckling establishes the prohibition (concerning marriage).' It was later abrogated with five, and the Messenger of Allah died while this statement was still recited as part of the Qur'an.'" A Hadith that Sahlah bint Suhayl narrated states that the

Messenger of Allah ordered her to suckle Salim the freed slave of Abu Hudhayfah with five." We should assert that the suckling mentioned here must occur before the age of two, as we stated when we explained the Ayah in Surat Al-Baqarah,

((The mothers) should suckle their children for two whole years, (that is) for those (parents) who desire to complete the term of suckling) (2:233). The Mother-in-Law and Stepdaughter are Prohibited in Marriage Allah said next,

(Your wives' mothers, your stepdaughters under your guardianship, born of your wives unto whom you have gone in - but there is no sin on you if you have not gone in unto them,) As for the mother of the wife, she becomes prohibited for marriage for her son-in-law when the marriage is conducted, whether the son-in-law has sexual relations with her daughter or not. As for the wife's daughter, she becomes prohibited for her stepfather when he has sexual relations with her mother, after the marriage contract is ratified. If the man divorces the mother before having sexual relations with her, he is allowed to marry her daughter. So Allah said;

(Your stepdaughters under your guardianship, born of your wives unto whom you have gone in -- but there is no sin on you if you have not gone in unto them,) to marry the stepdaughter.

The Stepdaughter is Prohibited in Marriage Even if She Was Not Under the Guardianship of Her Stepfather

Allah said,

(...your stepdaughters under your guardianship,) The majority of scholars state that the stepdaughter is prohibited in marriage for her stepfather (who consummated his marriage to her mother) whether she was under his guardianship or not. The Two Sahih recorded that Umm Habibah said, "O Messenger of Allah! Marry my sister, the daughter of Abu Sufyan (and in one narration `Azzah bint Abu Sufyan)." He said,

«أَوَ تُحِبِّينَ ذلِكِ»

("Do you like that I do that" She said, "I would not give you up for anything, but the best of whom I like to share with me in that which is righteously good, is my sister." He said,

«فَإِنَّ ذلِكِ لَا يَحِلُّ لِي»

"That is not allowed for me." She said, "We were told that you want to marry the daughter of Abu Salamah." He asked,

«بِنْتَ أُمِّ سَلَمَةَ»

"The daughter of Umm Salamah" She said, "Yes." He said,

«إِنَّهَا لَوْ لَمْ تَكُنْ رَبِيبَتِي فِي حِجْرِي مَا حَلَّتْ لِي، إِنَّهَا لَبِنْتُ أَخِي مِنَ الرَّضَاعَةِ، أَرْضَعَتْنِي وَأَبَا سَلَمَةَ ثُوَيْبَةُ، فَلَا تَعْرِضْنَ عَلَيَّ بَنَاتِكُنَّ وَلَا أَخَوَاتِكُنَّ»

"Even if she was not my stepdaughter and under my guardianship, she is still not allowed for me because she is my niece from suckling, for Thuwaybah suckled me and Abu Salamah. Therefore, do not offer me to marry your daughters or sisters. ") In another narration from Al-Bukhari,

«إِنِّي لَوْ لَمْ أَتَزَوَّجْ أُمَّ سَلَمَةَ مَا حَلَّتْ لِي»

(Had I not married Umm Salamah, her daughter would not have been allowed for me anyway.) Consequently, the Messenger stated that his marriage to Umm Salamah was the real reason behind that prohibition.

Meaning of `gone in unto them

The Ayah continues,

(Your wives unto whom you have gone in), meaning, had sexual relations with them, according to Ibn `Abbas and several others.

Prohibiting the Daughter-in-Law for Marriage

Allah said,

(The wives of your sons who (spring) from your own loins,) Therefore, you are prohibited to marry the wives of your own sons, but not the wives of your adopted sons, as adoption was common practice in Jahiliyyah. Allah said,

(So when Zayd had accomplished his desire from her (i.e. divorced her), We gave her to you in marriage, so that (in future) there may be no difficulty to the believers in respect of (the marriage of) the wives of their adopted sons when the latter have no desire to keep them (i.e. they had divorced them).) (33:37) Ibn Jurayj said, "I asked `Ata' about Allah's statement,

(The wives of your sons who (spring) from your own loins,) He said, `We were told that when the Prophet married the ex-wife of Zayd (who was the Prophet's adopted son before Islam prohibited this practice), the idolators in Makkah criticized him. Allah sent down the Ayat:

(The wives of your sons who (spring) from your own loins),

(nor has He made your adopted sons your real sons.) (33:4), and,

(Muhammad is not the father of any of your men) (33:40).'" Ibn Abi Hatim recorded that Al-Hasan bin Muhammad said, "These Ayat are encompassing,

(the wives of your sons), and,

(your wives' mothers). This is also the explanation of Tawus, Ibrahim, Az-Zuhri and Makhul. It means that these two Ayat encompass these types of women, whether the marriage was consummated or not, and there is a consensus on this ruling.

A Doubt and Rebuttal

Why is the wife of one's son from suckling prohibited for him for marriage - that is, if she is no longer married to his son from suckling - as the majority of scholars state, although they are not related by blood The answer is the Prophet's statement,

«يَحْرُمُ مِنَ الرَّضَاعِ مَا يَحْرُمُ مِنَ النَّسَبِ»

(Suckling prohibits what blood relations prohibit.)

The Prohibition of Taking Two Sisters as Rival Wives

Allah said,

(...and two sisters in wedlock at the same time, except for what has already passed;) The Ayah commands: you are prohibited to take two sisters as rival wives, or rival female-servants, except for what had happened to you during the time of Jahiliyyah, which We have forgiven and erased. Therefore, no one is allowed to take or keep two sisters as rival wives, according to the consensus of the scholars of the Companions, their followers, and the Imams of old and present. They all stated that taking two sisters as rival wives is prohibited, and that whoever embraces Islam while married to two sisters at the same time is given the choice to keep one of them and divorce the other. Imam Ahmad recorded that Ad-Dahhak bin Fayruz said that his father said, "I embraced Islam while married to two sisters at the same time and the Prophet commanded me to divorce one of them."

The Glorious Qur'an Juz' 5 (Part 5): Chapter (Surah) 4: An-Nisaa (The Women) 024 To Chapter (Surah) 4: An-Nisaa (The Women) 147

PART 5 FULL ARABIC TEXT

Chapter (Surah) 4: An-Nisaa 024-147

۞ وَٱلْمُحْصَنَٰتُ مِنَ ٱلنِّسَآءِ إِلَّا مَا مَلَكَتْ أَيْمَٰنُكُمْ ۖ كِتَٰبَ ٱللَّهِ عَلَيْكُمْ ۚ وَأُحِلَّ لَكُم مَّا
وَرَآءَ ذَٰلِكُمْ أَن تَبْتَغُوا۟ بِأَمْوَٰلِكُم مُّحْصِنِينَ غَيْرَ مُسَٰفِحِينَ ۚ فَمَا ٱسْتَمْتَعْتُم بِهِۦ مِنْهُنَّ
فَـَٔاتُوهُنَّ أُجُورَهُنَّ فَرِيضَةً ۚ وَلَا جُنَاحَ عَلَيْكُمْ فِيمَا تَرَٰضَيْتُم بِهِۦ مِنۢ بَعْدِ ٱلْفَرِيضَةِ ۚ
إِنَّ ٱللَّهَ كَانَ عَلِيمًا حَكِيمًا ﴿٢٤﴾ وَمَن لَّمْ يَسْتَطِعْ مِنكُمْ طَوْلًا أَن يَنكِحَ ٱلْمُحْصَنَٰتِ
ٱلْمُؤْمِنَٰتِ فَمِن مَّا مَلَكَتْ أَيْمَٰنُكُم مِّن فَتَيَٰتِكُمُ ٱلْمُؤْمِنَٰتِ ۚ وَٱللَّهُ أَعْلَمُ بِإِيمَٰنِكُم ۚ
بَعْضُكُم مِّنۢ بَعْضٍ ۚ فَٱنكِحُوهُنَّ بِإِذْنِ أَهْلِهِنَّ وَءَاتُوهُنَّ أُجُورَهُنَّ بِٱلْمَعْرُوفِ مُحْصَنَٰتٍ
غَيْرَ مُسَٰفِحَٰتٍ وَلَا مُتَّخِذَٰتِ أَخْدَانٍ ۚ فَإِذَآ أُحْصِنَّ فَإِنْ أَتَيْنَ بِفَٰحِشَةٍ فَعَلَيْهِنَّ
نِصْفُ مَا عَلَى ٱلْمُحْصَنَٰتِ مِنَ ٱلْعَذَابِ ۚ ذَٰلِكَ لِمَنْ خَشِىَ ٱلْعَنَتَ مِنكُمْ ۚ وَأَن تَصْبِرُوا۟
خَيْرٌ لَّكُمْ ۗ وَٱللَّهُ غَفُورٌ رَّحِيمٌ ﴿٢٥﴾ يُرِيدُ ٱللَّهُ لِيُبَيِّنَ لَكُمْ وَيَهْدِيَكُمْ سُنَنَ ٱلَّذِينَ مِن
قَبْلِكُمْ وَيَتُوبَ عَلَيْكُمْ ۗ وَٱللَّهُ عَلِيمٌ حَكِيمٌ ﴿٢٦﴾ وَٱللَّهُ يُرِيدُ أَن يَتُوبَ عَلَيْكُمْ وَيُرِيدُ
ٱلَّذِينَ يَتَّبِعُونَ ٱلشَّهَوَٰتِ أَن تَمِيلُوا۟ مَيْلًا عَظِيمًا ﴿٢٧﴾ يُرِيدُ ٱللَّهُ أَن يُخَفِّفَ عَنكُمْ ۚ وَخُلِقَ
ٱلْإِنسَٰنُ ضَعِيفًا ﴿٢٨﴾ يَٰٓأَيُّهَا ٱلَّذِينَ ءَامَنُوا۟ لَا تَأْكُلُوٓا۟ أَمْوَٰلَكُم بَيْنَكُم بِٱلْبَٰطِلِ إِلَّآ
أَن تَكُونَ تِجَٰرَةً عَن تَرَاضٍ مِّنكُمْ ۚ وَلَا تَقْتُلُوٓا۟ أَنفُسَكُمْ ۚ إِنَّ ٱللَّهَ كَانَ بِكُمْ رَحِيمًا ﴿٢٩﴾
وَمَن يَفْعَلْ ذَٰلِكَ عُدْوَٰنًا وَظُلْمًا فَسَوْفَ نُصْلِيهِ نَارًا ۚ وَكَانَ ذَٰلِكَ عَلَى ٱللَّهِ يَسِيرًا ﴿٣٠﴾
إِن تَجْتَنِبُوا۟ كَبَآئِرَ مَا تُنْهَوْنَ عَنْهُ نُكَفِّرْ عَنكُمْ سَيِّـَٔاتِكُمْ وَنُدْخِلْكُم مُّدْخَلًا كَرِيمًا ﴿٣١﴾
وَلَا تَتَمَنَّوْا۟ مَا فَضَّلَ ٱللَّهُ بِهِۦ بَعْضَكُمْ عَلَىٰ بَعْضٍ ۚ لِّلرِّجَالِ نَصِيبٌ مِّمَّا ٱكْتَسَبُوا۟ ۖ
وَلِلنِّسَآءِ نَصِيبٌ مِّمَّا ٱكْتَسَبْنَ ۚ وَسْـَٔلُوا۟ ٱللَّهَ مِن فَضْلِهِۦٓ ۗ إِنَّ ٱللَّهَ كَانَ بِكُلِّ شَىْءٍ

عَلِيمًا (٣٢) وَلِكُلٍّ جَعَلْنَا مَوَٰلِىَ مِمَّا تَرَكَ ٱلْوَٰلِدَانِ وَٱلْأَقْرَبُونَ ۚ وَٱلَّذِينَ عَقَدَتْ
أَيْمَـٰنُكُمْ فَـَٔاتُوهُمْ نَصِيبَهُمْ ۚ إِنَّ ٱللَّهَ كَانَ عَلَىٰ كُلِّ شَىْءٍ شَهِيدًا (٣٣) ٱلرِّجَالُ
قَوَّٰمُونَ عَلَى ٱلنِّسَآءِ بِمَا فَضَّلَ ٱللَّهُ بَعْضَهُمْ عَلَىٰ بَعْضٍ وَبِمَآ أَنفَقُوا۟ مِنْ أَمْوَٰلِهِمْ ۚ
فَٱلصَّـٰلِحَـٰتُ قَـٰنِتَـٰتٌ حَـٰفِظَـٰتٌ لِّلْغَيْبِ بِمَا حَفِظَ ٱللَّهُ ۚ وَٱلَّـٰتِى تَخَافُونَ نُشُوزَهُنَّ
فَعِظُوهُنَّ وَٱهْجُرُوهُنَّ فِى ٱلْمَضَاجِعِ وَٱضْرِبُوهُنَّ ۖ فَإِنْ أَطَعْنَكُمْ فَلَا تَبْغُوا۟ عَلَيْهِنَّ
سَبِيلًا ۗ إِنَّ ٱللَّهَ كَانَ عَلِيًّا كَبِيرًا (٣٤) وَإِنْ خِفْتُمْ شِقَاقَ بَيْنِهِمَا فَٱبْعَثُوا۟ حَكَمًا مِّنْ
أَهْلِهِۦ وَحَكَمًا مِّنْ أَهْلِهَآ إِن يُرِيدَآ إِصْلَـٰحًا يُوَفِّقِ ٱللَّهُ بَيْنَهُمَآ ۗ إِنَّ ٱللَّهَ كَانَ عَلِيمًا خَبِيرًا (٣٥)
۞ وَٱعْبُدُوا۟ ٱللَّهَ وَلَا تُشْرِكُوا۟ بِهِۦ شَيْـًٔا ۖ وَبِٱلْوَٰلِدَيْنِ إِحْسَـٰنًا وَبِذِى ٱلْقُرْبَىٰ وَٱلْيَتَـٰمَىٰ
وَٱلْمَسَـٰكِينِ وَٱلْجَارِ ذِى ٱلْقُرْبَىٰ وَٱلْجَارِ ٱلْجُنُبِ وَٱلصَّاحِبِ بِٱلْجَنۢبِ وَٱبْنِ ٱلسَّبِيلِ وَمَا
مَلَكَتْ أَيْمَـٰنُكُمْ ۗ إِنَّ ٱللَّهَ لَا يُحِبُّ مَن كَانَ مُخْتَالًا فَخُورًا (٣٦) ٱلَّذِينَ يَبْخَلُونَ وَيَأْمُرُونَ
ٱلنَّاسَ بِٱلْبُخْلِ وَيَكْتُمُونَ مَآ ءَاتَىٰهُمُ ٱللَّهُ مِن فَضْلِهِۦ ۗ وَأَعْتَدْنَا لِلْكَـٰفِرِينَ
عَذَابًا مُّهِينًا (٣٧) وَٱلَّذِينَ يُنفِقُونَ أَمْوَٰلَهُمْ رِئَآءَ ٱلنَّاسِ وَلَا يُؤْمِنُونَ بِٱللَّهِ وَلَا
بِٱلْيَوْمِ ٱلْـَٔاخِرِ ۗ وَمَن يَكُنِ ٱلشَّيْطَـٰنُ لَهُۥ قَرِينًا فَسَآءَ قَرِينًا (٣٨) وَمَاذَا عَلَيْهِمْ لَوْ ءَامَنُوا۟ بِٱللَّهِ
وَٱلْيَوْمِ ٱلْـَٔاخِرِ وَأَنفَقُوا۟ مِمَّا رَزَقَهُمُ ٱللَّهُ ۚ وَكَانَ ٱللَّهُ بِهِمْ عَلِيمًا (٣٩) إِنَّ ٱللَّهَ لَا يَظْلِمُ مِثْقَالَ
ذَرَّةٍ ۖ وَإِن تَكُ حَسَنَةً يُضَـٰعِفْهَا وَيُؤْتِ مِن لَّدُنْهُ أَجْرًا عَظِيمًا (٤٠) فَكَيْفَ إِذَا جِئْنَا مِن
كُلِّ أُمَّةٍۭ بِشَهِيدٍ وَجِئْنَا بِكَ عَلَىٰ هَـٰٓؤُلَآءِ شَهِيدًا (٤١) يَوْمَئِذٍ يَوَدُّ ٱلَّذِينَ كَفَرُوا۟ وَعَصَوُا۟
ٱلرَّسُولَ لَوْ تُسَوَّىٰ بِهِمُ ٱلْأَرْضُ وَلَا يَكْتُمُونَ ٱللَّهَ حَدِيثًا (٤٢) يَـٰٓأَيُّهَا ٱلَّذِينَ ءَامَنُوا۟ لَا تَقْرَبُوا۟
ٱلصَّلَوٰةَ وَأَنتُمْ سُكَـٰرَىٰ حَتَّىٰ تَعْلَمُوا۟ مَا تَقُولُونَ وَلَا جُنُبًا إِلَّا عَابِرِى سَبِيلٍ حَتَّىٰ
تَغْتَسِلُوا۟ ۚ وَإِن كُنتُم مَّرْضَىٰٓ أَوْ عَلَىٰ سَفَرٍ أَوْ جَآءَ أَحَدٌ مِّنكُم مِّنَ ٱلْغَآئِطِ أَوْ لَـٰمَسْتُمُ ٱلنِّسَآءَ
فَلَمْ تَجِدُوا۟ مَآءً فَتَيَمَّمُوا۟ صَعِيدًا طَيِّبًا فَٱمْسَحُوا۟ بِوُجُوهِكُمْ وَأَيْدِيكُمْ ۗ إِنَّ ٱللَّهَ كَانَ عَفُوًّا
غَفُورًا (٤٣) أَلَمْ تَرَ إِلَى ٱلَّذِينَ أُوتُوا۟ نَصِيبًا مِّنَ ٱلْكِتَـٰبِ يَشْتَرُونَ ٱلضَّلَـٰلَةَ وَيُرِيدُونَ أَن
تَضِلُّوا۟ ٱلسَّبِيلَ (٤٤) وَٱللَّهُ أَعْلَمُ بِأَعْدَآئِكُمْ ۚ وَكَفَىٰ بِٱللَّهِ وَلِيًّا وَكَفَىٰ بِٱللَّهِ نَصِيرًا (٤٥) مِّنَ

ٱلَّذِينَ هَادُوا۟ يُحَرِّفُونَ ٱلْكَلِمَ عَن مَّوَاضِعِهِۦ وَيَقُولُونَ سَمِعْنَا وَعَصَيْنَا وَٱسْمَعْ غَيْرَ مُسْمَعٍ
وَرَٰعِنَا لَيًّۢا بِأَلْسِنَتِهِمْ وَطَعْنًا فِى ٱلدِّينِ ۚ وَلَوْ أَنَّهُمْ قَالُوا۟ سَمِعْنَا وَأَطَعْنَا وَٱسْمَعْ وَٱنظُرْنَا لَكَانَ
خَيْرًا لَّهُمْ وَأَقْوَمَ وَلَٰكِن لَّعَنَهُمُ ٱللَّهُ بِكُفْرِهِمْ فَلَا يُؤْمِنُونَ إِلَّا قَلِيلًا ﴿٤٦﴾ يَٰٓأَيُّهَا ٱلَّذِينَ أُوتُوا۟
ٱلْكِتَٰبَ ءَامِنُوا۟ بِمَا نَزَّلْنَا مُصَدِّقًا لِّمَا مَعَكُم مِّن قَبْلِ أَن نَّطْمِسَ وُجُوهًا فَنَرُدَّهَا عَلَىٰٓ
أَدْبَارِهَآ أَوْ نَلْعَنَهُمْ كَمَا لَعَنَّآ أَصْحَٰبَ ٱلسَّبْتِ ۚ وَكَانَ أَمْرُ ٱللَّهِ مَفْعُولًا ﴿٤٧﴾ إِنَّ ٱللَّهَ لَا يَغْفِرُ أَن
يُشْرَكَ بِهِۦ وَيَغْفِرُ مَا دُونَ ذَٰلِكَ لِمَن يَشَآءُ ۚ وَمَن يُشْرِكْ بِٱللَّهِ فَقَدِ ٱفْتَرَىٰٓ إِثْمًا عَظِيمًا ﴿٤٨﴾
أَلَمْ تَرَ إِلَى ٱلَّذِينَ يُزَكُّونَ أَنفُسَهُم ۚ بَلِ ٱللَّهُ يُزَكِّى مَن يَشَآءُ وَلَا يُظْلَمُونَ فَتِيلًا ﴿٤٩﴾ ٱنظُرْ كَيْفَ
يَفْتَرُونَ عَلَى ٱللَّهِ ٱلْكَذِبَ ۖ وَكَفَىٰ بِهِۦٓ إِثْمًا مُّبِينًا ﴿٥٠﴾ أَلَمْ تَرَ إِلَى ٱلَّذِينَ أُوتُوا۟ نَصِيبًا مِّنَ
ٱلْكِتَٰبِ يُؤْمِنُونَ بِٱلْجِبْتِ وَٱلطَّٰغُوتِ وَيَقُولُونَ لِلَّذِينَ كَفَرُوا۟ هَٰٓؤُلَآءِ أَهْدَىٰ مِنَ ٱلَّذِينَ
ءَامَنُوا۟ سَبِيلًا ﴿٥١﴾ أُو۟لَٰٓئِكَ ٱلَّذِينَ لَعَنَهُمُ ٱللَّهُ ۖ وَمَن يَلْعَنِ ٱللَّهُ فَلَن تَجِدَ لَهُۥ نَصِيرًا ﴿٥٢﴾ أَمْ لَهُمْ
نَصِيبٌ مِّنَ ٱلْمُلْكِ فَإِذًا لَّا يُؤْتُونَ ٱلنَّاسَ نَقِيرًا ﴿٥٣﴾ أَمْ يَحْسُدُونَ ٱلنَّاسَ عَلَىٰ مَآ ءَاتَىٰهُمُ
ٱللَّهُ مِن فَضْلِهِۦ ۖ فَقَدْ ءَاتَيْنَآ ءَالَ إِبْرَٰهِيمَ ٱلْكِتَٰبَ وَٱلْحِكْمَةَ وَءَاتَيْنَٰهُم مُّلْكًا عَظِيمًا ﴿٥٤﴾
فَمِنْهُم مَّنْ ءَامَنَ بِهِۦ وَمِنْهُم مَّن صَدَّ عَنْهُ ۚ وَكَفَىٰ بِجَهَنَّمَ سَعِيرًا ﴿٥٥﴾ إِنَّ ٱلَّذِينَ كَفَرُوا۟ بِـَٔايَٰتِنَا
سَوْفَ نُصْلِيهِمْ نَارًا كُلَّمَا نَضِجَتْ جُلُودُهُم بَدَّلْنَٰهُمْ جُلُودًا غَيْرَهَا لِيَذُوقُوا۟ ٱلْعَذَابَ ۗ
إِنَّ ٱللَّهَ كَانَ عَزِيزًا حَكِيمًا ﴿٥٦﴾ وَٱلَّذِينَ ءَامَنُوا۟ وَعَمِلُوا۟ ٱلصَّٰلِحَٰتِ سَنُدْخِلُهُمْ جَنَّٰتٍ
تَجْرِى مِن تَحْتِهَا ٱلْأَنْهَٰرُ خَٰلِدِينَ فِيهَآ أَبَدًا ۖ لَّهُمْ فِيهَآ أَزْوَٰجٌ مُّطَهَّرَةٌ ۖ وَنُدْخِلُهُمْ
ظِلًّا ظَلِيلًا ﴿٥٧﴾ ۞ إِنَّ ٱللَّهَ يَأْمُرُكُمْ أَن تُؤَدُّوا۟ ٱلْأَمَٰنَٰتِ إِلَىٰٓ أَهْلِهَا وَإِذَا حَكَمْتُم بَيْنَ ٱلنَّاسِ
أَن تَحْكُمُوا۟ بِٱلْعَدْلِ ۚ إِنَّ ٱللَّهَ نِعِمَّا يَعِظُكُم بِهِۦٓ ۗ إِنَّ ٱللَّهَ كَانَ سَمِيعًۢا بَصِيرًا ﴿٥٨﴾ يَٰٓأَيُّهَا ٱلَّذِينَ
ءَامَنُوٓا۟ أَطِيعُوا۟ ٱللَّهَ وَأَطِيعُوا۟ ٱلرَّسُولَ وَأُو۟لِى ٱلْأَمْرِ مِنكُمْ ۖ فَإِن تَنَٰزَعْتُمْ فِى شَىْءٍ فَرُدُّوهُ إِلَى
ٱللَّهِ وَٱلرَّسُولِ إِن كُنتُمْ تُؤْمِنُونَ بِٱللَّهِ وَٱلْيَوْمِ ٱلْءَاخِرِ ۚ ذَٰلِكَ خَيْرٌ وَأَحْسَنُ تَأْوِيلًا ﴿٥٩﴾ أَلَمْ تَرَ
إِلَى ٱلَّذِينَ يَزْعُمُونَ أَنَّهُمْ ءَامَنُوا۟ بِمَآ أُنزِلَ إِلَيْكَ وَمَآ أُنزِلَ مِن قَبْلِكَ يُرِيدُونَ أَن
يَتَحَاكَمُوٓا۟ إِلَى ٱلطَّٰغُوتِ وَقَدْ أُمِرُوٓا۟ أَن يَكْفُرُوا۟ بِهِۦ وَيُرِيدُ ٱلشَّيْطَٰنُ أَن يُضِلَّهُمْ ضَلَٰلًۢا

بَعِيدًا (٦٠) وَإِذَا قِيلَ لَهُمْ تَعَالَوْا۟ إِلَىٰ مَآ أَنزَلَ ٱللَّهُ وَإِلَى ٱلرَّسُولِ رَأَيْتَ ٱلْمُنَٰفِقِينَ يَصُدُّونَ
عَنكَ صُدُودًا (٦١) فَكَيْفَ إِذَآ أَصَٰبَتْهُم مُّصِيبَةٌۢ بِمَا قَدَّمَتْ أَيْدِيهِمْ ثُمَّ جَآءُوكَ يَحْلِفُونَ
بِٱللَّهِ إِنْ أَرَدْنَآ إِلَّآ إِحْسَٰنًا وَتَوْفِيقًا (٦٢) أُو۟لَٰٓئِكَ ٱلَّذِينَ يَعْلَمُ ٱللَّهُ مَا فِى قُلُوبِهِمْ فَأَعْرِضْ
عَنْهُمْ وَعِظْهُمْ وَقُل لَّهُمْ فِىٓ أَنفُسِهِمْ قَوْلًۢا بَلِيغًا (٦٣) وَمَآ أَرْسَلْنَا مِن رَّسُولٍ إِلَّا لِيُطَاعَ
بِإِذْنِ ٱللَّهِ ۚ وَلَوْ أَنَّهُمْ إِذ ظَّلَمُوٓا۟ أَنفُسَهُمْ جَآءُوكَ فَٱسْتَغْفَرُوا۟ ٱللَّهَ وَٱسْتَغْفَرَ لَهُمُ ٱلرَّسُولُ
لَوَجَدُوا۟ ٱللَّهَ تَوَّابًا رَّحِيمًا (٦٤) فَلَا وَرَبِّكَ لَا يُؤْمِنُونَ حَتَّىٰ يُحَكِّمُوكَ فِيمَا شَجَرَ
بَيْنَهُمْ ثُمَّ لَا يَجِدُوا۟ فِىٓ أَنفُسِهِمْ حَرَجًا مِّمَّا قَضَيْتَ وَيُسَلِّمُوا۟ تَسْلِيمًا (٦٥) وَلَوْ أَنَّا كَتَبْنَا
عَلَيْهِمْ أَنِ ٱقْتُلُوٓا۟ أَنفُسَكُمْ أَوِ ٱخْرُجُوا۟ مِن دِيَٰرِكُم مَّا فَعَلُوهُ إِلَّا قَلِيلٌ مِّنْهُمْ ۖ وَلَوْ أَنَّهُمْ فَعَلُوا۟ مَا
يُوعَظُونَ بِهِۦ لَكَانَ خَيْرًا لَّهُمْ وَأَشَدَّ تَثْبِيتًا (٦٦) وَإِذًا لَّءَاتَيْنَٰهُم مِّن لَّدُنَّآ أَجْرًا عَظِيمًا (٦٧)
وَلَهَدَيْنَٰهُمْ صِرَٰطًا مُّسْتَقِيمًا (٦٨) وَمَن يُطِعِ ٱللَّهَ وَٱلرَّسُولَ فَأُو۟لَٰٓئِكَ مَعَ ٱلَّذِينَ أَنْعَمَ ٱللَّهُ
عَلَيْهِم مِّنَ ٱلنَّبِيِّۦنَ وَٱلصِّدِّيقِينَ وَٱلشُّهَدَآءِ وَٱلصَّٰلِحِينَ ۚ وَحَسُنَ أُو۟لَٰٓئِكَ رَفِيقًا (٦٩) ذَٰلِكَ
ٱلْفَضْلُ مِنَ ٱللَّهِ ۚ وَكَفَىٰ بِٱللَّهِ عَلِيمًا (٧٠) يَٰٓأَيُّهَا ٱلَّذِينَ ءَامَنُوا۟ خُذُوا۟ حِذْرَكُمْ فَٱنفِرُوا۟
ثُبَاتٍ أَوِ ٱنفِرُوا۟ جَمِيعًا (٧١) وَإِنَّ مِنكُمْ لَمَن لَّيُبَطِّئَنَّ فَإِنْ أَصَٰبَتْكُم مُّصِيبَةٌ قَالَ قَدْ أَنْعَمَ
ٱللَّهُ عَلَىَّ إِذْ لَمْ أَكُن مَّعَهُمْ شَهِيدًا (٧٢) وَلَئِنْ أَصَٰبَكُمْ فَضْلٌ مِّنَ ٱللَّهِ لَيَقُولَنَّ كَأَن لَّمْ تَكُنۢ
بَيْنَكُمْ وَبَيْنَهُۥ مَوَدَّةٌ يَٰلَيْتَنِى كُنتُ مَعَهُمْ فَأَفُوزَ فَوْزًا عَظِيمًا (٧٣) ۞ فَلْيُقَٰتِلْ فِى سَبِيلِ ٱللَّهِ
ٱلَّذِينَ يَشْرُونَ ٱلْحَيَوٰةَ ٱلدُّنْيَا بِٱلْءَاخِرَةِ ۚ وَمَن يُقَٰتِلْ فِى سَبِيلِ ٱللَّهِ فَيُقْتَلْ أَوْ يَغْلِبْ
فَسَوْفَ نُؤْتِيهِ أَجْرًا عَظِيمًا (٧٤) وَمَا لَكُمْ لَا تُقَٰتِلُونَ فِى سَبِيلِ ٱللَّهِ وَٱلْمُسْتَضْعَفِينَ مِنَ
ٱلرِّجَالِ وَٱلنِّسَآءِ وَٱلْوِلْدَٰنِ ٱلَّذِينَ يَقُولُونَ رَبَّنَآ أَخْرِجْنَا مِنْ هَٰذِهِ ٱلْقَرْيَةِ ٱلظَّالِمِ أَهْلُهَا
وَٱجْعَل لَّنَا مِن لَّدُنكَ وَلِيًّا وَٱجْعَل لَّنَا مِن لَّدُنكَ نَصِيرًا (٧٥) ٱلَّذِينَ ءَامَنُوا۟ يُقَٰتِلُونَ فِى
سَبِيلِ ٱللَّهِ ۖ وَٱلَّذِينَ كَفَرُوا۟ يُقَٰتِلُونَ فِى سَبِيلِ ٱلطَّٰغُوتِ فَقَٰتِلُوٓا۟ أَوْلِيَآءَ ٱلشَّيْطَٰنِ ۖ إِنَّ كَيْدَ
ٱلشَّيْطَٰنِ كَانَ ضَعِيفًا (٧٦) أَلَمْ تَرَ إِلَى ٱلَّذِينَ قِيلَ لَهُمْ كُفُّوٓا۟ أَيْدِيَكُمْ وَأَقِيمُوا۟ ٱلصَّلَوٰةَ وَءَاتُوا۟
ٱلزَّكَوٰةَ فَلَمَّا كُتِبَ عَلَيْهِمُ ٱلْقِتَالُ إِذَا فَرِيقٌ مِّنْهُمْ يَخْشَوْنَ ٱلنَّاسَ كَخَشْيَةِ ٱللَّهِ أَوْ أَشَدَّ خَشْيَةً ۚ

وَقَالُواْ رَبَّنَا لِمَ كَتَبْتَ عَلَيْنَا ٱلْقِتَالَ لَوْلَآ أَخَّرْتَنَآ إِلَىٰٓ أَجَلٍ قَرِيبٍۗ قُلْ مَتَٰعُ ٱلدُّنْيَا قَلِيلٌ
وَٱلْأَخِرَةُ خَيْرٌ لِّمَنِ ٱتَّقَىٰ وَلَا تُظْلَمُونَ فَتِيلًا ﴿٧٧﴾ أَيْنَمَا تَكُونُواْ يُدْرِككُّمُ ٱلْمَوْتُ وَلَوْ
كُنتُمْ فِي بُرُوجٍ مُّشَيَّدَةٍۗ وَإِن تُصِبْهُمْ حَسَنَةٌ يَقُولُواْ هَٰذِهِۦ مِنْ عِندِ ٱللَّهِۖ وَإِن تُصِبْهُمْ سَيِّئَةٌ
يَقُولُواْ هَٰذِهِۦ مِنْ عِندِكَۚ قُلْ كُلٌّ مِّنْ عِندِ ٱللَّهِۖ فَمَالِ هَٰٓؤُلَآءِ ٱلْقَوْمِ لَا يَكَادُونَ يَفْقَهُونَ
حَدِيثًا ﴿٧٨﴾ مَّآ أَصَابَكَ مِنْ حَسَنَةٍ فَمِنَ ٱللَّهِۖ وَمَآ أَصَابَكَ مِن سَيِّئَةٍ فَمِن نَّفْسِكَۚ
وَأَرْسَلْنَٰكَ لِلنَّاسِ رَسُولًاۚ وَكَفَىٰ بِٱللَّهِ شَهِيدًا ﴿٧٩﴾ مَّن يُطِعِ ٱلرَّسُولَ فَقَدْ أَطَاعَ ٱللَّهَۖ وَمَن
تَوَلَّىٰ فَمَآ أَرْسَلْنَٰكَ عَلَيْهِمْ حَفِيظًا ﴿٨٠﴾ وَيَقُولُونَ طَاعَةٌ فَإِذَا بَرَزُواْ مِنْ عِندِكَ بَيَّتَ
طَآئِفَةٌ مِّنْهُمْ غَيْرَ ٱلَّذِي تَقُولُۖ وَٱللَّهُ يَكْتُبُ مَا يُبَيِّتُونَۖ فَأَعْرِضْ عَنْهُمْ وَتَوَكَّلْ عَلَى ٱللَّهِۚ
وَكَفَىٰ بِٱللَّهِ وَكِيلًا ﴿٨١﴾ أَفَلَا يَتَدَبَّرُونَ ٱلْقُرْءَانَۚ وَلَوْ كَانَ مِنْ عِندِ غَيْرِ ٱللَّهِ لَوَجَدُواْ فِيهِ
ٱخْتِلَٰفًا كَثِيرًا ﴿٨٢﴾ وَإِذَا جَآءَهُمْ أَمْرٌ مِّنَ ٱلْأَمْنِ أَوِ ٱلْخَوْفِ أَذَاعُواْ بِهِۦۖ وَلَوْ رَدُّوهُ إِلَى
ٱلرَّسُولِ وَإِلَىٰٓ أُوْلِي ٱلْأَمْرِ مِنْهُمْ لَعَلِمَهُ ٱلَّذِينَ يَسْتَنۢبِطُونَهُۥ مِنْهُمْۗ وَلَوْلَا فَضْلُ ٱللَّهِ
عَلَيْكُمْ وَرَحْمَتُهُۥ لَٱتَّبَعْتُمُ ٱلشَّيْطَٰنَ إِلَّا قَلِيلًا ﴿٨٣﴾ فَقَٰتِلْ فِي سَبِيلِ ٱللَّهِ لَا تُكَلَّفُ إِلَّا
نَفْسَكَۚ وَحَرِّضِ ٱلْمُؤْمِنِينَۖ عَسَى ٱللَّهُ أَن يَكُفَّ بَأْسَ ٱلَّذِينَ كَفَرُواْۚ وَٱللَّهُ أَشَدُّ بَأْسًا وَأَشَدُّ
تَنكِيلًا ﴿٨٤﴾ مَّن يَشْفَعْ شَفَٰعَةً حَسَنَةً يَكُن لَّهُۥ نَصِيبٌ مِّنْهَاۖ وَمَن يَشْفَعْ شَفَٰعَةً سَيِّئَةً يَكُن
لَّهُۥ كِفْلٌ مِّنْهَاۗ وَكَانَ ٱللَّهُ عَلَىٰ كُلِّ شَيْءٍ مُّقِيتًا ﴿٨٥﴾ وَإِذَا حُيِّيتُم بِتَحِيَّةٍ فَحَيُّواْ بِأَحْسَنَ مِنْهَآ
أَوْ رُدُّوهَآۗ إِنَّ ٱللَّهَ كَانَ عَلَىٰ كُلِّ شَيْءٍ حَسِيبًا ﴿٨٦﴾ ٱللَّهُ لَآ إِلَٰهَ إِلَّا هُوَۚ لَيَجْمَعَنَّكُمْ إِلَىٰ يَوْمِ
ٱلْقِيَٰمَةِ لَا رَيْبَ فِيهِۗ وَمَنْ أَصْدَقُ مِنَ ٱللَّهِ حَدِيثًا ﴿٨٧﴾ ۞ فَمَا لَكُمْ فِي ٱلْمُنَٰفِقِينَ فِئَتَيْنِ وَٱللَّهُ
أَرْكَسَهُم بِمَا كَسَبُوٓاْۚ أَتُرِيدُونَ أَن تَهْدُواْ مَنْ أَضَلَّ ٱللَّهُۖ وَمَن يُضْلِلِ ٱللَّهُ فَلَن تَجِدَ
لَهُۥ سَبِيلًا ﴿٨٨﴾ وَدُّواْ لَوْ تَكْفُرُونَ كَمَا كَفَرُواْ فَتَكُونُونَ سَوَآءًۖ فَلَا تَتَّخِذُواْ مِنْهُمْ أَوْلِيَآءَ
حَتَّىٰ يُهَاجِرُواْ فِي سَبِيلِ ٱللَّهِۚ فَإِن تَوَلَّوْاْ فَخُذُوهُمْ وَٱقْتُلُوهُمْ حَيْثُ وَجَدتُّمُوهُمْۖ وَلَا
تَتَّخِذُواْ مِنْهُمْ وَلِيًّا وَلَا نَصِيرًا ﴿٨٩﴾ إِلَّا ٱلَّذِينَ يَصِلُونَ إِلَىٰ قَوْمِۭ بَيْنَكُمْ وَبَيْنَهُم مِّيثَٰقٌ أَوْ
جَآءُوكُمْ حَصِرَتْ صُدُورُهُمْ أَن يُقَٰتِلُوكُمْ أَوْ يُقَٰتِلُواْ قَوْمَهُمْۚ وَلَوْ شَآءَ ٱللَّهُ لَسَلَّطَهُمْ عَلَيْكُمْ

فَلَقَـٰتَلُوكُمْ ۚ فَإِنِ ٱعْتَزَلُوكُمْ فَلَمْ يُقَـٰتِلُوكُمْ وَأَلْقَوْا۟ إِلَيْكُمُ ٱلسَّلَمَ فَمَا جَعَلَ ٱللَّهُ لَكُمْ عَلَيْهِمْ
سَبِيلًا ﴿٩٠﴾ سَتَجِدُونَ ءَاخَرِينَ يُرِيدُونَ أَن يَأْمَنُوكُمْ وَيَأْمَنُوا۟ قَوْمَهُمْ كُلَّ مَا رُدُّوٓا۟ إِلَى
ٱلْفِتْنَةِ أُرْكِسُوا۟ فِيهَا ۚ فَإِن لَّمْ يَعْتَزِلُوكُمْ وَيُلْقُوٓا۟ إِلَيْكُمُ ٱلسَّلَمَ وَيَكُفُّوٓا۟ أَيْدِيَهُمْ فَخُذُوهُمْ
وَٱقْتُلُوهُمْ حَيْثُ ثَقِفْتُمُوهُمْ ۚ وَأُو۟لَـٰٓئِكُمْ جَعَلْنَا لَكُمْ عَلَيْهِمْ سُلْطَـٰنًا مُّبِينًا ﴿٩١﴾ وَمَا كَانَ
لِمُؤْمِنٍ أَن يَقْتُلَ مُؤْمِنًا إِلَّا خَطَـًٔا ۚ وَمَن قَتَلَ مُؤْمِنًا خَطَـًٔا فَتَحْرِيرُ رَقَبَةٍ مُّؤْمِنَةٍ وَدِيَةٌ
مُّسَلَّمَةٌ إِلَىٰٓ أَهْلِهِۦٓ إِلَّآ أَن يَصَّدَّقُوا۟ ۚ فَإِن كَانَ مِن قَوْمٍ عَدُوٍّ لَّكُمْ وَهُوَ مُؤْمِنٌ فَتَحْرِيرُ
رَقَبَةٍ مُّؤْمِنَةٍ ۖ وَإِن كَانَ مِن قَوْمٍۭ بَيْنَكُمْ وَبَيْنَهُم مِّيثَـٰقٌ فَدِيَةٌ مُّسَلَّمَةٌ إِلَىٰٓ أَهْلِهِۦ
وَتَحْرِيرُ رَقَبَةٍ مُّؤْمِنَةٍ ۖ فَمَن لَّمْ يَجِدْ فَصِيَامُ شَهْرَيْنِ مُتَتَابِعَيْنِ تَوْبَةً مِّنَ ٱللَّهِ ۗ وَكَانَ ٱللَّهُ
عَلِيمًا حَكِيمًا ﴿٩٢﴾ وَمَن يَقْتُلْ مُؤْمِنًا مُّتَعَمِّدًا فَجَزَآؤُهُۥ جَهَنَّمُ خَـٰلِدًا فِيهَا وَغَضِبَ ٱللَّهُ
عَلَيْهِ وَلَعَنَهُۥ وَأَعَدَّ لَهُۥ عَذَابًا عَظِيمًا ﴿٩٣﴾ يَـٰٓأَيُّهَا ٱلَّذِينَ ءَامَنُوٓا۟ إِذَا ضَرَبْتُمْ فِى سَبِيلِ ٱللَّهِ
فَتَبَيَّنُوا۟ وَلَا تَقُولُوا۟ لِمَنْ أَلْقَىٰٓ إِلَيْكُمُ ٱلسَّلَـٰمَ لَسْتَ مُؤْمِنًا تَبْتَغُونَ عَرَضَ ٱلْحَيَوٰةِ
ٱلدُّنْيَا فَعِندَ ٱللَّهِ مَغَانِمُ كَثِيرَةٌ ۚ كَذَٰلِكَ كُنتُم مِّن قَبْلُ فَمَنَّ ٱللَّهُ عَلَيْكُمْ
فَتَبَيَّنُوٓا۟ ۚ إِنَّ ٱللَّهَ كَانَ بِمَا تَعْمَلُونَ خَبِيرًا ﴿٩٤﴾ لَّا يَسْتَوِى ٱلْقَـٰعِدُونَ مِنَ ٱلْمُؤْمِنِينَ
غَيْرُ أُو۟لِى ٱلضَّرَرِ وَٱلْمُجَـٰهِدُونَ فِى سَبِيلِ ٱللَّهِ بِأَمْوَٰلِهِمْ وَأَنفُسِهِمْ ۚ فَضَّلَ ٱللَّهُ ٱلْمُجَـٰهِدِينَ
بِأَمْوَٰلِهِمْ وَأَنفُسِهِمْ عَلَى ٱلْقَـٰعِدِينَ دَرَجَةً ۚ وَكُلًّا وَعَدَ ٱللَّهُ ٱلْحُسْنَىٰ ۚ وَفَضَّلَ ٱللَّهُ ٱلْمُجَـٰهِدِينَ
عَلَى ٱلْقَـٰعِدِينَ أَجْرًا عَظِيمًا ﴿٩٥﴾ دَرَجَـٰتٍ مِّنْهُ وَمَغْفِرَةً وَرَحْمَةً ۚ وَكَانَ ٱللَّهُ
غَفُورًا رَّحِيمًا ﴿٩٦﴾ إِنَّ ٱلَّذِينَ تَوَفَّىٰهُمُ ٱلْمَلَـٰٓئِكَةُ ظَالِمِىٓ أَنفُسِهِمْ قَالُوا۟ فِيمَ كُنتُمْ ۖ قَالُوا۟ كُنَّا
مُسْتَضْعَفِينَ فِى ٱلْأَرْضِ ۚ قَالُوٓا۟ أَلَمْ تَكُنْ أَرْضُ ٱللَّهِ وَٰسِعَةً فَتُهَاجِرُوا۟ فِيهَا ۚ فَأُو۟لَـٰٓئِكَ مَأْوَىٰهُمْ
جَهَنَّمُ ۖ وَسَآءَتْ مَصِيرًا ﴿٩٧﴾ إِلَّا ٱلْمُسْتَضْعَفِينَ مِنَ ٱلرِّجَالِ وَٱلنِّسَآءِ وَٱلْوِلْدَٰنِ لَا
يَسْتَطِيعُونَ حِيلَةً وَلَا يَهْتَدُونَ سَبِيلًا ﴿٩٨﴾ فَأُو۟لَـٰٓئِكَ عَسَى ٱللَّهُ أَن يَعْفُوَ عَنْهُمْ ۚ وَكَانَ ٱللَّهُ
عَفُوًّا غَفُورًا ﴿٩٩﴾ ۞ وَمَن يُهَاجِرْ فِى سَبِيلِ ٱللَّهِ يَجِدْ فِى ٱلْأَرْضِ مُرَٰغَمًا كَثِيرًا وَسَعَةً ۚ وَمَن
يَخْرُجْ مِنۢ بَيْتِهِۦ مُهَاجِرًا إِلَى ٱللَّهِ وَرَسُولِهِۦ ثُمَّ يُدْرِكْهُ ٱلْمَوْتُ فَقَدْ وَقَعَ أَجْرُهُۥ عَلَى ٱللَّهِ ۗ

وَكَانَ ٱللَّهُ غَفُورًا رَّحِيمًا ﴿١٠٠﴾ وَإِذَا ضَرَبْتُمْ فِى ٱلْأَرْضِ فَلَيْسَ عَلَيْكُمْ جُنَاحٌ أَن تَقْصُرُوا۟ مِنَ
ٱلصَّلَوٰةِ إِنْ خِفْتُمْ أَن يَفْتِنَكُمُ ٱلَّذِينَ كَفَرُوٓا۟ ۚ إِنَّ ٱلْكَٰفِرِينَ كَانُوا۟ لَكُمْ عَدُوًّا مُّبِينًا ﴿١٠١﴾ وَإِذَا
كُنتَ فِيهِمْ فَأَقَمْتَ لَهُمُ ٱلصَّلَوٰةَ فَلْتَقُمْ طَآئِفَةٌ مِّنْهُم مَّعَكَ وَلْيَأْخُذُوٓا۟ أَسْلِحَتَهُمْ فَإِذَا
سَجَدُوا۟ فَلْيَكُونُوا۟ مِن وَرَآئِكُمْ وَلْتَأْتِ طَآئِفَةٌ أُخْرَىٰ لَمْ يُصَلُّوا۟ فَلْيُصَلُّوا۟ مَعَكَ
وَلْيَأْخُذُوا۟ حِذْرَهُمْ وَأَسْلِحَتَهُمْ ۗ وَدَّ ٱلَّذِينَ كَفَرُوا۟ لَوْ تَغْفُلُونَ عَنْ أَسْلِحَتِكُمْ وَأَمْتِعَتِكُمْ
فَيَمِيلُونَ عَلَيْكُم مَّيْلَةً وَٰحِدَةً ۚ وَلَا جُنَاحَ عَلَيْكُمْ إِن كَانَ بِكُمْ أَذًى مِّن مَّطَرٍ أَوْ كُنتُم
مَّرْضَىٰٓ أَن تَضَعُوٓا۟ أَسْلِحَتَكُمْ ۖ وَخُذُوا۟ حِذْرَكُمْ ۗ إِنَّ ٱللَّهَ أَعَدَّ لِلْكَٰفِرِينَ عَذَابًا مُّهِينًا ﴿١٠٢﴾
فَإِذَا قَضَيْتُمُ ٱلصَّلَوٰةَ فَٱذْكُرُوا۟ ٱللَّهَ قِيَٰمًا وَقُعُودًا وَعَلَىٰ جُنُوبِكُمْ ۚ فَإِذَا ٱطْمَأْنَنتُمْ
فَأَقِيمُوا۟ ٱلصَّلَوٰةَ ۚ إِنَّ ٱلصَّلَوٰةَ كَانَتْ عَلَى ٱلْمُؤْمِنِينَ كِتَٰبًا مَّوْقُوتًا ﴿١٠٣﴾ وَلَا تَهِنُوا۟ فِى
ٱبْتِغَآءِ ٱلْقَوْمِ ۖ إِن تَكُونُوا۟ تَأْلَمُونَ فَإِنَّهُمْ يَأْلَمُونَ كَمَا تَأْلَمُونَ ۖ وَتَرْجُونَ مِنَ ٱللَّهِ مَا
لَا يَرْجُونَ ۗ وَكَانَ ٱللَّهُ عَلِيمًا حَكِيمًا ﴿١٠٤﴾ إِنَّآ أَنزَلْنَآ إِلَيْكَ ٱلْكِتَٰبَ بِٱلْحَقِّ لِتَحْكُمَ بَيْنَ
ٱلنَّاسِ بِمَآ أَرَىٰكَ ٱللَّهُ ۚ وَلَا تَكُن لِّلْخَآئِنِينَ خَصِيمًا ﴿١٠٥﴾ وَٱسْتَغْفِرِ ٱللَّهَ ۖ إِنَّ ٱللَّهَ كَانَ
غَفُورًا رَّحِيمًا ﴿١٠٦﴾ وَلَا تُجَٰدِلْ عَنِ ٱلَّذِينَ يَخْتَانُونَ أَنفُسَهُمْ ۚ إِنَّ ٱللَّهَ لَا يُحِبُّ مَن كَانَ
خَوَّانًا أَثِيمًا ﴿١٠٧﴾ يَسْتَخْفُونَ مِنَ ٱلنَّاسِ وَلَا يَسْتَخْفُونَ مِنَ ٱللَّهِ وَهُوَ مَعَهُمْ إِذْ يُبَيِّتُونَ مَا
لَا يَرْضَىٰ مِنَ ٱلْقَوْلِ ۚ وَكَانَ ٱللَّهُ بِمَا يَعْمَلُونَ مُحِيطًا ﴿١٠٨﴾ هَٰٓأَنتُمْ هَٰٓؤُلَآءِ جَٰدَلْتُمْ عَنْهُمْ فِى
ٱلْحَيَوٰةِ ٱلدُّنْيَا فَمَن يُجَٰدِلُ ٱللَّهَ عَنْهُمْ يَوْمَ ٱلْقِيَٰمَةِ أَم مَّن يَكُونُ عَلَيْهِمْ وَكِيلًا ﴿١٠٩﴾ وَمَن
يَعْمَلْ سُوٓءًا أَوْ يَظْلِمْ نَفْسَهُۥ ثُمَّ يَسْتَغْفِرِ ٱللَّهَ يَجِدِ ٱللَّهَ غَفُورًا رَّحِيمًا ﴿١١٠﴾ وَمَن يَكْسِبْ
إِثْمًا فَإِنَّمَا يَكْسِبُهُۥ عَلَىٰ نَفْسِهِۦ ۚ وَكَانَ ٱللَّهُ عَلِيمًا حَكِيمًا ﴿١١١﴾ وَمَن يَكْسِبْ خَطِيٓـَٔةً أَوْ إِثْمًا
ثُمَّ يَرْمِ بِهِۦ بَرِيٓـًٔا فَقَدِ ٱحْتَمَلَ بُهْتَٰنًا وَإِثْمًا مُّبِينًا ﴿١١٢﴾ وَلَوْلَا فَضْلُ ٱللَّهِ عَلَيْكَ وَرَحْمَتُهُۥ
لَهَمَّت طَّآئِفَةٌ مِّنْهُمْ أَن يُضِلُّوكَ وَمَا يُضِلُّونَ إِلَّآ أَنفُسَهُمْ ۖ وَمَا يَضُرُّونَكَ مِن شَىْءٍ ۚ
وَأَنزَلَ ٱللَّهُ عَلَيْكَ ٱلْكِتَٰبَ وَٱلْحِكْمَةَ وَعَلَّمَكَ مَا لَمْ تَكُن تَعْلَمُ ۚ وَكَانَ فَضْلُ ٱللَّهِ
عَلَيْكَ عَظِيمًا ﴿١١٣﴾ ۞ لَّا خَيْرَ فِى كَثِيرٍ مِّن نَّجْوَىٰهُمْ إِلَّا مَنْ أَمَرَ بِصَدَقَةٍ أَوْ مَعْرُوفٍ أَوْ

إِصۡلَٰحِۭ بَيۡنَ ٱلنَّاسِۚ وَمَن يَفۡعَلۡ ذَٰلِكَ ٱبۡتِغَآءَ مَرۡضَاتِ ٱللَّهِ فَسَوۡفَ نُؤۡتِيهِ
أَجۡرًا عَظِيمٗا ﴿١١٤﴾ وَمَن يُشَاقِقِ ٱلرَّسُولَ مِنۢ بَعۡدِ مَا تَبَيَّنَ لَهُ ٱلۡهُدَىٰ وَيَتَّبِعۡ غَيۡرَ سَبِيلِ
ٱلۡمُؤۡمِنِينَ نُوَلِّهِۦ مَا تَوَلَّىٰ وَنُصۡلِهِۦ جَهَنَّمَۖ وَسَآءَتۡ مَصِيرًا ﴿١١٥﴾ إِنَّ ٱللَّهَ لَا يَغۡفِرُ أَن يُشۡرَكَ
بِهِۦ وَيَغۡفِرُ مَا دُونَ ذَٰلِكَ لِمَن يَشَآءُۚ وَمَن يُشۡرِكۡ بِٱللَّهِ فَقَدۡ ضَلَّ ضَلَٰلَۢا بَعِيدًا ﴿١١٦﴾ إِن
يَدۡعُونَ مِن دُونِهِۦٓ إِلَّآ إِنَٰثٗا وَإِن يَدۡعُونَ إِلَّا شَيۡطَٰنٗا مَّرِيدٗا ﴿١١٧﴾ لَّعَنَهُ ٱللَّهُۘ وَقَالَ
لَأَتَّخِذَنَّ مِنۡ عِبَادِكَ نَصِيبٗا مَّفۡرُوضٗا ﴿١١٨﴾ وَلَأُضِلَّنَّهُمۡ وَلَأُمَنِّيَنَّهُمۡ وَلَأٓمُرَنَّهُمۡ فَلَيُبَتِّكُنَّ
ءَاذَانَ ٱلۡأَنۡعَٰمِ وَلَأٓمُرَنَّهُمۡ فَلَيُغَيِّرُنَّ خَلۡقَ ٱللَّهِۚ وَمَن يَتَّخِذِ ٱلشَّيۡطَٰنَ وَلِيّٗا مِّن
دُونِ ٱللَّهِ فَقَدۡ خَسِرَ خُسۡرَانٗا مُّبِينٗا ﴿١١٩﴾ يَعِدُهُمۡ وَيُمَنِّيهِمۡۖ وَمَا يَعِدُهُمُ ٱلشَّيۡطَٰنُ إِلَّا
غُرُورًا ﴿١٢٠﴾ أُوْلَٰٓئِكَ مَأۡوَىٰهُمۡ جَهَنَّمُ وَلَا يَجِدُونَ عَنۡهَا مَحِيصٗا ﴿١٢١﴾ وَٱلَّذِينَ ءَامَنُواْ وَعَمِلُواْ
ٱلصَّٰلِحَٰتِ سَنُدۡخِلُهُمۡ جَنَّٰتٖ تَجۡرِي مِن تَحۡتِهَا ٱلۡأَنۡهَٰرُ خَٰلِدِينَ فِيهَآ أَبَدٗاۖ وَعۡدَ ٱللَّهِ حَقّٗاۚ
وَمَنۡ أَصۡدَقُ مِنَ ٱللَّهِ قِيلٗا ﴿١٢٢﴾ لَّيۡسَ بِأَمَانِيِّكُمۡ وَلَآ أَمَانِيِّ أَهۡلِ ٱلۡكِتَٰبِۗ مَن يَعۡمَلۡ سُوٓءٗا
يُجۡزَ بِهِۦ وَلَا يَجِدۡ لَهُۥ مِن دُونِ ٱللَّهِ وَلِيّٗا وَلَا نَصِيرٗا ﴿١٢٣﴾ وَمَن يَعۡمَلۡ مِنَ ٱلصَّٰلِحَٰتِ مِن
ذَكَرٍ أَوۡ أُنثَىٰ وَهُوَ مُؤۡمِنٞ فَأُوْلَٰٓئِكَ يَدۡخُلُونَ ٱلۡجَنَّةَ وَلَا يُظۡلَمُونَ نَقِيرٗا ﴿١٢٤﴾ وَمَنۡ أَحۡسَنُ
دِينٗا مِّمَّنۡ أَسۡلَمَ وَجۡهَهُۥ لِلَّهِ وَهُوَ مُحۡسِنٞ وَٱتَّبَعَ مِلَّةَ إِبۡرَٰهِيمَ حَنِيفٗاۗ وَٱتَّخَذَ ٱللَّهُ إِبۡرَٰهِيمَ
خَلِيلٗا ﴿١٢٥﴾ وَلِلَّهِ مَا فِي ٱلسَّمَٰوَٰتِ وَمَا فِي ٱلۡأَرۡضِۚ وَكَانَ ٱللَّهُ بِكُلِّ شَيۡءٖ مُّحِيطٗا ﴿١٢٦﴾
وَيَسۡتَفۡتُونَكَ فِي ٱلنِّسَآءِۖ قُلِ ٱللَّهُ يُفۡتِيكُمۡ فِيهِنَّ وَمَا يُتۡلَىٰ عَلَيۡكُمۡ فِي ٱلۡكِتَٰبِ فِي يَتَٰمَى
ٱلنِّسَآءِ ٱلَّٰتِي لَا تُؤۡتُونَهُنَّ مَا كُتِبَ لَهُنَّ وَتَرۡغَبُونَ أَن تَنكِحُوهُنَّ وَٱلۡمُسۡتَضۡعَفِينَ مِنَ
ٱلۡوِلۡدَٰنِ وَأَن تَقُومُواْ لِلۡيَتَٰمَىٰ بِٱلۡقِسۡطِۚ وَمَا تَفۡعَلُواْ مِنۡ خَيۡرٖ فَإِنَّ ٱللَّهَ كَانَ
بِهِۦ عَلِيمٗا ﴿١٢٧﴾ وَإِنِ ٱمۡرَأَةٌ خَافَتۡ مِنۢ بَعۡلِهَا نُشُوزًا أَوۡ إِعۡرَاضٗا فَلَا جُنَاحَ عَلَيۡهِمَآ أَن
يُصۡلِحَا بَيۡنَهُمَا صُلۡحٗاۚ وَٱلصُّلۡحُ خَيۡرٞۗ وَأُحۡضِرَتِ ٱلۡأَنفُسُ ٱلشُّحَّۚ وَإِن تُحۡسِنُواْ وَتَتَّقُواْ
فَإِنَّ ٱللَّهَ كَانَ بِمَا تَعۡمَلُونَ خَبِيرٗا ﴿١٢٨﴾ وَلَن تَسۡتَطِيعُوٓاْ أَن تَعۡدِلُواْ بَيۡنَ ٱلنِّسَآءِ وَلَوۡ
حَرَصۡتُمۡۖ فَلَا تَمِيلُواْ كُلَّ ٱلۡمَيۡلِ فَتَذَرُوهَا كَٱلۡمُعَلَّقَةِۚ وَإِن تُصۡلِحُواْ وَتَتَّقُواْ فَإِنَّ ٱللَّهَ

كَانَ غَفُورًا رَّحِيمًا ﴿١٢٩﴾ وَإِن يَتَفَرَّقَا يُغْنِ ٱللَّهُ كُلًّا مِّن سَعَتِهِۦ ۚ وَكَانَ ٱللَّهُ وَٰسِعًا
حَكِيمًا ﴿١٣٠﴾ وَلِلَّهِ مَا فِى ٱلسَّمَٰوَٰتِ وَمَا فِى ٱلْأَرْضِ ۗ وَلَقَدْ وَصَّيْنَا ٱلَّذِينَ أُوتُوا۟ ٱلْكِتَٰبَ مِن
قَبْلِكُمْ وَإِيَّاكُمْ أَنِ ٱتَّقُوا۟ ٱللَّهَ ۚ وَإِن تَكْفُرُوا۟ فَإِنَّ لِلَّهِ مَا فِى ٱلسَّمَٰوَٰتِ وَمَا فِى ٱلْأَرْضِ ۚ وَكَانَ
ٱللَّهُ غَنِيًّا حَمِيدًا ﴿١٣١﴾ وَلِلَّهِ مَا فِى ٱلسَّمَٰوَٰتِ وَمَا فِى ٱلْأَرْضِ ۚ وَكَفَىٰ بِٱللَّهِ وَكِيلًا ﴿١٣٢﴾ إِن يَشَأْ
يُذْهِبْكُمْ أَيُّهَا ٱلنَّاسُ وَيَأْتِ بِـَٔاخَرِينَ ۚ وَكَانَ ٱللَّهُ عَلَىٰ ذَٰلِكَ قَدِيرًا ﴿١٣٣﴾ مَّن كَانَ يُرِيدُ
ثَوَابَ ٱلدُّنْيَا فَعِندَ ٱللَّهِ ثَوَابُ ٱلدُّنْيَا وَٱلْءَاخِرَةِ ۚ وَكَانَ ٱللَّهُ سَمِيعًۢا بَصِيرًا ﴿١٣٤﴾ ۞ يَٰٓأَيُّهَا ٱلَّذِينَ
ءَامَنُوا۟ كُونُوا۟ قَوَّٰمِينَ بِٱلْقِسْطِ شُهَدَآءَ لِلَّهِ وَلَوْ عَلَىٰٓ أَنفُسِكُمْ أَوِ ٱلْوَٰلِدَيْنِ وَٱلْأَقْرَبِينَ ۚ إِن
يَكُنْ غَنِيًّا أَوْ فَقِيرًا فَٱللَّهُ أَوْلَىٰ بِهِمَا ۖ فَلَا تَتَّبِعُوا۟ ٱلْهَوَىٰٓ أَن تَعْدِلُوا۟ ۚ وَإِن تَلْوُۥٓا۟ أَوْ تُعْرِضُوا۟
فَإِنَّ ٱللَّهَ كَانَ بِمَا تَعْمَلُونَ خَبِيرًا ﴿١٣٥﴾ يَٰٓأَيُّهَا ٱلَّذِينَ ءَامَنُوٓا۟ ءَامِنُوا۟ بِٱللَّهِ وَرَسُولِهِۦ وَٱلْكِتَٰبِ
ٱلَّذِى نَزَّلَ عَلَىٰ رَسُولِهِۦ وَٱلْكِتَٰبِ ٱلَّذِىٓ أَنزَلَ مِن قَبْلُ ۚ وَمَن يَكْفُرْ بِٱللَّهِ وَمَلَٰٓئِكَتِهِۦ
وَكُتُبِهِۦ وَرُسُلِهِۦ وَٱلْيَوْمِ ٱلْءَاخِرِ فَقَدْ ضَلَّ ضَلَٰلًۢا بَعِيدًا ﴿١٣٦﴾ إِنَّ ٱلَّذِينَ ءَامَنُوا۟ ثُمَّ كَفَرُوا۟ ثُمَّ
ءَامَنُوا۟ ثُمَّ كَفَرُوا۟ ثُمَّ ٱزْدَادُوا۟ كُفْرًا لَّمْ يَكُنِ ٱللَّهُ لِيَغْفِرَ لَهُمْ وَلَا لِيَهْدِيَهُمْ سَبِيلًۢا ﴿١٣٧﴾ بَشِّرِ
ٱلْمُنَٰفِقِينَ بِأَنَّ لَهُمْ عَذَابًا أَلِيمًا ﴿١٣٨﴾ ٱلَّذِينَ يَتَّخِذُونَ ٱلْكَٰفِرِينَ أَوْلِيَآءَ مِن دُونِ ٱلْمُؤْمِنِينَ ۚ
أَيَبْتَغُونَ عِندَهُمُ ٱلْعِزَّةَ فَإِنَّ ٱلْعِزَّةَ لِلَّهِ جَمِيعًا ﴿١٣٩﴾ وَقَدْ نَزَّلَ عَلَيْكُمْ فِى ٱلْكِتَٰبِ أَنْ إِذَا
سَمِعْتُمْ ءَايَٰتِ ٱللَّهِ يُكْفَرُ بِهَا وَيُسْتَهْزَأُ بِهَا فَلَا تَقْعُدُوا۟ مَعَهُمْ حَتَّىٰ يَخُوضُوا۟ فِى حَدِيثٍ غَيْرِهِۦٓ ۚ
إِنَّكُمْ إِذًا مِّثْلُهُمْ ۗ إِنَّ ٱللَّهَ جَامِعُ ٱلْمُنَٰفِقِينَ وَٱلْكَٰفِرِينَ فِى جَهَنَّمَ جَمِيعًا ﴿١٤٠﴾ ٱلَّذِينَ يَتَرَبَّصُونَ
بِكُمْ فَإِن كَانَ لَكُمْ فَتْحٌ مِّنَ ٱللَّهِ قَالُوٓا۟ أَلَمْ نَكُن مَّعَكُمْ وَإِن كَانَ لِلْكَٰفِرِينَ نَصِيبٌ قَالُوٓا۟ أَلَمْ
نَسْتَحْوِذْ عَلَيْكُمْ وَنَمْنَعْكُم مِّنَ ٱلْمُؤْمِنِينَ ۚ فَٱللَّهُ يَحْكُمُ بَيْنَكُمْ يَوْمَ ٱلْقِيَٰمَةِ ۗ وَلَن يَجْعَلَ
ٱللَّهُ لِلْكَٰفِرِينَ عَلَى ٱلْمُؤْمِنِينَ سَبِيلًا ﴿١٤١﴾ إِنَّ ٱلْمُنَٰفِقِينَ يُخَٰدِعُونَ ٱللَّهَ وَهُوَ خَٰدِعُهُمْ وَإِذَا
قَامُوٓا۟ إِلَى ٱلصَّلَوٰةِ قَامُوا۟ كُسَالَىٰ يُرَآءُونَ ٱلنَّاسَ وَلَا يَذْكُرُونَ ٱللَّهَ إِلَّا قَلِيلًا ﴿١٤٢﴾
مُّذَبْذَبِينَ بَيْنَ ذَٰلِكَ لَآ إِلَىٰ هَٰٓؤُلَآءِ وَلَآ إِلَىٰ هَٰٓؤُلَآءِ ۚ وَمَن يُضْلِلِ ٱللَّهُ فَلَن تَجِدَ
لَهُۥ سَبِيلًا ﴿١٤٣﴾ يَٰٓأَيُّهَا ٱلَّذِينَ ءَامَنُوا۟ لَا تَتَّخِذُوا۟ ٱلْكَٰفِرِينَ أَوْلِيَآءَ مِن دُونِ ٱلْمُؤْمِنِينَ ۚ

أَتُرِيدُونَ أَن تَجْعَلُوا۟ لِلَّهِ عَلَيْكُمْ سُلْطَـٰنًا مُّبِينًا ﴿١٤٤﴾ إِنَّ ٱلْمُنَـٰفِقِينَ فِى ٱلدَّرْكِ ٱلْأَسْفَلِ مِنَ
ٱلنَّارِ وَلَن تَجِدَ لَهُمْ نَصِيرًا ﴿١٤٥﴾ إِلَّا ٱلَّذِينَ تَابُوا۟ وَأَصْلَحُوا۟ وَٱعْتَصَمُوا۟ بِٱللَّهِ وَأَخْلَصُوا۟
دِينَهُمْ لِلَّهِ فَأُو۟لَـٰٓئِكَ مَعَ ٱلْمُؤْمِنِينَ ۖ وَسَوْفَ يُؤْتِ ٱللَّهُ ٱلْمُؤْمِنِينَ أَجْرًا عَظِيمًا ﴿١٤٦﴾ مَّا
يَفْعَلُ ٱللَّهُ بِعَذَابِكُمْ إِن شَكَرْتُمْ وَءَامَنتُمْ ۚ وَكَانَ ٱللَّهُ شَاكِرًا عَلِيمًا ﴿١٤٧﴾

INTRODUCTION TO CHAPTER (SURAH) 4: AN-NISAA (THE WOMEN)

Maududi's Introduction

Period of Revelation

This Surah comprises several discourses which were revealed on different occasions during the period ranging probably between the end of A. H. 3 and the end of A. H. 4 or the beginning of A. H. 5. Although it is difficult to determine the exact dates of their revelations, yet it is possible to assign to them a fairly correct period with the help of the Commandments and the events mentioned therein and the Traditions concerning them. A few instances are given below by way of illustration :

1. We know that the instructions about the division of inheritance of the martyrs and for the safeguard of the rights of the orphans were sent down after the Battle of Uhd in which 70 Muslims were killed. Then naturally the question of the division of the inheritance of the martyrs and the safeguard of the rights of their orphans arose in many families at Al-Madinah. From this we conclude that vv. 1 -28 were revealed on that occasion.

2. We learn from the Traditions that the Commandment about salat during war time was given on the occasion of Zat-ur-Riqa'a, an expedition which took place in A. H. 4. From this we conclude that the discourse containing v. 102 was revealed on that occasion.

3. The last warning (v. 47) to the Jews was given before the Banu Nadir were exiled from Al- Madinah in Rabi'-ulAwwal, A. H. 4. From this it may safely be concluded that the discourse containing v. 47 must have been revealed some time before that date.

4. The permission about ***tayammum*** (the performance of ablutions with pure dust, in case no water be available) was given during the Bani-al-Mustaliq expedition, which took place in A. H. 5.. Therefore the probable period of the revelation of the discourse containing v. 43 was A. H. 5.

Topics and Their Background

Let us now consider the social and historical considerations of the period in order to understand the Surah. All the discourses in this Surah deal with three main problems which confronted the Holy Prophet at the time. First of all, he was engaged in bringing about an all round development of the Islamic Community that had been formed at the time of his migration to Al-Madinah. For this purpose he was introducing new moral, cultural, social, economic and political ways in place of the old ones of the pre-Islamic period. The second thing that occupied his attention and efforts was the bitter struggle that was going on with the

mushrik Arabs, the Jewish clans and the hypocrites who were opposing tooth and nail his mission of reform. Above all he had to propagate Islam in the face of the bitter opposition of these powers of evil with a view to capturing more and more minds and hearts.

Accordingly, detailed instructions have been given for the consolidation and strengthening of the Islamic Community in continuation of those given in Al-Baqarah. Principles for the smooth running of family life have been laid down and ways of settling family disputes have been taught. Rules have been prescribed for marriage and rights of wife and husband have been apportioned fairly and equitably. The status of women in the society has been determined and the declaration of the rights of orphans has been made laws and regulations have been laid down for the division of inheritance, and instructions have been given to reform economic affairs. The foundation of the penal code has been laid down drinking has been prohibited, and instructions have been given for cleanliness and purity. The Muslims have been taught the kind of relations good men should have with their Allah and fellow men. Instructions have been given for the maintenance of discipline in the Muslim Community.

The moral and religious condition of the people of the Book has been reviewed to teach lessons to the Muslims and to forewarn them to refrain from following in their footsteps. The conduct of the hypocrites has been criticized and the distinctive features of hypocrisy and true faith have been clearly marked off to enable the Muslims to distinguish between the two.

In order to cope with the aftermath of the Battle of Uhd, Inspiring discourses were sent down to urge the Muslims to face the enemy bravely, for the defeat in the Battle had so emboldened the ***mushrik*** Arab clans and the neighboring Jews and the hypocrites at home that they were threatening the Muslims on all sides. At this critical juncture, Allah filled the Muslims with courage and gave them such instructions as were needed during that period of war clouds. In order to counteract the fearful rumors that were being spread by the hypocrites and the Muslims of weak faith, they were asked to make a thorough enquiry into them and to inform the responsible people about them. Then they were experiencing some difficulties in offering their salat during the expeditions to some places where no water was available for performing their ablutions, etc. In such cases they were allowed to cleanse themselves with pure earth and to shorten the salat or to offer the "Salat of Fear", when they were faced with danger. Instructions were also given for the solution of the puzzling problem of those Muslims who were scattered among the unbelieving Arab clans and were often involved in war. They were asked to migrate to Al-Madinah, the abode of Islam.

This Surah also deals with the case of Bani Nadir who were showing a hostile and menacing attitude, in spite of the peace treaties they had made with the Muslims. They were openly siding with the enemies of Islam and hatching plots against the Holy Prophet and the Muslim Community even at AIMadinah itself. They were taken to task for their inimical behavior and given a final warning to change their attitude, and were at last exiled from Al-Madinah on account of their misconduct.

The problem of the hypocrites, who had become very troublesome at that time, was involving the Believers in difficulties-- Therefore they were divided into different categories to enable the Muslims to deal with them appropriately.

Clear instructions were also given regarding the attitude they should adopt towards the nonbelligerent clans. The most important thing needed at that time was to prepare the Muslims for the bitter struggle with the opponents of Islam. For this purpose greatest importance was attached to their character building, for it was obvious that the small Muslim

Community could only come out successful, nay, survive, if the Muslims possessed high moral character. They were, therefore, enjoined to adopt the highest moral qualities and were severely criticized whenever any moral weakness was detected in them.

Though this Surah mainly deals with the moral and social reforms, yet due attention has been paid to propagation of Islam. On the one hand, the superiority of the Islamic morality and culture has been established over that of the Jews, Christians and mushriks; on the other hand, their wrong religious conceptions, their wrong morality and their evil acts have been criticized to prepare the ground for inviting them to the way of the Truth.

Subject: Consolidation of the Islamic Community

The main object of this Surah is to teach the Muslims the ways that unite a people and make them firm and strong. Introductions for the stability of family, which is the nucleus of community have been given. Then they have been urged to prepare themselves for defence. Side by side with these, they have been taught the importance of the propagation of Islam. Above all, the importance of the highest moral character in the scheme of consolidation of the Community has been impressed.

Topics and their Interconnection

Just, fair and equitable laws and regulations for the smooth running of family life have been laid down for the husband and wife. Detailed instructions have been given for the division of inheritance and due regard has been paid to the rights of orphans. 1 - 35

In order to inculcate the right spirit for the observance of rules and regulations, the Muslims have been enjoined to show generosity to all around them and to be free from meanness, selfishness, stinginess of mind, because this is essential for the consolidation of the Communities and helpful for the propagation of Islam. 36 - 42

The ways of the purification of mind and body for the offering of Salat have been taught because it plays the most important part in every scheme of moral and social reform. 43

After moral preparation, instructions for defence have been given. First of all, the Muslims have been warned to be on their guard against the cunning machinations and vile practices of the local Jews who were hostile to the New Movement. This caution was necessary for removing some possible misunderstanding that might have arisen on account of the pre-Islamic alliance between the people of Al-Madinah and the Jews. 44 - 57

Then they have been enjoined to place their trusts and offices of trust in the custody of honest and qualified persons, and to do what is just and right, and to obey Allah and His Messenger and those among themselves entrusted with the conduct of their affairs and to turn to Allah and His Messenger for the settlement of their disputes. As such an attitude and behaviour alone can ensure consolidation, they have been strongly warned that any deviation from this path will lead to their disintegration. 58 - 72

After this pre-requisite, they have been exhorted to make preparation for defence and to fight bravely for the cause of Islam, without showing any kind of cowardice or weakness. They have also been warned to be on their guard against hypocrites. A line of demarcation has been drawn to distinguish the intentional shirkers from the helpless devotees. 73 - 100

Here again instructions have been given for the offering of Salat during military campaigns and actual fighting. This is to impress the importance of Salat even at the time of fear and danger. 101 - 103

Before proceeding on to the next topic, the Muslims have been exhorted to persevere in their fight without showing any kind of weakness. 104

In order to make the Islamic Community firm and strong for defence, the Muslims have been enjoined to observe the highest standard of justice. The Muslims are required to deal out strict justice even in case of the enemy, with whom they might be involved in war. They should also settle disputes between husband and wife with justice. In order to ensure this, they should keep their beliefs and deeds absolutely free from every kind of impurity and should become the standard bearers of justice. 105 - 135

Resuming the theme of defence, the Muslims have been warned to be on their guard against their enemies. They have been admonished to take necessary precautions against the machinations of the hypocrites and the unbelievers and the people of the Book. As belief in Allah, and Revelation and Life-after-death is the only safeguard against every kind of enemy, they should sincerely believe in and follow His Messenger, Muhammad (Allah's peace be upon him). 136 - 175

Though this verse also deals with the family laws contained in verses 1 - 35, it has been added as a supplement at the end of this Surah because it was revealed long after An-Nisa was being recited as a complete Surah. 17

Ibn Kathir's Introduction

Virtues of Surat An-Nisa, A Madinan Surah

Al-`Awfi reported that Ibn `Abbas said that Surat An-Nisa' was revealed in Al-Madinah. Ibn Marduwyah recorded similar statements from `Abdullah bin Az-Zubayr and Zayd bin Thabit. In his Mustadrak, Al-Hakim recorded that `Abdullah bin Mas`ud said, "There are five Ayat in Surat An-Nisa' that I would prefer to the life of this world and all that is in it,

(Surely, Allah wrongs not even the weight of an atom,) (4:40),

(If you avoid the great sins which you are forbidden to do) (4:31),

(Verily, Allah forgives not that partners should be set up with Him (in worship), but He forgives except that (anything else) to whom He wills) (4:48),

(If they (hypocrites), when they had been unjust to themselves, had come to you) (4:64), and,

(And whoever does evil or wrongs himself, but afterwards seeks Allah's forgiveness, he will find Allah Oft-Forgiving, Most Merciful) (4:110)." Al-Hakim recorded that Ibn `Abbas said, "Ask me about Surat An-Nisa', for I learned the Qur'an when I was still young." Al-Hakim said, "This Hadith is Sahih according to the criteria of the Two Sahihs, and they did not collect it."

CHAPTER (SURAH) 4: AN-NISAA (THE WOMEN), VERSES 024-147

Surah: 4 Ayah: 24

﴿ ۞ وَٱلۡمُحۡصَنَٰتُ مِنَ ٱلنِّسَآءِ إِلَّا مَا مَلَكَتۡ أَيۡمَٰنُكُمۡۖ كِتَٰبَ ٱللَّهِ عَلَيۡكُمۡۚ وَأُحِلَّ لَكُم مَّا
وَرَآءَ ذَٰلِكُمۡ أَن تَبۡتَغُواْ بِأَمۡوَٰلِكُم مُّحۡصِنِينَ غَيۡرَ مُسَٰفِحِينَۚ فَمَا ٱسۡتَمۡتَعۡتُم بِهِۦ مِنۡهُنَّ
فَـَٔاتُوهُنَّ أُجُورَهُنَّ فَرِيضَةٗۚ وَلَا جُنَاحَ عَلَيۡكُمۡ فِيمَا تَرَٰضَيۡتُم بِهِۦ مِنۢ بَعۡدِ ٱلۡفَرِيضَةِۚ
إِنَّ ٱللَّهَ كَانَ عَلِيمًا حَكِيمٗا ﴿٢٤﴾ ﴾

24. Also (forbidden are) women already married, except those (slaves) whom your right hands possess. Thus has Allâh ordained for you. All others are lawful, provided you seek (them in marriage) with Mahr (bridal money given by the husband to his wife at the time of marriage) from your property, desiring chastity, not committing illegal sexual intercourse, so with those of whom you have enjoyed sexual relations, give them their Mahr as prescribed; but if after a Mahr is prescribed, you agree mutually (to give more), there is no sin on you. Surely, Allâh is Ever All-Knowing, All-Wise.

Transliteration

24. Waalmuhsanatu mina alnnisa-i illa ma malakat aymanukum kitaba Allahi AAalaykum waohilla lakum ma waraa thalikum an tabtaghoo bi-amwalikum muhsineena ghayra musafiheena fama istamtaAAtum bihi minhunna faatoohunna ojoorahunna fareedatan wala junaha AAalaykum feema taradaytum bihi min baAAdi alfareedati inna Allaha kana AAaleeman hakeeman

Tafsir Ibn Kathir

Forbidding Women Already Married, Except for Female Slaves

Allah said,

(Also (forbidden are) women already married, except those whom your right hands possess.) The Ayah means, you are prohibited from marrying women who are already married,

(except those whom your right hands possess) except those whom you acquire through war, for you are allowed such women after making sure they are not pregnant. Imam Ahmad recorded that Abu Sa`id Al-Khudri said, "We captured some women from the area of Awtas who were already married, and we disliked having sexual relations with them because they already had husbands. So, we asked the Prophet about this matter, and this Ayah was revealed,

(Also (forbidden are) women already married, except those whom your right hands possess). Consequently, we had sexual relations with these women." This is the wording collected by At-Tirmidhi An-Nasa'i, Ibn Jarir and Muslim in his Sahih. Allah's statement,

(Thus has Allah ordained for you) means, this prohibition was ordained for you by Allah. Therefore, adhere to Allah's Book, do not transgress His set limits, and adhere to His legislation and decrees.

The Permission to Marry All Other Women

Allah said,

(All others are lawful) meaning, you are allowed to marry women other than the prohibited types mentioned here, as `Ata' and others have stated. Allah's statement,

(provided you seek them (with a dowry) from your property, desiring chastity, not fornication,) meaning, you are allowed to use your money to marry up to four wives and for (the purchase of) as many female slaves as you like, all through legal means,

((desiring) chastity, not fornication.) Allah's statement,

(So with those among them whom you have enjoyed, give them their required due,) means, to enjoy them sexually, surrender to them their rightful dowry as compensation. In other Ayat, Allah said,

(And how could you take it (back) while you have gone in unto each other),

(And give to the women (whom you marry) their dowry with a good heart), and,

(And it is not lawful for you (men) to take back (from your wives) any of what (dowry) you gave them)

Prohibiting the Mut`ah of Marriage

Mujahid stated that,

(So with those among them whom you have enjoyed, give them their required due,) was revealed about the Mut`ah marriage. A Mut`ah marriage is a marriage that ends upon a predeterminied date. In the Two Sahihs, it is recorded that the Leader of the Faithful `Ali bin Abi Talib said, "The Messenger of Allah prohibited Mut`ah marriage and eating the meat of domesticated donkeys on the day of Khaybar (battle)." In addition, in his Sahih, Muslim recorded that Ar-Rabi` bin Sabrah bin Ma`bad Al-Juhani said that his father said that he accompanied the Messenger of Allah during the conquest of Makkah, and that the Prophet said,

«يَا أَيُّهَا النَّاسُ إِنِّي كُنْتُ أَذِنْتُ لَكُمْ فِي الاسْتِمْتَاعِ مِنَ النِّسَاءِ، وَإِنَّ اللهَ قَدْ حَرَّمَ ذَلِكَ إِلى يَوْمِ الْقِيَامَةِ، فَمَنْ كَانَ عِنْدَهُ مِنْهُنَّ شَيْءٌ فَلْيُخلِّ سَبِيلَهُ، وَلَا تَأْخُذُوا مِمَّا آتَيْتُمُوهُنَّ شيئًا»

(O people! I allowed you the Mut`ah marriage with women before. Now, Allah has prohibited it until the Day of Resurrection. Therefore, anyone who has any women in Mut`ah, let him let them go, and do not take anything from what you have given them.) Allah's statement,

(but if you agree mutually (to give more) after the requirement (has been determined), there is no sin on you.) is similar to His other statement,

(And give to the women their dowry with a good heart). The meaning of these Ayat is: If you have stipulated a dowry for her, and she later forfeits it, either totally or partially, then this bears no harm on you or her in this case. Ibn Jarir said, "Al-Hadrami said that some men would designate a certain dowry, but then fall into financial difficulties. Therefore, Allah said that there is no harm on you, O people, concerning your mutual agreement after the requirement (has been determined)." meaning, if she gives up part of the dowry, then you men are allowed to accept that. Allah's statement,

(Surely, Allah is Ever All-Knowing, All-Wise.) is suitable here, after Allah mentioned these prohibitions.

Surah: 4 Ayah: 25

﴿ وَمَن لَّمْ يَسْتَطِعْ مِنكُمْ طَوْلًا أَن يَنكِحَ ٱلْمُحْصَنَٰتِ ٱلْمُؤْمِنَٰتِ فَمِن مَّا مَلَكَتْ
أَيْمَٰنُكُم مِّن فَتَيَٰتِكُمُ ٱلْمُؤْمِنَٰتِ ۚ وَٱللَّهُ أَعْلَمُ بِإِيمَٰنِكُم ۚ بَعْضُكُم مِّنۢ بَعْضٍ ۚ
فَٱنكِحُوهُنَّ بِإِذْنِ أَهْلِهِنَّ وَءَاتُوهُنَّ أُجُورَهُنَّ بِٱلْمَعْرُوفِ مُحْصَنَٰتٍ غَيْرَ
مُسَٰفِحَٰتٍ وَلَا مُتَّخِذَٰتِ أَخْدَانٍ ۚ فَإِذَآ أُحْصِنَّ فَإِنْ أَتَيْنَ بِفَٰحِشَةٍ فَعَلَيْهِنَّ
نِصْفُ مَا عَلَى ٱلْمُحْصَنَٰتِ مِنَ ٱلْعَذَابِ ۚ ذَٰلِكَ لِمَنْ خَشِىَ ٱلْعَنَتَ مِنكُمْ ۚ وَأَن
تَصْبِرُوا۟ خَيْرٌ لَّكُمْ ۗ وَٱللَّهُ غَفُورٌ رَّحِيمٌ ﴿٢٥﴾ ﴾

25. And whoever of you has not the means wherewith to wed free, believing women, they may wed believing girls from among those (slaves) whom your right hands possess, and Allâh has full knowledge about your Faith; you are one from another. Wed them with the permission of their own folk (guardians, Auliyâ' or masters) and give them their Mahr according to what is reasonable; they (the above said captive and slave-girls) should be chaste, not adulterous, nor taking boy-friends. And after they have been taken in wedlock, if they commit illegal sexual intercourse, their punishment is half that for free (unmarried) women. This is for him among you who is afraid of being harmed in his religion or in his body; but it is better for you that you practice self-restraint, and Allâh is Oft-Forgiving, Most Merciful.

Transliteration

25. Waman lam yastatiAA minkum tawlan an yankiha almuhsanati almu/minati famin ma malakat aymanukum min fatayatikumu almu/minati waAllahu aAAlamu bi-eemanikum baAAdukum min baAAdin fainkihoohunna bi-ithni ahlihinna waatoohunna ojoorahunna bialmaAAroofi muhsanatin ghayra masafihatin wala muttakhithati akhdanin fa-itha ohsinna fa-in atayna bifahishatin faAAalayhinna nisfu ma AAala almuhsanati mina alAAathabi thalika liman khashiya alAAanata minkum waan tasbiroo khayrun lakum waAllahu ghafoorun raheemun

Tafsir Ibn Kathir

Marrying a Female Slave, if One Cannot Marry a Free Woman

Allah said, those who do not have,

(the means), financial capability,

(Wherewith to wed free believing women) meaning, free faithful, chaste women.

(They may wed believing girls from among those whom your right hands possess,) meaning, they are allowed to wed believing slave girls owned by the believers.

(and Allah has full knowledge about your faith; you are one from another.) Allah knows the true reality and secrets of all things, but you people know only the apparent things. Allah then said,

(Wed them with the permission of their own folk) indicating that the owner is responsible for the slave girl, and consequently, she cannot marry without his permission. The owner is also responsible for his male slave and they cannot wed without his permission. A Hadith states,

«أَيُّمَا عَبْدٍتَزَوَّجَ بِغَيْرِ إِذْنِ مَوَالِيهِ،فَهُوَ عَاهِرٌ»

(Any male slave who marries without permission from his master, is a fornicator.) When the owner of the female slave is a female, those who are allowed to give away the free woman in marriage, with her permission, become responsible for giving away her female slave in marriage, as well. A Hadith states that

«لَا تُزَوِّجِ الْمَرْأَةُ الْمَرْأَةَ، وَلَا الْمَرْأَةُ نَفْسَهَا، فَإِنَّ الزَّانِيَةَ هِيَ الَّتِي تُزَوِّجُ نَفْسَهَا»

(The woman does not give away another woman, or herself in marriage, for only the adulteress gives herself away in marriage.) Allah's statement,

(And give them their due in a good manner;) meaning, pay them their dowry with a good heart, and do not keep any of it, belittling the matter due to the fact that they are owned slaves. Allah's statement,

(they should be chaste) means, they are honorable women who do not commit adultery, and this is why Allah said,

(not fornicators) referring to dishonorable women, who do not refrain from illicit sexual relations with those who ask. Ibn `Abbas said that the fornicating women are the whores, who do not object to having relations with whomever seeks it, while,

(nor promiscuous.) refers to taking boyfriends. Similar was said by Abu Hurayrah, Mujahid, Ash-Sha`bi, Ad-Dahhak, `Ata' Al-Khurasani, Yahya bin Abi Kathir, Muqatil bin Hayyan and As-Suddi.

The Slave Girl's Punishment for Adultery is Half that of a Free Unmarried Woman

Allah said,

(And after they have been taken in wedlock, if they commit Fahishah, their punishment is half of that for free (unmarried) women.) this is about the slave women who got married, as indicated by the Ayah;

(And whoever of you have not the means wherewith to wed free believing women, they may wed believing girls from among those whom your right hands possess,) Therefore, since the honorable Ayah is about believing slave girls, then,

(And after they have been taken in wedlock,) refers to when they (believing slave girls) get married, as Ibn `Abbas and others have said. Allah's statement,

(their punishment is half of that for free (unmarried) women.) indicates that the type of punishment prescribed here is the one that can be reduced to half, lashes in this case, not stoning to death, and Allah knows best. Allah's statement,

(This is for him among you who is afraid of being harmed in his religion or in his body;) indicates that marrying slave girls, providing one satisfies the required conditions, is for those who fear for their chastity and find it hard to be patient and refrain from sex. In this difficult circumstance, one is allowed to marry a slave girl. However, it is better to refrain from marrying slave girls and to observe patience, for otherwise, the offspring will become slaves to the girl's master. Allah said,

(but it is better for you that you practice self-restraint, and Allah is Oft-Forgiving, Most Merciful.)

Surah: 4 Ayah: 26, Ayah: 27 & Ayah: 28

﴿يُرِيدُ ٱللَّهُ لِيُبَيِّنَ لَكُمۡ وَيَهۡدِيَكُمۡ سُنَنَ ٱلَّذِينَ مِن قَبۡلِكُمۡ وَيَتُوبَ عَلَيۡكُمۡۗ وَٱللَّهُ عَلِيمٌ
حَكِيمٞ ٢٦﴾

26. Allâh wishes to make clear (what is lawful and what is unlawful) to you, and to show you the ways of those before you, and accept your repentance, and Allâh is All-Knower, All-Wise.

﴿وَٱللَّهُ يُرِيدُ أَن يَتُوبَ عَلَيۡكُمۡ وَيُرِيدُ ٱلَّذِينَ يَتَّبِعُونَ ٱلشَّهَوَٰتِ أَن تَمِيلُواْ مَيۡلًا
عَظِيمٗا ٢٧﴾

27. Allâh wishes to accept your repentance, but those who follow their lusts, wish that you (believers) should deviate tremendously away (from the Right Path).

﴿يُرِيدُ ٱللَّهُ أَن يُخَفِّفَ عَنكُمۡۚ وَخُلِقَ ٱلۡإِنسَٰنُ ضَعِيفٗا ٢٨﴾

28. Allâh wishes to lighten (the burden) for you; and man was created weak (cannot be patient to leave sexual intercourse with woman).

Transliteration

26. Yureedu Allahu liyubayyina lakum wayahdiyakum sunana allatheena min qablikum wayatooba AAalaykum waAllahu AAaleemun hakeemun 27. WaAllahu yureedu an yatooba AAalaykum wayureedu allatheena yattabiAAoona alshshahawati an tameeloo maylan AAatheeman 28. Yureedu Allahu an yukhaffifa AAankum wakhuliqa al-insanu daAAeefan

Tafsir Ibn Kathir

Allah explains to the believers what He has allowed and prohibited for them in this and other Surahs,

(And to show you the ways of those before you,) meaning their righteous ways and how to adhere to the commandments that He likes and is pleased with.

(and accept your repentance) from sin and error,

(and Allah is All-Knower, All-Wise.) in His commands, decrees, actions and statements. Allah's statement,

(but those who follow their lusts, wish that you (believers) should deviate tremendously away from the right path)) indicates that the followers of Shaytan among the Jews, Christians and the adulterous, wish that you would take the horrendous path of falsehood instead of the truth.

(Allah wishes to lighten (the burden) for you") His legislation, orders, what He prohibits and what He decrees for you. This is why Allah has allowed free men to marry slave girls under certain conditions, as Mujahid and others have stated.

(and man was created weak.) and this is why it is suitable in his case that the commands are made easy for him, because of his weakness and feebleness. Ibn Abi Hatim recorded that Tawus said that,

(and man was created weak), "Concerning women". Waki` said, "Man's mind leaves when women are involved."

Surah: 4 Ayah: 29, Ayah: 30 & Ayah: 31

﴿ يَٰٓأَيُّهَا ٱلَّذِينَ ءَامَنُواْ لَا تَأۡكُلُوٓاْ أَمۡوَٰلَكُم بَيۡنَكُم بِٱلۡبَٰطِلِ إِلَّآ أَن تَكُونَ تِجَٰرَةً
عَن تَرَاضٖ مِّنكُمۡۚ وَلَا تَقۡتُلُوٓاْ أَنفُسَكُمۡۚ إِنَّ ٱللَّهَ كَانَ بِكُمۡ رَحِيمٗا ٢٩ ﴾

29. O you who believe! Eat not up your property among yourselves unjustly except it be a trade amongst you, by mutual consent. And do not kill yourselves (nor kill one another). Surely, Allâh is Most Merciful to you.

﴿ وَمَن يَفۡعَلۡ ذَٰلِكَ عُدۡوَٰنٗا وَظُلۡمٗا فَسَوۡفَ نُصۡلِيهِ نَارٗاۚ وَكَانَ ذَٰلِكَ عَلَى ٱللَّهِ
يَسِيرًا ٣٠ ﴾

30. And whoever commits that through aggression and injustice, We shall cast him into the Fire, and that is easy for Allâh.

﴿ إِن تَجۡتَنِبُواْ كَبَآئِرَ مَا تُنۡهَوۡنَ عَنۡهُ نُكَفِّرۡ عَنكُمۡ سَيِّـَٔاتِكُمۡ وَنُدۡخِلۡكُم مُّدۡخَلٗا
كَرِيمٗا ٣١ ﴾

31. If you avoid the great sins which you are forbidden to do, We shall expiate from you your (small) sins, and admit you to a Noble Entrance (i.e. Paradise).

Transliteration

29. Ya ayyuha allatheena amanoo la ta/kuloo amwalakum baynakum bialbatili illa an takoona tijaratan AAan taradin minkum wala taqtuloo anfusakum inna Allaha kana bikum raheeman 30. Waman yafAAal thalika AAudwanan wathulman fasawfa nusleehi naran wakana thalika AAala Allahi yaseeran 31. In tajtaniboo kaba-ira ma tunhawna AAanhu nukaffir AAankum sayyi-atikum wanudkhilkum mudkhalan kareeman

Tafsir Ibn Kathir

Prohibiting Unlawfully Earned Money

Allah, the Exalted and Most Honored, prohibits His believing servants from illegally acquiring each other's property using various dishonest methods such as Riba, gambling and other wicked methods that appear to be legal, but Allah knows that, in reality, those involved seek to deal in interest. Ibn Jarir recorded that Ibn `Abbas commented on a man who buys a garment, saying that if he likes it he will keep it, or he will return it along with an extra Dirham, "This is what Allah meant, when He said,

(Eat not up your property among yourselves unjustly.") `Ali bin Abi Talhah reported that Ibn `Abbas said, "When Allah sent down,

(O you who believe! Eat not up your property among yourselves unjustly) some Muslims said, `Allah has forbidden us from eating up each other's property unjustly, and food is our best property. Therefore, none among us is allowed to eat from anyone else's food.' After that Allah sent down,

(There is no restriction on the blind) (until the end of the Ayah). (24:61).'" Qatadah said similarly. Allah's statement,

(except it be a trade amongst you, by mutual consent.) means, do not revert to illegal ways and means to acquire money. However, there is no harm in commercial transactions that transpire between the buyer and the seller with mutual consent, so that money is legally earned from these transactions. Mujahid said that,

(except it be a trade amongst you, by mutual consent.) means, "By selling and buying, or giving someone a gift." Ibn Jarir recorded this statement.

The Option to Buy or Sell Before Parting, is Part of `Mutual Consent' in Trading

Mutual agreement in various transactions is attained when both parties have the right to uphold or dissolve the agreement before they part. In the Two Sahihs, it is recorded that the Messenger of Allah said,

«الْبَيِّعَانِ بِالْخِيَارِ مَالَمْ يَتَفَرَّقَا»

(The seller and the buyer retain the (right to change their mind) as long as they have not parted.) Al-Bukhari's wording for this Hadith reads,

«إِذَا تَبَايَعَ الرَّجُلَانِ فَكُلُّ وَاحِدٍ مِنْهُمَا بِالْخِيَارِ، مَالَمْ يَتفرَّقَا»

(When two men conduct a transaction, they retain their (right to change their mind) as long as they have not parted.)

Forbidding Murder and Suicide

Allah said,

(And do not kill yourselves.) by committing Allah's prohibitions, falling into sin and eating up each other's property unjustly,

(Surely, Allah is Most Merciful to you.) in what He commanded you and prohibited you from. Imam Ahmad recorded that `Amr bin Al-`As said that when the Prophet sent him for the battle of Dhat As-Salasil, "I had a wet dream during a very cold night and feared that if I bathed, I would die. So I performed Tayammum (with pure earth) and led my company in the Dawn prayer. When I went back to the Messenger of Allah , I mentioned what had happened to me and he said,

«يَا عَمْرُو صَلَّيْتَ بِأَصْحَابِكَ وَأَنْتَ جُنُب»

(O `Amr! Have you led your people in prayer while you were in a state of sexual impurity) I said, 'O Messenger of Allah! I had a wet dream on a very cold night and feared that if I bathed I would perish, and I remembered Allah's statement,

(And do not kill yourselves. Surely, Allah is Most Merciful to you). So I performed Tayammum and prayed.' The Messenger of Allah smiled and did not say anything." This is the narration reported by Abu Dawud. Ibn Marduwyah mentioned this honorable Ayah and then reported that Abu Hurayrah said that the Messenger of Allah said,

«مَنْ قَتَلَ نَفْسَهُ بَحَدِيدَةٍ، فَحَدِيدَتُهُ فِي يَدِهِ، يَجَأُ بِهَا بطْنَهُ يَوْمَ الْقِيَامَةِ فِي نَارِ جَهَنَّمَ، خَالِدًا مُخَلَّدًا فِيهَا أَبَدًا، ومَنْ قَتَلَ نَفْسَهُ بِسُمَ فَسُمُّهُ فِي يَدِهِ، يَتَحَسَّاهُ فِي نَارِ جَهَنَّمَ، خَالِدًا مُخَلَّدًا فِيهَا أَبَدًا، وَمَنْ تَرَدَّى مِنْ جَبَلٍ فَقَتَلَ نَفْسَهُ، فَهُوَ مُتَرَدِ فِي نَارِ جَهَنَّمَ، خَالِدًا مُخَلَّدًا فِيهَا أَبَدًا»

(Whoever kills himself with an iron tool, then his tool will be in his hand and he will keep stabbing himself with it in the Fire of Jahannam, forever and ever. Whoever kills himself with poison, then his poison will be in his hand and he will keep taking it in the Fire of Jahannam forever and ever. Whoever kills himself by throwing himself from a mountain, will keep falling in the Fire of Jahannam forever and ever.) This Hadith was also collected in the Two Sahihs. Abu Qilabah said that Thabit bin Ad-Dahhak said that the Messenger of Allah said,

«مَنْ قَتَلَ نَفْسَهُ بِشَيْءٍ، عُذِّبَ بِهِ يَوْمَ الْقِيَامَةِ»

(Whoever kills himself with an instrument, will be punished with it on the Day of Resurrection.) This Hadith was collected by the Group. This is why Allah said,

(And whoever commits that through aggression and injustice,) meaning, whoever commits what Allah has forbidden for him transgression and injustice - while knowing that it is forbidden for him, yet he still dares to commit it,

(We shall cast him into the Fire,). This Ayah carries a stern warning and a truthful promise. Therefore, every sane person should beware of it, those who hear the speech with full comprehension.

Minor Sins Will be Pardoned if One Refrains from Major Sins

Allah said,

(If you avoid the great sins which you are forbidden to do, We shall remit from you your (small) sins,) meaning, if you avoid the major evil deeds that you were prohibited We will forgive you the minor evil deeds and will admit you into Paradise. This is why Allah said,

(and admit you to a Noble Entrance (i.e. Paradise).) There are several Hadiths on the subject of this honorable Ayah. Imam Ahmad recorded that Salman Al-Farisi said, "The Prophet said to me, `Do you know what the day of Al-Jumu`ah is' I said, `It is the day during which Allah brought together the creation of your father (Adam).' He said,

«لكِنْ أَدْرِي مَا يَوْمُ الْجُمُعَةِ، لَا يَتَطَهَّرُ الرَّجُلُ فَيُحْسِنُ طُهُورَهُ، ثُمَّ يَأْتِي الْجُمُعَةَ فَيُنْصِتُ حَتَّى يَقْضِيَ الْإِمَامُ صَلَاتَهُ، إِلَّا كَانَ كَفَّارَةً لَهُ مَا بَيْنَهُ وَبَيْنَ الْجُمُعَةِ الْمُقْبِلَةِ، مَا اجْتُنِبَتِ الْمَقْتَلَة»

(I know what the day of Jumu`ah is. Anyone who takes a bath and cleans himself as much as he can and then proceeds for the Friday prayer and remains quiet until the Imam finishes the prayer, all his sins in between the present and the next Friday will be forgiven, as long as major sins were avoided.)" Al-Bukhari recorded similar wording from Salman Al-Farisi.

The Seven Destructive Sins

What are the Seven Destructive Sins In the Two Sahihs, it is recorded that Abu Hurayrah said that the Messenger of Allah said,

«اجْتَنِبُوا السَّبْعَ الْمُوبِقَات»

(Avoid the seven great destructive sins.) The people inquired, 'O Allah's Messenger! What are they' He said,

«الشِّرْكُ بِاللهِ، وَقَتْلُ النَّفْسِ الَّتِي حَرَّمَ اللهُ إِلَّا بِالْحَقِّ، وَالسِّحْرُ، وَأَكْلُ الرِّبَا، وَأَكْلُ مَالِ الْيَتِيمِ، وَالتَّوَلِّي يَوْمَ الزَّحْفِ، وَقَذْفُ الْمُحْصَنَاتِ الْمُؤْمِنَاتِ الْغَافِلَاتِ»

(To join others in worship along with Allah, to kill the life which Allah has forbidden except for a just cause, magic, to consume Riba, to consume an orphan's wealth, to turn away from the enemy and flee from the battlefield when the battle begins, and to accuse chaste women, who never even think of anything that would tarnish their chastity and are good believers.) Another Hadith that mentions False Witness Imam Ahmad recorded that Anas bin Malik said, "The Messenger of Allah mentioned the major sins, or was asked about the major sins. He said,

«الشِّرْكُ بِاللهِ، وَقَتْلُ النَّفْسِ، وَعُقُوقُ الْوَالِدَيْنِ»

(Associating others with Allah in worship, killing the life, and being undutiful to the parents.) He then said,

«أَلَا أُنَبِّئُكُمْ بِأَكْبَرِ الْكَبَائِرِ؟»

(Should I tell you about the biggest of the major sins)

He said:

«قَوْلُ الزُّورِ أَوْ شَهَادَةُ الزُّورِ »

(The false statement - or the false testimony.)" Shu`bah - one of the narrators of the Hadith - said, "Most likely, in my opinion, he said, `False testimony.'" The Two Sahihs recorded this Hadith from Shu`bah from Anas. Another Hadith In the Two Sahihs, it is recorded that `Abdur-Rahman bin Abi Bakrah said that his father said, "The Prophet said,

«أَلَا أُنَبِّئُكُمْ بِأَكْبَرِ الْكَبَائِرِ؟»

(Should I inform you about the greatest of the great sins) We said, `Yes, O Allah's Messenger !' He said,

«الْإِشْرَاكُ بِاللهِ، وَعُقُوقُ الْوَالِدَيْنِ»

(To join others in worship with Allah and to be undutiful to one's parents.) He was reclining, then he sat up and said;

«أَلَا وَشَهَادَةُ الزُّورِ، أَلَا وَقَوْلُ الزُّورِ»

(And I warn you against false testimony and false speech.) and he continued repeating it until we wished that he would stop." Another Hadith that mentions killing the Offspring In the Two Sahihs, it is recorded that `Abdullah bin Mas`ud said, "I asked, `O Allah's Messenger! What is the greatest sin' ((in one narration) the biggest sin)' He said,

«أَنْ تَجْعَلَ للهِ نِدًّا وَهُوَ خَلَقَكَ»

(To make a rival for Allah while He Alone created you.) I said, `Then' He said,

«أَنْ تَقْتُلَ وَلَدَكَ خَشْيَةَ أَنْ يَطْعَمَ مَعَكَ»

(To kill your offspring for fear that he might share your food with you.) I said, `Then' He said,

«أَنْ تُزَانِيَ حَلِيلَةَ جَارِكَ»

(To commit adultery with your neighbor's wife.) He then recited,

(And those who invoke not any other god along with Allah), until,

(Except those who repent)." Another Hadith from `Abdullah bin `Amr Imam Ahmad recorded that `Abdullah bin `Amr said that the Prophet said,

«أَكْبَرُ الْكَبَائِرِ: الِإشْرَاكُ بِاللهِ، وَعُقُوقُ الْوَالِدَيْنِ أَوْ قَتْلُ النَّفْسِ شعبة الشاك وَالْيَمِينُ الْغَمُوس»

(The greatest sins are: To join others in worship with Allah, to be undutiful to one's parents - or to take a life) Shu`bah was uncertain of which one - (and the false oath). Recorded by Al-Bukhari, At-Tirmidhi, and An-Nasai. Another Hadith by `Abdullah bin `Amr about Causing one's Parents to be Cursed `Abdullah bin `Amr said that the Messenger of Allah said,

«إِنَّ مِنْ أَكْبَرِ الْكَبَائِرِ أَنْ يَلْعَنَ الرَّجُلُ وَالِدَيْه»

(Among the worst of the major sins is for a man to curse his own parents.) They said, "How can one curse his own parents" He said,

«يَسُبُّ الرَّجُلُ أَبَا الرَّجُلِ، فَيَسُبُّ أَبَاهُ، وَيَسُبُّ أُمَّهُ فَيَسُبُّ أُمَّه»

(One curses another man's father, and that man curses his father in retaliation, or he curses someone's mother and that man curses his mother.) This is the wording of Muslim. At-Tirmidhi said, "Sahih." It is recorded in the Sahih that the Messenger of Allah said,

«سِبَابُ الْمُسْلِمِ فُسُوقٌ، وَقِتَالُهُ كُفْرٌ»

(Cursing a Muslim is a sin and fighting him is Kufr.)

Surah: 4 Ayah: 32

﴿ وَلَا تَتَمَنَّوْا۟ مَا فَضَّلَ ٱللَّهُ بِهِۦ بَعْضَكُمْ عَلَىٰ بَعْضٍ ۚ لِّلرِّجَالِ نَصِيبٌ مِّمَّا ٱكْتَسَبُوا۟ ۖ
وَلِلنِّسَآءِ نَصِيبٌ مِّمَّا ٱكْتَسَبْنَ ۚ وَسْـَٔلُوا۟ ٱللَّهَ مِن فَضْلِهِۦٓ ۗ إِنَّ ٱللَّهَ كَانَ بِكُلِّ شَىْءٍ
عَلِيمًا ﴿٣٢﴾ ﴾

32. And wish not for the things in which Allâh has made some of you to excel others. For men there is reward for what they have earned, (and likewise) for women there is reward for what they have earned, and ask Allâh of His Bounty. Surely, Allâh is Ever All-Knower of everything.

Transliteration

32. Wala tatamannaw ma faddala Allahu bihi baAAdakum AAala baAAdin lilrrijali naseebun mimma iktasaboo walilnnisa-i naseebun mimma iktasabna wais-aloo Allaha min fadlihi inna Allaha kana bikulli shay-in AAaleeman

Tafsir Ibn Kathir

Do Not Wish for the Things Which Allah has Made Some Others to Excel In

Imam Ahmad recorded that Umm Salamah said, "O Messenger of Allah! Men go to battle, but we do not go to battle, and we earn one-half of the inheritance (that men get)." Allah sent down,

(And wish not for the things in which Allah has made some of you to excel others). At-Tirmidhi also recorded this Hadith. Allah's statement,

(For men there is reward for what they have earned, (and likewise) for women there is reward for what they have earned,) indicates, according to Ibn Jarir, that each person will earn his wages for his works, a reward if his deeds are good, and punishment if his deeds are evil. It was also reported that this Ayah is talking about inheritance, indicating the fact that each person will get his due share of the inheritance, as Al-Walibi reported from Ibn `Abbas. Allah then directed the servants to what benefits them,

(and ask Allah of His Bounty.)Therefore, the Ayah states, "Do not wish for what other people were endowed with over you, for this is a decision that will come to pass, and wishing does not change its decree. However, ask Me of My favor and I will grant it to you, for I Am Most Generous and Most Giving." Allah then said,

(Surely, Allah is Ever All-Knower of everything.) meaning, Allah knows who deserves this life, and so He gives him riches, and whoever deserves poverty, He makes him poor. He also knows who deserves the Hereafter, and He directs him to perform the deeds that will help him to be sucessful in it, and whoever deserves failure, He prevents him from achieving righteousness and what leads to it. Hence, Allah said,

(Surely, Allah is Ever All-Knower of everything).

Surah: 4 Ayah: 33

﴿ وَلِكُلٍّ جَعَلْنَا مَوَالِيَ مِمَّا تَرَكَ ٱلْوَالِدَانِ وَٱلْأَقْرَبُونَ ۚ وَٱلَّذِينَ عَقَدَتْ أَيْمَـٰنُكُمْ
فَـَٔاتُوهُمْ نَصِيبَهُمْ ۚ إِنَّ ٱللَّهَ كَانَ عَلَىٰ كُلِّ شَيْءٍ شَهِيدًا ﴿٣٣﴾ ﴾

33. And to everyone, We have appointed heirs of that (property) left by parents and relatives. To those also with whom you have made a pledge (brotherhood), give them their due portion (by Wasiyya - wills). Truly, Allâh is Ever a Witness over all things.

Transliteration

33. Walikullin jaAAalna mawaliya mimma taraka alwalidani waal-aqraboona waallatheena AAaqadat aymanukum faatoohum naseebahum inna Allaha kana AAala kulli shay-in shaheedan

Tafsir Ibn Kathir

Ibn `Abbas, Mujahid, Sa`id bin Jubayr, Abu Salih, Qatadah, Zayd bin Aslam, As-Suddi, Ad-Dahhak, Muqatil bin Hayyan, and others said that Allah's statement,

(And to everyone, We have appointed Mawali) means, "Heirs." Ibn `Abbas was also reported to have said that Mawali refers to relatives. Ibn Jarir commented, "The Arabs call the cousin a Mawla." Ibn Jarir continued, "Allah's statement,

(of that (property) left by parents and relatives.) means, from what he inherited from his parents and family members. Therefore, the meaning of the Ayah becomes: `To all of you, O people, We appointed relatives (such as children) who will later inherit what you inherited from your own parents and relatives." Allah's statement,

(To those also with whom you have made a pledge (brotherhood), give them their due portion.) means, "Those with whom you have a pledge of brotherhood, give them their share of inheritance, thus fulfilling the ratified pledges that you gave them. Allah has witnessed all of you when you gave these pledges and promises." This practice was followed in the beginning of Islam, but was later on abrogated when Muslims were commanded to fulfill the pledges (brotherhood) they had already given, but to refrain from making any new pledges after that. Al-Bukhari recorded that Ibn `Abbas said,

(And to everyone, We have appointed Mawali) "meaning, heirs;

(To those also with whom you have made a pledge (brotherhood)) When the emigrants came to Al-Madinah, the emigrant would inherit from the Ansari, while the latter's relatives would not inherit from him because of the bond of brotherhood which the Prophet established between them (the emigrants and the Ansar). When the verse,

(And to everyone We have appointed Mawali) was revealed, it cancelled (the pledge of brotherhood regarding inheritance)." Then he said, "The verse,

(To those also with whom you have made a pledge (brotherhood), give them their due portion.) remained valid for cases of co-operation and mutual advice, while the matter of inheritance was excluded and it became permissible to assign something in one's will to the person who had the right of inheriting before."

Surah: 4 Ayah: 34

﴿ ٱلرِّجَالُ قَوَّٰمُونَ عَلَى ٱلنِّسَآءِ بِمَا فَضَّلَ ٱللَّهُ بَعۡضَهُمۡ عَلَىٰ بَعۡضٖ وَبِمَآ أَنفَقُواْ مِنۡ
أَمۡوَٰلِهِمۡۚ فَٱلصَّٰلِحَٰتُ قَٰنِتَٰتٌ حَٰفِظَٰتٞ لِّلۡغَيۡبِ بِمَا حَفِظَ ٱللَّهُۚ وَٱلَّٰتِي تَخَافُونَ
نُشُوزَهُنَّ فَعِظُوهُنَّ وَٱهۡجُرُوهُنَّ فِي ٱلۡمَضَاجِعِ وَٱضۡرِبُوهُنَّۖ فَإِنۡ أَطَعۡنَكُمۡ فَلَا
تَبۡغُواْ عَلَيۡهِنَّ سَبِيلًاۗ إِنَّ ٱللَّهَ كَانَ عَلِيّٗا كَبِيرٗا ٣٤ ﴾

34. Men are the protectors and maintainers of women, because Allâh has made one of them to excel the other, and because they spend (to support them) from their means. Therefore the righteous women are devoutly obedient (to Allâh and to their husbands), and guard in the husband's absence what Allâh orders them to guard (e.g. their chastity, their husband's property). As to those women on whose part you see ill-conduct, admonish them (first), (next), refuse to share their beds, (and last) beat them (lightly, if it is useful); but if they return to obedience, seek not against them means (of annoyance). Surely, Allâh is Ever Most High, Most Great.

Transliteration

34. Alrrijalu qawwamoona AAala alnnisa-i bima faddala Allahu baAAdahum AAala baAAdin wabima anfaqoo min amwalihim faalssalihatu qanitatun hafithatun lilghaybi bima hafitha Allahu waallatee takhafoona nushoozahunna faAAithoohunna waohjuroohunna fee almadajiAAi waidriboohunna fa-in ataAAnakum fala tabghoo AAalayhinna sabeelan inna Allaha kana AAaliyyan kabeeran

Tafsir Ibn Kathir

Allah said,

(Men are the protectors and maintainers of women,) meaning, the man is responsible for the woman, and he is her maintainer, caretaker and leader who disciplines her if she deviates.

(because Allah has made one of them to excel the other,) meaning, because men excel over women and are better than them for certain tasks. This is why prophethood was exclusive of men, as well as other important positions of leadership. The Prophet said,

«لَنْ يُفْلِحَ قَوْمٌ وَلَّوْا أَمْرَهُمُ امْرَأَةً»

(People who appoint a woman to be their leader, will never achieve success.) Al-Bukhari recorded this Hadith. Such is the case with appointing women as judges or on other positions of leadership.

(and because they spend from their means.) meaning the dowry, expenditures and various expenses that Allah ordained in His Book and the Sunnah of His Messenger for men to spend on women. For these reasons it is suitable that he is appointed her maintainer, just as Allah said,

(But men have a degree (of responsibility) over them).

Qualities of the Righteous Wife

Allah said,

(Therefore, the righteous) women,

(are Qanitat), obedient to their husbands, as Ibn `Abbas and others stated.

(and guard in the husband's absence) As-Suddi and others said that it means she protects her honor and her husband's property when he is absent, and Allah's statement,

(what Allah orders them to guard.) means, the protected (husband) is the one whom Allah protects. Ibn Jarir recorded that Abu Hurayrah said that the Messenger of Allah said,

«خَيْرُ النِّسَاءِ امْرَأَةٌ إِذَا نَظَرْتَ إِلَيْهَا سَرَّتْكَ، وَإِذَا أَمَرْتَهَا أَطَاعَتْكَ، وَإِذَا غِبْتَ عَنْهَا حَفِظَتْكَ فِي نَفْسِهَا وَمَالِكَ»

(The best women is she who when you look at her, she pleases you, when you command her she obeys you, and when you are absent, she protects her honor and your property.) Then, the Messenger of Allah recited the Ayah,

(Men are the protectors and maintainers of women,) until its end. Imam Ahmad recorded that `Abdur-Rahman bin 'Awf said that the Messenger of Allah said,

«إِذَا صَلَّتِ الْمَرْأَةُ خَمْسَهَا، وَصَامَتْ شَهْرَهَا، وَحَفِظَتْ فَرْجَهَا، وَأَطَاعَتْ زَوْجَهَا، قِيلَ لَهَا: ادْخُلِي الْجَنَّةَ مِنْ أَيِّ الْأَبْوَابِ شِئْتِ»

(If the woman prayed her five daily prayers, fasted her month, protected her chastity and obeyed her husband, she will be told, 'Enter Paradise from any of its doors you wish.')

Dealing with the Wife's Ill-Conduct

Allah said,

(As to those women on whose part you see ill conduct,) meaning, the woman from whom you see ill conduct with her husband, such as when she acts as if she is above her husband, disobeys him, ignores him, dislikes him, and so forth. When these signs appear in a woman, her husband should advise her and remind her of Allah's torment if she disobeys him. Indeed, Allah ordered the wife to obey her husband and prohibited her from disobeying him, because of the enormity of his rights and all that he does for her. The Messenger of Allah said,

«لَوْ كُنْتُ آمِرًا أَحَدًا أَنْ يَسْجُدَ لِأَحَدٍ، لَأَمَرْتُ الْمَرْأَةَ أَنْ تَسْجُدَ لِزَوْجِهَا، مِنْ عِظَمِ حَقِّهِ عَلَيْهَا»

(If I were to command anyone to prostrate before anyone, I would have commanded the wife to prostrate before her husband, because of the enormity of his right upon her.) Al-Bukhari recorded that Abu Hurayrah said that the Messenger of Allah said,

«إِذَا دَعَا الرَّجُلُ امْرَأَتَهُ إِلى فِرَاشِهِ فَأَبَتْ عَلَيْهِ، لَعَنَتْهَا الْمَلَائِكَةُ حَتَّى تُصْبِح»

(If the man asks his wife to come to his bed and she declines, the angels will keep cursing her until the morning.) Muslim recorded it with the wording,

«إِذَا بَاتَتِ الْمَرْأَةُ هَاجِرَةً فِرَاشَ زَوْجِهَا، لَعَنَتْهَا الْمَلَائِكَةُ حَتَّى تُصْبِح»

(If the wife goes to sleep while ignoring her husband's bed, the angels will keep cursing her until the morning.) This is why Allah said,

(As to those women on whose part you see ill conduct, admonish them (first)). Allah's statement,

(abandon them in their beds,) `Ali bin Abi Talhah reported that Ibn `Abbas said "The abandonment refers to not having intercourse with her, to lie on her bed with his back to her." Several others said similarly. As-Suddi, Ad-Dahhak, `Ikrimah, and Ibn `Abbas, in another narration, added, "Not to speak with her or talk to her." The Sunan and Musnad compilers recorded that Mu`awiyah bin Haydah Al-Qushayri said, "O Allah's Messenger! What is the right that the wife of one of us has on him" The Prophet said,

«أَنْ تُطْعِمَهَا إِذَا طَعِمْتَ، وَتَكْسُوَهَا إِذَا اكْتَسَيْتَ، وَلَا تَضْرِبِ الْوَجْهَ، وَلَا تُقَبِّحْ، وَلَا تَهْجُرْ إِلَّا فِي الْبَيْت»

(To feed her when you eat, cloth her when you buy clothes for yourself, refrain from striking her face or cursing her, and to not abandon her, except in the house.) Allah's statement,

(beat them) means, if advice and ignoring her in the bed do not produce the desired results, you are allowed to discipline the wife, without severe beating. Muslim recorded that Jabir said that during the Farewell Hajj, the Prophet said;

«وَاتَّقُوا اللهَ فِي النِّسَاءِ، فَإِنَّهُنَّ عِنْدَكُمْ عَوَانٍ، وَلَكُمْ عَلَيْهِنَّ أَنْ لَا يُوطِئْنَ فُرُشَكُمْ أَحَدًا تَكْرَهُونَهُ،فَإِنْ فَعَلْنَ ذَلِكَ فَاضْرِبُوهُنَّ ضَرْبًا غَيْرَ مُبرِحٍ، وَلَهُنَّ عَلَيْكُمْ رِزْقُهُنَّ وَكِسْوَتُهُنَّ بِالْمَعْرُوف»

(Fear Allah regarding women, for they are your assistants. You have the right on them that they do not allow any person whom you dislike to step on your mat. However, if they do that, you are allowed to discipline them lightly. They have a right on you that you provide them with their provision and clothes, in a reasonable manner.) Ibn `Abbas and several others said that the Ayah refers to a beating that is not violent. Al-Hasan Al-Basri said that it means, a beating that is not severe.

When the Wife Obeys Her Husband, Means of Annoyance Against Her are Prohibited

Allah said,

(but if they return to obedience, seek not against them means (of annoyance),) meaning, when the wife obeys her husband in all that Allah has allowed, then no means of annoyance from the husband are allowed against his wife. Therefore, in this case, the husband does not have the right to beat her or shun her bed. Allah's statement,

(Surely, Allah is Ever Most High, Most Great.) reminds men that if they transgress against their wives without justification, then Allah, the Ever Most High, Most Great, is their Protector, and He will exert revenge on those who transgress against their wives and deal with them unjustly.

Surah: 4 Ayah: 35

﴿ وَإِنْ خِفْتُمْ شِقَاقَ بَيْنِهِمَا فَٱبْعَثُوا۟ حَكَمًا مِّنْ أَهْلِهِۦ وَحَكَمًا مِّنْ أَهْلِهَآ إِن يُرِيدَآ إِصْلَٰحًا
يُوَفِّقِ ٱللَّهُ بَيْنَهُمَآ ۗ إِنَّ ٱللَّهَ كَانَ عَلِيمًا خَبِيرًا ﴿٣٥﴾ ﴾

35. If you fear a breach between them twain (the man and his wife), appoint (two) arbitrators, one from his family and the other from her's; if they both wish for peace, Allâh will cause their reconciliation. Indeed Allâh is Ever All-Knower, Well-Acquainted with all things.

Transliteration

35. Wa-in khiftum shiqaqa baynihima faibAAathoo hakaman min ahlihi wahakaman min ahliha in yureeda islahan yuwaffiqi Allahu baynahuma inna Allaha kana AAaleeman khabeeran

Tafsir Ibn Kathir

Appointing Two Arbitrators When the Possibility of Estrangement Between Husband and Wife Occurs

Allah first mentioned the case of rebellion on the part of the wife. He then mentioned the case of estrangement and alienation between the two spouses. Allah said,

(If you fear a breach between the two, appoint (two) arbitrators, one from his family). The Fuqaha' (scholars of Fiqh) say that when estrangement occurs between the husband and wife, the judge refers them to a trusted person who examines their case in order to stop any wrongs commited between them. If the matter continues or worsens, the judge sends a trustworthy person from the woman's family and a trustworthy person from the man's family to meet with them and examine their case to determine whether it is best for them to part or to remain together. Allah gives preference to staying together, and this is why Allah said,

(if they both wish for peace, Allah will cause their reconciliation.) `Ali bin Abi Talhah reported that Ibn `Abbas said, "Allah commands that a righteous man from the husband's side of the family and the wife's side of the family are appointed, so that they find out who among the spouses is in the wrong. If the man is in the wrong, they prevent him from his wife, and he pays some restitution. If the wife is in the wrong, she remains with her husband, and he does not pay any restitution. If the arbitrators decide that the marriage should remain intact or be dissolved, then their decision is upheld. If they decide that the marriage remains intact, but one of the spouses disagrees while the other agrees, and one of them dies, then the one who agreed inherits from the other, while the spouse who did not agree does not inherit from the spouse who agreed." This was collected by Ibn Abi Hatim and Ibn Jarir. Shaykh Abu `Umar bin `Abdul-Barr said, "The scholars agree that when the two arbitrators disagree, then the opinion that dissolves the marriage will not be adopted. They also agree that the decision of the arbitrators is binding, even if the two spouses did not appoint them as agents. This is the case if it is decided that they should stay together, but they disagree whether it is binding or not when they decide for separation." Then he mentioned that the majority holds the view that the decision is still binding, even if they did not appoint them to make any decision.

Surah: 4 Ayah: 36

﴿ ۞ وَٱعْبُدُوا۟ ٱللَّهَ وَلَا تُشْرِكُوا۟ بِهِۦ شَيْـًٔا ۖ وَبِٱلْوَٰلِدَيْنِ إِحْسَـٰنًا وَبِذِى ٱلْقُرْبَىٰ وَٱلْيَتَـٰمَىٰ وَٱلْمَسَـٰكِينِ وَٱلْجَارِ ذِى ٱلْقُرْبَىٰ وَٱلْجَارِ ٱلْجُنُبِ وَٱلصَّاحِبِ بِٱلْجَنۢبِ وَٱبْنِ ٱلسَّبِيلِ وَمَا مَلَكَتْ أَيْمَـٰنُكُمْ ۗ إِنَّ ٱللَّهَ لَا يُحِبُّ مَن كَانَ مُخْتَالًا فَخُورًا ﴿٣٦﴾ ﴾

36. Worship Allâh and join none with Him in worship; and do good to parents, kinsfolk, orphans, Al-Masâkîn (the poor), the neighbor who is near of kin, the neighbor who is a stranger, the companion by your side, the wayfarer (you meet), and those (slaves) whom your right hands possess. Verily, Allâh does not like such as are proud and boastful.

Transliteration

36. WaoAAbudoo Allaha wala tushrikoo bihi shay-an wabialwalidayni ihsanan wabithee alqurba waalyatama waalmasakeeni waaljari thee alqurba waaljari aljunubi waalssahibi bialjanbi waibni alssabeeli wama malakat aymanukum inna Allaha la yuhibbu man kana mukhtalan fakhooran

Tafsir Ibn Kathir

The Order to Worship Allah Alone and to Be Dutiful to Parents

Allah orders that He be worshipped Alone without partners, because He Alone is the Creator and Sustainer Who sends His favors and bounties on His creation in all situations and instances. Therefore He deserves to be singled out, without associating anything or anyone from His creation with Him in worship. Indeed, the Prophet said to Mu`adh,

«أَتَدْرِي مَا حَقُّ اللهِ عَلَى الْعِبَادِ؟»

(Do you know what Allah's right on His servants is) Mu`adh replied, "Allah and His Messenger know better." He said,

«أَنْ يَعْبُدُوهُ وَلَا يُشْرِكُوا بِهِ شَيْئًا»

(That they should worship Him and should not worship any others with Him.) The Prophet then said,

«أَتَدْرِي مَا حَقُّ الْعِبَادِ عَلَى اللهِ إِذَا فَعَلُوا ذَلِكَ؟ أَنْ لَا يُعَذِّبَهُم»

(Do you know what the right of the servants on Allah is if they do this He should not punish them.) Allah then commands the servants to be dutiful to their parents, for Allah made parents the reason for the servants to come to existence, after they did not exist. Allah joins the order to worship Him with being dutiful to parents in many places. For example, He said,

(give thanks to Me and to your parents), and,

(And your Lord has decreed that you worship none but Him. And that you be dutiful to your parents). After Allah ordained being dutiful to parents, He ordained kind treatment of relatives, males and females. A Hadith states,

«الصَّدَقَةُ عَلَى الْمِسْكِينِ صَدَقَةٌ، وَعَلى ذِي الرَّحِمِ صَدَقَةٌ وَصِلَة»

(Charity given to the poor is Sadaqah, while charity given to relatives is both Sadaqah and Silah (keeping the relations).) Allah then said,

(orphans), because they lost their caretakers who would spend on them. So Allah commands that the orphans be treated with kindness and compassion. Allah then said,

(Al-Masakin (the poor)) who have various needs and cannot find what sustains these needs. Therefore, Allah commands they should be helped in acquiring their needs in a sufficient manner that will end their inadequacy. We will further elaborate on the matter of the destitute and the poor in Surah Bara'h (9:60).

The Right of the Neighbor

Allah said,

(the neighbor who is near of kin, the neighbor who is a stranger) `Ali bin Abi Talhah said that Ibn `Abbas said that,

(the neighbor who is near of kin) means, "The neighbor who is also a relative", while,

(The neighbor who is a stranger) means, "Who is not a relative." It was also reported that `Ikrimah, Mujahid, Maymun bin Mihran, Ad-Dahhak, Zayd bin Aslam, Muqatil bin Hayyan and Qatadah said similarly. Mujahid was also reported to have said that Allah's statement,

(the neighbor who is a stranger) means, "The companion during travel." There are many Hadiths that command kind treatment to the neighbors, and we will mention some of them here with Allah's help. The First Hadith Imam Ahmad recorded that `Abdullah bin `Umar said that the Messenger of Allah said,

«مَازَالَ جِبْرِيلُ يُوصِينِي بِالْجَارِ حَتَّى ظَنَنْتُ أَنَّهُ سَيُوَرِّثُه»

(Jibril kept reminding of the neighbor's right, until I thought that he was going to give him a share of the inheritance.) The Two Sahihs recorded this Hadith. The Second Hadith Imam Ahmad recorded that `Abdullah bin `Amr said that the Messenger of Allah said,

«مَازَالَ جِبْرِيلُ يُوصِينِي بِالْجَارِ حَتَّى ظَنَنْتُ أَنَّهُ سَيُوَرِّثُه»

(Jibril kept reminding me of the neighbor's right, until I thought he was going to appoint a share of the inheritance for him.) Abu Dawud and At-Tirmidhi recorded this Hadith, which At-Tirmidhi said was "Hasan Gharib through this route." The Third Hadith Imam Ahmad recorded that `Abdullah bin `Amr bin Al-`As said that the Prophet said,

«خَيْرُ الْأَصْحَابِ عِنْدَ اللهِ خَيْرُهُمْ لِصَاحِبِهِ، وَخَيْرُ الْجِيرَانِ عِنْدَ اللهِ خَيْرُهُمْ لِجَارِه»

(The best companions according to Allah are those who are the best with their friends, and the best neighbors according to Allah are the best with their neighbors.) At-Tirmidhi recorded this Hadith and said, "Hasan Gharib". The Fourth Hadith Imam Ahmad recorded that Al-Miqdad bin Al-Aswad said that the Messenger of Allah asked his Companions,

«مَا تَقُولُونَ فِي الزِّنَا؟»

(What do you say about adultery) They said, "It is prohibited, for Allah and His Messenger have prohibited it. So it is forbidden until the Day of Resurrection." The Messenger of Allah said,

«لَأَنْ يَزْنِيَ الرَّجُلُ بِعَشْرِ نِسْوَةٍ، أَيْسَرُ عَلَيْهِ مِنْ أَنْ يَزْنِيَ بِامْرَأَةِ جَارِه»

(For a man to commit adultery with his neighbor's wife is worse than if he commits adultery with ten women.) He then said,

«مَا تَقُولُونَ فِي السَّرِقَةِ؟»

(What do you say about theft) They said, "It is prohibited, for Allah and His Messenger prohibited it." He said,

«لَأَنْ يَسْرِقَ الرَّجُلُ مِنْ عَشْرَةِ أَبْيَاتٍ، أَيْسَرُ عَلَيْهِ مِنْ أَنْ يَسْرِقَ مِنْ جَارِه»

(If a man steals from his neighbor, it is worse for him than stealing from ten homes.) Only Ahmad recorded this Hadith. A similar Hadith is recorded in the Two Sahihs, Ibn Mas`ud said, "I asked, `O Allah's Messenger! What is the greatest sin' He said,

«أَنْ تَجْعَلَ للهِ نِدًّا وَهُوَ خَلَقَك»

(To make a rival for Allah while He Alone created you.) I said, `Then' He said,

«أَنْ تَقْتُلَ وَلَدَكَ خَشْيَةَ أَنْ يَطْعَمَ مَعَك»

(To kill your offspring for fear that he might share your food with you.) I said, `Then' He said,

«أَنْ تُزَانِيَ حَلِيلَةَ جَارِك»

(To commit adultery with your neighbor's wife.)" The Fifth Hadith Imam Ahmad recorded that `A'ishah asked the Messenger of Allah, "I have two neighbors, so whom among them should I give my gift" He said,

«إِلى أَقْرَبِهِمَا مِنْكِ بَابًا»

(The neighbor whose door is the closest to you.) Al-Bukhari narrated this Hadith We will elaborate on this subject in the Tafsir of Surah Bara'h, Allah willing and upon Him we depend.

Being Kind to Slaves and Servants

Allah said,

(and those (slaves) whom your right hands possess,) this is an order to be kind to them because they are weak, being held as captives by others. An authentic Hadith records that during the illness that preceded his death, the Messenger of Allah continued advising his Ummah:

«الصَّلَاةَ الصَّلَاةَ، وَمَا مَلَكَتْ أَيْمَانُكُم»

((Protect) the prayer, (protect) the prayer, and (those slaves) whom your hands possess.) He was repeating it until his tongue was still. Imam Ahmad recorded that Al-Miqdam bin Ma`dykarib said that the Messenger of Allah said,

«مَا أَطْعَمْتَ نَفْسَكَ فَهُوَ لَكَ صَدَقَةٌ، وَمَا أَطْعَمْتَ وَلَدَكَ فَهُوَ لَكَ صَدَقَةٌ، وَمَا أَطْعَمْتَ زَوْجَتَكَ فَهُوَ لَكَ صَدَقَةٌ، وَمَا أَطْعَمْتَ خَادِمَكَ فَهُوَ لَكَ صَدَقَة»

(What you feed yourself is a Sadaqah (charity) for you, what you feed your children is Sadaqah for you, what you feed your wife is Sadaqah for you and what you feed your servant is Sadaqah for you.) An-Nasa'i recorded this Hadith which has an authentic chain of narration, all the thanks are due to Allah. `Abdullah bin `Amr said to a caretaker of his, "Did you give the slaves their food yet" He said, "No." Ibn `Amr said, "Go and give it to them, for the Messenger of Allah said,

«كَفَى بِالْمَرْءِ إِثْمًا أَنْ يَحْبِسَ عَمَّنْ يَمْلِكُ قُوتَهُم»

(It is enough sin for someone to prevent whomever he is responsible for from getting their food.)" Muslim recorded this Hadith. Abu Hurayrah narrated that the Prophet said,

«لِلْمَمْلُوكِ طَعَامُهُ وَكِسْوَتُهُ، وَلَا يُكَلَّفُ مِنَ الْعَمَلِ إِلَّا مَا يُطِيق»

(The slave has the right to have food, clothing and to only be required to perform what he can bear of work.) Muslim also recorded this Hadith. Abu Hurayrah narrated that the Prophet said,

«إِذَا أَتَى أَحَدَكُمْ خَادِمُهُ بِطَعَامِه، فَإِنْ لَمْ يُجْلِسْهُ مَعَهُ فَلْيُنَاوِلْهُ لُقْمَةً أَوْ لُقْمَتَيْنِ أَوْ أُكْلَةً أَوْ أُكْلَتَيْنِ فَإِنَّهُ وَلِيَ حَرَّهُ وَعِلَاجَه»

(When your servant brings meals to one of you, if he does not let him sit and share the meal, then he should at least give him a mouthful or two mouthfuls of that meal or a meal or two, for he has prepared it.) This is the wording collected by Al-Bukhari.

Allah Does Not Like the Arrogant

Allah said,

(Verily, Allah does not like such as are proud and boastful.) meaning, one who is proud and arrogant, insolent and boasts to others. He thinks that he is better than other people, thus thinking high of himself, even though he is insignificant to Allah and hated by people. Mujahid said that Allah's statement,

(Verily, Allah does not like such as are proud) means arrogant, while,

(boastful) means boasting about what he has, while he does not thank Allah. This Ayah indicates that such a person boasts with people about the bounty that Allah has given him, but he is actually ungrateful to Allah for this bounty. Ibn Jarir recorded that `Abdullah bin Waqid Abu Raja' Al-Harawi said, "You will find that those who are mean are also proud and boasting. He then recited,

(and those (slaves) whom your right hands possess,) You will find that he who is undutiful (to parents) is also arrogant, and deprived. He then recited,

(And dutiful to my mother, and made me not arrogant, deprived.) Once a man asked the Prophet, "O Messenger of Allah, advise me.' The Prophet said,

«إِيَّاكَ وَإِسْبَالَ الْإِزَارِ، فَإِنَّ إِسْبَالَ الْإِزَارِ مِنَ الْمَخِيلَةِ، وَإِنَّ اللهَ لَا يُحِبُّ الْمَخِيلَة»

(Avoid lengthening the dress (below the ankles), for this practice is from arrogance. Verily, Allah does not like arrogance.)"

Surah: 4 Ayah: 37, Ayah: 38 & Ayah: 39

﴿ٱلَّذِينَ يَبۡخَلُونَ وَيَأۡمُرُونَ ٱلنَّاسَ بِٱلۡبُخۡلِ وَيَكۡتُمُونَ مَآ ءَاتَىٰهُمُ ٱللَّهُ مِن فَضۡلِهِۦۗ
وَأَعۡتَدۡنَا لِلۡكَٰفِرِينَ عَذَابٗا مُّهِينٗا ٣٧﴾

37. Those who are miserly and enjoin miserliness on other men and hide what Allâh has bestowed upon them of His Bounties. And We have prepared for the disbelievers a disgraceful torment.

﴿وَٱلَّذِينَ يُنفِقُونَ أَمۡوَٰلَهُمۡ رِئَآءَ ٱلنَّاسِ وَلَا يُؤۡمِنُونَ بِٱللَّهِ وَلَا بِٱلۡيَوۡمِ ٱلۡأٓخِرِۗ وَمَن
يَكُنِ ٱلشَّيۡطَٰنُ لَهُۥ قَرِينٗا فَسَآءَ قَرِينٗا ٣٨﴾

38. And (also) those who spend of their substance to be seen of men, and believe not in Allâh and the Last Day (they are the friends of Shaitân (Satan)) and whoever takes Shaitân (Satan) as an intimate; then what a dreadful intimate he has!

﴿وَمَاذَا عَلَيۡهِمۡ لَوۡ ءَامَنُواْ بِٱللَّهِ وَٱلۡيَوۡمِ ٱلۡأٓخِرِ وَأَنفَقُواْ مِمَّا رَزَقَهُمُ ٱللَّهُۚ وَكَانَ ٱللَّهُ بِهِمۡ
عَلِيمًا ٣٩﴾

39. And what loss have they if they had believed in Allâh and in the Last Day, and they spend out of what Allâh has given them for sustenance? And Allâh is Ever All-Knower of them.

Transliteration

37. Allatheena yabkhaloona waya/muroona alnnasa bialbukhli wayaktumoona ma atahumu Allahu min fadlihi waaAAtadna lilkafireena AAathaban muheenan 38. Waallatheena yunfiqoona amwalahum ri-aa alnnasi wala yu/minoona biAllahi wala bialyawmi alakhiri waman yakuni alshshaytanu lahu qareenan fasaa qareenan 39. Wamatha AAalayhim law amanoo biAllahi waalyawmi al-akhiri waanfaqoo mimma razaqahumu Allahu wakana Allahu bihim AAaleeman

Tafsir Ibn Kathir

The Censure of Stingy Behavior

Allah chastises the stingy behavior of those who refuse to spend their money for what Allah ordered them, such as being kind to parents and compassionate to relatives, orphans, the poor, the relative who is also a neighbor, the companion during travel, the needy wayfarer, the slaves and servants. Such people do not give Allah's right from their wealth, and they assist in the spread of stingy behavior. The Messenger of Allah said,

«وَأَيُّ دَاءٍ أَدْوَأُ مِنَ الْبُخْلِ»

(What disease is more serious than being stingy) He also said,

«إِيَّاكُمْ وَالشُّحَّ، فَإِنَّهُ أَهْلَكَ مَنْ كَانَ قَبْلَكُمْ، أَمَرَهُمْ بِالْقَطِيعَةِ فَقَطَعُوا، وَأَمَرَهُمْ بِالْفُجُورِ فَفَجَرُوا»

(Beware of being stingy, for it destroyed those who were before you, as it encouraged them to cut their relations and they did, and it encouraged them to commit sin and they did.) Allah said,

(and hide what Allah has bestowed upon them of His bounties,) Therefore, the miser is ungrateful for Allah's favor, for its effect does not appear on him, whether in his food, clothes or what he gives. Similarly, Allah said,

(Verily, man is ungrateful to his Lord. And to that he bears witness.) by his manners and conduct,

(And verily, he is violent in the love of wealth.) Allah said,

(and hide what Allah has bestowed upon them of His bounties) and this is why He threatened them,

(And We have prepared for the disbelievers a disgraceful torment.) Kufr means to cover something. Therefore, the Bakhil (miser) covers the favors that Allah has blessed him with, meaning he does not spread those favors. So he is described by the term Kafir (ungrateful) regarding the favors that Allah granted him. A Hadith states that,

«إِنَّ اللهَ إِذَا أَنْعَمَ نِعْمَةً عَلى عَبْدٍ،أَحَبَّ أَنْ يَظْهَرَ أَثَرُهَا عَلَيْه»

(When Allah grants a servant a favor, He likes that its effect appears on him.) Some of the Salaf stated that this Ayah (4:37) is describing the Jews who hid the knowledge they had about the description of Muhammad, and there is no doubt that the general meaning of the Ayah includes this. The apparent wording for this Ayah indicates that it is talking about being stingy with money, even though miserly conduct with knowledge is also included. The Ayah talks about spending on relatives and the weak, just as the Ayah after it,

(And (also) those who spend of their wealth to be seen of men,) Allah first mentions the punished misers who do not spend, then He mentions those who spend to show off to gain the reputation that they are generous, not for the Face of Allah. A Hadith states that the first three persons on whom the fire will feed are a scholar, a fighter and a spender who shows off with their actions. For instance,

«يَقُولُ صَاحِبُ الْمَالِ: مَا تَرَكْتُ مِنْ شَيْءٍ تُحِبُّ أَنْ يُنْفَقَ فِيهِ، إِلَّا أَنْفَقْتُ فِي سَبِيلِكَ، فَيَقُولُ اللهُ: كَذَبْتَ، إِنَّمَا أَرَدْتَ أَنْ يُقَالَ: جَوَادٌ، فَقَدْ قِيل»

(The wealthy will say, "I did not leave any area that You like to be spent on, but I spent on it in Your cause." Allah will say, "You lie, you only did that so that it is said, `He is generous.'

And it was said...") meaning you acquired your reward in the life, and this is indeed what you sought with your action. This is why Allah said,

(and believe not in Allah and the Last Day,) meaning, it is Shaytan who lured them to commit this evil action, instead of performing the good deed as it should be performed. Shaytan encouraged, excited and lured them by making the evil appear good,

(And whoever takes Shaytan as an intimate; then what a dreadful intimate he has!) Allah then said,

(And what loss have they if they had believed in Allah and in the Last Day, and they spend out of what Allah has given them for sustenance) This Ayah means, what harm would it cause them if they believe in Allah, go on the righteous path, replace showing off with sincerity, have faith in Allah, and await His promise in the Hereafter, for those who do good and spend what He has given them on what He likes and is pleased with. Allah's statement:

(And Allah is Ever All-Knower of them.) means, He has perfect knowledge of their intentions, whether good or evil. Indeed, Allah knows those who deserve success, and He grants them success and guidance, directing them to perform righteous actions that will earn them His pleasure. He also knows those who deserve failure and expulsion from His great mercy, which amounts to utter failure in this life and the Hereafter for them, we seek refuge in Allah from this evil end.

Surah: 4 Ayah: 40, Ayah: 41 & Ayah: 42

﴿ إِنَّ ٱللَّهَ لَا يَظۡلِمُ مِثۡقَالَ ذَرَّةٖۖ وَإِن تَكُ حَسَنَةٗ يُضَٰعِفۡهَا وَيُؤۡتِ مِن لَّدُنۡهُ أَجۡرًا
عَظِيمٗا ٤٠ ﴾

40. Surely! Allâh wrongs not even of the weight of an atom (or a small ant), but if there is any good (done), He doubles it, and gives from Him a great reward.

﴿ فَكَيۡفَ إِذَا جِئۡنَا مِن كُلِّ أُمَّةِۭ بِشَهِيدٖ وَجِئۡنَا بِكَ عَلَىٰ هَٰٓؤُلَآءِ شَهِيدٗا ٤١ ﴾

41. How (will it be) then, when We bring from each nation a witness and We bring you (O Muhammad (peace be upon him)) as a witness against these people?

﴿ يَوۡمَئِذٖ يَوَدُّ ٱلَّذِينَ كَفَرُواْ وَعَصَوُاْ ٱلرَّسُولَ لَوۡ تُسَوَّىٰ بِهِمُ ٱلۡأَرۡضُ وَلَا يَكۡتُمُونَ ٱللَّهَ
حَدِيثٗا ٤٢ ﴾

42. On that day those who disbelieved and disobeyed the Messenger (Muhammad (peace be upon him)) will wish that they were buried in the earth, but they will never be able to hide a single fact from Allâh.

Transliteration

40. Inna Allaha la yathlimu mithqala tharratin wa-in taku hasanatan yudaAAifha wayu/ti min ladunhu ajran AAatheeman 41. Fakayfa itha ji/na min kulli ommatin bishaheedin waji/na bika AAala haola-i shaheedan 42. Yawma-ithin yawaddu allatheena kafaroo waAAasawoo alrrasoola law tusawwa bihimu al-ardu wala yaktumoona Allaha hadeethan

Tafsir Ibn Kathir

Allah Wrongs Not Even the Weight of a Speck of Dust

Allah states that He does not treat any of His servants with injustice on the Day of Resurrection, be it the weight of a mustard seed or a speck of dust. Rather, Allah shall reward them for this action and multiply it, if it were a good deed. For instance, Allah said,

(And We shall set up balances of justice) Allah said that Luqman said,

(O my son! If it be (anything) equal to the weight of a mustard seed, and though it be in a rock, or in the heavens or in the earth, Allah will bring it forth). Allah said,

(That Day mankind will proceed in scattered groups that they may be shown their deeds. So whosoever does good equal to the weight of a speck of dust shall see it. And whosoever does evil equal to the weight of a speck of dust shall see it.) The Two Sahihs recorded the long Hadith about the intercession that Abu Sa`id Al-Khudri narrated, and in which the Messenger of Allah said,

«فَيَقُولُ اللهُ عَزَّ وَجَلَّ: ارْجِعُوا، فَمَنْ وَجَدْتُمْ فِي قَلْبِهِ مِثْقَالَ حَبَّةِ خَرْدَلٍ مِنْ إِيمَانٍ، فَأَخْرِجُوهُ مِنَ النَّارِ»

(Allah then says, "Go back, and take out of the Fire everyone in whose heart you find the weight of a mustard seed of faith") In another narration, Allah says,

«أَدْنَى أَدْنَى مِثْقَالِ ذَرَّةٍ مِنْ إِيمَانٍ، فَأَخْرِجُوهُ مِنَ النَّارِ، فَيُخْرِجُونَ خَلْقًا كَثِيرًا»

("Whosoever had the least, least, least speck of faith, take him out of the Fire," and they will take out many people.) Abu Sa`id then said, "Read, if you will,

(Surely! Allah wrongs not even of the weight of a speck of dust)."

Will Punishment be Diminished for the Disbelievers

Sa`id bin Jubayr commented about Allah's statement,

(but if there is any good (done), He doubles it,) "As for the disbeliever, his punishment will be lessened for him on the Day of Resurrection, but he will never depart the Fire." He used as evidence the authentic Hadith in which Al-`Abbas said, "O Messenger of Allah! Your uncle Abu Talib used to protect and support you, did you benefit him at all" The Messenger said,

«نَعَمْ هُوَ فِي ضَحْضَاحٍ مِنْ نَارٍ، وَلَوْلَا أَنَا، لَكَانَ فِي الدَّرْكِ الْأَسْفَلِ مِنَ النَّارِ»

(Yes. He is in a shallow area in Hell-fire, and were it not for me, he would have been in the deepest depths of the Fire.) However, this Hadith only applies to Abu Talib, not the rest of the disbelievers. To support this, we mention what Abu Dawud At-Tayalisi recorded in his Musnad that Anas said that the Messenger of Allah said,

«إِنَّ اللهَ لَا يَظْلِمُ الْمُؤْمِنَ حَسَنَةً، يُثَابُ عَلَيْهَا الرِّزْقَ فِي الدُّنْيَا، وَيُجْزَى بِهَا فِي الْآخِرَةِ، وَأَمَّا الْكَافِرُ فَيُطْعَمُ بِهَا فِي الدُّنْيَا، فَإِذَا كَانَ يَوْمُ الْقِيَامَةِ لَمْ يَكُنْ لَهُ حَسَنَةٌ»

(Allah does not wrong the faithful even concerning one good action, for he will be rewarded for it by provision in this life and awarded for it in the Hereafter. As for the disbeliever, he will be provided provision in this life for his good action, and on the Day of Resurrection, he will not have any good deed.)

What Does `Great Reward' Mean

Abu Hurayrah, `Ikrimah, Sa`id bin Jubayr, Al-Hasan, Qatadah and Ad-Dahhak said that Allah's statement,

(and gives from Him a great reward.) refers to Paradise. We ask Allah for His pleasure and Paradise. Ibn Abi Hatim recorded that Abu `Uthman An-Nahdi said, "No other person accompanied Abu Hurayrah more than I. One year, he went to Hajj before me, and I found the people of Al-Basrah saying that he narrated that he heard the Messenger of Allah saying,

«إِنَّ اللهَ يُضَاعِفُ الْحَسَنَةَ أَلْفَ أَلْفِ حَسَنَة»

(Allah rewards the good deed with a million deeds.) So I said, `Woe to you! No person accompanied Abu Hurayrah more than I, and I never heard him narrate this Hadith!' When I wanted to meet him, I found that he had left for Hajj so I followed him to Hajj to ask him about this Hadith." Ibn Abi Hatim also recorded this Hadith using another chain of narration leading to Abu `Uthman. In this narration, Abu `Uthman said, "I said, `O Abu Hurayrah! I heard my brethren in Al-Basrah claim that you narrated that you heard the Messenger of Allah saying,

«إِنَّ اللهَ يَجْزِي بِالْحَسَنَةِ أَلْفَ أَلْفِ حَسَنَة»

(Allah rewards the good deed with a million deeds.) Abu Hurayrah said, `By Allah! I heard the Messenger of Allah saying,

«إِنَّ اللهَ يَجْزِي بِالْحَسَنَةِ أَلْفَيْ أَلْفِ حَسَنَة»

(Allah rewards the good deed with two million deeds.) He then recited this Ayah,

(But little is the enjoyment of the life of this world as compared to the Hereafter)."

Our Prophet will be a Witness Against, or For his Ummah on the Day of Resurrection, When the Disbelievers Will Wish for Death

Allah said,

(How (will it be) then, when We bring from each nation a witness and We bring you (O Muhammad) as a witness against these people) Allah describes the horrors, hardships and difficulties of the Day of Resurrection, saying, how would it be on that Day when there will be a witness from every nation, meaning the Prophets, just as Allah said;

(And the earth will shine with the light of its Lord, and the Book will be placed (open); and the Prophets and the witnesses will be brought forward), and,

(And (remember) the Day when We shall raise up from every nation a witness against them from amongst themselves). Al-Bukhari recorded that `Abdullah bin Mas`ud said, "The Messenger of Allah said to me, `Recite to me.' I said, `O Messenger of Allah! Should I recite (the Qur'an) to you, while it was revealed to you' He said, `Yes, for I like to hear it from other people.' I recited Surat An-Nisa' until I reached this Ayah,

(How (will it be) then, when We bring from each nation a witness and We bring you (O Muhammad) as a witness against these people) He then said, `Stop now.' I found that his eyes were tearful." Allah's statement,

(On that day those who disbelieved and disobeyed the Messenger will wish that they were buried in the earth, but they will never be able to hide a single fact from Allah.) means, they will wish that the earth would open up and swallow them because of the horror of the gathering place and the disgrace, dishonor and humiliation they will suffer on that Day. This is similar to Allah's statement,

(The Day when man will see that (the deeds) which his hands have sent forth) Allah then said,

(but they will never be able to hide a single fact from Allah.) indicating that they will admit to everything they did and will not hide any of it. `Abdur-Razzaq recorded that Sa`id bin Jubayr said, "A man came to Ibn `Abbas and said to him, `There are things that confuse me in the Qur'an.' Ibn `Abbas said, `What things do you have doubts about in the Qur'an' He said, `Not doubts, but rather confusing things.' Ibn `Abbas said, `Tell me what caused you confusion.' He said, `I hear Allah's statement,

(There will then be no test for them but to say: "By Allah, our Lord, we were not those who joined others in worship with Allah.") but He also says,

(but they will never be able to hide a single fact from Allah.) They have indeed hid something.' Ibn `Abbas said, `As for Allah's statement,

(There will then be no test for them but to say: "By Allah, our Lord, we were not those who joined others in worship with Allah."), when they see that on the Day of Resurrection that Allah does not forgive, except for the people of Islam, and that He forgives the sins, no matter how big they are, except Shirk, then the Mushriks will lie. They will say,

("By Allah, our Lord, we were not those who joined others in worship with Allah."), hoping that Allah will forgive them. However, Allah will then seal their mouths, and their hands and feet will disclose what they used to do. Then,

(those who disbelieved and disobeyed the Messenger will wish that they were buried in the earth, but they will never be able to hide a single fact from Allah.)'"

Surah: 4 Ayah: 43

﴿ يَـٰٓأَيُّهَا ٱلَّذِينَ ءَامَنُوا۟ لَا تَقْرَبُوا۟ ٱلصَّلَوٰةَ وَأَنتُمْ سُكَـٰرَىٰ حَتَّىٰ تَعْلَمُوا۟ مَا تَقُولُونَ وَلَا جُنُبًا
إِلَّا عَابِرِى سَبِيلٍ حَتَّىٰ تَغْتَسِلُوا۟ ۚ وَإِن كُنتُم مَّرْضَىٰٓ أَوْ عَلَىٰ سَفَرٍ أَوْ جَآءَ أَحَدٌ مِّنكُم مِّنَ
ٱلْغَآئِطِ أَوْ لَـٰمَسْتُمُ ٱلنِّسَآءَ فَلَمْ تَجِدُوا۟ مَآءً فَتَيَمَّمُوا۟ صَعِيدًا طَيِّبًا فَٱمْسَحُوا۟ بِوُجُوهِكُمْ
وَأَيْدِيكُمْ ۗ إِنَّ ٱللَّهَ كَانَ عَفُوًّا غَفُورًا ﴿٤٣﴾ ﴾

43. O you who believe! Approach not As-Salât (the prayer) when you are in a drunken state until you know (the meaning) of what you utter, nor when you are in a state of Janâba, (i.e. in a state of sexual impurity and have not yet taken a bath) except when travelling on the road (without enough water, or just passing through a mosque), till you wash your whole body. And if you are ill, or on a journey, or one of you comes after answering the call of nature, or you have been in contact with women (by sexual relations) and you find no water, perform Tayammum with clean earth and rub therewith your faces and hands (Tayammum). Truly, Allâh is Ever Oft-Pardoning, Oft-Forgiving.

Transliteration

43. Ya ayyuha allatheena amanoo la taqraboo alssalata waantum sukara hatta taAAlamoo ma taqooloona wala junuban illa AAabiree sabeelin hatta taghtasiloo wa-in kuntum marda aw AAala safarin aw jaa ahadun minkum mina algha-iti aw lamastumu alnnisaa falam tajidoo maan fatayammamoo saAAeedan tayyiban faimsahoo biwujoohikum waaydeekum inna Allaha kana AAafuwwan ghafooran

Tafsir Ibn Kathir

The Prohibition of Approaching Prayer When Drunk or Junub

Allah forbade His believing servants from praying while drunk, for one does not know the meaning of what he is saying in that state, and He forbade them from attending the Masjids while sexually impure, except when one is just passing through the Masjid from one door to another. This Ayah was revealed before alcohol consumption was completely prohibited, as evident by the Hadith that we mentioned in Surat Al-Baqarah when we explained Allah's statement,

(They ask you about alcoholic drink and gambling). In that Hadith, the Messenger of Allah recited this Ayah to `Umar, who said, "O Allah! Explain the ruling about Khamr (intoxicants) for us in a plain manner." When this Ayah (4:43) was revealed, the Prophet recited it to `Umar, who still said, "O Allah! Explain the ruling about Khamr (intoxicants) for us in a plain manner." After that, they would not drink alcohol close to the time of prayer. When Allah's statement,

(O you who believe! alcoholic drinks, gambling, Al-Ansab, and Al-Azlam are an abomination of Shayatan's handiwork. So avoid that in order that you may be successful.) (5:90), until,

(So, will you not then abstain) (5:91) was revealed, `Umar said, "We abstain, we abstain." In another narration, when the Ayah in Surat An-Nisa' was revealed,

(O you who believe! Do not approach Salah while you are in a druken state until you know what you are saying,) at the time of prayer, the Messenger of Allah would have someone proclaim; "Let not any drunk approach the prayer." This is the wording collected by Abu Dawud.

Causes of Its Revelation

Ibn Abi Hatim has recorded some reports about the incident of its revelation: Sa`d said, "Four Ayat were revealed concerning me. A man from the Ansar once made some food and invited some Muhajirin and Ansar men to it, and we ate and drank until we became intoxicated. We then boasted about our status." Then a man held a camel's bone and injured Sa`d's nose, which was scarred ever since. This occurred before Al-Khamr was prohibited, and Allah later revealed,

(O you who believe! Approach not AsSalat (the prayer) when you are in a drunken state). Muslim recorded this Hadith, and the collectors of the Sunan recorded it, with the exception of Ibn Majah. Another Reason Ibn Abi Hatim narrated that `Ali bin Abi Talib said, "Abdur-Rahman bin `Awf made some food to which he invited us and served some alcohol to drink. When we became intoxicated, and the time for prayer came, they asked someone to lead us in prayer. He recited `Say, `O disbelievers! I do not worship that which you worship, but we worship that which you worship (refer to the correct wording of the Surah: 109).'" Allah then revealed,

(O you who believe! Do not approach Salah when you are in a drunken state until you know what you are saying). " This is the narration collected by Ibn Abi Hatim and At-Tirmidhi, who said "Hasan (Gharib) Sahih." Allah's statement,

(until you know what you are saying) is the best description for when one is intoxicated, that is, when he does not know the meaning of what he is saying. When a person is drunk, he makes obvious mistakes in the recitation and will not be able to be humble during the prayer. Imam Ahmad recorded that Anas said that the Messenger of Allah said,

«إِذَا نَعَسَ أَحَدُكُمْ وَهُوَ يُصَلِّي، فَلْيَنْصَرِفْ فَلْيَنَمْ، حَتَّى يَعْلَمَ مَا يَقُولُ»

(If one feels sleepy while he is praying, let him sleep for a while so that he knows the meaning of what he is saying.) This was also recorded by Al-Bukhari and An-Nasa'i. In some of the narrations of this Hadith, the Messenger said,

«فَلَعَلَّهُ يَذْهَبُ يَسْتَغْفِرُ فَيَسُبَّ نَفْسَه»

(...For he might want to ask for forgiveness, but instead curses himself!) Allah said,

(nor while Junub (sexually impure), except while passing through, until you bathe (your entire body),) Ibn Abi Hatim recorded that Ibn `Abbas said that Allah's statement,

(nor while Junub (sexually impure), except while passing through, until you bathe (your entire body,) means, "Do not enter the Masjid when you are Junub, unless you are just passing by, in which case, you pass through without sitting down." Ibn Abi Hatim said that similar is reported from `Abdullah bin Mas`ud, Anas, Abu `Ubaydah, Sa`id bin Al-Musayyib, Abu Ad-Duha, `Ata', Mujahid, Masruq, Ibrahim An-Nakha`i, Zayd bin Aslam, Abu Malik, `Amr bin Dinar, Al-Hakam bin `Utaybah, `Ikrimah, Al-Hasan Al-Basri, Yahya bin Sa`id Al-Ansari, Ibn Shihab and Qatadah. Ibn Jarir recorded that Yazid bin Abi Habib commented on Allah's statement,

(nor while Junub (sexually impure), except while passing through,) when some men from the Ansar, whose doors literally opened into the Masjid, were sexually impure, and they did not have water, their only way to get water was to pass through the Masjid. So, Allah sent down,

(nor while Junub (sexually impure), except while passing through,)." What supports this statement by Yazid bin Abi Habib, may Allah have mercy upon him, is Al-Bukhari's report in his Sahih, that the Messenger of Allah said,

«سُدُّوا كُلَّ خَوْخَةٍ فِي الْمَسْجِدِ إِلَّا خَوْخَةَ أَبِي بَكْرٍ»

(Close all the small doors in this Masjid, except that of Abu Bakr.) This is what the Prophet commanded at the end of his life, knowing that Abu Bakr will be the Khalifah after him, and that he would need to enter the Masjid on numerous occasions to manage the important affairs of the Muslims. Yet, the Messenger of Allah commanded that all the small doors that open into the Masjid be closed, except Abu Bakr's door. Some of the Sunan compilers recorded the Prophet saying that only `Ali's door should remain open, but this is an error, what is in the Sahih is what is correct. In his Sahih, Muslim recorded that `A'ishah said, "The Messenger of Allah said to me,

«نَاوِلِينِي الْخُمْرَةَ مِنَ الْمَسْجِدِ»

(Bring me the garment from the Masjid.) I said, `I am having my period.' He said,

«إِنَّ حَيْضَتَكِ لَيْسَتْ فِي يَدِكِ»

(Your period is not in your hand.) Muslim also collected a similar narration from Abu Hurayrah. This Hadith indicates that the woman is allowed to pass through the Masjid during menses or post-natal bleeding, and Allah knows best.

Description of Tayammum

Allah said,

(and if you are ill, or on a journey, or one of you comes from the Gha'it (toilet), or from Lamastum (touching) women, but you do not find water, then perform Tayammum with clean earth, rubbing your face and hands. Truly, Allah is Ever Oft-Pardoning, Oft-Forgiving.) As for the type of illness which would allow Tayammum, it is an illness that one fears would be aggravated by using water, which could be detrimental to a part of the body, or when doing so would prolong an illness. Some scholars said that any type of illness warrants Tayammum, because of the general indications of the Ayah. As for travelling on a journey, it is known, regardless of its length. Allah then said, (or comes from the Gha'it). The Gha'it is, literally, the flat land, and this part of the Ayah refers to the minor impurity. Allah then said,

(or you Lamastum women), which was recited Lamastum and Lamastum, referring to sexual intercourse. For instance, Allah said in another Ayah,

(And if you divorce them before you have touched them, and you have appointed unto them the dowry, then pay half of that) (2:237), and,

(O you who believe! When you marry believing women, and then divorce them before you have touched them, no `Iddah (period of waiting) have you to count in respect of them) (33:49). Ibn Abi Hatim recorded that Ibn `Abbas said that Allah's statement,

(or Lamastum women) refers to sexual intercourse. It was reported that `Ali, Ubayy bin Ka`b, Mujahid, Tawus, Al-Hasan, `Ubayd bin `Umayr, Sa`id bin Jubayr, Ash-Sha`bi, Qatadah and Muqatil bin Hayyan said similarly. Allah said,

(but you do not find water,them perform Tayammum with clean earth,) In the Two Sahihs, it is recorded that `Imran bin Husayn said,

(Allah's Messenger saw a person sitting away from the people and not praying with them. He asked him,

«يَا فُلَانُ مَا مَنَعَكَ أَنْ تُصَلِّيَ مَعَ الْقَوْمِ، أَلَسْتَ بِرَجُلٍ مُسْلِمٍ؟»

`O so-and-so! What prevented you from offering the prayer with the people, are not you Muslim' He replied, `Yes, O Allah's Messenger! I am Junub and there is no water.' The Prophet said,

«عَلَيْكَ بِالصَّعِيدِ، فَإِنَّهُ يَكْفِيك»

`Perform Tayammum with clean earth and that will be sufficient for you.') The linguistic meaning of Tayammum is to intend, as Arabs say, "May Allah Tayammamaka (direct at you) His care." `Clean earth' means dust. In his Sahih, Muslim recorded that Hudhayfah bin Al-Yaman said that the Messenger of Allah said,

«فُضِّلْنَا عَلَى النَّاسِ بِثَلَاثٍ: جُعِلَتْ صُفُوفُنَا كَصُفُوفِ الْمَلَائِكَةِ، وَجُعِلَتْ لَنَا الْأَرْضُ كُلُّهَا مَسْجِدًا، وَجُعِلَتْ تُرْبَتُهَا لَنَا طَهُورًا، إِذَا لَمْ نَجِدِ الْمَاءِ»

(We were given preference over people in three things. Our lines (in prayer) were arranged in rows to resemble the rows of the angels, all of the earth was made a Masjid for us, and its dust was made clean for us when there is no water.) The Messenger mentioned the favor of making dust a purifyer for us, and if there were any other substance to replace it for Tayammum, he would have mentioned it. Imam Ahmad and the collectors of Sunan, with the exception of Ibn Majah, recorded that Abu Dharr said that the Messenger of Allah said,

«الصَّعِيدُ الطَّيِّبُ طَهُورُ الْمُسْلِمِ، وَإِنْ لَمْ يَجِدِ الْمَاءَ عَشْرَ حِجَجٍ، فَإِذَا وَجَدَهُ فَلْيُمِسَّهُ بَشَرَتَهُ، فَإِنَّ ذَلِكَ خَيْرٌ»

(Clean earth is pure for the Muslim, even if he does not find water for ten years. When he finds water, let him use it for his skin, for this is better.) At-Tirmidhi said, "Hasan Sahih". Allah's statement,

(rubbing your faces and hands (Tayammum)) indicates that Tayammum is a substitute for normal ablution, not that it involves cleaning the parts that normal ablution does. Therefore, it is sufficient in Tayammum to just wipe the face and hands, as the consensus concurs. The face and hands are wiped with one strike on the sand in this case, as Imam Ahmad recorded that `Abdur-Rahman bin Abza said that a man came to `Umar and asked him, "I am Junub, but there is no water." `Umar said, "Then, do not pray." `Ammar said, "Do you not remember, O Leader of the Faithful! You and I were on a military expedition when we became Junub and did not find water. You did not pray, but I rolled myself in the sand and then prayed. When we went back to the Prophet, we mentioned to him what had happened. He said to me,

«إِنَّمَا كَانَ يَكْفِيك»

(This would have been sufficient for you), and the Prophet stroked his hand on the earth once, blew into it and wiped his face and hands." The Muslim Ummah, rather than all other nations, was favored with the allowance of Tayammum. In the Two Sahihs, it is recorded that Jabir bin `Abdullah said that the Messenger of Allah said,

«أُعْطِيتُ خَمْسًا لَمْ يُعْطَهُنَّ أَحَدٌ قَبْلِي: نُصِرْتُ بِالرُّعْبِ مَسِيرَةَ شَهْرٍ، وَجُعِلَتْ لِيَ الْأَرْضُ مَسْجِدًا وَطَهُورًا، فَأَيُّمَا رَجُلٍ مِنْ أُمَّتِي أَدْرَكَتْهُ الصَّلَاةُ فَلْيُصَل»

(I have been given five things which were not given to any (Prophet) before me: Allah made me victorious with fright that covers a month's distance. The earth has been made for me (and for my followers) a place for praying and an object to perform purification with. Therefore let my followers pray wherever the time of a prayer is due) - and in another narration –

«فَعِنْدَهُ طَهُورُهُ وَمَسْجِدُهُ، وَأُحِلَّتْ لِيَ الْغَنَائِمُ، وَلَمْ تَحِلَّ لِأَحَدٍ قَبْلِي، وَأُعْطِيتُ الشَّفَاعَةَ، وَكَانَ النَّبِيُّ يُبْعَثُ إِلَى قَوْمِهِ، وَبُعِثْتُ إِلَى النَّاسِ عَامَّة»

(he will have his means of purity and his Masjid. The spoils of war have been made lawful for me and it was not made so for anyone else before me. I have been given the right of intercession (on the Day of Resurrection.) Every Prophet used to be sent to his nation exclusively, but I have been sent to all mankind.) We also mentioned the Hadith of Hudhayfah that Muslim recorded;

«فُضِّلْنَا عَلَى النَّاسِ بِثَلَاثٍ، جُعِلَتْ صُفُوفُنَا كَصُفُوفِ الْمَلَائِكَةِ، وَجُعِلَتْ لَنَا الْأَرْضُ مَسْجِدًا، وَتُرْبَتُهَا طَهُورًا، إِذَا لَمْ نَجِدِ الْمَاءَ»

(We were preferred with three things over people. Our lines (in prayer) were arranged in rows to resemble the rows of the angels, all of the earth was made a Masjid for us, and its dust was made clean for us when there is no water.) Allah said in this Ayah,

(rubbing your faces and hands. Truly, Allah is Ever Oft-Pardoning, Oft-Forgiving.) meaning, a part of His pardoning and forgiving is that He allows you to use Tayammum and to pray after using it when there is no water, to make things easy for you. This Ayah sanctifies the position of the prayer, it being too sacred than to be performed in a defecient manner, like in a state of drunkenness, until one becomes aware of what he is saying, or sexually impure, until he bathes (Ghusl), or after answering the call of nature, until he performs ablution. There are exceptions when one is ill or when there is no water. In this case, Allah allows us to use Tayammum, out of His mercy and kindness for His servants, and to facilitate them, all praise is due to Allah.

The Reason behind allowing Tayammum

Al-Bukhari recorded that `A'ishah said, "We set out with Allah's Messenger on one of his journeys until we reached Al-Bayda' or Dhat-ul-Jaysh, where a necklace of mine was broken (and lost). Allah's Messenger stayed there to search for it, and so did the people along with him. There was no water source or any water with them at that place, so the people went to Abu Bakr As-Siddiq and said, `Don't you see what `A'ishah has done! She has made Allah's Messenger and the people stay where there is no source of water and they have no water with them.' Abu Bakr came while Allah's Messenger was sleeping with his head on my thigh. He said to me, `You have detained Allah's Messenger and the people where there is no source of water and they have no water with them.' So he admonished me and said what Allah wished him to say and hit me on my flank with his hand. Nothing prevented me from moving (because of pain) but the position of Allah's Messenger on my thigh. Allah's Messenger got up when dawn broke and there was no water. So Allah revealed the verses of Tayammum, and they all performed Tayammum. Usayd bin Hudayr said, `O the family of Abu Bakr! This is not the first blessing of yours.' Then the camel on which I was riding was moved from its place and the necklace was found beneath it." Al-Bukhari and Muslim recorded this Hadith.

Surah: 4 Ayah: 44, Ayah: 45 & Ayah: 46

﴿ أَلَمْ تَرَ إِلَى ٱلَّذِينَ أُوتُوا۟ نَصِيبًا مِّنَ ٱلْكِتَـٰبِ يَشْتَرُونَ ٱلضَّلَـٰلَةَ وَيُرِيدُونَ أَن تَضِلُّوا۟ ٱلسَّبِيلَ ﴿٤٤﴾ ﴾

44. Have you not seen those who were given a portion of the book (the Jews), purchasing the wrong path, and wish that you should go astray from the Right Path.

﴿ وَٱللَّهُ أَعۡلَمُ بِأَعۡدَآئِكُمۡۚ وَكَفَىٰ بِٱللَّهِ وَلِيّٗا وَكَفَىٰ بِٱللَّهِ نَصِيرٗا ٤٥ ﴾

45. Allâh has full knowledge of your enemies, and Allâh is Sufficient as a Walî (Protector), and Allâh is Sufficient as a Helper.

﴿ مِّنَ ٱلَّذِينَ هَادُواْ يُحَرِّفُونَ ٱلۡكَلِمَ عَن مَّوَاضِعِهِۦ وَيَقُولُونَ سَمِعۡنَا وَعَصَيۡنَا وَٱسۡمَعۡ غَيۡرَ
مُسۡمَعٖ وَرَٰعِنَا لَيَّۢا بِأَلۡسِنَتِهِمۡ وَطَعۡنٗا فِي ٱلدِّينِۚ وَلَوۡ أَنَّهُمۡ قَالُواْ سَمِعۡنَا وَأَطَعۡنَا وَٱسۡمَعۡ وَٱنظُرۡنَا
لَكَانَ خَيۡرٗا لَّهُمۡ وَأَقۡوَمَ وَلَٰكِن لَّعَنَهُمُ ٱللَّهُ بِكُفۡرِهِمۡ فَلَا يُؤۡمِنُونَ إِلَّا قَلِيلٗا ٤٦ ﴾

46. Among those who are Jews, there are some who displace words from (their) right places and say: "We hear your word (O Muhammad (peace be upon him)) and disobey," and "Hear and let you (O Muhammad (peace be upon him)) hear nothing." And Râ'ina with a twist of their tongues and as a mockery of the religion (Islâm). And if only they had said: "We hear and obey", and "Do make us understand," it would have been better for them, and more proper; but Allâh has cursed them for their disbelief, so they believe not except a few.

Transliteration

44. Alam tara ila allatheena ootoo naseeban mina alkitabi yashtaroona alddalalata wayureedoona an tadilloo alssabeela 45. WaAllahu aAAlamu bi-aAAda-ikum wakafa biAllahi waliyyan wakafa biAllahi naseeran 46. Mina allatheena hadoo yuharrifoona alkalima AAan mawadiAAihi wayaqooloona samiAAna waAAasayna waismaAA ghayra musmaAAin waraAAina layyan bi-alsinatihim wataAAnan fee alddeeni walaw annahum qaloo samiAAna waataAAna waismaAA waonthurna lakana khayran lahum waaqwama walakin laAAanahumu Allahu bikufrihim fala yu/minoona illa qaleelan

Tafsir Ibn Kathir

Chastising the Jews for Choosing Misguidance, Altering Allah's Words, and Mocking Islam

Allah states that the Jews, may Allah's continued curse fall on them until the Day of Resurrection, have purchased the wrong path instead of guidance, and ignored what Allah sent down to His Messenger Muhammad . They also ignored the knowledge that they inherited from previous Prophets, about the description of Muhammad , so that they may have a small amount of the delights of this life.

(and wishing that you should go astray from the right path.) for they would like that you disbelieve in what was sent down to you, O believers, and that you abandon the guidance and beneficial knowledge that you have.

(Allah has full knowledge of your enemies) meaning, Allah has better knowledge of your enemies, and He warns you against them.

(and Allah is sufficient as a Wali (Protector), and Allah is Sufficient as a Helper) He is a Sufficient Protector for those who seek refuge with Him and a Sufficient Supporter for those who seek His help. Allah then said, (there are some who displace words from (their) right places) meaning, they intentionally and falsely alter the meanings of the Words of Allah and explain them in a different manner than what Allah meant,

(And say: "We hear your word and disobey) saying, "We hear what you say, O Muhammad, but we do not obey you in it," as Mujahid and Ibn Zayd explained. This is the implied meaning of the Ayah, and it demonstrates the Jews' disbelief, stubbornness and disregard for Allah's Book after they understood it, all the while aware of the sin and punishment that this behavior will earn for them. Allah's statement,

(And "Hear and let you hear nothing.") means, hear our words, may you never hear anything, as Ad-Dahhak reported from Ibn `Abbas. This is the Jews' way of mocking and jesting, may Allah's curse descend on them.

(And Ra`ina, with a twist of their tongues and as a mockery of the religion.) meaning, they pretend to say, `Hear us,' when they say, Ra`ina (an insult in Hebrew, but in Arabic it means `Listen to us.').' Yet, their true aim is to curse the Prophet . We mentioned this subject when we explained Allah's statement,

(O you who believe! Say not Ra`ina but say Unzurna (make us understand)). Therefore, Allah said about them, while they pretend to say other than what they truly mean,

(With a twist of their tongues and as a mockery of the religion) because of their cursing the Prophet . Allah then said,

(And if only they had said: "We hear and obey", and "Do make us understand," it would have been better for them, and more proper; but Allah has cursed them for their disbelief, so they believe not except a few.) meaning, their hearts are cast away from the path of righteousness and therefore, no beneficial part of faith enters it. Earlier, when we explained,

(so little is that which they believe) which means they do not have beneficial faith.

Surah: 4 Ayah: 47 & Ayah: 48

﴿ يَٰٓأَيُّهَا ٱلَّذِينَ أُوتُواْ ٱلْكِتَٰبَ ءَامِنُواْ بِمَا نَزَّلْنَا مُصَدِّقًا لِّمَا مَعَكُم مِّن قَبْلِ أَن نَّطْمِسَ وُجُوهًا فَنَرُدَّهَا عَلَىٰٓ أَدْبَارِهَآ أَوْ نَلْعَنَهُمْ كَمَا لَعَنَّآ أَصْحَٰبَ ٱلسَّبْتِ ۚ وَكَانَ أَمْرُ ٱللَّهِ مَفْعُولًا ﴿٤٧﴾ ﴾

47. O you who have been given the Scripture (Jews and Christians)! Believe in what We have revealed (to Muhammad (peace be upon him)) confirming what is (already) with you, before We efface faces (by making them like the back of necks; without nose, mouth) and turn them hindwards, or curse them as We cursed the Sabbath-breakers. And the Commandment of Allâh is always executed.

﴿ إِنَّ ٱللَّهَ لَا يَغْفِرُ أَن يُشْرَكَ بِهِۦ وَيَغْفِرُ مَا دُونَ ذَٰلِكَ لِمَن يَشَآءُ ۚ وَمَن يُشْرِكْ بِٱللَّهِ فَقَدِ ٱفْتَرَىٰٓ إِثْمًا عَظِيمًا ﴿٤٨﴾ ﴾

48. Verily, Allâh forgives not that partners should be set up with Him (in worship), but He forgives except that (anything else) to whom He wills; and whoever sets up partners with Allâh in worship, he has indeed invented a tremendous sin.

Transliteration

47. Ya ayyuha allatheena ootoo alkitaba aminoo bima nazzalna musaddiqan lima maAAakum min qabli an natmisa wujoohan fanaruddaha AAala adbariha aw nalAAanahum kama laAAanna as-haba alssabti wakana amru Allahi mafAAoolan
48. Inna Allaha la yaghfiru an yushraka bihi wayaghfiru ma doona thalika liman yashao waman yushrik biAllahi faqadi iftara ithman AAatheeman

Tafsir Ibn Kathir

Calling the People of the Book to Embrace the Faith, Warning them Against Doing Otherwise

Allah commands the People of the Scriptures to believe in what He has sent down to His servant and Messenger, Muhammad , the Glorious Book that conforms to the good news that they already have about Muhammad . He also warns them,

(before We efface faces and turn them backwards) Al-`Awfi said that Ibn `Abbas said that `effacing' here refers to blindness,

(and turn them backwards) meaning, We put their faces on their backs, and make them walk backwards, since their eyes will be in their backs. Similar was said by Qatadah and `Atiyah Al-`Awfi. This makes the punishment even more severe, and it is a parable that Allah set for ignoring the truth, preferring the wrong way and turning away from the plain path for the paths of misguidance. Therefore, such people walk backwards. Similarly, some said that Allah's statement,

(Verily, We have put on their necks iron collars reaching to the chins, so that their heads are raised up. And We have put a barrier before them) that is a parable that Allah gave for their deviation and hindrance from guidance.

Ka`b Al-Ahbar Embraces Islam Upon Hearing this Ayah [4:47]

It was reported that Ka`b Al-Ahbar became Muslim when he heard this Ayah (4:47). Ibn Jarir recorded that `Isa bin Al-Mughirah said: We were with Ibrahim when we talked about the time when Ka`b became Muslim. He said, `Ka`b became Muslim during the reign of `Umar, for he passed by Al-Madinah intending to visit Jerusalem, and `Umar said to him, "Embrace Islam, O Ka`b.' Ka`b said, `Do you not read in your Book,

(The likeness of those who were entrusted with the Tawrah...) (62:5) until,

(Books) I am among those who were entrusted with the Tawrah.' `Umar left him alone and Ka`b went on to Hims (in Syria) and heard one of its inhabitants recite this Ayah while feeling sad,

(O you who have been given the Scripture (Jews and Christians)! Believe in what We have revealed confirming what is with you, before We efface faces and turn them backwards). Ka`b said, `I believe, O Lord! I embraced Islam, O Lord!' for He feared that this might be struck by this threat. He then went back to his family in Yemen and returned with them all as Muslims." Allah's statement,

(or curse them as We cursed the people of the Sabbath.) refers to those who breached the sanctity of the Sabbath, using deceit, for the purpose of doing more work. Allah changed these people into apes and swine, as we will come to know in the explanation of Surat Al-A`raf (7). Allah's statement,

(And the commandment of Allah is always executed.) means, when He commands something, then no one can dispute or resist His command.

Allah Does not Forgive Shirk, Except After Repenting From it

Allah said that He,

(forgives not that partners should be set up with Him (in worship),) meaning, He does not forgive a servant if he meets Him while he is associating partners with Him,

(but He forgives except that) of sins,

(to whom He wills) of His servants. Imam Ahmad recorded that Abu Dharr said that the Messenger of Allah said,

«إِنَّ اللهَ يَقُولُ: يَا عَبْدِي مَا عَبَدْتَنِي وَرَجَوْتَنِي، فَإِنِّي غَافِرٌ لَكَ عَلى مَا كَانَ فِيكَ، يَا عَبْدِي إِنَّكَ إِنْ لَقِيتَنِي بِقُرَابِ الْأَرْضِ خَطِيئَةً مَا لَمْ تُشْرِكْ بِي، لَقِيتُكَ بِقُرَابِهَا مَغْفِرَةً»

(Allah said, "O My servant! As long as you worship and beg Me, I will forgive you, no matter your shortcomings. O My servant! If you meet Me with the earth's fill of sin, yet you do not associate any partners with Me, I will meet you with its fill of forgiveness.") Only Ahmad recorded this Hadith with this chain of narration. Imam Ahmad recorded that Abu Dharr said, "I came to the Messenger of Allah and he said,

«مَا مِنْ عَبْدٍ قَالَ: لَا إِلهَ إِلَّا اللهُ ثُمَّ مَاتَ عَلَى ذَلِكَ، إِلَّا دَخَلَ الْجَنَّةَ»

("No servant proclaims,`There is no deity worthy of worship except Allah,' and dies on that belief, but will enter Paradise." I said, "Even if he committed adultery and theft" He said,

«وَإِنْ زَنَى وَإِنْ سَرَق»

"Even if he committed adultery and theft." I asked again, "Even if he committed adultery and theft" He said,

«وَإِنْ زَنَى وَإِنْ سَرَقَ»

"Even if he committed adultery and theft." The fourth time, he said,

«عَلَى رَغْمِ أَنْفِ أَبِي ذَر»

"Even if Abu Dharr's nose was put in the dust.") Abu Dharr departed while pulling his Izar and saying, "Even if Abu Dharr's nose was put in the dust." Ever since that happened, Abu Dharr used to narrate the Hadith and then comment, "Even if Abu Dharr's nose was put in dust." The Two Sahihs recorded this Hadith Al-Bazzar recorded that Ibn `Umar said, "We used to refrain from begging (Allah) for forgiveness for those who commit major sins until we heard our Prophet reciting,

(Verily, Allah forgives not that partners should be set up with Him (in worship), but He forgives except that (anything else) to whom He wills;), and his saying,

«أَخَّرْتُ شَفَاعَتِي لِأَهْلِ الْكَبَائِرِ مِنْ أُمَّتِي يَوْمَ الْقِيَامَة»

(I have reserved my intercession on the Day of Resurrection for those among my Ummah who commit major sins.)" Allah's statement,

(and whoever sets up partners with Allah in worship, he has indeed invented a tremendous sin.) is similar to His statement,

(Verily, joining others in worship with Allah is a great Zulm (wrong) indeed.) In the Two Sahihs, it is recorded that Ibn Mas`ud said, "I said, `O Messenger of Allah! Which is the greatest sin' He said,

«أَنْ تَجْعَلَ للهِ نِدًّا وَهُوَ خَلَقَك»

(To make a rival with Allah, while He Alone created you.)"

Surah: 4 Ayah: 49, Ayah: 50, Ayah: 51 & Ayah: 52

﴿ أَلَمْ تَرَ إِلَى ٱلَّذِينَ يُزَكُّونَ أَنفُسَهُم ۚ بَلِ ٱللَّهُ يُزَكِّى مَن يَشَآءُ وَلَا يُظْلَمُونَ فَتِيلًا ﴿٤٩﴾ ﴾

49. Have you not seen those (Jews and Christians) who claim sanctity for themselves. Nay, but Allâh sanctifies whom He wills, and they will not be dealt with injustice even equal to the extent of a scalish thread in the long slit of a date-stone.

﴿ ٱنظُرْ كَيْفَ يَفْتَرُونَ عَلَى ٱللَّهِ ٱلْكَذِبَ ۖ وَكَفَىٰ بِهِۦٓ إِثْمًا مُّبِينًا ﴿٥٠﴾ ﴾

50. Look, how they invent a lie against Allâh, and enough is that as a manifest sin.

﴿ أَلَمْ تَرَ إِلَى ٱلَّذِينَ أُوتُوا۟ نَصِيبًا مِّنَ ٱلْكِتَـٰبِ يُؤْمِنُونَ بِٱلْجِبْتِ وَٱلطَّـٰغُوتِ وَيَقُولُونَ
لِلَّذِينَ كَفَرُوا۟ هَـٰٓؤُلَآءِ أَهْدَىٰ مِنَ ٱلَّذِينَ ءَامَنُوا۟ سَبِيلًا ﴿٥١﴾ ﴾

51. Have you not seen those who were given a portion of the Scripture? They believe in Jibt and Tâghût and say to the disbelievers that they are better guided as regards the way than the believers (Muslims).

﴿ أُوْلَـٰٓئِكَ ٱلَّذِينَ لَعَنَهُمُ ٱللَّهُ ۖ وَمَن يَلْعَنِ ٱللَّهُ فَلَن تَجِدَ لَهُۥ نَصِيرًا ﴿٥٢﴾ ﴾

52. They are those whom Allâh curses, and he whom Allâh curses, you will not find for him (any) helper,

Transliteration

49. Alam tara ila allatheena yuzakkoona anfusahum bali Allahu yuzakkee man yashao wala yuthlamoona fateelan 50. Onthur kayfa yaftaroona AAala Allahi alkathiba wakafa bihi ithman mubeenan 51. Alam tara ila allatheena ootoo naseeban mina alkitabi yu/minoona bialjibti waalttaghooti wayaqooloona lillatheena kafaroo haola-i ahda mina allatheena amanoo sabeelan 52. Ola-ika allatheena laAAanahumu Allahu waman yalAAani Allahu falan tajida lahu naseeran

Tafsir Ibn Kathir

Chastising and Cursing the Jews for Claiming Purity for Themselves and Believing in Jibt and Taghut

Al-Hasan and Qatadah said, "This Ayah,

(Have you not seen those who claim sanctity for themselves) was revealed about the Jews and Christians when they said, `We are Allah's children and His loved ones.'" Ibn Zayd also said, "This Ayah was revealed concerning their statement,

(We are the children of Allah and His loved ones) and their statement,

(None shall enter Paradise unless he be a Jew or a Christian)." This is why Allah said,

(Nay, but Allah sanctifies whom He wills,) meaning, the decision in this matter is with Allah Alone, because He has perfect knowledge of the true reality and secrets of all things. Allah then said,

(And they will not be dealt with injustice even equal to the extent of a Fatil,) meaning, He does no injustice with anyone's compensation in any part of his reward, even if it was the weight of a Fatil. Ibn `Abbas, Mujahid, `Ikrimah, `Ata', Al-Hasan, Qatadah and others among the Salaf said that Fatil means, "The scalish thread in the long slit of the date-stone." Allah said,

(Look, how they invent a lie against Allah,) claiming purity for themselves, their claim that they are Allah's children and His loved ones, their statement;

(None shall enter Paradise unless he be a Jew or a Christian) their statement;

(The Fire shall not touch us but for a number of days) and their reliance on the righteous deeds of their forefathers. Allah has decreed that the good actions of the fathers do not help the children, when He said,

(That was a nation who has passed away. They shall receive the reward of what they earned and you of what you earn). Allah then said,

(and enough is that as a manifest sin.) meaning, these lies and fabrications of theirs are sufficent. Allah's statement,

(Have you not seen those who were given a portion of the Scripture They believe in Jibt and Taghut). Muhammad bin Ishaq said from Hassan bin Fa'id that `Umar bin Al-Khattab said, "Jibt is sorcery and Taghut is the Shaytan." Abu Nasr Isma`il bin Hammad Al-Jawhari, the renowned scholar, said in his book As-Sihah, "Al-Jibt means idol, soothsayer and sorcerer." Ibn Abi Hatim recorded that Jabir bin `Abdullah was asked about Taghut, and he said, "They are soothsayers upon whom the devils descend." Mujahid said "Taghut is a devil in the shape of man, and they refer to him for judgment." Imam Malik said, "Taghut is every object that is worshipped instead of Allah, the Exalted and Most Honored."

Disbelievers Are not Better Guided Than Believers

Allah said,

(and say to those who disbelieve, "These people are better guided on the way," than the believers.) preferring the disbelievers over Muslims, because of their ignorance, un-religious nature and disbelief in Allah's Book which is before them. Ibn Abi Hatim recorded that `Ikrimah said, "Huyay bin Akhtab and Ka`b bin Al-Ashraf (two Jewish leaders) came to the people of Makkah, who said to them, `You (Jews) are people of the Book and knowledge, so judge us and Muhammad.' They said, `Describe yourselves and describe Muhammad.' They said, `We keep relation with kith and kin, slaughter camels (for the poor), release the indebted and provide water for the pilgrims. As for Muhammad he is without male children, he severed our relations, and the thieves who rob pilgrims (the tribe of) Ghifar follow him. So who is better, we or him' They said, `You are more righteous and better guided.' Thereafter, Allah sent down,

(Have you not seen those who were given a portion)." This story was also reported from Ibn `Abbas and several others among the Salaf. Allah's Curse on the Jews This Ayah (4:52) contains a curse for the Jews and informs them that they have no supporter in this life or the Hereafter, because they sought the help of the idolators. They uttered this statement (in Ayah 4:51) to lure the disbelievers into supporting them, and they ultimately gathered their forces for the battle of Al-Ahzab, forcing the Prophet and his Companions to dig a defensive tunnel around Al-Madinah. But, Allah saved the Muslims from their evil,

(And Allah drove back those who disbelieved in their rage, they gained no advantage (booty). Allah sufficed for the believers in the fighting. And Allah is Ever All-Strong, All-Mighty).

Surah: 4 Ayah: 53, Ayah: 54 & Ayah: 55

﴿أَمْ لَهُمْ نَصِيبٌ مِّنَ ٱلْمُلْكِ فَإِذًا لَّا يُؤْتُونَ ٱلنَّاسَ نَقِيرًا ﴿٥٣﴾﴾

53. Or have they a share in the dominion? Then in that case they would not give mankind even a speck on the back of a date-stone.

﴿ أَمْ يَحْسُدُونَ ٱلنَّاسَ عَلَىٰ مَآ ءَاتَىٰهُمُ ٱللَّهُ مِن فَضْلِهِۦ ۖ فَقَدْ ءَاتَيْنَآ ءَالَ إِبْرَٰهِيمَ ٱلْكِتَـٰبَ
وَٱلْحِكْمَةَ وَءَاتَيْنَـٰهُم مُّلْكًا عَظِيمًا ﴿٥٤﴾ ﴾

54. Or do they envy men (Muhammad (peace be upon him) and his followers) for what Allâh has given them of His Bounty? Then We had already given the family of Ibrâhîm (Abraham) the Book and Al-Hikmah (As-Sunnah - Divine Revelation to those Prophets not written in the form of a book), and conferred upon them a great kingdom.

﴿ فَمِنْهُم مَّنْ ءَامَنَ بِهِۦ وَمِنْهُم مَّن صَدَّ عَنْهُ ۚ وَكَفَىٰ بِجَهَنَّمَ سَعِيرًا ﴿٥٥﴾ ﴾

55. Of them were (some) who believed in him (Muhammad (peace be upon him)) and of them were (some) who averted their faces from him (Muhammad (peace be upon him)) and enough is Hell for burning (them).

Transliteration

53. Am lahum naseebun mina almulki fa-ithan la yu/toona alnnasa naqeeran 54. Am yahsudoona alnnasa AAala ma atahumu Allahu min fadlihi faqad atayna ala ibraheema alkitaba waalhikmata waataynahum mulkan AAatheeman 55. Faminhum man amana bihi waminhum man sadda AAanhu wakafa bijahannama saAAeeran

Tafsir Ibn Kathir

The Envy and Miserly Conduct of the Jews

Allah asked the Jews if they have a share in the dominion. That is merely a statement of rebuke, since they do not have any share in the dominion. Allah then described them as misers,

(Then in that case they would not give mankind even a Naqir.) Meaning, if they had a share in the sovereignty and dominion, they would not give anyone anything, especially Muhammad , even if it was the speck on the back of a date-stone, which is the meaning of Naqir according to Ibn `Abbas and the majority of the scholars. This Ayah is similar to another of Allah's statements,

(Say: "If you possessed the treasure of the mercy of my Lord, then you would surely withold it out of fear of spending it.) meaning, for fear that what you have might end, although there is no such possibility here. This only demonstrates their greedy and stingy nature. This is why Allah said,

(And man is ever Qatur) meaning Bakhil (stingy). Allah then said,

(Or do they envy men for what Allah has given them of His Bounty) referring to their envy of the Prophet for the great prophethood that Allah entrusted him with. Their envy made them reject him, because he was an Arab and not from the Children of Israel. At-Tabarani recorded that Ibn `Abbas said that,

(Or do they envy men) means, "We are the worthy people, rather than the rest of the people." Allah said,

(Then, We have already given the family of Ibrahim the Book and Al-Hikmah, and conferred upon them a great kingdom.) meaning, We gave the prophethood to the tribes of the Children of Israel, who are among the offspring of Ibrahim and sent down the Books to them. These Prophets ruled the Jews with the prophetic tradition, and We made kings among them. Yet,

(Of them were (some) who believed in it;) referring to Allah's favor and bounty (Prophets, Books, kingship),

(and of them were (some) who rejected it) by disbelieving in it, ignoring it, and hindering the people from its path, although this bounty was from and for them, the Children of Israel. They disputed with their own Prophets; so what about you, O Muhammad , especially since you are not from the Children of Israel Mujahid said,

(Of them were (some) who believed in (him),) "Muhammad ,

(and of them were (some) who rejected (him).)" Therefore, O Muhammad, the rejection of you because of their disbelief is even more severe and they are even further from the truth that you brought them. This is why Allah threatened them,

(and enough is Hell for burning (them).), meaning, the Fire is a just punishment for them because of their disbelief, rebellion and defiance of Allah's Books and Messengers.

Surah: 4 Ayah: 56 & Ayah: 57

﴿ إِنَّ ٱلَّذِينَ كَفَرُوا۟ بِـَٔايَٰتِنَا سَوْفَ نُصْلِيهِمْ نَارًا كُلَّمَا نَضِجَتْ جُلُودُهُم بَدَّلْنَٰهُمْ جُلُودًا
غَيْرَهَا لِيَذُوقُوا۟ ٱلْعَذَابَ ۗ إِنَّ ٱللَّهَ كَانَ عَزِيزًا حَكِيمًا ﴿٥٦﴾ ﴾

56. Surely! Those who disbelieved in Our Ayât (proofs, evidences, verses, lessons, signs, revelations, etc.), We shall burn them in Fire. As often as their skins are roasted through, We shall change them for other skins that they may taste the punishment. Truly, Allâh is Ever Most Powerful, All-Wise.

﴿ وَٱلَّذِينَ ءَامَنُوا۟ وَعَمِلُوا۟ ٱلصَّٰلِحَٰتِ سَنُدْخِلُهُمْ جَنَّٰتٍ تَجْرِى مِن تَحْتِهَا ٱلْأَنْهَٰرُ خَٰلِدِينَ
فِيهَآ أَبَدًا ۖ لَّهُمْ فِيهَآ أَزْوَٰجٌ مُّطَهَّرَةٌ ۖ وَنُدْخِلُهُمْ ظِلًّا ظَلِيلًا ﴿٥٧﴾ ﴾

57. But those who believe (in the Oneness of Allâh - Islâmic Monotheism) and do deeds of righteousness, We shall admit them to Gardens under which rivers flow (Paradise), abiding therein forever. Therein they shall have Azwâjun Mutahharatun (purified mates or wives, and We shall admit them to shades wide and ever deepening (Paradise).

Transliteration

56. Inna allatheena kafaroo bi-ayatina sawfa nusleehim naran kullama nadijat julooduhum baddalnahum juloodan ghayraha liyathooqoo alAAathaba inna Allaha kana AAazeezan hakeeman 57. Waallatheena amanoo waAAamiloo alssalihati sanudkhiluhum jannatin tajree min tahtiha alanharu khalideena feeha abadan lahum feeha azwajun mutahharatun wanudkhiluhum thillan thaleelan

Tafsir Ibn Kathir

The Punishment of Those Who Disbelieve in Allah's Books and Messengers

Allah describes the torment in the Fire of Jahannam for those who disbelieve in His Ayat and hinder from the path of His Messengers. Allah said,

(Surely, those who disbelieved in Our Ayat ,) meaning, We will place them in the Fire which will encompass every part of their bodies. Allah then states that their punishment and torment are everlasting,

(We shall burn them in Fire. As often as their skins are roasted through, We shall change them for other skins that they may taste the punishment). Al-A`mash said that Ibn `Umar said, "When their skin are burned, they will be given another skin in replacement, and this skin will be as white as paper." This was collected by Ibn Abi Hatim, who also recorded that Al-Hasan said,

(As often as their skins are roasted through,) "Their skin will be roasted through, seventy thousand times every day." Husayn said; Fudayl added that Hisham said that Al-Hasan also said that,

(As often as their skins are roasted through,) means, "Whenever the Fire has roasted them through and consumed their flesh, they will be told, `Go back as you were before,' and they will."

The Wealth of the Righteous; Paradise and its Joy

Allah said,

(But those who believe and do deeds of righteousness, We shall admit them to Gardens under which rivers flow (Paradise), abiding therein forever.) describing the destination of the happy ones in the gardens of Eden, beneath which rivers flow in all of its areas, spaces and corners, wherever they desire and wish. They will reside in it for eternity, and they will not be transferred or removed from it, nor would they want to move from it. Allah said,

(Therein they shall have Azwajun Mutahharatun (purified mates),) free of menstruation, postnatal bleeding, filth, bad manners and shortcomings. Ibn `Abbas said that the Ayah means, "They are purified of filth and foul things." Similar was said by `Ata', Al-Hasan, Ad-Dahhak, An-Nakha`i, Abu Salih, `Atiyah, and As-Suddi. Mujahid said that they are, free of urine, menstruation, spit, mucous and pregnancies." Allah's statement,

(And We shall admit them to shades, wide and ever deepening (Paradise).) means, wide, extensive, pure and elegant shade. Ibn Jarir recorded that Abu Hurayrah said that the Prophet said,

«إِنَّ فِي الْجَنَّةِ لَشَجَرَةً يَسِيرُ الرَّاكِبُ فِي ظِلِّهَا مِائَةَ عَامٍ لَا يَقْطَعُهَا: شَجَرَةَ الْخُلْدِ»

(There is a tree in Paradise, that if a rider travels under its shade for a hundred years, he will not cross it. It is the Tree of Everlasting Life.)

Surah: 4 Ayah: 58

﴿ ۞ إِنَّ ٱللَّهَ يَأۡمُرُكُمۡ أَن تُؤَدُّواْ ٱلۡأَمَٰنَٰتِ إِلَىٰٓ أَهۡلِهَا وَإِذَا حَكَمۡتُم بَيۡنَ ٱلنَّاسِ أَن تَحۡكُمُواْ
بِٱلۡعَدۡلِۚ إِنَّ ٱللَّهَ نِعِمَّا يَعِظُكُم بِهِۦٓۗ إِنَّ ٱللَّهَ كَانَ سَمِيعَۢا بَصِيرٗا ۝٥٨ ﴾

58. Verily! Allâh commands that you should render back the trusts to those to whom they are due; and that when you judge between men, you judge with justice. Verily, how excellent is the teaching which He (Allâh) gives you! Truly, Allâh is Ever All-Hearer, All-Seer.

Transliteration

58. Inna Allaha ya/murukum an tu-addoo al-amanati ila ahliha wa-itha hakamtum bayna alnnasi an tahkumoo bialAAadli inna Allaha niAAimma yaAAithukum bihi inna Allaha kana sameeAAan baseeran

Tafsir Ibn Kathir

The Command to Return the Trusts to Whomever They Are Due

Allah commands that the trusts be returned to their rightful owners. Al-Hasan narrated that Samurah said that the Messenger of Allah said,

«أَدِّ الْأَمَانَةَ إِلى مَنِ ائْتَمَنَكَ، وَلَا تَخُنْ مَنْ خَانَكَ»

(Return the trust to those who entrusted you, and do not betray those who betrayed you.) Imam Ahmad and the collectors of Sunan recorded this Hadith. This command refers to all things that one is expected to look after, such as Allah's rights on His servants: praying, Zakah, fasting, penalties for sins, vows and so forth. The command also includes the rights of the servants on each other, such as what they entrust each other with, including the cases that are not recorded or documented. Allah commands that all types of trusts be fulfillled. Those who do not implement this command in this life, it will be extracted from them on the Day of Resurrection. It is recorded in the Sahih that the Messenger of Allah said,

«لَتُؤَدَّنَّ الْحُقُوقُ إِلى أَهْلِهَا حَتَّى يُقْتَصَّ لِلشَّاةِ الْجَمَّاءِ مِنَ الْقَرْنَاء»

(The rights will be rendered back to those to whom they are due, and even the sheep that does not have horns will take revenge from the horned sheep.) Ibn Jarir recorded that Ibn Jurayj said about this Ayah, "It was revealed concerning `Uthman bin Talhah from whom the Messenger of Allah took the key of the Ka`bah and entered it on the Day of the victory of Makkah. When the Prophet went out, he was reciting this Ayah,

(Verily, Allah commands that you should render back the trusts to those, to whom they are due). He then called `Uthman and gave the key back to him." Ibn Jarir also narrated that `Umar bin Al-Khattab said, "When the Messenger of Allah went out of the Ka`bah, he was reciting this Ayah,

(Verily, Allah commands that you should render back the trusts to those, to whom they are due). May I sacrifice my father and mother for him, I never heard him recite this Ayah before that." It is popular that this is the reason behind revealing the Ayah (4:58). Yet, the application of the Ayah is general, and this is why Ibn `Abbas and Muhammad bin Al-Hanafiyyah said, "This Ayah is for the righteous and wicked," meaning it is a command that encompasses everyone.

The Order to Be Just

Allah said,

(and that when you judge between men, you judge with justice.) commanding justice when judging between people. Muhammad bin Ka`b, Zayd bin Aslam and Shahr bin Hawshab said; "This Ayah was revealed about those in authority", meaning those who judge between people. A Hadith states,

«إِنَّ اللهَ مَعَ الْحَاكِمِ مَا لَمْ يَجُرْ، فَإِذَا جَارَ وَكَلَهُ اللهُ إِلَى نَفْسِه»

(Allah is with the judge as long as he does not commit injustice, for when he does, Allah will make him reliant on himself.) A statement goes, "One day of justice equals forty years of worship." Allah said,

(Verily, how excellent is the teaching which He (Allah) gives you!) meaning, His commands to return the trusts to their owners, to judge between people with justice, and all of His complete, perfect and great commandments and laws. Allah's statement,

(Truly, Allah is Ever All-Hearer, All-Seer.) means, He hears your statements and knows your actions.

Surah: 4 Ayah: 59

﴿ يَـٰٓأَيُّهَا ٱلَّذِينَ ءَامَنُوٓاْ أَطِيعُواْ ٱللَّهَ وَأَطِيعُواْ ٱلرَّسُولَ وَأُوْلِى ٱلْأَمْرِ مِنكُمْ ۖ فَإِن تَنَـٰزَعْتُمْ فِى شَىْءٍ فَرُدُّوهُ إِلَى ٱللَّهِ وَٱلرَّسُولِ إِن كُنتُمْ تُؤْمِنُونَ بِٱللَّهِ وَٱلْيَوْمِ ٱلْـَٔاخِرِ ۚ ذَٰلِكَ خَيْرٌ وَأَحْسَنُ تَأْوِيلًا ﴿٥٩﴾ ﴾

59. O you who believe! Obey Allâh and obey the Messenger (Muhammad (peace be upon him)) and those of you (Muslims) who are in authority. (And) if you differ in anything amongst yourselves, refer it to Allâh and His Messenger (peace be upon him), if you believe in Allâh and in the Last Day. That is better and more suitable for final determination.

Transliteration

59. Ya ayyuha allatheena amanoo ateeAAoo Allaha waateeAAoo alrrasoola waolee al-amri minkum fain tanazaAAtum fee shay-in faruddoohu ila Allahi waalrrasooli in kuntum tu/minoona biAllahi waalyawmi al-akhiri thalika khayrun waahsanu ta/weelan

Tafsir Ibn Kathir

The Necessity of Obeying the Rulers in Obedience to Allah

Al-Bukhari recorded that Ibn `Abbas said that the Ayah,

(Obey Allah and obey the Messenger, and those of you who are in authority.) "Was revealed about `Abdullah bin Hudhafah bin Qays bin `Adi, who the Messenger of Allah sent on a military expedition." This statement was collected by the Group, with the exception of Ibn Majah At-Tirmidhi said, "Hasan, Gharib". Imam Ahmad recorded that `Ali said, "The Messenger of Allah sent a troop under the command of a man from Al-Ansar. When they left, he became angry with them for some reason and said to them, `Has not the Messenger of Allah commanded you to obey me' They said, `Yes.' He said, `Collect some wood,' and then he started a fire with the wood, saying, `I command you to enter the fire.' The people almost entered the fire, but a young man among them said, `You only ran away from the Fire to Allah's Messenger. Therefore, do not rush until you go back to Allah's Messenger, and if he commands you to enter it, then enter it.' When they went back to Allah's Messenger , they told him what had happened, and the Messenger said,

«لَوْ دَخَلْتُمُوهَا مَا خَرَجْتُمْ مِنْهَا أَبَدًا، إِنَّمَا الطَّاعَةُ فِي الْمَعْرُوف»

(Had you entered it, you would never have departed from it. Obedience is only in righteousness.)" This Hadith is recorded in the Two Sahihs. Abu Dawud recorded that `Abdullah bin `Umar said that the Messenger of Allah said,

«السَّمْعُ وَالطَّاعَةُ عَلَى الْمَرْءِ الْمُسْلِمِ فِيمَا أَحَبَّ وَكَرِهَ، مَا لَمْ يُؤْمَرْ بِمَعْصِيَةٍ، فَإِذَا أُمِرَ بِمَعْصِيَةٍ فَلَا سَمْعَ وَلَا طَاعَة»

(The Muslim is required to hear and obey in that which he likes and dislikes, unless he was commanded to sin. When he is commanded with sin, then there is no hearing or obeying.) This Hadith is recorded in the Two Sahihs. `Ubadah bin As-Samit said, "We gave our pledge to Allah's Messenger to hear and obey (our leaders), while active and otherwise, in times of ease and times of difficulty, even if we were deprived of our due shares, and to not dispute this matter (leadership) with its rightful people. The Prophet said,

«إِلَّا أَنْ تَرَوْا كُفْرًا بَوَاحًا، عِنْدَكُمْ فِيهِ مِنَ اللهِ بُرْهَان»

(Except when you witness clear Kufr about which you have clear proof from Allah.)" This Hadith is recorded in the Two Sahihs. Another Hadith narrated by Anas states that the Messenger of Allah said,

«اسْمَعُوا وَأَطِيعُوا، وَإِنْ أُمِّرَ عَلَيْكُمْ عَبْدٌحَبَشِيٌّ كَأَنَّ رَأْسَهُ زَبِيبَة»

(Hear and obey (your leaders), even if an Ethiopian slave whose head is like a raisin, is made your chief.) Al-Bukhari recorded this Hadith. Umm Al-Husayn said that she heard the Messenger of Allah giving a speech during the Farewell Hajj, in which he said;

«وَلَوِ اسْتُعْمِلَ عَلَيْكُمْ عَبْدٌيَقُودُكُمْ بِكِتَابِ اللهِ، اسْمَعُوا لَهُ وَأَطِيعُوا»

(Even if a slave was appointed over you, and he rules you with Allah's Book, then listen to him and obey him.) Muslim recorded this Hadith. In another narration with Muslim, the Prophet said,

«عَبْدًا حَبَشِيًّا مَجْدُوعًا»

(Even if an Ethiopian slave, whose nose was mutilated...) In the Two Sahihs, it is recorded that Abu Hurayrah said that the Messenger of Allah said,

«مَنْ أَطَاعَنِي فَقَدْ أَطَاعَ اللهَ، وَمَنْ عَصَانِي فَقَدْ عَصَى اللهَ، وَمَنْ أَطَاعَ أَمِيرِي فَقَدْ أَطَاعَنِي، وَمَنْ عَصَى أَمِيرِي فَقَدْ عَصَانِي»

(Whoever obeys me, obeys Allah, and whoever disobeys me, disobeys Allah. Whoever obeys my commander, obeys me, and whoever disobeys my commander, disobeys me.) This is why Allah said,

(Obey Allah), adhere to His Book,

(and obey the Messenger), adhere to his Sunnah,

(And those of you who are in authority) in the obedience to Allah which they command you, not what constitutes disobedience of Allah, for there is no obedience to anyone in disobedience to Allah, as we mentioned in the authentic Hadith,

«إِنَّمَا الطَّاعَةُ فِي الْمَعْرُوف»

(Obedience is only in righteousness.)

The Necessity of Referring to the Qur'an and Sunnah for Judgment

Allah said,

((And) if you differ in anything amongst yourselves, refer it to Allah and His Messenger). Mujahid and several others among the Salaf said that the Ayah means, "(Refer) to the Book of Allah and the Sunnah of His Messenger." This is a command from Allah that whatever areas the people dispute about, whether major or minor areas of the religion, they are required to refer to the Qur'an and Sunnah for judgment concerning these disputes. In another Ayah, Allah said,

(And in whatsoever you differ, the decision thereof is with Allah). Therefore, whatever the Book and Sunnah decide and testify to the truth of, then it, is the plain truth. What is beyond truth, save falsehood This is why Allah said,

(if you believe in Allah and in the Last Day.) meaning, refer the disputes and conflicts that arise between you to the Book of Allah and the Sunnah of His Messenger for judgment. Allah's statement, (if you believe in Allah and in the Last Day.) indicates that those who do not refer to the Book and Sunnah for judgment in their disputes, are not believers in Allah or the Last Day. Allah said,

(That is better) meaning, referring to the Book of Allah and the Sunnah of His Messenger for judgment in various disputes is better,

(and more suitable for final determination.) meaning, "Has a better end and destination," as As-Suddi and several others have stated while Mujahid said, "Carries a better reward."

Surah: 4 Ayah: 60, Ayah: 61, Ayah: 62 & Ayah: 63

﴿ أَلَمْ تَرَ إِلَى ٱلَّذِينَ يَزْعُمُونَ أَنَّهُمْ ءَامَنُوا۟ بِمَآ أُنزِلَ إِلَيْكَ وَمَآ أُنزِلَ مِن قَبْلِكَ يُرِيدُونَ
أَن يَتَحَاكَمُوٓا۟ إِلَى ٱلطَّٰغُوتِ وَقَدْ أُمِرُوٓا۟ أَن يَكْفُرُوا۟ بِهِۦ وَيُرِيدُ ٱلشَّيْطَٰنُ أَن يُضِلَّهُمْ ضَلَٰلًۢا
بَعِيدًا ﴿٦٠﴾ ﴾

60. Have you seen those (hypocrites) who claim that they believe in that which has been sent down to you, and that which was sent down before you, and they wish to go for judgement (in their disputes) to the Tâghût (false judges) while they have been ordered to reject them. But Shaitân (Satan) wishes to lead them far astray.

﴿ وَإِذَا قِيلَ لَهُمْ تَعَالَوْا۟ إِلَىٰ مَآ أَنزَلَ ٱللَّهُ وَإِلَى ٱلرَّسُولِ رَأَيْتَ ٱلْمُنَٰفِقِينَ يَصُدُّونَ عَنكَ
صُدُودًا ﴿٦١﴾ ﴾

61. And when it is said to them: "Come to what Allâh has sent down and to the Messenger (Muhammad (peace be upon him))" you (Muhammad (peace be upon him)) see the hypocrites turn away from you (Muhammad (peace be upon him)) with aversion.

﴿ فَكَيْفَ إِذَآ أَصَٰبَتْهُم مُّصِيبَةٌۢ بِمَا قَدَّمَتْ أَيْدِيهِمْ ثُمَّ جَآءُوكَ يَحْلِفُونَ بِٱللَّهِ إِنْ أَرَدْنَآ إِلَّآ
إِحْسَٰنًا وَتَوْفِيقًا ﴿٦٢﴾ ﴾

62. How then, when a catastrophe befalls them because of what their hands have sent forth, they come to you swearing by Allâh, "We meant no more than goodwill and conciliation!"

﴿ أُو۟لَٰٓئِكَ ٱلَّذِينَ يَعْلَمُ ٱللَّهُ مَا فِى قُلُوبِهِمْ فَأَعْرِضْ عَنْهُمْ وَعِظْهُمْ وَقُل لَّهُمْ فِىٓ أَنفُسِهِمْ
قَوْلًۢا بَلِيغًا ﴿٦٣﴾ ﴾

63. They (hypocrites) are those of whom Allâh knows what is in their hearts; so turn aside from them (do not punish them) but admonish them, and speak to them an effective word (i.e. to believe in Allâh, worship Him, obey Him, and be afraid of Him) to reach their innerselves.

Transliteration

60. Alam tara ila allatheena yazAAumoona annahum amanoo bima onzila ilayka wama onzila min qablika yureedoona an yatahakamoo ila alttaghooti waqad omiroo an yakfuroo bihi wayureedu alshshaytanu an yudillahum dalalan baAAeedan 61. Wa-itha qeela lahum taAAalaw ila ma anzala Allahu wa-ila alrrasooli raayta almunafiqeena yasuddoona AAanka sudoodan 62. Fakayfa itha asabat-hum museebatun bima qaddamat aydeehim thumma jaooka yahlifoona biAllahi in aradna illa ihsanan watawfeeqan 63. Ola-ika allatheena yaAAlamu Allahu ma fee quloobihim faaAArid AAanhum waAAithhum waqul lahum fee anfusihim qawlan baleeghan

Kathir's Tafsir

Referring to Other than the Qur'an and Sunnah for Judgment is Characteristic of Non-Muslims

Allah chastises those who claim to believe in what Allah has sent down to His Messenger and to the earlier Prophets, yet they refer to other than the Book of Allah and the Sunnah of His Messenger for judgment in various disputes. It was reported that the reason behind revealing this Ayah was that a man from the Ansar and a Jew had a dispute, and the Jew said, "Let us refer to Muhammad to judge between us." However, the Muslim man said, "Let us refer to Ka`b bin Al-Ashraf (a Jew) to judge between us." It was also reported that the Ayah was revealed about some hypocrites who pretended to be Muslims, yet they sought to refer to the judgment of Jahiliyyah. Other reasons were also reported behind the revelation of the Ayah. However, the Ayah has a general meaning, as it chastises all those who refrain from referring to the Qur'an and Sunnah for judgment and prefer the judgment of whatever they chose of falsehood, which befits the description of Taghut here. This is why Allah said,

(and they wish to go for judgment to the Taghut) until the end of the Ayah. Allah's statement,

(turn away from you with aversion) means, they turn away from you in arrogance, just as Allah described the polytheists,

(When it is said to them: "Follow what Allah has sent down." They say: "Nay! We shall follow what we found our fathers following.") This is different from the conduct of the faithful believers, whom Allah describes as,

(The only saying of the faithful believers, when they are called to Allah and His Messenger, to judge between them, is that they say: "We hear and we obey.")

Chastising the Hypocrites

Chastising the hypocrites, Allah said,

(How then, when a catastrophe befalls them because of what their hands have sent forth,) meaning, how about it if they feel compelled to join you because of disasters that they suffer due to their sins, then they will be in need of you.

(They come to you swearing by Allah, "We meant no more than goodwill and conciliation!") apologizing and swearing that they only sought goodwill and reconciliation when they referred to other than the Prophet for judgment, not that they believe in such alternative judgment, as they claim. Allah describes these people to us further in His statement,

(And you see those in whose hearts there is a disease (of hypocrisy), they hurry to their friendship, saying: "We fear"), until,

(Then they will become regretful for what they have been keeping as a secret in themselves). At-Tabarani recorded that Ibn `Abbas said, "Abu Barzah Al-Aslami used to be a soothsayer who judged between the Jews in their disputes. When some Muslims came to him to judge between them, Allah sent down,

(Have you not seen those (hyprocrites) who claim that they believe in that which has been sent down to you, and that which was sent down before you), until,

("We meant no more than goodwill and conciliation!") Allah then said,

(They (hypocrites) are those of whom Allah knows what is in their hearts;) These people are hypocrites, and Allah knows what is in their hearts and will punish them accordingly, for nothing escapes Allah's watch. Consequently, O Muhammad! Let Allah be sufficient for you in this regard, because He has perfect knowledge of their apparent and hidden affairs. This is why Allah said,

(so turn aside from them (do not punish them)) meaning, do not punish them because of what is in their hearts.

(but admonish them) means, advise them against the hypocrisy and evil that reside in their hearts,

(and speak to them an effective word to reach their inner selves) advise them, between you and them, using effective words that might benefit them.

Surah: 4 Ayah: 64 & Ayah: 65

﴿ وَمَآ أَرْسَلْنَا مِن رَّسُولٍ إِلَّا لِيُطَاعَ بِإِذْنِ ٱللَّهِ ۚ وَلَوْ أَنَّهُمْ إِذ ظَّلَمُوٓا۟ أَنفُسَهُمْ جَآءُوكَ
فَٱسْتَغْفَرُوا۟ ٱللَّهَ وَٱسْتَغْفَرَ لَهُمُ ٱلرَّسُولُ لَوَجَدُوا۟ ٱللَّهَ تَوَّابًا رَّحِيمًا ﴿٦٤﴾ ﴾

64. We sent no Messenger, but to be obeyed by Allâh's Leave. If they (hypocrites), when they had been unjust to themselves, had come to you (Muhammad (peace be upon him)) and begged Allâh's Forgiveness, and the Messenger had begged forgiveness for them: indeed, they would have found Allâh All-Forgiving (One Who accepts repentance), Most Merciful.

﴿ فَلَا وَرَبِّكَ لَا يُؤْمِنُونَ حَتَّىٰ يُحَكِّمُوكَ فِيمَا شَجَرَ بَيْنَهُمْ ثُمَّ لَا يَجِدُوا۟ فِىٓ أَنفُسِهِمْ
حَرَجًا مِّمَّا قَضَيْتَ وَيُسَلِّمُوا۟ تَسْلِيمًا ﴿٦٥﴾ ﴾

65. But no, by your Lord, they can have no Faith, until they make you (O Muhammad (peace be upon him)) judge in all disputes between them, and find in themselves no resistance against your decisions, and accept (them) with full submission.

Transliteration

64. Wama arsalna min rasoolin illa liyutaAAa bi-ithni Allahi walaw annahum ith thalamoo anfusahum jaooka faistaghfaroo Allaha waistaghfara lahumu alrrasoolu lawajadoo Allaha

tawwaban raheeman 65. Fala warabbika la yu/minoona hatta yuhakkimooka feema shajara baynahum thumma la yajidoo fee anfusihim harajan mimma qadayta wayusallimoo tasleeman

Tafsir Ibn Kathir

The Necessity of Obeying the Messenger

Allah said,

(We sent no Messenger, but to be obeyed) meaning, obeying the Prophet was ordained for those to whom Allah sends the Prophet. Allah's statement,

(by Allah's leave) means, "None shall obey, except by My leave," according to Mujahid. This Ayah indicates that the Prophets are only obeyed by whomever Allah directs to obedience. In another Ayah, Allah said,

(And Allah did indeed fulfill His promise to you when you were killing them (your enemy) with His permission) meaning, by His command, decree, will and because He granted you superiority over them. Allah's statement,

(If they (hypocrites), when they had been unjust to themselves,) directs the sinners and evildoers, when they commit errors and mistakes, to come to the Messenger , so that they ask Allah for forgiveness in his presence and ask him to supplicate to Allah to forgive them. If they do this, Allah will forgive them and award them His mercy and pardon. This is why Allah said,

(they would have found Allah All-Forgiving (One Who forgives and accepts repentance), Most Merciful).

One Does not Become a Believer Unless He Refers to the Messenger for Judgment and Submits to his Decisions

Allah said,

(But no, by your Lord, they can have no faith, until they make you judge in all disputes between them,) Allah swears by His Glorious, Most Honorable Self, that no one shall attain faith until he refers to the Messenger for judgment in all matters. Thereafter, whatever the Messenger commands, is the plain truth that must be submitted to inwardly and outwardly. Allah said,

(and find in themselves no resistance against your decisions, and accept (them) with full submission.) meaning: they adhere to your judgment, and thus do not feel any hesitation over your decision, and they submit to it inwardly and outwardly. They submit to the Prophet's decision with total submission without any rejection, denial or dispute. Al-Bukhari recorded that `Urwah said, "Az-Zubayr quarreled with a man about a stream which both of them used for irrigation. Allah's Messenger said to Az-Zubayr,

«اسْقِ يَا زُبَيْرُ ثُمَّ أَرْسِلِ الْمَاءَ إِلَى جَارِكَ»

(O Zubayr! Irrigate (your garden) first, and then let the water flow to your neighbor.) The Ansari became angry and said, `O Allah's Messenger! Is it because he is your cousin' On that, the face of Allah's Messenger changed color (because of anger) and said,

«اسْقِ يَا زُبَيْرُ ثُمَّ احْبِسِ الْمَاءَ حَتَّى يَرْجِعَ إِلَى الْجَدْرِ، ثُمَّ أَرْسِلِ الْمَاءَ إِلَى جَارِكَ»

(Irrigate (your garden), O Zubayr, and then withhold the water until it reaches the walls (surrounding the palms). Then, release the water to your neighbor.) So, Allah's Messenger gave Az-Zubayr his full right when the Ansari made him angry. Before that, Allah's Messenger had given a generous judgment, beneficial for Az-Zubayr and the Ansari. Az-Zubayr said, `I think the following verse was revealed concerning that case,

(But no, by your Lord, they can have no faith, until they make you (O Muhammad) judge in all disputes between them.)'" Another Reason In his Tafsir, Al-Hafiz Abu Ishaq Ibrahim bin `Abdur-Rahman bin Ibrahim bin Duhaym recorded that Damrah narrated that two men took their dispute to the Prophet , and he gave a judgment to the benefit of whoever among them had the right. The person who lost the dispute said, "I do not agree." The other person asked him, "What do you want then" He said, "Let us go to Abu Bakr As-Siddiq." They went to Abu Bakr and the person who won the dispute said, "We went to the Prophet with our dispute and he issued a decision in my favor." Abu Bakr said, "Then the decision is that which the Messenger of Allah issued." The person who lost the dispute still rejected the decision and said, "Let us go to `Umar bin Al-Khattab." When they went to `Umar, the person who won the dispute said, "We took our dispute to the Prophet and he decided in my favor, but this man refused to submit to the decision." `Umar bin Al-Khattab asked the second man and he concurred. `Umar went to his house and emerged from it holding aloft his sword. He struck the head of the man who rejected the Prophet's decision with the sword and killed him. Consequently, Allah revealed,

(But no, by your Lord, they can have no faith).

Surah: 4 Ayah: 66, Ayah: 67, Ayah: 68, Ayah: 69 & Ayah: 70

﴿ وَلَوْ أَنَّا كَتَبْنَا عَلَيْهِمْ أَنِ ٱقْتُلُوٓا۟ أَنفُسَكُمْ أَوِ ٱخْرُجُوا۟ مِن دِيَٰرِكُم مَّا فَعَلُوهُ إِلَّا قَلِيلٌ مِّنْهُمْ ۖ
وَلَوْ أَنَّهُمْ فَعَلُوا۟ مَا يُوعَظُونَ بِهِۦ لَكَانَ خَيْرًا لَّهُمْ وَأَشَدَّ تَثْبِيتًا ﴿٦٦﴾ ﴾

66. And if We had ordered them (saying), "Kill yourselves (i.e. the innocent ones kill the guilty ones) or leave your homes," very few of them would have done it; but if they had done what they were told, it would have been better for them, and would have strengthened their (Faith);

﴿ وَإِذًا لَّءَاتَيْنَٰهُم مِّن لَّدُنَّآ أَجْرًا عَظِيمًا ﴿٦٧﴾ ﴾

67. And indeed We should then have bestowed upon them a great reward from Ourselves.

﴿ وَلَهَدَيْنَٰهُمْ صِرَٰطًا مُّسْتَقِيمًا ﴿٦٨﴾ ﴾

68. And indeed We should have guided them to a Straight Way.

﴿ وَمَن يُطِعِ ٱللَّهَ وَٱلرَّسُولَ فَأُو۟لَٰٓئِكَ مَعَ ٱلَّذِينَ أَنْعَمَ ٱللَّهُ عَلَيْهِم مِّنَ ٱلنَّبِيِّۦنَ وَٱلصِّدِّيقِينَ
وَٱلشُّهَدَآءِ وَٱلصَّٰلِحِينَ ۚ وَحَسُنَ أُو۟لَٰٓئِكَ رَفِيقًا ﴿٦٩﴾ ﴾

69. And whoso obey Allâh and the Messenger (Muhammad (peace be upon him)) then they will be in the company of those on whom Allâh has bestowed His Grace, of the Prophets, the Siddiqûn (those followers of the Prophets who were first and foremost to believe in them, like Abu Bakr As-Siddiq (may Allah be pleased with him), the martyrs, and the righteous. And how excellent these companions are!

﴿ذَٰلِكَ ٱلْفَضْلُ مِنَ ٱللَّهِ ۚ وَكَفَىٰ بِٱللَّهِ عَلِيمًا ٧٠﴾

70. Such is the Bounty from Allâh, and Allâh is Sufficient as All-Knower.

Transliteration

66. Walaw anna katabna AAalayhim ani oqtuloo anfusakum awi okhrujoo min diyarikum ma faAAaloohu illa qaleelun minhum walaw annahum faAAaloo ma yooAAathoona bihi lakana khayran lahum waashadda tathbeetan 67. Wa-ithan laataynahum min ladunna ajran AAatheeman 68. Walahadaynahum siratan mustaqeeman 69. Waman yutiAAi Allaha waalrrasoola faola-ika maAAa allatheena anAAama Allahu AAalayhim mina alnnabiyyeena waalssiddeeqeena waalshshuhada-i waalssaliheena wahasuna ola-ika rafeeqan 70. Thalika alfadlu mina Allahi wakafa biAllahi AAaleeman

Tafsir Ibn Kathir

Most People Disobey What They Are Ordered

Allah states that even if the people were commanded to commit what they were prohibited from doing, most of them would not submit to this command, for their wicked nature is such that they dispute orders. Allah has complete knowledge of what has not occured, and how it would be if and when it did occur. This is why Allah said,

(And if We had ordered them (saying), "Kill yourselves (i.e. the innnocent ones kill the guilty ones)) until the end of the Ayah. This is why Allah said,

(but if they had done what they were told,) meaning, if they do what they were commanded and refrain from what they were prohibited,

(it would have been better for them,) than disobeying the command and committing the prohibition,

(and would have strengthened their conviction), stronger Tasdiq (conviction of faith), according to As-Suddi.

(And indeed We should then have bestowed upon them from Ladunna) from Us,

(A great reward), Paradise,

(And indeed We should have guided them to the straight way.) in this life and the Hereafter.

Whoever Obeys Allah and His Messenger Will Be Honored by Allah

Allah then said,

(And whoever obeys Allah and the Messenger, then they will be in the company of those on whom Allah has bestowed His grace, of the Prophets, the Siddiqin, the martyrs, and the righteous. And how excellent these companions are!) Consequently, whosoever implements what Allah and His Messenger have commanded him and avoids what Allah and His Messenger have prohibited, then Allah will grant him a dwelling in the Residence of Honor. There, Allah will place him in the company of the Prophets, and those who are lesser in grade, the true believers, then the martyrs and then the righteous, who are righteous inwardly and outwardly. Allah then praised this company,

(And how excellent these companions are!) Al-Bukhari recorded that `A'ishah said, "I heard the Messenger of Allah saying,

«مَا مِنْ نَبِيَ يَمْرَضُ إِلَّا خُيِّرَ بَيْنَ الدُّنْيَا وَالْآخِرَة»

(Every Prophet who falls ill is given the choice between this life and the Hereafter.) During the illness that preceded his death, his voice became weak and I heard him saying,

[مَعَ الَّذِينَ أَنْعَمَ اللَّهُ عَلَيْهِم مِّنَ النَّبِيِّينَ وَالصِّدِّيقِينَ وَالشُّهَدَآءِ وَالصَّـلِحِينَ]

(in the company of those on whom Allah has bestowed His grace, the Prophets, the true believers (Siddiqin), the martyrs and the righteous) I knew then that he was being given the choice." Muslim recorded this Hadith. This Hadith explains the meaning of another Hadith; the Prophet said before his death;

«اللَّهُمَّ (فِي) الرَّفِيقِ الْأَعْلَى»

(O Allah! In the Most High Company) three times, and he then died, may Allah's best blessings be upon him.

The Reason Behind Revealing this Honorable Ayah

Ibn Jarir recorded that Sa`id bin Jubayr said, "An Ansari man came to the Messenger of Allah while feeling sad. The Prophet said to him, `Why do I see you sad' He said, `O Allah's Prophet! I was contemplating about something.' The Prophet said, `What is it' The Ansari said, `We come to you day and night, looking at your face and sitting by you. Tomorrow, you will be raised with the Prophets, and we will not be able to see you.' The Prophet did not say anything, but later Jibril came down to him with this Ayah,

(And whoever obeys Allah and the Messenger then they will be in the company of those on whom Allah has bestowed His grace, of the Prophets), and the Prophet sent the good news to the Ansari man." This Hadith was narrated in Mursal form from Masruq, `Ikrimah, `Amir Ash-Sha`bi, Qatadah and Ar-Rabi` bin Anas. This is the version with the best chain of narrators. Abu Bakr bin Marduwyah recorded it with a different chain from `A'ishah, who said; "A man came to the Prophet and said to him, `O Messenger of Allah! You are more beloved to me than myself, my family and children. Sometimes, when I am at home, I remember you, and I cannot wait until I come and look at you. When I contemplate about my death and your death, I know that you will be with the Prophets when you enter Paradise. I fear that I might not see you when I enter Paradise.' The Prophet did not answer him until the Ayah,

(And whoever obeys Allah and the Messenger, then they will be in the company of those on whom Allah has bestowed His grace, of the Prophets, the true believers, the martyrs, and the righteous. And how excellent these companions are!) was revealed to him." This was collected by Al-Hafiz Abu `Abdullah Al-Maqdisi in his book, Sifat Al-Jannah, he then commented, "I do not see problems with this chain." And Allah knows best. Muslim recorded that Rabi`ah bin Ka`b Al-Aslami said, "I used to sleep at the Prophet's house and bring him his water for ablution and his needs. He once said to me, `Ask me.' I said, `O Messenger of Allah! I ask that I be your companion in Paradise.' He said, `Anything except that' I said, `Only that.' He said,

«فَأَعِنِّي عَلى نَفْسِكَ بِكَثْرَةِ السُّجُود»

(Then help me (fulfill this wish) for you by performing many prostrations.)" Imam Ahmad recorded that `Amr bin Murrah Al-Juhani said, "A man came to the Prophet and said, `O Allah's Messenger! I bear witness that there is no deity worthy of worship except Allah and that you are the Messenger of Allah, pray the five (daily prayers), give the Zakah due on my wealth and fast the month of Ramadan.' The Messenger of Allah said,

«مَنْ مَاتَ عَلى هَذَا كَانَ مَعَ النَّبِيِّينَ وَالصِّدِّيقِينَ وَالشُّهَدَاءِ يَوْمَ الْقِيَامَةِ، هَكَذا وَنَصَبَ أُصْبُعَيْهِ مَا لَمْ يَعُقَّ وَالِدَيْه»

(Whoever dies in this state will be with the Prophets, the truthful and martyrs on the Day of Resurrection, as long as - and he raised his finger - he is not disobedient to his parents.)" Only Ahmad recorded this Hadith. Greater news than this is in the authentic Hadith collected in the Sahih and Musnad compilations, in Mutawatir form, narrated by several Companions that the Messenger of Allah was asked about the person who loves a people, but his status is not close to theirs. The Messenger said,

«الْمَرْءُ مَعَ مَنْ أَحَب»

(One is with those whom he loves.) Anas commented, "Muslims were never happier than with this Hadith." In another narration, Anas said, "I love the Messenger of Allah, Abu Bakr and `Umar, and I hope that Allah will resurrect me with them, even though I did not perform actions similar to theirs." Allah said,

(Such is the bounty from Allah) meaning, from Allah by His mercy, for it is He who made them suitable for this, not their good deeds.

(and Allah is sufficient as All-Knower), He knows those who deserve guidance and success.

Surah: 4 Ayah: 71, Ayah: 72, Ayah: 73 & Ayah: 74

﴿يَـٰٓأَيُّهَا ٱلَّذِينَ ءَامَنُواْ خُذُواْ حِذْرَكُمْ فَٱنفِرُواْ ثُبَاتٍ أَوِ ٱنفِرُواْ جَمِيعًا ﴿٧١﴾﴾

71. O you who believe! Take your precautions, and either go forth (on an expedition) in parties, or go forth all together.

﴿ وَإِنَّ مِنكُمْ لَمَن لَّيُبَطِّئَنَّ فَإِنْ أَصَابَتْكُم مُّصِيبَةٌ قَالَ قَدْ أَنْعَمَ ٱللَّهُ عَلَيَّ إِذْ لَمْ أَكُن مَّعَهُمْ
شَهِيدًا ﴿٧٢﴾ ﴾

72. There is certainly among you he who would linger behind (from fighting in Allâh's Cause). If a misfortune befalls you, he says, "Indeed Allâh has favored me in that I was not present among them."

﴿ وَلَئِنْ أَصَابَكُمْ فَضْلٌ مِّنَ ٱللَّهِ لَيَقُولَنَّ كَأَن لَّمْ تَكُنۢ بَيْنَكُمْ وَبَيْنَهُۥ مَوَدَّةٌ يَٰلَيْتَنِى كُنتُ
مَعَهُمْ فَأَفُوزَ فَوْزًا عَظِيمًا ﴿٧٣﴾ ﴾

73. But if a bounty (victory and booty) comes to you from Allâh, he would surely say - as if there had never been ties of affection between you and him - "Oh! I wish I had been with them; then I would have achieved a great success (a good share of booty)."

﴿ فَلْيُقَٰتِلْ فِى سَبِيلِ ٱللَّهِ ٱلَّذِينَ يَشْرُونَ ٱلْحَيَوٰةَ ٱلدُّنْيَا بِٱلْءَاخِرَةِ ۚ وَمَن يُقَٰتِلْ فِى سَبِيلِ
ٱللَّهِ فَيُقْتَلْ أَوْ يَغْلِبْ فَسَوْفَ نُؤْتِيهِ أَجْرًا عَظِيمًا ﴿٧٤﴾ ﴾

74. Let those (believers) who sell the life of this world for the Hereafter fight in the Cause of Allâh, and whoso fights in the Cause of Allâh, and is killed or gets victory, We shall bestow on him a great reward.

Transliteration

71. Ya ayyuha allatheena amanoo khuthoo hithrakum fainfiroo thubatin awi infiroo jameeAAan
72. Wa-inna minkum laman layubatti-anna fa-in asabatkum museebatun qala qad anAAama Allahu AAalayya ith lam akun maAAahum shaheedan 73. Wala-in asabakum fadlun mina Allahi layaqoolanna kaan lam takun baynakum wabaynahu mawaddatun ya laytanee kuntu maAAahum faafooza fawzan AAatheeman 74. Falyuqatil fee sabeeli Allahi allatheena yashroona alhayata alddunya bial-akhirati waman yuqatil fee sabeeli Allahi fayuqtal aw yaghlib fasawfa nu/teehi ajran AAatheeman

Tafsir Ibn Kathir

The Necessity of Taking Necessary Precautions Against the Enemy

Allah commands His faithful servants to take precautions against their enemies, by being prepared with the necessary weapons and supplies, and increasing the number of troops fighting in His cause.

(in parties) means, group after group, party after party, and expedition after expedition. `Ali bin Talhah reported that Ibn `Abbas said that,

(and either go forth in parties) means, "In groups, expedition after expedition,

(or go forth all together), means, all of you." Similar was reported from Mujahid, `Ikrimah, As-Suddi, Qatadah, Ad-Dahhak, `Ata' Al-Khurrasani, Muqatil bin Hayyan and Khusayf Al-Jazari.

Refraining from Joining Jihad is a Sign of Hypocrites

Allah said,

(There is certainly among you he who would linger behind.) Mujahid and others said that this Ayah was revealed about the hypocrites. Muqatil bin Hayyan said that,

(linger behind) means, stays behind and does not join Jihad. It is also possible that this person himself lingers behind, while luring others away from joining Jihad. For instance, `Abdullah bin Ubayy bin Salul, may Allah curse him, used to linger behind and lure other people to do the same and refrain from joining Jihad, as Ibn Jurayj and Ibn Jarir stated. This is why Allah said about the hypocrite, that when he lingers behind from Jihad, then:

(If a misfortune befalls you) death, martyrdom, or - by Allah's wisdom - being defeated by the enemy,

(he says, "Indeed Allah has favored me that I was not present among them.") meaning, since I did not join them in battle. Because he considers this one of Allah's favors on him, unaware of the reward that he might have gained from enduring war or martyrdom, if he was killed.

(But if a bounty comes to you from Allah) such as victory, triumph and booty,

(he would surely say - as if there had never been ties of affection between you and him,) meaning, as if he was not a follower of your religion,

("Oh! I wish I had been with them; then I would have achieved a great success.") by being assigned a share of the booty and taking possession of that share. This is his ultimate aim and objective.

The Encouragement to Participation in Jihad

Allah then said,

(So fight) the believer with an aversion (to fighting),

(those who trade the life of this world with the Hereafter) referring to those sell their religion for the meager goods of the world, and they only do this because of their disbelief and lack of faith. Allah then said;

(And whoever fights in the cause of Allah, and is killed or gets victory, We shall bestow on him a great reward.) meaning, whoever fights in the cause of Allah, whether he was killed or triumphant, he will earn an immense compensation and a great reward with Allah. The Two Sahihs recorded,

«وَتَكَفَّلَ اللهُ لِلْمُجَاهِدِ فِي سَبِيلِهِ، إِنْ تَوَفَّاهُ أَنْ يُدْخِلَهُ الْجَنَّةَ، أَوْ يَرْجِعَهُ إِلى مَسْكَنِهِ الَّذِي خَرَجَ مِنْهُ، بِمَا نَالَ مِنْ أَجْرٍ أَوْ غَنِيمَة»

(Allah has guaranteed the Mujahid in His cause that He will either bring death to him, admitting into Paradise; or, He will help him return safely to his home with whatever reward and booty he gained.)

Surah: 4 Ayah: 75 & Ayah: 76

﴿ وَمَا لَكُمْ لَا تُقَـٰتِلُونَ فِى سَبِيلِ ٱللَّهِ وَٱلْمُسْتَضْعَفِينَ مِنَ ٱلرِّجَالِ وَٱلنِّسَآءِ وَٱلْوِلْدَٰنِ ٱلَّذِينَ يَقُولُونَ رَبَّنَآ أَخْرِجْنَا مِنْ هَـٰذِهِ ٱلْقَرْيَةِ ٱلظَّالِمِ أَهْلُهَا وَٱجْعَل لَّنَا مِن لَّدُنكَ وَلِيًّا وَٱجْعَل لَّنَا مِن لَّدُنكَ نَصِيرًا ﴿٧٥﴾ ﴾

75. And what is wrong with you that you fight not in the Cause of Allâh, and for those weak, ill-treated and oppressed among men, women, and children, whose cry is: "Our Lord! Rescue us from this town whose people are oppressors; and raise for us from You one who will protect, and raise for us from You one who will help."

﴿ ٱلَّذِينَ ءَامَنُوا۟ يُقَـٰتِلُونَ فِى سَبِيلِ ٱللَّهِ ۖ وَٱلَّذِينَ كَفَرُوا۟ يُقَـٰتِلُونَ فِى سَبِيلِ ٱلطَّـٰغُوتِ فَقَـٰتِلُوٓا۟ أَوْلِيَآءَ ٱلشَّيْطَـٰنِ ۖ إِنَّ كَيْدَ ٱلشَّيْطَـٰنِ كَانَ ضَعِيفًا ﴿٧٦﴾ ﴾

76. Those who believe, fight in the Cause of Allâh, and those who disbelieve, fight in the cause of Tâghût (Satan). So fight you against the friends of Shaitân (Satan). Ever feeble indeed is the plot of Shaitân (Satan).

Transliteration

75. Wama lakum la tuqatiloona fee sabeeli Allahi waalmustadAAafeena mina alrrijali waalnnisa-i waalwildani allatheena yaqooloona rabbana akhrijna min hathihi alqaryati alththalimi ahluha waijAAal lana min ladunka waliyyan waijAAal lana min ladunka naseeran 76. Allatheena amanoo yuqatiloona fee sabeeli Allahi waallatheena kafaroo yuqatiloona fee sabeeli alttaghooti faqatiloo awliyaa alshshaytani inna kayda alshshaytani kana daAAeefan

Tafsir Ibn Kathir

Encouraging Jihad to Defend the Oppressed

Allah encouraged His believing servants to perform Jihad in His cause and to strive hard to save the oppressed Muslims in Makkah, men, women and children who were restless because of having to remain there. This is why Allah said,

(whose cry is: "Our Lord! Rescue us from this town), referring to Makkah. In a similar Ayah, Allah said,

(And many a town, stronger than your town which has driven you out) Allah then describes this town,

(whose people are oppressors; and raise for us from You one who will protect, and raise for us from You one who will help) meaning, send protectors and helpers for us. Al-Bukhari recorded that Ibn `Abbas said, "I and my mother were from the oppressed (in Makkah)." Allah then said,

(Those who believe, fight in the cause of Allah, and those who disbelieve, fight in the cause of the Taghut.) Therefore, the believers fight in obedience to Allah and to gain His pleasure, while the disbelievers fight in obedience to Shaytan. Allah then encourages the believers to fight His enemies,

(So fight against the friends of Shaytan; ever feeble indeed is the plot of Shaytan).

Surah: 4 Ayah: 77, Ayah: 78 & Ayah: 79

﴿ أَلَمۡ تَرَ إِلَى ٱلَّذِينَ قِيلَ لَهُمۡ كُفُّوٓاْ أَيۡدِيَكُمۡ وَأَقِيمُواْ ٱلصَّلَوٰةَ وَءَاتُواْ ٱلزَّكَوٰةَ فَلَمَّا كُتِبَ عَلَيۡهِمُ
ٱلۡقِتَالُ إِذَا فَرِيقٞ مِّنۡهُمۡ يَخۡشَوۡنَ ٱلنَّاسَ كَخَشۡيَةِ ٱللَّهِ أَوۡ أَشَدَّ خَشۡيَةٗۚ وَقَالُواْ رَبَّنَا لِمَ كَتَبۡتَ
عَلَيۡنَا ٱلۡقِتَالَ لَوۡلَآ أَخَّرۡتَنَآ إِلَىٰٓ أَجَلٖ قَرِيبٖۗ قُلۡ مَتَٰعُ ٱلدُّنۡيَا قَلِيلٞ وَٱلۡأٓخِرَةُ خَيۡرٞ لِّمَنِ ٱتَّقَىٰ
وَلَا تُظۡلَمُونَ فَتِيلًا ٧٧ ﴾

77. Have you not seen those who were told to hold back their hands (from fighting) and perform As-Salât (Iqâmat-as-Salât), and give Zakât, but when the fighting was ordained for them, behold! a section of them fear men as they fear Allâh or even more. They say: "Our Lord! Why have You ordained for us fighting? Would that You had granted us respite for a short period?" Say: "Short is the enjoyment of this world. The Hereafter is (far) better for him who fears Allâh, and you shall not be dealt with unjustly even equal to a scalish thread in the long slit of a date-stone.

﴿ أَيۡنَمَا تَكُونُواْ يُدۡرِككُّمُ ٱلۡمَوۡتُ وَلَوۡ كُنتُمۡ فِي بُرُوجٖ مُّشَيَّدَةٖۗ وَإِن تُصِبۡهُمۡ حَسَنَةٞ يَقُولُواْ
هَٰذِهِۦ مِنۡ عِندِ ٱللَّهِۖ وَإِن تُصِبۡهُمۡ سَيِّئَةٞ يَقُولُواْ هَٰذِهِۦ مِنۡ عِندِكَۚ قُلۡ كُلّٞ مِّنۡ عِندِ ٱللَّهِۖ
فَمَالِ هَٰٓؤُلَآءِ ٱلۡقَوۡمِ لَا يَكَادُونَ يَفۡقَهُونَ حَدِيثٗا ٧٨ ﴾

78. "Wheresoever you may be, death will overtake you even if you are in fortresses built up strong and high!" And if some good reaches them, they say, "This is from Allâh," but if some evil befalls them, they say, "This is from you (O Muhammad (peace be upon him))" Say: "All things are from Allâh," so what is wrong with these people that they fail to understand any word?

﴿ مَّآ أَصَابَكَ مِنۡ حَسَنَةٖ فَمِنَ ٱللَّهِۖ وَمَآ أَصَابَكَ مِن سَيِّئَةٖ فَمِن نَّفۡسِكَۚ وَأَرۡسَلۡنَٰكَ لِلنَّاسِ
رَسُولٗاۚ وَكَفَىٰ بِٱللَّهِ شَهِيدٗا ٧٩ ﴾

79. Whatever of good reaches you, is from Allâh, but whatever of evil befalls you, is from yourself. And We have sent you (O Muhammad (peace be upon him)) as a Messenger to mankind, and Allâh is Sufficient as a Witness.

Transliteration

77. Alam tara ila allatheena qeela lahum kuffoo aydiyakum waaqeemoo alssalata waatoo alzzakata falamma kutiba AAalayhimu alqitalu itha fareequn minhum yakhshawna alnnasa kakhashyati Allahi aw ashadda khashyatan waqaloo rabbana lima katabta AAalayna alqitala lawla akhkhartana ila ajalin qareebin qul mataAAu alddunya qaleelun waal-akhiratu khayrun limani ittaqa wala tuthlamoona fateelan 78. Aynama takoonoo yudrikkumu almawtu walaw kuntum fee buroojin mushayyadatin wa-in tusibhum hasanatun yaqooloo hathihi min AAindi Allahi wa-in tusibhum sayyi-atun yaqooloo hathihi min AAindika qul kullun min AAindi Allahi famali haola-i alqawmi la yakadoona yafqahoona hadeethan 79. Ma asabaka min hasanatin

famina Allahi wama asabaka min sayyi-atin famin nafsika waarsalnaka lilnnasi rasoolan wakafa biAllahi shaheedan

Tafsir Ibn Kathir

The Wish that the Order for Jihad be Delayed

In the beginning of Islam, Muslims in Makkah were commanded to perform the prayer and pay some charity, so as to comfort the poor among them. They were also commanded to be forgiving and forbearing with the idolators and to observe patience with them at the time. However, they were eager and anticipating the time when they would be allowed to fight, so that they could punish their enemies. The situation at that time did not permit armed conflict for many reasons. For instance, Muslims were few at the time, compared to their numerous enemies. The Muslims' city was a sacred one and the most honored area on the earth, and this is why the command to fight was not revealed in Makkah. Later on when the Muslims controlled a town of their own, Al-Madinah, and had strength, power and support, Jihad was then legislated. Yet, when the command to fight was revealed, just as Muslims wished, some of them became weary and were very fearful of facing the idolators in battle.

(They say: "Our Lord! Why have You ordained for us fighting Would that You had granted us respite for a short period") meaning, we wish that Jihad was delayed until a later time, because it means bloodshed, orphans and widows. In a similar Ayah, Allah said,

(Those who believe say: "Why is not a Surah sent down (for us) But when a decisive is sent down, and fighting is mentioned). Ibn Abi Hatim recorded that Ibn `Abbas said that `Abdur-Rahman bin `Awf and several of his companions came to the Prophet while in Makkah and said, "O Allah's Prophet! We were mighty when we were pagans, but when we embraced the faith, we became weak." The Prophet said,

«إِنِّي أُمِرْتُ بِالْعَفْوِ فَلَا تُقَاتِلُوا الْقَوْمَ»

(I was commanded to pardon the people, so do not fight them.) When Allah transferred the Prophet to Al-Madinah, He commanded him to fight (the idolators), but they (some Muslims) held back. So, Allah revealed the Ayah;

(Have you not seen those who were told to hold back their hands) This Hadith was collected by An-Nasa'i and Al-Hakim. Allah's statement,

(Say: "Short is the enjoyment of this world. The Hereafter is (far) better for him who fears Allah,) means, the destination of the one who with Taqwa is better for him than this life.

(and you shall not be dealt with unjustly even equal to the Fatil.) for your good deeds. Rather, you will earn your full rewards for them. This promise directs the focus of believers away from this life and makes them eager for the Hereafter, all the while encouraging them to fight in Jihad.

There is No Escaping Death

Allah said,

(Wheresoever you may be, death will overtake you even if you are in fortresses built up strong and high!) meaning, you shall certainly die and none of you shall ever escape death. Allah said,

(Whatsooever is on it (the earth) will perish),

(Everyone shall taste death), and,

(And We granted not to any human being immortality before you). Therefore, every soul shall taste death and nothing can save any person from it, whether he performed Jihad or not. Everyone has an appointed time, and a limited term of life. In the illness that preceded his death, Khalid bin Al-Walid said, while in his bed, "I participated in so and so number of battles, and every part of my body sustained an injury due to a stab or a shot. Yet here I am, I die in my bed! Let not the eyes of the cowards ever taste sleep." Allah's statement,

(even if you are in fortresses built up strong and high!) means, entrenched, fortified, high and towering. No caution or fortification can ever avert death.

The Hypocrites Sense a Bad Omen Because of the Prophet!

Allah said,

(And if some good reaches them) meaning, fertile years and provision of fruits, produce, children, etc., as said by Ibn `Abbas, Abu Al-`Aliyah and As-Suddi.

(they say, "This is from Allah," but if some evil befalls them) drought, famine, shortages of fruits and produce, death that strikes their children or animals, and so forth, as Abu Al-`Aliyah and As-Suddi stated.

(they say, "This is from you,") meaning, because of you and because we followed you and embraced your religion. Allah said about the people of Fir`awn,

(But whenever good came to them, they said: "Ours is this." And if evil afflicted them, they ascribed it to evil omens connected with Musa and those with him.) Allah said,

(And among mankind is he who worships Allah as it were upon the edge (i. e. in doubt)). The same is the statement uttered by the hypocrites, who embraced Islam outwardly, but disliked it inwardly. This is why when a calamity befell them, they attributed it to following the Prophet . Consequently, Allah revealed,

Say: All things are from Alla0h, Allah's statement that all things are from Him means, everything occurs by the decision and decree of Allah, and His decision shall come to pass for both the righteous and the wicked, the faithful and the disbelievers. Allah then said while addressing His Messenger , but refering to mankind in general,

(Whatever of good reaches you, is from Allah,) meaning, of Allah's bounty, favor, kindness and mercy.

(But whatever of evil befalls you, is from yourself.), meaning because of you and due to your actions. Similarly, Allah said,

(And whatever of misfortune befalls you, it is because of what your hands have earned. And He pardons much.) As-Suddi, Al-Hasan Al-Basri, Ibn Jurayj and Ibn Zayd said that, (from yourself) means, because of your errors. Qatadah said that,

(From yourself) means, as punishment for you, O son of Adam, because of your sins. Allah said,

(And We have sent you as a Messenger to mankind,) so that you convey to them Allah's commandments, what He likes and is pleased with, and what He dislikes and refuses.

(and Allah is sufficient as a Witness.) that He has sent you. He is also Witness over you and them, having full knowledge in what you convey to them and the disbelief and rebellion with which they respond to the truth.

Surah: 4 Ayah: 80 & Ayah: 81

﴿ مَّن يُطِعِ ٱلرَّسُولَ فَقَدۡ أَطَاعَ ٱللَّهَۖ وَمَن تَوَلَّىٰ فَمَآ أَرۡسَلۡنَٰكَ عَلَيۡهِمۡ حَفِيظٗا ﴿٨٠﴾ ﴾

80. He who obeys the Messenger (Muhammad (peace be upon him)) has indeed obeyed Allâh, but he who turns away, then we have not sent you (O Muhammad (peace be upon him)) as a watcher over them.

﴿ وَيَقُولُونَ طَاعَةٞ فَإِذَا بَرَزُواْ مِنۡ عِندِكَ بَيَّتَ طَآئِفَةٞ مِّنۡهُمۡ غَيۡرَ ٱلَّذِي تَقُولُۖ وَٱللَّهُ يَكۡتُبُ مَا يُبَيِّتُونَۖ فَأَعۡرِضۡ عَنۡهُمۡ وَتَوَكَّلۡ عَلَى ٱللَّهِۚ وَكَفَىٰ بِٱللَّهِ وَكِيلًا ﴿٨١﴾ ﴾

81. They say: "We are obedient," but when they leave you (Muhammad (peace be upon him)) a section of them spend all night in planning other than what you say. But Allâh records their nightly (plots). So turn aside from them (do not punish them), and put your trust in Allâh. And Allâh is Ever All-Sufficient as a Disposer of affairs.

Transliteration

80. Man yutiAAi alrrasoola faqad ataAAa Allaha waman tawalla fama arsalnaka AAalayhim hafeethan 81. Wayaqooloona taAAatun fa-itha barazoo min AAindika bayyata ta-ifatun minhum ghayra allathee taqoolu waAllahu yaktubu ma yubayyitoona faaAArid AAanhum watawakkal AAala Allahi wakafa biAllahi wakeelan

Tafsir Ibn Kathir

Obeying the Messenger is Obeying Allah

Allah states that whoever obeys His servant and Messenger, Muhammad , obeys Allah; and whoever disobeys him, disobeys Allah. Verily, whatever the Messenger utters is not of his own desire, but a revelation inspired to him. Ibn Abi Hatim recorded that Abu Hurayrah said that the Messenger of Allah said,

«مَنْ أَطَاعَنِي فَقَدْ أَطَاعَ اللهَ، وَمَنْ عَصَانِي فَقَدْ عَصَى اللهَ، وَمَنْ أَطَاعَ الْأَمِيرَ فَقَدْ أَطَاعَنِي، وَمَنْ عَصَى الْأَمِيرَ فَقَدْ عَصَانِي»

(Whoever obeys me, obeys Allah; and whoever disobeys me, disobeys Allah. Whoever obeys the Amir (leader, ruler), obeys me; and whoever disobeys the Amir, disobeys me.) This Hadith was recorded in the Two Sahihs. Allah's statement,

(But he who turns away, then We have not sent you as a watcher over them.) means, do not worry about him. Your job is only to convey, and whoever obeys you, he will acquire happiness and success and you will gain a similar reward to that he earns. As for the one who turns away from you, he will gain failure and loss and you will not carry a burden because of what he does. A Hadith states,

«مَنْ يُطِعِ اللهَ وَرَسُولَهُ فَقَدْ رَشَدَ، وَمَنْ يَعْصِ اللهَ وَرَسُولَهُ فَإِنَّهُ لَا يَضُرُّ إِلَّا نَفْسَه»

(Whoever obeys Allah and His Messenger, will acquire guidance; and whoever disobeys Allah and His Messenger, will only harm himself.)

The Foolishness of the Hypocrites

Allah said,

(They say: "We are obedient,"). Allah states that the hypocrites pretend to be loyal and obedient.

(but when they leave you), meaning, when they depart and are no longer with you,

(a section of them spends all night in planning other than what you say). They plot at night among themselves for other than what they pretend when they are with you. Allah said,

(But Allah records their nightly (plots).) meaning, He has full knowledge of their plots and records it through His command to His scribes, the angels who are responsible for recording the actions of the servants. This is a threat from Allah, stating that He knows what the hypocrites try to hide, their plotting in the night to defy the Messenger and oppose him, even though they pretend to be loyal and obedient to him. Allah will certainly punish them for this conduct. In a similar Ayah, Allah said,

(They (hypocrites) say: "We have believed in Allah and in the Messenger, and we obey,") until the end of the Ayah. Allah's statement,

(So turn aside from them) means, pardon them, be forbearing with them, do not punish them, do not expose them to the people and do not fear them.

(and put your trust in Allah. And Allah is Ever All-Sufficient as a Disposer of affairs.) meaning, He is sufficient as Protector, Supporter and Helper for those who rely on Him and return to Him.

Surah: 4 Ayah: 82 & Ayah: 83

﴿أَفَلَا يَتَدَبَّرُونَ ٱلْقُرْءَانَ ۚ وَلَوْ كَانَ مِنْ عِندِ غَيْرِ ٱللَّهِ لَوَجَدُوا۟ فِيهِ ٱخْتِلَٰفًا كَثِيرًا ﴿٨٢﴾﴾

82. Do they not then consider the Qur'ân carefully? Had it been from other than Allâh, they would surely have found therein many a contradiction.

﴿ وَإِذَا جَآءَهُمْ أَمْرٌ مِّنَ ٱلْأَمْنِ أَوِ ٱلْخَوْفِ أَذَاعُوا۟ بِهِۦ ۖ وَلَوْ رَدُّوهُ إِلَى ٱلرَّسُولِ وَإِلَىٰٓ أُو۟لِى
ٱلْأَمْرِ مِنْهُمْ لَعَلِمَهُ ٱلَّذِينَ يَسْتَنۢبِطُونَهُۥ مِنْهُمْ ۗ وَلَوْلَا فَضْلُ ٱللَّهِ عَلَيْكُمْ وَرَحْمَتُهُۥ لَٱتَّبَعْتُمُ
ٱلشَّيْطَٰنَ إِلَّا قَلِيلًا ﴿٨٣﴾ ﴾

83. When there comes to them some matter touching (public) safety or fear, they make it known (among the people); if only they had referred it to the Messenger or to those charged with authority among them, the proper investigators would have understood it from them (directly). Had it not been for the Grace and Mercy of Allâh upon you, you would have followed Shaitân (Satan), save a few of you.

Transliteration

82. Afala yatadabbaroona alqur-ana walaw kana min AAindi ghayri Allahi lawajadoo feehi ikhtilafan katheeran 83. Wa-itha jaahum amrun mina al-amni awi alkhawfi athaAAoo bihi walaw raddoohu ila alrrasooli waila olee al-amri minhum laAAalimahu allatheena yastanbitoonahu minhum walawla fadlu Allahi AAalaykum warahmatuhu laittabaAAtumu alshshaytana illa qaleelan

Tafsir Ibn Kathir

The Qur'an is True

Allah commands them to contemplate about the Qur'an and forbids them from ignoring it, or ignoring its wise meanings and eloquent words. Allah states that there are no inconsistencies, contradictions, conflicting statements or discrepancies in the Qur'an, because it is a revelation from the Most-Wise, Worthy of all praise. Therefore, the Qur'an is the truth coming from the Truth, Allah. This is why Allah said in another Ayah,

(Do they not then think deeply in the Qur'an, or are their hearts locked up (from understanding it)) Allah then said,

(Had it been from other than Allah,) meaning, had it been fraudulent and made up, as the ignorant idolators and hypocrites assert in their hearts,

(they would surely, have found therein contradictions), discrepancies and inconsistencies,

(in abundance). However, this Qur'an is free of shortcomings, and therefore, it is from Allah. Similarly, Allah describes those who are firmly grounded in knowledge,

(We believe in it, all of it is from our Lord.)(3:7) meaning, the Muhkam sections (entirely clear) and the Mutashabih sections (not entirely clear) of the Qur'an are all true. So they understand the not entirely clear from the clear, and thus gain guidance. As for those in whose heart is the disease of hypocrisy, they understand the Muhkam from the Mutashabih; thus only gaining misguidance. Allah praised those who have knowledge and criticized the wicked. Imam Ahmad recorded that `Amr bin Shu`ayb said that his father said that his grandfather said, "I and my brother were present in a gathering, which is more precious to me than red camels. My brother and I came and found that some of the leaders of the Companions of the Messenger of Allah were sitting close to a door of his. We did not like the idea of being separate from them, so we sat near the room. They then mentioned an Ayah and began disputing until they raised their voices. The Messenger of Allah was so angry that when he went out his face was red. He threw sand on them and said to them,

«مَهْلًا يَا قَوْمِ، بِهَذَا أُهْلِكَتِ الْأُمَمُ مِنْ قَبْلِكُمْ، بِاخْتِلَافِهِمْ عَلى أَنْبِيَائِهِمْ، وَضَرْبِهِم الْكُتُبَ بَعْضَهَا بِبَعْضٍ، إِنَّ الْقُرْآنَ لَمْ يَنْزِلْ يُكَذِّبُ بَعْضُهُ بَعْضًا، إِنَّمَا يُصَدِّقُ بَعْضُهُ بَعْضًا، فَمَا عَرَفْتُمْ مِنْهُ فَاعْمَلُوا بِهِ، وَمَا جَهِلْتُمْ مِنْهُ فَرُدُّوهُ إِلى عَالِمِهِ»

(Behold, O people! This is how the nations before you were destroyed, because of their disputing with their Prophets and their contradicting parts of the Books with other parts. The Qur'an does not contradict itself. Rather, it testifies to the truth of itself. Therefore, whatever of it you have knowledge in, then implement it, and whatever you do not know of it, then refer it to those who have knowledge in it.)" Ahmad recorded that `Abdullah bin `Amr said, "I went to the Messenger of Allah one day. When we were sitting, two men disputed about an Ayah, and their voices became loud. The Prophet said,

«إِنَّمَا هَلَكَتِ الْأُمَمُ قَبْلَكُمْ بِاخْتِلَافِهِمْ فِي الْكِتَابِ»

(Verily, the nations before you were destroyed because of their disagreements over the Book.) Muslim and An-Nasa'i recorded this Hadith.

The Prohibition of Disclosing Unreliable and Uninvestigated News

Allah said,

(When there comes to them some matter touching (public) safety or fear, they make it known (among the people);) chastising those who indulge in things before being sure of their truth, disclosing them, making them known and spreading their news, even though such news might not be true at all. In the introduction to his Sahih, Imam Muslim recorded that Abu Hurayrah said that the Prophet said,

«كَفَى بِالْمَرْءِ كَذِبًا أَنْ يُحَدِّثَ بِكُلِّ مَا سَمِعَ»

(Narrating everything one hears is sufficient to make a person a liar.) This is the same narration collected by Abu Dawud in the section of Adab (manners) in his Sunan. In the Two Sahihs, it is recorded that Al-Mughirah bin Shu`bah said that the Messenger of Allah prohibited, "It was said," and, "So-and-so said." This Hadith refers to those who often convey the speech that people utter without investigating the reliability and truth of what he is disclosing. The Sahih also records,

«مَنْ حَدَّثَ بِحَدِيثٍ وَهُوَ يُرَى أَنَّهُ كَذِبٌ، فَهُوَ أَحَدُ الْكَاذِبَيْنِ»

(Whoever narrates a Hadith while knowing it is false, then he is one of the two liars (who invents and who spreads the lie).) We should mention here the Hadith of `Umar bin Al-

Khattab collected in the Two Sahihs. When `Umar was informed that the Messenger of Allah divorced his wives, he came from his house, entered the Masjid and found the people talking about this news. He could not wait and went to the Prophet to ask him about what had truly happened, asking him, "Have you divorced your wives" The Prophet said, "No." `Umar said, "I said, Allahu Akbar..." and mentioned the rest of the Hadith. In the narration that Muslim collected, `Umar said, "I asked, `Have you divorced them' He said, `No.' So, I stood by the door of the Masjid and shouted with the loudest voice, `The Messenger of Allah did not divorce his wives.' Then, this Ayah was revealed,

(When there comes to them some matter touching (public) safety or fear, they make it known (among the people), if only they had referred it to the Messenger or to those charged with authority among them, the proper investigators would have understood it from them (directly).) So I properly investigated that matter." This Ayah refers to proper investigation, or extraction of matters from their proper resources. Allah's statement,

(you would have followed Shaytan except a few of you.) refers to the believers, as `Ali bin Abi Talhah reported from Ibn `Abbas.

Surah: 4 Ayah: 84, Ayah: 85, Ayah: 86 & Ayah: 87

﴿ فَقَٰتِلۡ فِي سَبِيلِ ٱللَّهِ لَا تُكَلَّفُ إِلَّا نَفۡسَكَۚ وَحَرِّضِ ٱلۡمُؤۡمِنِينَۖ عَسَى ٱللَّهُ أَن يَكُفَّ بَأۡسَ
ٱلَّذِينَ كَفَرُواْۚ وَٱللَّهُ أَشَدُّ بَأۡسٗا وَأَشَدُّ تَنكِيلٗا ٨٤ ﴾

84. Then fight (O Muhammad (peace be upon him)) in the Cause of Allâh, you are not tasked (held responsible) except for yourself, and incite the believers (to fight along with you), it may be that Allâh will restrain the evil might of the disbelievers. And Allâh is Stronger in Might and Stronger in punishing.

﴿ مَّن يَشۡفَعۡ شَفَٰعَةً حَسَنَةٗ يَكُن لَّهُۥ نَصِيبٞ مِّنۡهَاۖ وَمَن يَشۡفَعۡ شَفَٰعَةٗ سَيِّئَةٗ يَكُن لَّهُۥ كِفۡلٞ
مِّنۡهَاۗ وَكَانَ ٱللَّهُ عَلَىٰ كُلِّ شَيۡءٖ مُّقِيتٗا ٨٥ ﴾

85. Whosoever intercedes for a good cause will have the reward thereof, and whosoever intercedes for an evil cause will have a share in its burden. And Allâh is Ever All-Able to do (and also an All-Witness to) everything.

﴿ وَإِذَا حُيِّيتُم بِتَحِيَّةٖ فَحَيُّواْ بِأَحۡسَنَ مِنۡهَآ أَوۡ رُدُّوهَآۗ إِنَّ ٱللَّهَ كَانَ عَلَىٰ كُلِّ شَيۡءٍ حَسِيبًا ٨٦
﴾

86. When you are greeted with a greeting, greet in return with what is better than it, or (at least) return it equally. Certainly, Allâh is Ever a Careful Account Taker of all things.

﴿ ٱللَّهُ لَآ إِلَٰهَ إِلَّا هُوَۚ لَيَجۡمَعَنَّكُمۡ إِلَىٰ يَوۡمِ ٱلۡقِيَٰمَةِ لَا رَيۡبَ فِيهِۗ وَمَنۡ أَصۡدَقُ مِنَ ٱللَّهِ
حَدِيثٗا ٨٧ ﴾

87. Allâh! Lâ ilâha illa Huwa (none has the right to be worshipped but He). Surely, He will gather you together on the Day of Resurrection about which there is no doubt. And who is truer in statement than Allâh?

Transliteration

84. Faqatil fee sabeeli Allahi la tukallafu illa nafsaka waharridi almu/mineena AAasa Allahu an yakuffa ba/sa allatheena kafaroo waAllahu ashaddu ba/san waashaddu tankeelan 85. Man yashfaAA shafaAAatan hasanatan yakun lahu naseebun minha waman yashfaAA shafaAAatan sayyi-atan yakun lahu kiflun minha wakana Allahu AAala kulli shay-in muqeetan 86. Wa-itha huyyeetum bitahiyyatin fahayyoo bi-ahsana minha aw ruddooha inna Allaha kana AAala kulli shay-in haseeban 87. Allahu la ilaha illa huwa layajmaAAannakum ila yawmi alqiyamati la rayba feehi waman asdaqu mina Allahi hadeethan

Tafsir Ibn Kathir

Allah Commands His Messenger to Perform Jihad

Allah commands His servant and Messenger, Muhammad , to himself fight in Jihad and not to be concerned about those who do not join Jihad. Hence Allah's statement,

(you are not tasked (held responsible except for yourself,) Ibn Abi Hatim recorded that Abu Ishaq said, "I asked Al-Bara bin `Azib about a man who meets a hundred enemies and still fights them, would he be one of those referred to in Allah's statement,

(And do not throw yourselves into destruction (by not spending your wealth in the cause of Allah)) He said, `Allah said to His Prophet,

(Then fight in the cause of Allah, you are not tasked (held responsible) except for yourself, and incite the believers (to fight along with you))." Imam Ahmad recorded Sulayman bin Dawud saying that Abu Bakr bin `Ayyash said that Abu Ishaq said, "I asked Al-Bara', `If a man attacks the lines of the idolators, would he be throwing himself to destruction' He said, `No because Allah has sent His Messenger and commanded him,

(Then fight in the cause of Allah, you are not tasked (held responsible) except for yourself,) That Ayah is about spending (in Allah's cause)."

Inciting the Believers to Fight

Allah said,

(and incite the believers) to fight, by encouraging them and strengthening their resolve in this regard. For instance, the Prophet said to the believers at the battle of Badr, while organizing their lines,

«قُومُوا إِلَى جَنَّةٍ عَرْضُهَا السَّموَاتُ وَالْأَرْضُ»

(Stand up and march forth to a Paradise, as wide as the heavens and Earth.) There are many Hadiths that encourage Jihad. Al-Bukhari recorded that Abu Hurayrah said that the Messenger of Allah said,

«مَنْ آمَنَ بِاللهِ وَرَسُولِهِ، وَأَقَامَ الصَّلَاةَ، وَآتَى الزَّكَاةَ، وَصَامَ رَمَضَانَ، كَانَ حَقًّا عَلَى اللهِ أَنْ يُدْخِلَهُ الْجَنَّــــةَ، هَاجَرَ فِي سَبِيلِ اللهِ أَوْ جَلَسَ فِي أَرْضِهِ الَّتِي وُلِدَ فِيهَا»

(Whoever believes in Allah and His Messenger, offers prayer, pays the Zakah and fasts the month of Ramadan, will rightfully be granted Paradise by Allah, no matter whether he migrates in Allah's cause or remains in the land where he is born.) The people said, `O Allah's Messenger! Shall we acquaint the people with this good news' He said,

«إِنَّ فِي الْجَنَّــــةِ مِائَةَ دَرَجَةٍ أَعَدَّهَا اللهُ لِلْمُجَاهِدِينَ فِي سَبِيلِ اللهِ، بَيْنَ كُلِّ دَرَجَتَيْنِ كَمَا بَيْنَ السَّمَاءِ وَالْأَرْضِ، فَإِذَا سَأَلْتُمُ اللهَ فَاسْأَلُوهُ الْفِرْدَوْسَ، فَإِنَّهُ وَسَطُ الْجَنَّةِ، وَأَعْلَى الْجَنَّةِ، وَفَوْقَهُ عَرْشُ الرَّحْمنِ، وَمِنْهُ تَفَجَّرُ أَنْهَارُ الْجَنَّة»

(Paradise has one hundred grades which Allah has reserved for the Mujahidin who fight in His cause, the distance between each two grades is like the distance between the heaven and the Earth. So, when you ask Allah, ask for Al-Firdaws, which is the best and highest part of Paradise, above it is the Throne of the Most Beneficent (Allah) and from it originate the rivers of Paradise.) There are various narrations for this Hadith from `Ubadah, Mu`adh, and Abu Ad-Darda'. Abu Sa`id Al-Khudri narrated that the Messenger of Allah said,

«يَا أَبَا سَعِيدٍ مَنْ رَضِيَ بِاللهِ رَبًّا، وَبِالْإِسْلَامِ دِينًا، وَبِمُحَمَّدٍصلى الله عليه وسلّم نَبِيًّا، وَجَبَتْ لَهُ الْجَنَّــــة»

(O Abu Sa`id! Whoever accepts Allah as his Lord, Islam as his religion and Muhammad as the Prophet, then he would rightfully acquire Paradise.) Abu Sa`id liked these words and said, "O Allah's Messenger! Repeat them for me." The Prophet repeated his words, then said,

«وَأُخْرَى يَرْفَعُ اللهُ الْعَبْدَبِهَا مِائَةَ دَرَجَةٍ فِي الْجَنَّــــةِ، مَا بَيْنَ كُلِّ دَرَجَتَيْنِ كَمَا بَيْنَ السَّمَاءِ وَالْأَرْض»

(And (there is) another deed for which Allah raises the servant a hundred grades in Paradise, between each two grades is the distance between heaven and Earth.) Abu Sa`id said, "What is it, O Allah's Messenger " He said,

«الْجِهَادُ فِي سَبِيلِ الله»

(Jihad in Allah's cause.) This Hadith was collected by Muslim. Allah's statement,

(it may be that Allah will restrain the evil might of the disbelievers.) means, by your encouraging them to fight, their resolve will be strengthened to meet the enemy in battle, to defend Islam and its people and to endure and be patient against the enemy. Allah's statement,

(And Allah is Stronger in might and Stronger in punishing.) means, He is able over them in this life and the Hereafter, just as He said in another Ayah,

(But if it had been Allah's will, He Himself could certainly have punished them (without you). But (He lets you fight) in order to test some of you with others) (47:4).

Interceding for a Good or an Evil Cause

Allah said,

(Whosoever intercedes for a good cause, will have the reward thereof;) meaning, whoever intercedes in a matter that produces good results, will acquire a share in that good.

(And whosoever intercedes for an evil cause, will have a share in its burden.) meaning, he will carry a burden due to what resulted from his intercession and intention. For instance, it is recorded in the Sahih that the Prophet said,

«اشْفَعُوا تُؤْجَرُوا، وَيَقْضِي اللهُ عَلى لِسَانِ نَبِيِّهِ مَا شَاء»

(Intercede and you will gain a reward of it. Yet, Allah shall decide whatever He wills by the words of His Prophet.) Mujahid bin Jabr said, "This Ayah was revealed about the intercession of people on behalf of each other." Allah then said,

(And Allah is Ever Muqit over everything.) Ibn `Abbas, `Ata', `Atiyah, Qatadah and Matar Al-Warraq said that,

(Muqit) means, "Watcher." Mujahid said that Muqit means, `Witness', and in another narration, `Able to do.'

Returning the Salam, With a Better Salam

Allah said,

(When you are greeted with a greeting, greet in return with what is better than it, or (at least) return it equally.) meaning, if the Muslim greets you with the Salam, then return the greeting with a better Salam, or at least equal to the Salam that was given. Therefore, the better Salam is recommended, while returning it equally is an obligation. Imam Ahmad recorded that Abu Raja' Al-`Utaridi said that `Imran bin Husayn said that a man came to the Messenger of Allah and said, "As-Salamu `Alaykum". The Prophet returned the greeting, and after the man sat down he said, "Ten." Another man came and said, "As-Salamu `Alaykum wa Rahmatullah, O Allah's Messenger." The Prophet returned the greeting, and after the man sat down he said, "Twenty." Then another man came and said, "As-Salamu `Alaykum wa Rahmatullah wa Barakatuh." The Prophet returned the greeting, and after the man sat down he said, "Thirty." This is the narration recorded by Abu Dawud. At-Tirmidhi, An-Nasa'i and Al-Bazzar also recorded it. At-Tirmidhi said, "Hasan Gharib". There are several other Hadiths on this subject from Abu Sa`id, `Ali, and Sahl bin Hanif. When the Muslim is greeted with the full form of Salam, he is obliged to return the greeting equally. As for Ahl Adh-Dhimmah the Salam should not be initiated nor should the greeting be added to when returning their greeting. Rather, as recorded in the Two Sahihs their greeting is returned to them equally. Ibn `Umar narrated that the Messenger of Allah said,

«إِذَا سَلَّمَ عَلَيْكُمُ الْيَهُودُ، فَإِنَّمَا يَقُولُ أَحَدُهُمْ: السَّامُ عَلَيْكَ، فَقُلْ: وَعَلَيْكَ»

(When the Jews greet you, one of them would say, `As-Samu `Alayka (death be unto you).' Therefore, say, `Wa `Alayka (and the same to you).') In his Sahih, Muslim recorded that Abu Hurayrah said that the Messenger of Allah said,

«لَا تَبْدَأُوا الْيَهُودَ وَالنَّصَارَى بِالسَّلَامِ، وَإِذَا لَقِيتُمُوهُمْ فِي طَرِيقٍ فَاضْطَرُّوهُمْ إِلَى أَضْيَقِهِ»

(Do not initiate greeting the Jews and Christians with the Salam, and when you pass by them on a road, force them to its narrowest path.) Abu Dawud recorded that Abu Hurayrah said that the Messenger of Allah said,

«وَالَّذِي نَفْسِي بِيَدِهِ، لَا تَدْخُلُوا الْجَنَّـــةَ حَتَّى تُؤْمِنُوا، وَلَا تُؤْمِنُوا حَتَّى تَحَابُّوا، أَفَلَا أَدُلُّكُمْ عَلَى أَمْرٍ إِذَا فَعَلْتُمُوهُ تَحَابَبْتُمْ؟ أَفْشُوا السَّلَامَ بَيْنَكُم»

(By He in Whose Hand is my soul! You will not enter Paradise until you believe, and you will not believe until you love each other. Should I direct you to an action that would direct you to love each other Spread the Salam among yourselves.) Allah said,

(Allah! none has the right to be worshipped but He) informing that He is singled out as the sole God of all creation. Allah then said,

(Surely, He will gather you together on the Day of Resurrection about which there is no doubt.) swearing that He will gather the earlier and latter generations in one area, rewarding or punishing each person according to his or her actions. Allah said,

(And who is truer in statement than Allah) meaning, no one utters more truthful statements than Allah, in His promise, warning, stories of the past and information of what is to come; there is no deity worthy of worship nor Lord except Him.

Surah: 4 Ayah: 88, Ayah: 89, Ayah: 90 & Ayah: 91

﴿ فَمَا لَكُمْ فِي ٱلْمُنَـٰفِقِينَ فِئَتَيْنِ وَٱللَّهُ أَرْكَسَهُم بِمَا كَسَبُوٓا۟ ۚ أَتُرِيدُونَ أَن تَهْدُوا۟ مَنْ أَضَلَّ ٱللَّهُ ۖ وَمَن يُضْلِلِ ٱللَّهُ فَلَن تَجِدَ لَهُۥ سَبِيلًا ﴿٨٨﴾ ﴾

88. Then what is the matter with you that you are divided into two parties about the hypocrites? Allâh has cast them back (to disbelief) because of what they have earned. Do you want to guide him whom Allâh has made to go astray? And he whom Allâh has made to go astray, you will never find for him any way (of guidance).

﴿ وَدُّوا۟ لَوْ تَكْفُرُونَ كَمَا كَفَرُوا۟ فَتَكُونُونَ سَوَآءً ۖ فَلَا تَتَّخِذُوا۟ مِنْهُمْ أَوْلِيَآءَ حَتَّىٰ يُهَاجِرُوا۟ فِى
سَبِيلِ ٱللَّهِ ۚ فَإِن تَوَلَّوْا۟ فَخُذُوهُمْ وَٱقْتُلُوهُمْ حَيْثُ وَجَدتُّمُوهُمْ ۖ وَلَا تَتَّخِذُوا۟ مِنْهُمْ وَلِيًّا وَلَا
نَصِيرًا ٨٩ ﴾

89. They wish that you reject Faith, as they have rejected (Faith), and thus that you all become equal (like one another). So take not Auliyâ' (protectors or friends) from them, till they emigrate in the Way of Allâh (to Muhammad (peace be upon him)) But if they turn back (from Islâm), take (hold) of them and kill them wherever you find them, and take neither Auliyâ' (protectors or friends) nor helpers from them.

﴿ إِلَّا ٱلَّذِينَ يَصِلُونَ إِلَىٰ قَوْمٍۭ بَيْنَكُمْ وَبَيْنَهُم مِّيثَٰقٌ أَوْ جَآءُوكُمْ حَصِرَتْ صُدُورُهُمْ أَن
يُقَٰتِلُوكُمْ أَوْ يُقَٰتِلُوا۟ قَوْمَهُمْ ۚ وَلَوْ شَآءَ ٱللَّهُ لَسَلَّطَهُمْ عَلَيْكُمْ فَلَقَٰتَلُوكُمْ ۚ فَإِنِ ٱعْتَزَلُوكُمْ فَلَمْ
يُقَٰتِلُوكُمْ وَأَلْقَوْا۟ إِلَيْكُمُ ٱلسَّلَمَ فَمَا جَعَلَ ٱللَّهُ لَكُمْ عَلَيْهِمْ سَبِيلًا ٩٠ ﴾

90. Except those who join a group, between you and whom there is a treaty (of peace), or those who approach you with their breasts restraining from fighting you as well as fighting their own people. Had Allâh willed, indeed He would have given them power over you, and they would have fought you. So if they withdraw from you, and fight not against you, and offer you peace, then Allâh has opened no way for you against them.

﴿ سَتَجِدُونَ ءَاخَرِينَ يُرِيدُونَ أَن يَأْمَنُوكُمْ وَيَأْمَنُوا۟ قَوْمَهُمْ كُلَّ مَا رُدُّوٓا۟ إِلَى ٱلْفِتْنَةِ أُرْكِسُوا۟
فِيهَا ۚ فَإِن لَّمْ يَعْتَزِلُوكُمْ وَيُلْقُوٓا۟ إِلَيْكُمُ ٱلسَّلَمَ وَيَكُفُّوٓا۟ أَيْدِيَهُمْ فَخُذُوهُمْ وَٱقْتُلُوهُمْ حَيْثُ
ثَقِفْتُمُوهُمْ ۚ وَأُو۟لَٰٓئِكُمْ جَعَلْنَا لَكُمْ عَلَيْهِمْ سُلْطَٰنًا مُّبِينًا ٩١ ﴾

91. You will find others that wish to have security from you and security from their people. Every time they are sent back to temptation, they yield thereto. If they withdraw not from you, nor offer you peace, nor restrain their hands, take (hold) of them and kill them wherever you find them. In their case, We have provided you with a clear warrant against them.

Transliteration

88. Fama lakum fee almunafiqeena fi-atayni waAllahu arkasahum bima kasaboo atureedoona an tahdoo man adalla Allahu waman yudlili Allahu falan tajida lahu sabeelan 89. Waddoo law takfuroona kama kafaroo fatakoonoona sawaan fala tattakhithoo minhum awliyaa hatta yuhajiroo fee sabeeli Allahi fa-in tawallaw fakhuthoohum waoqtuloohum haythu wajadtumoohum wala tattakhithoo minhum waliyyan wala naseeran 90. Illa allatheena yasiloona ila qawmin baynakum wabaynahum meethaqun aw jaookum hasirat sudooruhum an

yuqatilookum aw yuqatiloo qawmahum walaw shaa Allahu lasallatahum AAalaykum falaqatalookum fa-ini iAAtazalookum falam yuqatilookum waalqaw ilaykumu alssalama fama jaAAala Allahu lakum AAalayhim sabeelan 91. Satajidoona akhareena yureedoona an ya/manookum waya/manoo qawmahum kulla ma ruddoo ila alfitnati orkisoo feeha fa-in lam yaAAtazilookum wayulqoo ilaykumu alssalama wayakuffoo aydiyahum fakhuthoohum waoqtuloohum haythu thaqiftumoohum waola-ikum jaAAalna lakum AAalayhim sultanan mubeenan

Tafsir Ibn Kathir

Censuring the Companions for Disagreeing over the Hypocrites who Returned to Al-Madinah Before Uhud

Allah criticizes the believers for disagreeing over the hypocrites. There are conflicting opinions over the reason behind revealing this Ayah. Imam Ahmad recorded that Zayd bin Thabit said that Messenger of Allah marched towards Uhud. However, some people who accompanied him went back to Al-Madinah, and the Companions of the Messenger of Allah divided into two groups concerning them, one saying they should be killed and the other objecting. Allah sent down,

(Then what is the matter with you that you are divided into two parties about the hypocrites) The Messenger of Allah said,

«إِنَّهَا طَيْبَةُ، وَإِنَّهَا تَنْفِي الْخَبَثَ، كَمَا يَنْفِي الْكِيرُ خَبَثَ الْحَدِيد»

(She (Al-Madinah) is Taybah, and she expels filth, just as the billow expels rust from iron.) The Two Sahihs also recorded this Hadith. Al-`Awfi reported that Ibn `Abbas said that the Ayah was revealed about some people in Makkah who said they embraced Islam, yet they gave their support to the idolators. One time, theses people went out of Makkah to fulfill some needs and said to each other, "If we meet the Companions of Muhammad, there will be no harm for us from their side." When the believers got news that these people went out of Makkah, some of them said, "Let us march to these cowards and kill them, because they support your enemy against you." However, another group from the believers said, "Glory be to Allah! Do you kill a people who say as you have said, just because they did not perform Hijrah or leave their land Is it allowed to shed their blood and confiscate their money in this case" So they divided to two groups, while the Messenger was with them, and did not prohibit either group from reiterating their argument. Thereafter, Allah revealed,

(Then what is the matter with you that you are divided into two parties about the hypocrites) Ibn Abi Hatim recorded this Hadith. Allah said,

(Allah has cast them back because of what they have earned.) meaning, He made them revert to, and fall into error. Ibn `Abbas said that,

(Arkasahum) means, `cast them' . Allah's statement,

(because of what they have earned) means, because of their defiance and disobedience to the Messenger and following falsehood.

(Do you want to guide him whom Allah has made to go astray And he whom Allah has made to go astray, you will never find for him a way.) meaning, there will be no path for him, or way to guidance. Allah's statement,

(They wish that you reject faith, as they have rejected, and thus that you all become equal.) means, they wish that you fall into misguidance, so that you and they are equal in that regard. This is because of their extreme enmity and hatred for you. Therefore, Allah said,

(So take not Awliya' from them, till they emigrate in the way of Allah. But if they turn back,) if they abandon Hijrah, as Al-`Awfi reported from Ibn `Abbas. As-Suddi said that this part of the Ayah means, "If they make their disbelief public."

Combatants and Noncombatants

Allah excluded some people;

(Except those who join a group, between you and whom there is a treaty (of peace),) meaning, except those who join and take refuge with a people with whom you have a pact of peace, or people of Dhimmah, then treat them as you treat the people with whom you have peace. This is the saying of As-Suddi, Ibn Zayd and Ibn Jarir. In his Sahih, Al-Bukhari recorded the story of the treaty of Al-Hudaybiyyah, where it was mentioned that whoever liked to have peace with Quraysh and conduct a pact with them, then they were allowed. Those who liked to have peace with Muhammad and his Companions and enter a pact with them were allowed. It was reported that Ibn `Abbas said that this Ayah was later abrogated by Allah's statement,

(Then when the Sacred Months have passed, kill the idolators wherever you find them) Allah said,

(or those who approach you with their breasts restraining) referring to another type of people covered by the exclusion from fighting. They are those who approach the Muslims with hesitation in their hearts because of their aversion to fighting the Muslims. They do not have the heart to fight with the Muslims against their own people. Therefore, they are neither with nor against Muslims.

(Had Allah willed, indeed He would have given them power over you, and they would have fought you.) meaning, it is from Allah's mercy that He has stopped them from fighting you.

(So, if they withdraw from you, and fight not against you, and offer you peace,) meaning, they revert to peace,

(then Allah has opened no way for you against them), you do not have the right to kill them, as long as they take this position. This was the position of Banu Hashim (the tribe of the Prophet), such as Al-`Abbas, who accompanied the idolators in the battle of Badr, for they joined the battle with great hesitation. This is why the Prophet commanded that Al-`Abbas not be killed, but only captured. Allah's statement,

(You will find others that wish to have security from you and security from their people.) refers to a type of people who on the surface appear to be like the type we just mentioned. However, the intention of each type is different, for the latter are hypocrites. They pretend to be Muslims with the Prophet and his Companions, so that they could attain safety with the Muslims for their blood, property and families. However, they support the idolators in secret and worship what they worship, so that they are at peace with them also. These people have secretly sided with the idolators, just as Allah described them,

(But when they are alone with their Shayatin, they say: "Truly, we are with you."). In this Ayah, Allah said,

(Every time they are sent back to Fitnah, they yield thereto.) meaning, they dwell in Fitnah. As-Suddi said that the Fitnah mentioned here refers to Shirk. Ibn Jarir recorded that Mujahid said that the Ayah was revealed about a group from Makkah who used to go to the Prophet (in Al-Madinah) pretending to be Muslims. However, when they went back to Quraysh, they reverted to worshipping idols. They wanted to be at peace with both sides. Allah commanded they should be fought against, unless they withdraw from combat and resort to peace. This is why Allah said,

(If they withdraw not from you, nor offer you peace) meaning, revert to peaceful and complacent behavior,

(nor restrain their hands) refrain from fighting you,

(take (hold of) them), capture them,

(and kill them wherever you Thaqiftumuhum.), wherever you find them,

(In their case, We have provided you with a clear warrant against them), meaning an unequivocal and plain warrant.

Surah: 4 Ayah: 92 & Ayah: 93

﴿ وَمَا كَانَ لِمُؤْمِنٍ أَنْ يَقْتُلَ مُؤْمِنًا إِلَّا خَطَأً ۚ وَمَنْ قَتَلَ مُؤْمِنًا خَطَأً فَتَحْرِيرُ رَقَبَةٍ
مُؤْمِنَةٍ وَدِيَةٌ مُسَلَّمَةٌ إِلَىٰ أَهْلِهِ إِلَّا أَنْ يَصَّدَّقُوا ۚ فَإِنْ كَانَ مِنْ قَوْمٍ عَدُوٍّ لَكُمْ وَهُوَ
مُؤْمِنٌ فَتَحْرِيرُ رَقَبَةٍ مُؤْمِنَةٍ ۖ وَإِنْ كَانَ مِنْ قَوْمٍ بَيْنَكُمْ وَبَيْنَهُمْ مِيثَاقٌ فَدِيَةٌ
مُسَلَّمَةٌ إِلَىٰ أَهْلِهِ وَتَحْرِيرُ رَقَبَةٍ مُؤْمِنَةٍ ۖ فَمَنْ لَمْ يَجِدْ فَصِيَامُ شَهْرَيْنِ مُتَتَابِعَيْنِ تَوْبَةً مِنَ اللَّهِ ۗ
وَكَانَ اللَّهُ عَلِيمًا حَكِيمًا ﴿٩٢﴾ ﴾

92. It is not for a believer to kill a believer except (that it be) by mistake; and whosoever kills a believer by mistake, (it is ordained that) he must set free a believing slave and a compensation (blood money, i.e. Diya) be given to the deceased's family, unless they remit it. If the deceased belonged to a people at war with you and he was a believer, the freeing of a believing slave (is prescribed); and if he belonged to a people with whom you have a treaty of mutual alliance, compensation (blood money - Diya) must be paid to his family, and a believing slave must be freed. And whoso finds this (the penance of freeing a slave) beyond his means, he must fast for two consecutive months in order to seek repentance from Allâh. And Allâh is Ever All-Knowing, All-Wise.

﴿ وَمَن يَقْتُلْ مُؤْمِنًا مُّتَعَمِّدًا فَجَزَآؤُهُۥ جَهَنَّمُ خَٰلِدًا فِيهَا وَغَضِبَ ٱللَّهُ عَلَيْهِ وَلَعَنَهُۥ وَأَعَدَّ
لَهُۥ عَذَابًا عَظِيمًا ﴿٩٣﴾ ﴾

93. And whoever kills a believer intentionally, his recompense is Hell to abide therein; and the Wrath and the Curse of Allâh are upon him, and a great punishment is prepared for him.

Transliteration

92. Wama kana limu/minin an yaqtula mu/minan illa khataan waman qatala mu/minan khataan fatahreeru raqabatin mu/minatin wadiyatun musallamatun ila ahlihi illa an yassaddaqoo fa-in kana min qawmin AAaduwwin lakum wahuwa mu/minun fatahreeru raqabatin mu/minatin wa-in kana min qawmin baynakum wabaynahum meethaqun fadiyatun musallamatun ila ahlihi watahreeru raqabatin mu/minatin faman lam yajid fasiyamu shahrayni mutatabiAAayni tawbatan mina Allahi wakana Allahu AAaleeman hakeeman 93. Waman yaqtul mu/minan mutaAAammidan fajazaohu jahannamu khalidan feeha waghadiba Allahu AAalayhi walaAAanahu waaAAadda lahu AAathaban AAatheeman

Tafsir Ibn Kathir

The Ruling Concerning Killing a Believer by Mistake

Allah states that the believer is not allowed to kill his believing brother under any circumstances. In the Two Sahihs, it is recorded that Ibn Mas\`ud said that the Messenger of Allah said,

«لَا يَحِلُّ دَمُ امْرِىءٍ مُسْلِمٍ يَشْهَدُ أَنْ لَا إِلٰهَ إِلَّا اللهُ، وَأَنِّي رَسُولُ اللهِ، إِلَّا بِإِحْدَى
ثَلَاثٍ: النَّفْسُ بِالنَّفْسِ، وَالثَّيِّبُ الزَّانِي، وَالتَّارِكُ لِدِينِهِ الْمُفَارِقُ لِلْجَمَاعَةِ»

(The blood of a Muslim who testifies that there is no deity worthy of worship except Allah and that I am the Messenger of Allah, is sacred, except in three instances. (They are:) life for life, the married adulterer, and whoever reverts from the religion and abandons the Jama\`ah (community of the faithful believers).) When one commits any of these three offenses, it is not up to ordinary citizens to kill him or her, because this is the responsibility of the Muslim Leader or his deputy. Allah said,

(except by mistake). There is a difference of opinion concerning the reason behind revealing this part of the Ayah. Mujahid and others said that it was revealed about \`Ayyash bin Abi Rabi\`ah, Abu Jahl's half brother, from his mother's side, Asma' bint Makhrabah. \`Ayyash killed a man called Al-Harith bin Yazid Al-\`Amiri, out of revenge for torturing him and his brother because of their Islam. That man later embraced Islam and performed Hijrah, but \`Ayyash did not know this fact. On the Day of the Makkan conquest, \`Ayyash saw that man and thought that he was still a disbeliever, so he attacked and killed him. Later, Allah sent down this Ayah. \`Abdur-Rahman bin Zayd bin Aslam said that this Ayah was revealed about Abu Ad-Darda' because he killed a man after he embraced the faith, just as Abu Ad-Darda' held the sword above him. When this matter was conveyed to the Messenger of Allah , Abu Ad-Darda' said, "He only said that to avert death." The Prophet said to him,

«هَلَّا شَقَقْتَ عَنْ قَلْبِه»

(Have you opened his heart) The basis for this story is in the Sahih, but it is not about Abu Ad-Darda'. Allah said,

(and whosoever kills a believer by mistake, he must set free a believing slave and submit compensation (blood money) to the deceased's family) thus, ordaining two requirements for murder by mistake. The first requirement is the Kaffarah (fine) for the great sin that has been committed, even if it was a mistake. The Kaffarah is to free a Muslim slave, not a non-Muslim slave. Imam Ahmad recorded that a man from the Ansar said that he brought a slave and said, "O Messenger of Allah! I have to free a believing slave, so if you see that this slave is a believer, I will free her." The Messenger of Allah asked her,

«أَتَشْهَدِينَ أَنْ لَا إِلَهَ إِلَّا اللهُ؟»

(Do you testify that there is no deity worthy of worship except Allah) She said, "Yes." He asked her,

«أَتَشْهَدِينَ أَنِّي رَسُولُ اللهِ؟»

(Do you testify that I am the Messenger of Allah) She said, "Yes." He asked,

«أَتُؤْمِنِينَ بِالْبَعْثِ بَعْدَ الْمَوْتِ؟»

(Do you believe in Resurrection after death) She said, "Yes." The Prophet said,

«أَعْتِقْهَا»

(Then free her.) This is an authentic chain of narration, and not knowing the name of the Ansari Companion does not lessen its authenticity. Allah's statement,

(and submit compensation (blood money) to the deceased's family) is the second obligation which involves the killer and the family of the deceased, who will receive blood money as compensation for their loss. The compensation is only obligatory for the one who possesses one of five; as Imam Ahmad, and the Sunan compilers recorded from Ibn Mas`ud. He said; "Allah's Messenger determined that the Diyah (blood money) for unintentional murder is twenty camels which entered their fourth year, twenty camels which entered their fifth year, twenty camels which entered their second year, and twenty camels which entered their third year." This is the wording of An-Nasa'i. This Diyah is required from the elders of the killer's tribe, not from his own money. In the Two Sahihs, it is recorded that Abu Hurayrah said, "Two women from Hudhayl quarreled and one of them threw a stone at the other and killed her and her unborn fetus. They disputed before the Messenger of Allah and he decided that the Diyah of the fetus should be to free a male or a female slave. He also decided that the Diyah of the deceased is required from the elders of the killer's tribe." This Hadith indicates that in the case of what appears to be intentional murder, the Diyah is the same as that for killing by virtual mistake. The former type requires three types of Diyah, just like intentional murder, because it is somewhat similar to intentional murder. Al-Bukhari recorded in his Sahih that `Abdullah bin `Umar said, "The Messenger of Allah sent Khalid bin Al-Walid to Banu Jadhimah and he called them to Islam, but they did not know how to say, `We became Muslims.' They started saying, `Saba'na, Saba'na (we became Sabians). Khalid started killing them, and when this news was conveyed to the Messenger of Allah , he raised his hands and said,

«اللَّهُمَّ إِنِّي أَبْرَأُ إِلَيْكَ مِمَّا صَنَعَ خَالِد»

(O Allah! I declare my innocence before You of what Khalid did.) The Messenger sent `Ali to pay the Diyah of those who were killed and to compensate for the property that was destroyed, to the extent of replacing the dog's bowl. This Hadith indicates that the mistake of the Leader or his deputy (Khalid in this case) is paid from the Muslim Treasury. Allah said,

(unless they remit it), meaning, the Diyah must be delivered to the family of the deceased, unless they forfeit their right, in which case the Diyah does not become necessary. Allah's statement,

(If the deceased belonged to a people at war with you and he was a believer, the freeing of a believing slave (is prescribed);) means, if the murdered person was a believer, yet his family were combatant disbelievers, then they will receive no Diyah. In this case, the murderer only has to free a believing slave. Allah's statement,

(and if he belonged to a people with whom you have a treaty of mutual alliance,) meaning, if the family of the deceased were from Ahl Adh-Dhimmah or with whom there is a peace treaty, then they deserve his Diyah; full Diyah if the deceased was a believer, in which case the killer is required to free a believing slave also.

(And whoso finds this beyond his means, he must fast for two consecutive months) without breaking the fast (in the days of) the two months. If he breaks the fast without justification, i.e. illness, menstruation, post-natal bleeding, then he has to start all over again. Allah's statement,

(to seek repentance from Allah. And Allah is Ever All-Knowing, All-Wise.) means, this is how the one who kills by mistake can repent, he fasts two consecutive months if he does not find a slave to free.

(And Allah is Ever All-Knowing, All-Wise), we mentioned the explanation of this before.

Warning Against Intentional Murder

After Allah mentioned the ruling of unintentional murder, He mentioned the ruling for intentional murder. Allah said,

(And whoever kills a believer intentionally,) This Ayah carries a stern warning and promise for those who commit so grave a sin that it is mentioned along with Shirk in several Ayat of Allah's Book. For instance, in Surat Al-Furqan, Allah said,

(And those who invoke not any other god along with Allah, nor kill such person as Allah has forbidden, except for just cause). Allah said,

(Say: "Come, I will recite what your Lord has prohibited you from: Join not anything in worship with Him.) (6:151). There are many Ayat and Hadiths that prohibit murder. In the Two Sahihs, it is recorded that Ibn Mas`ud said that the Messenger of Allah said,

«أَوَّلُ مَا يُقْضَى بَيْنَ النَّاسِ يَوْمَ الْقِيَامَةِ فِي الدِّمَاءِ»

(Blood offenses are the first disputes to be judged between the people on the Day of Resurrection.) In a Hadith that Abu Dawud recorded, `Ubadah bin As-Samit states that the Messenger of Allah said,

«لَا يَزَالُ الْمُؤْمِنُ مُعْنِقًا صَالِحًا، مَا لَمْ يُصِبْ دَمًا حَرَامًا، فَإِذَا أَصَابَ دَمًا حَرَامًا بَلَّح»

(The believer will remain unburdened in righteousness as long as he does not shed prohibited blood. When he sheds forbidden blood, he will become burdened.) Another Hadith, states,

«لَزَوَالُ الدُّنْيَا أَهْوَنُ عِنْدَ اللهِ مِنْ قَتْلِ رَجُلٍ مُسْلِم»

(The destruction of this earthly life is less significant before Allah than killing a Muslim man (or woman).)

Will the Repentance of those who Commit Intentional Murder be Accepted

Ibn `Abbas held the view that the repentance of one who intentionally murders a believer, will not be accepted. Al-Bukhari recorded that Ibn Jubayr said, "The people of knowledge of Al-Kufah differed on this subject, I traveled to Ibn `Abbas to ask him about it. He said, `This Ayah,

(And whoever kills a believer intentionally, his recompense is Hell) was the last revealed (on this subject) and nothing abrogated it.'" Muslim and An-Nasa'i also recorded it. However, the majority of scholars of the earlier and later generations said that the killer's repentance can be accepted. If he repents, and goes back to Allah humbly, submissively, and performing righteous deeds, then Allah will change his evil deeds into good deeds and compensate the deceased for his loss by rewarding him for his suffering. Allah said, R

(And those who invoke not any other god along with Allah), until,

(Except those who repent and believe, and do righteous deeds). The Ayah we just mentioned should not be considered abrogated or only applicable to the disbelievers (who become Muslim), for this contradicts the general, encompassing indications of the Ayah and requires evidence to support it. Allah knows best. Allah said,

(Say: "O My servants who have transgressed against themselves! Despair not of the mercy of Allah). This Ayah is general, covering all types of sins, including Kufr, Shirk, doubt, hypocrisy, murder, sin, and so forth. Therefore, everyone who repents sincerely from any of these errors, then Allah will forgive him. Allah said,

(Verily, Allah forgives not that partners should be set up with Him (in worship), but He forgives except that (anything else) to whom He wills). This Ayah is general and includes every sin except Shirk, and it has been mentioned in this Surah, both after this Ayah and before it, in order to encourage hope in Allah, and Allah knows best. It is confirmed in the Two Sahihs, that an Israeli killed one hundred people then he asked a scholar, "Is it possible for me to repent" So he replied, "What is there that would prevent you from repentance" So he told him to go to another land where Allah was worshipped. He began to emigrate to it but died on the way, and the angel of mercy was the one to take him. Although this Hadith is about an Israeli, it is even more suitable for the Muslim community that their repentance be accepted. Indeed, Allah relieved Muslims from the burdens and restrictions that were placed on the Jews, and He sent our Prophet with the easy Hanifiyyah way (Islamic Monotheism). As for the honorable Ayah,

(And whoever kills a believer intentionally), Abu Hurayrah and several among the Salaf said that this is his punishment, if Allah decides to punish him. And this is the case with every threat that is issued for every sin. For instance, there could be good deeds that this person has done that would prevent him from being punished for that, and Allah knows best. Even if the murderer inevitably enters the Fire -- as Ibn `Abbas stated because his repentance was not accepted, or he did not have good deeds to save him, he will not remain there for eternity, but only for a long time. There are Mutawatir Hadiths stating that the Messenger of Allah said,

«إِنَّهُ يَخْرُجُ مِنَ النَّارِ مَنْ كَانَ فِي قَلْبِهِ أَدْنَى ذَرَّةٍ مِنْ إِيمَانٍ»

(Whoever has the least speck of faith in his heart shall ultimately depart the Fire.)

Surah: 4 Ayah: 94

﴿ يَٰٓأَيُّهَا ٱلَّذِينَ ءَامَنُوٓاْ إِذَا ضَرَبۡتُمۡ فِي سَبِيلِ ٱللَّهِ فَتَبَيَّنُواْ وَلَا تَقُولُواْ لِمَنۡ أَلۡقَىٰٓ إِلَيۡكُمُ ٱلسَّلَٰمَ لَسۡتَ مُؤۡمِنٗا تَبۡتَغُونَ عَرَضَ ٱلۡحَيَوٰةِ ٱلدُّنۡيَا فَعِندَ ٱللَّهِ مَغَانِمُ كَثِيرَةٞۚ كَذَٰلِكَ كُنتُم مِّن قَبۡلُ فَمَنَّ ٱللَّهُ عَلَيۡكُمۡ فَتَبَيَّنُوٓاْۚ إِنَّ ٱللَّهَ كَانَ بِمَا تَعۡمَلُونَ خَبِيرٗا ٩٤ ﴾

94. O you who believe! When you go (to fight) in the Cause of Allâh, verify (the truth), and say not to anyone who greets you (by embracing Islâm): "You are not a believer"; seeking the perishable goods of the worldly life. There are much more profits and booties with Allâh. Even as he is now, so were you yourselves before till Allâh conferred on you His Favors (i.e. guided you to Islâm), therefore, be cautious in discrimination. Allâh is Ever Well-Aware of what you do.

Transliteration

94. Ya ayyuha allatheena amanoo itha darabtum fee sabeeli Allahi fatabayyanoo wala taqooloo liman alqa ilaykumu alssalama lasta mu/minan tabtaghoona AAarada alhayati alddunya faAAinda Allahi maghanimu katheeratun kathalika kuntum min qablu famanna Allahu AAalaykum fatabayyanoo inna Allaha kana bima taAAmaloona khabeeran

Tafsir Ibn Kathir

Greeting with the Salam is a Sign of Islam

Imam Ahmad recorded that `Ikrimah said that Ibn `Abbas said, "A man from Bani Sulaym, who was tending a flock of sheep, passed by some of the Companions of the Prophet and said Salam to them. They said (to each other), `He only said Salam to protect himself from us.' Then they attacked him and killed him. They brought his sheep to the Prophet , and this Ayah was revealed,

(O you who believe!), until the end of the Ayah." At-Tirmidhi recorded this in his (chapter on) Tafsir, and said, "This Hadith is Hasan, and it is also reported from Usamah bin Zayd." Al-Hakim also recorded it and said, "Its chain is Sahih, but they did not collect it." Al-Bukhari recorded that Ibn `Abbas commented;

(and say not to anyone who greets you: "You are not a believer;"), "A man was tending his sheep and the Muslims caught up with him. He said, `As-Salamu `Alaykum.' However, they killed him and took his sheep. Allah revealed the Ayah;

(And say not to anyone who greets you: "You are not a believer; seeking the perishable goods of the worldly life)." Ibn `Abbas said; "The goods of this world were those sheep." And he recited,

(Peace) Imam Ahmad recorded that Al-Qa`qa` bin Abdullah bin Abi Hadrad narrated that his father `Abdullah bin Abi Hadrad said, "The Messenger of Allah sent us to (the area of) Idam. I rode out with a group of Muslims that included Abu Qatadah, Al-Harith bin Rab`i and Muhallam bin Juthamah bin Qays. We continued on until we reached the area of Idam, where `Amr bin Al-Adbat Al-Ashja`i passed by us on his camel. When he passed by us he said Salam to us, and we did not attack him. Because of some previous problems with him, Muhallam bin Juthamah killed him and took his camel. When we went back to the Messenger of Allah and told him what had happened, a part of the Qur'an was revealed about us,

(O you who believe! When you go (to fight) in the cause of Allah), until,

(Well-Aware)." Only Ahmad recorded this Hadith. Al-Bukhari recorded that Ibn `Abbas said that the Messenger of Allah said to Al-Miqdad,

«إِذَا كَانَ رَجُلٌ مُؤْمِنٌ يُخْفِي إِيمَانَهُ مَعَ قَوْمٍ كُفَّارٍ فَأَظْهَرَ إِيمَانَهُ فَقَتَلْتَهُ، فَكَذلِكَ كُنْتَ أَنْتَ تُخْفِي إِيمَانَكَ بِمَكَّةَ مِنْ قَبْلُ»

(You killed a believing man who hid his faith with disbelieving people, after he had announced his faith to you. Remember that you used to hide your faith in Makkah before.) Al-Bukhari recorded this shorter version without a complete chain of narrators. However a longer version with a connected chain of narrators has also been recorded. Al-Hafiz Abu Bakr Al-Bazzar recorded that Ibn `Abbas said, "The Messenger of Allah sent a military expedition under the authority of Al-Miqdad bin Al-Aswad and when they reached the designated area, they found the people had dispersed. However, a man with a lot of wealth did not leave and said, `I bear witness that there is no deity worthy of worship except Allah.' Yet, Al-Miqdad killed him, and a man said to him, `You killed a man after he proclaimed: "There is no deity worthy of worship except Allah. By Allah I will mention what you did to the Prophet .' When they went back to the Messenger of Allah, they said, `O Messenger of Allah! Al-Miqdad killed a man who testified that there is no deity worthy of worship except Allah.' He said,

«ادْعُوا لِيَ الْمِقْدَادَ، يَا مِقْدَادُ أَقَتَلْتَ رَجُلًا يَقُولُ: لَا إِلَهَ إِلَّا اللهُ، فَكَيْفَ لَكَ بِلَا إِلَهَ إِلَّا اللهُ غَدًا؟»

(Summon Al-Miqdad before me. O Miqdad! Did you kill a man who proclaimed, "There is no deity worthy of worship except Allah" What would you do when you face, "There is no deity worthy of worship except Allah tomorrow") Allah then revealed;

(O you who believe! When you go (to fight) in the cause of Allah, verify (the truth), and say not to anyone who greets you: "You are not a believer;" seeking the perishable goods of the worldly life. There are much more profits and booties with Allah. Even as he is now, so were you yourselves before till Allah conferred on you His Favors, therefore, be cautious in discrimination). The Messenger of Allah said to Al-Miqdad,

«كَانَ رَجُلٌ مُؤْمِنٌ يُخْفِي إِيمَانَهُ مَعَ قَوْمٍ كُفَّارٍ فَأَظْهَرَ إِيمَانَهُ فَقَتَلْتَهُ، فَكَذَلِكَ كُنْتَ أَنْتَ تُخْفِي إِيمَانَكَ بِمَكَّةَ مِنْ قَبْلُ»

(He was a believing man who hid his faith among disbelieving people, and he announced his faith to you, but you killed him, although you used to hide your faith before, in Makkah.)" Allah's statement,

(There is much more benefit with Allah.) means, better than what you desired of worldly possessions which made you kill the one who greeted you with the Salam and pronounced his faith to you. Yet, you ignored all this and accused him of hypocrisy, to acquire the gains of this life. However, the pure wealth with Allah is far better than what you acquired. Allah's statement,

(so were you yourselves before, till Allah conferred on you His Favors.) means, beforehand, you used to be in the same situation like this person who hid his faith from his people. We mentioned the relevant Hadiths above. Allah said,

(And remember when you were few and were reckoned weak in the land). `Abdur-Razzaq recorded that Sa`id bin Jubayr commented about Allah's statement,

(so were you yourselves before), "You used to hide your faith, just as this shepherd hid his faith." Allah said,

(therefore, be cautious in discrimination), then said,

(Allah is Ever Well-Aware of what you do.) and this part of the Ayah contains a threat and a warning, as Sa`id bin Jubayr stated.

Surah: 4 Ayah: 95 & Ayah: 96

﴿ لَّا يَسْتَوِى ٱلْقَـٰعِدُونَ مِنَ ٱلْمُؤْمِنِينَ غَيْرُ أُو۟لِى ٱلضَّرَرِ وَٱلْمُجَـٰهِدُونَ فِى سَبِيلِ ٱللَّهِ
بِأَمْوَٰلِهِمْ وَأَنفُسِهِمْ ۚ فَضَّلَ ٱللَّهُ ٱلْمُجَـٰهِدِينَ بِأَمْوَٰلِهِمْ وَأَنفُسِهِمْ عَلَى ٱلْقَـٰعِدِينَ دَرَجَةً ۚ وَكُلًّا
وَعَدَ ٱللَّهُ ٱلْحُسْنَىٰ ۚ وَفَضَّلَ ٱللَّهُ ٱلْمُجَـٰهِدِينَ عَلَى ٱلْقَـٰعِدِينَ أَجْرًا عَظِيمًا ﴿٩٥﴾ ﴾

95. Not equal are those of the believers who sit (at home), except those who are disabled (by injury or are blind or lame), and those who strive hard and fight in the Cause of Allâh with their wealth and their lives. Allâh has preferred in grades those who strive hard and fight with their wealth and their lives above those who sit (at home). Unto each, Allâh has promised good (Paradise), but Allâh has preferred those who strive hard and fight, above those who sit (at home) by a huge reward.

﴿ دَرَجَـٰتٍ مِّنْهُ وَمَغْفِرَةً وَرَحْمَةً ۚ وَكَانَ ٱللَّهُ غَفُورًا رَّحِيمًا ﴿٩٦﴾ ﴾

96. Degrees of (higher) grades from Him, and Forgiveness and Mercy. And Allâh is Ever Oft-Forgiving, Most Merciful.

Transliteration

95. La yastawee alqaAAidoona mina almu/mineena ghayru olee alddarari waalmujahidoona fee sabeeli Allahi bi-amwalihim waanfusihim faddala Allahu almujahideena bi-amwalihim waanfusihim AAala alqaAAideena darajatan wakullan waAAada Allahu alhusna wafaddala Allahu almujahideena AAala alqaAAideena ajran AAatheeman 96. Darajatin minhu wamaghfiratan warahmatan wakana Allahu ghafooran raheeman

Tafsir Ibn Kathir

The Mujahid and those Who Do not Join Jihad are Not the Same, [and Jihad is Fard Kifayah]

Al-Bukhari recorded that Al-Bara' said, "When the Ayah,

(Not equal are those of the believers who sit (at home),) was revealed, the Messenger of Allah called Zayd and commanded him to write it. Then, Ibn Umm Maktum came and mentioned that he was blind. Allah revealed,

(except those who are disabled (by injury or are blind or lame))." Al-Bukhari recorded that Sahl bin Sa`d As-Sa`di said, "I saw Marwan bin Al-Hakam sitting in the Masjid. I came and sat by his side. He told us that Zayd bin Thabit told him that Allah's Messenger dictated this Ayah to him,

(Not equal are those of the believers who sit (at home), except those who are disabled, and those who strive hard and fight in the cause of Allah) Ibn Umm Maktum came to the Prophet as he was dictating that very Ayah to me. Ibn Umm Maktum said, `O Allah's Messenger! By Allah, if I had power, I would surely take part in Jihad.' He was a blind man. So Allah sent down revelation to His Messenger while his thigh was on mine and it became so heavy for me that I feared that my thigh would be broken. That ended after Allah revealed, (except those who are disabled)." This was recorded by Al-Bukhari. At-Tirmidhi recorded that Ibn `Abbas said,

(Not equal are those of the believers who sit (at home), except those who are disabled), refers to those who did not go to the battle of Badr and those who went to Badr. When the battle of Badr was about to occur, Abu Ahmad bin Jahsh and Ibn Umm Maktum said, `We are blind, O Messenger of Allah! Do we have an excuse' The Ayah,

(Not equal are those of the believers who sit (at home), except those who are disabled) was revealed. Allah made those who fight, above those who sit in their homes not hindered by disability.

(but Allah has preferred those who strive hard and fight, above those who sit (at home), by a huge reward. Degrees of (higher) grades from Him), above the believers who sit at home without a disability hindering them." This is the wording recorded by At-Tirmidhi, who said, "Hasan Gharib. Allah's statement,

(Not equal are those of the believers who sit (at home),) this is general. Soon after, the revelation came down with,

(except those who are disabled). So whoever has a disability, such as blindness, a limp, or an illness that prevents them from joining Jihad, they were not compared to the Mujahidin who strive in Allah's cause with their selves and wealth, as those who are not disabled and did not join the Jihad were. In his Sahih, Al-Bukhari recorded that Anas said that the Messenger of Allah said,

«إِنَّ بِالْمَدِينَةِ أَقْوَامًا مَا سِرْتُمْ مِنْ مَسِيرٍ، وَلَا قَطَعْتُمْ مِنْ وَادٍ، إِلَّا وَهُمْ مَعَكُمْ فِيهِ»

(There are people who remained in Al-Madinah, who were with you in every march you marched and every valley you crossed.) They said, "While they are still in Al-Madinah, O Messenger of Allah" He said,

«نَعَمْ حَبَسَهُمُ الْعُذْرُ»

(Yes. Only their disability hindered them (from joining you).) Allah said,

(Unto each, Allah has promised good) meaning, Paradise and tremendous rewards. This Ayah indicates that Jihad is not Fard on each and every individual, but it is Fard Kifayah (which is a collective duty). Allah then said,

(but Allah has preferred those who strive hard and fight, above those who sit (at home), by a huge reward). Allah mentions what He has given them rooms in Paradise, along with His forgiveness and the descent of mercy and blessing on them, as a favor and honor from Him. So He said;

(Degrees of (higher) grades from Him, and forgiveness and mercy. And Allah is Ever Oft-Forgiving, Most Merciful.). In the Two Sahihs, it is recorded that Abu Sa`id Al-Khudri said that the Messenger of Allah said,

«إِنَّ فِي الْجَنَّةِ مِائَةَ دَرَجَةٍ، أَعَدَّهَا اللهُ لِلْمُجَاهِدِينَ فِي سَبِيلِهِ، مَا بَيْنَ كُلِّ دَرَجَتَيْنِ كَمَا بَيْنَ السَّمَاءِ وَالْأَرْضِ»

(There are a hundred grades in Paradise that Allah has prepared for the Mujahidin in His cause, between each two grades is the distance between heaven and Earth.)

Surah: 4 Ayah: 97, Ayah: 98, Ayah: 99 & Ayah: 100

﴿ إِنَّ ٱلَّذِينَ تَوَفَّىٰهُمُ ٱلْمَلَـٰٓئِكَةُ ظَالِمِىٓ أَنفُسِهِمْ قَالُوا۟ فِيمَ كُنتُمْ ۖ قَالُوا۟ كُنَّا مُسْتَضْعَفِينَ فِى ٱلْأَرْضِ ۚ قَالُوٓا۟ أَلَمْ تَكُنْ أَرْضُ ٱللَّهِ وَٰسِعَةً فَتُهَاجِرُوا۟ فِيهَا ۚ فَأُو۟لَـٰٓئِكَ مَأْوَىٰهُمْ جَهَنَّمُ ۖ وَسَآءَتْ مَصِيرًا ﴿٩٧﴾ ﴾

97. Verily! As for those whom the angels take (in death) while they are wronging themselves (as they stayed among the disbelievers even though emigration was obligatory for them), they (angels) say (to them): "In what (condition) were you?" They reply: "We were weak and oppressed on earth." They (angels) say: "Was not the earth of Allâh spacious enough for you to emigrate therein?" Such men will find their abode in Hell - What an evil destination!

﴿ إِلَّا ٱلْمُسْتَضْعَفِينَ مِنَ ٱلرِّجَالِ وَٱلنِّسَآءِ وَٱلْوِلْدَٰنِ لَا يَسْتَطِيعُونَ حِيلَةً وَلَا يَهْتَدُونَ سَبِيلًا ﴿٩٨﴾ ﴾

98. Except the weak ones among men, women and children who cannot devise a plan, nor are they able to direct their way.

﴿ فَأُو۟لَـٰٓئِكَ عَسَى ٱللَّهُ أَن يَعْفُوَ عَنْهُمْ ۚ وَكَانَ ٱللَّهُ عَفُوًّا غَفُورًا ﴿٩٩﴾ ﴾

99. These are they whom Allâh is likely to forgive them, and Allâh is Ever Oft Pardoning, Oft-Forgiving.

﴿ ۞ وَمَن يُهَاجِرْ فِى سَبِيلِ ٱللَّهِ يَجِدْ فِى ٱلْأَرْضِ مُرَٰغَمًا كَثِيرًا وَسَعَةً ۚ وَمَن يَخْرُجْ مِنۢ بَيْتِهِۦ مُهَاجِرًا إِلَى ٱللَّهِ وَرَسُولِهِۦ ثُمَّ يُدْرِكْهُ ٱلْمَوْتُ فَقَدْ وَقَعَ أَجْرُهُۥ عَلَى ٱللَّهِ ۗ وَكَانَ ٱللَّهُ غَفُورًا رَّحِيمًا ﴿١٠٠﴾ ﴾

100. He who emigrates (from his home) in the Cause of Allâh, will find on earth many dwelling places and plenty to live by. And whosoever leaves his home as an emigrant unto Allâh and His Messenger, and death overtakes him, his reward is then surely incumbent upon Allâh. And Allâh is Ever Oft-Forgiving, Most Merciful.

Transliteration

97. Inna allatheena tawaffahumu almala-ikatu thalimee anfusihim qaloo feema kuntum qaloo kunna mustadAAafeena fee al-ardi qaloo alam takun ardu Allahi wasiAAatan fatuhajiroo feeha faola-ika ma/wahum jahannamu wasaat maseeran 98. Illa almustadAAafeena mina alrrijali waalnnisa-i waalwildani la yastateeAAoona heelatan wala yahtadoona sabeelan 99. Faola-ika AAasa Allahu an yaAAfuwa AAanhum wakana Allahu AAafuwwan ghafooran 100. Waman yuhajir fee sabeeli Allahi yajid fee al-ardi muraghaman katheeran wasaAAatan waman yakhruj min baytihi muhajiran ila Allahi warasoolihi thumma yudrik-hu almawtu faqad waqaAAa ajruhu AAala Allahi wakana Allahu ghafooran raheeman

Tafsir Ibn Kathir

The Prohibition of Residing Among the Disbelievers While Able to Emigrate

Al-Bukhari recorded that Muhammad bin `Abdur-Rahman, Abu Al-Aswad, said, "The people of Al-Madinah were forced to prepare an army (to fight against the people of Ash-Sham during the Khilafah of Abdullah bin Az-Zubayir at Makkah), and I was enlisted in it. Then I met `Ikrimah, the freed slave of Ibn `Abbas, and informed him (about it), and he forbade me strongly from doing so (i.e., to enlist in that army), and then he said to me, `Ibn `Abbas told me that some Muslims used to go out with the idolators increasing the size of their army against the Messenger of Allah . Then, an arrow would hit one of them and kill him, or he would be struck on his neck (with a sword) and killed, and Allah sent down the Ayah,

(Verily, as for those whom the angels take (in death) while they are wronging themselves)." Ad-Dahhak stated that this Ayah was revealed about some hypocrites who did not join the Messenger of Allah but remained in Makkah and went out with the idolators for the battle of Badr. They were killed among those who were killed. Thus, this honorable Ayah was revealed about those who reside among the idolators, while able to perform Hijrah and unable to practice the faith. Such people will be committing injustice against themselves and falling into a prohibition according to the consensus and also according to this Ayah,

(Verily, as for those whom the angels take (in death) while they are wronging themselves,) by refraining from Hijrah,

(They (angels) say (to them): "In what (condition) were you") meaning, why did you remain here and not perform Hijrah

(They reply: "We were weak and oppressed on the earth.") meaning, we are unable to leave the land or move about in the earth,

(They (angels) say: "Was not the earth of Allah spacious enough for you). Abu Dawud recorded that Samurah bin Jundub said that the Messenger of Allah said,

«مَنْ جَامَعَ الْمُشْرِكَ وَسَكَنَ مَعَهُ فَإِنَّهُ مِثْلُه»

(Whoever mingles with the idolator and resides with him, he is just like him.) Allah's statement,

(Except the weak) until the end of the Ayah, is an excuse that Allah gives for this type of people not to emigrate, because they are unable to free themselves from the idolators. And even if they did, they would not know which way to go. This is why Allah said,

(Who cannot devise a plan, nor are they able to direct their way), meaning, they do not find the way to emigrate, as Mujahid, `Ikrimah and As-Suddi stated. Allah's statement,

(These are they whom Allah is likely to forgive them,) means, pardon them for not migrating, and here, `likely' means He shall,

(and Allah is Ever Oft-Pardoning, Oft-Forgiving). Al-Bukhari recorded that Abu Hurayrah said, "While the Messenger of Allah was praying `Isha', he said, `Sami` Allahu Liman Hamidah.' He then said before he prostrated,

«اللَّهُمَّ أَنْجِ عَيَّاشَ بْنَ أَبِي رَبِيعَةَ، اللَّهُمَّ أَنْجِ سَلَمَةَ بْنَ هِشَامٍ، اللَّهُمَّ أَنْجِ الْوَلِيدَ بْنَ الْوَلِيدِ، اللَّهُمَّ أَنْجِ الْمُسْتَضْعَفِينَ مِنَ الْمُؤْمِنِينَ، اللَّهُمَّ اشْدُدْ وَطْأَتَكَ عَلَى مُضَرَ، اللَّهُمَّ اجْعَلْهَا سِنِينَ كَسِنِي يُوسُفَ»

(O Allah! Save `Ayyash bin Abi Rabi`ah. O Allah! Save Salamah bin Hisham. O Allah! Save Al-Walid bin Al-Walid. O Allah! Save the weak Muslims. O Allah! Be very hard on Mudar tribe. O Allah! Afflict them with years (of famine) similar to the (famine) years of the time of Prophet Yusuf.)" Al-Bukhari recorded that Abu An-Nu`man said that Hammad bin Zayd said that Ayyub narrated that Ibn Abi Mulaykah said that Ibn `Abbas commented on the verse,

(Except the weak ones among men), "I and my mother were among those (weak ones) whom Allah excused." Allah's statement,

(He who emigrates in the cause of Allah, will find on earth many dwelling places and plenty to live by.) this encourages the believers to perform Hijrah and abandon the idolators, for wherever the believer emigrates, he will find a safe refuge to resort to. Mujahid said that,

(many dwelling places) means, he will find a way out of what he dislikes. Allah's statement,

(and plenty to live by.) refers to provision. Qatadah also said that,

(...will find on earth many dwelling places and plenty to live by.) means, Allah will take him from misguidance to guidance and from poverty to richness. Allah's statement,

(And whosoever leaves his home as an emigrant unto Allah and His Messenger, and death overtakes him, his reward is then surely, incumbent upon Allah.) means, whoever starts emigrating and dies on the way, he will acquire the reward of those who emigrate for Allah. The Two Sahihs, along with the Musnad and Sunan compilers, recorded that `Umar bin Al-Khattab said that the Messenger of Allah said,

«إِنَّمَا الْأَعْمَالُ بِالنِّــــيَّاتِ، وَإِنَّمَا لِكُلِّ امْرِىءٍ مَا نَوَى، فَمَنْ كَانَتْ هِجْرَتُهُ إِلَى اللهِ وَرَسُولِهِ، فَهِجْرَتُهُ إِلَى اللهِ وَرَسُولِهِ، وَمَنْ كَانَتْ هِجْرَتُهُ إِلَى دُنْيَا يُصِيبُهَا، أَوِ امْرَأَةٍ يَتَزَوَّجُهَا، فَهِجْرَتُهُ إِلَى مَا هَاجَرَ إِلَيْهِ»

(The reward of deeds depends upon the intentions, and every person will be rewarded according to what he has intended. So, whoever emigrated to Allah and His Messenger, then his emigration is for Allah and His Messenger. And whoever emigrated for worldly benefits or for a woman to marry, his emigration is for what he emigrated for.) This Hadith is general, it applies to Hijrah as well as every other deed. In the Two Sahihs, it is recorded that a man killed ninety-nine people and completed the number one hundred when he killed a worshipper. He then asked a scholar if he has a chance to repent. The scholar said, "What prevents you from repentance" The scholar told the killer to emigrate from his land to another land where Allah is worshipped. When he left his land and started on the migration to the other land, death overtook him on the way. The angels of mercy and the angels of torment disputed about the man, whereas the former said that he went out in repentance, while the latter said that he did not arrive at his destination. They were commanded to measure the distance between the two lands and to whichever land he is closer to, he will be considered part of that land. Allah commanded that the righteous land to move closer and the land of evil to move farther. The angels found that he died closer to the land that he intended to emigrate to by a hand-span, and thus the angels of mercy captured his soul. In another narration, when death came to that man, he moved his chest towards the righteous village that he emigrated to.

Surah: 4 Ayah: 101

﴿ وَإِذَا ضَرَبْتُمْ فِى ٱلْأَرْضِ فَلَيْسَ عَلَيْكُمْ جُنَاحٌ أَن تَقْصُرُواْ مِنَ ٱلصَّلَوٰةِ إِنْ خِفْتُمْ أَن يَفْتِنَكُمُ ٱلَّذِينَ كَفَرُوٓاْ ۚ إِنَّ ٱلْكَـٰفِرِينَ كَانُواْ لَكُمْ عَدُوًّا مُّبِينًا ﴿١٠١﴾ ﴾

101. And when you (Muslims) travel in the land, there is no sin on you if you shorten As-Salât (the prayer) if you fear that the disbelievers may put you in trial (attack you etc.), verily, the disbelievers are ever unto you open enemies.

Transliteration

101. Wa-itha darabtum fee al-ardi falaysa AAalaykum junahun an taqsuroo mina alssalati in khiftum an yaftinakumu allatheena kafaroo inna alkafireena kanoo lakum AAaduwwan mubeenan

Tafsir Ibn Kathir

Salat Al-Qasr, Shortening the Prayer

Allah said,

(And when you Darabtum in the land,) meaning if you travel in the land. In another Ayah, Allah said,

(He knows that there will be some among you sick, others Yadribuna (traveling) through the land, seeking of Allah's bounty...) (73:20). Allah's statement,

(there is no sin on you if you shorten the Salah (prayer)) by reducing (the units of the prayer) from four to two. Allah's statement,

(if you fear that the disbelievers may put you in trial (attack you)), refers to the typical type of fear prevalent when this Ayah was revealed. In the beginning of Islam, and after the Hijrah, Muslims used to experience fear during most of their travels. Rather, they restricted their movements to large or short military expeditions. During that era, most areas were areas of combatant enemies of Islam and its people. But when the prevalent circumstances cease, or a new situation is prevalent, decrees of this nature may not be understood, as Allah said;

(And force not your slave girls to prostitution, if they desire chastity). And His saying;

(And your stepdaughters, under your guardianship, born of your wives whom you have gone into) Imam Ahmad recorded that Ya`la bin Umayyah said, "I asked `Umar bin Al-Khattab about the verse:

(there is no sin on you if you shorten the prayer. If you fear that the disbelievers may put you in trial,) e `Allah granted Muslims safety now' `Umar said to me, `I wondered about the same thing and asked the Messenger of Allah about it and he said,

«صَدَقَـــــةٌ تَصَدَّقَ اللهُ بِهَا عَلَيْكُمْ فَاقْبَلُوا صَدَقَتَه»

(A gift that Allah has bestowed on you, so accept His gift)." Muslim and the collectors of Sunan recorded this Hadith. At-Tirmidhi said, "Hasan Sahih". `Ali bin Al-Madini said, "This Hadith is Hasan Sahih from the narration of `Umar, and it is not preserved by any other route besides this one, and its narrators are all known." Abu Bakr Ibn Abi Shaybah recorded that Abu Hanzalah Al-Hadha' said, "I asked Ibn `Umar about the Qasr prayer and he said, `It consists of two Rak`ahs.' I said, what about Allah's statement,

(if you fear that the disbelievers may put you in trial (attack you),) `We are safe now.' He said, `This is the Sunnah of the Messenger of Allah .'". Al-Bukhari recorded that Anas said, "We went out with the Messenger of Allah from Al-Madinah to Makkah; he used to pray two Rak`ahs until we went back to Al-Madinah." When he was asked how long they remained in Makkah, he said, "We remained in Makkah for ten days." This was recorded by the Group. Imam Ahmad recorded that Harithah bin Wahb Al-Khuza`i said, "I prayed behind the Prophet for the Zuhr and `Asr prayers in Mina, when the people were numerous and very safe, and he prayed two Rak`ahs." This was recorded by the Group, with the exception of Ibn Majah. Al-Bukhari's narration of this Hadith reads, "The Prophet led us in the prayer at Mina during the peace period by offering two Rak`ahs. "

Surah: 4 Ayah: 102

﴿ وَإِذَا كُنتَ فِيهِمْ فَأَقَمْتَ لَهُمُ ٱلصَّلَوٰةَ فَلْتَقُمْ طَآئِفَةٌ مِّنْهُم مَّعَكَ وَلْيَأْخُذُوٓا۟ أَسْلِحَتَهُمْ فَإِذَا
سَجَدُوا۟ فَلْيَكُونُوا۟ مِن وَرَآئِكُمْ وَلْتَأْتِ طَآئِفَةٌ أُخْرَىٰ لَمْ يُصَلُّوا۟ فَلْيُصَلُّوا۟ مَعَكَ

وَلْيَأْخُذُوا۟ حِذْرَهُمْ وَأَسْلِحَتَهُمْ ۗ وَدَّ ٱلَّذِينَ كَفَرُوا۟ لَوْ تَغْفُلُونَ عَنْ أَسْلِحَتِكُمْ وَأَمْتِعَتِكُمْ
فَيَمِيلُونَ عَلَيْكُم مَّيْلَةً وَٰحِدَةً ۚ وَلَا جُنَاحَ عَلَيْكُمْ إِن كَانَ بِكُمْ أَذًى مِّن مَّطَرٍ أَوْ كُنتُم
مَّرْضَىٰٓ أَن تَضَعُوٓا۟ أَسْلِحَتَكُمْ ۖ وَخُذُوا۟ حِذْرَكُمْ ۗ إِنَّ ٱللَّهَ أَعَدَّ لِلْكَٰفِرِينَ عَذَابًا مُّهِينًا ﴿١٠٢﴾

102. When you (O Messenger Muhammad (peace be upon him)) are among them, and lead them in As-Salât (the prayer), let one party of them stand up (in Salât (prayer)) with you taking their arms with them; when they finish their prostrations, let them take their positions in the rear and let the other party come up which have not yet prayed, and let them pray with you taking all the precautions and bearing arms. Those who disbelieve wish, if you were negligent of your arms and your baggage, to attack you in a single rush, but there is no sin on you if you put away your arms because of the inconvenience of rain or because you are ill, but take every precaution for yourselves. Verily, Allâh has prepared a humiliating torment for the disbelievers.

Transliteration

102. Wa-itha kunta feehim faaqamta lahumu alssalata faltaqum ta-ifatun minhum maAAaka walya/khuthoo aslihatahum fa-itha sajadoo falyakoonoo min wara-ikum walta/ti ta-ifatun okhra lam yusalloo falyusalloo maAAaka walya/khuthoo hithrahum waaslihatahum wadda allatheena kafaroo law taghfuloona AAan aslihatikum waamtiAAatikum fayameeloona AAalaykum maylatan wahidatan wala junaha AAalaykum in kana bikum athan min matarin aw kuntum marda an tadaAAoo aslihatakum wakhuthoo hithrakum inna Allaha aAAadda lilkafireena AAathaban muheenan

Tafsir Ibn Kathir

The Description of The Fear Prayer

The Fear prayer has different forms, for the enemy is sometimes in the direction of the Qiblah and sometimes in another direction. The Fear prayer consists sometimes of four Rak`ahs, three Rak`ahs, as for Maghrib, and sometimes two Rak`ah like Fajr and prayer during travel. The Fear prayer is sometimes prayed in congregation, but when the battle is raging, congregational prayer may not be possible. In this case, they pray each by himself, facing the Qiblah or otherwise, riding or on foot. In this situation, they are allowed to walk and fight, all the while performing the acts of the prayer. Some scholars said that in the latter case, they pray only one Rak`ah, for Ibn `Abbas narrated, "By the words of your Prophet , Allah has ordained the prayer of four Rak`ah while residing, two Rak`ah during travel, and one Rak`ah during fear." Muslim, Abu Dawud, An-Nasa'i and Ibn Majah recorded it. This is also the view of Ahmad bin Hanbal. Al-Mundhiri said, "This is the saying of `Ata', Jabir, Al-Hasan, Mujahid, Al-Hakam, Qatadah and Hammad; and Tawus and Ad-Dahhak also prefered it." Abu `Asim Al-`Abadi mentioned that Muhammad bin Nasr Al-Marwazi said the Fajr prayer also becomes one Rak`ah during fear. This is also the opinion of Ibn Hazm. Ishaq bin Rahwayh said, "When a battle is raging, one Rak`ah during which you nod your head is sufficient for you. If you are unable, then one prostration is sufficient, because the prostration is remembrance of Allah."

The Reason behind Revealing this Ayah

Imam Ahmad recorded that Abu `Ayyash Az-Zuraqi said, "We were with the Messenger of Allah in the area of `Usfan (a well known place near Makkah), when the idolators met us under the command of Khalid bin Al-Walid, and they were between us and the Qiblah. The

Messenger of Allah led us in Zuhr prayer, and the idolators said, `They were busy with something during which we had a chance to attack them.' They then said, `Next, there will come a prayer (`Asr) that is dearer to them than their children and themselves.' However, Jibril came down with these Ayat between the prayers of Zuhr and `Asr,

(When you (O Messenger Muhammad) are among them, and lead them in Salah (prayer)). When the time for prayer came, the Messenger of Allah commanded Muslims to hold their weapons and he made us stand in two lines behind him. When he bowed, we all bowed behind him. When he raised his head, we all raised our heads. The Prophet then prostrated with the line that was behind him while the rest stood in guard. When they finished with the prostration and stood up, the rest sat and performed prostration, while those who performed it stood up in guard after the two lines exchanged position. The Prophet then bowed and they all bowed after him, then raised their heads after he raised his head. Then the Prophet performed prostration with the line that was behind him, while the rest stood in guard. When those who made prostration sat, the rest prostrated. The Prophet then performed the Taslim and ended the prayer. The Messenger of Allah performed this prayer twice, once in `Usfan and once in the land of Banu Sulaym.'" This is the narration recorded by Abu Dawud and An-Nasa'i, and it has an authentic chain of narration and many other texts to support it. Al-Bukhari recorded that Ibn `Abbas said, "Once the Prophet led the Fear prayer and the people stood behind him. He said Allahu-Akbar and the people said the same. He bowed and some of them bowed. Then he prostrated and they also prostrated. Then he stood for the second Rak`ah and those who had prayed the first Rak`ah left and guarded their brothers. The second party joined him and performed bowing and prostration with him. All the people were in prayer, but they were guarding one another during the prayer." Imam Ahmad recorded that Jabir bin `Abdullah said that the Messenger of Allah led them in the Fear prayer. A group of them stood before him and a group behind him. The Prophet led those who were behind him with one Rak`ah and two prostrations. They then moved to the position of those who did not pray, while the others stood in their place, and the Messenger of Allah performed one Rak`ah and two prostrations and then said the Salam. Therefore, the Prophet prayed two Rak`ah while they prayed one. An-Nasa'i recorded this Hadith, while Muslim collected other wordings for it. Collectors of the Sahih, Sunan and Musnad collections recorded this in a Hadith from Jabir. Ibn Abi Hatim recorded that Salim said that his father said,

(When you (O Messenger Muhammad) are among them, and lead them in Salah (prayer)) refers to the Fear prayer. The Messenger of Allah led one group and prayed one Rak`ah, while the second group faced the enemy. Then the second group that faced the enemy came and Allah's Messenger led them, praying one Rak`ah, and then said the Salam. Each of the two groups then stood up and prayed one more Rak`ah each (while the other group stood in guard)." The Group collected this Hadith with Ma`mar in its chain of narrators. This Hadith also has many other chains of narration from several Companions, and Al-Hafiz Abu Bakr Ibn Marduwyah collected these various narrations, as did Ibn Jarir. As for the command to hold the weapons during the Fear prayer, a group of scholars said that it is obligatory according to the Ayah. What testifies to this is that Allah said;

(But there is no sin on you if you put away your arms because of the inconvenience of rain or because you are ill, but take every precaution for yourselves) meaning, so that when necessary, you will be able to get to your weapons easily,

(Verily, Allah has prepared a humiliating torment for the disbelievers).

Surah: 4 Ayah: 103 & Ayah: 104

﴿ فَإِذَا قَضَيْتُمُ ٱلصَّلَوٰةَ فَٱذْكُرُوا۟ ٱللَّهَ قِيَـٰمًا وَقُعُودًا وَعَلَىٰ جُنُوبِكُمْ ۚ فَإِذَا ٱطْمَأْنَنتُمْ
فَأَقِيمُوا۟ ٱلصَّلَوٰةَ ۚ إِنَّ ٱلصَّلَوٰةَ كَانَتْ عَلَى ٱلْمُؤْمِنِينَ كِتَـٰبًا مَّوْقُوتًا ﴿١٠٣﴾ ﴾

103. When you have finished As-Salât (the congregational prayer), remember Allâh standing, sitting down, and (lying down) on your sides, but when you are free from danger, perform As-Salât (Iqâmat-as- Salât). Verily, As-Salât (the prayer) is enjoined on the believers at fixed hours.

﴿ وَلَا تَهِنُوا۟ فِى ٱبْتِغَآءِ ٱلْقَوْمِ ۖ إِن تَكُونُوا۟ تَأْلَمُونَ فَإِنَّهُمْ يَأْلَمُونَ كَمَا تَأْلَمُونَ ۖ
وَتَرْجُونَ مِنَ ٱللَّهِ مَا لَا يَرْجُونَ ۗ وَكَانَ ٱللَّهُ عَلِيمًا حَكِيمًا ﴿١٠٤﴾ ﴾

104. And don't be weak in the pursuit of the enemy; if you are suffering (hardships) then surely, they (too) are suffering (hardships) as you are suffering, but you have a hope from Allâh (for the reward, i.e. Paradise) that for which they hope not; and Allâh is Ever All-Knowing, All-Wise.

Transliteration

103. Fa-itha qadaytumu alssalata faothkuroo Allaha qiyaman waquAAoodan waAAala junoobikum faitha itma/nantum faaqeemoo alssalata inna alssalata kanat AAala almu/mineena kitaban mawqootan 104. Wala tahinoo fee ibtigha-i alqawmi in takoonoo ta/lamoona fa-innahum ya/lamoona kama ta/lamoona watarjoona mina Allahi ma la yarjoona wakana Allahu AAaleeman hakeeman

Tafsir Ibn Kathir

The Order for Ample Remembrance After the Fear Prayer

Allah commands Dhikr after finishing the Fear prayer, in particular, even though such Dhikr is encouraged after finishing other types of prayer in general. In the case of Fear prayer, Dhikr is encouraged even more because the pillars of the prayer are diminished since they move about while performing it, etc., unlike other prayers. Allah said about the Sacred Months,

(so wrong not yourselves therein), even though injustice is prohibited all year long. However, injustice is particularly outlawed during the Sacred Months due to their sanctity and honor. So Allah's statement,

(When you have finished Salah, remember Allah standing, sitting down, and on your sides,) means, in all conditions,

(But when you are free from danger perform the Salah.) when you are safe, tranquil and fear subsides,

(perform the Salah) by performing it as you were commanded; fulfilling its obligations, with humbleness, completing the bowing and prostration positions etc. Allah's statement,

(Verily, the Salah is Kitaban on the believers at fixed hours.) means, enjoined, as Ibn \`Abbas stated. Ibn \`Abbas also said, "The prayer has a fixed time, just as the case with Hajj." Similar is reported from Mujahid, Salim bin `Abdullah, `Ali bin Al-Husayn, Muhammad bin `Ali, Al-Hasan, Muqatil. As-Suddi and `Atiyah Al-`Awfi.

The Encouragement to Pursue the Enemy Despite Injuries

Allah's statement,

(And don't be weak in the pursuit of the enemy;) means, do not weaken your resolve in pursuit of your enemy. Rather, pursue them vigorously, fight them and be wary of them.

(if you are suffering then surely they are suffering as you are suffering,) meaning, just as you suffer from injuries and death, the same happens to the enemy. In another Ayah, Allah said,

(If you suffer a harm, be sure a similar harm has struck the others). Allah then said,

(but you have a hope from Allah that for which they hope not;) meaning, you and they are equal regarding the injuries and pain that you suffer from. However, you hope for Allah's reward, victory and aid, just as He has promised you in His Book and by the words of his Messenger . Surely, Allah's promise is true. On the other hand, your enemies do not have hope for any of this. So, it is you, not they, who should be eager to fight so that you establish the Word of Allah and raise it high. i

(And Allah is Ever All-Knowing, All-Wise.) means, He is most knowledgeable and wise in all what He decides, decrees, wills and acts on concerning various worldly and religious ordainments, and He is worthy of praise in all conditions.

Surah: 4 Ayah: 105, Ayah: 106, Ayah: 107, Ayah: 108 & Ayah: 109

﴿ إِنَّآ أَنزَلۡنَآ إِلَيۡكَ ٱلۡكِتَٰبَ بِٱلۡحَقِّ لِتَحۡكُمَ بَيۡنَ ٱلنَّاسِ بِمَآ أَرَىٰكَ ٱللَّهُۚ وَلَا تَكُن لِّلۡخَآئِنِينَ
خَصِيمٗا ١٠٥ ﴾

105. Surely, We have sent down to you (O Muhammad) the Book (this Qur'ân) in truth that you might judge between men by that which Allâh has shown you (i.e. has taught you through Divine Revelation), so be not a pleader for the treacherous)

﴿ وَٱسۡتَغۡفِرِ ٱللَّهَۖ إِنَّ ٱللَّهَ كَانَ غَفُورٗا رَّحِيمٗا ١٠٦ ﴾

106. And seek the Forgiveness of Allâh, certainly, Allâh is Ever Oft-Forgiving, Most Merciful.

﴿ وَلَا تُجَٰدِلۡ عَنِ ٱلَّذِينَ يَخۡتَانُونَ أَنفُسَهُمۡۚ إِنَّ ٱللَّهَ لَا يُحِبُّ مَن كَانَ خَوَّانًا أَثِيمٗا ١٠٧ ﴾

107. And argue not on behalf of those who deceive themselves. Verily, Allâh does not like anyone who is a betrayer, sinner.

﴿ يَسۡتَخۡفُونَ مِنَ ٱلنَّاسِ وَلَا يَسۡتَخۡفُونَ مِنَ ٱللَّهِ وَهُوَ مَعَهُمۡ إِذۡ يُبَيِّتُونَ مَا لَا يَرۡضَىٰ مِنَ
ٱلۡقَوۡلِۚ وَكَانَ ٱللَّهُ بِمَا يَعۡمَلُونَ مُحِيطًا ١٠٨ ﴾

108. They may hide (their crimes) from men, but they cannot hide (them) from Allâh; for He is with them (by His Knowledge), when they plot by night in words that He does not approve. And Allâh ever encompasses what they do.

﴿ هَٰٓأَنتُمْ هَٰٓؤُلَآءِ جَٰدَلْتُمْ عَنْهُمْ فِى ٱلْحَيَوٰةِ ٱلدُّنْيَا فَمَن يُجَٰدِلُ ٱللَّهَ عَنْهُمْ يَوْمَ ٱلْقِيَٰمَةِ أَم مَّن يَكُونُ عَلَيْهِمْ وَكِيلًا ﴿١٠٩﴾ ﴾

109. Lo! You are those who have argued for them in the life of this world, but who will argue for them on the Day of Resurrection against Allâh, or who will then be their defender?

Transliteration

105. Inna anzalna ilayka alkitaba bialhaqqi litahkuma bayna alnnasi bima araka Allahu wala takun lilkha-ineena khaseeman 106. Waistaghfiri Allaha inna Allaha kana ghafooran raheeman 107. Wala tujadil AAani allatheena yakhtanoona anfusahum inna Allaha la yuhibbu man kana khawwanan atheeman 108. Yastakhfoona mina alnnasi wala yastakhfoona mina Allahi wahuwa maAAahum ith yubayyitoona ma la yarda mina alqawli wakana Allahu bima yaAAmaloona muheetan 109. Haantum haola-i jadaltum AAanhum fee alhayati alddunya faman yujadilu Allaha AAanhum yawma alqiyamati am man yakoonu AAalayhim wakeelan

Tafsir Ibn Kathir

The Necessity of Referring to What Allah has Revealed for Judgement

Allah says to His Messenger, Muhammad ,

(Surely, We have sent down to you the Book in truth) meaning, it truly came from Allah and its narrations and commandments are true. Allah then said,

(that you might judge between men by that which Allah has shown you,) In the Two Sahihs, it is recorded that Zaynab bint Umm Salamah said that Umm Salamah said that the Messenger of Allah heard the noise of disputing people close to the door of his room, and he went out to them saying,

«أَلَا إِنَّمَا أَنَا بَشَرٌ، وَإِنَّمَا أَقْضِي بِنَحْوٍ مِمَّا أَسْمَعُ، وَلَعَلَّ أَحَدَكُمْ أَنْ يَكُونَ أَلْحَنَ بِحُجَّتِهِ مِنْ بَعْضٍ فَأَقْضِيَ لَهُ، فَمَنْ قَضَيْتُ لَهُ بِحَقِّ مُسْلِمٍ، فَإِنَّمَا هِيَ قِطْعَةٌ مِنْ نَارٍ، فَلْيَحْمِلْهَا أَوْ لِيَذَرْهَا»

(Verily, I am only human and I judge based on what I hear. Some of you might be more eloquent in presenting his case than others, so that I judge in his favor. If I judge in one's favor concerning the right of another Muslim, then it is a piece of the Fire. So let one take it or leave it.) Imam Ahmad recorded that Umm Salamah said, "Two men from the Ansar came to the Messenger of Allah with a dispute regarding some old inheritance, but they did not have evidence. The Messenger of Allah said,

«إِنَّكُمْ تَخْتَصِمُونَ إِلَيَّ، وَإِنَّمَا أَنَا بَشَرٌ، وَلَعَلَّ بَعْضَكُمْ أَلْحَنُ بِحُجَّتِهِ مِنْ بَعْضٍ، وَإِنَّما أَقْضِي بَيْنَكُمْ عَلى نَحْوٍ مِمَّا أَسْمَعُ، فَمَنْ قَضَيْتُ لَهُ مِنْ حَقِّ أَخِيهِ شَيْئًا فَلَا يَأْخُذْهُ، فَإِنَّمَا أَقْطَعُ لَهُ قِطْعَةً مِنَ النَّارِ، يَأْتِي بِهَا إِسْطَامًا فِي عُنُقِهِ يَوْمَ الْقِيَامَةِ»

(You bring your disputes to me, but I am only human. Some of you might be more persuasive in their arguments than others. I only judge between you according to what I hear. Therefore, whomever I judge in his favor and give him a part of his brother's right, let him not take it, for it is a part of the Fire that I am giving him and it will be tied around his neck on the Day of Resurrection.) The two men cried and each one of them said, `I forfeit my right to my brother.' The Messenger of Allah said,

«أَمَا إِذْ قُلْتُمَا فَاذْهَبَا فَاقْتَسِمَا، ثُمَّ تَوَخَّيَا الْحَقَّ ثُمَّ اسْتَهِمَا، ثُم لِيُحْلِلْ كُلُّ وَاحِدٍ مِنْكُمَا صَاحِبَه»

(Since you said that, then go and divide the inheritance, and try to be just in your division. Then draw lots, and each one of you should forgive his brother thereafter (regardless of who got the best share).)" Allah's statement,

(They may hide (their crimes) from men, but they cannot hide (them) from Allah;) chastises the hypocrites because they hide their evil works from the people so that they will not criticize them. Yet, the hypocrites disclose this evil with Allah, Who has perfect watch over their secrets and knows what is in their hearts. This is why Allah said,

(for He is with them (by His knowledge), when they plot by night in words that He does not approve. And Allah ever encompasses what they do) threatening and warning them. Allah then said,

(Lo! You are those who have argued for them in the life of this world,) meaning, suppose these people gain the verdict from the rulers in their favor in this life, since the rulers judge according to what is apparent to them. However, what will their condition be on the Day of Resurrection before Allah, Who knows the secret and what is even more hidden Who will be his advocate on that Day Verily, none will support them that Day. Hence, Allah's statement,

(or who will then be their defender)

Surah: 4 Ayah: 110, Ayah: 111, Ayah: 112 & Ayah: 113

﴿ وَمَن يَعْمَلْ سُوٓءًا أَوْ يَظْلِمْ نَفْسَهُۥ ثُمَّ يَسْتَغْفِرِ ٱللَّهَ يَجِدِ ٱللَّهَ غَفُورًا رَّحِيمًا ١١٠ ﴾

110. And whoever does evil or wrongs himself but afterwards seeks Allâh's Forgiveness, he will find Allâh Oft-Forgiving, Most Merciful.

﴿ وَمَن يَكْسِبْ إِثْمًا فَإِنَّمَا يَكْسِبُهُۥ عَلَىٰ نَفْسِهِۦ ۚ وَكَانَ ٱللَّهُ عَلِيمًا حَكِيمًا ١١١ ﴾

111. And whoever earns sin, he earns it only against himself. And Allâh is Ever All-Knowing, All-Wise.

﴿ وَمَن يَكْسِبْ خَطِيٓـَٔةً أَوْ إِثْمًا ثُمَّ يَرْمِ بِهِۦ بَرِيٓـًٔا فَقَدِ ٱحْتَمَلَ بُهْتَـٰنًا وَإِثْمًا مُّبِينًا ﴿١١٢﴾ ﴾

112. And whoever earns a fault or a sin and then throws it on to someone innocent, he has indeed burdened himself with falsehood and a manifest sin.

﴿ وَلَوْلَا فَضْلُ ٱللَّهِ عَلَيْكَ وَرَحْمَتُهُۥ لَهَمَّت طَّآئِفَةٌ مِّنْهُمْ أَن يُضِلُّوكَ وَمَا يُضِلُّونَ إِلَّآ
أَنفُسَهُمْ ۖ وَمَا يَضُرُّونَكَ مِن شَىْءٍ ۚ وَأَنزَلَ ٱللَّهُ عَلَيْكَ ٱلْكِتَـٰبَ وَٱلْحِكْمَةَ وَعَلَّمَكَ مَا لَمْ
تَكُن تَعْلَمُ ۚ وَكَانَ فَضْلُ ٱللَّهِ عَلَيْكَ عَظِيمًا ﴿١١٣﴾ ﴾

113. Had not the Grace of Allâh and His Mercy been upon you (O Muhammad (peace be upon him)) a party of them would certainly have made a decision to mislead you, but (in fact) they mislead none except their own selves, and no harm can they do to you in the least. Allâh has sent down to you the Book (The Qur'ân), and Al-Hikmah (Islâmic laws, knowledge of legal and illegal things i.e. the Prophet's Sunnah - legal ways), and taught you that which you knew not. And Ever Great is the Grace of Allâh unto you (O Muhammad (peace be upon him))

Transliteration

110. Waman yaAAmal soo-an aw yathlim nafsahu thumma yastaghfiri Allaha yajidi Allaha ghafooran raheeman 111. Waman yaksib ithman fa-innama yaksibuhu AAala nafsihi wakana Allahu AAaleeman hakeeman 112. Waman yaksib khatee-atan aw ithman thumma yarmi bihi baree-an faqadi ihtamala buhtanan waithman mubeenan 113. Walawla fadlu Allahi AAalayka warahmatuhu lahammat ta-ifatun minhum an yudillooka wama yudilloona illa anfusahum wama yadurroonaka min shay-in waanzala Allahu AAalayka alkitaba waalhikmata waAAallamaka ma lam takun taAAlamu wakana fadlu Allahi AAalayka AAatheeman

Tafsir Ibn Kathir

The Encouragement to Seek Allah's Forgiveness, and Warning those who Falsely Accuse Innocent People

Allah emphasizes His generosity and kindness, in that He forgives whoever repents to Him from whatever evil they commit. Allah said,

(And whoever does evil or wrongs himself but afterwards seeks Allah's forgiveness, he will find Allah Oft-Forgiving, Most Merciful.) `Ali bin Abi Talhah said that Ibn `Abbas commented about this Ayah, "Allah informs His servants of His forgiveness, forbearing generosity and expansive mercy. So whoever commits a sin, whether minor or major,

(but afterwards seeks Allah's forgiveness, he will find Allah Oft-Forgiving, Most Merciful.) even if his sins were greater than the heavens, the earth and the mountains." Imam Ahmad recorded that `Ali said, "Whenever I hear anything from the Messenger of Allah, Allah benefits me with whatever He wills of that. Abu Bakr told me, and Abu Bakr has said the truth, that the Messenger of Allah said,

«مَا مِنْ مُسْلِمٍ يُذْنِبُ ذَنْبًا، ثُمَّ يَتَوَضَّأُ فَيُصَلِّي رَكْعَتَيْنِ، ثُمَّ يَسْتَغْفِرُ اللهَ لِذلِكَ الذَّنْبِ، إِلَّا غَفَرَ لَه»

(No Muslim commits a sin and then performs ablution, prays two Rak`ahs and begs Allah for forgiveness for that sin, but He forgives him.) He then recited these two Ayat,

(And whoever does evil or wrongs himself), and,

(And those who, when they have committed Fahishah or wronged themselves with evil)." Allah's statement,

(And whoever earns sin, he earns it only against himself.) is similar to His statement,

(And no bearer of burdens shall bear the burden of another). So no one will avail anyone else. Rather, every soul, and none else, shall carry its own burden. This is why Allah said,

(And Allah is Ever All-Knowing, All-Wise.) meaning, this occurs due to His knowledge, wisdom, fairness and mercy.

(and taught you that which you knew not.), before this revelation was sent down to you. Similarly, Allah said,

(And thus We have sent to you (O Muhammad) a Ruh (a revelation, and a mercy) of Our command. You knew not what is the Book) until the end of the Surah. Allah said,

(And you were not expecting that the Book (this Qur'an) would be sent down to you, but it is a mercy from your Lord). So Allah said;

(And ever great is the grace of Allah unto you (O Muhammad)).

Surah: 4 Ayah: 114 & Ayah: 115

﴿ لَّا خَيْرَ فِى كَثِيرٍ مِّن نَّجْوَىٰهُمْ إِلَّا مَنْ أَمَرَ بِصَدَقَةٍ أَوْ مَعْرُوفٍ أَوْ إِصْلَٰحٍۭ بَيْنَ ٱلنَّاسِ ۚ وَمَن يَفْعَلْ ذَٰلِكَ ٱبْتِغَآءَ مَرْضَاتِ ٱللَّهِ فَسَوْفَ نُؤْتِيهِ أَجْرًا عَظِيمًا ﴿١١٤﴾ ﴾

114. There is no good in most of their secret talks save (in) him who orders Sadaqah (charity in Allâh's Cause), or Ma'rûf (Islâmic Monotheism and all the good and righteous deeds which Allâh has ordained), or conciliation between mankind; and he who does this, seeking the good Pleasure of Allâh, We shall give him a great reward.

﴿ وَمَن يُشَاقِقِ ٱلرَّسُولَ مِنۢ بَعْدِ مَا تَبَيَّنَ لَهُ ٱلْهُدَىٰ وَيَتَّبِعْ غَيْرَ سَبِيلِ ٱلْمُؤْمِنِينَ نُوَلِّهِۦ مَا تَوَلَّىٰ وَنُصْلِهِۦ جَهَنَّمَ ۖ وَسَآءَتْ مَصِيرًا ﴿١١٥﴾ ﴾

115. And whoever contradicts and opposes the Messenger (Muhammad (peace be upon him)) after the right path has been shown clearly to him, and follows other than the believers' way. We shall keep him in the path he has chosen, and burn him in Hell - what an evil destination!

Transliteration

114. La khayra fee katheerin min najwahum illa man amara bisadaqatin aw maAAroofin aw islahin bayna alnnasi waman yafAAal thalika ibtighaa mardati Allahi fasawfa nu/teehi ajran AAatheeman 115. Waman yushaqiqi alrrasoola min baAAdi ma tabayyana lahu alhuda wayattabiAA ghayra sabeeli almu/mineena nuwallihi ma tawalla wanuslihi jahannama wasaat maseeran

Tafsir Ibn Kathir

Righteous Najwa, Secret Talk

Allah said,

(There is no good in most of their secret talks) meaning, what the people say to each other.

(save him who orders Sadaqah (charity), or goodness, or reconciliation between mankind;) meaning, except for this type of talk. Imam Ahmad recorded that Umm Kulthum bint `Uqbah said that she heard the Messenger of Allah saying,

«لَيْسَ الْكَذَّابُ الَّذِي يُصْلِحُ بَيْنَ النَّاسِ فَيَنْمِي خَيْرًا، أَوْ يَقُولُ خَيْرًا»

(He who brings about reconciliation between people by embellishing good or saying good things, is not a liar.) She also said, "I never heard him allow what the people say (lies) except in three cases: in war, bringing peace between people and the man's speech (invented compliments) to his wife and her speech to her husband." Umm Kulthum bint `Uqbah was among the immigrant women who gave their pledge of allegiance to the Messenger of Allah . The Group also recorded this Hadith, with the exception of Ibn Majah. Imam Ahmad recorded that Abu Ad-Darda' said that the Messenger of Allah said,

«أَلَا أُخْبِرُكُمْ بِأَفْضَلَ مِنْ دَرَجَةِ الصِّيَامِ، وَالصَّلَاةِ، وَالصَّدَقَةِ؟»

(Should I tell you what is better than the grade of fasting, praying and Sadaqah) They said, "Yes, O Allah's Messenger!" He said,

«إِصْلَاحُ ذَاتِ الْبَيْنِ»

(Bringing reconciliation between people.) He also said,

«وَفَسَادُ ذَاتِ الْبَيْنِ هِيَ الْحَالِقَةُ»

(Spoiling the relationship (between people) is the destroyer.) Abu Dawud and At-Tirmidhi also recorded this Hadith, and At-Tirmidhi said, "Hasan Sahih". Allah said,

(and he who does this, seeking the good pleasure of Allah,) with sincerity and awaiting the reward with Allah, the Exalted and Most Honored,

(We shall give him a great reward.) meaning, an immense, enormous and tremendous reward.

The Punishment for Contradicting and Opposing the Messenger and Following a Path Other than That of the Believers

Allah's statement,

(And whoever contradicts and opposes the Messenger after the right path has been shown clearly to him.) refers to whoever intentionally takes a path other than the path of the Law revealed to the Messenger, after the truth has been made clear, apparent and plain to him. Allah's statement,

(and follows other than the believers' way,) refers to a type of conduct that is closely related to contradicting the Messenger . This contradiction could be in the form of contradicting a text (from the Qur'an or Sunnah) or contradicting what the Ummah of Muhammad has agreed on. The Ummah of Muhammad is immune from error when they all agree on something, a miracle that serves to increase their honor, due to the greatness of their Prophet. There are many authentic Hadiths on this subject. Allah warned against the evil of contradicting the Prophet and his Ummah, when He said, e

(We shall keep him in the path he has chosen, and burn him in Hell --- what an evil destination!) meaning, when one goes on this wicked path, We will punish him by making the evil path appear good in his heart, and will beautify it for him so that he is tempted further. For instance, Allah said,

(Then leave Me Alone with such as belie this Qur'an. We shall punish them gradually from directions they perceive not),

(So when they turned away (from the path of Allah), Allah turned their hearts away), and,

(And We shall leave them in their trespass to wander blindly). Allah made the Fire the destination of such people in the Hereafter. Indeed, the path of those who avoid the right guidance will only lead to the Fire on the Day of Resurrection, as evident by Allah's statements,

((It will be said to the angels): "Assemble those who did wrong, together with their companions (from the devils)), and,

(And the criminals, shall see the Fire and apprehend that they have to fall therein. And they will find no way of escape from there).

Surah: 4 Ayah: 116, Ayah: 117, Ayah: 118, Ayah: 119, Ayah: 120, Ayah: 121 & Ayah: 122

﴿ إِنَّ ٱللَّهَ لَا يَغْفِرُ أَن يُشْرَكَ بِهِۦ وَيَغْفِرُ مَا دُونَ ذَٰلِكَ لِمَن يَشَآءُ ۚ وَمَن يُشْرِكْ بِٱللَّهِ فَقَدْ ضَلَّ ضَلَـٰلًا بَعِيدًا ﴿١١٦﴾ ﴾

116. Verily! Allâh forgives not (the sin of) setting up partners (in worship) with Him, but He forgives whom He wills sins other than that, and whoever sets up partners in worship with Allâh, has indeed strayed far away.

﴿ إِن يَدْعُونَ مِن دُونِهِۦٓ إِلَّآ إِنَٰثًا وَإِن يَدْعُونَ إِلَّا شَيْطَٰنًا مَّرِيدًا ﴿١١٧﴾ ﴾

117. They (all those who worship others than Allâh) invoke nothing but female deities besides Him (Allâh), and they invoke nothing but Shaitân (Satan), a persistent rebel!

﴿ لَّعَنَهُ ٱللَّهُ وَقَالَ لَأَتَّخِذَنَّ مِنْ عِبَادِكَ نَصِيبًا مَّفْرُوضًا ﴿١١٨﴾ ﴾

118. Allâh cursed him. And he (Shaitân (Satan)) said: "I will take an appointed portion of your slaves.

﴿ وَلَأُضِلَّنَّهُمْ وَلَأُمَنِّيَنَّهُمْ وَلَءَامُرَنَّهُمْ فَلَيُبَتِّكُنَّ ءَاذَانَ ٱلْأَنْعَٰمِ وَلَءَامُرَنَّهُمْ فَلَيُغَيِّرُنَّ
خَلْقَ ٱللَّهِ ۚ وَمَن يَتَّخِذِ ٱلشَّيْطَٰنَ وَلِيًّا مِّن دُونِ ٱللَّهِ فَقَدْ خَسِرَ خُسْرَانًا مُّبِينًا ﴿١١٩﴾ ﴾

119. Verily, I will mislead them, and surely, I will arouse in them false desires; and certainly, I will order them to slit the ears of cattle, and indeed I will order them to change the nature created by Allâh." And whoever takes Shaitân (Satan) as a Walî (protector or helper) instead of Allâh, has surely suffered a manifest loss.

﴿ يَعِدُهُمْ وَيُمَنِّيهِمْ ۖ وَمَا يَعِدُهُمُ ٱلشَّيْطَٰنُ إِلَّا غُرُورًا ﴿١٢٠﴾ ﴾

120. He (Shaitan (Satan)) makes promises to them, and arouses in them false desires; and Shaitan's (Satan) promises are nothing but deceptions.

﴿ أُو۟لَٰٓئِكَ مَأْوَىٰهُمْ جَهَنَّمُ وَلَا يَجِدُونَ عَنْهَا مَحِيصًا ﴿١٢١﴾ ﴾

121. The dwelling of such (people) is Hell, and they will find no way of escape from it.

﴿ وَٱلَّذِينَ ءَامَنُوا۟ وَعَمِلُوا۟ ٱلصَّٰلِحَٰتِ سَنُدْخِلُهُمْ جَنَّٰتٍ تَجْرِى مِن تَحْتِهَا ٱلْأَنْهَٰرُ
خَٰلِدِينَ فِيهَآ أَبَدًا ۖ وَعْدَ ٱللَّهِ حَقًّا ۚ وَمَنْ أَصْدَقُ مِنَ ٱللَّهِ قِيلًا ﴿١٢٢﴾ ﴾

122. But those who believe (in the Oneness of Allâh - Islâmic Monotheism) and do deeds of righteousness, We shall admit them to the Gardens under which rivers flow (i.e. in Paradise) to dwell therein forever. Allâh's Promise is the Truth; and whose words can be truer than those of Allâh? (Of course, none).

Transliteration

116. Inna Allaha la yaghfiru an yushraka bihi wayaghfiru ma doona thalika liman yashao
waman yushrik biAllahi faqad dalla dalalan baAAeedan 117. In yadAAoona min doonihi illa
inathan wa-in yadAAoona illa shaytanan mareedan 118. LaAAanahu Allahu waqala
laattakhithanna min AAibadika naseeban mafroodan 119. Walaodillannahum
walaomanniyannahum walaamurannahum falayubattikunna athana alanAAami
walaamurannahum falayughayyirunna khalqa Allahi waman yattakhithi alshshaytana waliyyan
min dooni Allahi faqad khasira khusranan mubeenan 120. YaAAiduhum wayumanneehim
wama yaAAiduhumu alshshaytanu illa ghurooran 121. Ola-ika ma/wahum jahannamu wala
yajidoona AAanha maheesan 122. Waallatheena amanoo waAAamiloo alssalihati
sanudkhiluhum jannatin tajree min tahtiha alanharu khalideena feeha abadan waAAda Allahi
haqqan waman asdaqu mina Allahi qeelan

Tafsir Ibn Kathir

Shirk Shall not be Forgiven, in Reality the Idolators Worship Shaytan

We talked about Allah's statement,

(Verily, Allah forgives not (the sin of) setting up partners (in worship) with Him, but He forgives whom He wills, sins other than that,) before and mentioned the relevant Hadiths in the beginning of this Surah. Allah's statement,

(and whoever sets up partners in worship with Allah, has indeed strayed far away.) means, he will have taken other than the true path, deviated from guidance and righteousness, destroyed himself in this life and the Hereafter, and lost contentment in this life and the Hereafter. Juwaybir said that Ad-Dahhak said about Allah's statement,

(They invoke nothing but female deities besides Him (Allah),) "The idolators claimed that the angels are Allah's daughters, saying, `We only worship them so that they bring us closer to Allah.' So they took the angels as gods, made the shapes of girls and decided, `These (idols) resemble the daughters of Allah (i.e., the angels), Whom we worship. '" This is similar to Allah's statements,

(Have you then considered Al-Lat and Al-`Uzza)

(And they make the angels who themselves are servants of the Most Gracious (Allah) females) and,

(And they have invented a kinship between Him and the Jinn). Allah's statement,

(and they invoke nothing but Shaytan, a persistent rebel!) means, Shaytan has commanded them to do this and made it seem fair and beautiful in their eyes. Consequently, they are worshipping Shaytan in reality, just as Allah said in another Ayah,

(Did I not command you, O Children of Adam, that you should not worship Shaytan) Allah said that, on the Day of Resurrection, the angels shall proclaim about the idolators who worshipped them in this life:

(Nay, but they used to worship the Jinn; most of them were believers in them). Allah's statement,

(Allah cursed him), means, He expelled him and banished him from His mercy and His grace.

(I will take an appointed portion of your servants) means, a fixed and known share. Muqatil bin Hayyan commented, "From every one thousand, nine hundred and ninety-nine will go to the Fire and one to Paradise."

(Verily, I will mislead them) from the true path,

(and surely, I will arouse in them false desires;) tempting them to feign repentance, arousing false hopes in them, encouraging them to delay and procrastinate with righteous deeds, deceiving them.

(and certainly, I will order them to slit the ears of cattle,) meaning, slitting their ears to designate them as Bahirah, Sa'ibah, and a Wasilah, as Qatadah and As-Suddi stated.

(And indeed I will order them to change the nature created by Allah.) means tattooing, according to Al-Hasan bin Abi Al-Hasan Al-Basri. In his Sahih, Muslim recorded the prohibition of tattooing the face, which in one of its wordings states: "May Allah curse whoever does this." It is also recorded in the Sahih that Ibn Mas`ud said, "May Allah curse those who have tattoos and those who do it, who pluck their (facial) hairs and the one who does it for them, and those who make spaces between their teeth for the purpose of beauty, changing what Allah has created." He then said, "Why should not I curse whom the Messenger of Allah has cursed, when the Book of Allah commands it," referring to the Ayah,

(And whatsoever the Messenger gives you, take it; and whatsoever he forbids you, abstain (from it)). Allah's statement,

(And whoever takes Shaytan as a Wali (protector or helper) instead of Allah, has surely suffered a manifest loss.) means, he will have lost this life and the Hereafter. Indeed, this is a type of loss that cannot be compensated or restored. Allah's statement,

(He (Shaytan) makes promises to them, and arouses in them false desires;) explains the true reality. Surely, Shaytan deceitfully promises his supporters and tempts them into believing that they are winners in this and the Hereafter. This is why Allah said,

(and Shaytan's promises are nothing but deceptions.) Allah states that on the Day of Return,

(And Shaytan will say when the matter has been decided: "Verily, Allah promised you a promise of truth. And I too promised you, but I betrayed you. I had no authority over you), until,

(Verily, there is a painful torment for the wrongdoers.) Allah's statement,

(of such (people)) refers to those who like and prefer what Shaytan is promising and assuring them of,

(The dwelling of such (people) is Hell), as their destination and abode on the Day of Resurrection,

(and they will find no way of escape from it.), meaning, they will not be able to avoid, avert, evade or elude the Hellfire.

The Reward of Righteous Believers

Allah then mentions the condition of the content righteous believers and the perfect honor they will earn in the end. Allah said,

(And those who believe and do righteous good deeds,) meaning, their hearts were truthful and their limbs obedient with the righteous acts they were commanded, all the while abandoning the evil they were prohibited from doing.

(We shall admit them to Gardens under which rivers flow (Paradise)) meaning, they will think of where they want these rivers to flow and they will flow there,

(to dwell therein forever), without end or being removed from it.

(Allah's promise is the truth), meaning, this is a true promise from Allah, and verily, Allah's promise shall come to pass. Allah then said, (and whose words can be truer than those of Allah) meaning, none is more truthful in statement and narration than Allah. There is no deity worthy of worship, or Lord except Him. The Messenger of Allah used to proclaim in his speech,

«إِنَّ أَصْدَقَ الْحَدِيثِ كَلَامُ اللهِ، وَخَيْرَ الْهَدْيِ هَدْيُ مُحَمَّدٍ صلى الله عليه وسلّم، وَشَرَّ الْأُمُورِ مُحْدَثَاتُهَا، وَكُلَّ مُحْدَثَةٍ بِدْعَةٌ، وَكُلَّ بِدْعَةٍ ضَلَالَةٌ، وَكُلَّ ضَلَالَةٍ فِي النَّارِ»

(The most truthful speech is Allah's Speech, and the best guidance is the guidance of Muhammad. The worst matters are the newly invented (in religion), every newly invented matter is an innovation, and every innovation is a heresy, and every heresy is in the Fire.)

Surah: 4 Ayah: 123, Ayah: 124, Ayah: 125 & Ayah: 126

﴿ لَّيْسَ بِأَمَانِيِّكُمْ وَلَآ أَمَانِيِّ أَهْلِ ٱلْكِتَـٰبِ ۗ مَن يَعْمَلْ سُوٓءًا يُجْزَ بِهِۦ وَلَا يَجِدْ لَهُۥ مِن دُونِ ٱللَّهِ وَلِيًّا وَلَا نَصِيرًا ﴿١٢٣﴾ ﴾

123. It will not be in accordance with your desires (Muslims), nor those of the people of the Scripture (Jews and Christians), whosoever works evil, will have the recompense thereof, and he will not find any protector or helper besides Allâh.

﴿ وَمَن يَعْمَلْ مِنَ ٱلصَّـٰلِحَـٰتِ مِن ذَكَرٍ أَوْ أُنثَىٰ وَهُوَ مُؤْمِنٌ فَأُو۟لَـٰٓئِكَ يَدْخُلُونَ ٱلْجَنَّةَ وَلَا يُظْلَمُونَ نَقِيرًا ﴿١٢٤﴾ ﴾

124. And whoever does righteous good deeds, male or female, and is a (true) believer (in the Oneness of Allâh (Muslim)) such will enter Paradise and not the least injustice, even to the size of a speck on the back of a date-stone, will be done to them.

﴿ وَمَنْ أَحْسَنُ دِينًا مِّمَّنْ أَسْلَمَ وَجْهَهُۥ لِلَّهِ وَهُوَ مُحْسِنٌ وَٱتَّبَعَ مِلَّةَ إِبْرَٰهِيمَ حَنِيفًا ۗ وَٱتَّخَذَ ٱللَّهُ إِبْرَٰهِيمَ خَلِيلًا ﴿١٢٥﴾ ﴾

125. And who can be better in religion than one who submits his face (himself) to Allâh (i.e. follows Allâh's Religion of Islâmic Monotheism); and he is a Muhsin (a good-doer - see V.2:112). And follows the religion of Ibrâhîm (Abraham) Hanîfa (Islâmic Monotheism - to worship none but Allâh Alone). And Allâh did take Ibrâhîm (Abraham) as a Khalil (an intimate friend)!

﴿ وَلِلَّهِ مَا فِى ٱلسَّمَـٰوَٰتِ وَمَا فِى ٱلْأَرْضِ ۚ وَكَانَ ٱللَّهُ بِكُلِّ شَىْءٍ مُّحِيطًا ﴿١٢٦﴾ ﴾

126. And to Allâh belongs all that is in the heavens and all that is in the earth. And Allâh is Ever Encompassing all things.

Transliteration

123. Laysa bi-amaniyyikum wala amaniyyi ahli alkitabi man yaAAmal soo-an yujza bihi wala yajid lahu min dooni Allahi waliyyan wala naseeran 124. Waman yaAAmal mina alssalihati min thakarin aw ontha wahuwa mu/minun faola-ika yadkhuloona aljannata wala yuthlamoona naqeeran 125. Waman ahsanu deenan mimman aslama wajhahu lillahi wahuwa muhsinun waittabaAAa millata ibraheema haneefan waittakhatha Allahu ibraheema khaleelan 126. Walillahi ma fee alssamawati wama fee al-ardi wakana Allahu bikulli shay-in muheetan

Tafsir Ibn Kathir

Success is Only Achieved by Performing Righteous Deeds, not Wishful Thinking

Qatadah said, "We were told that the Muslims and the People of the Scriptures mentioned their own virtues to each other. People of the Scriptures said, `Our Prophet came before your Prophet and our Book before your Book. Therefore, we should have more right to Allah than you have.' Muslims said, `Rather, we have more right to Allah than you, our Prophet is the Final Prophet and our Book supersedes all the Books before it.' Allah sent down,

(It will not be in accordance with your desires (Muslims), nor those of the People of the Scripture (Jews and Christians), whosoever works evil, will have the recompense thereof),

(And who can be better in religion than one who submits his face (himself) to Allah; and he is a Muhsin.) Allah then supported the argument of the Muslims against their opponents of the other religions." Similar statements were attributed to As-Suddi, Masruq, Ad-Dahhak and Abu Salih. Al-`Awfi reported that Ibn `Abbas commented on this Ayah (4:123), "The followers of various religions disputed, the people of the Tawrah said, `Our Book is the best Book and our Prophet (Musa) is the best Prophet. ' The people of the Injil said similarly, the people of Islam said, `There is no religion except Islam, our Book has abrogated every other Book, our Prophet is the Final Prophet, and you were commanded to believe in your Books and adhere to our Book.' Allah judged between them, saying,

(It will not be in accordance with your desires, nor those of the People of the Scripture, whosoever works evil, will have the recompense thereof)." This Ayah indicates that the religion is not accepted on account of wishful thinking or mere hopes. Rather, the accepted religion relies on what resides in the heart and which is made truthful through actions. It is not true that when one utters a claim to something, he attains it merely on account of his claim. It is not true that every person who claims to be on the truth is considered as such, merely on account of his words, until his claim gains merit with proof from Allah. Hence Allah's statement,

(It will not be in accordance with your desires, nor those of the People of the Scripture, whosoever works evil, will have the recompense thereof), meaning safety will not be acquired by you or them just by wishful thinking. Rather, the key is in obeying Allah and following what He has legislated through the words of His honorable Messengers. This is why Allah said afterwards,

(whosoever works evil, will have the recompense thereof,) Similarly, Allah said,

(So whosoever does good equal to the weight of an atom, shall see it. And whosoever does evil equal to the weight of an atom, shall see it.) and it was reported that when these Ayat were revealed, they became hard on many Companions. Ibn Abi Hatim recorded that `A'ishah said, "I said, `O Messenger of Allah! I know the hardest Ayah in the Qur'an.' He said, `What is it, O `A'ishah!' I said,

(whoever works evil, will have the recompense thereof,) He said,

«هُوَ مَا يُصِيبُ الْعَبْدَالْمُؤْمِنَ، حَتَّى النَّكْبَةِ يُنْكَبُهَا»

(That is what strikes the believing servant, even the problems that bother him.)" Ibn Jarir and Abu Dawud also recorded this Hadith. Sa`id bin Mansur recorded that Abu Hurayrah said, "When the Ayah,

(whosoever works evil, will have the recompense thereof,) was revealed, it was hard on Muslims. The Messenger of Allah said to them,

«سَدِّدُوا وَقَارِبُوا، فَإِنَّ فِي كُلِّ مَا يُصَابُ بِهِ الْمُسْلِمُ كَفَّارَةً، حَتَّى الشَّوْكَةِ يُشَاكُهَا، وَالنَّكْبَةِ يُنْكَبُهَا»

(Be steadfast and seek closeness. Everything that afflicts the Muslim, even the thorn that pierces his skin and the hardship he suffers, will be an expiation for him.)" This is the wording collected by Ahmad through Sufyan bin `Uyaynah. Muslim and At-Tirmidhi also recorded it. Allah's statement,

(and he will not find any protector or helper besides Allah,) `Ali bin Abi Talhah reported that Ibn `Abbas said; "Unless he repents and Allah forgives him." Ibn Abi Hatim recorded it. Allah then said,

(And whoever does righteous good deeds, male or female, and is a believer). Allah mentions the recompense for evil actions and that He will surely inflict its punishment on the servant, either in this life, which is better for him, or in the Hereafter, we seek refuge with Allah from this end. We also beg Allah for our well-being in this life and the Hereafter and for His forgiveness, mercy and pardon. Allah then mentions His kindness, generosity and mercy in accepting the good deeds from His servants, whether male or female, with the condition that they embrace the faith. He also stated that He will admit the believers into Paradise and will not withhold any of their righteous deeds, even the weight of a Naqir - speck on the back of a date-stone. Earlier, we discussed the Fatil - the scalish thread in the long slit of a date-stone, and both of these, along with the Qitmir -- the thin membrane over the date-stone were mentioned in the Qur'an. Allah then said,

(And who can be better in religion than one who submits his face to Allah.) meaning, performs the good actions in sincerity for his Lord with faith and awaiting the reward with Allah,

(and he is a Muhsin) following the correct guidance that Allah legislated in the religion of truth which He sent His Messenger with. These are the two conditions, in the absence of which no deed will be accepted from anyone; sincerity and correctness. The work is sincere when it is performed for Allah alone and it becomes correct when it conforms to the Shari`ah. So, the deed becomes outwardly correct with following the Sunnah and inwardly correct with sincerity. When any deed lacks either of these two conditions, the deed becomes null and void. For instance, when one lacks the pillar of sincerity in his work, he becomes a hypocrite who shows off for people. Whoever does not follow the Shari`ah, he becomes an ignorant, wicked person. When one combines both pillars, his actions will be the deeds of the faithful believers whose best deeds are accepted from them and their errors erased. Consequently, Allah said,

(And follows the religion of Ibrahim the Hanif (Monotheist).) referring to Muhammad and his following, until the Day of Resurrection. Allah said,

(Verily, among mankind who have the best claim to Ibrahim are those who followed him, and this Prophet), and,

(Then, We have sent the Revelation to you (saying): "Follow the religion of Ibrahim the Hanif (Monotheist) and he was not of the Mushrikin). The Hanif, intentionally and with knowledge, avoids Shirk, he goes attentively to the truth, allowing no one to hinder him or stop him from it.

Ibrahim is Allah's Khalil

Allah's statement,

(And Allah did take Ibrahim as a Khalil (an intimate friend)!) encourages following Ibrahim Al-Khalil, because he was and still is an Imam whose conduct is followed and imitated. Indeed, Ibrahim reached the ultimate closeness to Allah that the servants seek, for he attained the grade of Khalil, which is the highest grade of love. He acquired all this due to his obedience to His Lord, just as Allah has described him,

(And of Ibrahim, the one who fulfilled),

(And (remember) when the Lord of Ibrahim tried him with (certain) commands, which he fulfilled), and,

(Verily, Ibrahim was an Ummah, obedient to Allah, a Hanif, and he was not one of the Mushrikin). Al-Bukhari recorded that `Amr bin Maymun said that when Mu`adh came back from Yemen, he led them in the Fajr prayer and recited,

(And Allah did take Ibrahim as a Khalil!) One of the men present commented, "Surely, the eye of Ibrahim's mother has been comforted." Ibrahim was called Allah's Khalil due to his Lord's great love towards him, on account of the acts of obedience he performed that Allah loves and prefers. We should mention here that in the Two Sahihs, it is recorded that Abu Sa`id Al-Khudri said that when the Messenger of Allah gave them his last speech, he said,

«أَمَّا بَعْدُ، أَيُّهَا النَّاسُ فَلَوْ كُنْتُ مُتَّخِذًا مِنْ أَهْلِ الْأَرْضِ خَلِيلًا، لَاتَّخَذْتُ أَبَا بَكْرِ ابْنَ أَبِي قُحَافَةَ خَلِيلًا، وَلَكِنْ صَاحِبُكُمْ خَلِيلُ اللهِ»

(O people! If I were to take a Khalil from the people of the earth, I would have taken Abu Bakr bin Abi Quhafah as my Khalil. However, your companion (meaning himself) is the Khalil of Allah.) Jundub bin `Abdullah Al-Bajali, `Abdullah bin `Amr bin Al-`As and `Abdullah bin Mas`ud narrated that the Prophet said,

«إِنَّ اللهَ اتَّخَذَنِي خَلِيلًا، كَمَا اتَّخَذَ إِبْرَاهِيمَ خَلِيلًا»

(Allah has chosen me as His Khalil, just as He has chosen Ibrahim as His Khalil.) Allah's statement,

(And to Allah belongs all that is in the heavens and all that is in the earth.) means, everything and everyone are His property, servants and creation, and He has full authority over all of this. There is no one who can avert Allah's decision or question His judgment. He is never asked about what He does due to His might, ability, fairness, wisdom, compassion and mercy. Allah's statement,

(And Allah is Ever Encompassing all things.) means, His knowledge encompasses everything and nothing concerning His servants is ever hidden from Him. Nothing, even the weight of an atom, ever escapes His observation in the heavens and earth, nor anything smaller or bigger than that.

Surah: 4 Ayah: 127

﴿ وَيَسْتَفْتُونَكَ فِي ٱلنِّسَآءِ ۖ قُلِ ٱللَّهُ يُفْتِيكُمْ فِيهِنَّ وَمَا يُتْلَىٰ عَلَيْكُمْ فِي ٱلْكِتَـٰبِ فِي يَتَـٰمَى ٱلنِّسَآءِ ٱلَّـٰتِى لَا تُؤْتُونَهُنَّ مَا كُتِبَ لَهُنَّ وَتَرْغَبُونَ أَن تَنكِحُوهُنَّ وَٱلْمُسْتَضْعَفِينَ مِنَ ٱلْوِلْدَٰنِ وَأَن تَقُومُوا۟ لِلْيَتَـٰمَىٰ بِٱلْقِسْطِ ۚ وَمَا تَفْعَلُوا۟ مِنْ خَيْرٍ فَإِنَّ ٱللَّهَ كَانَ بِهِۦ عَلِيمًا ﴿١٢٧﴾ ﴾

127. They ask your legal instruction concerning women, say: Allâh instructs you about them, and about what is recited unto you in the Book concerning the orphan girls whom you give not the prescribed portions (as regards Mahr and inheritance) and yet whom you desire to marry, and (concerning) the children who are weak and oppressed, and that you stand firm for justice to orphans. And whatever good you do, Allâh is Ever All-Aware of it.

Transliteration

127. Wayastaftoonaka fee alnnisa-i quli Allahu yufteekum feehinna wama yutla AAalaykum fee alkitabi fee yatama alnnisa-i allatee la tu/toonahunna ma kutiba lahunna watarghaboona an tankihoohunna waalmustadAAafeena mina alwildani waan taqoomoo lilyatama bialqisti wama tafAAaloo min khayrin fa-inna Allaha kana bihi AAaleeman

Tafsir Ibn Kathir

The Ruling Concerning Female Orphans

Al-Bukhari recorded that `A'ishah said about the Ayah,

(They ask your instruction concerning women. Say, "Allah instructs you about them...) until,

(whom you desire to marry...) "It is about the man who is taking care of a female orphan, being her caretaker and inheritor. Her money is joined with his money to such an extent, that she shares with him even the branch of a date that he has. So he likes (for material gain) to marry her himself, and hates to marry her to another man who would have a share in his money, on account of her share in his money. Therefore, he refuses to let her marry anyone else. So, this Ayah was revealed." Muslim also recorded it. Ibn Abi Hatim recorded that `A'ishah said, "The people asked Allah's Messenger (about orphan girls), so Allah revealed,

(They ask your instruction concerning women. Say, "Allah instructs you about them and about what is recited unto you in the Book...") What is meant by Allah's saying, `And about what is recited unto you in the Book' is the former verse which said,

(If you fear that you shall not be able to deal justly with the orphan girls, then marry (other) women of your choice.)" `A'ishah said, "Allah's statement,

(whom you desire to marry...) also refers to the desire of the guardian not to marry an orphan girl under his supervision when she lacks property or beauty. The guardians were forbidden to marry their orphan girls possessing property and beauty without being just to them, as they generally refrain from marrying them (when they are neither beautiful nor wealthy)." The basis of this is recorded in Two Sahihs. Consequently, when a man is the caretaker of a female orphan, he might like to marry her himself. In this case, Allah commands him to give her a suitable dowry that other women of her status get. If he does not want to do that, then let him marry other women, for Allah has made this matter easy for Muslims. Sometimes, the caretaker does not desire to marry the orphan under his care, because she is not attractive to his eye. In this case, Allah forbids the caretaker from preventing the female orphan from marrying another man for fear that her husband would share in the money that is mutually shared between the caretaker and the girl. `Ali bin Abi Talhah said that Ibn `Abbas said, "During the time of Jahiliyyah, the caretaker of a female orphan would cover her with his rope, and when he did that, no man would marry her. If she was beautiful and he desired to marry her, he married her and took control of her wealth. If she was not beautiful, he did not allow her to marry until she died, and when she died he inherited her money. Allah prohibited and outlawed this practice. " He also said about Allah's statement,

(and the children who are weak and oppressed,) that during the time of Jahiliyyah, they used to deny young children and females a share of inheritance. So Allah's statement,

(you give not what they deserve) thus prohibiting this practice and designating a fixed share for each,

(To the male, a portion equal to that of two females..) whether they were young or old, as Sa`id bin Jubayr and others stated. Sa`id bin Jubayr said about Allah's statement,

(and that you stand firm for justice to orphans.) "Just as when she is beautiful and wealthy you would want to marry her and have her for yourself, so when she is not wealthy or beautiful, marry her and have her for yourself." Allah's statement,

r(And whatever good you do, Allah is Ever All-Aware of it.) encourages performing the good deeds and fulfilling the commandments, and states that Allah is knowledgeable of all of this and He will reward for it in the best and most perfect manner.

Surah: 4 Ayah: 128, Ayah: 129 & Ayah: 130

﴿وَإِنِ ٱمۡرَأَةٌ خَافَتۡ مِنۢ بَعۡلِهَا نُشُوزًا أَوۡ إِعۡرَاضٗا فَلَا جُنَاحَ عَلَيۡهِمَآ أَن يُصۡلِحَا بَيۡنَهُمَا
صُلۡحٗاۚ وَٱلصُّلۡحُ خَيۡرٞۗ وَأُحۡضِرَتِ ٱلۡأَنفُسُ ٱلشُّحَّۚ وَإِن تُحۡسِنُواْ وَتَتَّقُواْ فَإِنَّ ٱللَّهَ
كَانَ بِمَا تَعۡمَلُونَ خَبِيرٗا ١٢٨﴾

128. And if a woman fears cruelty or desertion on her husband's part, there is no sin on them both if they make terms of peace between themselves; and making peace is better. And human inner-selves are swayed by greed. But if you do good and keep away from evil, verily, Allâh is Ever Well-Acquainted with what you do.

﴿وَلَن تَسۡتَطِيعُوٓاْ أَن تَعۡدِلُواْ بَيۡنَ ٱلنِّسَآءِ وَلَوۡ حَرَصۡتُمۡۖ فَلَا تَمِيلُواْ كُلَّ ٱلۡمَيۡلِ فَتَذَرُوهَا
كَٱلۡمُعَلَّقَةِۚ وَإِن تُصۡلِحُواْ وَتَتَّقُواْ فَإِنَّ ٱللَّهَ كَانَ غَفُورٗا رَّحِيمٗا ١٢٩﴾

129. You will never be able to do perfect justice between wives even if it is your ardent desire, so do not incline too much to one of them (by giving her more of your time and provision) so as to leave the other hanging (i.e. neither divorced nor married). And if you do justice, and do all that is right and fear Allâh by keeping away from all that is wrong, then Allâh is Ever Oft-Forgiving, Most Merciful.

﴿وَإِن يَتَفَرَّقَا يُغۡنِ ٱللَّهُ كُلّٗا مِّن سَعَتِهِۦۚ وَكَانَ ٱللَّهُ وَٰسِعًا حَكِيمٗا ١٣٠﴾

130. But if they separate (by divorce), Allâh will provide abundance for everyone of them from His Bounty. And Allâh is Ever All-Sufficient for His creatures' need, All-Wise.

Transliteration

128. Wa-ini imraatun khafat min baAAliha nushoozan aw iAAradan fala junaha AAalayhima an yusliha baynahuma sulhan waalssulhu khayrun waohdirati al-anfusu alshshuhha wa-in tuhsinoo watattaqoo fa-inna Allaha kana bima taAAmaloona khabeeran 129. Walan tastateeAAoo an taAAdiloo bayna alnnisa-i walaw harastum fala tameeloo kulla almayli fatatharooha kaalmuAAallaqati wa-in tuslihoo watattaqoo fa-inna Allaha kana ghafooran raheeman 130. Wa-in yatafarraqa yughni Allahu kullan min saAAatihi wakana Allahu wasiAAan hakeeman

Tafsir Ibn Kathir

The Ruling Concerning Desertion on the Part of the Husband

Allah states, and thus legislates accordingly, that sometimes, the man inclines away from his wife, sometimes towards her and sometimes he parts with her. In the first case, when the wife fears that her husband is steering away from her or deserting her, she is allowed to forfeit all or part of her rights, such as provisions, clothing, dwelling, and so forth, and the husband is allowed to accept such concessions from her. Hence, there is no harm if she offers such concessions, and if her husband accepts them. This is why Allah said,

(there is no sin on them both if they make terms of peace between themselves;) He then said, (and making peace is better) than divorce. Allah's statement,

(And human souls are swayed by greed.) means, coming to peaceful terms, even when it involves forfeiting some rights, is better than parting. Abu Dawud At-Tayalisi recorded that Ibn `Abbas said, "Sawdah feared that the Messenger of Allah might divorce her and she said, `O Messenger of Allah! Do not divorce me; give my day to `A'ishah.' And he did, and later on Allah sent down,

(And if a woman fears cruelty or desertion on her husband's part, there is no sin on them both) Ibn `Abbas said, "Whatever (legal agreement) the spouses mutually agree to is allowed.". At-Tirmidhi recorded it and said, "Hasan Gharib". In the Two Sahihs, it is recorded that `A'ishah said that when Sawdah bint Zam`ah became old, she forfeited her day to `A'ishah, and the Prophet used to spend Sawdah's night with `A'ishah. There is a similar narration also collected by Al-Bukhari. Al-Bukhari also recorded that `A'ishah commented;

(And if a woman fears cruelty or desertion on her husband's part), that it refers to, "A man who is married to an old woman, and he does not desire her and wants to divorce her. So she says, `I forfeit my right on you.' So this Ayah was revealed."

Meaning of "Making Peace is Better

Allah said,

(And making peace is better). `Ali bin Abi Talhah related that Ibn `Abbas said that the Ayah refers to, "When the husband gives his wife the choice between staying with him or leaving him, as this is better than the husband preferring other wives to her." However, the apparent wording of the Ayah refers to the settlement where the wife forfeits some of the rights she has over her husband, with the husband agreeing to this concession, and that this settlement is better than divorce. For instance, the Prophet kept Sawdah bint Zam`ah as his wife after she offered to forfeit her day for `A'ishah. By keeping her among his wives, his Ummah may follow this kind of settlement. Since settlement and peace are better with Allah than parting, Allah said,

(and making peace is better). Divorce is not preferred with Allah. The meaning of Allah's statement,

(But if you do good and have Taqwa, verily, Allah is Ever Well-Acquainted with what you do) if you are patient with the wife you dislike and treat her as other wives are treated, then Allah knows what you do and will reward you for it perfectly. Allah's statement,

(You will never be able to do perfect justice between wives even if it is your ardent desire,) means, O people! You will never be able to be perfectly just between wives in every respect. Even when one divides the nights justly between wives, there will still be various degrees concerning love, desire and sexual intimacy, as Ibn `Abbas, `Ubaydah As-Salmani, Mujahid, Al-Hasan Al-Basri and Ad-Dahhak bin Muzahim stated. Imam Ahmad and the collectors of the Sunan recorded that `A'ishah said, "The Messenger of Allah used to treat his wives equally and proclaim,

«اللَّهُمَّ هَذَا قَسْمِي فِيمَا أَمْلِكُ، فَلَا تَلُمْنِي فِيمَا تَمْلِكُ وَلَا أَمْلِكُ»

(O Allah! This is my division in what I own, so do not blame me for what You own and I do not own) referring to his heart. This was the wording that Abu Dawud collected, and its chain of narrators is Sahih. Allah's statement,

(so do not incline too much to one of them) means, when you like one of your wives more than others, do not exaggerate in treating her that way,

(so as to leave the other hanging.) referring to the other wives. Ibn `Abbas, Mujahid, Sa`id bin Jubayr, Al-Hasan, Ad-Dahhak, Ar-Rabi` bin Anas, As-Suddi and Muqatil bin Hayyan said that Mu`allaqah (hanging) means, "She is neither divorced nor married." Abu Dawud At-Tayalisi recorded that Abu Hurayrah said that the Messenger of Allah said,

«مَنْ كَانَتْ لَهُ امْرَأَتَانِ فَمَالَ إِلَى إِحْدَاهُمَا، جَاءَ يَوْمَ الْقِيَامَةِ وَأَحَدُ شِقَّيْهِ سَاقِطٌ»

(Whoever has two wives and inclines to one of them (too much), will come on the Day of Resurrection with one of his sides dragging.) Allah's statement,

(And if you do justice, and do all that is right and have Taqwa, then Allah is Ever Oft-Forgiving, Most Merciful.) The Ayah states: If you do justice and divide equally in what you have power over, while fearing Allah in all conditions, then Allah will forgive you the favoritism that you showed to some of your wives. Allah then said,

(But if they separate (divorce), Allah will provide abundance for everyone of them from His bounty. And Allah is Ever All-Sufficient for His creatures' needs, All-Wise.) This is the third case between husband and wife, in which divorce occurs. Allah states that if the spouses separate by divorce, then Allah will suffice them by giving him a better wife and her a better husband. The meaning of,

(And Allah is Ever All-Sufficient for His creatures' needs, All-Wise.) is: His favor is tremendous, His bounty is enormous and He is All-Wise in all His actions, decisions and commandments.

Surah: 4 Ayah: 131, Ayah: 132, Ayah: 133 & Ayah: 134

﴿ وَلِلَّهِ مَا فِي ٱلسَّمَـٰوَٰتِ وَمَا فِي ٱلْأَرْضِ ۗ وَلَقَدْ وَصَّيْنَا ٱلَّذِينَ أُوتُوا۟ ٱلْكِتَـٰبَ مِن قَبْلِكُمْ وَإِيَّاكُمْ أَنِ ٱتَّقُوا۟ ٱللَّهَ ۚ وَإِن تَكْفُرُوا۟ فَإِنَّ لِلَّهِ مَا فِي ٱلسَّمَـٰوَٰتِ وَمَا فِي ٱلْأَرْضِ ۚ وَكَانَ ٱللَّهُ غَنِيًّا حَمِيدًا ﴿١٣١﴾ ﴾

131. And to Allâh belongs all that is in the heavens and all that is in the earth. And verily, We have recommended to the people of the Scripture before you, and to you (O Muslims) that you (all) fear Allâh, and keep your duty to Him. But if you disbelieve, then unto Allâh belongs all that is in the heavens and all that is in the earth, and Allâh is Ever Rich (Free of all wants), Worthy of all praise.

﴿ وَلِلَّهِ مَا فِي ٱلسَّمَـٰوَٰتِ وَمَا فِي ٱلْأَرْضِ ۚ وَكَفَىٰ بِٱللَّهِ وَكِيلًا ﴿١٣٢﴾ ﴾

132. And to Allâh belongs all that is in the heavens and all that is in the earth. And Allâh is Ever All-Sufficient as a Disposer of affairs.

﴿إِن يَشَأْ يُذْهِبْكُمْ أَيُّهَا ٱلنَّاسُ وَيَأْتِ بِـَٔاخَرِينَ ۚ وَكَانَ ٱللَّهُ عَلَىٰ ذَٰلِكَ قَدِيرًا ﴿١٣٣﴾﴾

133. If He wills, He can take you away, O people, and bring others. And Allâh is Ever All-Potent over that.

﴿مَّن كَانَ يُرِيدُ ثَوَابَ ٱلدُّنْيَا فَعِندَ ٱللَّهِ ثَوَابُ ٱلدُّنْيَا وَٱلْـَٔاخِرَةِ ۚ وَكَانَ ٱللَّهُ سَمِيعًۢا بَصِيرًا ﴿١٣٤﴾﴾

134. Whoever desires a reward in this life of the world, then with Allâh (Alone and none else) is the reward of this worldly life and of the Hereafter. And Allâh is Ever All-Hearer, All-Seer.

Transliteration

131. Walillahi ma fee alssamawati wama fee al-ardi walaqad wassayna allatheena ootoo alkitaba min qablikum wa-iyyakum ani ittaqoo Allaha wa-in takfuroo fa-inna lillahi ma fee alssamawati wama fee alardi wakana Allahu ghaniyyan hameedan 132. Walillahi ma fee alssamawati wama fee al-ardi wakafa biAllahi wakeelan 133. In yasha/ yuthhibkum ayyuha alnnasu waya/ti bi-akhareena wakana Allahu AAala thalika qadeeran 134. Man kana yureedu thawaba alddunya faAAinda Allahi thawabu alddunya waal-akhirati wakana Allahu sameeAAan baseeran

Tafsir Ibn Kathir

The Necessity of Taqwa of Allah

Allah states that He is the Owner of the heavens and earth and that He is the Supreme Authority over them. Hence Allah's statement,

(And verily, We have recommended to the People of the Scripture before you, and to you) meaning, We have recommended to you what We recommended to the People of Scriptures; Taqwa of Allah, by worshipping Him Alone without partners. Allah then said,

(But if you disbelieve, then unto Allah belongs all that is in the heavens and all that is in the earth). In another Ayah, Allah said that Musa said to his people,

("If you disbelieve, you and all on the earth together, then verily, Allah is Rich (free of any need), Owner of all praise."). Allah said,

(So they disbelieved and turned away. But Allah was not in need (of them). And Allah is Rich (free of any need), Worthy of all praise) meaning, He is far too Rich than to need His servants, and worthy of all praise in all His decisions and commandments. The meaning of Allah's statement,

(And to Allah belongs all that is in the heavens and all that is in the earth. And Allah is Ever All-Sufficient as a Disposer of affairs.) He has perfect watch over every soul, knowing what it deserves, He is the Watcher, and Witness of all things. Allah's statement,

(If He wills, He can take you away, O people, and bring others. And Allah is Ever All-Potent over that.) means, He is able to take you away and replace you with other people if you disobey Him. In a similar Ayah, Allah said,

(And if you turn away, He will exchange you for some other people and they will not be your likes) Allah's statement,

(Whoever desires the rewards of this life, then with Allah is the reward of this worldly life and of the Hereafter.) means, O those whose ultimate desire is this life, know that Allah owns the rewards of this life and the Hereafter. Therefore, if you ask Allah for both, He will enrich you, award you and suffice for you. As Allah said,

(But of mankind there are some who say: "Our Lord! Give us in this world!" and for such there will be no portion in the Hereafter. And of them there are some who say: "Our Lord! Give us in this world that which is good and in the Hereafter that which is good, and save us from the torment of the Fire!" For them there will be alloted a share for what they have earned),

(Whosoever desires (by his deeds) the reward of the Hereafter, We give him increase in his reward), and

(Whoever desires the quick-passing (transitory enjoyment of this world), We readily grant him what We will for whom We like) until,

(See how We prefer one above another (in this world)). So Allah said here,

(And Allah is Ever All-Hearer, All-Seer.)

Surah: 4 Ayah: 135

﴿ ۞ يَـٰٓأَيُّهَا ٱلَّذِينَ ءَامَنُوا۟ كُونُوا۟ قَوَّٰمِينَ بِٱلْقِسْطِ شُهَدَآءَ لِلَّهِ وَلَوْ عَلَىٰٓ أَنفُسِكُمْ أَوِ ٱلْوَٰلِدَيْنِ
وَٱلْأَقْرَبِينَ ۚ إِن يَكُنْ غَنِيًّا أَوْ فَقِيرًا فَٱللَّهُ أَوْلَىٰ بِهِمَا ۖ فَلَا تَتَّبِعُوا۟ ٱلْهَوَىٰٓ أَن تَعْدِلُوا۟ ۚ وَإِن
تَلْوُۥٓا۟ أَوْ تُعْرِضُوا۟ فَإِنَّ ٱللَّهَ كَانَ بِمَا تَعْمَلُونَ خَبِيرًا ﴿١٣٥﴾ ﴾

135. O you who believe! Stand out firmly for justice, as witnesses to Allâh, even though it be against yourselves, or your parents, or your kin, be he rich or poor, Allâh is a Better Protector to both (than you). So follow not the lusts (of your hearts), lest you avoid justice; and if you distort your witness or refuse to give it, verily, Allâh is Ever Well-Acquainted with what you do.

Transliteration

135. Ya ayyuha allatheena amanoo koonoo qawwameena bialqisti shuhadaa lillahi walaw AAala anfusikum awi alwalidayni waal-aqrabeena in yakun ghaniyyan aw faqeeran faAllahu awla bihima fala tattabiAAoo alhawa an taAAdiloo wa-in talwoo aw tuAAridoo fa-inna Allaha kana bima taAAmaloona khabeeran

Tafsir Ibn Kathir

Commanding Justice and Conveying the Witness for Allah

Allah commands His believing servants to stand up for justice and fairness and not to deviate from it, right or left. They should not fear the blame of anyone or allow anyone to prevent them from doing something for the sake of Allah. They are also required to help, support and aid each other for Allah's sake. Allah's statement, (as witnesses to Allah) is similar to His statement,

(And establish the testimony for Allah). Testimony should be delivered precisely, for the sake of Allah, thus making the testimony correct, truly just, and free of alterations, changes or deletions. This is why Allah said,

(even though it be against yourselves,) meaning, give correct testimony, and say the truth when you are asked about it, even if harm will effect you as a consequence. Indeed, Allah shall make a way out and give relief for those who obey Him in every matter. Allah's statement,

(or your parents, or your kin,) means, even if you have to testify against your parents and kin, do not compromise for their sake. Rather, give the correct and just witness even if they are harmed in the process, for the truth presides above everyone and is preferred to everyone. Allah's statement,

(be he rich or poor, Allah is a better Protector to both.) means, do not favor someone (in your testimony) because he is rich, or feel pity for him because he is poor, for Allah is their caretaker, a better Protector of them than you, and has better knowledge of what is good for them. Allah's statement,

(So follow not the lusts, lest you may avoid justice;) means, let not desire, lust or the hatred you have against others, lure you into injustice in your affairs. Rather, stand for justice in all situations. Allah said;

(And let not the enmity and hatred of others make you avoid justice. Be just: that is nearer to piety) when the Prophet sent `Abdullah bin Rawahah to collect the tax on the fruits and produce of the Jews of Khaybar, they offered him a bribe so that he would go easy on them. He said; "By Allah! I have come to you from the dearest of the creation to me (Muhammad), and you are more hated by me than an equivelent number of apes and swine. However, my love for him (the Prophet) and hatred for you shall not prevent me from being just with you." On that, they said, "This (justice) is the basis which the heavens and earth were created. " We will mention this Hadith later in Surat Al-Ma'idah (chapter 5) Allah willing. Allah's statement afterwards,

(and if you Talwu or Tu`ridu) means, "Distort your testimony and change it", according to Mujahid and several others among the Salaf. Talwu, includes distortion and intentional lying. For instance, Allah said,

(And verily, among them is a party who Yalwuna (distort) the Book with their tongues (as they read)). Tu`ridu, includes hiding and withholding the testimony. Allah said,

(Who hides it, surely, his heart is sinful) The Prophet said,

«خَيْرُ الشُّهَدَاءِ الَّذِي يَأْتِي بِشَهَادَتِهِ قَبْلَ أَنْ يُسْأَلَهَا»

(The best witness is he who discloses his testimony before being asked to do so.) Allah then warned,

(Verily, Allah is Ever Well-Acquainted with what you do.) and will reward or punish you accordingly.

Surah: 4 Ayah: 136

﴿ يَٰٓأَيُّهَا ٱلَّذِينَ ءَامَنُوٓاْ ءَامِنُواْ بِٱللَّهِ وَرَسُولِهِۦ وَٱلۡكِتَٰبِ ٱلَّذِي نَزَّلَ عَلَىٰ رَسُولِهِۦ وَٱلۡكِتَٰبِ
ٱلَّذِيٓ أَنزَلَ مِن قَبۡلُۚ وَمَن يَكۡفُرۡ بِٱللَّهِ وَمَلَٰٓئِكَتِهِۦ وَكُتُبِهِۦ وَرُسُلِهِۦ وَٱلۡيَوۡمِ ٱلۡأٓخِرِ فَقَدۡ ضَلَّ
ضَلَٰلَۢا بَعِيدًا ١٣٦ ﴾

136. O you who believe! Believe in Allâh, and His Messenger (Muhammad (peace be upon him)) and the Book (the Qur'ân) which He has sent down to His Messenger, and the Scripture which He sent down to those before (him); and whosoever disbelieves in Allâh, His Angels, His Books, His Messengers, and the Last Day, then indeed he has strayed far away.

Transliteration

136. Ya ayyuha allatheena amanoo aminoo biAllahi warasoolihi waalkitabi allathee nazzala AAala rasoolihi waalkitabi allathee anzala min qablu waman yakfur biAllahi wamala-ikatihi wakutubihi warusulihi waalyawmi al-akhiri faqad dalla dalalan baAAeedan

Tafsir Ibn Kathir

The Order to Have Faith after Believing

Allah commands His faithful servants to adhere to all the elements of faith, its branches, pillars and cornerstones. This is not stated as mere redundancy, but from the view of completing faith and the continual maintenence of it. For instance, the believer proclaims in every prayer,

(Guide us to the straight way.) which means, make us aware of the straight path and increase us in guidance and strengthen us on it. In this Ayah (4:136), Allah commands the believers to believe in Him and in His Messenger, just as He said elsewhere,

(O you who believe! Have Taqwa of Allah, and believe in His Messenger,). Allah's statement,

(and the Book which He has sent down to His Messenger,) refers to the Qur'an, while,

(and the Scripture which He sent down to those before (him);) refers to the previously revealed divine Books. Allah then said,

(and whosoever disbelieves in Allah, His Angels, His Books, His Messengers, and the Last Day, then indeed he has strayed far away.) meaning, he will have deviated from the correct guidance and strayed far away from its path.

Surah: 4 Ayah: 137, Ayah: 138, Ayah: 139 & Ayah: 140

﴿ إِنَّ ٱلَّذِينَ ءَامَنُواْ ثُمَّ كَفَرُواْ ثُمَّ ءَامَنُواْ ثُمَّ كَفَرُواْ ثُمَّ ٱزۡدَادُواْ كُفۡرٗا لَّمۡ يَكُنِ ٱللَّهُ لِيَغۡفِرَ لَهُمۡ
وَلَا لِيَهۡدِيَهُمۡ سَبِيلَۢا ١٣٧ ﴾

137. Verily, those who believe, then disbelieve, then believe (again), and (again) disbelieve, and go on increasing in disbelief; Allâh will not forgive them, nor guide them on the (Right) Way.

﴿ بَشِّرِ ٱلۡمُنَـٰفِقِينَ بِأَنَّ لَهُمۡ عَذَابًا أَلِيمًا ﴿١٣٨﴾ ﴾

138. Give to the hypocrites the tidings that there is for them a painful torment.

﴿ ٱلَّذِينَ يَتَّخِذُونَ ٱلۡكَـٰفِرِينَ أَوۡلِيَآءَ مِن دُونِ ٱلۡمُؤۡمِنِينَ ۚ أَيَبۡتَغُونَ عِندَهُمُ ٱلۡعِزَّةَ فَإِنَّ ٱلۡعِزَّةَ لِلَّهِ جَمِيعًا ﴿١٣٩﴾ ﴾

139. Those who take disbelievers for Auliyâ' (protectors or helpers or friends) instead of believers, do they seek honor, power and glory with them? Verily, then to Allâh belongs all honor, power and glory.

﴿ وَقَدۡ نَزَّلَ عَلَيۡكُمۡ فِى ٱلۡكِتَـٰبِ أَنۡ إِذَا سَمِعۡتُمۡ ءَايَـٰتِ ٱللَّهِ يُكۡفَرُ بِهَا وَيُسۡتَهۡزَأُ بِهَا فَلَا تَقۡعُدُواْ مَعَهُمۡ حَتَّىٰ يَخُوضُواْ فِى حَدِيثٍ غَيۡرِهِۦٓ ۚ إِنَّكُمۡ إِذًا مِّثۡلُهُمۡ ۗ إِنَّ ٱللَّهَ جَامِعُ ٱلۡمُنَـٰفِقِينَ وَٱلۡكَـٰفِرِينَ فِى جَهَنَّمَ جَمِيعًا ﴿١٤٠﴾ ﴾

140. And it has already been revealed to you in the Book (this Qur'ân) that when you hear the Verses of Allâh being denied and mocked at, then sit not with them, until they engage in a talk other than that; (but if you stayed with them) certainly in that case you would be like them. Surely, Allâh will collect the hypocrites and disbelievers all together in Hell.

Transliteration

137. Inna allatheena amanoo thumma kafaroo thumma amanoo thumma kafaroo thumma izdadoo kufran lam yakuni Allahu liyaghfira lahum wala liyahdiyahum sabeelan 138. Bashshiri almunafiqeena bi-anna lahum AAathaban aleeman 139. Allatheena yattakhithoona alkafireena awliyaa min dooni almu/mineena ayabtaghoona AAindahumu alAAizzata fa-inna alAAizzata lillahi jameeAAan 140. Waqad nazzala AAalaykum fee alkitabi an itha samiAAtum ayati Allahi yukfaru biha wayustahzao biha fala taqAAudoo maAAahum hatta yakhoodoo fee hadeethin ghayrihi innakum ithan mithluhum inna Allaha jamiAAu almunafiqeena waalkafireena fee jahannama jameeAAan

Tafsir Ibn Kathir

Characteristics of the Hypocrites and Their Destination

Allah states that whoever embraces the faith, reverts from it, embraces it again, reverts from it and remains on disbelief and increases in it until death, then he will never have a chance to gain accepted repentance after death. Nor will Allah forgive him, or deliver him from his plight to the path of correct guidance. This is why Allah said,

(Allah will not forgive them, nor guide them on the (right) way). Ibn Abi Hatim recorded that his father said that Ahmad bin `Abdah related that Hafs bin Jami' said that Samak said that `Ikrimah reported that Ibn `Abbas commented;

(and go on increasing in disbelief), "They remain on disbelief until they die." Mujahid said similarly. Allah then said,

(Give to the hypocrites the tidings that there is for them a painful torment.) Hence, the hypocrites have this characteristic, for they believe, then disbelieve, and this is why their hearts become sealed. Allah describes the hypocrites as taking the disbelievers as friends instead of the believers, meaning they are the disbelievers' supporters in reality, for they give them their loyalty and friendship in secret. They also say to disbelievers when they are alone with them, "We are with you, we only mock the believers by pretending to follow their religion." Allah said, while chastising them for being friends with the disbelievers,

(do they seek honor, with them) Allah then states that honor, power and glory is for Him Alone without partners, and for those whom Allah grants such qualities to. Allah said,

(Whosoever desires honor, then to Allah belong all honor), and,

(But honor belongs to Allah, and to His Messenger, and to the believers, but the hypocrites know not). The statement that honor is Allah's Alone, is meant to encourage the servants to adhere to their servitude to Allah and to be among His faithful servants who will gain victory in this life and when the Witnesses stand up to testify on the Day of Resurection. Allah's statement,

(And it has already been revealed to you in the Book that when you hear the verses of Allah being denied and mocked at, then sit not with them, until they engage in talk other than that; certainly in that case you would be like them.) The Ayah means, if you still commit this prohibition after being aware of its prohibition, sitting with them where Allah's Ayat are rejected, mocked at and denied, and you sanction such conduct, then you have participated with them in what they are doing. So Allah said,

((But if you stayed with them) certainly in that case you would be like them.) concerning the burden they will earn. What has already been revealed in the Book -- as the Ayah says -- is the Ayah in Surat Al-An`am (6), which was revealed in Makkah,

(And when you see those who engage in false conversation about Our verses (of the Qur'an) by mocking at them, stay away from them). Muqatil bin Hayyan said that this Ayah (4:140) abrogated the Ayah in Surat Al-An`am, referring to the part that says here,

((But if you stayed with them) certainly in that case you would be like them), and Allah's statement in Al-An`am,

(Those who fear Allah, keep their duty to Him and avoid evil, are not responsible for them (the disbelievers) in any case, but (their duty) is to remind them, that they may have Taqwa). Allah's statement,

(Surely, Allah will collect the hypocrites and disbelievers all together in Hell.) means, just as the hypocrites participate in the Kufr of disbelievers, Allah will join them all together to reside in the Fire for eternity, dwelling in torment, punishment, enchained, restrained and in drinking boiling water.

Surah: 4 Ayah: 141

﴿ ٱلَّذِينَ يَتَرَبَّصُونَ بِكُمْ فَإِن كَانَ لَكُمْ فَتْحٌ مِّنَ ٱللَّهِ قَالُوٓاْ أَلَمْ نَكُن مَّعَكُمْ وَإِن كَانَ
لِلْكَـٰفِرِينَ نَصِيبٌ قَالُوٓاْ أَلَمْ نَسْتَحْوِذْ عَلَيْكُمْ وَنَمْنَعْكُم مِّنَ ٱلْمُؤْمِنِينَ ۚ فَٱللَّهُ يَحْكُمُ
بَيْنَكُمْ يَوْمَ ٱلْقِيَـٰمَةِ ۗ وَلَن يَجْعَلَ ٱللَّهُ لِلْكَـٰفِرِينَ عَلَى ٱلْمُؤْمِنِينَ سَبِيلًا ﴿١٤١﴾

141. Those (hypocrites) who wait and watch about you; if you gain a victory from Allâh, they say: "Were we not with you?" but if the disbelievers gain a success, they say (to them): "Did we not gain mastery over you and did we not protect you from the believers?" Allâh will judge between you (all) on the Day of Resurrection. And never will Allâh grant to the disbelievers a way (to triumph) over the believers.

Transliteration

141. Allatheena yatarabbasoona bikum fa-in kana lakum fathun mina Allahi qaloo alam nakun maAAakum wa-in kana lilkafireena naseebun qaloo alam nastahwith AAalaykum wanamnaAAkum mina almu/mineena faAllahu yahkumu baynakum yawma alqiyamati walan yajAAala Allahu lilkafireena AAala almu/mineena sabeelan

Tafsir Ibn Kathir

Hypocrites Wait and Watch what Happens to Muslims

Allah states that the hypocrites watch and await the harm that occurs to the believers, awaiting the time when the Muslim circumstances and religion are dissolved and the state of Kufr takes over.

(if you gain a victory from Allah) triumph, aid and booty,

(they say, "Were we not with you") trying to come closer to the believers with this statement. However,

(But if the disbelievers gain a success,) by gaining victory over the believers sometimes, just as occurred during Uhud, for surely, the Messengers are tested, but the final victory is theirs.

(they say (to them), "Did we not gain mastery over you and did we not protect you from the believers") meaning, did we not help you in secret and try our best to confuse the believers and weaken their resolve, until you gained victory over them This statement of the hypocrites is an attempt to strengthen relations with the disbelievers, because they pretend to be friends with both parties so that they will be safe from their harm, due to their weak faith and lack of certainty. Allah said,

(Allah will judge between you (all) on the Day of Resurrection) meaning, by what He knows about you, O hypocrites. Therefore, do not be deceived by being shaded under the protection of Islamic Law in this life, which is such only out of Allah's wisdom. Surely, on the Day of Resurrection, your pretending shall not benefit you, because on that Day, the secrets of the souls will be disclosed and the contents of the hearts will be collected. Allah said,

(And never will Allah grant to the disbelievers a way (to triumph) over the believers). `Abdur-Razzaq recorded that Yasi` Al-Kindi said, "A man came to `Ali bin Abi Talib and said, `What about this Ayah,

(And never will Allah grant to the disbelievers a way (to triumph) over the believers.) `Ali said, `Come closer, come closer. Allah will judge between you on the Day of Resurrection, and He will not grant victory for the disbelievers over the believers.' " Ibn Jurayj recorded that `Ata' Al-Khurasani said that Ibn `Abbas said that,

(And never will Allah grant to the disbelievers a way (to triumph) over the believers.) "Will occur on the Day of Resurrection." As-Suddi recorded that Abu Malik Al-Ashja`i said that it occurs on the Day of Resurrection. As-Suddi said that "way" means, proof. It is possible that the meaning of, `and never will Allah grant to the disbelievers a way (to triumph) over the believers', is in this life by being unable to exterminate the believers completely, although they sometimes gain victory over some Muslims. However, the Final Triumph will be for the believers in this life and the Hereafter. Allah said,

(Verily, We will indeed make victorious Our Messengers and those who believe in the worldly life) This provides a rebuttal to the wishes of the hypocrites for the destruction of the believers, and their loyalty to the disbelievers, fearing for themselves if they are victorious.

Surah: 4 Ayah: 142 & Ayah: 143

﴿ إِنَّ ٱلْمُنَٰفِقِينَ يُخَٰدِعُونَ ٱللَّهَ وَهُوَ خَٰدِعُهُمْ وَإِذَا قَامُوٓا۟ إِلَى ٱلصَّلَوٰةِ قَامُوا۟ كُسَالَىٰ
يُرَآءُونَ ٱلنَّاسَ وَلَا يَذْكُرُونَ ٱللَّهَ إِلَّا قَلِيلًا ﴿١٤٢﴾ ﴾

142. Verily, the hypocrites seek to deceive Allâh, but it is He Who deceives them. And when they stand up for As-Salât (the prayer), they stand with laziness and to be seen of men, and they do not remember Allâh but little.

﴿ مُّذَبْذَبِينَ بَيْنَ ذَٰلِكَ لَآ إِلَىٰ هَٰٓؤُلَآءِ وَلَآ إِلَىٰ هَٰٓؤُلَآءِ ۚ وَمَن يُضْلِلِ ٱللَّهُ فَلَن تَجِدَ لَهُۥ
سَبِيلًا ﴿١٤٣﴾ ﴾

143. (They are) swaying between this and that, belonging neither to these nor to those; and he whom Allâh sends astray, you will not find for him a way (to the truth - Islâm).

Transliteration

142. Inna almunafiqeena yukhadiAAoona Allaha wahuwa khadiAAuhum wa-itha qamoo ila alssalati qamoo kusala yuraoona alnnasa wala yathkuroona Allaha illa qaleelan 143. Muthabthabeena bayna thalika la ila haola-i wala ila haola-i waman yudlili Allahu falan tajida lahu sabeelan

Tafsir Ibn Kathir

The Hypocrites Try to Deceive Allah and Sway Between Believers and Disbelievers

In the beginning of Surat Al-Baqarah (2), we mentioned Allah's statement,

(They (think to) deceive Allah and those who believe). Here, Allah states,

(Verily, the hypocrites seek to deceive Allah, but it is He Who deceives them.) There is no doubt that Allah can never be deceived, for He has perfect knowledge of the secrets and what the hearts conceal. However, the hypocrites, due to their ignorance, scarce knowledge and weak minds, think that since they were successful in deceiving people, using Islamic Law as a cover of safety for themselves, they will acquire the same status with Allah on the Day of Resurrection and deceive Him too. Allah states that on that Day, the hypocrites will swear to Him that they were on the path of righteousness and correctness thinking that such statement will benefit them with Allah. For instance, Allah said,

(On the Day when Allah will resurrect them all together; then they will swear to Him as they swear to you) Allah's statement,

(but it is He Who deceives them) means, He lures them further into injustice and misguidance. He also prevents them from reaching the truth in this life and on the Day of Resurrection. Allah said,

(On the Day when the hypocrites - men and women - will say to the believers: "Wait for us! Let us get something from your light!" It will be said: "Go back to your rear! Then seek a light!") until,

(And worst indeed is that destination). A Hadith states;

«مَن سَمَّعَ سَمَّعَ اللهُ بِهِ، وَمَنْ رَاءَى رَاءَى اللهُ بِه»

(Whoever wants to be heard of, Allah will make him heard of, and whoever wants to be seen, Allah will show him.) Allah's statement,

(And when they stand up for Salah, they stand with laziness). This is the characteristic of the hypocrites with the most honored, best and righteous act of worship, the prayer. When they stand for prayer, they stand in laziness because they neither truly intend to perform it nor do they believe in it, have humility in it, or understand it. This is the description of their outward attitude! As for their hearts, Allah said,

(to be seen of men) meaning, they do not have sincerity when worshipping Allah. Rather, they show off to people so that they gain closeness to them. They are often absent from the prayers that they can hide away from, such as the `Isha' prayer and the Dawn prayer that are prayed in darkness. In the Two Sahihs, it is recorded that the Messenger of Allah said,

«أَثْقَلُ الصَّلَاةِ عَلَى الْمُنَافِقِينَ صَلَاةُ الْعِشَاءِ وَصَلَاةُ الْفَجْرِ، وَلَوْ يَعْلَمُونَ مَا فِيهِمَا لَأَتَوْهُمَا وَلَوْ حَبْوًا، وَلَقَدْ هَمَمْتُ أَنْ آمُرَ بِالصَّلَاةِ فَتُقَامُ، ثُمَّ آمُرَ رَجُلًا فَيُصَلِّي بِالنَّاسِ، ثُمَّ أَنْطَلِقَ مَعِيَ بِرِجَالٍ مَعَهُمْ حُزَمٌ مِنْ حَطَبٍ، إِلَى قَوْمٍ لَا يَشْهَدُونَ الصَّلَاةَ، فَأُحَرِّقَ عَلَيْهِمْ بُيُوتَهُمْ بِالنَّار»

(The heaviest prayers on the hypocrites are the `Isha' and Dawn prayers. If they know their rewards, they will attend them even if they have to crawl. I was about to order someone to pronounce the Adhan for the prayer, then order someone to lead the prayer for the people, then order some men to collect fire-wood (fuel); then I would burn the houses around men who did not attend the (compulsory congregational) prayer.) In another narration, the Prophet said,

«وَالَّذِي نَفْسِي بِيَدِهِ، لَوْ عَلِمَ أَحَدُهُمْ أَنَّهُ يَجِدُ عَرْقًا سَمِينًا أَوْ مِرْمَاتَيْنِ حَسَنَتَيْنِ، لَشَهِدَ الصَّلَاةَ، وَلَوْلَا مَا فِي الْبُيُوتِ مِنَ النِّسَاءِ وَالذُّرِّيَّـــةِ لَحَرَّقْتُ عَلَيْهِمْ بُيُوتَهُمْ بِالنَّارِ»

(By Him, in Whose Hand my soul is, if anyone of them had known that he would get a bone covered with good meat or two (small) pieces of meat between two ribs, he would have turned up for the prayer, and had it not been that the houses have women and children in them, I would burn their homes around them.) Allah's statement,

(And they do not remember Allah but little) means, during the prayer they do not feel humbleness or pay attention to what they are reciting. Rather, during their prayer, they are inattentive, jesting and avoid the good that they are meant to receive from prayer. Imam Malik reported that Al-`Ala' bin `Abdur-Rahman said that Anas bin Malik said that the Messenger of Allah said,

«تِلْكَ صَلَاةُ الْمُنَافِقِ، تِلْكَ صَلَاةُ الْمُنَافِقِ، تِلْكَ صَلَاةُ الْمُنَافِقِ، يَجْلِسُ يَرْقُبُ الشَّمْسَ، حَتَّى إِذَا كَانَتْ بَيْنَ قَرْنَيِ الشَّيْطَانِ، قَامَ فَنَقَرَ أَرْبَعًا، لَا يَذْكُرُ اللهَ فِيهَا إِلَّا قَلِيلًا»

(This is the prayer of the hypocrite, this is the prayer of the hypocrite, this is the prayer of the hypocrite. He sits watching the sun until when it goes down between the two horns of the devil, he stands up pecks out four Rak`ahs (for `Asr) without remembering Allah during them except little.) Muslim, At-Tirmidhi and An-Nasa'i also recorded it. At-Tirmidhi said "Hasan Sahih". Allah's statement,

((They are) swaying between this and that, belonging neither to these) means that the hypocrites are swaying between faith and disbelief. So they are neither with believers inwardly or outwardly nor with disbelievers inwardly or outwardly. Rather, they are with the believers outwardly and with the disbelievers inwardly. Some of them would suffer fits of doubt, leaning towards these sometimes and towards those sometimes,

(Whenever it flashes for them, they walk therein, and when darkness covers them, they stand still). Mujahid said;

((They are) swaying between this and that, belonging neither to these) "The Companions of Muhammad , (nor to those): the Jews." Ibn Jarir recorded that Ibn `Umar said that the Prophet said,

«مَثَلُ الْمُنَافِقِ كَمَثَلِ الشَّاةِ الْعَائِرَةِ بَيْنَ الْغَنَمَيْنِ، تَعِيرُ إِلَى هَذِهِ مَرَّةً، وَإِلَى هَذِهِ مَرَّةً، وَلَا تَدْرِي أَيَّتَهُمَا تَتْبَع»

(The example of the hypocrite is the example of the sheep wandering between two herds, sometimes she goes to one of them, and sometimes the other, confused over whom she should follow.) Muslim also recorded it. This is why Allah said afterwards,

(and he whom Allah sends astray, you will not find for him a way.) meaning, whomever He leads astray from the guidance,

(For him you will find no Wali (guiding friend) to lead him (to the right path)) because,

(Whomsoever Allah sends astray, none can guide him). So the hypocrites whom Allah has led astray from the paths of safety will never find a guide to direct them, nor someone to save them. There is none who can resist Allah's decision, and He is not asked about what He does, while they all will be asked.

Surah: 4 Ayah: 144, Ayah: 145, Ayah: 146 & Ayah: 147

﴿ يَٰٓأَيُّهَا ٱلَّذِينَ ءَامَنُواْ لَا تَتَّخِذُواْ ٱلْكَٰفِرِينَ أَوْلِيَآءَ مِن دُونِ ٱلْمُؤْمِنِينَ ۚ أَتُرِيدُونَ أَن تَجْعَلُواْ لِلَّهِ عَلَيْكُمْ سُلْطَٰنًا مُّبِينًا ﴿١٤٤﴾ ﴾

144. O you who believe! Take not for Auliyâ' (protectors or helpers or friends) disbelievers instead of believers. Do you wish to offer Allâh a manifest proof against yourselves?

﴿ إِنَّ ٱلْمُنَٰفِقِينَ فِى ٱلدَّرْكِ ٱلْأَسْفَلِ مِنَ ٱلنَّارِ وَلَن تَجِدَ لَهُمْ نَصِيرًا ﴿١٤٥﴾ ﴾

145. Verily, the hypocrites will be in the lowest depth (grade) of the Fire; no helper will you find for them.

﴿ إِلَّا ٱلَّذِينَ تَابُواْ وَأَصْلَحُواْ وَٱعْتَصَمُواْ بِٱللَّهِ وَأَخْلَصُواْ دِينَهُمْ لِلَّهِ فَأُوْلَٰٓئِكَ مَعَ ٱلْمُؤْمِنِينَ ۖ وَسَوْفَ يُؤْتِ ٱللَّهُ ٱلْمُؤْمِنِينَ أَجْرًا عَظِيمًا ﴿١٤٦﴾ ﴾

146. Except those who repent (from hypocrisy), do righteous good deeds, hold fast to Allâh, and purify their religion for Allâh (by worshipping none but Allâh, and do good for Allâh's sake only, not to show-off), then they will be with the believers. And Allâh will grant the believers a great reward.

﴿ مَّا يَفْعَلُ ٱللَّهُ بِعَذَابِكُمْ إِن شَكَرْتُمْ وَءَامَنتُمْ ۚ وَكَانَ ٱللَّهُ شَاكِرًا عَلِيمًا ﴿١٤٧﴾ ﴾

147. Why should Allâh punish you if you have thanked (Him) and have believed in Him. And Allâh is Ever All-Appreciative (of good), All-Knowing.

Transliteration

144. Ya ayyuha allatheena amanoo la tattakhithoo alkafireena awliyaa min dooni almu/mineena atureedoona an tajAAaloo lillahi AAalaykum sultanan mubeenan 145. Inna almunafiqeena fee alddarki al-asfali mina alnnari walan tajida lahum naseeran 146. Illa allatheena taboo waaslahoo waiAAtasamoo biAllahi waakhlasoo deenahum lillahi faola-ika maAAa almu/mineena wasawfa yu/ti Allahu almu/mineena ajran AAatheeman 147. Ma yafAAalu Allahu biAAathabikum in shakartum waamantum wakana Allahu shakiran AAaleeman

Tafsir Ibn Kathir

The Prohibition of Wilayah with the Disbelievers

Allah forbids His believing servants from taking the disbelievers as friends instead of the believers. This includes being friends and associates of the disbelievers, advising them, being intimate with them and exposing the secrets of the believers to them. In another Ayah, Allah said,

(Let not the believers take the disbelievers as friends instead of the believers, and whoever does that, will never be helped by Allah in any way, except if you indeed fear a danger from them. And Allah warns you against Himself). meaning, He warns you against His punishment if you fall into what He has prohibited. This is why Allah said here,

(Do you wish to offer Allah a manifest Sultan against yourselves) meaning, proof against you that warrants receiving His torment. Ibn Abi Hatim narrated that Ibn `Abbas commented;

(manifest Sultan), "The word Sultan in the Qur'an means proof. " There is an authentic chain of narration for this statement, which is also the saying of Mujahid, `Ikrimah, Sa`id bin Jubayr, Muhammad bin Ka`b Al-Qurazi, Ad-Dahhak, As-Suddi and An-Nadr bin `Arabi.

The Hypocrites and the Friends of Disbelievers are in the Lowest Depth of the Fire, Unless they Repent

Allah then states that,

(Verily, the hypocrites will be in the lowest depths of the Fire;) on the Day of Resurrection due to their tremendous Kufr. Al-Walibi (`Ali bin Abi Talhah) said that Ibn `Abbas said,

(in the lowest depths (grade) of the Fire;) means, in the bottom of the Fire. Other scholars said that the Fire has ever lower depths just as Paradise had ever higher grades. Ibn Jarir recorded that `Abdullah bin Mas`ud said that,

(Verily, the hypocrites will be in the lowest depths (grade) of the Fire), "Inside coffins of Fire that surround them, for they are closed and sealed in them." Ibn Abi Hatim recorded that when Ibn Mas`ud was asked about the hypocrites, he said, "They will be placed in coffins made of fire and they will be closed in them in the lowest depth of the Fire."

(no helper will you find for them.) to save them from their misery and painful torment. Allah then states that whoever among the hypocrites repents in this life, Allah will accept his repentance and sorrow, if his repentance were sincere and he then follows it by performing righteous deeds, all the while depending on his Lord. Allah said, a

(Except those who repent (from hypocrisy), do righteous good deeds, depend on Allah, and purify their religion for Allah) replacing showing off with sincerity, so that their good deeds will benefit them, even if they were minute.

(then they will be with the believers.) on the Day of Resurrection,

(And Allah will grant to the believers a great reward.) Allah then states that He is too Rich to need anyone and that He only punishes the servants because of their sins,

(Why should Allah punish you if you have thanked (Him) and have believed in Him.) by correcting your actions and having faith in Allah and His Messenger ,

(And Allah is Ever All-Appreciative (of good), All-Knowing.) Allah appreciates those who appreciate Him, and has knowledge of those whose hearts believe in Him, and He will give them perfect reward

The Glorious Qur'an Juz' 6 (Part 6): Chapter (Surah) 4: An-Nisaa (The Women) 148 To Chapter (Surah) 5: Al-Ma'idah (The Table, The Table Spread) 081

PART 6 FULL ARABIC TEXT

Chapter (Surah) 4: An-Nisaa 148-176

۞ لَّا يُحِبُّ ٱللَّهُ ٱلْجَهْرَ بِٱلسُّوٓءِ مِنَ ٱلْقَوْلِ إِلَّا مَن ظُلِمَ ۚ وَكَانَ ٱللَّهُ سَمِيعًا عَلِيمًا ﴿١٤٨﴾ إِن
تُبْدُوا۟ خَيْرًا أَوْ تُخْفُوهُ أَوْ تَعْفُوا۟ عَن سُوٓءٍ فَإِنَّ ٱللَّهَ كَانَ عَفُوًّا قَدِيرًا ﴿١٤٩﴾ إِنَّ ٱلَّذِينَ
يَكْفُرُونَ بِٱللَّهِ وَرُسُلِهِۦ وَيُرِيدُونَ أَن يُفَرِّقُوا۟ بَيْنَ ٱللَّهِ وَرُسُلِهِۦ وَيَقُولُونَ نُؤْمِنُ
بِبَعْضٍ وَنَكْفُرُ بِبَعْضٍ وَيُرِيدُونَ أَن يَتَّخِذُوا۟ بَيْنَ ذَٰلِكَ سَبِيلًا ﴿١٥٠﴾ أُو۟لَٰٓئِكَ هُمُ
ٱلْكَٰفِرُونَ حَقًّا ۚ وَأَعْتَدْنَا لِلْكَٰفِرِينَ عَذَابًا مُّهِينًا ﴿١٥١﴾ وَٱلَّذِينَ ءَامَنُوا۟ بِٱللَّهِ وَرُسُلِهِۦ وَلَمْ
يُفَرِّقُوا۟ بَيْنَ أَحَدٍ مِّنْهُمْ أُو۟لَٰٓئِكَ سَوْفَ يُؤْتِيهِمْ أُجُورَهُمْ ۗ وَكَانَ ٱللَّهُ غَفُورًا رَّحِيمًا ﴿١٥٢﴾
يَسْـَٔلُكَ أَهْلُ ٱلْكِتَٰبِ أَن تُنَزِّلَ عَلَيْهِمْ كِتَٰبًا مِّنَ ٱلسَّمَآءِ ۚ فَقَدْ سَأَلُوا۟ مُوسَىٰٓ أَكْبَرَ مِن
ذَٰلِكَ فَقَالُوٓا۟ أَرِنَا ٱللَّهَ جَهْرَةً فَأَخَذَتْهُمُ ٱلصَّٰعِقَةُ بِظُلْمِهِمْ ۚ ثُمَّ ٱتَّخَذُوا۟ ٱلْعِجْلَ مِنۢ بَعْدِ
مَا جَآءَتْهُمُ ٱلْبَيِّنَٰتُ فَعَفَوْنَا عَن ذَٰلِكَ ۚ وَءَاتَيْنَا مُوسَىٰ سُلْطَٰنًا مُّبِينًا ﴿١٥٣﴾ وَرَفَعْنَا

فَوۡقَهُمُ ٱلطُّورَ بِمِيثَٰقِهِمۡ وَقُلۡنَا لَهُمُ ٱدۡخُلُواْ ٱلۡبَابَ سُجَّدٗا وَقُلۡنَا لَهُمۡ لَا تَعۡدُواْ فِي ٱلسَّبۡتِ
وَأَخَذۡنَا مِنۡهُم مِّيثَٰقًا غَلِيظٗا ١٥٤ فَبِمَا نَقۡضِهِم مِّيثَٰقَهُمۡ وَكُفۡرِهِم بِـَٔايَٰتِ ٱللَّهِ وَقَتۡلِهِمُ
ٱلۡأَنۢبِيَآءَ بِغَيۡرِ حَقّٖ وَقَوۡلِهِمۡ قُلُوبُنَا غُلۡفُۢۚ بَلۡ طَبَعَ ٱللَّهُ عَلَيۡهَا بِكُفۡرِهِمۡ فَلَا يُؤۡمِنُونَ إِلَّا
قَلِيلٗا ١٥٥ وَبِكُفۡرِهِمۡ وَقَوۡلِهِمۡ عَلَىٰ مَرۡيَمَ بُهۡتَٰنًا عَظِيمٗا ١٥٦ وَقَوۡلِهِمۡ إِنَّا قَتَلۡنَا ٱلۡمَسِيحَ
عِيسَى ٱبۡنَ مَرۡيَمَ رَسُولَ ٱللَّهِ وَمَا قَتَلُوهُ وَمَا صَلَبُوهُ وَلَٰكِن شُبِّهَ لَهُمۡۚ وَإِنَّ ٱلَّذِينَ ٱخۡتَلَفُواْ
فِيهِ لَفِي شَكّٖ مِّنۡهُۚ مَا لَهُم بِهِۦ مِنۡ عِلۡمٍ إِلَّا ٱتِّبَاعَ ٱلظَّنِّۚ وَمَا قَتَلُوهُ يَقِينَۢا ١٥٧ بَل رَّفَعَهُ
ٱللَّهُ إِلَيۡهِۚ وَكَانَ ٱللَّهُ عَزِيزًا حَكِيمٗا ١٥٨ وَإِن مِّنۡ أَهۡلِ ٱلۡكِتَٰبِ إِلَّا لَيُؤۡمِنَنَّ بِهِۦ قَبۡلَ
مَوۡتِهِۦۖ وَيَوۡمَ ٱلۡقِيَٰمَةِ يَكُونُ عَلَيۡهِمۡ شَهِيدٗا ١٥٩ فَبِظُلۡمٖ مِّنَ ٱلَّذِينَ هَادُواْ حَرَّمۡنَا
عَلَيۡهِمۡ طَيِّبَٰتٍ أُحِلَّتۡ لَهُمۡ وَبِصَدِّهِمۡ عَن سَبِيلِ ٱللَّهِ كَثِيرٗا ١٦٠ وَأَخۡذِهِمُ ٱلرِّبَوٰاْ وَقَدۡ نُهُواْ
عَنۡهُ وَأَكۡلِهِمۡ أَمۡوَٰلَ ٱلنَّاسِ بِٱلۡبَٰطِلِۚ وَأَعۡتَدۡنَا لِلۡكَٰفِرِينَ مِنۡهُمۡ عَذَابًا أَلِيمٗا ١٦١ لَّٰكِنِ
ٱلرَّٰسِخُونَ فِي ٱلۡعِلۡمِ مِنۡهُمۡ وَٱلۡمُؤۡمِنُونَ يُؤۡمِنُونَ بِمَآ أُنزِلَ إِلَيۡكَ وَمَآ أُنزِلَ مِن قَبۡلِكَۚ
وَٱلۡمُقِيمِينَ ٱلصَّلَوٰةَۚ وَٱلۡمُؤۡتُونَ ٱلزَّكَوٰةَ وَٱلۡمُؤۡمِنُونَ بِٱللَّهِ وَٱلۡيَوۡمِ ٱلۡأٓخِرِ أُوْلَٰٓئِكَ
سَنُؤۡتِيهِمۡ أَجۡرًا عَظِيمًا ١٦٢ ۞ إِنَّآ أَوۡحَيۡنَآ إِلَيۡكَ كَمَآ أَوۡحَيۡنَآ إِلَىٰ نُوحٖ وَٱلنَّبِيِّـۧنَ مِنۢ
بَعۡدِهِۦۚ وَأَوۡحَيۡنَآ إِلَىٰٓ إِبۡرَٰهِيمَ وَإِسۡمَٰعِيلَ وَإِسۡحَٰقَ وَيَعۡقُوبَ وَٱلۡأَسۡبَاطِ وَعِيسَىٰ وَأَيُّوبَ
وَيُونُسَ وَهَٰرُونَ وَسُلَيۡمَٰنَۚ وَءَاتَيۡنَا دَاوُۥدَ زَبُورٗا ١٦٣ وَرُسُلٗا قَدۡ قَصَصۡنَٰهُمۡ عَلَيۡكَ مِن
قَبۡلُ وَرُسُلٗا لَّمۡ نَقۡصُصۡهُمۡ عَلَيۡكَۚ وَكَلَّمَ ٱللَّهُ مُوسَىٰ تَكۡلِيمٗا ١٦٤ رُّسُلٗا مُّبَشِّرِينَ
وَمُنذِرِينَ لِئَلَّا يَكُونَ لِلنَّاسِ عَلَى ٱللَّهِ حُجَّةُۢ بَعۡدَ ٱلرُّسُلِۚ وَكَانَ ٱللَّهُ عَزِيزًا حَكِيمٗا ١٦٥
لَّٰكِنِ ٱللَّهُ يَشۡهَدُ بِمَآ أَنزَلَ إِلَيۡكَۖ أَنزَلَهُۥ بِعِلۡمِهِۦۖ وَٱلۡمَلَٰٓئِكَةُ يَشۡهَدُونَۚ وَكَفَىٰ بِٱللَّهِ
شَهِيدًا ١٦٦ إِنَّ ٱلَّذِينَ كَفَرُواْ وَصَدُّواْ عَن سَبِيلِ ٱللَّهِ قَدۡ ضَلُّواْ ضَلَٰلَۢا بَعِيدًا ١٦٧ إِنَّ
ٱلَّذِينَ كَفَرُواْ وَظَلَمُواْ لَمۡ يَكُنِ ٱللَّهُ لِيَغۡفِرَ لَهُمۡ وَلَا لِيَهۡدِيَهُمۡ طَرِيقًا ١٦٨ إِلَّا طَرِيقَ جَهَنَّمَ
خَٰلِدِينَ فِيهَآ أَبَدٗاۚ وَكَانَ ذَٰلِكَ عَلَى ٱللَّهِ يَسِيرٗا ١٦٩ يَٰٓأَيُّهَا ٱلنَّاسُ قَدۡ جَآءَكُمُ ٱلرَّسُولُ
بِٱلۡحَقِّ مِن رَّبِّكُمۡ فَـَٔامِنُواْ خَيۡرٗا لَّكُمۡۚ وَإِن تَكۡفُرُواْ فَإِنَّ لِلَّهِ مَا فِي ٱلسَّمَٰوَٰتِ وَٱلۡأَرۡضِۚ

وَكَانَ ٱللَّهُ عَلِيمًا حَكِيمًا ﴿١٧٠﴾ يَٰٓأَهۡلَ ٱلۡكِتَٰبِ لَا تَغۡلُواْ فِي دِينِكُمۡ وَلَا تَقُولُواْ عَلَى
ٱللَّهِ إِلَّا ٱلۡحَقَّۚ إِنَّمَا ٱلۡمَسِيحُ عِيسَى ٱبۡنُ مَرۡيَمَ رَسُولُ ٱللَّهِ وَكَلِمَتُهُۥٓ أَلۡقَىٰهَآ إِلَىٰ
مَرۡيَمَ وَرُوحٞ مِّنۡهُۖ فَـَٔامِنُواْ بِٱللَّهِ وَرُسُلِهِۦۖ وَلَا تَقُولُواْ ثَلَٰثَةٌۚ ٱنتَهُواْ خَيۡرٗا لَّكُمۡۚ إِنَّمَا ٱللَّهُ
إِلَٰهٞ وَٰحِدٞۖ سُبۡحَٰنَهُۥٓ أَن يَكُونَ لَهُۥ وَلَدٞۘ لَّهُۥ مَا فِي ٱلسَّمَٰوَٰتِ وَمَا فِي ٱلۡأَرۡضِۗ وَكَفَىٰ
بِٱللَّهِ وَكِيلٗا ﴿١٧١﴾ لَّن يَسۡتَنكِفَ ٱلۡمَسِيحُ أَن يَكُونَ عَبۡدٗا لِّلَّهِ وَلَا ٱلۡمَلَٰٓئِكَةُ ٱلۡمُقَرَّبُونَۚ
وَمَن يَسۡتَنكِفۡ عَنۡ عِبَادَتِهِۦ وَيَسۡتَكۡبِرۡ فَسَيَحۡشُرُهُمۡ إِلَيۡهِ جَمِيعٗا ﴿١٧٢﴾ فَأَمَّا ٱلَّذِينَ
ءَامَنُواْ وَعَمِلُواْ ٱلصَّٰلِحَٰتِ فَيُوَفِّيهِمۡ أُجُورَهُمۡ وَيَزِيدُهُم مِّن فَضۡلِهِۦۖ وَأَمَّا ٱلَّذِينَ
ٱسۡتَنكَفُواْ وَٱسۡتَكۡبَرُواْ فَيُعَذِّبُهُمۡ عَذَابًا أَلِيمٗا وَلَا يَجِدُونَ لَهُم مِّن دُونِ ٱللَّهِ وَلِيّٗا وَلَا
نَصِيرٗا ﴿١٧٣﴾ يَٰٓأَيُّهَا ٱلنَّاسُ قَدۡ جَآءَكُم بُرۡهَٰنٞ مِّن رَّبِّكُمۡ وَأَنزَلۡنَآ إِلَيۡكُمۡ نُورٗا مُّبِينٗا ﴿١٧٤﴾
فَأَمَّا ٱلَّذِينَ ءَامَنُواْ بِٱللَّهِ وَٱعۡتَصَمُواْ بِهِۦ فَسَيُدۡخِلُهُمۡ فِي رَحۡمَةٖ مِّنۡهُ وَفَضۡلٖ وَيَهۡدِيهِمۡ
إِلَيۡهِ صِرَٰطٗا مُّسۡتَقِيمٗا ﴿١٧٥﴾ يَسۡتَفۡتُونَكَ قُلِ ٱللَّهُ يُفۡتِيكُمۡ فِي ٱلۡكَلَٰلَةِۚ إِنِ ٱمۡرُؤٌاْ هَلَكَ
لَيۡسَ لَهُۥ وَلَدٞ وَلَهُۥٓ أُخۡتٞ فَلَهَا نِصۡفُ مَا تَرَكَۚ وَهُوَ يَرِثُهَآ إِن لَّمۡ يَكُن لَّهَا وَلَدٞۚ فَإِن كَانَتَا
ٱثۡنَتَيۡنِ فَلَهُمَا ٱلثُّلُثَانِ مِمَّا تَرَكَۚ وَإِن كَانُوٓاْ إِخۡوَةٗ رِّجَالٗا وَنِسَآءٗ فَلِلذَّكَرِ مِثۡلُ حَظِّ ٱلۡأُنثَيَيۡنِۗ
يُبَيِّنُ ٱللَّهُ لَكُمۡ أَن تَضِلُّواْۗ وَٱللَّهُ بِكُلِّ شَيۡءٍ عَلِيمُۢ ﴿١٧٦﴾

Chapter (Surah) 5: Al-Maidah 001-081

بِسۡمِ ٱللَّهِ ٱلرَّحۡمَٰنِ ٱلرَّحِيمِ

يَٰٓأَيُّهَا ٱلَّذِينَ ءَامَنُوٓاْ أَوۡفُواْ بِٱلۡعُقُودِۚ أُحِلَّتۡ لَكُم بَهِيمَةُ ٱلۡأَنۡعَٰمِ إِلَّا مَا يُتۡلَىٰ عَلَيۡكُمۡ غَيۡرَ
مُحِلِّي ٱلصَّيۡدِ وَأَنتُمۡ حُرُمٌۗ إِنَّ ٱللَّهَ يَحۡكُمُ مَا يُرِيدُ ﴿١﴾ يَٰٓأَيُّهَا ٱلَّذِينَ ءَامَنُواْ لَا تُحِلُّواْ شَعَٰٓئِرَ ٱللَّهِ
وَلَا ٱلشَّهۡرَ ٱلۡحَرَامَ وَلَا ٱلۡهَدۡيَ وَلَا ٱلۡقَلَٰٓئِدَ وَلَآ ءَآمِّينَ ٱلۡبَيۡتَ ٱلۡحَرَامَ يَبۡتَغُونَ فَضۡلٗا مِّن رَّبِّهِمۡ
وَرِضۡوَٰنٗاۚ وَإِذَا حَلَلۡتُمۡ فَٱصۡطَادُواْۚ وَلَا يَجۡرِمَنَّكُمۡ شَنَـَٔانُ قَوۡمٍ أَن صَدُّوكُمۡ عَنِ ٱلۡمَسۡجِدِ
ٱلۡحَرَامِ أَن تَعۡتَدُواْۘ وَتَعَاوَنُواْ عَلَى ٱلۡبِرِّ وَٱلتَّقۡوَىٰۖ وَلَا تَعَاوَنُواْ عَلَى ٱلۡإِثۡمِ وَٱلۡعُدۡوَٰنِۚ وَٱتَّقُواْ

ٱللَّهَ ۖ إِنَّ ٱللَّهَ شَدِيدُ ٱلْعِقَابِ ﴿٢﴾ حُرِّمَتْ عَلَيْكُمُ ٱلْمَيْتَةُ وَٱلدَّمُ وَلَحْمُ ٱلْخِنزِيرِ وَمَآ أُهِلَّ لِغَيْرِ
ٱللَّهِ بِهِۦ وَٱلْمُنْخَنِقَةُ وَٱلْمَوْقُوذَةُ وَٱلْمُتَرَدِّيَةُ وَٱلنَّطِيحَةُ وَمَآ أَكَلَ ٱلسَّبُعُ إِلَّا مَا ذَكَّيْتُمْ وَمَا
ذُبِحَ عَلَى ٱلنُّصُبِ وَأَن تَسْتَقْسِمُوا۟ بِٱلْأَزْلَـٰمِ ۚ ذَٰلِكُمْ فِسْقٌ ۗ ٱلْيَوْمَ يَئِسَ ٱلَّذِينَ كَفَرُوا۟ مِن
دِينِكُمْ فَلَا تَخْشَوْهُمْ وَٱخْشَوْنِ ۚ ٱلْيَوْمَ أَكْمَلْتُ لَكُمْ دِينَكُمْ وَأَتْمَمْتُ عَلَيْكُمْ نِعْمَتِى
وَرَضِيتُ لَكُمُ ٱلْإِسْلَـٰمَ دِينًا ۚ فَمَنِ ٱضْطُرَّ فِى مَخْمَصَةٍ غَيْرَ مُتَجَانِفٍ لِّإِثْمٍ ۙ فَإِنَّ ٱللَّهَ غَفُورٌ
رَّحِيمٌ ﴿٣﴾ يَسْـَٔلُونَكَ مَاذَآ أُحِلَّ لَهُمْ ۖ قُلْ أُحِلَّ لَكُمُ ٱلطَّيِّبَـٰتُ ۙ وَمَا عَلَّمْتُم مِّنَ ٱلْجَوَارِحِ
مُكَلِّبِينَ تُعَلِّمُونَهُنَّ مِمَّا عَلَّمَكُمُ ٱللَّهُ ۖ فَكُلُوا۟ مِمَّآ أَمْسَكْنَ عَلَيْكُمْ وَٱذْكُرُوا۟ ٱسْمَ ٱللَّهِ عَلَيْهِ ۖ وَٱتَّقُوا۟
ٱللَّهَ ۚ إِنَّ ٱللَّهَ سَرِيعُ ٱلْحِسَابِ ﴿٤﴾ ٱلْيَوْمَ أُحِلَّ لَكُمُ ٱلطَّيِّبَـٰتُ ۖ وَطَعَامُ ٱلَّذِينَ أُوتُوا۟ ٱلْكِتَـٰبَ
حِلٌّ لَّكُمْ وَطَعَامُكُمْ حِلٌّ لَّهُمْ ۖ وَٱلْمُحْصَنَـٰتُ مِنَ ٱلْمُؤْمِنَـٰتِ وَٱلْمُحْصَنَـٰتُ مِنَ ٱلَّذِينَ أُوتُوا۟
ٱلْكِتَـٰبَ مِن قَبْلِكُمْ إِذَآ ءَاتَيْتُمُوهُنَّ أُجُورَهُنَّ مُحْصِنِينَ غَيْرَ مُسَـٰفِحِينَ وَلَا مُتَّخِذِىٓ
أَخْدَانٍ ۗ وَمَن يَكْفُرْ بِٱلْإِيمَـٰنِ فَقَدْ حَبِطَ عَمَلُهُۥ وَهُوَ فِى ٱلْـَٔاخِرَةِ مِنَ ٱلْخَـٰسِرِينَ ﴿٥﴾ يَـٰٓأَيُّهَا
ٱلَّذِينَ ءَامَنُوٓا۟ إِذَا قُمْتُمْ إِلَى ٱلصَّلَوٰةِ فَٱغْسِلُوا۟ وُجُوهَكُمْ وَأَيْدِيَكُمْ إِلَى ٱلْمَرَافِقِ
وَٱمْسَحُوا۟ بِرُءُوسِكُمْ وَأَرْجُلَكُمْ إِلَى ٱلْكَعْبَيْنِ ۚ وَإِن كُنتُمْ جُنُبًا فَٱطَّهَّرُوا۟ ۚ وَإِن كُنتُم
مَّرْضَىٰٓ أَوْ عَلَىٰ سَفَرٍ أَوْ جَآءَ أَحَدٌ مِّنكُم مِّنَ ٱلْغَآئِطِ أَوْ لَـٰمَسْتُمُ ٱلنِّسَآءَ فَلَمْ تَجِدُوا۟ مَآءً
فَتَيَمَّمُوا۟ صَعِيدًا طَيِّبًا فَٱمْسَحُوا۟ بِوُجُوهِكُمْ وَأَيْدِيكُم مِّنْهُ ۚ مَا يُرِيدُ ٱللَّهُ لِيَجْعَلَ
عَلَيْكُم مِّنْ حَرَجٍ وَلَـٰكِن يُرِيدُ لِيُطَهِّرَكُمْ وَلِيُتِمَّ نِعْمَتَهُۥ عَلَيْكُمْ لَعَلَّكُمْ
تَشْكُرُونَ ﴿٦﴾ وَٱذْكُرُوا۟ نِعْمَةَ ٱللَّهِ عَلَيْكُمْ وَمِيثَـٰقَهُ ٱلَّذِى وَاثَقَكُم بِهِۦٓ إِذْ قُلْتُمْ سَمِعْنَا
وَأَطَعْنَا ۖ وَٱتَّقُوا۟ ٱللَّهَ ۚ إِنَّ ٱللَّهَ عَلِيمٌۢ بِذَاتِ ٱلصُّدُورِ ﴿٧﴾ يَـٰٓأَيُّهَا ٱلَّذِينَ ءَامَنُوا۟ كُونُوا۟
قَوَّٰمِينَ لِلَّهِ شُهَدَآءَ بِٱلْقِسْطِ ۖ وَلَا يَجْرِمَنَّكُمْ شَنَـَٔانُ قَوْمٍ عَلَىٰٓ أَلَّا تَعْدِلُوا۟ ۚ ٱعْدِلُوا۟ هُوَ
أَقْرَبُ لِلتَّقْوَىٰ ۖ وَٱتَّقُوا۟ ٱللَّهَ ۚ إِنَّ ٱللَّهَ خَبِيرٌۢ بِمَا تَعْمَلُونَ ﴿٨﴾ وَعَدَ ٱللَّهُ ٱلَّذِينَ ءَامَنُوا۟
وَعَمِلُوا۟ ٱلصَّـٰلِحَـٰتِ ۙ لَهُم مَّغْفِرَةٌ وَأَجْرٌ عَظِيمٌ ﴿٩﴾ وَٱلَّذِينَ كَفَرُوا۟ وَكَذَّبُوا۟ بِـَٔايَـٰتِنَآ
أُو۟لَـٰٓئِكَ أَصْحَـٰبُ ٱلْجَحِيمِ ﴿١٠﴾ يَـٰٓأَيُّهَا ٱلَّذِينَ ءَامَنُوا۟ ٱذْكُرُوا۟ نِعْمَتَ ٱللَّهِ عَلَيْكُمْ إِذْ هَمَّ

قَوْمٌ أَن يَبْسُطُوٓا۟ إِلَيْكُمْ أَيْدِيَهُمْ فَكَفَّ أَيْدِيَهُمْ عَنكُمْ ۖ وَٱتَّقُوا۟ ٱللَّهَ ۚ وَعَلَى ٱللَّهِ فَلْيَتَوَكَّلِ
ٱلْمُؤْمِنُونَ ﴿١١﴾ ۞ وَلَقَدْ أَخَذَ ٱللَّهُ مِيثَـٰقَ بَنِىٓ إِسْرَٰٓءِيلَ وَبَعَثْنَا مِنْهُمُ ٱثْنَىْ عَشَرَ نَقِيبًا ۖ
وَقَالَ ٱللَّهُ إِنِّى مَعَكُمْ ۖ لَئِنْ أَقَمْتُمُ ٱلصَّلَوٰةَ وَءَاتَيْتُمُ ٱلزَّكَوٰةَ وَءَامَنتُم بِرُسُلِى وَعَزَّرْتُمُوهُمْ
وَأَقْرَضْتُمُ ٱللَّهَ قَرْضًا حَسَنًا لَّأُكَفِّرَنَّ عَنكُمْ سَيِّـَٔاتِكُمْ وَلَأُدْخِلَنَّكُمْ جَنَّـٰتٍ تَجْرِى مِن
تَحْتِهَا ٱلْأَنْهَـٰرُ ۚ فَمَن كَفَرَ بَعْدَ ذَٰلِكَ مِنكُمْ فَقَدْ ضَلَّ سَوَآءَ ٱلسَّبِيلِ ﴿١٢﴾ فَبِمَا
نَقْضِهِم مِّيثَـٰقَهُمْ لَعَنَّـٰهُمْ وَجَعَلْنَا قُلُوبَهُمْ قَـٰسِيَةً ۖ يُحَرِّفُونَ ٱلْكَلِمَ عَن مَّوَاضِعِهِۦ ۙ
وَنَسُوا۟ حَظًّا مِّمَّا ذُكِّرُوا۟ بِهِۦ ۚ وَلَا تَزَالُ تَطَّلِعُ عَلَىٰ خَآئِنَةٍ مِّنْهُمْ إِلَّا قَلِيلًا مِّنْهُمْ ۖ فَٱعْفُ عَنْهُمْ
وَٱصْفَحْ ۚ إِنَّ ٱللَّهَ يُحِبُّ ٱلْمُحْسِنِينَ ﴿١٣﴾ وَمِنَ ٱلَّذِينَ قَالُوٓا۟ إِنَّا نَصَـٰرَىٰٓ أَخَذْنَا
مِيثَـٰقَهُمْ فَنَسُوا۟ حَظًّا مِّمَّا ذُكِّرُوا۟ بِهِۦ فَأَغْرَيْنَا بَيْنَهُمُ ٱلْعَدَاوَةَ وَٱلْبَغْضَآءَ إِلَىٰ يَوْمِ
ٱلْقِيَـٰمَةِ ۚ وَسَوْفَ يُنَبِّئُهُمُ ٱللَّهُ بِمَا كَانُوا۟ يَصْنَعُونَ ﴿١٤﴾ يَـٰٓأَهْلَ ٱلْكِتَـٰبِ قَدْ
جَآءَكُمْ رَسُولُنَا يُبَيِّنُ لَكُمْ كَثِيرًا مِّمَّا كُنتُمْ تُخْفُونَ مِنَ ٱلْكِتَـٰبِ وَيَعْفُوا۟
عَن كَثِيرٍ ۚ قَدْ جَآءَكُم مِّنَ ٱللَّهِ نُورٌ وَكِتَـٰبٌ مُّبِينٌ ﴿١٥﴾ يَهْدِى بِهِ ٱللَّهُ مَنِ
ٱتَّبَعَ رِضْوَٰنَهُۥ سُبُلَ ٱلسَّلَـٰمِ وَيُخْرِجُهُم مِّنَ ٱلظُّلُمَـٰتِ إِلَى ٱلنُّورِ بِإِذْنِهِۦ وَيَهْدِيهِمْ إِلَىٰ
صِرَٰطٍ مُّسْتَقِيمٍ ﴿١٦﴾ لَّقَدْ كَفَرَ ٱلَّذِينَ قَالُوٓا۟ إِنَّ ٱللَّهَ هُوَ ٱلْمَسِيحُ ٱبْنُ مَرْيَمَ ۚ قُلْ فَمَن
يَمْلِكُ مِنَ ٱللَّهِ شَيْـًٔا إِنْ أَرَادَ أَن يُهْلِكَ ٱلْمَسِيحَ ٱبْنَ مَرْيَمَ وَأُمَّهُۥ وَمَن فِى
ٱلْأَرْضِ جَمِيعًا ۗ وَلِلَّهِ مُلْكُ ٱلسَّمَـٰوَٰتِ وَٱلْأَرْضِ وَمَا بَيْنَهُمَا ۚ يَخْلُقُ مَا يَشَآءُ ۚ وَٱللَّهُ عَلَىٰ كُلِّ
شَىْءٍ قَدِيرٌ ﴿١٧﴾ وَقَالَتِ ٱلْيَهُودُ وَٱلنَّصَـٰرَىٰ نَحْنُ أَبْنَـٰٓؤُا۟ ٱللَّهِ وَأَحِبَّـٰٓؤُهُۥ ۚ قُلْ فَلِمَ يُعَذِّبُكُم
بِذُنُوبِكُم ۖ بَلْ أَنتُم بَشَرٌ مِّمَّنْ خَلَقَ ۚ يَغْفِرُ لِمَن يَشَآءُ وَيُعَذِّبُ مَن يَشَآءُ ۚ وَلِلَّهِ مُلْكُ
ٱلسَّمَـٰوَٰتِ وَٱلْأَرْضِ وَمَا بَيْنَهُمَا ۖ وَإِلَيْهِ ٱلْمَصِيرُ ﴿١٨﴾ يَـٰٓأَهْلَ ٱلْكِتَـٰبِ قَدْ جَآءَكُمْ رَسُولُنَا
يُبَيِّنُ لَكُمْ عَلَىٰ فَتْرَةٍ مِّنَ ٱلرُّسُلِ أَن تَقُولُوا۟ مَا جَآءَنَا مِنۢ بَشِيرٍ وَلَا نَذِيرٍ ۖ فَقَدْ جَآءَكُم بَشِيرٌ
وَنَذِيرٌ ۗ وَٱللَّهُ عَلَىٰ كُلِّ شَىْءٍ قَدِيرٌ ﴿١٩﴾ وَإِذْ قَالَ مُوسَىٰ لِقَوْمِهِۦ يَـٰقَوْمِ ٱذْكُرُوا۟ نِعْمَةَ ٱللَّهِ
عَلَيْكُمْ إِذْ جَعَلَ فِيكُمْ أَنۢبِيَآءَ وَجَعَلَكُم مُّلُوكًا وَءَاتَىٰكُم مَّا لَمْ يُؤْتِ أَحَدًا مِّنَ ٱلْعَـٰلَمِينَ ﴿٢٠﴾

يَٰقَوۡمِ ٱدۡخُلُواْ ٱلۡأَرۡضَ ٱلۡمُقَدَّسَةَ ٱلَّتِي كَتَبَ ٱللَّهُ لَكُمۡ وَلَا تَرۡتَدُّواْ عَلَىٰٓ أَدۡبَارِكُمۡ فَتَنقَلِبُواْ
خَٰسِرِينَ ﴿٢١﴾ قَالُواْ يَٰمُوسَىٰٓ إِنَّ فِيهَا قَوۡمٗا جَبَّارِينَ وَإِنَّا لَن نَّدۡخُلَهَا حَتَّىٰ يَخۡرُجُواْ مِنۡهَا فَإِن
يَخۡرُجُواْ مِنۡهَا فَإِنَّا دَٰخِلُونَ ﴿٢٢﴾ قَالَ رَجُلَانِ مِنَ ٱلَّذِينَ يَخَافُونَ أَنۡعَمَ ٱللَّهُ عَلَيۡهِمَا
ٱدۡخُلُواْ عَلَيۡهِمُ ٱلۡبَابَ فَإِذَا دَخَلۡتُمُوهُ فَإِنَّكُمۡ غَٰلِبُونَۚ وَعَلَى ٱللَّهِ فَتَوَكَّلُوٓاْ إِن كُنتُم
مُّؤۡمِنِينَ ﴿٢٣﴾ قَالُواْ يَٰمُوسَىٰٓ إِنَّا لَن نَّدۡخُلَهَآ أَبَدٗا مَّا دَامُواْ فِيهَاۖ فَٱذۡهَبۡ أَنتَ وَرَبُّكَ
فَقَٰتِلَآ إِنَّا هَٰهُنَا قَٰعِدُونَ ﴿٢٤﴾ قَالَ رَبِّ إِنِّي لَآ أَمۡلِكُ إِلَّا نَفۡسِي وَأَخِيۖ فَٱفۡرُقۡ بَيۡنَنَا
وَبَيۡنَ ٱلۡقَوۡمِ ٱلۡفَٰسِقِينَ ﴿٢٥﴾ قَالَ فَإِنَّهَا مُحَرَّمَةٌ عَلَيۡهِمۡۛ أَرۡبَعِينَ سَنَةٗۛ يَتِيهُونَ فِي
ٱلۡأَرۡضِۚ فَلَا تَأۡسَ عَلَى ٱلۡقَوۡمِ ٱلۡفَٰسِقِينَ ﴿٢٦﴾ ۞وَٱتۡلُ عَلَيۡهِمۡ نَبَأَ ٱبۡنَيۡ ءَادَمَ بِٱلۡحَقِّ إِذۡ
قَرَّبَا قُرۡبَانٗا فَتُقُبِّلَ مِنۡ أَحَدِهِمَا وَلَمۡ يُتَقَبَّلۡ مِنَ ٱلۡأٓخَرِ قَالَ لَأَقۡتُلَنَّكَۖ قَالَ إِنَّمَا يَتَقَبَّلُ ٱللَّهُ
مِنَ ٱلۡمُتَّقِينَ ﴿٢٧﴾ لَئِنۢ بَسَطتَ إِلَيَّ يَدَكَ لِتَقۡتُلَنِي مَآ أَنَا۠ بِبَاسِطٖ يَدِيَ إِلَيۡكَ لِأَقۡتُلَكَۖ إِنِّيٓ
أَخَافُ ٱللَّهَ رَبَّ ٱلۡعَٰلَمِينَ ﴿٢٨﴾ إِنِّيٓ أُرِيدُ أَن تَبُوٓأَ بِإِثۡمِي وَإِثۡمِكَ فَتَكُونَ مِنۡ أَصۡحَٰبِ ٱلنَّارِۚ
وَذَٰلِكَ جَزَٰٓؤُاْ ٱلظَّٰلِمِينَ ﴿٢٩﴾ فَطَوَّعَتۡ لَهُۥ نَفۡسُهُۥ قَتۡلَ أَخِيهِ فَقَتَلَهُۥ فَأَصۡبَحَ مِنَ
ٱلۡخَٰسِرِينَ ﴿٣٠﴾ فَبَعَثَ ٱللَّهُ غُرَابٗا يَبۡحَثُ فِي ٱلۡأَرۡضِ لِيُرِيَهُۥ كَيۡفَ يُوَٰرِي سَوۡءَةَ أَخِيهِۚ
قَالَ يَٰوَيۡلَتَىٰٓ أَعَجَزۡتُ أَنۡ أَكُونَ مِثۡلَ هَٰذَا ٱلۡغُرَابِ فَأُوَٰرِيَ سَوۡءَةَ أَخِيۖ فَأَصۡبَحَ مِنَ
ٱلنَّٰدِمِينَ ﴿٣١﴾ مِنۡ أَجۡلِ ذَٰلِكَ كَتَبۡنَا عَلَىٰ بَنِيٓ إِسۡرَٰٓءِيلَ أَنَّهُۥ مَن قَتَلَ نَفۡسَۢا بِغَيۡرِ نَفۡسٍ أَوۡ
فَسَادٖ فِي ٱلۡأَرۡضِ فَكَأَنَّمَا قَتَلَ ٱلنَّاسَ جَمِيعٗا وَمَنۡ أَحۡيَاهَا فَكَأَنَّمَآ أَحۡيَا ٱلنَّاسَ
جَمِيعٗاۚ وَلَقَدۡ جَآءَتۡهُمۡ رُسُلُنَا بِٱلۡبَيِّنَٰتِ ثُمَّ إِنَّ كَثِيرٗا مِّنۡهُم بَعۡدَ ذَٰلِكَ فِي ٱلۡأَرۡضِ
لَمُسۡرِفُونَ ﴿٣٢﴾ إِنَّمَا جَزَٰٓؤُاْ ٱلَّذِينَ يُحَارِبُونَ ٱللَّهَ وَرَسُولَهُۥ وَيَسۡعَوۡنَ فِي ٱلۡأَرۡضِ فَسَادًا أَن
يُقَتَّلُوٓاْ أَوۡ يُصَلَّبُوٓاْ أَوۡ تُقَطَّعَ أَيۡدِيهِمۡ وَأَرۡجُلُهُم مِّنۡ خِلَٰفٍ أَوۡ يُنفَوۡاْ مِنَ ٱلۡأَرۡضِۚ ذَٰلِكَ
لَهُمۡ خِزۡيٞ فِي ٱلدُّنۡيَاۖ وَلَهُمۡ فِي ٱلۡأٓخِرَةِ عَذَابٌ عَظِيمٌ ﴿٣٣﴾ إِلَّا ٱلَّذِينَ تَابُواْ مِن قَبۡلِ أَن
تَقۡدِرُواْ عَلَيۡهِمۡۖ فَٱعۡلَمُوٓاْ أَنَّ ٱللَّهَ غَفُورٞ رَّحِيمٞ ﴿٣٤﴾ يَٰٓأَيُّهَا ٱلَّذِينَ ءَامَنُواْ ٱتَّقُواْ ٱللَّهَ
وَٱبۡتَغُوٓاْ إِلَيۡهِ ٱلۡوَسِيلَةَ وَجَٰهِدُواْ فِي سَبِيلِهِۦ لَعَلَّكُمۡ تُفۡلِحُونَ ﴿٣٥﴾ إِنَّ ٱلَّذِينَ كَفَرُواْ

لَوْ أَنَّ لَهُم مَّا فِى ٱلْأَرْضِ جَمِيعًا وَمِثْلَهُۥ مَعَهُۥ لِيَفْتَدُوا۟ بِهِۦ مِنْ عَذَابِ يَوْمِ ٱلْقِيَٰمَةِ مَا
تُقُبِّلَ مِنْهُمْ ۖ وَلَهُمْ عَذَابٌ أَلِيمٌ ﴿٣٦﴾ يُرِيدُونَ أَن يَخْرُجُوا۟ مِنَ ٱلنَّارِ وَمَا هُم بِخَٰرِجِينَ
مِنْهَا ۖ وَلَهُمْ عَذَابٌ مُّقِيمٌ ﴿٣٧﴾ وَٱلسَّارِقُ وَٱلسَّارِقَةُ فَٱقْطَعُوٓا۟ أَيْدِيَهُمَا جَزَآءًۢ بِمَا كَسَبَا نَكَٰلًا
مِّنَ ٱللَّهِ ۗ وَٱللَّهُ عَزِيزٌ حَكِيمٌ ﴿٣٨﴾ فَمَن تَابَ مِنۢ بَعْدِ ظُلْمِهِۦ وَأَصْلَحَ فَإِنَّ ٱللَّهَ يَتُوبُ
عَلَيْهِ ۗ إِنَّ ٱللَّهَ غَفُورٌ رَّحِيمٌ ﴿٣٩﴾ أَلَمْ تَعْلَمْ أَنَّ ٱللَّهَ لَهُۥ مُلْكُ ٱلسَّمَٰوَٰتِ وَٱلْأَرْضِ يُعَذِّبُ مَن
يَشَآءُ وَيَغْفِرُ لِمَن يَشَآءُ ۗ وَٱللَّهُ عَلَىٰ كُلِّ شَىْءٍ قَدِيرٌ ﴿٤٠﴾ ۞ يَٰٓأَيُّهَا ٱلرَّسُولُ لَا يَحْزُنكَ
ٱلَّذِينَ يُسَٰرِعُونَ فِى ٱلْكُفْرِ مِنَ ٱلَّذِينَ قَالُوٓا۟ ءَامَنَّا بِأَفْوَٰهِهِمْ وَلَمْ تُؤْمِن قُلُوبُهُمْ ۛ
وَمِنَ ٱلَّذِينَ هَادُوا۟ ۛ سَمَّٰعُونَ لِلْكَذِبِ سَمَّٰعُونَ لِقَوْمٍ ءَاخَرِينَ لَمْ يَأْتُوكَ ۖ
يُحَرِّفُونَ ٱلْكَلِمَ مِنۢ بَعْدِ مَوَاضِعِهِۦ ۖ يَقُولُونَ إِنْ أُوتِيتُمْ هَٰذَا فَخُذُوهُ وَإِن لَّمْ تُؤْتَوْهُ
فَٱحْذَرُوا۟ ۚ وَمَن يُرِدِ ٱللَّهُ فِتْنَتَهُۥ فَلَن تَمْلِكَ لَهُۥ مِنَ ٱللَّهِ شَيْـًٔا ۚ أُو۟لَٰٓئِكَ ٱلَّذِينَ لَمْ يُرِدِ ٱللَّهُ
أَن يُطَهِّرَ قُلُوبَهُمْ ۚ لَهُمْ فِى ٱلدُّنْيَا خِزْىٌ ۖ وَلَهُمْ فِى ٱلْءَاخِرَةِ عَذَابٌ عَظِيمٌ ﴿٤١﴾ سَمَّٰعُونَ
لِلْكَذِبِ أَكَّٰلُونَ لِلسُّحْتِ ۚ فَإِن جَآءُوكَ فَٱحْكُم بَيْنَهُمْ أَوْ أَعْرِضْ عَنْهُمْ ۖ وَإِن تُعْرِضْ
عَنْهُمْ فَلَن يَضُرُّوكَ شَيْـًٔا ۖ وَإِنْ حَكَمْتَ فَٱحْكُم بَيْنَهُم بِٱلْقِسْطِ ۚ إِنَّ ٱللَّهَ يُحِبُّ
ٱلْمُقْسِطِينَ ﴿٤٢﴾ وَكَيْفَ يُحَكِّمُونَكَ وَعِندَهُمُ ٱلتَّوْرَىٰةُ فِيهَا حُكْمُ ٱللَّهِ ثُمَّ يَتَوَلَّوْنَ مِنۢ
بَعْدِ ذَٰلِكَ ۚ وَمَآ أُو۟لَٰٓئِكَ بِٱلْمُؤْمِنِينَ ﴿٤٣﴾ إِنَّآ أَنزَلْنَا ٱلتَّوْرَىٰةَ فِيهَا هُدًى وَنُورٌ ۚ يَحْكُمُ بِهَا
ٱلنَّبِيُّونَ ٱلَّذِينَ أَسْلَمُوا۟ لِلَّذِينَ هَادُوا۟ وَٱلرَّبَّٰنِيُّونَ وَٱلْأَحْبَارُ بِمَا ٱسْتُحْفِظُوا۟ مِن كِتَٰبِ
ٱللَّهِ وَكَانُوا۟ عَلَيْهِ شُهَدَآءَ ۚ فَلَا تَخْشَوُا۟ ٱلنَّاسَ وَٱخْشَوْنِ وَلَا تَشْتَرُوا۟ بِـَٔايَٰتِى ثَمَنًا قَلِيلًا ۚ
وَمَن لَّمْ يَحْكُم بِمَآ أَنزَلَ ٱللَّهُ فَأُو۟لَٰٓئِكَ هُمُ ٱلْكَٰفِرُونَ ﴿٤٤﴾ وَكَتَبْنَا عَلَيْهِمْ فِيهَآ أَنَّ ٱلنَّفْسَ
بِٱلنَّفْسِ وَٱلْعَيْنَ بِٱلْعَيْنِ وَٱلْأَنفَ بِٱلْأَنفِ وَٱلْأُذُنَ بِٱلْأُذُنِ وَٱلسِّنَّ بِٱلسِّنِّ وَٱلْجُرُوحَ
قِصَاصٌ ۚ فَمَن تَصَدَّقَ بِهِۦ فَهُوَ كَفَّارَةٌ لَّهُۥ ۚ وَمَن لَّمْ يَحْكُم بِمَآ أَنزَلَ ٱللَّهُ فَأُو۟لَٰٓئِكَ
هُمُ ٱلظَّٰلِمُونَ ﴿٤٥﴾ وَقَفَّيْنَا عَلَىٰٓ ءَاثَٰرِهِم بِعِيسَى ٱبْنِ مَرْيَمَ مُصَدِّقًا لِّمَا بَيْنَ يَدَيْهِ مِنَ
ٱلتَّوْرَىٰةِ ۖ وَءَاتَيْنَٰهُ ٱلْإِنجِيلَ فِيهِ هُدًى وَنُورٌ وَمُصَدِّقًا لِّمَا بَيْنَ يَدَيْهِ مِنَ ٱلتَّوْرَىٰةِ وَهُدًى

وَمَوْعِظَةً لِّلْمُتَّقِينَ (٤٦) وَلْيَحْكُمْ أَهْلُ ٱلْإِنجِيلِ بِمَآ أَنزَلَ ٱللَّهُ فِيهِ ۚ وَمَن لَّمْ يَحْكُم بِمَآ
أَنزَلَ ٱللَّهُ فَأُو۟لَـٰٓئِكَ هُمُ ٱلْفَـٰسِقُونَ (٤٧) وَأَنزَلْنَآ إِلَيْكَ ٱلْكِتَـٰبَ بِٱلْحَقِّ مُصَدِّقًا لِّمَا
بَيْنَ يَدَيْهِ مِنَ ٱلْكِتَـٰبِ وَمُهَيْمِنًا عَلَيْهِ ۖ فَٱحْكُم بَيْنَهُم بِمَآ أَنزَلَ ٱللَّهُ ۖ وَلَا تَتَّبِعْ
أَهْوَآءَهُمْ عَمَّا جَآءَكَ مِنَ ٱلْحَقِّ ۚ لِكُلٍّ جَعَلْنَا مِنكُمْ شِرْعَةً وَمِنْهَاجًا ۚ وَلَوْ شَآءَ ٱللَّهُ
لَجَعَلَكُمْ أُمَّةً وَٰحِدَةً وَلَـٰكِن لِّيَبْلُوَكُمْ فِى مَآ ءَاتَىٰكُمْ ۖ فَٱسْتَبِقُوا۟ ٱلْخَيْرَٰتِ ۚ إِلَى ٱللَّهِ
مَرْجِعُكُمْ جَمِيعًا فَيُنَبِّئُكُم بِمَا كُنتُمْ فِيهِ تَخْتَلِفُونَ (٤٨) وَأَنِ ٱحْكُم بَيْنَهُم بِمَآ أَنزَلَ ٱللَّهُ
وَلَا تَتَّبِعْ أَهْوَآءَهُمْ وَٱحْذَرْهُمْ أَن يَفْتِنُوكَ عَنۢ بَعْضِ مَآ أَنزَلَ ٱللَّهُ إِلَيْكَ ۖ فَإِن تَوَلَّوْا۟
فَٱعْلَمْ أَنَّمَا يُرِيدُ ٱللَّهُ أَن يُصِيبَهُم بِبَعْضِ ذُنُوبِهِمْ ۗ وَإِنَّ كَثِيرًا مِّنَ ٱلنَّاسِ لَفَـٰسِقُونَ (٤٩)
أَفَحُكْمَ ٱلْجَـٰهِلِيَّةِ يَبْغُونَ ۚ وَمَنْ أَحْسَنُ مِنَ ٱللَّهِ حُكْمًا لِّقَوْمٍ يُوقِنُونَ (٥٠) ۞ يَـٰٓأَيُّهَا ٱلَّذِينَ
ءَامَنُوا۟ لَا تَتَّخِذُوا۟ ٱلْيَهُودَ وَٱلنَّصَـٰرَىٰٓ أَوْلِيَآءَ ۘ بَعْضُهُمْ أَوْلِيَآءُ بَعْضٍ ۚ وَمَن يَتَوَلَّهُم مِّنكُمْ
فَإِنَّهُۥ مِنْهُمْ ۗ إِنَّ ٱللَّهَ لَا يَهْدِى ٱلْقَوْمَ ٱلظَّـٰلِمِينَ (٥١) فَتَرَى ٱلَّذِينَ فِى قُلُوبِهِم مَّرَضٌ
يُسَـٰرِعُونَ فِيهِمْ يَقُولُونَ نَخْشَىٰٓ أَن تُصِيبَنَا دَآئِرَةٌ ۚ فَعَسَى ٱللَّهُ أَن يَأْتِىَ بِٱلْفَتْحِ أَوْ أَمْرٍ مِّنْ
عِندِهِۦ فَيُصْبِحُوا۟ عَلَىٰ مَآ أَسَرُّوا۟ فِىٓ أَنفُسِهِمْ نَـٰدِمِينَ (٥٢) وَيَقُولُ ٱلَّذِينَ ءَامَنُوٓا۟ أَهَـٰٓؤُلَآءِ
ٱلَّذِينَ أَقْسَمُوا۟ بِٱللَّهِ جَهْدَ أَيْمَـٰنِهِمْ ۙ إِنَّهُمْ لَمَعَكُمْ ۚ حَبِطَتْ أَعْمَـٰلُهُمْ فَأَصْبَحُوا۟ خَـٰسِرِينَ (٥٣)
يَـٰٓأَيُّهَا ٱلَّذِينَ ءَامَنُوا۟ مَن يَرْتَدَّ مِنكُمْ عَن دِينِهِۦ فَسَوْفَ يَأْتِى ٱللَّهُ بِقَوْمٍ يُحِبُّهُمْ وَيُحِبُّونَهُۥٓ أَذِلَّةٍ
عَلَى ٱلْمُؤْمِنِينَ أَعِزَّةٍ عَلَى ٱلْكَـٰفِرِينَ يُجَـٰهِدُونَ فِى سَبِيلِ ٱللَّهِ وَلَا يَخَافُونَ لَوْمَةَ لَآئِمٍ ۚ
ذَٰلِكَ فَضْلُ ٱللَّهِ يُؤْتِيهِ مَن يَشَآءُ ۚ وَٱللَّهُ وَٰسِعٌ عَلِيمٌ (٥٤) إِنَّمَا وَلِيُّكُمُ ٱللَّهُ وَرَسُولُهُۥ وَٱلَّذِينَ
ءَامَنُوا۟ ٱلَّذِينَ يُقِيمُونَ ٱلصَّلَوٰةَ وَيُؤْتُونَ ٱلزَّكَوٰةَ وَهُمْ رَٰكِعُونَ (٥٥) وَمَن يَتَوَلَّ ٱللَّهَ وَرَسُولَهُۥ
وَٱلَّذِينَ ءَامَنُوا۟ فَإِنَّ حِزْبَ ٱللَّهِ هُمُ ٱلْغَـٰلِبُونَ (٥٦) يَـٰٓأَيُّهَا ٱلَّذِينَ ءَامَنُوا۟ لَا تَتَّخِذُوا۟ ٱلَّذِينَ
ٱتَّخَذُوا۟ دِينَكُمْ هُزُوًا وَلَعِبًا مِّنَ ٱلَّذِينَ أُوتُوا۟ ٱلْكِتَـٰبَ مِن قَبْلِكُمْ وَٱلْكُفَّارَ أَوْلِيَآءَ ۚ وَٱتَّقُوا۟
ٱللَّهَ إِن كُنتُم مُّؤْمِنِينَ (٥٧) وَإِذَا نَادَيْتُمْ إِلَى ٱلصَّلَوٰةِ ٱتَّخَذُوهَا هُزُوًا وَلَعِبًا ۚ ذَٰلِكَ بِأَنَّهُمْ قَوْمٌ
لَّا يَعْقِلُونَ (٥٨) قُلْ يَـٰٓأَهْلَ ٱلْكِتَـٰبِ هَلْ تَنقِمُونَ مِنَّآ إِلَّآ أَنْ ءَامَنَّا بِٱللَّهِ وَمَآ أُنزِلَ إِلَيْنَا وَمَآ

أُنزِلَ مِن قَبْلُ وَأَنَّ أَكْثَرَكُمْ فَـٰسِقُونَ ﴿٥٩﴾ قُلْ هَلْ أُنَبِّئُكُم بِشَرٍّ مِّن ذَٰلِكَ مَثُوبَةً عِندَ ٱللَّهِ ۚ مَن
لَّعَنَهُ ٱللَّهُ وَغَضِبَ عَلَيْهِ وَجَعَلَ مِنْهُمُ ٱلْقِرَدَةَ وَٱلْخَنَازِيرَ وَعَبَدَ ٱلطَّـٰغُوتَ ۚ أُو۟لَـٰٓئِكَ شَرٌّ مَّكَانًا
وَأَضَلُّ عَن سَوَآءِ ٱلسَّبِيلِ ﴿٦٠﴾ وَإِذَا جَآءُوكُمْ قَالُوٓا۟ ءَامَنَّا وَقَد دَّخَلُوا۟ بِٱلْكُفْرِ وَهُمْ قَدْ
خَرَجُوا۟ بِهِۦ ۚ وَٱللَّهُ أَعْلَمُ بِمَا كَانُوا۟ يَكْتُمُونَ ﴿٦١﴾ وَتَرَىٰ كَثِيرًا مِّنْهُمْ يُسَـٰرِعُونَ فِى ٱلْإِثْمِ
وَٱلْعُدْوَٰنِ وَأَكْلِهِمُ ٱلسُّحْتَ ۚ لَبِئْسَ مَا كَانُوا۟ يَعْمَلُونَ ﴿٦٢﴾ لَوْلَا يَنْهَىٰهُمُ ٱلرَّبَّـٰنِيُّونَ
وَٱلْأَحْبَارُ عَن قَوْلِهِمُ ٱلْإِثْمَ وَأَكْلِهِمُ ٱلسُّحْتَ ۚ لَبِئْسَ مَا كَانُوا۟ يَصْنَعُونَ ﴿٦٣﴾ وَقَالَتِ
ٱلْيَهُودُ يَدُ ٱللَّهِ مَغْلُولَةٌ ۚ غُلَّتْ أَيْدِيهِمْ وَلُعِنُوا۟ بِمَا قَالُوا۟ ۘ بَلْ يَدَاهُ مَبْسُوطَتَانِ يُنفِقُ كَيْفَ يَشَآءُ ۚ
وَلَيَزِيدَنَّ كَثِيرًا مِّنْهُم مَّآ أُنزِلَ إِلَيْكَ مِن رَّبِّكَ طُغْيَـٰنًا وَكُفْرًا ۚ وَأَلْقَيْنَا بَيْنَهُمُ ٱلْعَدَٰوَةَ
وَٱلْبَغْضَآءَ إِلَىٰ يَوْمِ ٱلْقِيَـٰمَةِ ۚ كُلَّمَآ أَوْقَدُوا۟ نَارًا لِّلْحَرْبِ أَطْفَأَهَا ٱللَّهُ ۚ وَيَسْعَوْنَ فِى ٱلْأَرْضِ
فَسَادًا ۚ وَٱللَّهُ لَا يُحِبُّ ٱلْمُفْسِدِينَ ﴿٦٤﴾ وَلَوْ أَنَّ أَهْلَ ٱلْكِتَـٰبِ ءَامَنُوا۟ وَٱتَّقَوْا۟ لَكَفَّرْنَا
عَنْهُمْ سَيِّـَٔاتِهِمْ وَلَأَدْخَلْنَـٰهُمْ جَنَّـٰتِ ٱلنَّعِيمِ ﴿٦٥﴾ وَلَوْ أَنَّهُمْ أَقَامُوا۟ ٱلتَّوْرَىٰةَ وَٱلْإِنجِيلَ وَمَآ
أُنزِلَ إِلَيْهِم مِّن رَّبِّهِمْ لَأَكَلُوا۟ مِن فَوْقِهِمْ وَمِن تَحْتِ أَرْجُلِهِم ۚ مِّنْهُمْ أُمَّةٌ مُّقْتَصِدَةٌ ۖ وَكَثِيرٌ
مِّنْهُمْ سَآءَ مَا يَعْمَلُونَ ﴿٦٦﴾ ۞ يَـٰٓأَيُّهَا ٱلرَّسُولُ بَلِّغْ مَآ أُنزِلَ إِلَيْكَ مِن رَّبِّكَ ۖ وَإِن لَّمْ تَفْعَلْ
فَمَا بَلَّغْتَ رِسَالَتَهُۥ ۚ وَٱللَّهُ يَعْصِمُكَ مِنَ ٱلنَّاسِ ۗ إِنَّ ٱللَّهَ لَا يَهْدِى ٱلْقَوْمَ ٱلْكَـٰفِرِينَ ﴿٦٧﴾
قُلْ يَـٰٓأَهْلَ ٱلْكِتَـٰبِ لَسْتُمْ عَلَىٰ شَىْءٍ حَتَّىٰ تُقِيمُوا۟ ٱلتَّوْرَىٰةَ وَٱلْإِنجِيلَ وَمَآ أُنزِلَ إِلَيْكُم مِّن
رَّبِّكُمْ ۗ وَلَيَزِيدَنَّ كَثِيرًا مِّنْهُم مَّآ أُنزِلَ إِلَيْكَ مِن رَّبِّكَ طُغْيَـٰنًا وَكُفْرًا ۖ فَلَا تَأْسَ عَلَى ٱلْقَوْمِ
ٱلْكَـٰفِرِينَ ﴿٦٨﴾ إِنَّ ٱلَّذِينَ ءَامَنُوا۟ وَٱلَّذِينَ هَادُوا۟ وَٱلصَّـٰبِـُٔونَ وَٱلنَّصَـٰرَىٰ مَنْ ءَامَنَ
بِٱللَّهِ وَٱلْيَوْمِ ٱلْـَٔاخِرِ وَعَمِلَ صَـٰلِحًا فَلَا خَوْفٌ عَلَيْهِمْ وَلَا هُمْ يَحْزَنُونَ ﴿٦٩﴾ لَقَدْ أَخَذْنَا
مِيثَـٰقَ بَنِىٓ إِسْرَٰٓءِيلَ وَأَرْسَلْنَآ إِلَيْهِمْ رُسُلًا ۖ كُلَّمَا جَآءَهُمْ رَسُولٌۢ بِمَا لَا تَهْوَىٰٓ أَنفُسُهُمْ
فَرِيقًا كَذَّبُوا۟ وَفَرِيقًا يَقْتُلُونَ ﴿٧٠﴾ وَحَسِبُوٓا۟ أَلَّا تَكُونَ فِتْنَةٌ فَعَمُوا۟ وَصَمُّوا۟ ثُمَّ تَابَ
ٱللَّهُ عَلَيْهِمْ ثُمَّ عَمُوا۟ وَصَمُّوا۟ كَثِيرٌ مِّنْهُمْ ۚ وَٱللَّهُ بَصِيرٌۢ بِمَا يَعْمَلُونَ ﴿٧١﴾ لَقَدْ كَفَرَ
ٱلَّذِينَ قَالُوٓا۟ إِنَّ ٱللَّهَ هُوَ ٱلْمَسِيحُ ٱبْنُ مَرْيَمَ ۖ وَقَالَ ٱلْمَسِيحُ يَـٰبَنِىٓ إِسْرَٰٓءِيلَ ٱعْبُدُوا۟

ٱللَّهَ رَبِّى وَرَبَّكُمْ ۖ إِنَّهُۥ مَن يُشْرِكْ بِٱللَّهِ فَقَدْ حَرَّمَ ٱللَّهُ عَلَيْهِ ٱلْجَنَّةَ وَمَأْوَىٰهُ ٱلنَّارُ ۖ وَمَا
لِلظَّٰلِمِينَ مِنْ أَنصَارٍ ﴿٧٢﴾ لَّقَدْ كَفَرَ ٱلَّذِينَ قَالُوٓا۟ إِنَّ ٱللَّهَ ثَالِثُ ثَلَٰثَةٍ ۘ وَمَا مِنْ إِلَٰهٍ
إِلَّآ إِلَٰهٌ وَٰحِدٌ ۚ وَإِن لَّمْ يَنتَهُوا۟ عَمَّا يَقُولُونَ لَيَمَسَّنَّ ٱلَّذِينَ كَفَرُوا۟ مِنْهُمْ عَذَابٌ
أَلِيمٌ ﴿٧٣﴾ أَفَلَا يَتُوبُونَ إِلَى ٱللَّهِ وَيَسْتَغْفِرُونَهُۥ ۚ وَٱللَّهُ غَفُورٌ رَّحِيمٌ ﴿٧٤﴾ مَّا ٱلْمَسِيحُ
ٱبْنُ مَرْيَمَ إِلَّا رَسُولٌ قَدْ خَلَتْ مِن قَبْلِهِ ٱلرُّسُلُ وَأُمُّهُۥ صِدِّيقَةٌ ۖ كَانَا يَأْكُلَانِ
ٱلطَّعَامَ ۗ ٱنظُرْ كَيْفَ نُبَيِّنُ لَهُمُ ٱلْءَايَٰتِ ثُمَّ ٱنظُرْ أَنَّىٰ يُؤْفَكُونَ ﴿٧٥﴾ قُلْ
أَتَعْبُدُونَ مِن دُونِ ٱللَّهِ مَا لَا يَمْلِكُ لَكُمْ ضَرًّا وَلَا نَفْعًا ۚ وَٱللَّهُ هُوَ
ٱلسَّمِيعُ ٱلْعَلِيمُ ﴿٧٦﴾ قُلْ يَٰٓأَهْلَ ٱلْكِتَٰبِ لَا تَغْلُوا۟ فِى دِينِكُمْ غَيْرَ ٱلْحَقِّ وَلَا تَتَّبِعُوٓا۟
أَهْوَآءَ قَوْمٍ قَدْ ضَلُّوا۟ مِن قَبْلُ وَأَضَلُّوا۟ كَثِيرًا وَضَلُّوا۟ عَن سَوَآءِ ٱلسَّبِيلِ ﴿٧٧﴾ لُعِنَ
ٱلَّذِينَ كَفَرُوا۟ مِنۢ بَنِىٓ إِسْرَٰٓءِيلَ عَلَىٰ لِسَانِ دَاوُۥدَ وَعِيسَى ٱبْنِ مَرْيَمَ ۚ ذَٰلِكَ بِمَا عَصَوا۟
وَّكَانُوا۟ يَعْتَدُونَ ﴿٧٨﴾ كَانُوا۟ لَا يَتَنَاهَوْنَ عَن مُّنكَرٍ فَعَلُوهُ ۚ لَبِئْسَ مَا
كَانُوا۟ يَفْعَلُونَ ﴿٧٩﴾ تَرَىٰ كَثِيرًا مِّنْهُمْ يَتَوَلَّوْنَ ٱلَّذِينَ كَفَرُوا۟ ۚ لَبِئْسَ مَا قَدَّمَتْ
لَهُمْ أَنفُسُهُمْ أَن سَخِطَ ٱللَّهُ عَلَيْهِمْ وَفِى ٱلْعَذَابِ هُمْ خَٰلِدُونَ ﴿٨٠﴾ وَلَوْ كَانُوا۟ يُؤْمِنُونَ
بِٱللَّهِ وَٱلنَّبِىِّ وَمَآ أُنزِلَ إِلَيْهِ مَا ٱتَّخَذُوهُمْ أَوْلِيَآءَ وَلَٰكِنَّ كَثِيرًا مِّنْهُمْ فَٰسِقُونَ ﴿٨١﴾

INTRODUCTION TO CHAPTER (SURAH) 4: AN-NISAA (THE WOMEN)

Maududi's Introduction

Period of Revelation

This Surah comprises several discourses which were revealed on different occasions during the period ranging probably between the end of A. H. 3 and the end of A. H. 4 or the beginning of A. H. 5. Although it is difficult to determine the exact dates of their revelations, yet it is possible to assign to them a fairly correct period with the help of the Commandments and the events mentioned therein and the Traditions concerning them. A few instances are given below by way of illustration :

1. We know that the instructions about the division of inheritance of the martyrs and for the safeguard of the rights of the orphans were sent down after the Battle of Uhd in which 70 Muslims were killed. Then naturally the question of the division of the inheritance of the martyrs and the safeguard of the rights of their orphans arose in many families at Al-Madinah. From this we conclude that vv. 1 -28 were revealed on that occasion.

2. We learn from the Traditions that the Commandment about salat during war time was given on the occasion of Zat-ur-Riqa'a, an expedition which took place in A. H. 4. From this we conclude that the discourse containing v. 102 was revealed on that occasion.

3. The last warning (v. 47) to the Jews was given before the Banu Nadir were exiled from Al- Madinah in Rabi'-ulAwwal, A. H. 4. From this it may safely be concluded that the discourse containing v. 47 must have been revealed some time before that date.

4. The permission about ***tayammum*** (the performance of ablutions with pure dust, in case no water be available) was given during the Bani-al-Mustaliq expedition, which took place in A. H. 5.. Therefore the probable period of the revelation of the discourse containing v. 43 was A. H. 5.

Topics and Their Background

Let us now consider the social and historical considerations of the period in order to understand the Surah. All the discourses in this Surah deal with three main problems which confronted the Holy Prophet at the time. First of all, he was engaged in bringing about an all round development of the Islamic Community that had been formed at the time of his migration to Al-Madinah. For this purpose he was introducing new moral, cultural, social, economic and political ways in place of the old ones of the pre-Islamic period. The second thing that occupied his attention and efforts was the bitter struggle that was going on with the ***mushrik*** Arabs, the Jewish clans and the hypocrites who were opposing tooth and nail his mission of reform. Above all he had to propagate Islam in the face of the bitter opposition of these powers of evil with a view to capturing more and more minds and hearts.

Accordingly, detailed instructions have been given for the consolidation and strengthening of the Islamic Community in continuation of those given in Al-Baqarah. Principles for the smooth running of family life have been laid down and ways of settling family disputes have been taught. Rules have been prescribed for marriage and rights of wife and husband have been apportioned fairly and equitably. The status of women in the society has been determined and the declaration of the rights of orphans has been made laws and regulations have been laid down for the division of inheritance, and instructions have been given to reform economic affairs. The foundation of the penal code has been laid down drinking has been prohibited, and instructions have been given for cleanliness and purity. The Muslims have been taught the kind of relations good men should have with their Allah and fellow men. Instructions have been given for the maintenance of discipline in the Muslim Community.

The moral and religious condition of the people of the Book has been reviewed to teach lessons to the Muslims and to forewarn them to refrain from following in their footsteps. The conduct of the hypocrites has been criticized and the distinctive features of hypocrisy and true faith have been clearly marked off to enable the Muslims to distinguish between the two.

In order to cope with the aftermath of the Battle of Uhd, Inspiring discourses were sent down to urge the Muslims to face the enemy bravely, for the defeat in the Battle had so emboldened the ***mushrik*** Arab clans and the neighboring Jews and the hypocrites at home that they were threatening the Muslims on all sides. At this critical juncture, Allah filled the Muslims with courage and gave them such instructions as were needed during that period of war clouds. In order to counteract the fearful rumors that were being spread by the hypocrites and the Muslims of weak faith, they were asked to make a thorough enquiry into them and to inform the responsible people about them. Then they were experiencing some difficulties in offering their salat during the expeditions to some places where no water was available for performing their ablutions, etc. In such cases they were allowed to cleanse themselves with pure earth and to shorten the salat or to offer the "Salat of Fear", when they were faced with danger. Instructions were also given for the solution of the puzzling problem of those Muslims who were scattered among the unbelieving Arab clans and were often involved in war. They were asked to migrate to Al-Madinah, the abode of Islam.

This Surah also deals with the case of Bani Nadir who were showing a hostile and menacing attitude, in spite of the peace treaties they had made with the Muslims. They were openly siding with the enemies of Islam and hatching plots against the Holy Prophet and the Muslim Community even at AIMadinah itself. They were taken to task for their inimical behavior and given a final warning to change their attitude, and were at last exiled from Al-Madinah on account of their misconduct.

The problem of the hypocrites, who had become very troublesome at that time, was involving the Believers in difficulties-- Therefore they were divided into different categories to enable the Muslims to deal with them appropriately.

Clear instructions were also given regarding the attitude they should adopt towards the nonbelligerent clans. The most important thing needed at that time was to prepare the Muslims for the bitter struggle with the opponents of Islam. For this purpose greatest importance was attached to their character building, for it was obvious that the small Muslim Community could only come out successful, nay, survive, if the Muslims possessed high moral character. They were, therefore, enjoined to adopt the highest moral qualities and were severely criticized whenever any moral weakness was detected in them.

Though this Surah mainly deals with the moral and social reforms, yet due attention has been paid to propagation of Islam. On the one hand, the superiority of the Islamic morality and culture has been established over that of the Jews, Christians and mushriks; on the other hand, their wrong religious conceptions, their wrong morality and their evil acts have been criticized to prepare the ground for inviting them to the way of the Truth.

Subject: Consolidation of the Islamic Community

The main object of this Surah is to teach the Muslims the ways that unite a people and make them firm and strong. Introductions for the stability of family, which is the nucleus of community have been given. Then they have been urged to prepare themselves for defence. Side by side with these, they have been taught the importance of the propagation of Islam. Above all, the importance of the highest moral character in the scheme of consolidation of the Community has been impressed.

Topics and their Interconnection

Just, fair and equitable laws and regulations for the smooth running of family life have been laid down for the husband and wife. Detailed instructions have been given for the division of inheritance and due regard has been paid to the rights of orphans. 1 - 35

In order to inculcate the right spirit for the observance of rules and regulations, the Muslims have been enjoined to show generosity to all around them and to be free from meanness, selfishness, stinginess of mind, because this is essential for the consolidation of the Communities and helpful for the propagation of Islam. 36 - 42

The ways of the purification of mind and body for the offering of Salat have been taught because it plays the most important part in every scheme of moral and social reform. 43

After moral preparation, instructions for defence have been given. First of all, the Muslims have been warned to be on their guard against the cunning machinations and vile practices of the local Jews who were hostile to the New Movement. This caution was necessary for removing some possible misunderstanding that might have arisen on account of the pre-Islamic alliance between the people of Al-Madinah and the Jews. 44 - 57

Then they have been enjoined to place their trusts and offices of trust in the custody of honest and qualified persons, and to do what is just and right, and to obey Allah and His Messenger and those among themselves entrusted with the conduct of their affairs and to turn to Allah and His Messenger for the settlement of their disputes. As such an attitude and behaviour alone can ensure consolidation, they have been strongly warned that any deviation from this path will lead to their disintegration. 58 - 72

After this pre-requisite, they have been exhorted to make preparation for defence and to fight bravely for the cause of Islam, without showing any kind of cowardice or weakness. They have also been warned to be on their guard against hypocrites. A line of demarcation has been drawn to distinguish the intentional shirkers from the helpless devotees. 73 - 100

Here again instructions have been given for the offering of Salat during military campaigns and actual fighting. This is to impress the importance of Salat even at the time of fear and danger. 101 - 103

Before proceeding on to the next topic, the Muslims have been exhorted to persevere in their fight without showing any kind of weakness. 104

In order to make the Islamic Community firm and strong for defence, the Muslims have been enjoined to observe the highest standard of justice. The Muslims are required to deal out strict justice even in case of the enemy, with whom they might be involved in war. They should also settle disputes between husband and wife with justice. In order to ensure this, they should keep their beliefs and deeds absolutely free from every kind of impurity and should become the standard bearers of justice. 105 - 135

Resuming the theme of defence, the Muslims have been warned to be on their guard against their enemies. They have been admonished to take necessary precautions against the machinations of the hypocrites and the unbelievers and the people of the Book. As belief in Allah, and Revelation and Life-after-death is the only safeguard against every kind of enemy, they should sincerely believe in and follow His Messenger, Muhammad (Allah's peace be upon him). 136 - 175

Though this verse also deals with the family laws contained in verses 1 - 35, it has been added as a supplement at the end of this Surah because it was revealed long after An-Nisa was being recited as a complete Surah. 17

Ibn Kathir's Introduction

Virtues of Surat An-Nisa, A Madinan Surah

Al-`Awfi reported that Ibn `Abbas said that Surat An-Nisa' was revealed in Al-Madinah. Ibn Marduwyah recorded similar statements from `Abdullah bin Az-Zubayr and Zayd bin Thabit. In his Mustadrak, Al-Hakim recorded that `Abdullah bin Mas`ud said, "There are five Ayat in Surat An-Nisa' that I would prefer to the life of this world and all that is in it,

(Surely, Allah wrongs not even the weight of an atom,) (4:40),

(If you avoid the great sins which you are forbidden to do) (4:31),

(Verily, Allah forgives not that partners should be set up with Him (in worship), but He forgives except that (anything else) to whom He wills) (4:48),

(If they (hypocrites), when they had been unjust to themselves, had come to you) (4:64), and,

(And whoever does evil or wrongs himself, but afterwards seeks Allah's forgiveness, he will find Allah Oft-Forgiving, Most Merciful) (4:110)." Al-Hakim recorded that Ibn `Abbas said, "Ask me about Surat An-Nisa', for I learned the Qur'an when I was still young." Al-Hakim said, "This Hadith is Sahih according to the criteria of the Two Sahihs, and they did not collect it."

CHAPTER (SURAH) 4: AN-NISAA (THE WOMEN), VERSES 148 - 176

Surah: 4 Ayah: 148 & Ayah: 149

﴿ لَّا يُحِبُّ ٱللَّهُ ٱلْجَهْرَ بِٱلسُّوٓءِ مِنَ ٱلْقَوْلِ إِلَّا مَن ظُلِمَ ۚ وَكَانَ ٱللَّهُ سَمِيعًا عَلِيمًا ﴿١٤٨﴾ ﴾

148. Allâh does not like that the evil should be uttered in public except by him who has been wronged. And Allâh is Ever All-Hearer, All-Knower.

﴿ إِن تُبْدُوا۟ خَيْرًا أَوْ تُخْفُوهُ أَوْ تَعْفُوا۟ عَن سُوٓءٍ فَإِنَّ ٱللَّهَ كَانَ عَفُوًّا قَدِيرًا ﴿١٤٩﴾ ﴾

149. Whether you (mankind) disclose (by good words of thanks) a good deed (done to you in the form of a favor by someone), or conceal it, or pardon an evil, ... verily, Allâh is Ever Oft-Pardoning, All-Powerful.

Transliteration

148. La yuhibbu Allahu aljahra bialssoo-i mina alqawli illa man thulima wakana Allahu sameeAAan AAaleeman 149. In tubdoo khayran aw tukhfoohu aw taAAfoo AAan soo-in fa-inna Allaha kana AAafuwwan qadeeran

Tafsir Ibn Kathir

The Permission to Utter Evil in Public, For One Who Was Wronged

`Ali bin Abi Talhah said that Ibn `Abbas commented on the Ayah,

(Allah does not like that the evil should be uttered in public) "Allah does not like that any one should invoke Him against anyone else, unless one was wronged. In this case, Allah allows one to invoke Him against whoever wronged him. Hence Allah's statement,

(except by him who has been wronged.) Yet, it is better for one if he observes patience." Al-Hasan Al-Basri commented, "One should not invoke Allah (for curses) against whoever wronged him. Rather, he should supplicate, `O Allah! Help me against him and take my right from him.'" In another narration, Al-Hasan said, "Allah has allowed one to invoke Him against whoever wronged him without transgressing the limits." `Abdul-Karim bin Malik Al-Jazari said about this Ayah; "When a man curses you, you could curse him in retaliation. But if he lies about you, you may not lie about him.

(And indeed whosoever takes revenge after he has suffered wrong, for such there is no way (of blame) against them.)" Abu Dawud recorded that Abu Hurayrah said that the Messenger of Allah said,

«الْمُسْتَبَّانِ مَا قَالَا، فَعَلَى الْبَادِئ مِنْهُمَا مَا لَمْ يَعْتَدِ الْمَظْلُوم»

(Whatever words are uttered by those who curse each other, then he who started it will carry the burden thereof, unless the one who was wronged transgresses the limit.) Allah said,

(Whether you disclose a good deed, or conceal it, or pardon an evil; verily, Allah is Ever Pardoning, All-Powerful.) Meaning when you, mankind, admit to a good favor done to you, or conceal it, and forgive those who wrong you, then this will bring you closer to Allah and increase your reward with Him. Among Allah's attributes is that He forgives and pardons His servants, although He is able to punish them. Hence Allah's statement,

(Verily, Allah is Ever Pardoning, All-Powerful.) It was reported that some of the angels who carry Allah's Throne praise Him saying, "All praise is due to You for Your forbearing even though You have perfect knowledge (in all evil committed)." Some of them supplicate, "All praise is due to You for Your forgiving even though You have perfect ability (to punish)." An authentic Hadith states,

«مَا نَقَصَ مَالٌ مِنْ صَدَقَةٍ، وَلَا زَادَ اللهُ عَبْدًا بِعَفْوٍ إِلَّا عِزًّا، وَمَنْ تَوَاضَعَ للهِ رَفَعَهُ اللهُ»

(No charity shall ever decrease wealth, and Allah will only increase the honor of a servant who pardons, and he who is humble for Allah's sake, then Allah will elevate his grade.)

Surah: 4 Ayah: 150, Ayah: 151 & Ayah: 152

﴿ إِنَّ ٱلَّذِينَ يَكۡفُرُونَ بِٱللَّهِ وَرُسُلِهِۦ وَيُرِيدُونَ أَن يُفَرِّقُواْ بَيۡنَ ٱللَّهِ وَرُسُلِهِۦ وَيَقُولُونَ نُؤۡمِنُ بِبَعۡضٖ وَنَكۡفُرُ بِبَعۡضٖ وَيُرِيدُونَ أَن يَتَّخِذُواْ بَيۡنَ ذَٰلِكَ سَبِيلًا ١٥٠ ﴾

150. Verily, those who disbelieve in Allâh and His Messengers and wish to make distinction between Allâh and His Messengers (by believing in Allâh and disbelieving in His

Messengers) saying, "We believe in some but reject others," and wish to adopt a way in between.

﴿ أُوْلَٰٓئِكَ هُمُ ٱلۡكَٰفِرُونَ حَقّٗاۚ وَأَعۡتَدۡنَا لِلۡكَٰفِرِينَ عَذَابٗا مُّهِينٗا ١٥١ ﴾

151. They are in truth disbelievers. And We have prepared for the disbelievers a humiliating torment.

﴿ وَٱلَّذِينَ ءَامَنُواْ بِٱللَّهِ وَرُسُلِهِۦ وَلَمۡ يُفَرِّقُواْ بَيۡنَ أَحَدٖ مِّنۡهُمۡ أُوْلَٰٓئِكَ سَوۡفَ يُؤۡتِيهِمۡ أُجُورَهُمۡۚ وَكَانَ ٱللَّهُ غَفُورٗا رَّحِيمٗا ١٥٢ ﴾

152. And those who believe in Allâh and His Messengers and make no distinction between any of them (Messengers), We shall give them their rewards; and Allâh is Ever Oft-Forgiving, Most Merciful.

Transliteration

150. Inna allatheena yakfuroona biAllahi warusulihi wayureedoona an yufarriqoo bayna Allahi warusulihi wayaqooloona nu/minu bibaAAdin wanakfuru bibaAAdin wayureedoona an yattakhithoo bayna thalika sabeelan 151. Ola-ika humu alkafiroona haqqan waaAAtadna lilkafireena AAathaban muheenan 152. Waallatheena amanoo biAllahi warusulihi walam yufarriqoo bayna ahadin minhum ola-ika sawfa yu/teehim ojoorahum wakana Allahu ghafooran raheeman

Tafsir Ibn Kathir

Believing in Some Prophets and Rejecting Others is Pure Kufr

Allah threatens those who disbelieve in Him and in His Messengers, such as the Jews and Christians, who differentiate between Allah and His Messengers regarding faith. They believe in some Prophets and reject others, following their desires, lusts and the practices of their forefathers. They do not follow any proof for such distinction, because there is no such proof. Rather, they follow their lusts and prejudices. The Jews, may Allah curse them, believe in the Prophets, except `Isa and Muhammad, peace be upon them. The Christians believe in the Prophets but reject their Final and Seal, and the most honored among the prophets, Muhammad, peace be upon him. In addition, the Samirah (Samaritans) do not believe in any Prophet after Yuwsha` (Joshua), the successor of Musa bin `Imran. The Majus (Zoroastrians) are said to believe only in a Prophet called Zoroaster, although they do not believe in the law he brought them casting it behind them, and Allah knows best. Therefore, whoever rejects only one of Allah's Prophets, he will have disbelieved in all of them, because it is required from mankind to believe in every prophet whom Allah sent to the people of the earth. And whoever rejects one Prophet, out of envy, bias and personal whim, he only demonstrates that his faith in other Prophets is not valid, but an act of following desire and whim. This is why Allah said,

(Verily, those who disbelieve in Allah and His Messengers...) Thus, Allah describes these people as disbelievers in Allah and His Messengers;

(and wish to make distinction between Allah and His Messengers) in faith,

(saying, "We believe in some but reject others," and wish to adopt a way in between.) Allah then describes them;

(They are in truth disbelievers.) meaning, their disbelief in the Prophet they claim to believe in is clear. This is because their claimed faith in a certain Messenger is not true, for had they truly believed in him, they would have believed in other Messengers, especially if the other Messenger has a stronger proof for his truthfulness. Or at least, they would have strived hard to acquire knowledge of the truth of the other Messenger. Allah said,

(And We have prepared for the disbelievers a humiliating torment.) This is just punishment for belittling the Prophets whom they disbelieved in, by ignoring what the Prophet brought to them from Allah, and because they are interested in the insignificant possessions of this world. Or, their behavior could be the result of their disbelief in the Prophet after they were aware of his truth, just as the Jewish rabbis did during the time of Muhammad, the Messenger of Allah . The Jews envied the Messenger because of the great prophethood that Allah gave him, and as a consequence, they denied the Messenger, defied him, became his enemies and fought against him. Allah sent humiliation upon them in this life, that shall be followed by disgrace in the Hereafter,

(And they were covered with humiliation and misery, and they drew on themselves the wrath of Allah.) in this life and the Hereafter. Allah's statement,

(And those who believe in Allah and His Messengers and make no distinction between any of them,) This refers to the Ummah of Muhammad who believe in every Book that Allah has revealed and in every Prophet whom Allah has sent. Allah said,

(The Messenger believes in what has been revealed to him from his Lord, and (so do) the believers. All of them believe in Allah.) (2:285). Allah then states that He has prepared great rewards for them, tremendous favor and a handsome bounty,

(We shall give them their rewards;) because of their faith in Allah and His Messengers,

(and Allah is Ever Forgiving, Most Merciful.) for their sin, if they have any.

Surah: 4 Ayah: 153 & Ayah: 154

﴿ يَسْـَٔلُكَ أَهْلُ ٱلْكِتَـٰبِ أَن تُنَزِّلَ عَلَيْهِمْ كِتَـٰبًا مِّنَ ٱلسَّمَآءِ ۚ فَقَدْ سَأَلُوا۟ مُوسَىٰٓ أَكْبَرَ مِن
ذَٰلِكَ فَقَالُوٓا۟ أَرِنَا ٱللَّهَ جَهْرَةً فَأَخَذَتْهُمُ ٱلصَّـٰعِقَةُ بِظُلْمِهِمْ ۚ ثُمَّ ٱتَّخَذُوا۟ ٱلْعِجْلَ مِنۢ بَعْدِ مَا
جَآءَتْهُمُ ٱلْبَيِّنَـٰتُ فَعَفَوْنَا عَن ذَٰلِكَ ۚ وَءَاتَيْنَا مُوسَىٰ سُلْطَـٰنًا مُّبِينًا ﴿١٥٣﴾ ﴾

153. The people of the Scripture (Jews) ask you to cause a book to descend upon them from heaven. Indeed they asked Mûsâ (Moses) for even greater than that, when they said: "Show us Allâh in public," but they were struck with thunderclap and lightning for their wickedness. Then they worshipped the calf even after clear proofs, evidences, and signs had come to them. (Even) so We forgave them. And We gave Mûsâ (Moses) a clear proof of authority.

﴿ وَرَفَعْنَا فَوْقَهُمُ ٱلطُّورَ بِمِيثَـٰقِهِمْ وَقُلْنَا لَهُمُ ٱدْخُلُوا۟ ٱلْبَابَ سُجَّدًا وَقُلْنَا لَهُمْ لَا تَعْدُوا۟ فِى
ٱلسَّبْتِ وَأَخَذْنَا مِنْهُم مِّيثَـٰقًا غَلِيظًا ﴿١٥٤﴾ ﴾

154. And for their covenant, We raised over them the Mount and (on the other occasion) We said: "Enter the gate prostrating (or bowing) with humility;" and We commanded them: "Transgress not (by doing worldly works) on the Sabbath (Saturday)." And We took from them a firm covenant.

Transliteration

153. Yas-aluka ahlu alkitabi an tunazzila AAalayhim kitaban mina alssama-i faqad saaloo moosa akbara min thalika faqaloo arina Allaha jahratan faakhathat-humu alssaAAiqatu bithulmihim thumma ittakhathoo alAAijla min baAAdi ma jaat-humu albayyinatu faAAafawna AAan thalika waatayna moosa sultanan mubeenan
154. WarafaAAna fawqahumu alttoora bimeethaqihim waqulna lahumu odkhuloo albaba sujjadan waqulna lahum la taAAdoo fee alssabti waakhathna minhum meethaqan ghaleethan

Tafsir Ibn Kathir

The Stubbornness of the Jews

Muhammad bin Ka`b Al-Qurazi, As-Suddi and Qatadah said that the Jews asked the Messenger of Allah to cause a book to come down to them from heaven, just as the Tawrah was sent down to Musa. Ibn Jurayj said that the Jews asked the Messenger to cause books to come down to them addressed to so-and-so among them, testifying to the truth of what he was sent with. The Jews only asked for this because of their stubbornness, defiance, rejection and disbelief. The disbelievers of Quraysh also asked for similar things from the Prophet, as is mentioned in Surat Al-Isra',

(And they say: "We shall not believe in you, until you cause a spring to gush forth from the earth for us;) (17:90) Allah said,

(Indeed, they asked Musa for even greater than that, when they said, "Show us Allah in public," but they were struck with a bolt of lightning for their wickedness.) injustice, transgression, defiance and rebellion. This part was explained in Surat Al-Baqarah,

(And (remember) when you said: "O Musa! We shall never believe in you until we see Allah plainly." But you were struck by a bolt of lightning while you were looking. Then We raised you up after your death, so that you might be grateful.) (2:55,56) Allah's statement,

(Then they worshipped the calf even after Al-Bayyinat had come to them.) meaning, after they witnessed the tremendous miracles and unequivocal proofs at the hand of Musa in Egypt. They also witnessed the demise of their enemy, Fir`awn and his soldiers, when they all drowned in the sea. Yet soon after, when they passed by a people who were worshipping idols, they said to Musa,

(Make for us a god as they have gods.) Allah explains the story of the Jews worshipping the calf in Surat Al-A`raf (7) and Surah Ta Ha (20) after Musa went to meet with his Lord. When Musa returned, Allah decreed that in order for the Jews to earn accepted repentance, then those who did not worship the calf would have to kill those who worshipped it. They complied with this command, and Allah resurrected them afterwards. Allah said here,

((Even) so We forgave them. And We gave Musa a clear proof of authority.) Allah then said,

(And for their covenant, We raised over them the mount,) This was when they refrained from implementing the rulings of the Tawrah and refused what Musa brought them from Allah. So

Allah raised the mountain above their heads and they were ordered to prostrate, which they did. Even so, they were looking above when they were prostrating for fear that the mountain might fall on them,

(And (remember) when We raised the mountain over them as if it had been a canopy, and they thought that it was going to fall on them. (We said): "Hold firmly to what We have given you.") Allah then said,

(and We said, "Enter the gate prostrating (or bowing) with humility;") meaning that they also defied this command in word and action. They were commanded to enter Bayt Al-Quds (in Jerusalem) while bowing and saying "Hittah", meaning: `O Allah! take from us our sin of abandoning Jihad.' This was the cause of their wandering in the desert of Tih for forty years. Yet, they entered the House while crawling on their rear ends and saying `Hintah (a wheat grain) in Sha`rah (the hair)'.

(and We commanded them, "Transgress not the Sabbath (Saturday).") meaning, We commanded them to honor the Sabbath and honor what Allah prohibited them on that day.

t(And We took from them a firm covenant.) meaning, strong covenant. They rebelled, transgressed and committed what Allah prohibited by using deceit and trickery, as is mentioned in Surat Al-A`raf (7), (And ask them about the town that was by the sea.)

Surah: 4 Ayah: 155, Ayah: 156, Ayah: 157, Ayah: 18 & Ayah: 159

﴿ فَبِمَا نَقْضِهِم مِّيثَٰقَهُمْ وَكُفْرِهِم بِـَٔايَٰتِ ٱللَّهِ وَقَتْلِهِمُ ٱلْأَنۢبِيَآءَ بِغَيْرِ حَقٍّ وَقَوْلِهِمْ قُلُوبُنَا
غُلْفٌۢ ۚ بَلْ طَبَعَ ٱللَّهُ عَلَيْهَا بِكُفْرِهِمْ فَلَا يُؤْمِنُونَ إِلَّا قَلِيلًا ﴿١٥٥﴾ ﴾

155. Because of their breaking the covenant, and of their rejecting the Ayât (proofs, evidences, verses, lessons, signs, revelations, etc.) of Allâh, and of their killing the Prophets unjustly, and of their saying: "Our hearts are wrapped (with coverings, i.e. we do not understand what the Messengers say)" - nay, Allâh has set a seal upon their hearts because of their disbelief, so they believe not but a little.

﴿ وَبِكُفْرِهِمْ وَقَوْلِهِمْ عَلَىٰ مَرْيَمَ بُهْتَٰنًا عَظِيمًا ﴿١٥٦﴾ ﴾

156. And because of their (Jews) disbelief and uttering against Maryam (Mary (peace be upon her)) a grave false charge (that she has committed illegal sexual intercourse);

﴿ وَقَوْلِهِمْ إِنَّا قَتَلْنَا ٱلْمَسِيحَ عِيسَى ٱبْنَ مَرْيَمَ رَسُولَ ٱللَّهِ وَمَا قَتَلُوهُ وَمَا صَلَبُوهُ وَلَٰكِن شُبِّهَ
لَهُمْ ۚ وَإِنَّ ٱلَّذِينَ ٱخْتَلَفُوا۟ فِيهِ لَفِى شَكٍّ مِّنْهُ ۚ مَا لَهُم بِهِۦ مِنْ عِلْمٍ إِلَّا ٱتِّبَاعَ ٱلظَّنِّ ۚ وَمَا قَتَلُوهُ
يَقِينًۢا ﴿١٥٧﴾ ﴾

157. And because of their saying (in boast), "We killed Messiah 'Isâ (Jesus), son of Maryam (Mary), the Messenger of Allâh," - but they killed him not, nor crucified him, but the resemblance of 'Isâ (Jesus) was put over another man (and they killed that man), and those who differ therein are full of doubts. They have no (certain) knowledge, they follow

nothing but conjecture. For surely; they killed him not (i.e. 'Isâ (Jesus), son of Maryam (Mary) (peace be upon them))

﴿ بَل رَّفَعَهُ ٱللَّهُ إِلَيۡهِۚ وَكَانَ ٱللَّهُ عَزِيزًا حَكِيمًا ١٥٨ ﴾

158. But Allâh raised him ('Isâ (Jesus)) up (with his body and soul) unto Himself (and he (peace be upon him) is in the heavens). And Allâh is Ever All-Powerful, All-Wise.

﴿ وَإِن مِّنۡ أَهۡلِ ٱلۡكِتَٰبِ إِلَّا لَيُؤۡمِنَنَّ بِهِۦ قَبۡلَ مَوۡتِهِۦۖ وَيَوۡمَ ٱلۡقِيَٰمَةِ يَكُونُ عَلَيۡهِمۡ
شَهِيدٗا ١٥٩ ﴾

159. And there is none of the people of the Scripture (Jews and Christians), but must believe in him ('Isâ (Jesus), son of Maryam (Mary), as only a Messenger of Allâh and a human being), before his ('Isâ (Jesus) (peace be upon him)or a Jew's or a Christian's) death (at the time of the appearance of the angel of death). And on the Day of Resurrection, he ('Isâ (Jesus)) will be a witness against them.

Transliteration

155. Fabima naqdihim meethaqahum wakufrihim bi-ayati Allahi waqatlihimu al-anbiyaa bighayri haqqin waqawlihim quloobuna ghulfun bal tabaAAa Allahu AAalayha bikufrihim fala yu/minoona illa qaleelan 156. Wabikufrihim waqawlihim AAala maryama buhtanan AAatheeman 157. Waqawlihim inna qatalna almaseeha AAeesa ibna maryama rasoola Allahi wama qataloohu wama salaboohu walakin shubbiha lahum wa-inna allatheena ikhtalafoo feehi lafee shakkin minhu ma lahum bihi min AAilmin illa ittibaAAa alththanni wama qataloohu yaqeenan 158. Bal rafaAAahu Allahu ilayhi wakana Allahu AAazeezan hakeeman 159. Wa-in min ahli alkitabi illa layu/minanna bihi qabla mawtihi wayawma alqiyamati yakoonu AAalayhim shaheedan

Tafsir Ibn Kathir

The Crimes of the Jews

The sins mentioned here are among the many sins that the Jews committed, which caused them to be cursed and removed far away from right guidance. The Jews broke the promises and vows that Allah took from them, and also rejected Allah's Ayat, meaning His signs and proofs, and the miracles that they witnessed at the hands of their Prophets. Allah said,

(and their killing the Prophets unjustly,) because their many crimes and offenses against the Prophets of Allah, for they killed many Prophets, may Allah's peace be upon them Their saying:

("Our hearts are Ghulf,") meaning, wrapped with covering, according to Ibn `Abbas, Mujahid, Sa`id bin Jubayr, `Ikrimah, As-Suddi and Qatadah. This is similar to the what the idolators said,

(And they say: "Our hearts are under coverings (screened) from that to which you invite us.") Allah said,

(nay, Allah has set a seal upon their hearts because of their disbelief,) It is as if they had given an excuse that their hearts do not understand what the Prophet says since their hearts are wrapped with coverings, so they claim. Allah said that their hearts are sealed because of their disbelief, as we mentioned before in the explanation of Surat Al-Baqarah. Allah then said,

(so they believe not but a little.) for their hearts became accustomed to Kufr, transgression and weak faith.

The Evil Accusation the Jews Uttered Against Maryam and Their Claim that They Killed `Isa

Allah said,

(And because of their (Jews) disbelief and uttering against Maryam a grave false charge.) `Ali bin Abi Talhah said that Ibn `Abbas stated that the Jews accused Maryam of fornication.This is also the saying of As-Suddi, Juwaybir, Muhammad bin Ishaq and several others. This meaning is also apparent in the Ayah, as the Jews accused Maryam and her son of grave accusations: They accused her of fornication and claimed that `Isa was an illegitimate son. Some of them even claimed that she was menstruating while fornicating. May Allah's continued curse be upon them until the Day of Resurrection. The Jews also said,

("We killed Al-Masih, `Isa, son of Maryam, the Messenger of Allah,") meaning, we killed the person who claimed to be the Messenger of Allah. The Jews only uttered these words in jest and mockery, just as the polytheists said,

(O you to whom the Dhikr (the Qur'an) has been sent down! Verily, you are a mad man!) When Allah sent `Isa with proofs and guidance, the Jews, may Allah's curses, anger, torment and punishment be upon them, envied him because of his prophethood and obvious miracles; curing the blind and leprous and bringing the dead back to life, by Allah's leave. He also used to make the shape of a bird from clay and blow in it, and it became a bird by Allah's leave and flew. `Isa performed other miracles that Allah honored him with, yet the Jews defied and bellied him and tried their best to harm him. Allah's Prophet `Isa could not live in any one city for long and he had to travel often with his mother, peace be upon them. Even so, the Jews were not satisfied, and they went to the king of Damascus at that time, a Greek polytheist who worshipped the stars. They told him that there was a man in Bayt Al-Maqdis misguiding and dividing the people in Jerusalem and stirring unrest among the king's subjects. The king became angry and wrote to his deputy in Jerusalem to arrest the rebel leader, stop him from causing unrest, crucify him and make him wear a crown of thorns. When the king's deputy in Jerusalem received these orders, he went with some Jews to the house that `Isa was residing in, and he was then with twelve, thirteen or seventeen of his companions. That day was a Friday, in the evening. They surrounded `Isa in the house, and when he felt that they would soon enter the house or that he would sooner or later have to leave it, he said to his companions, "Who volunteers to be made to look like me, for which he will be my companion in Paradise" A young man volunteered, but `Isa thought that he was too young. He asked the question a second and third time, each time the young man volunteering, prompting `Isa to say, "Well then, you will be that man." Allah made the young man look exactly like `Isa, while a hole opened in the roof of the house, and `Isa was made to sleep and ascended to heaven while asleep. Allah said,

(And (remember) when Allah said: "O `Isa! I will take you and raise you to Myself.") When `Isa ascended, those who were in the house came out. When those surrounding the house saw the man who looked like `Isa, they thought that he was `Isa. So they took him at night, crucified him and placed a crown of thorns on his head. The Jews then boasted that they killed

`Isa and some Christians accepted their false claim, due to their ignorance and lack of reason. As for those who were in the house with `Isa, they witnessed his ascension to heaven, while the rest thought that the Jews killed `Isa by crucifixion. They even said that Maryam sat under the corpse of the crucified man and cried, and they say that the dead man spoke to her. All this was a test from Allah for His servants out of His wisdom. Allah explained this matter in the Glorious Qur'an which He sent to His honorable Messenger, whom He supported with miracles and clear, unequivocal evidence. Allah is the Most Truthful, and He is the Lord of the worlds Who knows the secrets, what the hearts conceal, the hidden matters in heaven and earth, what has occurred, what will occur, and what would occur if it was decreed. He said,

(but they killed him not, nor crucified him, but it appeared as that to them,) referring to the person whom the Jews thought was `Isa. This is why Allah said afterwards,

(and those who differ therein are full of doubts. They have no (certain) knowledge, they follow nothing but conjecture.) referring to the Jews who claimed to kill `Isa and the ignorant Christians who believed them. Indeed they are all in confusion, misguidance and bewilderment. This is why Allah said,

(For surely; they killed him not.) meaning they are not sure that `Isa was the one whom they killed. Rather, they are in doubt and confusion over this matter.

(But Allah raised him up unto Himself. And Allah is Ever All-Powerful,) meaning, He is the Almighty, and He is never weak, nor will those who seek refuge in Him ever be subjected to disgrace,

(All-Wise.) in all that He decides and ordains for His creatures. Indeed, Allah's is the clearest wisdom, unequivocal proof and the most glorious authority. Ibn Abi Hatim recorded that Ibn `Abbas said, "Just before Allah raised `Isa to the heavens, `Isa went to his companions, who were twelve inside the house. When he arrived, his hair was dripping water and he said, `There are those among you who will disbelieve in me twelve times after he had believed in me.' He then asked, `Who volunteers that his image appear as mine, and be killed in my place. He will be with me (in Paradise)' One of the youngest ones among them volunteered and `Isa asked him to sit down. `Isa again asked for a volunteer, and the young man kept volunteering and `Isa asking him to sit down. Then the young man volunteered again and `Isa said, `You will be that man,' and the resemblance of `Isa was cast over that man while `Isa ascended to heaven from a hole in the house. When the Jews came looking for `Isa, they found that young man and crucified him. Some of `Isa's followers disbelieved in him twelve times after they had believed in him. They then divided into three groups. One group, Al-Ya`qubiyyah (Jacobites), said, `Allah remained with us as long as He willed and then ascended to heaven.' Another group, An-Nasturiyyah (Nestorians), said, `The son of Allah was with us as long as he willed and Allah took him to heaven.' Another group, Muslims, said, `The servant and Messenger of Allah remained with us as long as Allah willed, and Allah then took him to Him.' The two disbelieving groups cooperated against the Muslim group and they killed them. Ever since that happened, Islam was then veiled until Allah sent Muhammad ." This statement has an authentic chain of narration leading to Ibn `Abbas, and An-Nasa'i narrated it through Abu Kurayb who reported it from Abu Mu`awiyah. Many among the Salaf stated that `Isa asked if someone would volunteer for his appearance to be cast over him, and that he will be killed instead of `Isa, for which he would be his companion in Paradise.

All Christians Will Believe in `Isa Before He Dies

Allah said,

(And there is none of the People of the Scripture, but must believe in him, before his death. And on the Day of Resurrection, he will be a witness against them.) Ibn Jarir recorded that Ibn `Abbas commented,

(And there is none of the People of the Scripture, but must believe in him, before his death.) before the death of `Isa, son of Maryam, peace be upon him. Al-`Awfi reported similar from Ibn `Abbas. Abu Malik commented;

(but must believe in him, before his death.) "This occurs after `Isa returns and before he dies, as then, all of the People of the Scriptures will believe in him."

The Hadiths Regarding the Descent of `Isa Just Before the Day of Judgement, and his Mission

In the chapter about the Prophets in his Sahih, under, "The Descent of `Isa, Son of Maryam," Al-Bukhari recorded that Abu Hurayrah said that the Messenger of Allah said,

«وَالَّذِي نَفْسِي بِيَدِهِ، لَيُوشِكَنَّ أَنْ يَنْزِلَ فِيكُمُ ابْنُ مَرْيَمَ حَكَمًا عَدْلًا، فَيَكْسِرَ الصَّلِيبَ، وَيَقْتُلَ الْخِنْزِيرَ، وَيَضَعَ الْجِزْيَةَ، وَيَفِيضَ الْمَالُ حَتَّى لَا يَقْبَلَهُ أَحَدٌ، حَتَّى تَكُونَ السَّجْدَةُ خَيْرًا لَهُمْ مِنَ الدُّنْيَا وَمَا فِيهَا»

(By Him in Whose Hands my soul is, the son of Maryam (`Isa) will shortly descend among you as a just ruler, and will break the cross, kill the pig and abolish the Jizyah. Then there will be an abundance of wealth and nobody will accept charitable gifts any more. At that time, one prostration will be better for them than this life and all that is in it.) Abu Hurayrah then said, "Read if you will,

(And there is none of the People of the Scripture, but must believe in him, before his death. And on the Day of Resurrection, he will be a witness against them.)" Muslim recorded this Hadith. So, Allah's statement,

(before his death) refers to the death of `Isa, son of Maryam.

Another Hadith by Abu Hurayrah

Imam Ahmad recorded that Abu Hurayrah said that the Messenger of Allah said,

«لَيُهِلَّنَّ عِيسَى بِفَجِّ الرَّوْحَاءِ بِالْحَجِّ أَوِ الْعُمْرَةِ، أَوْ لَيَثْنِيَنَّهُمَا جَمِيعًا»

(`Isa will say Ihlal from the mountain highway of Ar-Rawha' for Hajj, `Umrah or both.) Muslim also recorded it. Ahmad recorded that Abu Hurayrah said that the Prophet said,

«يَنْزِلُ عِيسَى ابْنُ مَرْيَمَ فَيَقْتُلُ الْخِنْزِيرَ، وَيَمْحُو الصَّلِيبَ، وَتُجْمَعُ لَهُ الصَّلَاةُ، وَيُعْطَى الْمَالُ حَتَّى لَا يُقْبَلَ، وَيَضَعُ الْخَرَاجَ، وَيَنْزِلُ الرَّوْحَاءَ فَيَحُجُّ مِنْهَا أَوْ يَعْتَمِرُ أَوْ يَجْمَعُهُمَا»

(`Isa, son of Maryam, will descend and will kill the pig, break the cross, lead the prayer in congregation and give away wealth until it is no longer accepted by anyone. He will also abolish the Jizyah and go to Ar-Rawha' from where he will go to perform Hajj, `Umrah or both.) Abu Hurayrah then recited,

(And there is none of the People of the Scripture, but must believe in him, before his death.) Hanzalah said, "Abu Hurayrah added, `Will believe in `Isa before `Isa dies,' but I do not know if this was a part of the Prophet's Hadith or if it was something that Abu Hurayrah said on his own. " Ibn Abi Hatim also recorded this Hadith.

Another Hadith

Al-Bukhari recorded that Abu Hurayrah said that the Messenger of Allah said,

«كَيْفَ بِكُمْ إِذَا نَزَلَ فِيكُمُ الْمَسِيحُ ابْنُ مَرْيَمَ وَإِمَامُكُمْ مِنْكُم»

(How will you be when Al-Masih, son of Maryam (`Isa) descends among you while your Imam is from among yourselves) Imam Ahmad and Muslim also recorded this Hadith.

Another Hadith

Imam Ahmad recorded that Abu Hurayrah said that the Prophet said,

«الْأَنْبِيَاءُ إِخْوَةٌ لِعَلَّاتٍ، أُمَّهَاتُهُمْ شَتَّى، وَدِينُهُمْ وَاحِدٌ، وَإِنِّي أَوْلَى النَّاسِ بِعِيسَى ابْنِ مَرْيَمَ، لِأَنَّهُ لَمْ يَكُنْ نَبِيٌّ بَيْنِي وَبَيْنَهُ، وَإِنَّهُ نَازِلٌ فَإِذَا رَأَيْتُمُوهُ فَاعْرِفُوهُ: رَجُلٌ مَرْبُوعٌ إِلَى الْحُمْرَةِ وَالْبَيَاضِ، عَلَيْهِ ثَوْبَانِ مُمَصَّرَانِ، كَأَنَّ رَأْسَهُ يَقْطُرُ، وَإِنْ لَمْ يُصِبْهُ بَلَلٌ، فَيَدُقُّ الصَّلِيبَ، وَيَقْتُلُ الْخِنْزِيرَ، وَيَضَعُ الْجِزْيَةَ، وَيَدْعُو النَّاسَ إِلَى الْإِسْلَامِ، وَيُهْلِكُ اللهُ فِي زَمَانِهِ الْمِلَلَ كُلَّهَا إِلَّا الْإِسْلَامَ، وَيُهْلِكُ اللهُ فِي زَمَانِهِ الْمَسِيحَ الدَّجَّالَ،ثُمَّ تَقَعُ الْأَمَنَةُ عَلَى الْأَرْضِ حَتَّى تَرْتَعَ الْأُسُودُ مَعَ الْإِبِلِ، وَالنِّمَارُ مَعَ الْبَقَرِ، وَالذِّئَابُ مَعَ

الْغَنَمِ، وَيَلْعَبُ الصِّبْيَانُ بِالْحَيَّاتِ لَا تَضُرُّهُمْ، فَيَمْكُثُ أَرْبَعِينَ سَنَةً ثُمَّ يُتَوَفَّى، وَيُصَلِّي عَلَيْهِ الْمُسْلِمُونَ»

(The Prophets are paternal brothers; their mothers are different, but their religion is one. I, more than any of mankind, have more right to `Isa, son of Maryam, for there was no Prophet between him and I. He will descend, and if you see him, know him. He is a well-built man, (the color of his skin) between red and white. He will descend while wearing two long, light yellow garments. His head appears to be dripping water, even though no moisture touched it. He will break the cross, kill the pig, and banish the Jizyah and will call the people to Islam. During his time, Allah will destroy all religions except Islam and Allah will destroy Al-Masih Ad-Dajjal (the False Messiah). Safety will then fill the earth, so much so that the lions will mingle with camels, tigers with cattle and wolves with sheep. Children will play with snakes, and they will not harm them. `Isa will remain for forty years and then will die, and Muslims will offer the funeral prayer for him.) Abu Dawud also recorded it.

Another Hadith

In his Sahih, Muslim recorded that Abu Hurayrah related to the Messenger of Allah that he said,

«لَا تَقُومُ السَّاعَةُ حَتَّى يَنْزِلَ الرُّومُ بِالْأَعْمَاقِ أَوْ بِدَابِقَ، فَيَخْرُجُ إِلَيْهِمْ جَيْشٌ مِنَ الْمَدِينَةِ مِنْ خِيَارِ أَهْلِ الْأَرْضِ يَوْمَئِذٍ، فَإِذَا تَصَافُّوا، قَالَتِ الرُّومُ: خَلُّوا بَيْنَنَا وَبَيْنَ الَّذِينَ سَبَوْا مِنَّا نُقَاتِلْهُمْ، فَيَقُولُ الْمُسْلِمُونَ: لَا وَاللهِ، لَا نُخَلِّي بَيْنَكُمْ وَبَيْنَ إِخْوَانِنَا، فَيُقَاتِلُونَهُمْ، (فَيَنْهَزِمُ) ثُلُثٌ لَا يَتُوبُ اللهُ عَلَيْهِمْ أَبَدًا، وَيُقْتَلُ ثُلُثُهُ أَفْضَلُ الشُّهَدَاءِ عِنْدَ اللهِ، وَيَفْتَتِحُ الثُّلُثُ لَا يُفْتَنُونَ أَبَدًا، فَيَفْتَتِحُونَ قُسْطُنْطِينِيَّةَ، فَبَيْنَمَا هُمْ يَقْسِمُونَ الْغَنَائِمَ قَدْ عَلَّقُوا سُيُوفَهُمْ بِالزَّيْتُونِ، إِذْ صَاحَ فِيهِمُ الشَّيْطَانُ: إِنَّ الْمَسِيحَ قَدْ خَلَفَكُمْ فِي أَهْلِيكُمْ، فَيَخْرُجُونَ، وَذَلِكَ بَاطِلٌ، فَإِذَا جَاءُوا الشَّامَ خَرَجَ، فَبَيْنَمَا هُمْ يُعِدُّونَ لِلْقِتَالِ يُسَوُّونَ الصُّفُوفَ، إِذْ أُقِيمَتِ الصَّلَاةُ فَيَنْزِلُ عِيسَى ابْنُ مَرْيَمَ، فَأَمَّهُمْ، فَإِذَا رَآهُ عَدُوُّ اللهِ، ذَابَ كَمَا يَذُوبُ الْمِلْحُ فِي الْمَاءِ، فَلَوْ تَرَكَهُ لَانْذَابَ حَتَّى يَهْلِكَ، وَلَكِنْ يَقْتُلُهُ اللهُ بِيَدِهِ، فَيُرِيهِمْ دَمَهُ فِي حَرْبَتِهِ»

(The (Last) Hour will not start until the Romans occupy Al-A`maq or Dabiq. An army, comprised of the best of the people of the earth then, will come from Al-Madinah and challenge them. When they camp face to face, the Romans will say, `Let us fight those who captured some of us.' The Muslims will say, `Nay! By Allah, we will never let you get to our brothers.' They will fight them. A third of the (Muslim) army will flee in defeat, and those are the ones whom Allah will never forgive. Another third will be killed, and those are the best martyrs before Allah. The last third will be victorious, and this third will never be stricken with Fitnah, and they will capture Constantinople (Istanbul). While they are dividing war booty, after hanging their swords on olive trees, Shaytan will shout among them, saying, `Al-Masih (Ad-Dajjal) has cornered your people'. They will leave to meet Ad-Dajjal in Ash-Sham. This will be a false warning, and when they reach Ash-Sham, Ad-Dajjal will then appear. When the Muslims are arranging their lines for battle and the prayer is called for, `Isa, son of Maryam, will descend and lead them in prayer. When the enemy of Allah (the False Messiah) sees him, he will dissolve just as salt dissolves in water, and if any of him were left, he would continue dissolving until he died. Allah will kill him with the hand of `Isa and will show the Muslims his blood on his spear.) Muslim recorded that `Abdullah bin `Amr said that the Messenger of Allah said,

«لَتُقَاتِلُنَّ الْيَهُودَ فَلَتَقْتُلُنَّهُمْ، حَتَّى يَقُولَ الْحَجَرُ: يَامُسْلِمُ هَذَا يَهُودِيٌّ فَتَعَال فَاقْتُلْه»

(You will fight the Jews and will kill them, until the stone will say, `O Muslim! There is a Jew here, so come and kill him.') Muslim recorded that Abu Hurayrah said that the Messenger of Allah said,

«لَا تَقُومُ السَّاعَةُ حَتَّى يُقَاتِلَ الْمُسْلِمُونَ الْيَهُودَ، فَيَقْتُلُهُمُ الْمُسْلِمُونَ حَتَّى يَخْتَبِىءَ الْيَهُودِيُّ مِنْ وَرَاءِ الْحَجَرِ وَالشَّجَرِ، فَيَقُولُ الْحَجَرُ وَالشَّجَرُ: يَامُسْلِمُ يَاعَبْدَاللهِ هَذَا يَهُودِيٌّ خَلْفِي فَتَعَال فَاقْتُلْهُ إِلَّا الْغَرْقَدَ فَإِنَّهُ مِنْ شَجَرِ الْيَهُود»

(The Hour will not start, until after the Muslims fight the Jews and the Muslims kill them. The Jew will hide behind a stone or tree, and the tree will say, `O Muslim! O servant of Allah! This is a Jew behind me, come and kill him.' Except Al-Gharqad, for it is a tree of the Jews.) Muslim bin Al-Hajjaj recorded in his Sahih that An-Nawwas bin Sam`an said, "The Messenger of Allah , mentioned Ad-Dajjal one day and kept belittling him (because being blind, yet claiming to be Allah) and speaking in grave terms about him until we thought that he was hiding in gardens of date-trees (in Al-Madinah). When we went by the Messenger, he sensed this anxiety in us and said,

«مَا شَأْنُكُمْ؟»

(What is the matter with you) We said, `O Messenger of Allah! Earlier, you mentioned Ad-Dajjal and while belittling him you spoke gravely about him until we thought that he was hiding in gardens of date-trees (of Al-Madinah).' He said,

«غَيْرُ الدَّجَّالِ أَخْوَفُني عَلَيكُمْ، إِنْ يَخْرُجْ وَأَنَا فِيكُمْ فَأَنَا حَجِيجُهُ دُونَكُمْ، وَإِنْ يَخْرُجْ وَلَسْتُ فِيكُمْ فَامْرُؤٌ حَجِيجُ نَفْسِهِ، واللهُ خَلِيفَتِي عَلى كُلِّ مُسْلِمٍ. إِنَّهُ شَابٌّ قَطَطٌ، عَيْنُهُ طافِيَةٌ كَأَنِّي أُشَبِّهُهُ بِعَبْدِالعُزَّى بْنِ قَطَنٍ، مَنْ أَدْرَكَهُ مِنْكُمْ فَلْيَقْرَأْ عَلَيْهِ فَوَاتِحَ سُورَةِ الْكَهْفِ، إِنَّه خَارِجٌ مِنْ خَلَّةٍ بَيْنَ الشَّامِ والعِرَاقِ، فَعَاثَ يَمِينًا وَعَاثَ شِمَالًا، يَاعِبَادَ اللهِ فَاثْبُتوا»

(I fear other than Ad-Dajjal for you! If he appears while I am still among you, I will be his adversary on your behalf. If he appears while I am not among you, each one will depend on himself and Allah will be the Helper of every Muslim after me. He is young, with very curly hair and his eye is smashed. I thought that he looked like `Abdul-`Uzza bin Qatan. Whoever lives long and meets Ad-Dajjal, then let him recite the beginnings of Surat Al-Kahf. He will appear on a pass between Ash-Sham (Syria) and Al-`Iraq. He will wreak havoc to the right and left. O Servants of Allah! Hold fast.) We said, `O Messenger of Allah! How long will he stay on earth' He said,

«أَرْبَعُونَ يَوْمًا، يومٌ كَسَنَةٍ، وَيَوْمٌ كَشَهْرٍ، وَيَوْمٌ كَجُمُعَةٍ، وَسَائِرُ أَيَّامِهِ كَأَيَّامِكُم»

(Forty days: One day as long as a year, one day as long as a month and one day as long as a week. The rest of his days will be as long as one of your ordinary days.) We said, `O Messenger of Allah! As for the day that is like a year, will the prayers of one day suffice for it' He said,

«لَا، اقْدُرُوا لَهُ قَدْرَه»

(No. Count for its due measure.) We said, `O Messenger of Allah, how will his speed be on earth' He said,

«كَالْغَيْثِ اسْتَدْبَرَتْهُ الرِّيحُ فَيَأْتِي عَلى قَوْمٍ فَيَدْعُوهُمْ فَيُؤْمِنُون بِهِ، وَيَسْتَجِيبُونَ لَهُ، فَيَأْمُرُ السَّمَاءَ فَتُمْطِرُ، وَالأَرْضَ فَتُنْبِتُ، فَتَرُوحُ عَلَيْهِمْ سَارِحَتُهُمْ أَطْوَلَ مَا كَانَتْ ذُرًى، وَأَسْبَغَهُ ضُرُوعًا، وَأَمَدَّهُ خَوَاصِرَ، ثُمَّ يَأْتِي الْقَوْمَ فَيَدْعُوهُمْ فَيَرُدُّونَ عَلَيْهِ قَوْلَهُ، فَيَنْصَرِفُ عَنْهُمْ فَيُصْبِحُونَ مُمْحِلِينَ لَيْسَ بِأَيْدِيهِمْ شَيْءٌ مِنْ أَمْوَالِهِمْ وَيَمُرُّ بِالْخَرِبَةِ فَيَقُولُ لَهَا: أَخْرِجِي كُنُوزَكِ، فَتَتْبَعُهُ كُنُوزُهَا كَيَعَاسِيبِ النَّحْلِ، ثُمَّ يَدْعُو رَجُلًا

مُمْتَلِئًا شَبَابًا فَيَضْرِبُهُ بِالسَّيْفِ، فَيَقْطَعُهُ جِزْلَتَيْنِ رَمْيَةَ الْغَرَضِ، ثُمَّ يَدْعُوهُ، فَيُقْبِلُ وَيَتَهَلَّلُ وَجْهُهُ وَيَضْحَكُ، فَبَيْنَمَا هُوَ كَذَلِكَ إِذْ بَعَثَ اللهُ الْمَسِيحَ ابْنَ مَرْيَمَ عَلَيْهِ السَّلَامُ، فَيَنْزِلُ عِنْدَ الْمَنَارَةِ الْبَيْضَاءِ شَرْقِيَّ دِمَشْقَ بَيْنَ مَهْرُودَتَيْنِ، وَاضِعًا كَفَّيْهِ عَلَى أَجْنِحَةِ مَلَكَيْنِ، إِذَا طَأْطَأَ رَأْسَهُ قَطَرَ،وَإِذَا رَفَعَهُ تَحَدَّرَ مِنْهُ جُمَانٌ كَاللُّؤْلُؤِ، وَلَا يَحِلُّ لِكَافِرٍ يَجِدُ رِيحَ نَفَسِهِ إِلَّا مَاتَ، وَنَفَسُهُ يَنْتَهِي حَيْثُ يَنْتَهِي طَرْفُهُ، فَيَطْلُبُهُ حَتَّى يُدْرِكَهُ بِبَابِ لُدَ، فَيَقْتُلُهُ، ثُمَّ يَأْتِي عِيسَى عَلَيْهِ السَّلَامُ قَوْمًا قَدْ عَصَمَهُمُ اللهُ مِنْهُ، فَيَمْسَحُ عَنْ وُجُوهِهِمْ، وَيُحَدِّثُهُمْ بِدَرَجَاتِهِمْ فِي الْجَنَّةِ، فَبَيْنَمَا هُوَ كَذَلِكَ إِذْ أَوْحَى اللهُ عَزَّ وَجَلَّ إِلَى عِيسَى: إِنِّي قَدْ أَخْرَجْتُ عِبَادًا لِي لَا يَدَانِ لِأَحَدٍ بِقِتَالِهِمْ، فَحَرِّزْ عِبَادِي إِلَى الطُّورِ، وَيَبْعَثُ اللهُ يَأْجُوجَ وَمَأْجُوجَ وَهُمْ مِنْ كُلِّ حَدَبٍ يَنْسِلُونَ، فَيَمُرُّ أَوَّلُهُمْ عَلَى بُحَيْرَةِ طَبَرِيَّةَ فَيَشْرَبُونَ مَا فِيهَا، وَيَمُرُّ آخِرُهُمْ فَيَقُولُونَ: لَقَدْ كَانَ بِهَذِهِ مَرَّةً مَاءٌ، وَيُحْصَرُ نَبِيُّ اللهِ عِيسَى وَأَصْحَابُهُ، حَتَّى يَكُونَ رَأْسُ الثَّوْرِ لِأَحَدِهِمْ خَيْرٌ مِنْ مِائَةِ دِينَارٍ لِأَحَدِكُمُ الْيَوْمَ، فَيَرْغَبُ نَبِيُّ اللهِ عِيسَى وَأَصْحَابُهُ، فَيُرْسِلُ اللهُ عَلَيْهِمُ النَّغَفَ فِي رِقَابِهِمْ، فَيُصْبِحُونَ فَرْسَى كَمَوْتِ نَفْسٍ وَاحِدَةٍ، ثُمَّ يَهْبِطُ نَبِيُّ اللهِ عِيسَى وَأَصْحَابُهُ إِلَى الْأَرْضِ، فَلَا يَجِدُونَ فِي الْأَرْضِ مَوْضِعَ شِبْرٍ إِلَّا مَلَأَهُ زَهَمُهُمْ وَنَتْنُهُمْ، فَيَرْغَبُ نَبِيُّ اللهِ عِيسَى وَأَصْحَابُهُ إِلَى اللهِ، فَيُرْسِلُ اللهُ، طَيْرًا كَأَعْنَاقِ الْبُخْتِ، فَتَحْمِلُهُمْ فَتَطْرَحُهُمْ حَيْثُ شَاءَ اللهُ، ثُمَّ يُرْسِلُ اللهُ مَطَرًا لَا يَكُنُّ مِنْهُ بَيْتُ مَدَرٍ، وَلَا وَبَرٍ، فَيَغْسِلُ الْأَرْضَ حَتَّى يَتْرُكَهَا كَالزَّلَفَةِ، ثُمَّ يُقَالُ لِلْأَرْضِ: أَخْرِجِي ثَمَرَكِ وَرُدِّي بَرَكَتَكِ، فَيَوْمَئِذٍ تَأْكُلُ الْعِصَابَةُ مِنَ الرُّمَّانَةِ، وَيَسْتَظِلُّونَ بِقِحْفِهَا، وَيُبَارِكُ اللهُ فِي الرِّسْلِ حَتَّى إِنَّ اللِّقْحَةَ مِنَ الْإِبِلِ لَتَكْفِي الْفِئَامَ، (مِنَ النَّاسِ وَاللُّقْمَةَ مِنَ الْفَمِ لَتَكْفِي الْفَخِذَ مِنَ النَّاسِ)، فَبَيْنَمَا هُمْ كَذَلِكَ إِذْ بَعَثَ اللهُ رِيحًا

طَيِّبَةً، فَتَأْخُذُهُمْ تَحْتَ آبَاطِهِمْ، فَتَقْبِضُ رُوحَ كُلِّ مُؤْمِنٍ وَكُلِّ مُسْلِمٍ، وَيَبْقَى شِرَارُ النَّاسِ يَتَهَارَجُونَ فِيهَا تَهَارُجَ الْحُمُرِ،فَعَلَيْهِمْ تَقُومُ السَّاعَةُ»

(Like the storm when driven by the wind. He will come to a people and will call them (to his worship), and they will believe in him and accept his call. He will order the sky and it will rain, the land and it will grow (vegetation). Their cattle will return to them with their hair the longest, their udders the fullest (with milk) and their stomachs the fattest. He will come to a different people and will call them (to his worship), and they will reject his call. He will then leave them. They will wake up in the morning destitute, missing all of their possessions. He will pass by a deserted land and will say to it, `Bring out your treasures', and its treasures will follow him just like swarms of bees. He will summon a man full of youth and will strike him with the sword once and will cut him into two pieces (and will separate between them like) the distance (between the hunter and) the game. He will call the dead man and he will come, and his face will radiant with pleasure and laughter. Afterwards (while all this is happening with Ad-Dajjal), Allah will send Al-Masih (`Isa), son of Maryam down. He will descend close to the white minaret to the east of Damascus. He will be wearing garments lightly colored with saffron and his hands will be placed on the wings of two angels. Whenever he lowers his head droplets fall. Whenever he raises his head, precious stones that look like pearls fall. No disbeliever can survive `Isa's breath, which reaches the distance of his sight. He will pursue Ad-Dajjal and will follow him to the doors of (the Palestinian city of) Ludd where he will kill him. A group of people who, by Allah's help, resisted and survived Ad-Dajjal, will pass by `Isa and he will anoint their faces and inform them about their grades in Paradise. Shortly afterwards, while this is happening with `Isa, Allah will reveal to him, `I raised a people of My creation that no one can fight. Therefore, gather My servants to At-Tur (the mountain of Musa in Sinai).' Then, Allah will raise Gog and Magog and they will swiftly swarm from every mound. Their front forces will reach Lake Tabariah (Sea of Galilee) and will drink all its water. The last of their forces will say as they pass by the lake, `This lake once had water!'

Meanwhile, `Isa, Allah's Prophet, will be cornered along with his companions until the head of a bull will be more precious to them than a hundred Dinars to you today. `Isa, Allah's Prophet, and his companions will invoke Allah for help and Allah will send An-Naghaf (a worm) into the necks of Gog and Magog! The morning will come, and they will all be dead as if it was the death of one soul. Afterwards, `Isa, the Prophet of Allah, will come down with his companions to the low grounds (from Mount At-Tur). They will find that no space of a hand-span on the earth was free of their fat and rot (rotten corpses). `Isa, the Prophet of Allah, and his companions will seek Allah in supplication. Allah will send birds as large as the necks of camels. They will carry them (the corpses of Gog and Magog) and will throw them wherever Allah wills. Afterwards, Allah will send rain that no house made of mud or animal hair will be saved from, and it will cleanse the earth until it is as clean as a mirror. The earth will be commanded (by Allah), `Produce your fruits and regain your blessing.' Then, the group will eat from a pomegranate and will take shelter under the shade of its skin. Milk will be blessed, so much so that the milk-producing camel will yield large amounts that suffice for a large group of people. Meanwhile, Allah will send a pure wind that will overcome Muslims from under their arms and will take the soul of every believer and Muslim. Only the evildoers among people will remain. They will indulge in shameless public sex like that of donkeys. On them, the Hour will begin.)

Imam Ahmad and the collectors of the Sunan also recorded this Hadith. We will mention this Hadith again using the chain of narration collected by Ahmad explaining Allah's statement in Surat Al-Anbiya' (chapter 21),

(Until, when Ya`juj and Ma`juj (Gog and Magog people) are let loose (from their barrier).) In our time, in the year seven hundred and forty-one, a white minaret was built in the Umayyad Masjid (in Damascus) made of stone, in place of the minaret that was destroyed by a fire which the Christians were suspected to have started. May Allah's continued curses descend on the Christians until the Day of Resurrection. There is a strong feeling that this minaret is the one that `Isa will descend on, according to this Hadith.

Another Hadith

Muslim recorded in his Sahih that Ya`qub bin `Asim bin `Urwah bin Mas`ud Ath-Thaqafi said, "I heard `Abdullah bin `Amr saying to a man who asked him, `What is this Hadith that you are narrating You claim that the Hour will start on such and such date.' He said, `Subhan Allah (glory be to Allah),' or he said, `There is no deity worthy of worship except Allah.' I almost decided to never narrate anything to anyone. I only said, "Soon, you will witness tremendous incidents, the House (the Ka`bah) will be destroyed by fire, and such and such things will occur." He then said, `The Messenger of Allah said,

«يَخْرُجُ الدَّجَّالُ فِي أُمَّتِي فَيَمْكُثُ أَرْبَعِينَ، لَا أَدْرِي أَرْبَعِينَ يَوْمًا أَوْ أَرْبَعِينَ شَهْرًا أَوْ أَرْبَعِينَ عَامًا، فَيَبْعَثُ اللهُ تَعَالَى عِيسَى ابْنَ مَرْيَمَ كَأَنَّهُ عُرْوَةُ بْنُ مَسْعُودٍ، فَيَطْلُبُهُ فَيُهْلِكُهُ، ثُمَّ يَمْكُثُ النَّاسُ سَبْعَ سِنِينَ لَيْسَ بَيْنَ اثْنَيْنِ عَدَاوَةٌ، ثُمَّ يُرْسِلُ اللهُ رِيحًا بَارِدَةً مِنْ قِبَلِ الشَّامِ، فَلَا يَبْقَى عَلَى وَجْهِ الْأَرْضِ أَحَدٌ فِي قَلْبِهِ مِثْقَالُ ذَرَّةٍ مِنْ خَيْرٍ أَوْ إِيمَانٍ إِلَّا قَبَضَتْهُ، حَتَّى لَوْ أَنَّ أَحَدَكُمْ دَخَلَ فِي كَبِدِ جَبَلٍ لَدَخَلَتْه عَلَيْهِ حَتَّى تَقْبِضَه»

(Ad-Dajjal will appear in my nation and will remain for forty. (The narrator doubts whether it is forty days, months, or years).Then, Allah will send down `Isa, son of Maryam, looking just like `Urwah bin Mas`ud and he will seek Ad-Dajjal and will kill him. People will remain for seven years with no enmity between any two. Allah will send a cool wind from As-Sham that will leave no man on the face of the earth who has even the weight of an atom of good or faith, but will capture (his soul). Even if one of you takes refuge in the middle of a mountain, it will find him and capture (his soul).

«فَيَبْقَى شِرَارُ النَّاسِ فِي خِفَّةِ الطَّيْرِ وَأَحْلَامِ السِّبَاعِ، لَا يَعْرِفُونَ مَعْرُوفًا، وَلَا يُنْكِرُون مُنْكَرًا، فَيَتَمَثَّلُ لَهُمُ الشَّيْطَانُ فَيَقُولُ: أَلَا تَسْتَجِيبُونَ؟ فَيَقُولُونَ: فَمَا تَأْمُرُنَا؟ فَيَأْمُرُهُمْ

بِعِبَادَةِ الْأَوْثَانِ، وَهُمْ فِي ذٰلِكَ دَارٌّ رِزْقُهُمْ، حَسَنٌ عَيْشُهُمْ، ثُمَّ يُنْفَخُ فِي الصُّورِ فَلَا يَسْمَعُهُ أَحَدٌ إِلَّا أَصْغَى لِيتًا وَرَفَعَ لِيتًا،قَالَ: وَأَوَّلُ مَنْ يَسْمَعُهُ رَجُلٌ يَلُوطُ حَوْضَ إِبِلِهِ، قَالَ: فَيَصْعَقُ وَيَصْعَقُ النَّاسُ، ثُمَّ يُرْسِلُ اللهُ أَوْ قَالَ: يُنْزِلُ اللهُ مَطَرًا كَأَنَّهُ الطَّلُّ أَوْ قَالَ الظِّلُّ نُعْمَانُ الشَّاكُّ فَتَنْبُتُ مِنْهُ أَجْسَادُ النَّاسِ، ثُمَّ يُنَفَخُ فِيهِ أُخْرَى فَإِذَا هُمْ قِيَامٌ يَنْظُرُونَ. ثُمَّ يُقَالُ: أَيُّهَا النَّاسُ: هَلُمُّوا إِلَى رَبِّكُم»

Afterwards, only the most evil people will remain. They will be as light as birds, with the comprehension of beasts. They will not know or enjoin righteousness or forbid or know evil. Shaytan will appear to them and will say to them, `Would you follow me.' They will say, `What do you command us' He will command them to worship the idols. Meanwhile, their provision will come to them in abundance and their life will be good. Then the Trumpet will be blown and every person who hears it, will lower one side of his head and raise the other side (trying to hear that distant sound). The first man who will hear the Trumpet is someone who is preparing the water pool for his camels, and he and the people will swoon away. Allah will send down heavy rain and the bodies of people will grow with it. The Trumpet will be blown in again and the people will be resurrected and looking all about, staring. It will be said to them, `O people! Come to your Lord,'

(But stop them, verily, they are to be questioned.)

«ثم يقال: أخرجوا بعث النار، فيقال: من كم؟ فيقال: من كل ألف تسعمائة وتسعة وتسعين، قال: فذلك يوم»

(It will then be said, `Bring forth the share of the Fire.' It will be asked, `How many' It will be said, `From every one thousand, nine hundred and ninety-nine.' That Day is when,)

(the children will turn grey-headed,) and,

(The Day when the Shin shall be laid bare).)"

The Description of `Isa, upon him be Peace

As mentioned earlier, `Abdur-Rahman bin Adam narrated that Abu Hurayrah said that the Prophet said,

«فَإِذَا رَأَيْتُمُوهُ فَاعْرِفُوهُ: رَجُلٌ مَرْبُوعٌ إِلَى الْحُمْرَةِ وَالْبَيَاضِ، عَلَيْهِ ثَوْبَانِ مُمَصَّرَانِ، كَأَنَّ رَأْسَهُ يَقْطُرُ وَإِنْ لَمْ يُصِبْهُ بَلَل»

(If you see `Isa, know him. He is a well-built man, (the color of his skin) between red and white. He will descend while wearing light yellow garments. His head looks like it is dripping water, even though no moisture touched it.) In the Hadith that An-Nawwas bin Sam`an narrated,

«فَيَنْزِلُ عِنْدَ الْمَنَارَةِ الْبَيْضَاءِ شَرْقِيَّ دِمَشْقَ بَيْنَ مَهْرُودَتَيْنِ وَاضِعًا كَفَّيْهِ عَلَى أَجْنِحَةِ مَلَكَيْنِ، إِذَا طَأْطَأَ رَأْسَهُ قَطَرَ، وَإِذَا رَفَعهُ تَحَدَّرَ مِنْهُ مِثْلُ جُمَانِ اللُّؤْلُؤِ، لَا يَحِلُّ لِكَافِرٍ يَجِدُ رِيحَ نَفَسِهِ إِلَّا مَاتَ، وَنَفَسُهُ يَنْتَهِي حَيْثُ يَنْتَهِي طَرَفُه»

(He will descend close to the white minaret to the east of Damascus. He will be wearing two garments lightly colored with saffron, having his hands on the wings of two angels. Whenever he lowers his head, drops will fall off of it. Whenever he raises his head, precious jewels like pearls will fall off of it. No disbeliever can survive `Isa's breath, and his breath reaches the distance of his sight.) Al-Bukhari and Muslim recorded that Abu Hurayrah said that the Messenger of Allah said,

«لَيْلَةَ أُسْرِيَ بِي لَقِيتُ مُوسَى»

(I met Musa on the night of my Ascension to heaven.) The Prophet then described him saying, as I think,

«مُضْطَرِبٌ، رَجِلُ الرَّأْسِ كَأَنَّهُ مِنْ رِجَالِ شَنُوءَة»

(He was a tall person with hair as if he was one of the men from the tribe of Shanu'ah.) The Prophet further said,

«وَلَقِيتُ عِيسَى»

(`I met `Isa.' The Prophet described him saying,

«رَبْعَةٌ أَحْمَرُ كَأَنَّهُ خَرَجَ مِنْ دِيمَاس»

`He was of moderate height and was red-faced as if he had just come out of a bathroom.

«وَرَأَيْتُ إِبْرَاهِيمَ وَأَنَا أَشْبَهُ وَلَدِهِ بِه»

I saw Ibrahim whom I resembled more than any of his children did.') Al-Bukhari recorded that Mujahid said that Ibn `Umar said that the Messenger of Allah said,

«رَأَيْتُ مُوسَى وَعِيسَى وَإِبْرَاهِيمَ، فَأَمَّا عِيسَى فَأَحْمَرُ جَعْدٌ عَرِيضُ الصَّدْرِ، وَأَمَّا مُوسَى فَآدَمُ جَسِيمٌ سَبْطٌ، كَأَنَّهُ مِنْ رِجَالِ الزُّطِّ»

(I saw Musa, `Isa and Ibrahim. `Isa was of red complexion and had curly hair and a broad chest. Musa was of brown complexion and had straight hair and a tall stature, as if he was from the people of Az-Zutt.) Al-Bukhari and Muslim recorded that Ibrahim said that `Abdullah bin `Umar said, "The Prophet once mentioned the False Messiah (Al-Masih Ad-Dajjal) to people, saying,

«إِنَّ اللهَ لَيْسَ بِأَعْوَرَ، أَلَا إِنَّ الْمَسِيحَ الدَّجَّالَ أَعْوَرُ الْعَيْنِ الْيُمْنَى، كَأَنَّ عَيْنَهُ عِنَبَةٌ طَافِيَةٌ»

(Allah is not blind in His Eye. Al-Masih Ad-Dajjal is blind in his right eye. His eye is like a protruding grape.)" Muslim recorded that the Messenger of Allah said,

«وَأَرَانِي اللهُ عِنْدَ الْكَعْبَةِ فِي الْمَنَامِ، فَإِذَا رَجُلٌ آدَمُ كَأَحْسَنِ مَا تَرَى مِنْ أُدْمِ الرِّجَالِ، تَضْرِبُ لِمَّتُهُ بَيْنَ مَنْكِبَيْهِ، رَجِلُ الشَّعْرِ، يَقْطُرُ رَأْسُهُ مَاءً،وَاضِعًا يَدَيْهِ عَلَى مَنْكِبَيْ رَجُلَيْنِ، وَهُوَ يَطُوفُ بِالْبَيْتِ، فَقُلْتُ: مَنْ هَذَا؟ فَقَالُوا: هُوَ الْمَسِيحُ ابْنُ مَرْيَمَ، ثُمَّ رَأَيْتُ وَرَاءَهُ رَجُلًا جَعْدًا قَطِطًا، أَعْوَرَ الْعَيْنِ الْيُمْنَى، كَأَشْبَهِ مَنْ رَأَيْتُ بِابْنِ قَطَنٍ، وَاضِعًا يَدَيْهِ عَلَى مَنْكِبَي رَجُلٍ، يَطُوفُ بِالْبَيْتِ، فَقُلْتُ: مَنْ هَذَا؟ قَالُوا: الْمَسِيحُ الدَّجَّالُ»

(In a dream, I was at the Ka`bah and Allah made me see a light - colored man, a color that is as beautiful as a light - colored man could be, with combed hair that reached his shoulders. His hair was dripping water, and he was leaning on the shoulders of two men while circling the Ka`bah. I asked, `Who is this man' I was told, `This is the Al-Masih, son of Maryam.' Behind him, I saw a man with very curly hair who was blind in his right eye. He looked exactly as Ibn Qatan, and he was leaning on the shoulder of a man while circling the House. I asked, `Who is this man' I was told, `He is Al-Masih Ad-Dajjal.') Al-Bukhari recorded that Salim said that his father said, "No, By Allah! The Prophet did not say that `Isa was of red complexion but said,

«بَيْنَمَا أَنَا نَائِمٌ أَطُوفُ بِالْكَعْبَةِ، فَإِذَا رَجُلٌ آدَمُ سَبْطُ الشَّعْرِ، يَتَهَادَى بَيْنَ رَجُلَيْنِ، يَنْطُفُ رَأْسُهُ مَاءً أَوْ يُهَرَاقُ رَأْسُهُ مَاءً فَقُلْتُ: مَنْ هَذَا؟ فَقَالُوا: ابْنُ مَرْيَمَ، فَذَهَبْتُ

أَلْتَفِتُ، فَإِذَا رَجُلٌ أَحْمَرُ جَسِيمٌ، جَعْدُ الرَّأْسِ، أَعْوَرُ عَيْنِهِ الْيُمْنَى، كَأَنَّ عَيْنَهُ عِنَبَةٌ طَافِيَةٌ، قُلْتُ: مَنْ هَذَا؟ قَالُو: الدَّجَّالُ، وَأَقْرَبُ النَّاسِ بِهِ شَبَهًا ابْنُ قَطَنٍ»

(While I was asleep circumambulating the Ka`bah (in my dream), I suddenly saw a man of brown complexion and ample hair walking between two men with water dripping from his head. I asked, `Who is this' The people said, `He is the son of Maryam.' Then I looked behind and I saw a red-complexioned, fat, curly-haired man, blind in the right eye, which looked like a bulging out grape. I asked, `Who is this' They replied, `He is Ad-Dajjal.' The person he most resembled is Ibn Qatan.)" Az-Zuhri commented that Ibn Qatan was a man from the tribe of Khuza`ah who died during the time of Jahiliyyah. This is the wording of Al-Bukhari. Allah's statement,

(And on the Day of Resurrection, he (`Isa) will be a witness against them) Qatadah said, "He will bear witness before them that he has delivered the Message from Allah and that he is but a servant of His." In a similar statement in the end of Surat Al-Ma'idah,

And (remember) when Allâh will say (on the Day of Resurrection): "O 'Iesa (Jesus), son of Maryam (Mary)! Did you say unto men: 'Worship me and my mother as two gods besides Allâh?' " He will say: "Glory be to You! It was not for me to say what I had no right (to say). Had I said such a thing, You would surely have known it. You know what is in my inner-self though I do not know what is in Yours, truly, You, only You, are the AllKnower of all that is hidden and unseen

Surah: 4 Ayah: 160, Ayah: 161 & Ayah: 162

﴿ فَبِظُلْمٍ مِّنَ ٱلَّذِينَ هَادُواْ حَرَّمْنَا عَلَيْهِمْ طَيِّبَٰتٍ أُحِلَّتْ لَهُمْ وَبِصَدِّهِمْ عَن سَبِيلِ ٱللَّهِ كَثِيرًا ﴿١٦٠﴾ ﴾

160. For the wrong-doing of the Jews, We made unlawful to them certain good foods which had been lawful to them, and for their hindering many from Allâh's Way;

﴿ وَأَخْذِهِمُ ٱلرِّبَوٰاْ وَقَدْ نُهُواْ عَنْهُ وَأَكْلِهِمْ أَمْوَٰلَ ٱلنَّاسِ بِٱلْبَٰطِلِ ۚ وَأَعْتَدْنَا لِلْكَٰفِرِينَ مِنْهُمْ عَذَابًا أَلِيمًا ﴿١٦١﴾ ﴾

161. And their taking of Ribâ (usury) though they were forbidden from taking it and their devouring of men's substance wrongfully (bribery). And We have prepared for the disbelievers among them a painful torment.

﴿ لَّٰكِنِ ٱلرَّٰسِخُونَ فِي ٱلْعِلْمِ مِنْهُمْ وَٱلْمُؤْمِنُونَ يُؤْمِنُونَ بِمَآ أُنزِلَ إِلَيْكَ وَمَآ أُنزِلَ مِن قَبْلِكَ ۚ وَٱلْمُقِيمِينَ ٱلصَّلَوٰةَ ۚ وَٱلْمُؤْتُونَ ٱلزَّكَوٰةَ وَٱلْمُؤْمِنُونَ بِٱللَّهِ وَٱلْيَوْمِ ٱلْءَاخِرِ أُوْلَٰٓئِكَ سَنُؤْتِيهِمْ أَجْرًا عَظِيمًا ﴿١٦٢﴾ ﴾

162. But those among them who are well-grounded in knowledge, and the believers, believe in what has been sent down to you (Muhammad (peace be upon him)) and what was sent down before you; and those who perform As-Salât (Iqâmat-as-Salât), and give Zakât and believe in Allâh and in the Last Day, it is they to whom We shall give a great reward.

Transliteration

160. Fabithulmin mina allatheena hadoo harramna AAalayhim tayyibatin ohillat lahum wabisaddihim AAan sabeeli Allahi katheeran 161. Waakhthihimu alrriba waqad nuhoo AAanhu waaklihim amwala alnnasi bialbatili waaAAtadna lilkafireena minhum AAathaban aleeman 162. Lakini alrrasikhoona fee alAAilmi minhum waalmu/minoona yu/minoona bima onzila ilayka wama onzila min qablika waalmuqeemeena alssalata waalmu/toona alzzakata waalmu/minoona biAllahi waalyawmi al-akhiri ola-ika sanu/teehim ajran AAatheeman

Tafsir Ibn Kathir

Some Foods Were Made Unlawful for the Jews Because of their Injustice and Wrongdoing

Allah states that because of the injustice and transgression of the Jews, demonstrated by committing major sins, He prohibited some of the lawful, pure things which were previously allowed for them. This prohibition could be only that of decree, meaning that Allah allowed the Jews to falsely interpret their Book and change and alter the information about what was allowed for them. They thus, out of exaggeration and extremism in the religion, prohibited some things for themselves. It could also mean that in the Tawrah, Allah prohibited things that were allowed for them before. Allah said,

(All food was lawful to the Children of Israel, except what Isra'il made unlawful for himself before the Tawrah was revealed.) We mentioned this Ayah before, which means that all types of food were allowed for the Children of Israel before the Tawrah was revealed, except the camel's meat and milk that Isra'il prohibited for himself. Later, Allah prohibited many things in the Tawrah. Allah said in Surat Al-An`am (chapter 6),

(And unto those who are Jews, We forbade every (animal) with undivided hoof, and We forbade them the fat of the ox and the sheep except what adheres to their backs or their entrails, or is mixed up with a bone. Thus We recompensed them for their rebellion. And verily, We are Truthful.) This means, We prohibited these things for them because they deserved it due to their transgression, injustice, defying their Messenger and disputing with him. So Allah said;

(For the wrongdoing of the Jews, We made unlawful to them certain good foods which had been lawful to them, and for their hindering many from Allah's way.) This Ayah states that they hindered themselves and others from following the truth, and this is the behavior that they brought from the past to the present. This is why they were and still are the enemies of the Messengers, killing many of the Prophets. They also denied Muhammad and `Isa, peace be upon them. mAllah said,

(And their taking of Riba' though they were forbidden from taking it,) Allah prohibited them from taking Riba', yet they did so using various kinds of tricks, ploys and cons, thus devouring people's property unjustly. Allah said,

(And We have prepared for the disbelievers among them a painful torment.) Allah then said,

(But those among them who are well-grounded in knowledge...) firm in the religion and full of beneficial knowledge. We mentioned this subject when we explained Surah Al `Imran (3). The Ayah;

(and the believers...) refers to the well-grounded in knowledge;

(believe in what has been sent down to you and what was sent down before you;) Ibn `Abbas said, "This Ayah was revealed concerning `Abdullah bin Salam, Tha`labah bin Sa`yah, Zayd bin Sa`yah and Asad bin `Ubayd who embraced Islam and believed what Allah sent Muhammad with. Allah said,

(and give Zakah,) This could be referring to the obligatory charity due on one's wealth and property, or those who purify themselves, or both. Allah knows best.

(and believe in Allah and in the Last Day,) They believe that there is no deity worthy of worship except Allah, believe in Resurrection after death and the reward or punishment for the good or evil deeds. Allah's statement,

(It is they,) those whom the Ayah described above,

(To whom We shall give a great reward.) means Paradise.

Surah: 4 Ayah: 163, Ayah: 164 & Ayah: 165

﴿ ۞ إِنَّآ أَوۡحَيۡنَآ إِلَيۡكَ كَمَآ أَوۡحَيۡنَآ إِلَىٰ نُوحٖ وَٱلنَّبِيِّـۧنَ مِنۢ بَعۡدِهِۦۚ وَأَوۡحَيۡنَآ إِلَىٰٓ إِبۡرَٰهِيمَ
وَإِسۡمَٰعِيلَ وَإِسۡحَٰقَ وَيَعۡقُوبَ وَٱلۡأَسۡبَاطِ وَعِيسَىٰ وَأَيُّوبَ وَيُونُسَ وَهَٰرُونَ وَسُلَيۡمَٰنَۚ
وَءَاتَيۡنَا دَاوُۥدَ زَبُورٗا ١٦٣ ﴾

163. Verily, We have sent the revelation to you (O Muhammad (peace be upon him)) as We sent the revelation to Nûh (Noah) and the Prophets after him; We (also) sent the revelation to Ibrâhîm (Abraham), Ismâ'îl (Ishmael), Ishâque (Isaac), Ya'qûb (Jacob), and Al-Asbât (the twelve sons of Ya'qûb (Jacob)) 'Isâ (Jesus), Ayyûb (Job), Yûnus (Jonah), Hârûn (Aaron), and Sulaimân (Solomon), and to Dawûd (David) We gave the Zabûr (Psalms).

﴿ وَرُسُلٗا قَدۡ قَصَصۡنَٰهُمۡ عَلَيۡكَ مِن قَبۡلُ وَرُسُلٗا لَّمۡ نَقۡصُصۡهُمۡ عَلَيۡكَۚ وَكَلَّمَ ٱللَّهُ مُوسَىٰ
تَكۡلِيمٗا ١٦٤ ﴾

164. And Messengers We have mentioned to you before, and Messengers We have not mentioned to you, - and to Mûsâ (Moses) Allâh spoke directly.

﴿ رُّسُلٗا مُّبَشِّرِينَ وَمُنذِرِينَ لِئَلَّا يَكُونَ لِلنَّاسِ عَلَى ٱللَّهِ حُجَّةُۢ بَعۡدَ ٱلرُّسُلِۚ وَكَانَ ٱللَّهُ عَزِيزًا
حَكِيمٗا ١٦٥ ﴾

165. Messengers as bearers of good news as well as of warning in order that mankind should have no plea against Allâh after the (coming of) Messengers. And Allâh is Ever All-Powerful, All-Wise.

Transliteration

163. Inna awhayna ilayka kama awhayna ila noohin waalnnabiyyeena min baAAdihi waawhayna ila ibraheema wa-ismaAAeela wa-ishaqa wayaAAqooba waal-asbati waAAeesa waayyooba wayoonusa waharoona wasulaymana waatayna dawooda zabooran 164. Warusulan qad qasasnahum AAalayka min qablu warusulan lam naqsushum AAalayka wakallama Allahu moosa takleeman 165. Rusulan mubashshireena wamunthireena li-alla yakoona lilnnasi AAala Allahi hujjatun baAAda alrrusuli wakana Allahu AAazeezan hakeeman

Tafsir Ibn Kathir

Revelation Came to Prophet Muhammad , Just as it Came to the Prophets Before Him

Muhammad bin Ishaq narrated that Muhammad bin Abi Muhammad said that `Ikrimah, or Sa`id bin Jubayr, related to Ibn `Abbas that he said, "Sukayn and `Adi bin Zayd said, `O Muhammad! We do not know that Allah sent down anything to any human after Musa.' Allah sent down a rebuttal of their statement,

(Verily, We have inspired you (O Muhammad) as We inspired Nuh and the Prophets after him.)" Allah states that He sent down revelation to His servant and Messenger Muhammad just as He sent down revelation to previous Prophets. Allah said,

(Verily, We have inspired you (O Muhammad) as We inspired Nuh and the Prophets after him,) until,

(...and to Dawud We gave the Zabur.) The `Zabur' (Psalms) is the name of the Book revealed to Prophet Dawud, peace be upon him.

Twenty-Five Prophets Are Mentioned in the Qur'an

Allah said,

(And Messengers We have mentioned to you before, and Messengers We have not mentioned to you) Before the revelation of this Ayah. The following are the names of the Prophets whom Allah named in the Qur'an. They are: Adam, Idris, Nuh (Noah), Hud, Salih, Ibrahim (Abraham), Lut, Isma`il (Ishmael), Ishaq (Isaac), Ya`qub (Jacob), Yusuf (Joesph), Ayyub (Job), Shu`ayb, Musa (Moses), Harun (Aaron), Yunus (Jonah), Dawud (David), Sulayman (Solomon), Ilyas (Elias), Al-Yasa` (Elisha), Zakariya (Zachariya), Yahya (John) and `Isa (Jesus), and their leader, Muhammad . Several scholars of Tafsir also listed Dhul-Kifl among the Prophets. Allah's statement,

(and Messengers We have not mentioned to you,) means, `there are other Prophets whom We did not mention to you in the Qur'an.'

The Virtue of Musa

Allah said,

(and to Musa Allah spoke directly.) This is an honor to Musa, and this is why he is called the Kalim, he whom Allah spoke to directly. Al-Hafiz Abu Bakr bin Marduwyah recorded that `Abdul-Jabbar bin `Abdullah said, "A man came to Abu Bakr bin `Ayyash and said, `I heard a man recite (this Ayah this way): "and to Allah, Musa spoke directly." Abu Bakr said, `Only a disbeliever would recite it like this.' Al-A`mash recited it with Yahya bin Withab, who recited it with Abu `Abdur-Rahman As-Sulami who recited it with `Ali bin Abi Talib who recited with the Messenger of Allah ,

(and to Musa Allah spoke directly.)"' Abu Bakr bin Abi Ayyash was so angry with the man who recited the Ayah differently, because he altered its words and meanings. That person was from the group of Mu`tazilah who denied that Allah spoke to Musa or that He speaks to any of His creation. We were told that some of the Mu`tazilah once recited the Ayah that way, so one teacher present said to him, "O son of a stinking woman! What would you do concerning Allah's statement,

(And when Musa came at the time and place appointed by Us, and his Lord spoke to him,) (7:143)" The Shaykh meant that the later Ayah cannot be altered or changed.

The Reason Behind Sending the Prophets is to Establish the Proof

Allah said,

(Messengers as bearers of good news as well as of warning,) meaning, the Prophets bring good news to those who obey Allah and practice the good things that please Him. They also warn against His punishment and torment for those who defy His commandments. Allah said next,

(in order that mankind should have no plea against Allah after the Messengers. And Allah is Ever All-Powerful, All-Wise.) Allah sent down His Books and sent His Messengers with good news and warnings. He explained what He likes and is pleased with and what He dislikes and is displeased with. This way, no one will have an excuse with Allah. Allah said in other Ayat,

(And if We had destroyed them with a torment before this, they would surely have said: "Our Lord! If only You had sent us a Messenger, we should certainly have followed Your Ayat, before we were humiliated and disgraced.") and,

(And if (We had) not (sent you to the people of Makkah) in case a calamity should seize them for (the deeds) that their hands have sent forth.) It is recorded in the Two Sahihs that Ibn Mas`ud said that the Messenger of Allah said,

«لَا أَحَدَ أَغْيَرُ مِنَ اللهِ، مِنْ أَجْلِ ذٰلِكَ حَرَّمَ الْفَوَاحِشَ مَا ظَهَرَ مِنْهَا وَمَا بَطَنَ، وَلَا أَحَدْ أَحَبُّ إِلَيْهِ الْمَدْحُ مِنَ اللهِ عَزَّ وَجَلَّ، مِنْ أَجْلِ ذٰلِكَ مَدَحَ نَفْسَهُ، وَلَا أَحَدَ أَحَبُّ إِلَيْهِ الْعُذْرُ مِنَ اللهِ، مِنْ أَجْلِ ذٰلِكَ بَعَثَ النَّبِيِّينَ مُبَشِّرِينَ وَمُنْذِرِين»

(No one is more jealous than Allah. This is why He prohibited all types of sin committed in public or secret. No one likes praise more than Allah, and this is why He has praised Himself. No one likes to give excuse more than Allah, and this is why He sent the Prophets as bearers of good news and as warners.) In another narration, the Prophet said,

«مِنْ أَجْلِ ذٰلِكَ أَرْسَلَ رُسُلَهُ وَأَنْزَلَ كُتُبَه»

(And this is why He sent His Messengers and revealed His Books.)

Surah: 4 Ayah: 166, Ayah: 167, Ayah: 168, Ayah: 169 & Ayah: 170

﴿ لَّٰكِنِ ٱللَّهُ يَشْهَدُ بِمَآ أَنزَلَ إِلَيْكَ ۖ أَنزَلَهُۥ بِعِلْمِهِۦ ۖ وَٱلْمَلَٰٓئِكَةُ يَشْهَدُونَ ۚ وَكَفَىٰ بِٱللَّهِ
شَهِيدًا ﴿١٦٦﴾ ﴾

166. But Allâh bears witness to that which He has sent down (the Qur'ân) unto you (O Muhammad (peace be upon him)) He has sent it down with His Knowledge, and the angels bear witness. And Allâh is All-Sufficient as a Witness.

﴿ إِنَّ ٱلَّذِينَ كَفَرُوا۟ وَصَدُّوا۟ عَن سَبِيلِ ٱللَّهِ قَدْ ضَلُّوا۟ ضَلَٰلًۢا بَعِيدًا ﴿١٦٧﴾ ﴾

167. Verily, those who disbelieve (by concealing the truth about Prophet Muhammad (peace be upon him) and his message of true Islâmic Monotheism written in the Taurât (Torah) and the Injeel (Gospel) with them) and prevent (mankind) from the Path of Allâh (Islâmic Monotheism); they have certainly strayed far away. (Tafsir Al-Qurtubî).

﴿ إِنَّ ٱلَّذِينَ كَفَرُوا۟ وَظَلَمُوا۟ لَمْ يَكُنِ ٱللَّهُ لِيَغْفِرَ لَهُمْ وَلَا لِيَهْدِيَهُمْ طَرِيقًا ﴿١٦٨﴾ ﴾

168. Verily, those who disbelieve and did wrong (by concealing the truth about Prophet Muhammad (peace be upon him) and his message of true Islâmic Monotheism written in the Taurât (Torah) and the Injeel (Gospel) with them); Allâh will not forgive them, nor will He guide them to any way - (Tafsir Al-Qurtubî).

﴿ إِلَّا طَرِيقَ جَهَنَّمَ خَٰلِدِينَ فِيهَآ أَبَدًا ۚ وَكَانَ ذَٰلِكَ عَلَى ٱللَّهِ يَسِيرًا ﴿١٦٩﴾ ﴾

169. Except the way of Hell, to dwell therein forever; and this is ever easy for Allâh.

﴿ يَٰٓأَيُّهَا ٱلنَّاسُ قَدْ جَآءَكُمُ ٱلرَّسُولُ بِٱلْحَقِّ مِن رَّبِّكُمْ فَـَٔامِنُوا۟ خَيْرًا لَّكُمْ ۚ وَإِن تَكْفُرُوا۟ فَإِنَّ
لِلَّهِ مَا فِى ٱلسَّمَٰوَٰتِ وَٱلْأَرْضِ ۚ وَكَانَ ٱللَّهُ عَلِيمًا حَكِيمًا ﴿١٧٠﴾ ﴾

170. O mankind! Verily, there has come to you the Messenger (Muhammad (peace be upon him)) with the truth from your Lord. So believe in him, it is better for you. But if you disbelieve, then certainly to Allâh belongs all that is in the heavens and the earth. And Allâh is Ever All-Knowing, All-Wise.

Transliteration

166. Lakini Allahu yashhadu bima anzala ilayka anzalahu biAAilmihi waalmala-ikatu yashhadoona wakafa biAllahi shaheedan 167. Inna allatheena kafaroo wasaddoo AAan sabeeli Allahi qad dalloo dalalan baAAeedan 168. Inna allatheena kafaroo wathalamoo lam yakuni Allahu liyaghfira lahum wala liyahdiyahum tareeqan 169. Illa tareeqa jahannama khalideena feeha abadan wakana thalika AAala Allahi yaseeran 170. Ya ayyuha alnnasu qad jaakumu alrrasoolu bialhaqqi min rabbikum faaminoo khayran lakum wa-in takfuroo fa-inna lillahi ma fee alssamawati waal-ardi wakana Allahu AAaleeman hakeeman

Tafsir Ibn Kathir

(Verily, We have inspired you...) emphasized the Prophet's prophethood and refuted the idolators and People of the Scripture who denied him. Allah said,

(But Allah bears witness to that which He has sent down unto you,) meaning, even if they deny, defy and disbelieve in you, O Muhammad, Allah testifies that you are His Messenger to whom He sent down His Book, the Glorious Qur'an that,

(Falsehood cannot come to it from before it or behind it, (it is) sent down by the All-Wise, Worthy of all praise.) Allah then said,

(He has sent it down with His knowledge,) The knowledge of His that He willed His servants to have access to. Knowledge about the clear signs of guidance and truth, what Allah likes and is pleased with, what He dislikes and is displeased with, and knowledge of the Unseen, such as the past and the future. This also includes knowledge about His honorable attributes that no sent Messenger or illustrious angel can even know without Allah's leave. Similarly, Allah said,

(And they will never compass anything of His knowledge except that which He wills.) and,

(but they will never compass anything of His knowledge.) Allah's statement,

(and the angels bear witness.) to the truth of what you came with and what was revealed and sent down to you, along with Allah's testimony to the same,

(And Allah is All-Sufficient as a Witness.) Allah said,

(Verily, those who disbelieve and prevent (others) from the path of Allah, they have certainly strayed far away.) For they are disbelievers themselves and do not follow the truth. They strive hard to prevent people from following and embracing Allah's path. Therefore, they have defied the truth, deviated, and strayed far away from it. Allah also mentions His judgment against those who disbelieve in His Ayat, Book and Messenger, those who wrong themselves by their disbelief and hindering others from His path, committing sins and violating His prohibitions. Allah states that He will not forgive them;

(nor will He guide them to a way (that is, of good).)

(Except the way of Hell, to dwell therein forever...) and this is the exception. Allah then said,

(O mankind! Verily, there has come to you the Messenger with the truth from your Lord, so believe in him, it is better for you.) This Ayah means, Muhammad has come to you with guidance, the religion of truth and clear proof from Allah. Therefore, believe in what he has brought you and follow him, for this is better for you. Allah then said,

(But if you disbelieve, then certainly to Allah belongs all that is in the heavens and the earth.) Allah is far too rich than to need you or your faith, and no harm could ever affect Him because of your disbelief. Allah said in another Ayah,

(And Musa said: "If you disbelieve, you and all on earth together, then verily, Allah is Rich (Free of all needs), Owner of all praise.") Allah said here,

(And Allah is Ever All-Knowing,) He knows those who deserve to be guided, and He will guide them. He also knows those who deserve deviation, and He leads them to it,

(All-Wise) in His statements, actions, legislation and all that He decrees.

Surah: 4 Ayah: 171

﴿ يَـٰٓأَهْلَ ٱلْكِتَـٰبِ لَا تَغْلُوا۟ فِى دِينِكُمْ وَلَا تَقُولُوا۟ عَلَى ٱللَّهِ إِلَّا ٱلْحَقَّ ۚ إِنَّمَا ٱلْمَسِيحُ
عِيسَى ٱبْنُ مَرْيَمَ رَسُولُ ٱللَّهِ وَكَلِمَتُهُۥٓ أَلْقَىٰهَآ إِلَىٰ مَرْيَمَ وَرُوحٌ مِّنْهُ ۖ فَـَٔامِنُوا۟ بِٱللَّهِ
وَرُسُلِهِۦ ۖ وَلَا تَقُولُوا۟ ثَلَـٰثَةٌ ۚ ٱنتَهُوا۟ خَيْرًا لَّكُمْ ۚ إِنَّمَا ٱللَّهُ إِلَـٰهٌ وَٰحِدٌ ۖ سُبْحَـٰنَهُۥٓ أَن يَكُونَ
لَهُۥ وَلَدٌ ۘ لَّهُۥ مَا فِى ٱلسَّمَـٰوَٰتِ وَمَا فِى ٱلْأَرْضِ ۗ وَكَفَىٰ بِٱللَّهِ وَكِيلًا ﴿١٧١﴾ ﴾

171. O people of the Scripture! Do not exceed the limits in your religion, nor say of Allâh aught but the truth. The Messiah 'Isâ (Jesus), son of Maryam (Mary), was (no more than) a Messenger of Allâh and His Word, ("Be!" - and he was) which He bestowed on Maryam (Mary) and a spirit (Rûh) created by Him; so believe in Allâh and His Messengers. Say not: "Three (trinity)!" Cease! (it is) better for you. For Allâh is (the only) One Ilâh (God), Glory be to Him (Far Exalted is He) above having a son. To Him belongs all that is in the heavens and all that is in the earth. And Allâh is All-Sufficient as a Disposer of affairs.

Transliteration

171. Ya ahla alkitabi la taghloo fee deenikum wala taqooloo AAala Allahi illa alhaqqa innama almaseehu AAeesa ibnu maryama rasoolu Allahi wakalimatuhu alqaha ila maryama waroohun minhu faaminoo biAllahi warusulihi wala taqooloo thalathatun intahoo khayran lakum innama Allahu ilahun wahidun subhanahu an yakoona lahu waladun lahu ma fee alssamawati wama fee al-ardi wakafa biAllahi wakeelan

Tafsir Ibn Kathir

Prohibiting the People of the Book From Going to Extremes in Religion

Allah forbids the People of the Scriptures from going to extremes in religion, which is a common trait of theirs, especially among the Christians. The Christians exaggerated over `Isa until they elevated him above the grade that Allah gave him. They elevated him from the rank of prophethood to being a god, whom they worshipped just as they worshipped Allah. They exaggerated even more in the case of those who they claim were his followers, claiming that they were inspired, thus following every word they uttered whether true or false, be it guidance or misguidance, truth or lies. This is why Allah said,

(They took their rabbis and their monks to be their lords besides Allah.) Imam Ahmad recorded that Ibn `Abbas said that `Umar said that the Messenger of Allah said,

«لَا تُطْرُونِي كَمَا أَطْرَتِ النَّصَارَى عِيسَى ابْنَ مَرْيَمَ. فَإِنَّمَا أَنَا عَبْدٌفَقُولُوا: عَبْدُاللهِ وَرَسُولُه»

(Do not unduly praise me like the Christians exaggerated over `Isa, son of Maryam. Verily, I am only a servant, so say, `Allah's servant and His Messenger.') This is the wording of Al-Bukhari. Imam Ahmad recorded that Anas bin Malik said that a man once said, "O

Muhammad! You are our master and the son of our master, our most righteous person and the son of our most righteous person..." The Messenger of Allah said,

«يَا أَيُّهَا النَّاسُ عَلَيْكُمْ بِقَوْلِكُمْ، وَلَا يَسْتَهْوِيَنَّكُمُ الشَّيْطَانُ،أَنَا مُحَمَّدُ بْنُ عَبْدِاللهِ، عَبْدُاللهِ وَرَسُولُهُ، وَاللهِ مَا أُحِبُّ أَنْ تَرْفَعُونِي فَوْقَ مَنْزِلَتِي الَّتِي أَنْزَلَنِي اللهُ عَزَّ وَجَلَ»

(O people! Say what you have to say, but do not allow Shaytan to trick you. I am Muhammad bin `Abdullah, Allah's servant and Messenger. By Allah! I do not like that you elevate me above the rank that Allah has granted me.) Allah's statement,

(nor say of Allah except the truth.) means, do not lie and claim that Allah has a wife or a son, Allah is far holier than what they attribute to Him. Allah is glorified, praised, and honored in His might, grandure and greatness, and there is no deity worthy of worship nor Lord but Him. Allah said;

(Al-Masih `Isa, son of Maryam, was (no more than) a Messenger of Allah and His Word, which He bestowed on Maryam and a spirit from (created by) Him;) `Isa is only one of Allah's servants and one of His creatures. Allah said to him, `Be', and he was, and He sent him as a Messenger. `Isa was a word from Allah that He bestowed on Maryam, meaning He created him with the word `Be' that He sent with Jibril to Maryam. Jibril blew the life of `Isa into Maryam by Allah's leave, and `Isa came to existence as a result. This incident was in place of the normal conception between man and woman that results in children. This is why `Isa was a word and a Ruh (spirit) created by Allah, as he had no father to conceive him. Rather, he came to existence through the word that Allah uttered, `Be,' and he was, through the life that Allah sent with Jibril. Allah said,

(Al-Masih (`Isa), son of Maryam, was no more than a Messenger; many were the Messengers that passed away before him. His mother (Maryam) was a Siddiqah. They both ate food.) And Allah said,

(Verily, the likeness of `Isa before Allah is the likeness of Adam. He created him from dust, then (He) said to him: "Be! - and he was.)

(And she who guarded her chastity, We breathed into her (garment) and We made her and her son (`Isa) a sign for all that exits.) (21:91)

(And Maryam, the daughter of `Imran who guarded her chastity,) and Allah said concerning the Messiah,

(He (`Isa) was not more than a servant. We granted Our favor to him.)

The Meaning of "His Word and a spirit from Him

`Abdur-Razzaq narrated that Ma`mar said that Qatadah said that the Ayah,

(And His Word, which He bestowed on Maryam and a spirit from (created by) Him;) means, He said,

(Be) and he was. Ibn Abi Hatim recorded that Ahmad bin Sinan Al-Wasiti said that he heard Shadh bin Yahya saying about Allah's statement, (and His Word, which He bestowed on Maryam and a spirit from (created by Him;) "`Isa was not the word. Rather, `Isa came to existence because of the word." Al-Bukhari recorded that `Ubadah bin As-Samit said that the Prophet said,

«مَنْ شَهِدَ أَنْ لَا إِلٰهَ إِلَّا اللهُ، وَحْدَهُ لَا شَرِيكَ لَهُ، وَأَنَّ مُحَمَّدًا عَبْدُهُ وَرَسُولُهُ، وَأَنَّ عِيسَى عَبْدُاللهِ وَرَسُولُهُ وَكَلِمَتُهُ أَلْقَاهَا إِلَى مَرْيَمَ وَرُوحٌ مِنْهُ، وَأَنَّ الْجَنَّةَ حَقٌّ، وَالنَّارَ حَقٌّ، أَدْخَلَهُ اللهُ الْجَنَّةَ عَلَى مَا كَانَ مِنَ الْعَمَلِ»

(If anyone testifies that none has the right to be worshipped but Allah Alone Who has no partners, and that Muhammad is His servant and Messenger, and that `Isa is Allah's servant and Messenger and His Word which He bestowed on Maryam and a spirit created by Him, and that Paradise is true and Hell is true, then Allah will admit him into Paradise with the deeds which he performed.) In another narration, the Prophet said,

«مِنْ أَبْوَابِ الْجَنَّةِ الثَّمَانِيَّةِ يَدْخُلُ مِنْ أَيِّهَا شَاءَ»

(...through any of the eight doors of Paradise he wishes.) Muslim also recorded it. Therefore, `Ruh from Allah', in the Ayah and the Hadith is similar to Allah's statement,

(And has subjected to you all that is in the heavens and all that is in the earth; it is all from Him.) meaning, from His creation. `from Him' does not mean that it is a part of Him, as the Christians claim, may Allah's continued curses be upon them. Saying that something is from Allah, such as the spirit of Allah, the she-camel of Allah or the House of Allah, is meant to honor such items. Allah said,

(This is the she-camel of Allah...) and,

(and sanctify My House for those who circumambulate it.) An authentic Hadith states,

«فَأَدْخُلُ عَلَى رَبِّي فِي دَارِه»

(I will enter on my Lord in His Home) All these examples are meant to honor such items when they are attributed to Allah in this manner. Allah said,

(so believe in Allah and His Messengers.) believe that Allah is One and Alone and that He does not have a son or wife. Know and be certain that `Isa is the servant and Messenger of Allah. Allah said after that,

(Say not: "Three!") do not elevate `Isa and his mother to be gods with Allah. Allah is far holier than what they attribute to Him. In Surat Al-Ma'idah (chapter 5), Allah said,

(Surely, disbelievers are those who said: "Allah is the third of the three." But there is none who has the right to be worshipped but One God.) Allah said at the end of the same Surah,

(And (remember) when Allah will say (on the Day of Resurrection): "O `Isa, son of Maryam! Did you say unto men: `Worship me'") and in its beginning,

(Surely, in disbelief are they who say that Allah is the Messiah, son of Maryam.) The Christians, may Allah curse them, have no limit to their disbelief because of their ignorance, so their deviant statements and their misguidance grows. Some of them believe that `Isa is Allah, some believe that he is one in a trinity and some believe that he is the son of Allah. Their beliefs and creeds are numerous and contradict each other, prompting some people to say that if ten Christians meet, they would end up with eleven sects!

The Christian Sects

Sa`id bin Batriq, the Patriarch of Alexandria and a famous Christian scholar, mentioned in the year four hundred after the Hijrah, that a Christian Council convened during the reign of Constantine, who built the city that bears his name. In this Council, the Christians came up with what they called the Great Trust, which in reality is the Great Treachery. There were more than two thousand patriarchs in this Council, and they were in such disarray that they divided into many sects, where some sects had twenty, fifty or a hundred members, etc.! When the king saw that there were more than three hundred Patriarchs who had the same idea, he agreed with them and adopted their creed. Constantine who was a deviant philosopher -- gave his support to this sect for which, as an honor, churches were built and doctrines were taught to young children, who were baptized on this creed, and books were written about it. Meanwhile, the king oppressed all other sects. Another Council produced the sect known as the Jacobites, while the Nestorians were formed in a third Council. These three sects agreed that `Isa was divine, but disputed regarding the manner in which `Isa's divinity was related to his humanity; were they in unity or did Allah incarnate in `Isa! All three of these sects accuse each other of heresy and, we believe that all three of them are disbelievers. Allah said,

(Cease! (it is) better for you.) meaning, it will be better for you,

(For Allah is (the only) One God, hallowed be He above having a son.) and He is holier than such claim,

(To Him belongs all that is in the heavens and all that is in the earth. And Allah is All-Sufficient as a Disposer of affairs,) for all are creatures, property and servants under His control and disposal, and He is the Disposer of the affairs. Therefore, how can He have a wife or a son among them,

(He is the originator of the heavens and the earth. How can He have children.) and

(And they say: "The Most Gracious (Allah) has begotten a son. Indeed you have brought forth (said) a terrible evil thing.") Up to His saying,

(Alone.)

Surah: 4 Ayah: 172 & Ayah: 173

﴿ لَّن يَسْتَنكِفَ ٱلْمَسِيحُ أَن يَكُونَ عَبْدًا لِّلَّهِ وَلَا ٱلْمَلَٰٓئِكَةُ ٱلْمُقَرَّبُونَ ۚ وَمَن يَسْتَنكِفْ عَنْ
عِبَادَتِهِۦ وَيَسْتَكْبِرْ فَسَيَحْشُرُهُمْ إِلَيْهِ جَمِيعًا ﴿١٧٢﴾ ﴾

172. The Messiah will never be proud to reject to be a slave to Allâh, nor the angels who are the near (to Allâh). And whosoever rejects His worship and is proud, then He will gather them all together unto Himself.

﴿ فَأَمَّا ٱلَّذِينَ ءَامَنُوا۟ وَعَمِلُوا۟ ٱلصَّٰلِحَٰتِ فَيُوَفِّيهِمْ أُجُورَهُمْ وَيَزِيدُهُم مِّن فَضْلِهِۦ ۖ
وَأَمَّا ٱلَّذِينَ ٱسْتَنكَفُوا۟ وَٱسْتَكْبَرُوا۟ فَيُعَذِّبُهُمْ عَذَابًا أَلِيمًا وَلَا يَجِدُونَ لَهُم مِّن دُونِ ٱللَّهِ
وَلِيًّا وَلَا نَصِيرًا ﴿١٧٣﴾ ﴾

173. So, as for those who believed (in the Oneness of Allâh - Islâmic Monotheism) and did deeds of righteousness, He will give them their (due) rewards - and more out of His Bounty. But as for those who refused His worship and were proud, He will punish them with a painful torment . And they will not find for themselves besides Allâh any protector or helper.

Transliteration

172. Lan yastankifa almaseehu an yakoona AAabdan lillahi wala almala-ikatu almuqarraboona waman yastankif AAan AAibadatihi wayastakbir fasayahshuruhum ilayhi jameeAAan 173. Faamma allatheena amanoo waAAamiloo alssalihati fayuwaffeehim ojoorahum wayazeeduhum min fadlihi waamma allatheena istankafoo waistakbaroo fayuAAaththibuhum AAathaban aleeman wala yajidoona lahum min dooni Allahi waliyyan wala naseeran

Tafsir Ibn Kathir

The Prophets and Angels Are Never too Proud to Worship Allah

Ibn Abi Hatim recorded that Ibn `Abbas said that, `proud', means insolent. Qatadah said that,

(Al-Masih will never be too proud to be a servant of Allah nor the angels who are near (to Allah).) (they) will never be arrogant, Allah then said,

(And whosoever rejects His worship and is proud, then He will gather them all together unto Himself.) on the Day of Resurrection. Then, Allah will judge between them with His just judgment that is never unjust or wrong.

(So, as for those who believed and did deeds of righteousness, He will give their (due) rewards, and more out of His bounty.) Allah will award them their full rewards for their righteous actions and will give them more of His bounty, kindness, ample mercy and favor.

(But as for those who refused His worship and were proud,) out of arrogance, they refused to obey and worship Him,

(He will punish them with a painful torment. And they will not find for themselves besides Allah any protector or helper.) In another Ayah, Allah said,

(Verily! Those who scorn My worship, they will surely enter Hell in humiliation,) degradation, disgrace and dishonor, for they were arrogant and rebellious.

Surah: 4 Ayah: 174 & Ayah: 175

﴿ يَٰٓأَيُّهَا ٱلنَّاسُ قَدْ جَآءَكُم بُرْهَٰنٌ مِّن رَّبِّكُمْ وَأَنزَلْنَآ إِلَيْكُمْ نُورًا مُّبِينًا ﴿١٧٤﴾ ﴾

174. O mankind! Verily, there has come to you a convincing proof (Prophet Muhammad (peace be upon him)) from your Lord; and We sent down to you a manifest light (this Qur'ân).

﴿ فَأَمَّا ٱلَّذِينَ ءَامَنُوا۟ بِٱللَّهِ وَٱعْتَصَمُوا۟ بِهِۦ فَسَيُدْخِلُهُمْ فِى رَحْمَةٍ مِّنْهُ وَفَضْلٍ وَيَهْدِيهِمْ
إِلَيْهِ صِرَٰطًا مُّسْتَقِيمًا ﴿١٧٥﴾ ﴾

175. So, as for those who believed in Allâh and held fast to Him, He will admit them to His Mercy and Grace (i.e. Paradise), and guide them to Himself by the Straight Path.

Transliteration

174. Ya ayyuha alnnasu qad jaakum burhanun min rabbikum waanzalna ilaykum nooran mubeenan 175. Faamma allatheena amanoo biAllahi waiAAtasamoo bihi fasayudkhiluhum fee rahmatin minhu wafadlin wayahdeehim ilayhi siratan mustaqeeman

Tafsir Ibn Kathir

The Description of the Revelation that Came From Allah

Allah informs all people that a plain, unequivocal proof has come to them from Him. One that eradicates all possibility of having an excuse, or falling prey to evil doubts. Allah said,

(and We sent down to you a manifest light.) that directs to the Truth. Ibn Jurayj and others said, "It is the Qur'an."

(So, as for those who believed in Allah and held fast to (depend on) Him,) by worshipping Him and relying on Him for each and every thing. Ibn Jurayj said that this part of the Ayah means, "They believe in Allah and hold fast to the Qur'an."

(He will admit them to His mercy and grace,) meaning, He will grant them His mercy and admit them into Paradise, and will increase and multiply their rewards and their ranks, as a favor and bounty from Him.

(and guide them to Himself by a straight path.) and a clear way that has no wickedness in it or deviation. This, indeed, is the description of the believers in this life and the Hereafter, as they are on the straight and safe path in matters of action and creed. In the Hereafter, they are on the straight path of Allah that leads to the gardens of Paradise.

Surah: 4 Ayah: 176

﴿ يَسْتَفْتُونَكَ قُلِ ٱللَّهُ يُفْتِيكُمْ فِى ٱلْكَلَٰلَةِ ۚ إِنِ ٱمْرُؤٌا۟ هَلَكَ لَيْسَ لَهُۥ وَلَدٌ وَلَهُۥٓ أُخْتٌ فَلَهَا
نِصْفُ مَا تَرَكَ ۚ وَهُوَ يَرِثُهَآ إِن لَّمْ يَكُن لَّهَا وَلَدٌ ۚ فَإِن كَانَتَا ٱثْنَتَيْنِ فَلَهُمَا ٱلثُّلُثَانِ مِمَّا تَرَكَ ۚ

وَإِن كَانُوٓاْ إِخْوَةً رِّجَالًا وَنِسَآءً فَلِلذَّكَرِ مِثْلُ حَظِّ ٱلْأُنثَيَيْنِ ۗ يُبَيِّنُ ٱللَّهُ لَكُمْ أَن تَضِلُّواْ ۗ وَٱللَّهُ
بِكُلِّ شَىْءٍ عَلِيمٌۢ ﴿١٧٦﴾

176. They ask you for a legal verdict. Say: "Allâh directs (thus) about Al-Kalâlah (those who leave neither descendants nor ascendants as heirs). If it is a man that dies leaving a sister, but no child, she shall have half the inheritance. If (such a deceased was) a woman, who left no child, her brother takes her inheritance. If there are two sisters, they shall have two-thirds of the inheritance; if there are brothers and sisters, the male will have twice the share of the female. (Thus) does Allâh make clear to you (His Law) lest you go astray. And Allâh is the All-Knower of everything."

Transliteration

176. Yastaftoonaka quli Allahu yufteekum fee alkalalati ini imruon halaka laysa lahu waladun walahu okhtun falaha nisfu ma taraka wahuwa yarithuha in lam yakun laha waladun fa-in kanata ithnatayni falahuma alththuluthani mimma taraka wa-in kanoo ikhwatan rijalan wanisaan falilththakari mithlu haththi alonthayayni yubayyinu Allahu lakum an tadilloo waAllahu bikulli shay-in AAaleemun

Tafsir Ibn Kathir

This is the Last Ayah Ever Revealed, the Ruling on Al-Kalalah

Al-Bukhari recorded that Al-Bara' said that the last Surah to be revealed was Surah Bara'ah (chapter 9) and the last Ayah to be revealed was, (They ask you for a legal verdict...) Imam Ahmad recorded that Jabir bin `Abdullah said, "The Messenger of Allah came visiting me when I was so ill that I fell unconscious. He performed ablution and poured the remaining water on me, or had it poured on me. When I regained consciousness, I said, `I will only leave inheritance through Kalalah, so what about the inheritance that I leave behind' Allah later revealed the Ayah about Fara'id (inheritance (4:11))."' The Two Sahihs and also the Group recorded it. In one of the wordings, Jabir said that the Ayah on inheritance was revealed;

(They ask you for a legal verdict. Say: "Allah directs (thus) about Al-Kalalah.) The wording of the Ayah indicates that the question was about the Kalalah, (Say: "Allah directs (thus)...) We mentioned the meaning of Kalalah before, that it means the crown that surrounds the head from all sides. This is why the scholars stated that Kalalah pertains to one who dies and leaves behind neither descendants, nor ascendants. Some said that the Kalalah pertains to one who has no offspring, as the Ayah states, (If it is a man that dies, leaving no child,) The meaning and ruling of Kalalah was somewhat confusing to the Leader of the Faithful `Umar bin Al-Khattab. It is recorded in the Two Sahihs that `Umar said, "There are three matters that I wished the Messenger of Allah had explained to us, so that we could abide by his explanation. (They are: the share in the inheritance of) the grandfather, the Kalalah and a certain type of Riba." Imam Ahmad recorded that Ma`dan bin Abi Talhah said that `Umar bin Al-Khattab said, "There is nothing that I asked the Messenger of Allah about its meaning more than the Kalalah, until he stabbed me with his finger in my chest and said,

«يَكْفِيكَ آيَةُ الصَّيْفِ الَّتِي فِي آخِرِ سُورَةِ النِّسَاء»

(The Ayah that is in the end of Surat An-Nisa' should suffice for you.)" Ahmad mentioned this short narration for this Hadith, Muslim recorded a longer form of it.

The Meaning of This Ayah

Allah said, (If it is a man that dies.) Allah said in another Ayah, (Everything will perish save His Face.) Therefore, everything and everyone dies and perishes except Allah, the Exalted and Most Honored. Allah said, (Whatsoever is on it (the earth) will perish. And the Face of your Lord full of majesty and honor will remain forever.) Allah said here, (leaving no child,) referring to the person who has neither children, nor parents. What testifies to this, is that Allah said afterwards, (Leaving a sister, she shall have half the inheritance.) Had there been a surviving ascendant, the sister would not have inherited anything, and there is a consensus on this point. Therefore, this Ayah is referring to the man who dies leaving behind neither descendants nor ascendants, as is apparent for those who contemplate its meaning. This is because when there is a surviving parent, the sister does not inherit anything, let alone half of the inheritance. Ibn Jarir and others mentioned that Ibn `Abbas and Ibn Az-Zubayr used to judge that if a person dies and leaves behind a daughter and a sister, the sister does not inherit anything. They would recite,

(If it is a man that dies, leaving a sister, but no child, she shall have half the inheritance.) They said that if one leaves behind a daughter, then he has left behind a child. Therefore the sister does not get anything. The majority of scholars disagreed with them, saying the daughter gets one half and the sister the other half, relying on other evidence. This Ayah (4:176 above) gives the sister half of the inheritance in the case that it specifies. As for giving the sister half in other cases, Al-Bukhari recorded that Sulayman said that Ibrahim reported to Al-Aswad that he said, "During the time of the Messenger of Allah , Mu`adh bin Jabal gave a judgment that the daughter gets one half and the sister the other half." Al-Bukhari recorded that Huzayl bin Shurahbil said, "Abu Musa Al-Ash`ari was asked about the case when there was a daughter, grand-daughter and sister to inherit. He said, `The daughter gets one-half and the sister one-half.' Go and ask Ibn Mas`ud, although I think he is going to agree with me.' So Ibn Mas`ud was asked and was told about Abu Musa's answer, and Ibn Mas`ud commented, `I would have deviated then and would not have become among those who are rightly guided. I will give a judgment similar to the judgment given by the Prophet . The daughter gets one-half, the grand-daughter gets one-sixth, and these two shares will add up to two-thirds. Whatever is left will be for the sister.' We went back to Abu Musa and conveyed to him Ibn Mas`ud's answer and he said, `Do not ask me (for legal verdicts) as long as this scholar is still among you.'" Allah then said,

(... and he will be her heir if she has no children.) This Ayah means, the brother inherits all of that his sister leaves behind if she has no surviving offspring or parents. If she has a surviving parent, her brother would not inherit anything. If there is someone who gets a fixed share in the inheritance, such as a husband or half brother from the mother's side, they take their share and the rest goes to the brother. It is recorded in the Two Sahihs that Ibn `Abbas said that the Messenger of Allah said,

«أَلْحِقُوا الْفَرَائِضَ بِأَهْلِهَا، فَمَا أَبْقَتِ الْفَرَائِضُ فَلِأَوْلَى رَجُلٍ ذَكَرٍ»

(Give the Farai'd to its people, and whatever is left is the share of the nearest male relative.) Allah said,

(If there are two sisters, they shall have two-thirds of the inheritance;) meaning, if the person who dies in Kalalah has two sisters, they get two-thirds of the inheritance. More than two sisters share in the two-thirds. From this Ayah, the scholars took the ruling regarding the two daughters, or more, that they share in the two-thirds, just as the share of the sisters (two or more) was taken from the Ayah about the daughters, (if (there are) only daughters, two or more, their share is two thirds of the inheritance.) (4:11). Allah said,

(if there are brothers and sisters, the male will have twice the share of the female.) This is the share that the male relatives (sons, grandsons, brothers) regularly get, that is, twice as much as the female gets. Allah said, ((Thus) does Allah make clear to you...) His Law and set limits, clarifying His legislation,

(Lest you go astray.) from the truth after this explanation,

(And Allah is the All-Knower of everything.) Allah has perfect knowledge in the consequences of everything and in the benefit that each matter carries for His servants. He also knows what each of the relatives deserves from the inheritance, according to the degree of relation he or she has with the deceased. Ibn Jarir recorded that Tariq bin Shihab said that `Umar gathered the Companions of the Messenger of Allah once and said, "I will give a ruling concerning the Kalalah that even women will talk about it in their bedrooms." A snake then appeared in the house and the gathering had to disperse. `Umar commented, `Had Allah willed this (`Umar's verdict regarding the Kalalah) to happen, it would have happened." The chain of narration for this story is authentic. Al-Hakim, Abu `Abdullah An-Naysaburi recorded that `Umar bin Al-Khattab said, `Had I asked the Messenger of Allah regarding three things, it would have been better for me than red camels. (They are:) who should be the Khalifah after him; about a people who said, `We agree to pay Zakah, but not to you (meaning to the Khalifah),' if we are allowed to fight them; and about the Kalalah." Al-Hakim said, "Its chain is Sahih according to the Two Shaykhs, and they did not recorded it." Ibn Jarir also said that it was reported that `Umar said, "I feel shy to change a ruling that Abu Bakr issued. Abu Bakr used to say that the Kalalah is the person who has no descendants or ascendants." Abu Bakr's saying is what the majority of scholars among the Companions, their followers and the earlier and later Imams agree with. This is also the ruling that the Qur'an indicates. For Allah stated that He has explained and made plain the ruling of the Kalalah, when He said,

((Thus) does Allah makes clear to you (His Law) lest you go astray. And Allah is the All-Knower of everything.) And Allah knows best.

INTRODUCTION TO CHAPTER (SURAH) 5: AL-MAIDAH (THE TABLE, THE TABLE SPREAD)

Maududi's Introduction

Name

This Sarah takes its' name from verse 112 in which the word mai'dah occurs. Like the names of many other surahs, this name has no special relation to the subject of the Surah but has been used merely as a symbol to distinguish it from other surahs.

Period of Revelation

The theme of this Surah indicates, and traditions support it, that it was revealed after the treaty of Hudaibiyah at the end of 6 A. H. or in the beginning of 7 A. H. That is why it deals with those problems that arose from this treaty.

The Holy Prophet with 1400 Muslims went to Makkah in Zil-Qaadah 6 A. H. to perform `Umrah, but the Quraish spurred by their enmity, prevented him from its performance, though it was utterly against all the ancient religious traditions of Arabia. After a good deal of hard and harsh negotiations, a treaty was concluded at Hudaibiyah according to which it was agreed that he could perform `Umrah the following year. That was a very appropriate occasion for teaching the Muslims the right way of performing a pilgrimage to Makkah with the true Islamic dignity, and enjoining that they should not prevent the disbelievers from performing pilgrimage to Makkah as a retaliation for their misbehavior. This was not difficult at all as many disbelievers had to pass through Muslim territory on their way to Makkah. This is why the introductory verses deal with the things connected with pilgrimage to Makkah and the same theme has been resumed in vv. 101-104. The other topics of this Surah also appear to belong to the same period.

The continuity of the subject shows that most probably the whole of the surah was revealed as a single discourse at one and the same time. It is also possible that some of its verses were revealed at a later period and inserted in this Surah at different places where they fitted in. But there appears to be not the least gap anywhere in the surah to show that it might have comprised two or more discourses.

Occasion of Revelation

This Surah was revealed to suit the requirements of the changed conditions which were now different from those prevailing at the time of the revelation of Al-i-'Imran and An- Nisa. Then the shock of the set-back at Uhd had made the very surroundings of Al-Madinah dangerous for the Muslims, but now Islam had become an invulnerable power and the Islamic State had extended to Najd on the east, to the Red Sea on the west, to Syria on the north and to Makkah on the south. This set-back which the Muslims had suffered at Uhd had not broken their determination. It had rather spurred them to action. As a result of their continuous struggle and unparalleled sacrifices, the power of. the surrounding clans, within a radius of 200 miles or so, had been broken. The Jewish menace which was always threatening Al-Madinah had been totally removed and the Jews in the other parts of Hijaz had-become tributaries of the State of Al-Madinah. The last effort of the Quraish to suppress Islam had been thwarted in the Battle of the Ditch. After this, it had become quite obvious to the Arabs that no power could suppress the Islamic movement. Now Islam was not merely a creed which ruled over the minds and hearts of the people but had also become a State which dominated over every aspect of the life of the people who lived within its boundaries. This had enabled the Muslims to live their lives without let or hindrance, in accordance with their beliefs.

Another development had also taken place during this period. The Muslim civilization had developed in accordance with the principles of Islam and the Islamic viewpoint. This civilization was quite distinct from all other civilizations in all its' details, and distinguished the Muslims clearly from the non Muslims in their moral, social and cultural behavior. Mosques had been built in all territories, prayer had been established and' Imam (leader) for every habitation and clan had been appointed. The Islamic civil and criminal laws had been formulated in detail and were being enforced through the Islamic courts. New and reformed ways of trade and commerce had taken the place of the old ones. The Islamic laws of marriage and divorce, of the segregation of the sexes, of the punishment for adultery and calumny and the like had cast the social life of the Muslims in a special mould. Their social behavior, their conversation, their dress, their very mode of living, their culture etc., had taken a definite shape of its own. As a result of all these changes, the non-Muslims could not expect that the Muslims would ever return to their former fold.

Before the treaty of Hudaibiyah, the Muslims were so engaged in their struggle with the non-Muslim Quraish that they got no time to propagate their message. This hindrance was removed by what was apparently a defeat but in reality a victory at Hudaibiyah. This gave the Muslims not only peace in their own territory but also respite to spread their message in the surrounding territories. Accordingly the Holy Prophet addressed letters to the rulers of Iran, Egypt and the Roman Empire and the chiefs of Arabia, inviting them to Islam. At the same time the missionaries of Islam spread among the clans and tribes and invited them to accept the Divine Way of Allah. These were the circumstances at the time when Al-Ma'idah was revealed.

Topics

It deals with the following three main topics:

1. Commandments and instructions about the religious, cultural and political life of the Muslims.

In this connection, a code of ceremonial rules concerning the journey for Haj has been prescribed; the observance of strict respect for the emblems of Allah has been enjoined; and any kind of obstruction or interference with the pilgrims to the Kaabah has been prohibited. Definite rules and regulations have been laid down for what is lawful and unlawful in the matter of food, and self-imposed foolish restrictions of the pre-Islamic age have been abolished. Permission has been given to. take food with the people of the Book and to marry their women. Rules and regulations for the performance of Wudu (ablutions) and bath and purification and tayammum (ablutions with dust) havebeen prescribed. Punishment for rebellion, disturbance of peace and theft have been specified. Drinking and gambling have absolutely been made unlawful. Expiation for the breaking of oath has been laid down and a few more things have been added to the law of evidence.

2. Admonition to the Muslims.

Now that the Muslims had become a ruling body, it was feared that power might corrupt them. At this period of great trial, Allah had admonished them over and over again to stick to justice and to guard against the wrong behavior of their predecessors, the people of the Book. They have been enjoined to remain steadfast to the Covenant of obedience to Allah and His Messenger, and to observe strictly their commands and prohibitions in order to save themselves from the evil consequences which. befell the Jews and the Christians who had violated them. They have been instructed to observe the dictates of the Holy Quran in the conduct of all their affairs and warned against the attitude of hypocrisy.

3. Admonition to the Jews and the Christians.

As the power of the Jews had been totally weakened and almost all their habitations in north Arabia had come under the rule of the Muslims, they have been warned again about their wrong attitude and invited to follow the Right Way. At the same time a detailed invitation has also been extended to the Christians. The errors of their creeds have been clearly pointed out and they have been admonished to accept the guidance of the Holy Prophet. . Incidentally, it may be noted that no direct invitation has been made to the Majusis and idolaters living in the adjoining countries, because there was no need for a separate address for them as their condition. had already been covered by the addresses to the mushrik Arabs.

Subject:Consolidation of the Islamic Community

In continuation of the instructions about the consolidation of the Islamic Community given in Surah AN-NISA, the Muslims have been directed to observe and fulfill all their obligations: further regulations have been prescribed to train the Muslims for that purpose.

They have also been particularly warned as rulers to guard against the corruption, ofpower and directed to observe the Covenant of the Quran. They have also been exhorted to learn lessons from the failings of their predecessors, the Jews and the Christians, who in their turn have been admonished to give up their wrong attitudes towards the Right Way and accept the guidance taught by Prophet Muhammad (God's peace be upon him).

Topics and their Interconnection

The Believers have been exhorted to fulfill scrupulously all of their obligations andfollow the regulations prescribed by the Divine Law about food, sex, Salat, justice, etc. 1 - 10

The Muslims have been warned to guard against the errors of their predecessors; they should follow the Right Path and avoid the bad example of the Jews and the Christians, who broke their Covenants and went astray into evil ways. They, in their turn, have been admonished to give up their wrong ways and accept Islam. 11 - 26

The story of the two sons of Adam has been related to reproach the Jews for their plot to kill the Holy Prophet and his Companions. (v. 11 & E.N. 30). The story has also been used to emphasize the sanctity of human life. 27 - 32

To achieve this object, punishments have been prescribed for those who create chaos in the Islamic State, and the Believers have been urged to exert their utmost to establish the Right Way; the sanctity of property has also been emphasized. 33 - 40

The Holy Prophet (and through him the Muslims) has been reassured that he should not mind the enmity, the evil designs and the machinations of the Jews, but continue exerting his utmost to establish the Right Way in accordance with the Guidance of the Quran; for nothing better could be expected from those who had forsaken their own Torah. He should deal with the Christians likewise, for they, too, had forsaken their Gospel. 41 - 50

In view of the degenerate moral condition of the Jews and the Christians, the Believers have been warned not to make them their friends and confidants. Likewise they should be on their guard against the evil designs of the hypocrites, the disbelievers and the like and should rely on the true Believers alone. The people of the Book have, in their turn been exhorted to give up their enmity and adopt the right attitude, for they cannot get salvation without this. 51 - 69

The theme of the corruptions of the Jews and Christians has been resumed. The Christians especially have been reproved for their errors in regard to the doctrine of Tauhid. At the same time they have been preferred to the hard hearted Jews, for there are among them some who are more inclined towards the Truth. 70 - 86

In this portion of the Surah, further regulations about the lawful and the un-lawful, in addition to those contained in vv. 1 - 10, have been given. 87 - 108

At the end of the Surah, the mention of the conversation that will take place between Allah and His Prophets on the Day of Judgment, has been made for the benefit of the erring people to serve as a corrective to their creeds. The conversation with Prophet Christ has been cited as a specimen to warn particularly the Christians, who profess to believe in him, and generally all those people who put false hopes in their Prophets, etc. 109 - 119

Conclusion: "O man-kind! The Sovereignty of the heavens and the earth belongs to Allah: therefore you should become His true servants and fear Him, for He has full powers over everything." 120

Ibn kathir's Introduction

The Virtues of Surat Al-Ma'idah; When It was Revealed

At-Tirmidhi recorded that `Abdullah bin `Amr said, "The last Surahs to be revealed were Surat Al-Ma'idah and Surat Al-Fath (chapter 48)." At-Tirmidhi commented, "This Hadith is Hasan, Gharib." and it was also reported that Ibn `Abbas said that the last Surah to be revealed was,

(When there comes the help of Allah and the Conquest,) Al-Hakim collected a narration similar to that of At-Tirmidhi in his Mustadrak, and he said, "It is Sahih according to the criteria of the Two Shaykhs and they did not record it." Al-Hakim narrated that Jubayr bin Nufayr said, "I performed Hajj once and visited `A'ishah and she said to me, `O Jubayr! Do you read (or memorize) Al-Ma'idah ' I answered `Yes.' She said, `It was the last Surah to be revealed. Therefore, whatever permissible matters you find in it, then consider (treat) them permissible. And whatever impermissible matters you find in it, then consider (treat) them impermissible.'" Al-Hakim said, "It is Sahih according to the criteria of the Two Shaykhs and they did not record it. " Imam Ahmad recorded that `Abdur-Rahman bin Mahdi related that Mu`awiyah bin Salih added this statement in the last Hadith, "I (Jubayr) also asked `A'ishah about the Messenger of Allah's conduct and she answered by saying, `The Qur'an.'" An-Nasa'i also recorded it.

CHAPTER (SURAH) 5: AL-MAIDAH (THE TABLE, THE TABLE SPREAD), VERSES 001-081

﴿ بِسْمِ ٱللَّهِ ٱلرَّحْمَٰنِ ٱلرَّحِيمِ ۝١ ﴾

In the Name of Allâh, the Most Gracious, the Most Merciful.

Surah: 5 Ayah: 1 & Ayah: 2

﴿ يَٰٓأَيُّهَا ٱلَّذِينَ ءَامَنُوٓا۟ أَوْفُوا۟ بِٱلْعُقُودِ ۚ أُحِلَّتْ لَكُم بَهِيمَةُ ٱلْأَنْعَٰمِ إِلَّا مَا يُتْلَىٰ عَلَيْكُمْ غَيْرَ مُحِلِّى ٱلصَّيْدِ وَأَنتُمْ حُرُمٌ ۗ إِنَّ ٱللَّهَ يَحْكُمُ مَا يُرِيدُ ۝١ ﴾

1. O you who believe! Fulfill (your) obligations. Lawful to you (for food) are all the beasts of cattle except that which will be announced to you (herein), game (also) being unlawful

when you assume Ihrâm for Hajj or 'Umrah (pilgrimage). Verily, Allâh commands that which He wills.

﴿ يَٰٓأَيُّهَا ٱلَّذِينَ ءَامَنُواْ لَا تُحِلُّواْ شَعَٰٓئِرَ ٱللَّهِ وَلَا ٱلشَّهۡرَ ٱلۡحَرَامَ وَلَا ٱلۡهَدۡيَ وَلَا ٱلۡقَلَٰٓئِدَ وَلَآ
ءَآمِّينَ ٱلۡبَيۡتَ ٱلۡحَرَامَ يَبۡتَغُونَ فَضۡلٗا مِّن رَّبِّهِمۡ وَرِضۡوَٰنٗاۚ وَإِذَا حَلَلۡتُمۡ فَٱصۡطَادُواْۚ وَلَا
يَجۡرِمَنَّكُمۡ شَنَـَٔانُ قَوۡمٍ أَن صَدُّوكُمۡ عَنِ ٱلۡمَسۡجِدِ ٱلۡحَرَامِ أَن تَعۡتَدُواْۘ وَتَعَاوَنُواْ عَلَى ٱلۡبِرِّ
وَٱلتَّقۡوَىٰۖ وَلَا تَعَاوَنُواْ عَلَى ٱلۡإِثۡمِ وَٱلۡعُدۡوَٰنِۚ وَٱتَّقُواْ ٱللَّهَۖ إِنَّ ٱللَّهَ شَدِيدُ ٱلۡعِقَابِ ٢ ﴾

2. O you who believe! Violate not the sanctity of the Symbols of Allâh, nor of the Sacred Month, nor of the animals brought for sacrifice, nor the garlanded people or animals, and others nor the people coming to the Sacred House (Makkah), seeking the bounty and good pleasure of their Lord. But when you finish the Ihrâm (of Hajj or 'Umrah), you may hunt, and let not the hatred of some people in (once) stopping you from Al-Masjid-al-Harâm (at Makkah) lead you to transgression (and hostility on your part). Help you one another in Al-Birr and At-Taqwa (virtue, righteousness and piety); but do not help one another in sin and transgression. And fear Allâh. Verily, Allâh is Severe in punishment.

Transliteration

1. Ya ayyuha allatheena amanoo awfoo bialAAuqoodi ohillat lakum baheematu al-anAAami illa ma yutla AAalaykum ghayra muhillee alssaydi waantum hurumun inna Allaha yahkumu ma yureedu 2. Ya ayyuha allatheena amanoo la tuhilloo shaAAa-ira Allahi wala alshshahra alharama wala alhadya wala alqala-ida wala ammeena albayta alharama yabtaghoona fadlan min rabbihim waridwanan wa-itha halaltum faistadoo wala yajrimannakum shanaanu qawmin an saddookum AAani almasjidi alharami an taAAtadoo wataAAawanoo AAala albirri waalttaqwa wala taAAawanoo AAala al-ithmi waalAAudwani waittaqoo Allaha inna Allaha shadeedu alAAiqabi

Tafsir Ibn Kathir

Ibn Abi Hatim recorded that a man came to `Abdullah bin Mas`ud and said to him, "Advise me." He said, "When you hear Allah's statement,

(O you who believe!) then pay full attention, for it is a righteous matter that He is ordaining or an evil thing that He is forbidding." Khaythamah said, "Everything in the Qur'an that reads,

(O you who believe!) reads in the Tawrah, `O you who are in need.'" Allah said,

(Fulfill (your) obligations.) Ibn `Abbas, Mujahid and others said that `obligations' here means treaties. Ibn Jarir mentioned that there is a consensus for this view. Ibn Jarir also said that it means treaties, such as the alliances that they used to conduct. `Ali bin Abi Talhah reported that Ibn `Abbas commented:

(O you who believe! Fulfill (your) obligations.) "Refers to the covenants, meaning, what Allah permitted, prohibited, ordained and set limits for in the Qur'an. Therefore, do not commit treachery or break the covenants. Allah emphasized this command when He said,

(And those who break the covenant of Allah, after its ratification, and sever that which Allah has commanded to be joined,) until,

(unhappy (evil) home (i.e. Hell).)" Ad-Dahhak said that,

(Fulfill your obligations.) "Refers to what Allah has permitted and what He has prohibited. Allah has taken the covenant from those who proclaim their faith in the Prophet and the Book to fulfill the obligations that He has ordered for them in the permissible and the impermissible."

Explaining the Lawful and the Unlawful Beasts

Allah said,

(Lawful to you (for food) are all the beasts of cattle) camels, cows and sheep, as Al-Hasan, Qatadah and several others stated. Ibn Jarir said that this Tafsir conforms to the meaning of (`beasts of cattle') that the Arabs had. We should mention that Ibn `Umar, Ibn `Abbas and others relied on this Ayah as evidence to allow eating the meat of the fetus if it is found dead in the belly of its slaughtered mother. There is a Hadith to the same effect collected in the Sunan of Abu Dawud, At-Tirmidhi and Ibn Majah and narrated by Abu Sa`id who said, "We asked, `O Messenger of Allah! When we slaughter a camel, cow or sheep, we sometimes find a fetus in its belly, should we discard it or eat its meat' He said,

«كُلُوهُ إِنْ شِئْتُمْ فَإِنَّ ذَكَاتَهُ ذَكَاةُ أُمِّه»

(Eat it if you want, because its slaughter was fulfilled when its mother was slaughtered.)" At-Tirmidhi said, "This Hadith is Hasan." Abu Dawud recorded that Jabir bin `Abdullah said that the Messenger of Allah said,

«ذَكَاةُ الْجَنِينِ ذَكَاةُ أُمِّه»

(Proper slaughter of the fetus is fulfilled with the slaughter of its mother.) Only Abu Dawud collected this narration. Allah's statement,

(except that which will be announced to you (herein),) `Ali bin Abi Talhah reported that Ibn `Abbas said that it refers to, "The flesh of dead animals, blood and the meat of swine." Qatadah said, "The meat of dead animals and animals slaughtered without Allah's Name being pronounced at the time of slaughtering." It appears, and Allah knows best, that the Ayah refers to Allah's other statement,

(Forbidden to you (for food) are: Al-Maytah (the dead animals), blood, the flesh of swine, and what has been slaughtered as a sacrifice for others than Allah, and that which has been killed by strangling, or by a violent blow, or by a headlong fall, or by the goring of horns - and that which has been (partly) eaten by a wild animal.)(5:3), for although the animals mentioned in this Ayah are types of permissible cattle (except for swine), they become impermissible under the circumstances that the Ayah (5:3) specifies. This is why Allah said afterwards,

(Unless you are able to slaughter it (before its death) and that which is sacrificed (slaughtered) on An-Nusub (stone altars)) as the latter type is not permissible, because it can no longer be slaughtered properly. Hence, Allah's statement,

(Lawful to you are all the beasts of cattle except that which will be announced to you,) means, except the specific circumstances that prohibit some of these which will be announced to you. Allah said,

(game (also) being unlawful when you assume Ihram.) Some scholars said that the general meaning of `cattle' includes domesticated cattle, such as camels, cows and sheep, and wild cattle, such as gazzelle, wild cattle and wild donkeys. Allah made the exceptions mentioned above (dead animals blood, flesh of swine etc.), and prohibited hunting wild beasts while in the state of Ihram. It was also reported that the meaning here is, "We have allowed for you all types of cattle in all circumstances, except what We excluded herewith for the one hunting game while in the state of Ihram." Allah said,

(But if one is forced by necessity, without willful disobedience, and not transgressing, then, Allah is Oft-Forgiving, Most Merciful.) This Ayah means, "We allowed eating the meat of dead animals, when one is forced by necessity, under the condition that one is not transgressing the limits or overstepping them." Here, Allah states, "Just as We allowed the meat of cattle in all conditions and circumstances, then do not hunt game when in the state of Ihram, for this is the decision of Allah, Who is the Most Wise in all that He commands and forbids." So Allah said;

(Verily, Allah commands that which He wills.)

The Necessity of Observing the Sanctity of the Sacred Area and the Sacred Months

Allah continues,

(O you who believe! Violate not the sanctity of Sha'a'ir Allah (the symbols of Allah),) Ibn `Abbas said, "Sha`a'ir Allah means the rituals of Hajj." Mujahid said, "As-Safa and Al-Marwah, and the sacrificial animal are the symbols of Allah." It was also stated that Sha`a'ir Allah is what He prohibited. Therefore, it means, do not violate what Allah prohibited. Allah said afterwards,

(nor of the Sacred Month,) for you are required to respect and honor the Sacred Month and to refrain from what Allah forbade during it, such as fighting. This also lays emphasis on avoiding sins during that time. As Allah said;

(They ask you concerning fighting in the Sacred Month. Say, "Fighting therein is a great (transgression).") and,

(Verily, the number of months with Allah is twelve months (in a year).) Al-Bukhari recorded in his Sahih that Abu Bakrah said that the Messenger of Allah said during the Farewell Hajj,

«إِنَّ الزَّمَانَ قَدِ اسْتَدَارَ كَهَيْئَتِهِ يَوْمَ خَلَقَ اللهُ السَّمَوَاتِ وَالْأَرْضَ السَّنَةُ اثْنَا عَشَرَ شَهْرًا، مِنْهَا أَرْبَعَةٌ حُرُمٌ، ثَلَاثٌ مُتَوَالِيَاتٌ: ذُو الْقَعْدَةِ وَذُو الْحِجَّةِ وَالْمُحَرَّمُ، وَرَجَبُ مُضَرَ الَّذِي بَيْنَ جُمَادَى وَشَعْبَانَ»

(The division of time has returned as it was when Allah created the Heavens and the earth. The year is twelve months, four of which are sacred: Three are in succession, (they are:) Dhul-Qa'dah, Dhul-Hijjah and Muharram, and (the fourth is) Rajab of (the tribe of) Mudar which comes between Jumada (Ath-Thaniyah) and Sha'ban.) This Hadith testifies to the continued sanctity of these months until the end of time.

Taking the Hady to the Sacred House of Allah, Al-Ka`bah

Allah's statement,

(nor of the Hady brought for sacrifice, nor the garlands,) means, do not abandon the practice of bringing the Hady (sacrificial animals) to the Sacred House, as this ritual is a form of honoring the symbols of Allah. Do not abandon the practice of garlanding these animals on their necks, so that they are distinguished from other cattle. This way, it will be known that these animals are intended to be offered as Hady at the Ka`bah, and thus those who might intend some harm to them would refrain from doing so. Those who see the Hady might be encouraged to imitate this ritual, and indeed, he who calls to a type of guidance, will earn rewards equal to the rewards of those who follow his lead, without decrease in their own rewards. When the Messenger of Allah intended to perform Hajj, he spent the night at Dhul-Hulayfah, which is also called Wadi Al-`Aqiq. In the morning, the Prophet made rounds with his wives, who were nine at that time, performed Ghusl (bath), applied some perfume and performed a two Rak`ah prayer. He then garlanded the Hady and announced aloud his intention to perform Hajj and `Umrah. The Prophet's Hady at the time consisted of plenty of camels, more than sixty, and they were among the best animals, the healthiest and most physically acceptable, just as Allah's statement proclaims,

(Thus it is, and whosoever honors the symbols of Allah, then it is truly, from the piety of the hearts.) Muqatil bin Hayyan said that Allah's statement,

(nor the garlands) means, "Do not breach their sanctity." During the time of Jahiliyyah, the people used to garland themselves with animal hair and pelts when they left their areas in months other than the Sacred Months. The idolators of the Sacred House Area used to garland themselves with the tree-stems of the Sacred Area, so that they were granted safe passage." This statement was collected by Ibn Abi Hatim, who also recorded that Ibn `Abbas said, "There are two Ayat in this Surah (Al-Ma'idah) that were abrogated, the Ayah about the garlands (5:2), and

(So if they come to you (O Muhammad), either judge between them, or turn away from them.)"

The Necessity of Preserving the Sanctity and Safety of those who Intend to Travel to the Sacred House

Allah said,

(nor the people coming to the Sacred House (Makkah), seeking the bounty and good pleasure of their Lord.) The Ayah commands: Do not fight people who are heading towards the Sacred House of Allah, which if anyone enters it, he must be granted safe refuge. Likewise, those who are heading towards the Sacred House seeking the bounty and good pleasure of Allah, must not be stopped, prevented, or frightened away from entering the Sacred House. Mujahid, `Ata', Abu Al-`Aliyah, Mutarrif bin `Abdullah, `Abdullah bin `Ubayd bin `Umayr, Ar-Rabi` bin Anas, Muqatil bin Hayyan, Qatadah and several others said that,

(seeking the bounty of their Lord.) refers to trading. A similar discussion preceded concerning the Ayah;

(There is no sin on you if you seek the bounty of your Lord (during pilgrimage by trading).) Allah said;

(and pleasure.) Ibn `Abbas said that the word `pleasure' in the Ayah refers to, "seeking Allah's pleasure by their Hajj." `Ikrimah, As-Suddi and Ibn Jarir mentioned that this Ayah was revealed concerning Al-Hutam bin Hind Al-Bakri, who had raided the cattle belonging to the people of Al-Madinah. The following year, he wanted to perform `Umrah to the House of Allah and some of the Companions wanted to attack him on his way to the House. Allah revealed,

(nor the people coming to the Sacred House (Makkah), seeking the bounty and good pleasure of their Lord.)

Hunting Game is Permissible After Ihram Ends

Allah said,

(But when you finish the Ihram, then hunt,) When you end your Ihram, it is permitted for you to hunt game, which was prohibited for you during Ihram. Although this Ayah contains a command that takes effect after the end of a state of prohibition (during Ihram in this case), the Ayah, in fact, brings back the ruling that was previously in effect. If the previous ruling was an obligation, the new command will uphold that obligation, and such is the case with recommended and permissible matters. There are many Ayat that deny that the ruling in such cases is always an obligation. Such is also the case against those who say that it is always merely allowed. What we mentioned here is the correct opinion that employs the available evidence, and Allah knows best.

Justice is Always Necessary

Allah said,

(and let not the hatred of some people in (once) stopping you from Al-Masjid Al-Haram (at Makkah) lead you to transgression (and hostility on your part).) The meaning of this Ayah is apparent, as it commands: Let not the hatred for some people, who prevented you from reaching the Sacred House in the year of Hudaybiyyah, make you transgress Allah's Law and commit injustice against them in retaliation. Rather, rule as Allah has commanded you, being just with every one. We will explain a similar Ayah later on,

(And let not the enmity and hatred of others make you avoid justice. Be just: that is nearer to piety,) which commands: do not be driven by your hatred for some people into abandoning justice, for justice is ordained for everyone, in all situations. Ibn Abi Hatim recorded that Zayd bin Aslam said, "The Messenger of Allah and his Companions were in the area of Al-Hudaybiyyah when the idolators prevented them from visiting the House, and that was especially hard on them. Later on, some idolators passed by them from the east intending to perform `Umrah. So the Companions of the Prophet said, `Let us prevent those (from `Umrah) just as their fellow idolators prevented us.' Thereafter, Allah sent down this Ayah." Ibn Abbas and others said that "Shana'an" refers to enmity and hate. Allah said next,

(Help you one another in Al-Birr and At-Taqwa; but do not help one another in sin and transgression.) Allah commands His believing servants to help one another perform righteous, good deeds, which is the meaning of `Al-Birr', and to avoid sins, which is the meaning of `At-Taqwa'. Allah forbids His servants from helping one another in sin, `Ithm' and committing the prohibitions. Ibn Jarir said that, "Ithm means abandoning what Allah has ordained, while transgression means overstepping the limits that Allah set in your religion, along with overstepping what Allah has ordered concerning yourselves and others." Imam Ahmad recorded that Anas bin Malik said that the Messenger of Allah said,

«انْصُرْ أَخَاكَ ظَالِمًا أَوْ مَظْلُومًا»

(Support your brother whether he was unjust or the victim of injustice.) He was asked, "O Messenger of Allah! We know about helping him when he suffers injustice, so what about helping him when he commits injustice" He said,

«تَحْجُزُهُ وَتَمْنَعُهُ مِنَ الظُّلْمِ فَذَاكَ نَصْرُهُ»

(Prevent and stop him from committing injustice, and this represents giving support to him.) Al-Bukhari recorded this Hadith through Hushaym. Ahmad recorded that one of the Companions of the Prophet narrated the Hadith,

«الْمُؤْمِنُ الَّذِي يُخَالِطُ النَّاسَ وَيَصْبِرُ عَلَى أَذَاهُمْ أَعْظَمُ أَجْرًا مِنَ الَّذِي لَا يُخَالِطُ النَّاسَ وَلَا يَصْبِرُ عَلى أَذَاهُم»

(The believer who mingles with people and is patient with their annoyance, earns more reward than the believer who does not mingle with people and does not observe patience with their annoyance.) Muslim recorded a Hadith that states,

«مَنْ دَعَا إِلَى هُدًى كَانَ لَهُ مِنَ الْأَجْرِ مِثْلُ أُجُورِ مَنِ اتَّبَعَهُ إِلى يَوْمِ الْقِيَامَةِ لَا يَنْقُصُ ذلِكَ مِنْ أُجُورِهِمْ شَيْئًا، وَمَنْ دَعَا إِلَى ضَلَالَةٍ كَانَ عَلَيْهِ مِنَ الْإِثْمِ مِثْلُ آثَامِ مَنِ اتَّبَعَهُ إِلَى يَوْمِ الْقِيَامَةِ، لَا يَنْقُصُ ذلِكَ مِنْ آثَامِهِمْ شَيْئًا»

(He who calls to a guidance, will earn a reward similar to the rewards of those who accept his call, until the Day of Resurrection, without decreasing their rewards. Whoever calls to a heresy, will carry a burden similar to the burdens of those who accept his call, until the Day of Resurrection, without decreasing their own burdens.)

Surah: 5 Ayah: 3

﴿ حُرِّمَتْ عَلَيْكُمُ ٱلْمَيْتَةُ وَٱلدَّمُ وَلَحْمُ ٱلْخِنزِيرِ وَمَآ أُهِلَّ لِغَيْرِ ٱللَّهِ بِهِۦ وَٱلْمُنْخَنِقَةُ
وَٱلْمَوْقُوذَةُ وَٱلْمُتَرَدِّيَةُ وَٱلنَّطِيحَةُ وَمَآ أَكَلَ ٱلسَّبُعُ إِلَّا مَا ذَكَّيْتُمْ وَمَا ذُبِحَ عَلَى ٱلنُّصُبِ وَأَن
تَسْتَقْسِمُوا۟ بِٱلْأَزْلَٰمِ ۚ ذَٰلِكُمْ فِسْقٌ ۗ ٱلْيَوْمَ يَئِسَ ٱلَّذِينَ كَفَرُوا۟ مِن دِينِكُمْ فَلَا تَخْشَوْهُمْ
وَٱخْشَوْنِ ۚ ٱلْيَوْمَ أَكْمَلْتُ لَكُمْ دِينَكُمْ وَأَتْمَمْتُ عَلَيْكُمْ نِعْمَتِى وَرَضِيتُ لَكُمُ ٱلْإِسْلَٰمَ دِينًا ۚ
فَمَنِ ٱضْطُرَّ فِى مَخْمَصَةٍ غَيْرَ مُتَجَانِفٍ لِّإِثْمٍ ۙ فَإِنَّ ٱللَّهَ غَفُورٌ رَّحِيمٌ ﴿٣﴾

3. Forbidden to you (for food) are: Al-Maitah (the dead animals - cattle-beast not slaughtered), blood, the flesh of swine, and that on which Allâh's Name has not been mentioned while slaughtering, (that which has been slaughtered as a sacrifice for others than Allâh, or has been slaughtered for idols) and that which has been killed by strangling, or by a violent blow, or by a headlong fall, or by the goring of horns - and that which has been (partly) eaten by a wild animal - unless you are able to slaughter it (before its death) - and that which is sacrificed (slaughtered) on An-Nusub (stone altars). (Forbidden) also is to use arrows seeking luck or decision; (all) that is Fisqun (disobedience of Allâh and sin). This day, those who disbelieved have given up all hope of your religion; so fear them not, but fear Me. This day, I have perfected your religion for you, completed My Favor upon you, and have chosen for you Islâm as your religion. But as for him who is forced by severe hunger, with no inclination to sin (such can eat these above-mentioned meats), then surely, Allâh is Oft-Forgiving, Most Merciful.

Transliteration

3. Hurrimat AAalaykumu almaytatu waalddamu walahmu alkhinzeeri wama ohilla lighayri Allahi bihi waalmunkhaniqatu waalmawqoothatu waalmutaraddiyatu waalnnateehatu wama akala alssabuAAu illa ma thakkaytum wama thubiha AAala alnnusubi waan tastaqsimoo bial-azlami thalikum fisqun alyawma ya-isa allatheena kafaroo min deenikum fala takhshawhum waikhshawni alyawma akmaltu lakum deenakum waatmamtu AAalaykum niAAmatee waradeetu lakumu al-islama deenan famani idturra fee makhmasatin ghayra mutajanifin li-ithmin fa-inna Allaha ghafoorun raheemun

Tafsir Ibn Kathir

The Animals that are Unlawful to Eat

Allah informs His servants that He forbids consuming the mentioned types of foods, such as the Maytah, which is the animal that dies before being properly slaughtered or hunted. Allah forbids this type of food due to the harm it causes, because of the blood that becomes clogged in the veins of the dead animal. Therefore, the Maytah is harmful, religiously and physically, and this is why Allah has prohibited it. The only exception to this ruling is fish, for fish is allowed, even when dead, by slaughtering or otherwise. Malik in his Muwatta, also Abu

Dawud, At-Tirmidhi, An-Nasa'i and Ibn Majah in their Sunan, Ibn Khuzaymah and Ibn Hibban in their Sahihs, all recorded that Abu Hurayrah said that the Messenger of Allah was asked about seawater. He said,

«هُوَ الطَّهُورُ مَاؤُهُ الْحِلُّ مَيْتَتُه»

(Its water is pure and its dead are permissible.) The same ruling applies to locusts, as proven in a Hadith that we will mention later. Allah's statement,

(blood...) This refers to flowing blood, according to Ibn `Abbas and Sa`id bin Jubayr, and it is similar to Allah's other statement,

(Blood poured forth...) Ibn Abi Hatim recorded that Ibn `Abbas was asked about the spleen and he said, "Eat it." They said, "It is blood." He said, "You are only prohibited blood that was poured forth." Abu `Abdullah, Muhammad bin Idris Ash-Shafi`i recorded that Ibn `Umar said that the Messenger of Allah said,

«أُحِلَّ لَنَا مَيْتَتَانِ وَدَمَانِ، فَأَمَّا الْمَيْتَتَانِ فَالسَّمَكُ وَالْجَرَادُ، وَأَمَّا الدَّمَانِ فَالْكَبِدُ وَالطِّحَال»

(We were allowed two dead animals and two (kinds of) blood. As for the two dead animals, they are fish and locust. As for the two bloods, they are liver and spleen.) Imam Ahmad bin Hanbal, Ibn Majah, Ad-Daraqutni and Al-Bayhaqi also recorded this Hadith through `Abdur-Rahman bin Zayd bin Aslam, who is a weak narrator. Allah's statement,

(the flesh of swine...) includes domesticated and wild swine, and also refers to the whole animal, including its fat, for this is what the Arabs mean by Lahm or `flesh'. Muslim recorded that Buraydah bin Al-Husayb Al-Aslami said that the Messenger of Allah said,

«مَنْ لَعِبَ بِالنَّرْدَشِيرِ، فَكَأَنَّمَا صَبَغَ يَدَهُ فِي لَحْمِ الْخِنْزِيرِ وَدَمِه»

(He who plays Nardshir (a game with dice that involves gambling) is just like the one who puts his hand in the flesh and blood of swine.) If this is the case with merely touching the flesh and blood of swine, so what about eating and feeding on it This Hadith is a proof that Lahm means the entire body of the animal, including its fat. In is recorded in the Two Sahihs that the Messenger of Allah said,

«إِنَّ اللهَ حَرَّمَ بَيْعَ الْخَمْرِ وَالْمَيْتَةِ وَالْخِنْزِيرِ وَالْأَصْنَام»

(Allah made the trade of alcohol, dead animals, pigs and idols illegal.) The people asked, "O Allah's Messenger! What about the fat of dead animals, for it was used for greasing the boats and the hides; and people use it for lanterns" He said,

«لَا، هُوَ حَرَامٌ»

(No, it is illegal.) In the Sahih of Al-Bukhari, Abu Sufyan narrated that he said to Heraclius, Emperor of Rome, "He (Muhammad) prohibited us from eating dead animals and blood." Allah said,

(And that which has been slaughtered as a sacrifice for other than Allah.) Therefore, the animals on which a name other than Allah was mentioned upon slaughtering it, is impermissible, because Allah made it necessary to mention His Glorious Name upon slaughtering the animals, which He created. Whoever does not do so, mentioning other than Allah's Name, such as the name of an idol, a false deity or a monument, when slaughtering, he makes this meat unlawful, according to the consensus. Allah's statement,

(and that which has been killed by strangling...) either intentionally or by mistake, such as when an animal moves while restrained and dies by strangulation because of its struggling, this animal is also unlawful to eat.

(or by a violent blow...) This refers to the animal that is hit with a heavy object until it dies. Ibn `Abbas and several others said it is the animal that is hit with a staff until it dies. Qatadah said, "The people of Jahiliyyah used to strike the animal with sticks and when it died, they would eat it." It is recorded in the Sahih that `Adi bin Hatim said, "I asked, `O Allah's Messenger! I use the Mi`rad for hunting and catch game with it.' He replied,

«إِذَا رَمَيْتَ بِالْمِعْرَاضِ فَخَزَق فَكُلْهُ، وَإِنْ أَصَابَ بِعَرْضِهِ فَإِنَّمَا هُوَ وَقِيذٌ فَلَا تَأْكُلْه»

(If the game is hit by its sharp edge, eat it. But, if it is hit by its broad side, do not eat it, for it has been beaten to death.) Therefore, the Prophet made a distinction between killing the animal with the sharp edge of an arrow or a hunting stick, and rendered it lawful, and what is killed by the broad side of an object, and rendered it unlawful because it was beaten to death. There is a consensus among the scholars of Fiqh on this subject. rAs for the animal that falls headlong from a high place and dies as a result, it is also prohibited. `Ali bin Abi Talhah reported that Ibn `Abbas said that an animal that dies by a headlong fall, "Is that which falls from a mountain." Qatadah said that it is the animal that falls in a well. As-Suddi said that it is the animal that falls from a mountain or in a well. As for the animal that dies by being gorged by another animal, it is also prohibited, even if the horn opens a flesh wound and it bleeds to death from its neck. Allah's statement,

(and that which has been (partly) eaten by a wild animal,) refers to the animal that was attacked by a lion, leopard, tiger, wolf or dog, then the wild beast eats a part of it and it dies because of that. This type is also prohibited, even if the animal bled to death from its neck. There is also a consensus on this ruling. During the time of Jahiliyyah, the people used to eat the sheep, camel, or cow that were partly eaten by a wild animal. Allah prohibited this practice for the believers. Allah's statement,

(unless you are able to slaughter it,) before it dies, due to the causes mentioned above. This part of the Ayah is connected to, (and that which has been killed by strangling, or by a violent blow, or by a headlong fall, or by the goring of horns - and that which has been (partly) eaten by a wild animal.) `Ali bin Abi Talhah reported that Ibn `Abbas commented on Allah's statement,

(unless you are able to slaughter it,) "Unless you are able to slaughter the animal in the cases mentioned in the Ayah while it is still alive, then eat it, for it was properly slaughtered." Similar was reported from Sa`id bin Jubayr, Al-Hasan Al-Basri and As-Suddi. Ibn Jarir recorded that `Ali, may Allah be pleased with him, said, "If you are able to slaughter the animal that has been hit by a violent blow, or by a headlong fall, or by the gorging of horns while it still moves a foot or a leg, then eat from its meat." Similar was reported from Tawus, Al-Hasan, Qatadah, `Ubayd bin `Umayr, Ad-Dahhak and several others, that if the animal that is being slaughtered still moves, thus demonstrating that it is still alive while slaughtering, then it is lawful. The Two Sahihs recorded that Rafi` bin Khadij said, "I asked, `O Allah's Messenger! We fear that we may meet our enemy tomorrow and we have no knives, could we slaughter the animals with reeds' The Prophet said,

«مَا أَنْهَرَ الدَّمَ، وَذُكِرَ اسْمُ اللهِ عَلَيْهِ، فَكُلُوهُ، لَيْسَ السِّنَّ وَالظُّفُرَ، وَسَأُحَدِّثُكُمْ عَنْ ذَلِكَ: أَمَّا السِّنُّ فَعَظْمٌ، وَأَمَّا الظُّفُرُ فَمُدَى الْحَبَشَةِ»

(You can use what makes blood flow and you can eat what is slaughtered with the Name of Allah. But do not use teeth or claws (in slaughtering). I will tell you why, as for teeth, they are bones, and claws are used by Ethiopians for slaughtering.)" Allah said next,

(and that which is sacrificed on An-Nusub.) Nusub were stone altars that were erected around the Ka`bah, as Mujahid and Ibn Jurayj stated. Ibn Jurayj said, "There were three hundred and sixty Nusub (around the Ka`bah) that the Arabs used to slaughter in front of, during the time of Jahiliyyah. They used to sprinkle the animals that came to the Ka`bah with the blood of slaughtered animals, whose meat they cut to pieces and placed on the altars." Allah forbade this practice for the believers. He also forbade them from eating the meat of animals that were slaughtered in the vicinity of the Nusub, even if Allah's Name was mentioned on these animals when they were slaughtered, because it is a type of Shirk that Allah and His Messenger have forbidden.

The Prohibition of Using Al-Azlam for Decision Making

Allah said,

((Forbidden) also is to make decisions with Al-Azlam) The Ayah commands, "O believers! You are forbidden to use Al-Azlam (arrows) for decision making," which was a practice of the Arabs during the time of Jahiliyyah. They would use three arrows, one with the word `Do' written on it, another that says `Do not', while the third does not say anything. Some of them would write on the first arrow, `My Lord commanded me,' and, `My Lord forbade me,' on the second arrow and they would not write anything on the third arrow. If the blank arrow was picked, the person would keep trying until the arrow that says do or do not was picked, and the person would implement the command that he picked. Ibn `Abbas said that the Azlam were arrows that they used to seek decisions through. Muhammad bin Ishaq and others said that the major idol of the tribe of Quraysh was Hubal, which was erected on the tip of a well inside the Ka`bah, where gifts were presented and where the treasure of the Ka`bah was kept.

There, they also had seven arrows that they would use to seek a decision concerning matters of dispute. Whatever the chosen arrow would tell them, they would abide by it! Al-Bukhari recorded that when the Prophet entered Al-Ka`bah (after Makkah was conquered), he found pictures of Ibrahim and Isma`il in it holding the Azlam in their hands. The Prophet commented,

«قَاتَلَهُمُ اللهُ لَقَدْ عَلِمُوا أَنَّهُمَا لَمْ يَسْتَقْسِمَا بِهَا أَبَدًا»

(May Allah fight them (the idolaters)! They know that they never used the Azlam to make decisions.) Mujahid commented on Allah's statement,

((Forbidden) also is to make decisions with Al-Azlam,) "These were arrows that the Arabs used, and dice that the Persians and Romans used in gambling." This statement by Mujahid, that these arrows were used in gambling, is doubtful unless we say that they used the arrows for gambling sometimes and for decisions other times, and Allah knows best. We should also state that Allah mentioned Azlam and gambling in His statement before the end of the Surah (5:90, 91),

(O you who believe! Intoxicants (all kinds of alcoholic drinks), and gambling, and Al-Ansab, and Al-Azlam are an abomination of Shaytan's handiwork. So avoid that in order that you may be successful. Shaytan wants only to excite enmity and hatred between you with intoxicants (alcoholic drinks) and gambling, and hinder you from the remembrance of Allah and from the Salah (the prayer). So, will you not then abstain) In this Ayah, Allah said,

((Forbidden) also is to make decisions with Al-Azlam, (all) that is Fisq.) meaning, all these practices constitute disobedience, sin, misguidance, ignorance and, above all, Shirk. Allah has commanded the believers to seek decisions from Him when they want to do something, by first worshipping Him and then asking Him for the best decision concerning the matter they seek. Imam Ahmad, Al-Bukhari and the collectors of Sunan recorded that Jabir bin `Abdullah said, "The Prophet used to teach us how to make Istikharah (asking Allah to guide one to the right action), in all matters, as he taught us the Surahs of the Qur'an. He said,

«إِذَا هَمَّ أَحَدُكُمْ بِالْأَمْرِ فَلْيَرْكَعْ رَكْعَتَيْنِ مِنْ غَيْرِ الْفَرِيضَةِ، ثُمَّ لْيَقُلْ: اللَّهُمَّ إِنِّي أَسْتَخِيرُكَ بِعِلْمِكَ، وَأَسْتَقْدِرُكَ بِقُدْرَتِكَ، وَأَسْأَلُكَ مِنْ فَضْلِكَ الْعَظِيمِ، فَإِنَّكَ تَقْدِرُ وَلَا أَقْدِرُ وَتَعْلَمُ وَلَا أَعْلَمُ، وَأَنْتَ عَلَّامُ الْغُيُوبِ، اللَّهُمَّ إِنْ كُنْتَ تَعْلَمُ أَنَّ هَذَا الْأَمْرَ ويسميه باسمه خَيْرٌ لِي فِي دِينِي وَدُنْيَايَ وَمَعَاشِي وعَاقِبَةِ أَمْرِي أَوْ قَالَ: عَاجِلِ أَمْرِي وَآجِلِهِ فَاقْدُرْهُ لِي، وَيَسِّرْهُ لِي، ثُمَّ بَارِكْ لِي فِيهِ، اللَّهُمَّ وَإِنْ كُنْتَ تَعْلَمُ أَنَّهُ شَرٌّ لِي فِي دِينِي وَدُنْيَايَ وَمَعَاشِي وَعَاقِبَةِ أَمْرِي، فَاصْرِفْنِي عَنْهُ، وَاصْرِفْهُ عَنِّي، وَاقْدُرْ لِيَ الْخَيْرَ حَيْثُ كَانَ، ثُمَّ رَضِّنِي بِهِ»

(If anyone of you thinks of doing any matter, he should offer a two Rak'ah prayer, other than the compulsory, and say (after the prayer) `O Allah! I ask guidance from Your knowledge, from Your ability and I ask for Your great bounty, for You are capable and I am not, You know and I do not, and You know the Unseen. O Allah! If You know that this matter (and one should mention the matter or deed here) is good for my religion, my livelihood and the Hereafter (or he said, `for my present and later needs') then ordain it for me, make it easy for me to have, and then bless it for me. O Allah! And if You know that this is harmful to me in my religion and livelihood and for the Hereafter then keep it away from me and let me be away from it. And ordain whatever is good for me, and make me satisfied with it.') This is the wording collected by Ahmad, and At-Tirmidhi said, "Hasan Sahih Gharib."

Shaytan and the Disbelievers Do Not Hope that Muslims Will Ever Follow Them

Allah said,

(This day, those who disbelieved have given up all hope of your religion;) `Ali bin Abi Talhah reported that Ibn `Abbas said that the Ayah means, "They gave up hope that Muslims would revert to their religion." This is similar to the saying of `Ata' bin Abi Rabah, As-Suddi and Muqatil bin Hayyan. This meaning is supported by a Hadith recorded in the Sahih that states,

«إِنَّ الشَّيْطَانَ قَدْ يَئِسَ أَنْ يَعْبُدَهُ الْمُصَلُّونَ فِي جَزِيرَةِ الْعَرَبِ، وَلَكِنْ بِالتَّحْرِيشِ بَيْنَهُم»

(Verily, Shaytan has given up hope that those who pray in the Arabian Peninsula, will worship him. But he will still stir trouble among them.) It is also possible that the Ayah negates the possibility that the disbelievers and Shaytan will ever be like Muslims, since Muslims have various qualities that contradict Shirk and its people. This is why Allah commanded His believing servants to observe patience, to be steadfast in defying and contradicting the disbelievers, and to fear none but Allah. Allah said,

(So fear them not, but fear Me.) meaning, `do not fear them when you contradict them. Rather, fear Me and I will give you victory over them, I will eradicate them, and make you prevail over them, I will please your hearts and raise you above them in this life and the Hereafter.

Islam Has Been Perfected For Muslims

Allah said,

(This day, I have perfected your religion for you, completed My favor upon you, and have chosen for you Islam as your religion.) This, indeed, is the biggest favor from Allah to this Ummah, for He has completed their religion for them, and they, thus, do not need any other religion or any other Prophet except Muhammad . This is why Allah made Muhammad the Final Prophet and sent him to all humans and Jinn. Therefore, the permissible is what he allows, the impermissible is what he prohibits, the Law is what he legislates and everything that he conveys is true and authentic and does not contain lies or contradictions. Allah said;

(And the Word of your Lord has been fulfilled in truth and in justice,) meaning, it is true in what it conveys and just in what it commands and forbids. When Allah completed the religion for Muslims, His favor became complete for them as well. Allah said,

(This day, I have perfected your religion for you, completed My favor upon you, and have chosen for you Islam as your religion.) meaning, accept Islam for yourselves, for it is the religion that Allah likes and which He chose for you, and it is that with which He sent the best of the honorable Messengers and the most glorious of His Books. Ibn Jarir recorded that Harun bin `Antarah said that his father said, "When the Ayah, (This day, I have perfected your religion for you...) was revealed, during the great day of Hajj (the Day of `Arafah, the ninth day of Dhul-Hijjah) `Umar cried. The Prophet said, `What makes you cry' He said, `What made me cry is that our religion is being perfected for us. Now it is perfect, nothing is perfect, but it is bound to deteriorate.' The Prophet said,

«صَدَقْتَ»

(You have said the truth.)" What supports the meaning of this Hadith is the authentic Hadith,

«إِنَّ الْإِسْلَامَ بَدَأَ غَرِيبًا، وَسَيَعُودُ غَرِيبًا، فَطُوبَى لِلْغُرَبَاء»

(Islam was strange in its beginning and will return strange once more. Therefore, Tuba for the strangers.) Imam Ahmad recorded that Tariq bin Shihab said, "A Jewish man said to `Umar bin Al-Khattab, `O Leader of the Believers! There is a verse in your Book, which is read by all of you (Muslims), and had it been revealed to us, we would have taken that day (on which it was revealed) as a day of celebration.' `Umar bin Al-Khattab asked, `Which is that verse' The Jew replied, (This day, I have perfected your religion for you, completed My favor upon you...) `Umar replied, `By Allah! I know when and where this verse was revealed to Allah's Messenger . It was the evening on the Day of `Arafah on a Friday."' Al-Bukhari recorded this Hadith through Al-Hasan bin As-Sabbah from Ja`far bin `Awn. Muslim, At-Tirmidhi and An-Nasa'i also recorded this Hadith. In the narration collected by Al-Bukhari in the book of Tafsir, through Tariq, he said, "The Jews said to `Umar, `By Allah! There is a verse that is read by all of you (Muslims), and had it been revealed to us, we would have taken that day (on which it was revealed) as a day of celebration.' `Umar said, `By Allah! I know when and where this verse was revealed and where the Messenger of Allah was at that time. It was the day of `Arafah, and I was at `Arafah, by Allah." Sufyan (one of the narrators) doubted if Friday was mentioned in this narration. Sufyan's confusion was either because he was unsure if his teacher included this statement in the Hadith or not. Otherwise, if it was because he doubted that the particular day during the Farewell Hajj was a Friday, it would be a mistake that could not and should not have come from someone like Sufyan Ath-Thawri. The fact that it was a Friday, is agreed on by the scholars of Sirah and Fiqh. There are numerous Hadiths that support this fact that are definitely authentic and of the Mutawatir type. This Hadith was also reported from `Umar through various chains of narration.

Permitting the Dead Animals in Conditions of Necessity

Allah said,

(But as for him who is forced by severe hunger, with no inclination to sin (such can eat these above mentioned animals), then surely, Allah is Oft-Forgiving, Most Merciful.) Therefore, when one is forced to take any of the impermissible things that Allah mentioned to meet a necessity, he is allowed and Allah is Oft-Forgiving, Most Merciful with him. Allah is well aware of His servant's needs during dire straits, and He will forgive and pardon His servant in this case. In the Musnad and the Sahih of Ibn Hibban, it is recorded that Ibn `Umar said that Messenger of Allah said,

«إِنَّ اللهَ يُحِبُّ أَنْ تُؤْتَى رُخْصَتُهُ كَمَا يَكْرَهُ أَنْ تُؤْتَى مَعْصِيَتُه»

(Allah likes that His Rukhsah (allowance) be used, just as He dislikes that disobedience to Him is committed.) We should mention here that it is not necessary for one to wait three days before eating the meat of dead animals, as many unlettered Muslims mistakenly think. Rather, one can eat such meat when the dire need arises. Imam Ahmad recorded that Abu Waqid Al-Laythi said that the Companions asked, "O Messenger of Allah! We live in a land where famine often strikes us. Therefore, when are we allowed to eat the meat of dead animals" The Prophet replied,

«إِذَا لَمْ تَصْطَبِحُوا، وَلَمْ تَغْتَبِقُوا،وَلَمْ تَحْتَفِئُوا بَقْلًا فَشَأْنُكُمْ بِهَا»

(When you neither find food for lunch and dinner nor have any produce to eat, then eat from it.) Only Imam Ahmad collected this narration and its chain meets the criteria of the Two Sahihs. Allah said,

(with no inclination to sin,) meaning, one does not incline to commit what Allah has prohibited. Allah has allowed one when necessity arises to eat from what He otherwise prohibits, under the condition that his heart does not incline to eat what Allah prohibited. Allah said in Surat Al-Baqarah,

(But if one is forced by necessity without willful disobedience nor transgressing due limits, then there is no sin on him. Truly, Allah is Oft-Forgiving, Most Merciful.) Some scholars used this Ayah as evidence that those who travel for the purpose of committing an act of disobedience are not allowed to use any of the legal concessions of travel, because these concessions are not earned through sin, and Allah knows best.

Surah: 5 Ayah: 4

﴿ يَسْـَٔلُونَكَ مَاذَآ أُحِلَّ لَهُمْ ۖ قُلْ أُحِلَّ لَكُمُ ٱلطَّيِّبَٰتُ ۙ وَمَا عَلَّمْتُم مِّنَ ٱلْجَوَارِحِ مُكَلِّبِينَ تُعَلِّمُونَهُنَّ مِمَّا عَلَّمَكُمُ ٱللَّهُ ۖ فَكُلُوا۟ مِمَّآ أَمْسَكْنَ عَلَيْكُمْ وَٱذْكُرُوا۟ ٱسْمَ ٱللَّهِ عَلَيْهِ ۖ وَٱتَّقُوا۟ ٱللَّهَ ۚ إِنَّ ٱللَّهَ سَرِيعُ ٱلْحِسَابِ ﴿٤﴾ ﴾

4. They ask you (O Muhammad (peace be upon him)) what is lawful for them (as food). Say: "Lawful unto you are At-Tayyibât (all kind of Halâl (lawful-good) foods which Allâh has made lawful (meat of slaughtered eatable animals, milk products, fats, vegetables and fruits)). And those beasts and birds of prey which you have trained as hounds, training and teaching them (to catch) in the manner as directed to you by Allâh; so eat of what they catch for you, but pronounce the Name of Allâh over it, and fear Allâh. Verily, Allâh is Swift in reckoning."

Transliteration

4. Yas-aloonaka matha ohilla lahum qul ohilla lakumu alttayyibatu wama AAallamtum mina aljawarihi mukallibeena tuAAallimoonahunna mimma AAallamakumu Allahu fakuloo mimma amsakna AAalaykum waothkuroo isma Allahi AAalayhi waittaqoo Allaha inna Allaha sareeAAu alhisabi

Tafsir Ibn Kathir

Clarifying the Lawful

In the previous Ayah Allah mentioned the prohibited types of food, the impure and unclean things, harmful for those who eat them, either to their bodies, religion or both, except out of necessity,

(while He has explained to you in detail what is forbidden to you, except under compulsion of necessity) After that, Allah said,

(They ask you what is lawful for them. Say, "Lawful unto you are At-Tayyibat...") In Surat Al-A`raf Allah describes Muhammad allowing the good things and prohibiting the filthy things. Muqatil said, "At-Tayyibat includes everything Muslims are allowed and the various types of legally earned provision." Az-Zuhri was once asked about drinking urine for medicinal purposes and he said that it is not a type of Tayyibat." Ibn Abi Hatim also narrated this statement. Using Jawarih to Hunt Game is Permissible Allah said,

(And those Jawarih (beasts and birds of prey) which you have trained as hounds...) That is, lawful for you are the animals slaughtered in Allah's Name, and the good things for sustenance. (The game you catch) with the Jawarih are also lawful for you. This refers to trained dogs and falcons, as is the opinion of the majority of the Companions, their followers, and the Imams. `Ali bin Abi Talhah reported that Ibn `Abbas said that,

(And those Jawarih (beasts and birds of prey) which you have trained as hounds...) refers to trained hunting dogs, falcons and all types of birds and beasts that are trained to hunt, including dogs, wild cats, falcons, and so forth. Ibn Abi Hatim collected this and said, "Similar was reported from Khaythamah, Tawus, Mujahid, Makhul and Yahya bin Abi Kathir." Ibn Jarir recorded that Ibn `Umar said, "You are permitted the animal that the trained birds, such as falcons, hunt for you if you catch it (before it eats from it). Otherwise, do not eat from it." I say, the majority of scholars say that hunting with trained birds is just like hunting with trained dogs, because bird's of prey catch the game with their claws, just like dogs. Therefore, there is no difference between the two. Ibn Jarir recorded that `Adi bin Hatim said that he asked the Messenger of Allah about the game that the falcon hunts and the Messenger said,

«مَا أَمْسَكَ عَلَيْكَ فَكُلْ»

(Whatever it catches for you, eat from it.) These carnivores that are trained to catch game are called Jawarih in Arabic, a word that is derived from Jarh, meaning, what one earns. The Arabs would say, "So-and-so has Jaraha something good for his family," meaning, he has earned them something good. The Arabs would say, "So-and-so does not have a Jarih for him," meaning, a caretaker. Allah also said,

(And He knows what you have done during the day...) meaning, the good or evil you have earned or committed. Allah's statement,

(trained as hounds,) those Jawarih that have been trained to hunt as hounds with their claws or talons. Therefore, if the game is killed by the weight of its blow, not with its claws, then we are not allowed to eat from the game. Allah said,

(training them in the manner as directed to you by Allah,) as when the beast is sent, it goes after the game, and when it catches it, it keeps it until its owner arrives and does not catch it to eat it itself. This is why Allah said here,

(so eat of what they catch for you, but pronounce the Name of Allah over it,) When the beast is trained, and it catches the game for its owner who mentioned Allah's Name when he sent the beast after the game, then this game is allowed according to the consensus of scholars, even if it was killed. There are Hadiths in the Sunnah that support this statement. The Two Sahihs recorded that `Adi bin Hatim said, "I said, `O Allah's Messenger! I send hunting dogs and mention Allah's Name.' He replied,

«إِذَا أَرْسَلْتَ كَلْبَكَ الْمُعَلَّمَ وَذَكَرْتَ اسْمَ اللهِ فَكُلْ مَا أَمْسَكَ عَلَيْك»

(If, with mentioning Allah's Name, you let loose your tamed dog after a game and it catches it, you may eat what it catches.) I said, `Even if it kills the game' He replied,

«وَإِنْ قَتَلْنَ، مَا لَمْ يَشْرَكْهَا كَلْبٌ لَيسَ مِنْهَا، فَإِنَّكَ إِنَّمَا سَمَّيْتَ عَلى كَلْبِكَ وَلَمْ تُسَمِّ عَلى غَيْرِه»

(Even if it kills the game, unless another dog joins the hunt, for you mentioned Allah's Name when sending your dog, but not the other dog.) I said, `I also use the Mi`rad and catch game with it.' He replied,

«إِذَا رَمَيْتَ بِالْمِعْرَاضِ فَخزق فَكُلْهُ، وَإِنْ أَصَابَهُ بِعَرْضٍ فَإِنَّهُ وَقِيذٌ فَلَا تَأْكُلْه»

(If the game is hit by its sharp edge, eat it, but if it is hit by its broad side, do not eat it, for it has been beaten to death.) In another narration, the Prophet said,

«وَإِذَا أَرْسَلْتَ كَلْبَكَ فَاذْكُرِ اسْمَ اللهِ، فَإِنْ أَمْسَكَ عَلَيْكَ، فَأَدْرَكْتَهُ حَيًّا فَاذْبَحْهُ، وَإِنْ أَدْرَكْتَهُ قَدْ قَتَلَ وَلَمْ يَأْكُلْ مِنْهُ فَكُلْهُ، فَإِنَّ أَخْذَ الْكَلْبِ ذَكَاتُه»

(If you send your hunting dog, then mention Allah's Name and whatever it catches for you and you find alive, slaughter it. If you catch the game dead and the dog did not eat from it, then eat from it, for the dog has caused its slaughter to be fulfilled.) In yet another narration of two Sahihs, the Prophet said,

«فَإِنْ أَكَلَ فَلَا تَأْكُلْ، فَإِنِّي أَخَافُ أَنْ يَكُونَ أَمْسَكَ عَلَى نَفْسِهِ»

(If the dog eats from the game, do not eat from it for I fear that it has caught it as prey for itself.)

Mention Allah's Name Upon Sending the Predators to Catch the Game

Allah said,

(so eat of what they catch for you, but pronounce the Name of Allah over it,) meaning, upon sending it. The Prophet said to `Adi bin Hatim,

«إِذَا أَرْسَلْتَ كَلْبَكَ الْمُعَلَّمَ، وَذَكَرْتَ اسْمَ اللهِ، فَكُلْ مَا أَمْسَكَ عَلَيْكَ»

(When you send your trained dog and mention Allah's Name, eat from what it catches for you.) It is recorded in the Two Sahihs that Abu Tha`labah related that the Prophet said,

«إِذَا أَرْسَلْتَ كَلْبَكَ فَاذْكُرِ اسْمَ اللهِ، وَإِذَا رَمَيْتَ بِسَهْمِكَ فَاذْكُرِ اسْمَ اللهِ»

(If you send your hunting dog, mention Allah's Name over it. If you shoot an arrow, mention Allah's Name over it.) `Ali bin Abi Talhah reported that Ibn `Abbas commented,

[وَاذْكُرُواْ اسْمَ اللَّهِ عَلَيْهِ]

(but pronounce the Name of Allah over it,) "When you send a beast of prey, say, `In the Name of Allah!' If you forget, then there is no harm." It was also reported that this Ayah commands mentioning Allah's Name upon eating. It is recorded in the Two Sahihs that the Messenger of Allah taught his stepson `Umar bin Abu Salamah saying,

«سَمِّ اللهَ وَكُلْ بِيَمِينِكَ وَكُلْ مِمَّا يَلِيكَ»

(Mention Allah's Name, eat with your right hand and eat from the part of the plate that is in front of you.) Al-Bukhari recorded that `A'ishah said, "They asked, `O Allah's Messenger! Some people, - recently converted from disbelief - bring us some meats that we do not know if Allah's Name was mentioned over or not.' He replied,

«سَمُّوا اللهَ أَنْتُمْ وَكُلُوا»

(Mention Allah's Name on it and eat from it.)"

Surah: 5 Ayah: 5

﴿ ٱلْيَوْمَ أُحِلَّ لَكُمُ ٱلطَّيِّبَٰتُ ۖ وَطَعَامُ ٱلَّذِينَ أُوتُوا۟ ٱلْكِتَٰبَ حِلٌّ لَّكُمْ وَطَعَامُكُمْ حِلٌّ لَّهُمْ ۖ
وَٱلْمُحْصَنَٰتُ مِنَ ٱلْمُؤْمِنَٰتِ وَٱلْمُحْصَنَٰتُ مِنَ ٱلَّذِينَ أُوتُوا۟ ٱلْكِتَٰبَ مِن قَبْلِكُمْ إِذَآ
ءَاتَيْتُمُوهُنَّ أُجُورَهُنَّ مُحْصِنِينَ غَيْرَ مُسَٰفِحِينَ وَلَا مُتَّخِذِىٓ أَخْدَانٍ ۗ وَمَن يَكْفُرْ بِٱلْإِيمَٰنِ
فَقَدْ حَبِطَ عَمَلُهُۥ وَهُوَ فِى ٱلْءَاخِرَةِ مِنَ ٱلْخَٰسِرِينَ ﴿٥﴾

5. Made lawful to you this day are At-Tayyibât (all kinds of Halâl (lawful) foods, which Allâh has made lawful (meat of slaughtered eatable animals, milk products, fats, vegetables and fruits). The food (slaughtered cattle, eatable animals) of the people of the Scripture (Jews and Christians) is lawful to you and yours is lawful to them. (Lawful to you in marriage) are chaste women from the believers and chaste women from those who were given the Scripture (Jews and Christians) before your time when you have given their due Mahr (bridal-money given by the husband to his wife at the time of marriage), desiring chastity (i.e. taking them in legal wedlock) not committing illegal sexual intercourse, nor taking them as girl-friends. And whosoever disbelieves in Faith (i.e. in the Oneness of Allâh and in all the other Articles of Faith i.e. His (Allâh's), Angels, His Holy Books, His Messengers, the Day of Resurrection and Al-Qadar (Divine Preordainments)), then fruitless is his work; and in the Hereafter he will be among the losers.

Transliteration

5. Alyawma ohilla lakumu alttayyibatu wataAAamu allatheena ootoo alkitaba hillun lakum wataAAamukum hillun lahum waalmuhsanatu mina almu/minati waalmuhsanatu mina allatheena ootoo alkitaba min qablikum itha ataytumoohunna ojoorahunna muhsineena ghayra musafiheena wala muttakhithee akhdanin waman yakfur bial-eemani faqad habita AAamaluhu wahuwa fee al-akhirati mina alkhasireena

Tafsir Ibn Kathir

Permitting the Slaughtered Animals of the People of the Book

After Allah mentioned the filthy things that He prohibited for His believing servants and the good things that He allowed for them, He said next,

(Made lawful to you this day are At-Tayyibat.) Allah then mentioned the ruling concerning the slaughtered animals of the People of the Book, the Jews and Christians,

(The food of the People of the Scripture is lawful to you..) meaning, their slaughtered animals, as Ibn `Abbas, Abu Umamah, Mujahid, Sa`id bin Jubayr, `Ikrimah, `Ata', Al-Hasan, Makhul, Ibrahim An-Nakha`i, As-Suddi and Muqatil bin Hayyan stated. This ruling, that the slaughtered animals of the People of the Book are permissible for Muslims, is agreed on by the scholars, because the People of the Book believe that slaughtering for other than Allah is prohibited. They mention Allah's Name upon slaughtering their animals, even though they have deviant beliefs about Allah that do not befit His majesty. It is recorded in the Sahih that `Abdullah bin Mughaffal said, "While we were attacking the fort of Khaybar, a person threw a leather bag containing fat, and I ran to take it and said, `I will not give anyone anything from this container today.' But when I turned I saw the Prophet (standing behind) while smiling." The scholars rely on this Hadith as evidence that we are allowed to eat what we need of foods from the booty before it is divided. The scholars of the Hanafi, the Shafi`i and the Hanbali Madhhabs rely on this Hadith to allow eating parts of the slaughtered animals of the Jews that they prohibit for themselves, such as the fat. They used this Hadith as evidence against the scholars of the Maliki Madhhab who disagreed with this ruling. A better proof is the Hadith recorded in the Sahih that the people of Khaybar gave the Prophet a gift of a roasted leg of sheep, which they poisoned. The Prophet used to like eating the leg of the sheep and he took a bite from it, but it told the Prophet that it was poisoned, so he discarded that bite. The bite that the Prophet took effected the palate of his mouth, while Bishr bin Al-Bara' bin Ma`rur died from eating from that sheep. The Prophet had the Jewish woman, Zaynab, who poisoned the sheep, killed. Therefore, the Prophet and his Companions wanted to eat from that sheep and did not ask the Jews if they removed what the Jews believed was prohibited for them, such as its fat. Allah's statement,

(and your food is lawful to them.) means, you are allowed to feed them from your slaughtered animals. Therefore, this part of the Ayah is not to inform the People of the Scriptures that they are allowed to eat our food -- unless we consider it information for us about the ruling that they have -- i. e, that they are allowed all types of foods over which Allah's Name was mentioned, whether slaughtered according to their religion or otherwise. The first explanation is more plausible. So it means: you are allowed to feed them from your slaughtered animals just as you are allowed to eat from theirs, as equal compensation and fair treatment. The Prophet gave his robe to `Abdullah bin Ubayy bin Salul, who was wrapped with it when he died. They say that he did that because `Abdullah had given his robe to Al-`Abbas when Al-`Abbas came to Al-Madinah. As for the Hadith,

«لَا تَصْحَبْ إِلَّا مُؤْمِنًا، وَلَا يَأْكُلْ طَعَامَكَ إِلَّا تَقِي»

(Do not befriend but a believer, nor should other than a Taqi (pious person) eat your food.), This is to encourage such behavior, and Allah knows best.

The Permission to Marry Chaste Women From the People of the Scriptures

Allah said,

((Lawful to you in marriage) are chaste women from the believers) The Ayah states: you are allowed to marry free, chaste believing women. This Ayah is talking about women who do not commit fornication, as evident by the word `chaste'. Allah said in another Ayah,

(Desiring chastity not committing illegal sexual intercourse, nor taking them as boyfriends (lovers).) (4:25) `Abdullah Ibn `Umar used to advise against marrying Christian women saying, "I do not know of a worse case of Shirk than her saying that `Isa is her lord, while Allah said,

(And do not marry idolatresses till they believe.)" Ibn Abi Hatim recorded that Abu Malik Al-Ghifari said that Ibn `Abbas said that when this Ayah was revealed,

(And do not marry idolatresses till they believe,) the people did not marry the pagan women. When the following Ayah was revealed,

((Lawful to you in marriage) are chaste women from the believers and chaste women from those who were given the Scripture before your time) they married women from the People of the Book. " Some of the Companions married Christian women and did not see any problem in this, relying on the honorable Ayah,

((Lawful to you in marriage) are chaste women from those who were given the Scripture before your time) Therefore, they made this Ayah an exception to the Ayah in Surat Al-Baqarah,

(And do not marry the idolatresses till they believe,) considering the latter Ayah to include the People of the Book in its general meaning. Otherwise, there is no contradiction here, since the People of the Book were mentioned alone when mentioning the rest of the idolators. Allah said,

(Those who disbelieve from among the People of the Scripture and the idolators, were not going to leave (their disbelief) until there came to them clear evidence.) and,

(And say to those who were given the Scripture and to those who are illiterates: "Do you (also) submit yourselves" If they do, they are rightly guided.) Allah said next,

(When you have given them their due), This refers to the Mahr, so just as these women are chaste and honorable, then give them their Mahr with a good heart. We should mention here that Jabir bin `Abdullah, `Amir Ash-Sha`bi, Ibrahim An-Nakha`i and Al-Hasan Al-Basri stated that when a man marries a woman and she commits illegal sexual intercourse before the marriage is consummated, the marriage is annulled. In this case, she gives back the Mahr that he paid her. Allah said,

(Desiring chastity, not illegal sexual intercourse, nor taking them as girl-friends (or lovers).) And just as women must be chaste and avoid illegal sexual activity, such is the case with men, who must also be chaste and honorable. Therefore, Allah said,

(...not illegal sexual intercourse') as adulterous people do, those who do not avoid sin, nor reject adultery with whomever offers it to them.

(nor taking them as girl-friends (or lovers),) meaning those who have mistresses and girlfriends who commit illegal sexual intercourse with them, as we mentioned in the explanation of Surat An-Nisa'.

Surah: 5 Ayah: 6

﴿ يَٰٓأَيُّهَا ٱلَّذِينَ ءَامَنُوٓاْ إِذَا قُمۡتُمۡ إِلَى ٱلصَّلَوٰةِ فَٱغۡسِلُواْ وُجُوهَكُمۡ وَأَيۡدِيَكُمۡ إِلَى
ٱلۡمَرَافِقِ وَٱمۡسَحُواْ بِرُءُوسِكُمۡ وَأَرۡجُلَكُمۡ إِلَى ٱلۡكَعۡبَيۡنِۚ وَإِن كُنتُمۡ جُنُبٗا فَٱطَّهَّرُواْۚ
وَإِن كُنتُم مَّرۡضَىٰٓ أَوۡ عَلَىٰ سَفَرٍ أَوۡ جَآءَ أَحَدٞ مِّنكُم مِّنَ ٱلۡغَآئِطِ أَوۡ لَٰمَسۡتُمُ ٱلنِّسَآءَ
فَلَمۡ تَجِدُواْ مَآءٗ فَتَيَمَّمُواْ صَعِيدٗا طَيِّبٗا فَٱمۡسَحُواْ بِوُجُوهِكُمۡ وَأَيۡدِيكُم مِّنۡهُۚ مَا
يُرِيدُ ٱللَّهُ لِيَجۡعَلَ عَلَيۡكُم مِّنۡ حَرَجٖ وَلَٰكِن يُرِيدُ لِيُطَهِّرَكُمۡ وَلِيُتِمَّ نِعۡمَتَهُۥ عَلَيۡكُمۡ
لَعَلَّكُمۡ تَشۡكُرُونَ ٦ ﴾

6. O you who believe! When you intend to offer As-Salât (the prayer), wash your faces and your hands (forearms) up to the elbows, rub (by passing wet hands over) your heads, and (wash) your feet up to ankles. If you are in a state of Janâba (i.e. aftwer a sexual discharge), purify yourself (bathe your whole body). But if you are ill or on a journe, or any of you comes after answering the call of nature, or you have been in contact with women (i.e. sexual intercourse) , and you find no water, then perform Tayammum with clean earth and rub therewith your faces and hands. Allâh does not want to place you in difficulty, but He wants to purify you, and to complete His Favor on you that you may be thankful.

Transliteration

6. Ya ayyuha allatheena amanoo itha qumtum ila alssalati faighsiloo wujoohakum waaydiyakum ila almarafiqi waimsahoo biruoosikum waarjulakum ila alkaAAbayni wa-in kuntum junuban faittahharoo wa-in kuntum marda aw AAala safarin aw jaa ahadun minkum mina algha-iti aw lamastumu alnnisaa falam tajidoo maan fatayammamoo saAAeedan tayyiban faimsahoo biwujoohikum waaydeekum minhu ma yureedu Allahu liyajAAala AAalaykum min harajin walakin yureedu liyutahhirakum waliyutimma niAAmatahu AAalaykum laAAallakum tashkuroona

Tafsir Ibn Kathir

The Order to Perform Wudu'

Allah said,

(When you stand for (intend to offer) the Salah,) Allah commanded performing Wudu' for the prayer. This is a command of obligation in the case of impurity, and in the case of purity, it is merely a recommendation. It was said that in the beginning of Islam, Muslims had to perform Wudu' for every prayer, but later on, this ruling was abrogated. Imam Ahmad bin Hanbal recorded that Sulayman bin Buraydah said that his father said, "The Prophet used to perform Wudu' before every prayer. On the Day of Victory, he performed Wudu' and wiped on his Khuffs and prayed the five prayers with one Wudu'. `Umar said to him, `O Messenger of Allah! You did something new that you never did before.' The Prophet said,

«إني عمدا فعلته يا عمر»

(`I did that intentionally O `Umar!)'" Muslim and the collectors of the Sunan also recorded this Hadith. At-Tirmidhi said,"Hasan Sahih." Ibn Jarir recorded that Al-Fadl bin Al-Mubashshir said, "I saw Jabir bin `Abdullah perform several prayers with only one Wudu'. When he would answer the call of nature, he performed Wudu' and wiped the top of his Khuffs with his wet hand. I said, `O Abu `Abdullah! Do you do this according to your own opinion' He said, `Rather, I saw the Prophet do the same thing. So, I do what I saw the Messenger of Allah doing.'" Ibn Majah also recorded this Hadith. Ahmad recorded that `Ubaydullah bin `Abdullah bin `Umar was asked; "Did you see `Abdullah bin `Umar perform Wudu' for every prayer, whether he was in a state of purity or not," So he replied, "Asma' bint Zayd bin Al-Khattab told him that `Abdullah bin Hanzalah bin Abi `Amir Al-Ghasil told her that the Messenger of Allah was earlier commanded to perform Wudu' for every prayer, whether he needed it or not. When that became hard on him, he was commanded to use Siwak for every prayer, and to perform Wudu' when Hadath (impurity) occurs. `Abdullah (Ibn `Umar) thought that he was able to do that (perform Wudu' for every prayer) and he kept doing that until he died." Abu

Dawud also collected this narration. This practice by Ibn `Umar demonstrates that it is encouraged, not obligatory, to perform Wudu' for every prayer, and this is also the opinion of the majority of scholars. Abu Dawud recorded that `Abdullah bin `Abbas said that when the Messenger of Allah once left the area where he answered the call of nature, he was brought something to eat. They said, "Should we bring you your water for Wudu" He said,

«إِنَّمَا أُمِرْتُ بِالْوُضُوءِ إِذَا قُمْتُ إِلَى الصَّلَاةِ»

(I was commanded to perform Wudu' when I stand up for prayer.) At-Tirmidhi and An-Nasa'i also recorded this Hadith and At-Tirmidhi said, "This Hadith is Hasan." Muslim recorded that Ibn `Abbas said, "We were with the Prophet when he went to answer the call of nature and when he came back, he was brought some food. He was asked, `O Messenger of Allah! Do you want to perform Wudu" He said,

«لِمَ؟ أَأُصَلِّي فَأَتَوَضَّأ»

(`Why? Am I about to pray so that I have to make Wudu'.?)'"

The Intention and Mentioning Allah's Name for Wudu'

Allah said;

(then wash your faces...) The obligation for the intention before Wudu' is proven by this Ayah;

(When you stand (intend) to offer the Salah then wash your faces...) This is because it is just like the Arabs saying; "When you see the leader, then stand." Meaning stand for him. And the Two Sahihs recorded the Hadith,

«الْأَعْمَالُ بِالنِّـــيَّاتِ وَإِنَّمَا لِكُلِّ امْرِىءٍ مَانَوَى»

(Actions are judged by their intentions, and each person will earn what he intended.) It is also recommended before washing the face that one mentions Allah's Name for the Wudu'. A Hadith that was narrated by several Companions states that the Prophet said,

«لَا وُضُوءَ لِمَنْ لَمْ يَذْكُرِ اسْمَ اللهِ عَلَيْه»

(There is no Wudu' for he who does not mention Allah's Name over it.) It is also recommended that one washes his hands before he puts his hands in the vessel of water, especially after one wakes up from sleep, for the Two Sahihs recorded that Abu Hurayrah said that the Messenger of Allah said,

«إِذَا اسْتَيْقَظَ أَحَدُكُمْ مِنْ نَوْمِهِ فَلَا يُدْخِلْ يَدَهُ فِي الْإِنَاءِ قَبْلَ أَنْ يَغْسِلَهَا ثَلَاثًا، فَإِنَّ أَحَدَكُمْ لَا يَدْرِي أَيْنَ بَاتَتْ يَدُه»

(If one of you wakes up from his sleep, let him not put his hand in the pot until he washes it thrice, for one of you does not know where his hand spent the night.) The face according to the scholars of Fiqh starts where the hair line on the head starts, regardless of one's lack or abundance of hair, until the end of the cheeks and chin, and from ear to ear.

Passing the Fingers through the Beard While Performing Wudu'

Imam Ahmad recorded that Abu Wa'il said, "I saw `Uthman when he was performing Wudu'... When he washed his face, he passed his fingers through his beard three times. He said, `I saw the Messenger of Allah do what you saw me doing.'" At-Tirmidhi and Ibn Majah also recorded this Hadith. At-Tirmidhi said "Hasan Sahih." while Al-Bukhari graded it Hasan.

How to Perform Wudu'

Imam Ahmad recorded that Ibn `Abbas once performed Wudu' and took a handful of water and rinsed his mouth and nose with it. He took another handful of water and joined both hands and washed his face. He took another handful of water and washed his right hand, and another handful and washed his left hand with it. He next wiped his head. Next, he took a handful of water and sprinkled it on his right foot and washed it and took another handful of water and washed his left foot. When he finished, he said, "This is how I saw the Messenger of Allah (performing Wudu')." Al-Bukhari also recorded it. Allah said,

(and your hands (forearms) up to (Ila) the elbows...) meaning, including the elbows. Allah said in another Ayah (using Ila),

(And devour not their substance to (Ila) your substance (by adding or including it in your property). Surely, this is a great sin.) It is recommended that those who perform Wudu' should wash a part of the upper arm with the elbow. Al-Bukhari and Muslim recorded that Abu Hurayrah said that the Messenger of Allah said,

«إِنَّ أُمَّتِي يُدْعَوْنَ يَوْمَ الْقِيَامَةِ غُرًّا مُحَجَّلِينَ مِنْ آثَارِ الْوُضُوءِ، فَمَنِ اسْتَطَاعَ مِنْكُمْ أَنْ يُطِيلَ غُرَّتَهُ فَلْيَفْعَلْ»

(On the Day of Resurrection, my Ummah will be called "those with the radiant appendages" because of the traces of Wudu'. Therefore, whoever can increase the area of his radiance should do so.) Muslim recorded that Abu Hurayrah said, "I heard my intimate friend (the Messenger) saying,

«تَبْلُغُ الْحِلْيَةُ مِنَ الْمُؤْمِنِ حَيْثُ يَبْلُغُ الْوَضُوءُ»

(The radiance of the believer reaches the areas that the water of (his) Wudu' reaches.)" Allah said next,

(Rub your heads.) It is recorded in the Two Sahihs that Malik bin `Amr bin Yahya Al-Mazini said that his father said that a man said to `Abdullah bin Zayd bin `Asim, the grandfather of `Amr bin Yahya and one of the Companions of the Messenger , "Can you show me how the Messenger of Allah used to perform Wudu'" `Abdullah bin Zayd said, "Yes." He then asked for a pot of water. He poured from it on his hands and washed them twice, then he rinsed his mouth and washed his nose (with water) thrice (by putting water in it and blowing it out). He washed his face thrice and after that he washed his forearms up to the elbows twice. He then passed his wet hands over his head from its front to its back and vice versa, beginning from the front and taking them to the back of his head up to the nape of the neck and then brought them to the front again from where he had started. He next washed his feet. A similar description of the Wudu' of the Messenger of Allah was performed by `Ali in the Hadith by `Abdu Khayr. Abu Dawud recorded that Mu`awiyah and Al-Miqdad bin Ma`dikarib narrated similar descriptions of the Wudu' of the Messenger of Allah . These Hadiths indicate that it is necessary to wipe the entire head. `Abdur-Razzaq recorded that Humran bin Aban said, "I saw `Uthman bin `Affan performing Wudu', and he poured water over his hands and washed them thrice, and then rinsed his mouth and washed his nose (by putting water in it, and then blowing it out). Then he washed his face thrice, and then his right forearm up to the elbows thrice, and washed the left forearm thrice. Then he passed his wet hands over his head, then he washed his right foot thrice, and next his left foot thrice. After that `Uthman said, `I saw the Prophet performing Wudu' like this, and said,

«مَنْ تَوَضَّأَ نَحْوَ وُضُوئِي هَذَا، ثُمَّ صَلَّى رَكْعَتَيْنِ لَا يُحَدِّثُ فِيهِمَا نَفْسَهُ، غُفِرَ لَهُ مَا تَقَدَّمَ مِنْ ذَنْبِه»

(If anyone performs Wudu' like that of mine and offers a two-Rak`ah prayer during which he does not think of anything else, then his past sins will be forgiven.)'" Al-Bukhari and Muslim also recorded this Hadith in the Two Sahihs. In his Sunan, Abu Dawud also recorded it from `Uthman, under the description of Wudu', and in it, that he wiped his head one time.

The Necessity of Washing the Feet

Allah said,

(and your feet up to ankles.) Ibn Abi Hatim recorded that Ibn `Abbas stated that the Ayah refers to washing (the feet). `Abdullah bin Mas`ud, `Urwah, `Ata', `Ikrimah, Al-Hasan, Mujahid, Ibrahim, Ad-Dahhak, As-Suddi, Muqatil bin Hayyan, Az-Zuhri and Ibrahim At-Taymi said similarly. This clearly indicates the necessity of washing the feet, just as the Salaf have said, and not only wiping over the top of the bare foot.

The Hadiths that Indicate the Necessity of Washing the Feet

We mentioned the Hadiths by the two Leaders of the Faithful, `Uthman and `Ali, and also by Ibn `Abbas, Mu`awiyah, `Abdullah bin Zayd bin `Asim and Al-Miqdad bin Ma`dikarib, that the Messenger of Allah washed his feet for Wudu', either once, twice or thrice. It is recorded in the Two Sahihs that `Abdullah bin `Amr said, "The Messenger of Allah was once late during a trip we were taking, and he caught up with us when the time remaining for the `Asr prayer was short. We were still performing Wudu' (in a rush) and we were wiping our feet. He shouted at the top of his voice,

«أَسْبِغُوا الْوُضُوءَ وَيْلٌ لِلْأَعْقَابِ مِنَ النَّار»

(Perform Wudu' thoroughly. Save your heels from the Fire.)" The same narration was also collected in the Two Sahihs from Abu Hurayrah. Muslim recorded that `A'ishah said that the Prophet said,

«أَسْبِغُوا الْوُضُوءَ وَيْلٌ لِلْأَعْقَابِ مِنَ النَّارِ»

(Perform Wudu' thoroughly. Save your heels from the Fire.) `Abdullah bin Al-Harith bin Jaz' said that he heard the Messenger of Allah saying,

«وَيْلٌ لِلْأَعْقَابِ وَبُطُونِ الْأَقْدَامِ مِنَ النَّارِ»

(Save your heels and the bottom of the feet from the Fire.) It was recorded by Al-Bayhaqi and Al-Hakim, and this chain is Sahih. Muslim recorded that `Umar bin Al-Khattab said that a man once performed Wudu' and left a dry spot the size of a fingernail on his foot. The Prophet saw that and he said to him,

«ارْجِعْ فَأَحْسِنْ وُضُوءَكَ»

(Go back and perform proper Wudu'.) Al-Hafiz Abu Bakr Al-Bayhaqi also recorded that Anas bin Malik said that a man came to the Prophet , after he performed Wudu' and left a dry spot the size of a fingernail on his foot. The Messenger of Allah said to him,

«ارْجِعْ فَأَحْسِنْ وُضُوءَكَ»

(Go back and perform proper Wudu'.) Imam Ahmad recorded that some of the wives of the Prophet said that the Prophet saw a man praying, but noticed a dry spot on his foot, the size of a Dirham. The Messenger of Allah ordered that man to perform Wudu' again. This Hadith was also collected by Abu Dawud from Baqiyyah, who added in his narration, "And (the Prophet ordered him) to repeat the prayer." This Hadith has a strong, reasonably good chain of narrators. Allah knows best.

The Necessity of Washing Between the Fingers

In the Hadith that Humran narrated, `Uthman washed between his fingers when he was describing the Wudu' of the Prophet . The collectors of the Sunan recorded that Laqit bin Sabrah said, "I said, `O Messenger of Allah! Tell me about Wudu'.' The Messenger replied,

«أَسْبِغِ الْوُضُوءَ، وَخَلِّلْ بَيْنَ الْأَصَابِعِ، وَبَالِغْ فِي الِاسْتِنْشَاقِ إِلَّا أَنْ تَكُونَ صَائِمًا»

(Perform Wudu' thoroughly, wash between the fingers and exaggerate in rinsing your nose, unless you are fasting.)"

Wiping Over the Khuffs is an Established Sunnah

Imam Ahmad bin Hanbal recorded that Aws bin Abi Aws said, "I saw the Messenger of Allah perform Wudu' and wipe over his Khuffs. He then stood up for prayer." Abu Dawud recorded this Hadith by Aws bin Abi Aws, who said in this narration, "I saw the Messenger of Allah , after he answered the call of nature, perform Wudu' and wipe over his Khuffs and feet." Imam Ahmad recorded that Jarir bin `Abdullah Al-Bajali said, "I embraced Islam after Surat Al-Ma'idah was revealed and I saw the Messenger of Allah wipe after I became Muslim." It is recorded in the Two Sahihs that Hammam said, "Jarir answered the call of nature and then performed Wudu' and wiped over his Khuffs. He was asked, `Do you do this' He said, `Yes. I saw the Messenger of Allah , after he answered the call of nature, perform Wudu' and wipe on his Khuffs.'" Al-A`mash commented that Ibrahim said, "They liked this Hadith because Jarir embraced Islam after Surat Al-Ma'idah was revealed." This is the wording collected by Muslim. The subject of the Messenger of Allah wiping over his Khuffs, instead of washing the feet, if he had worn his Khuffs while having Wudu', reaches the Mutawatir grade of narration, and they describe this practice by his words and actions.

Performing Tayammum with Clean earth When There is no Water and When One is Ill

Allah said,

(But if you are ill or on a journey or any of you comes from the Gha'it (toilet), or you have touched women and you find no water, then perform Tayammum with clean earth and rub therewith your faces and hands.) We discussed all of this in Surat An-Nisa', and thus we do not need to repeat it here. We also mentioned the reason behind revealing this Ayah. Yet, Al-Bukhari mentioned an honorable Hadith here specifically about the Tafsir of this noble Ayah. He recorded that `A'ishah said, "Upon returning to Al-Madinah, a necklace of mine was broken (and lost) in Al-Bayda' area. Allah's Messenger stayed there and went to sleep with his head on my lap. Abu Bakr (`A'ishah's father) came and hit me on my flank with his hand saying, `You have detained the people because of a necklace' So I wished I were dead because (I could not move) the Messenger was sleeping on my lap and because of the pain Abu Bakr caused me. Allah's Messenger got up when dawn broke and there was no water. So Allah revealed,

(O you who believe! When you stand (intend) to offer As-Salah (the prayer), then wash your faces) iuntil the end of the Ayah. Usayd bin Al-Hudayr said, `O the family of Abu Bakr! Allah has blessed the people because of you. Therefore, you are only a blessing for the people." Allah said,

(Allah does not want to place you in difficulty,) This is why He made things easy and lenient for you. This is why He allowed you to use Tayammum when you are ill and when you do not find water, to make things comfortable for you and as mercy for you. Allah made Tayammum in place of Wudu', and Allah made it the same as ablution with water for the one who it is legitimate for, except for certain things, as we mentioned before. For example; Tayammum only involves one strike with the hand on the sand and wiping the face and hands. Allah said,

(but He wants to purify you, and to complete His favor on you that you may be thankful.) for His bounties on you, such as His easy, kind, merciful, comfortable and lenient legislation.

Supplicating to Allah after Wudu'

The Sunnah encourages supplicating to Allah after Wudu' and states that those who do so are among those who seek to purify themselves, as the Ayah above states. Imam Ahmad, Muslim and the collectors of Sunan narrated that `Uqbah bin `Amir said, "We were on watch, guarding camels, and when my turn to guard came, I took the camels back at night. I found that the Messenger of Allah was giving a speech to the people. I heard these words from that speech:

«مَا مِنْ مُسْلِمٍ يَتَوَضَّأُ فَيُحْسِنُ وُضُوءَهُ، ثُمَّ يَقُومُ فَيُصَلِّي رَكْعَتَيْنِ مُقْبِلًا عَلَيْهِمَا بِقَلْبِهِ وَوَجْهِهِ، إِلَّا وَجَبَتْ لَهُ الْجَنَّة»

(Any Muslim who performs Wudu' properly, then stands up and prays a two Rak'ah prayer with full attention in his heart and face, will earn Paradise.) I said, `What a good statement this is!' A person who was close by said, `The statement he said before it is even better.' When I looked, I found that it was `Umar, who said, `I saw that you just came. The Prophet said,

«مَا مِنْكُمْ مِنْ أَحَدٍ يَتَوَضَّأُ فَيُبْلِغُ أَوْفَيُسْبِغُ الْوُضُوءَ، يَقُولُ: أَشْهَدُ أَنْ لَا إِلَهَ إِلَّا اللهُ وَأَنَّ مُحَمَّدًا عَبْدُهُ وَرَسُولُهُ، إِلَّا فُتِحَتْ لَهُ أَبْوَابُ الْجَنَّةِ الثَّمَانِيَةِ، يَدْخُلُ مِنْ أَيِّهَا شَاء»

(When any of you performs Wudu' properly and says, `I bear witness that there is no deity worthy of worship except Allah and that Muhammad is His servant and Messenger', the eight doors of Paradise will be opened for him so that he can enter from any door he wishes.)" This is the wording collected by Muslim.

The Virtue of Wudu'

Malik recorded that Abu Hurayrah said that the Messenger of Allah said,

«إِذَا تَوَضَّأَ الْعَبْدُ الْمُسْلِمُ أَوِ الْمُؤْمِنُ فَغَسَلَ وَجْهَهُ، خَرَجَ مِنْ وَجْهِهِ، كُلُّ خَطِيئَةٍ نَظَرَ إِلَيْهَا بِعَيْنَيْهِ مَعَ الْمَاءِ أَوْ مَعَ آخِرِ قَطْرِ الْمَاءِ، فَإِذَا غَسَلَ يَدَيهِ خَرَجَ مِنْ يَدَيْهِ كُلُّ خَطِيئَةٍ بَطَشَتْهَا يَدَاهُ مَعَ الْمَاءِ أَوْ مَعَ آخِرِ قَطْرِ الْمَاءِ، فَإِذَا غَسَلَ رِجْلَيْهِ خَرَجَتْ كُلُّ خَطِيئَةٍ مَشَتْهَا رِجْلَاهُ مَعَ الْمَاءِ أَوْ مَعَ آخِرِ قَطْرِ الْمَاءِ، حَتَّى يَخْرُجَ نَقِيًّا مِنَ الذُّنُوب»

(When the Muslim or the believing servant performs Wudu' and washes his face, every sin that he looked at with his eyes will depart from his face with the water, or with the last drop of water. When he washes his hands, every sin that his hands committed will depart from his hands with the water, or with the last drop of water. When he washes his feet, every sin to which his feet took him will depart with the water, or with the last drop of water. Until, he ends up sinless.) Muslim also recorded it.

Muslim recorded that Abu Malik Al-Ash`ari said that the Messenger of Allah said,

«الطُّهُور شَطْرُ الْإِيمَانِ، وَالْحَمْدُ للهِ تَمْلَأُ الْمِيزَانَ، وَسُبْحَانَ اللهِ وَاللهُ أَكْبَرُ تَمْلَأُ مَا
بَيْنَ السَّمَاءِ وَالْأَرْضِ، وَالصَّوْمُ جُنَّةٌ، وَالصَّبْرُ ضِيَاءٌ، وَالصَّدَقَةُ بُرْهَانٌ، وَالْقُرْآنُ حُجَّةٌ
لَكَ أَوْ عَلَيْكَ، كُلُّ النَّاسِ يَغْدُو، فَبَائِعٌ نَفْسَهُ فَمُعْتِقُهَا أَوْ مُوبِقُهَا»

(Purity is half of faith and Al-Hamdu Lillah (all the thanks are due to Allah) fills the Mizan (the Scale). And Subhan Allah and Allahu Akbar (all praise is due to Allah, and Allah is the Most Great) fills what is between the heaven and earth. As-Sawm (the fast) is a Junnah (a shield), Sabr (patience) is a light, Sadaqah (charity) is evidence (of faith) and the Qur'an is proof for, or against you. Every person goes out in the morning and ends up selling himself, he either frees his soul or destroys it.)

Muslim recorded that Ibn `Umar said that the Messenger of Allah said,

«لَا يَقْبَلُ اللهُ صَدَقَةً مِنْ غُلُولٍ، وَلَا صَلَاةً بِغَيْرِ طُهُورٍ»

(Allah does not accept charity from one who commits Ghulul, or prayer without purity.)

Surah: 5 Ayah: 7, Ayah: 8, Ayah: 9, Ayah: 10 & Ayah: 11

﴿وَاذْكُرُوا نِعْمَةَ اللَّهِ عَلَيْكُمْ وَمِيثَاقَهُ الَّذِي وَاثَقَكُم بِهِ إِذْ قُلْتُمْ سَمِعْنَا وَأَطَعْنَا ۖ وَاتَّقُوا
اللَّهَ ۚ إِنَّ اللَّهَ عَلِيمٌ بِذَاتِ الصُّدُورِ (٧)﴾

7. And remember Allâh's Favor to you and His Covenant with which He bound you when you said: "We hear and we obey." And fear Allâh. Verily, Allâh is All-Knower of that which is in (the secrets of your) breasts.

﴿يَا أَيُّهَا الَّذِينَ آمَنُوا كُونُوا قَوَّامِينَ لِلَّهِ شُهَدَاءَ بِالْقِسْطِ ۖ وَلَا يَجْرِمَنَّكُمْ شَنَآنُ
قَوْمٍ عَلَىٰ أَلَّا تَعْدِلُوا ۚ اعْدِلُوا هُوَ أَقْرَبُ لِلتَّقْوَىٰ ۖ وَاتَّقُوا اللَّهَ ۚ إِنَّ اللَّهَ خَبِيرٌ بِمَا
تَعْمَلُونَ (٨)﴾

8. O you who believe! Stand out firmly for Allâh as just witnesses; and let not the enmity and hatred of others make you avoid justice. Be just: that is nearer to piety; and fear Allâh. Verily, Allâh is Well-Acquainted with what you do.

﴿وَعَدَ اللَّهُ الَّذِينَ آمَنُوا وَعَمِلُوا الصَّالِحَاتِ ۙ لَهُم مَّغْفِرَةٌ وَأَجْرٌ عَظِيمٌ (٩)﴾

9. Allâh has promised those who believe (in the Oneness of Allâh - Islâmic Monotheism) and do deeds of righteousness, that for them there is forgiveness and a great reward (i.e. Paradise).

﴿ وَٱلَّذِينَ كَفَرُواْ وَكَذَّبُواْ بِـَٔايَٰتِنَآ أُوْلَٰٓئِكَ أَصۡحَٰبُ ٱلۡجَحِيمِ ١٠ ﴾

10. They who disbelieve and deny our Ayât (proofs, evidences, verses, lessons, signs, revelations, etc.) are those who will be the dwellers of the Hell-fire.

﴿ يَٰٓأَيُّهَا ٱلَّذِينَ ءَامَنُواْ ٱذۡكُرُواْ نِعۡمَتَ ٱللَّهِ عَلَيۡكُمۡ إِذۡ هَمَّ قَوۡمٌ أَن يَبۡسُطُوٓاْ إِلَيۡكُمۡ
أَيۡدِيَهُمۡ فَكَفَّ أَيۡدِيَهُمۡ عَنكُمۡۖ وَٱتَّقُواْ ٱللَّهَۚ وَعَلَى ٱللَّهِ فَلۡيَتَوَكَّلِ ٱلۡمُؤۡمِنُونَ ١١ ﴾

11. O you who believe! Remember the Favor of Allâh unto you when some people desired (made a plan) to stretch out their hands against you, but (Allâh) held back their hands from you. So fear Allâh. And in Allâh let believers put their trust.

Transliteration

7. Waothkuroo niAAmata Allahi AAalaykum wameethaqahu allathee wathaqakum bihi ith qultum samiAAna waataAAna waittaqoo Allaha inna Allaha AAaleemun bithati alssudoori 8. Ya ayyuha allatheena amanoo koonoo qawwameena lillahi shuhadaa bialqisti wala yajrimannakum shanaanu qawmin AAala alla taAAdiloo iAAdiloo huwa aqrabu lilttaqwa waittaqoo Allaha inna Allaha khabeerun bima taAAmaloona 9. WaAAada Allahu allatheena amanoo waAAamiloo alssalihati lahum maghfiratun waajrun AAatheemun 10. Waallatheena kafaroo wakaththaboo bi-ayatina ola-ika as-habu aljaheemi 11. Ya ayyuha allatheena amanoo othkuroo niAAmata Allahi AAalaykum ith hamma qawmun an yabsutoo ilaykum aydiyahum fakaffa aydiyahum AAankum waittaqoo Allaha waAAala Allahi falyatawakkali almu/minoona

Tafsir Ibn Kathir

Reminding the Believers of the Bounty of the Message and Islam

Allah reminds His believing servants of His bounty by legislating this glorious religion and sending them this honorable Messenger. He also reminds them of the covenant and pledges that He took from them to follow the Messenger , support and aid him, implement his Law and convey it on his behalf, while accepting it themselves. Allah said,

(And remember Allah's favor upon you and His covenant with which He bound you when you said, "We hear and we obey.") This is the pledge that they used to give to the Messenger of Allah when they embraced Islam. They used to say, "We gave our pledge of obedience to the Messenger of Allah to hear and obey, in times when we are active and otherwise, even if we were passed on for rights, and not to dispute leadership with its rightful people." Allah also said,

(And what is the matter with you that you believe not in Allah! While the Messenger invites you to believe in your Lord; and He has indeed taken your covenant, if you are real believers.) It was also said that this Ayah (5:7) reminds the Jews of the pledges and promises Allah took from them to follow Muhammad and adhere to his Law, as `Ali bin Abi Talhah reported that Ibn `Abbas stated. Allah then said,

(And have Taqwa of Allah.) in all times and situations. Allah says that He knows the secrets and thoughts that the hearts conceal,

(Verily, Allah is All-Knower of the secrets of (your) breasts.)

The Necessity of Observing Justice

Allah said,

(O you who believe! Stand out firmly for Allah...) meaning, in truth for the sake of Allah, not for the sake of people or for fame,

(as just witnesses) observing justice and not transgression. It is recorded in the Two Sahihs that An-Nu`man bin Bashir said, "My father gave me a gift, but `Amrah bint Rawahah, my mother, said that she would not agree to it unless he made Allah's Messenger as a witness to it. So, my father went to Allah's Messenger to ask him to be a witness to his giving me the gift. Allah's Messenger asked,

«أكل ولدك نحلت مثله؟»

(`Have you given the like of it to everyone of your offspring') He replied in the negative. Allah's Messenger said,

«اتَّقُوا اللهَ وَاعْدِلُوا فِي أَوْلَادِكُم»

(Have Taqwa of Allah and treat your children equally.) And said;

«إِنِّي لَا أَشْهَدُ عَلى جَوْر»

(I shall not be witness to injustice.) My father then returned and took back his gift." Allah said;

(and let not the enmity and hatred of others make you avoid justice.) The Ayah commands: Do not be carried away by your hatred for some people to avoid observing justice with them. Rather, be just with every one, whether a friend or an enemy. This is why Allah said,

(Be just: that is nearer to Taqwa) this is better than if you abandon justice in this case. Although Allah said that observing justice is `nearer to Taqwa', there is not any other course of action to take, therefore `nearer' here means `is'. Allah said in another Ayah,

(The dwellers of Paradise will, on that Day, have the best abode, and have the fairer of places for repose.) Some of the female Companions said to `Umar, "You are more rough and crude than the Messenger of Allah ," meaning, you are rough, not that the Prophet is rough at all. Allah said next,

(and have Taqwa of Allah. Verily, Allah is WellAcquainted with what you do.) and consequently, He will reward or punish you according to your actions, whether good or evil. Hence Allah's statement afterwards,

(Allah has promised those who believe and do deeds of righteousness, that for them there is forgiveness) for their sins,

(and a great reward.) which is Paradise, that is part of Allah's mercy for His servants. They will not earn Paradise on account of their good actions, but rather on account of His mercy and favor, even though they will qualify to earn this mercy on account of their good actions. Allah has made these actions the cause and path that lead to His mercy, favor, pardon and acceptance. Therefore, all this is from Allah Alone and all thanks are due to Him. Allah said next,

(And they who disbelieve and deny our Ayat are those who will be the dwellers of the Hell-fire.) This only demonstrates Allah's perfect justice, wisdom and judgment, He is never wrong, for He is the Most Wise, Most Just and Most Able.

Among Allah's Favors is that He Prevented the Disbelievers from Fighting the Muslims

Allah said,

(O you who believe! Remember the favor of Allah unto you when some people desired (made a plan) to stretch out their hands against you, but (Allah) withheld their hands from you.) `Abdur-Razzaq recorded that Jabir said, "The Prophet once stayed at an area and the people spread out seeking shade under various trees. The Prophet hung his weapon on a tree, and a bedouin man came and took possession of the Prophet's weapon and held it aloft. He came towards the Prophet and said, `Who can protect you from me' He replied, `Allah, the Exalted, Most Honored.' The bedouin man repeated his question twice or thrice, each time the Prophet answering him by saying, `Allah.' The bedouin man then lowered the sword, and the Prophet called his Companions and told them what had happened while the bedouin was sitting next to him, for the Prophet did not punish him.' Ma`mar said that Qatadah used to mention that some Arabs wanted to have the Prophet killed, so they sent that bedouin. Qatadah would then mention this Ayah,

(Remember the favor of Allah unto you when some people desired (made a plan) to stretch out their hands against you...) The story of this bedouin man, whose name is Ghawrath bin Al-Harith, is mentioned in the Sahih. Muhammad bin Ishaq bin Yasar, Mujahid and `Ikrimah said that this Ayah was revealed about Bani An-Nadir, who plotted to drop a stone on the head of the Messenger when he came to them for help to pay the blood money of two persons whom Muslims killed. The Jews left the execution of this plot to `Amr bin Jihash bin Ka`b and ordered him to throw a stone on the Prophet from above, when he came to them and sat under the wall. Allah told His Prophet about their plot, and he went back to Al-Madinah and his Companions followed him later on. Allah sent down this Ayah concerning this matter. Allah's statement,

(And in Allah let the believers put their trust.) and those who do so, then Allah shall suffice for them and shall protect them from the evil plots of the people. Thereafter, Allah commanded His Messenger to expel Bani An-Nadir, and he laid siege to their area and forced them to evacuate Al-Madinah.

Surah: 5 Ayah: 12, Ayah: 13 & Ayah: 14

﴿ ۞ وَلَقَدْ أَخَذَ ٱللَّهُ مِيثَٰقَ بَنِىٓ إِسْرَٰٓءِيلَ وَبَعَثْنَا مِنْهُمُ ٱثْنَىْ عَشَرَ نَقِيبًا ۖ وَقَالَ ٱللَّهُ إِنِّى
مَعَكُمْ ۖ لَئِنْ أَقَمْتُمُ ٱلصَّلَوٰةَ وَءَاتَيْتُمُ ٱلزَّكَوٰةَ وَءَامَنتُم بِرُسُلِى وَعَزَّرْتُمُوهُمْ وَأَقْرَضْتُمُ

ٱللَّهَ قَرْضًا حَسَنًا لَّأُكَفِّرَنَّ عَنكُمْ سَيِّـَٔاتِكُمْ وَلَأُدْخِلَنَّكُمْ جَنَّـٰتٍ تَجْرِى مِن تَحْتِهَا
ٱلْأَنْهَـٰرُ ۚ فَمَن كَفَرَ بَعْدَ ذَٰلِكَ مِنكُمْ فَقَدْ ضَلَّ سَوَآءَ ٱلسَّبِيلِ ﴿١٢﴾

12. Indeed Allâh took the covenant from the Children of Israel (Jews), and We appointed twelve leaders among them. And Allâh said: "I am with you if you perform As-Salât (Iqâmat-as-Salât) and give Zakât and believe in My Messengers; honor and assist them, and lend a good loan to Allâh, verily, I will expiate your sins and admit you to Gardens under which rivers flow (in Paradise). But if any of you after this, disbelieved, he has indeed gone astray from the Straight Path."

﴿ فَبِمَا نَقْضِهِم مِّيثَـٰقَهُمْ لَعَنَّـٰهُمْ وَجَعَلْنَا قُلُوبَهُمْ قَـٰسِيَةً ۖ يُحَرِّفُونَ ٱلْكَلِمَ عَن
مَّوَاضِعِهِۦ ۙ وَنَسُوا۟ حَظًّا مِّمَّا ذُكِّرُوا۟ بِهِۦ ۚ وَلَا تَزَالُ تَطَّلِعُ عَلَىٰ خَآئِنَةٍ مِّنْهُمْ إِلَّا قَلِيلًا مِّنْهُمْ
فَٱعْفُ عَنْهُمْ وَٱصْفَحْ ۚ إِنَّ ٱللَّهَ يُحِبُّ ٱلْمُحْسِنِينَ ﴿١٣﴾

13. So because of their breach of their covenant, We cursed them and made their hearts grow hard. They change the words from their (right) places and have abandoned a good part of the Message that was sent to them. And you will not cease to discover deceit in them, except a few of them. But forgive them, and overlook (their misdeeds). Verily, Allâh loves Al-Muhsinûn (good-doers - see V.2:112).

﴿ وَمِنَ ٱلَّذِينَ قَالُوٓا۟ إِنَّا نَصَـٰرَىٰٓ أَخَذْنَا مِيثَـٰقَهُمْ فَنَسُوا۟ حَظًّا مِّمَّا ذُكِّرُوا۟ بِهِۦ
فَأَغْرَيْنَا بَيْنَهُمُ ٱلْعَدَاوَةَ وَٱلْبَغْضَآءَ إِلَىٰ يَوْمِ ٱلْقِيَـٰمَةِ ۚ وَسَوْفَ يُنَبِّئُهُمُ ٱللَّهُ بِمَا كَانُوا۟
يَصْنَعُونَ ﴿١٤﴾

14. And from those who call themselves Christians, We took their covenant, but they have abandoned a good part of the Message that was sent to them. So We planted amongst them enmity and hatred till the Day of Resurrection (when they discarded Allâh's Book, disobeyed Allâh's Messengers and His Orders and transgressed beyond bounds in Allâh's disobedience); and Allâh will inform them of what they used to do.

Transliteration

12. Walaqad akhatha Allahu meethaqa banee isra-eela wabaAAathna minhumu ithnay
AAashara naqeeban waqala Allahu innee maAAakum la-in aqamtumu alssalata waataytumu
alzzakata waamantum birusulee waAAazzartumoohum waaqradtumu Allaha qardan hasanan
laokaffiranna AAankum sayyi-atikum walaodkhilannakum jannatin tajree min tahtiha al-anharu
faman kafara baAAda thalika minkum faqad dalla sawaa alssabeeli 13. Fabima naqdihim
meethaqahum laAAannahum wajaAAalna quloobahum qasiyatan yuharrifoona alkalima AAan
mawadiAAihi wanasoo haththan mimma thukkiroo bihi wala tazalu tattaliAAu AAala kha-inatin
minhum illa qaleelan minhum faoAAfu AAanhum waisfah inna Allaha yuhibbu almuhsineena
14. Wamina allatheena qaloo inna nasara akhathna meethaqahum fanasoo haththan mimma
thukkiroo bihi faaghrayna baynahumu alAAadawata waalbaghdaa ila yawmi alqiyamati
wasawfa yunabbi-ohumu Allahu bima kanoo yasnaAAoona

Tafsir Ibn Kathir

Cursing the People of the Book for Breaking the Covenant

Allah commanded His believing servants to fullfil the promises and pledges that He took from them and which they gave His servant and Messenger, Muhammad, peace be upon him. Allah also commanded them to stand for the truth and give correct testimony. He also reminded them of the obvious and subtle favors of the truth and guidance that He granted them. Next, Allah informed them of the pledges and promises that He took from the People of the Book, who were before them, the Jews and Christians. When they broke these promises and covenants, Allah cursed them as a consequence and expelled them from His grace and mercy. He also sealed their hearts from receiving guidance and the religion of truth, beneficial knowledge and righteous actions. Allah said,

(Indeed Allah took the covenant from the Children of Israel and We appointed twelve leaders among them.) These twelve people were leaders who gave the pledge to Allah to listen and obey Allah, His Messenger and His Book on behalf of their tribes. Muhammad bin Ishaq and Ibn `Abbas said that this occurred when Musa went to fight the mighty enemy (in Palestine), and Allah commanded him to choose a leader from every tribe.

The Leaders of Ansar on the Night of `Aqabah

Likewise, when the Messenger of Allah took the pledge from the Ansar in the `Aqabah area, there were twelve leaders from the Ansar. There were three men from the tribe of Aws: Usayd bin Al-Hudayr, Sa`d bin Khaythamah and Rifa`ah bin `Abdul-Mundhir, or Abu Al-Haytham bin At-Tayhan. There were nine people from the tribe of Khazraj: Abu Umamah As`ad bin Zurarah, Sa`d bin Ar-Rabi`, `Abdullah bin Rawahah, Rafi` bin Malik bin Al-`Ajlan, Al-Bara' bin Ma`rur, `Ubadah bin As-Samit, Sa`d bin `Ubadah, `Abdullah bin `Amr bin Haram and Al-Mundhir bin `Umar bin Khunays. Ka`b bin Malik mentioned these men in his poem, as recorded by Ibn Ishaq.On that night, these men were the leaders or representatives of their tribes by the command of the Prophet . They gave the pledge and promise of allegiance and obedience to the Prophet on behalf of their people. Allah said,

(And Allah said, "I am with you...) with My protection, support and aid,

(if you perform the Salah and give the Zakah and believe in My Messengers;) concerning what they bring you of the revelation,

(honor and assist them...) and support them on the truth,

(and lend to Allah a good loan...) by spending in His cause, seeking to please Him.

(verily, I will remit your sins) and errors, I will erase them, cover them, and will not punish you for them,

(and admit you to Gardens under which rivers flow (in Paradise).) thus, protecting you from what you fear and granting you what you seek.

Breaking the Covenant

Allah said,

(But if any of you after this, disbelieved, he has indeed gone astray from the straight way.) Therefore, those who break this covenant, even though they pledged and vowed to keep it, yet, they broke it and denied it ever existed, they have avoided the clear path and deviated from the path of guidance to the path of misguidance. Allah then mentioned the punishment that befell those who broke His covenant and the pledge they gave Him,

(So because of their breach of their covenant, We cursed them...) Allah states, because of their breaking the promise that We took from them, We cursed them, deviated them away from the truth, and expelled them from guidance,

(and made their hearts grow hard...) and they do not heed any word of advice that they hear, because of the hardness of their hearts.

(They change the words from their (right) places...) Since their comprehension became corrupt, they behaved treacherously with Allah's Ayat, altering His Book from its apparent meanings which He sent down, and distorting its indications. They attributed to Allah what He did not say, and we seek refuge with Allah from such behavior.

(and have abandoned a good part of the Message that was sent to them.) by not implementing it and by ignoring it. Allah said next,

(And you will not cease to discover deceit in them,) such as their plots and treachery against you, O Muhammad, and your Companions. Mujahid said that this Ayah refers to their plot to kill the Messenger of Allah .

(But forgive them, and overlook (their misdeeds).) This, indeed, is the ultimate victory and triumph. Some of the Salaf said, "You would never treat those who disobey Allah with you better than obeying Allah with them." This way, their hearts will gather around the truth and Allah might lead them to the right guidance. This is why Allah said,

(Verily, Allah loves the doers of good.) Therefore, forgive those who err against you. Qatadah said that this Ayah was abrogated with Allah's statement,

(Fight against those who believe not in Allah, nor in the Last Day).

The Christians Also Broke their Covenant with Allah and the Repercussion of this Behavior

Allah said, (And from those who call themselves Christians, We took their covenant,) Meaning: `From those who call themselves Christians and followers of `Isa, son of Maryam, while in fact they are not as they claim. We took from them the covenant and pledges that they would follow the Prophet , aid him, honor him and follow his footsteps.' And that they would believe in every Prophet whom Allah sends to the people of the earth. They imitated the Jews and broke the promises and the pledges. This is why Allah said,

(but they have abandoned a good part of the Message that was sent to them. So We planted amongst them enmity and hatred till the Day of Resurrection;) Meaning: `We planted enmity and hatred between them, and they will remain like this until the Day of Resurrection.' Indeed, the numerous Christian sects have always been enemies and adversaries of each other, accusing each other of heresy and cursing each other. Each sect among them excommunicates the other sects and does not allow them entrance to their places of worship. The Monarchist sect accuses the Jacobite sect of heresy, and such is the case with the Nestorians and the

Arians. Each sect among them will continue to accuse the other of disbelief and heresy in this life and on the Day when the Witnesses will come forth. Allah then said,

(and Allah will inform them of what they used to do.) warning and threatening the Christians because of their lies against Allah and His Messenger and their false claims about Allah, hallowed be He above what they say about Him. The Christians attribute a companion and a son to Allah, while He is the One and Only, the All-Sufficient, Who neither begets nor was He begotten, and there is none like unto Him.

Surah: 5 Ayah: 15 & Ayah: 16

﴿ يَٰٓأَهۡلَ ٱلۡكِتَٰبِ قَدۡ جَآءَكُمۡ رَسُولُنَا يُبَيِّنُ لَكُمۡ كَثِيرٗا مِّمَّا كُنتُمۡ
تُخۡفُونَ مِنَ ٱلۡكِتَٰبِ وَيَعۡفُواْ عَن كَثِيرٖۚ قَدۡ جَآءَكُم مِّنَ ٱللَّهِ نُورٞ
وَكِتَٰبٞ مُّبِينٞ ١٥ ﴾

15. O people of the Scripture (Jews and Christians)! Now has come to you Our Messenger (Muhammad (peace be upon him)) explaining to you much of that which you used to hide from the Scripture and passing over (i.e. leaving out without explaining) much. Indeed, there has come to you from Allâh a light (Prophet Muhammad (peace be upon him)) and a plain Book (this Qur'ân).

﴿ يَهۡدِي بِهِ ٱللَّهُ مَنِ ٱتَّبَعَ رِضۡوَٰنَهُۥ سُبُلَ ٱلسَّلَٰمِ وَيُخۡرِجُهُم مِّنَ ٱلظُّلُمَٰتِ إِلَى ٱلنُّورِ
بِإِذۡنِهِۦ وَيَهۡدِيهِمۡ إِلَىٰ صِرَٰطٖ مُّسۡتَقِيمٖ ١٦ ﴾

16. Wherewith Allâh guides all those who seek His Good Pleasure to ways of peace, and He brings them out of darkness by His Will unto light and guides them to a Straight Way (Islâmic Monotheism).

Transliteration

15. Ya ahla alkitabi qad jaakum rasooluna yubayyinu lakum katheeran mimma kuntum tukhfoona mina alkitabi wayaAAfoo AAan katheerin qad jaakum mina Allahi noorun wakitabun mubeenun 16. Yahdee bihi Allahu mani ittabaAAa ridwanahu subula alssalami wayukhrijuhum mina alththulumati ila alnnoori bi-ithnihi wayahdeehim ila siratin mustaqeemin

Tafsir Ibn Kathir

Explaining the Truth Through the Messenger and the Qur'an

Allah states that He sent His Messenger Muhammad with the guidance and the religion of truth to all the people of the earth, the Arabs and non-Arabs, lettered and unlettered. Allah also states that He sent Muhammad with clear evidences and the distinction between truth and falsehood. Allah said,

(O People of the Scripture! Now has come to you Our Messenger explaining to you much of that which you used to hide from the Scripture and passing over much.) So the Prophet explained where they altered, distorted, changed and lied about Allah. He also ignored much of what they changed, since it would not bring about any benefit if it was explained. In his

Mustadrak, Al-Hakim recorded that Ibn `Abbas said, "He who disbelieves in stoning (the adulterer to death) will have inadvertently disbelieved in the Qur'an, for Allah said,

(O People of the Scripture! Now has come to you Our Messenger explaining to you much of that which you used to hide from the Scripture) and stoning was among the things that they used to hide." Al-Hakim said, "Its chain is Sahih, and they did not record it." Allah next mentions the Glorious Qur'an that He sent down to His honorable Prophet ,

(Indeed, there has come to you from Allah a light and a plain Book. Wherewith Allah guides all those who seek His pleasure to ways of peace.) meaning, ways of safety and righteousness,

(and He brings them out of darkness by His permission unto light and guides them to a straight path.) He thus saves them from destruction and explains to them the best, most clear path. Therefore, He protects them from what they fear, and brings about the best of what they long for, all the while ridding them of misguidance and directing them to the best, most righteous state of being.

Surah: 5 Ayah: 17 & Ayah: 18

﴿ لَّقَدْ كَفَرَ ٱلَّذِينَ قَالُوٓا۟ إِنَّ ٱللَّهَ هُوَ ٱلْمَسِيحُ ٱبْنُ مَرْيَمَ ۚ قُلْ فَمَن يَمْلِكُ مِنَ ٱللَّهِ
شَيْـًٔا إِنْ أَرَادَ أَن يُهْلِكَ ٱلْمَسِيحَ ٱبْنَ مَرْيَمَ وَأُمَّهُۥ وَمَن فِى ٱلْأَرْضِ جَمِيعًا ۗ وَلِلَّهِ
مُلْكُ ٱلسَّمَٰوَٰتِ وَٱلْأَرْضِ وَمَا بَيْنَهُمَا ۚ يَخْلُقُ مَا يَشَآءُ ۚ وَٱللَّهُ عَلَىٰ كُلِّ شَىْءٍ قَدِيرٌ ﴿١٧﴾ ﴾

17. Surely, in disbelief are they who say that Allâh is the Messiah, son of Maryam (Mary). Say (O Muhammad (peace be upon him)) "Who then has the least power against Allâh, if He were to destroy the Messiah, son of Maryam (Mary), his mother, and all those who are on the earth together?" And to Allâh belongs the dominion of the heavens and the earth, and all that is between them. He creates what He wills. And Allâh is Able to do all things.

﴿ وَقَالَتِ ٱلْيَهُودُ وَٱلنَّصَٰرَىٰ نَحْنُ أَبْنَٰٓؤُا۟ ٱللَّهِ وَأَحِبَّٰٓؤُهُۥ ۚ قُلْ فَلِمَ يُعَذِّبُكُم بِذُنُوبِكُم ۖ بَلْ
أَنتُم بَشَرٌ مِّمَّنْ خَلَقَ ۚ يَغْفِرُ لِمَن يَشَآءُ وَيُعَذِّبُ مَن يَشَآءُ ۚ وَلِلَّهِ مُلْكُ ٱلسَّمَٰوَٰتِ وَٱلْأَرْضِ وَمَا
بَيْنَهُمَا ۖ وَإِلَيْهِ ٱلْمَصِيرُ ﴿١٨﴾ ﴾

18. And (both) the Jews and the Christians say: "We are the children of Allâh and His loved ones." Say: "Why then does He punish you for your sins?" Nay, you are but human beings, of those He has created, He forgives whom He wills and He punishes whom He wills. And to Allâh belongs the dominion of the heavens and the earth and all that is between them; and to Him is the return (of all).

Transliteration

17. Laqad kafara allatheena qaloo inna Allaha huwa almaseehu ibnu maryama qul faman yamliku mina Allahi shay-an in arada an yuhlika almaseeha ibna maryama waommahu waman fee al-ardi jameeAAan walillahi mulku alssamawati waal-ardi wama baynahuma yakhluqu ma yashao waAllahu AAala kulli shay-in qadeerun 18. Waqalati alyahoodu waalnnasara nahnu abnao Allahi waahibbaohu qul falima yuAAaththibukum bithunoobikum bal antum basharun

mimman khalaqa yaghfiru liman yashao wayuAAaththibu man yashao walillahi mulku alssamawati waal-ardi wama baynahuma wa-ilayhi almaseeru

Tafsir Ibn Kathir

The Polytheism and Disbelief of the Christians

Allah states that the Christians are disbelievers because of their claim that `Isa, son of Maryam, one of Allah's servants and creatures, is Allah. Allah is holier than what they attribute to Him. Allah then reminds them of His perfect ability over everything and that everything is under His complete control and power,

(Say: "Who then has the least power against Allah, if He were to destroy the Messiah, son of Maryam, his mother, and all those who are on the earth together") Therefore, if Allah wills to do that, who would be able to stop Him or prevent Him from doing it Allah then said,

(And to Allah belongs the dominion of the heavens and the earth, and all that is between them. He creates what He wills.) All things in existence are Allah's property and creation and He is able to do everything. He is never asked about what He does with His power, domain, justice and greatness so this refutes the Christian creed, may Allah's continued curses be upon them until the Day of Resurrection.

Refuting the People of the Book's Claim that they are Allah's Children

Allah then refutes the Christians' and Jews' false claims and lies,

(And the Jews and the Christians say, "We are the children of Allah and His loved ones.") They claim: "We are the followers of Allah's Prophets, who are His children, whom He takes care of. He also loves us." The People of the Book claim in their Book that Allah said to His servant Isra'il, "You are my firstborn." But they explained this statement in an improper manner and altered its meaning. Some of the People of the Book who later became Muslims refuted this false statement saying, "This statement only indicates honor and respect, as is common in their speech at that time." The Christians claim that `Isa said to them, "I will go back to my father and your father," meaning, my Lord and your Lord. It is a fact that the Christians did not claim that they too are Allah's sons as they claimed about `Isa. Rather this statement by `Isa only meant to indicate a closeness with Allah. This is why when they said that they are Allah's children and loved ones, Allah refuted their claim,

(Say, "Why then does He punish you for your sins") meaning, if you were truly as you claim, Allah's children and loved ones, then why did He prepare the Fire because of your disbelief, lies and false claims

(Nay, you are but human beings, of those He has created,) Allah states: you are just like the rest of the children of Adam, and Allah is the Lord of all His creation,

(He forgives whom He wills and punishes whom He wills.) Allah does what He wills, there is none who can escape His judgement, and He is swift in reckoning.

(And to Allah belongs the dominion of the heavens and the earth and all that is between them;) Therefore, everything is Allah's property and under His power and control,

(and to Him is the return.) In the end, the return will be to Allah and He will judge between His servants as He will, and He is the Most Just Who is never wrong in His judgment.

Surah: 5 Ayah: 19

﴿ يَٰٓأَهۡلَ ٱلۡكِتَٰبِ قَدۡ جَآءَكُمۡ رَسُولُنَا يُبَيِّنُ لَكُمۡ عَلَىٰ فَتۡرَةٖ مِّنَ ٱلرُّسُلِ أَن تَقُولُواْ مَا جَآءَنَا
مِنۢ بَشِيرٖ وَلَا نَذِيرٖۖ فَقَدۡ جَآءَكُم بَشِيرٞ وَنَذِيرٞۗ وَٱللَّهُ عَلَىٰ كُلِّ شَيۡءٖ قَدِيرٞ ١٩ ﴾

19. O people of the Scripture (Jews and Christians)! Now has come to you Our Messenger (Muhammad (peace be upon him)) making (things) clear unto you, after a break in (the series of) Messengers, lest you say: "There came unto us no bringer of glad tidings and no warner." But now has come unto you a bringer of glad tidings and a warner. And Allâh is Able to do all things.

Transliteration

19. Ya ahla alkitabi qad jaakum rasooluna yubayyinu lakum AAala fatratin mina alrrusuli an taqooloo ma jaana min basheerin wala natheerin faqad jaakum basheerun wanatheerun waAllahu AAala kulli shay-in qadeerun

Tafsir Ibn Kathir

Allah is addressing the People of the Book -- the Jews and the Christians, saying that He has sent His Messenger Muhammad to them, the Final Prophet, after whom there will be no Prophet or Messenger. Rather, He is the Final Messenger who came after a long time passed between him and `Isa, son of Maryam peace be upon them. There is a difference of opinion about the length of time between `Isa and Muhammad . Abu `Uthman An-Nahdi and Qatadah were reported to have said that this period was six hundred years. Al-Bukhari also recorded this opinion from Salman Al-Farisi. Qatadah said that this period was five hundred and sixty years, while Ma`mar said that it is five hundred and forty years. Some said that this period is six hundred and twenty years. There is no contradiction here if we consider the fact that those who said that this period was six hundred years were talking about solar years, while the second refers to lunar years, since there is a difference of about three years between every one hundred lunar and solar years. As in Allah's statement,

(And they stayed in their Cave three hundred years, adding nine.) meaning, nine more lunar years to substitute for the difference between lunar and solar years, thus agreeing with the three hundred years that the People of the Book knew about. We should assert again that the time period we mentioned here was between `Isa, the last Prophet to the Children of Israel, and Muhammad , the Last Prophet and Messenger among the children of Adam. In the Sahih collected by Al-Bukhari, Abu Hurayrah said that the Messenger of Allah said,

«إِنَّ أَوْلَى النَّاسِ بِابْنِ مَرْيَمَ لَأَنَا، لَيْسَ بَيْنِي وَبَيْنَهُ نَبِي»

(I, among all people, have the most right to the son of Maryam, for there was no Prophet between Him and I.) This Hadith refutes the opinion of Al-Quda`i and others, that there was a Prophet after `Isa called Khalid bin Sinan. Allah sent Muhammad after a period of time during which there was no Prophet, clear path, or unchanged religions. Idol worshipping, fire worshipping and cross worshipping flourished during this time. Therefore, the bounty of sending Muhammad was the perfect bounty at a time when he was needed the most. Evil had filled the earth by then, and tyranny and ignorance had touched all the servants, except a few of those who remained loyal to the true teachings of previous Prophets, such as some Jewish rabbis, Christian priests and Sabian monks. Imam Ahmad recorded that `Iyad bin Himar Al-Mujash`i said that the Prophet gave a speech one day and said,

«وَإِنَّ رَبِّي أَمَرَنِي أَنْ أُعَلِّمَكُمْ مَا جَهِلْتُمْ مِمَّا عَلَّمَنِي فِي يَوْمِي هَذَا، كُلُّ مَالٍ نَحَلْتُهُ عِبَادِي حَلَالٌ، وَإِنِّي خَلَقْتُ عِبَادِي حُنَفَاءَ كُلَّهُمْ، وَإِنَّ الشَّيَاطِينَ أَتَتْهُمْ فَأَضَلَّتْهُمْ عَنْ دِينِهِمْ، وَحَرَّمَتْ عَلَيْهِمْ مَا أَحْلَلْتُ لَهُمْ، وَأَمَرَتْهُمْ أَنْ يُشْرِكُوا بِي مَا لَمْ أُنَزِّلْ بِهِ سُلْطَانًا، ثُمَّ إِنَّ اللهَ عَزَّ وَجَلَّ نَظَرَ إِلَى أَهْلِ الْأَرْضِ فَمقَتَهُمْ عَرَبَهُمْ وعَجَمَهُمْ، إِلَّا بَقَايَا مِنْ بَنِي إِسْرَائِيلَ، وقَالَ: إِنَّمَا بَعَثْتُكَ لِأَبْتَلِيَكَ وَأَبْتَلِيَ بِكَ، وَأَنْزَلْتُ عَلَيْكَ كِتَابًا لَا يَغْسِلُهُ الْمَاءُ،تَقْرَأُهُ نَائِمًا وَيَقْظَانَ، ثُمَّ إِنَّ اللهَ أَمَرَنِي أَنْ أُحَرِّقَ قُرَيْشًا فَقُلْتُ: يَارَبِّ إِذَنْ يَثْلَغُوا رَأْسِي، فَيَدَعُوهُ خُبْزَةً، فَقَالَ: اسْتَخْرِجْهُمْ كَمَا اسْتَخْرَجُوكَ، واغْزُهُمْ نُغْزِكَ، وَأَنْفِقْ عَلَيْهِمْ فَسَنُنْفِقَ عَلَيْكَ، وَابْعَثْ جَيْشًا نَبْعَثْ خَمْسًا أَمْثَالَهُ، وَقَاتِلْ بِمَنْ أَطَاعَكَ مَنْ عَصَاكَ، وَأَهْلُ الْجَنَّةِ ثَلَاثَةٌ: ذو سُلْطَانٍ مُقْسِطٌ مُوَفَّقٌ مُتَصَدِّقٌ، وَرَجُلٌ رَحِيمٌ رَقِيقُ الْقَلْبِ بِكُلِّ ذِي قُرْبَى وَمُسْلِمٍ، وَرَجُلٌ عَفِيفٌ فَقِيرٌ ذُو عِيَالٍ (مُتَصَدِّقٌ). وَأَهْلُ النَّارِ خَمْسَةٌ: الضَّعِيفُ الَّذِي لَا دِينَ لَهُ، وَالَّذِين هُمْ فِيكُمْ تَبَعٌ أَوْ تَبَعًا شَكَّ يَحْيى لَا يَبْتَغُون أَهْلًا وَلَا مَالًا، وَالْخَائِنُ الَّذِي لَا يَخْفَى لَهُ طَمَعٌ وَإِنْ دَقَّ إِلَّا خَانَهُ، وَرَجُلٌ لَا يُصْبِحُ وَلَا يُمْسِي إِلَّا وَهُوَ يُخَادِعُكَ عَنْ أَهْلِكَ وَمَالِكَ وَذَكَرَ الْبَخِيلَ أَوِ الْكَذَّابَ وَالشِّنْظِيرَ: الفَاحِش»

(My Lord has commanded me to teach you what you have no knowledge of and of which He taught me this day, `All the wealth that I gave to My servants is permissible. I created all My servants Hunafa (monotheists). But, the devils came to them and deviated them from their religion, prohibited for them what I allowed and commanded them to associate others with Me (in worship), which I gave no permission for.' Then Allah looked at the people of the earth and disliked them all, the Arabs and non-Arabs among them, except a few from among the Children of Israel. Allah said (to me), `I only sent you to test you and to test with you. I sent to you a Book that cannot be washed by water (it is eternal), and you will read it while asleep and while awake.' Allah has also Commanded me to burn (destroy) Quraysh. So I said, `O Lord! They will smash my head and leave it like a piece of bread.' He said, `I will drive them out as they drove you out, and when you invade them We will help you. Spend on them (your companions) and We will spend on you, send an army and We will send five armies like it (in its support). Fight with those who obey you, against those who disobey you. And the inhabitants of Paradise are three: a just, prosperous, and charitable ruler; A merciful man who has a kind heart toward every relative and every Muslim; a forgiving, poor man with dependants (who is charitable). And the inhabitants of the Fire are five: the weak one with no religion; those who follow after you not for family reasons nor wealth; and the treacherous who does not hide his treachery, acting treacherous in even the most insignificant matters; and a person who comes every morning and every evening, is cheating your family or your wealth.') And he mentioned the stingy, or the liar, and the foulmouthed person." Therefore, the Hadith states that Allah looked at the people of the earth and disliked them all, both the Arabs and non-Arabs among them, except a few among the Children of Israel, or a few among the People of the Book as Muslim recorded. The religion was distorted and changed for the people of the earth until Allah sent Muhammad , and Allah, thus, guided the creatures and took them away from the darkness to the light and placed them on a clear path and a glorious Law. Allah said,

(lest you say, "There came unto us no bringer of glad tidings and no warner.") meaning, so that you, who changed the true religion, do not make it an excuse and say, "No Messenger came to us bringing glad tidings and warning against evil." There has come to you a bringer of good news and a warner, Muhammad .

(And Allah is able to do all things.) Ibn Jarir said this part of the Ayah means, "I am able to punish those who disobey Me and to reward those who obey Me."

Surah: 5 Ayah: 20, Ayah: 21, Ayah: 22, Ayah: 23, Ayah: 24, Ayah: 25, Ayah: 26

﴿ وَإِذْ قَالَ مُوسَىٰ لِقَوْمِهِۦ يَـٰقَوْمِ ٱذْكُرُوا۟ نِعْمَةَ ٱللَّهِ عَلَيْكُمْ إِذْ جَعَلَ فِيكُمْ أَنۢبِيَآءَ وَجَعَلَكُم
مُّلُوكًا وَءَاتَىٰكُم مَّا لَمْ يُؤْتِ أَحَدًا مِّنَ ٱلْعَـٰلَمِينَ ﴿٢٠﴾ ﴾

20. And (remember) when Mûsâ (Moses) said to his people: "O my people! Remember the Favor of Allâh to you, when He made Prophets among you, made you kings and gave you what He had not given to any other among the 'Alamîn (mankind and jinn, in the past)."

﴿ يَـٰقَوْمِ ٱدْخُلُوا۟ ٱلْأَرْضَ ٱلْمُقَدَّسَةَ ٱلَّتِى كَتَبَ ٱللَّهُ لَكُمْ وَلَا تَرْتَدُّوا۟ عَلَىٰٓ أَدْبَارِكُمْ فَتَنقَلِبُوا۟
خَـٰسِرِينَ ﴿٢١﴾ ﴾

21. "O my people! Enter the holy land (Palestine) which Allâh has assigned to you and turn not back (in flight); for then you will be returned as losers."

﴿ قَالُوا۟ يَـٰمُوسَىٰٓ إِنَّ فِيهَا قَوْمًا جَبَّارِينَ وَإِنَّا لَن نَّدْخُلَهَا حَتَّىٰ يَخْرُجُوا۟ مِنْهَا فَإِن
يَخْرُجُوا۟ مِنْهَا فَإِنَّا دَٰخِلُونَ ﴿٢٢﴾ ﴾

22. They said: "O Mûsâ (Moses)! In it (this holy land) are a people of great strength, and we shall never enter it, till they leave it; when they leave, then we will enter."

﴿ قَالَ رَجُلَانِ مِنَ ٱلَّذِينَ يَخَافُونَ أَنْعَمَ ٱللَّهُ عَلَيْهِمَا ٱدْخُلُوا۟ عَلَيْهِمُ ٱلْبَابَ فَإِذَا
دَخَلْتُمُوهُ فَإِنَّكُمْ غَٰلِبُونَ ۚ وَعَلَى ٱللَّهِ فَتَوَكَّلُوٓا۟ إِن كُنتُم مُّؤْمِنِينَ ﴿٢٣﴾ ﴾

23. Two men of those who feared (Allâh and) on whom Allâh had bestowed His Grace (they were Yûsha' (Joshua) and Kâlab (Caleb)) said: "Assault them through the gate; for when you are in, victory will be yours; and put your trust in Allâh if you are believers indeed."

﴿ قَالُوا۟ يَٰمُوسَىٰٓ إِنَّا لَن نَّدْخُلَهَآ أَبَدًا مَّا دَامُوا۟ فِيهَا ۖ فَٱذْهَبْ أَنتَ وَرَبُّكَ فَقَٰتِلَآ إِنَّا
هَٰهُنَا قَٰعِدُونَ ﴿٢٤﴾ ﴾

24. They said: "O Mûsâ (Moses)! We shall never enter it as long as they are there. So go you and your Lord and fight you two, we are sitting right here."

﴿ قَالَ رَبِّ إِنِّى لَآ أَمْلِكُ إِلَّا نَفْسِى وَأَخِى ۖ فَٱفْرُقْ بَيْنَنَا وَبَيْنَ ٱلْقَوْمِ ٱلْفَٰسِقِينَ ﴿٢٥﴾ ﴾

25. He (Mûsâ (Moses)) said: "O my Lord! I have power only over myself and my brother, so separate us from the people who are the Fâsiqûn (rebellious and disobedient to Allâh)!"

﴿ قَالَ فَإِنَّهَا مُحَرَّمَةٌ عَلَيْهِمْ ۛ أَرْبَعِينَ سَنَةً ۛ يَتِيهُونَ فِى ٱلْأَرْضِ ۚ فَلَا تَأْسَ عَلَى ٱلْقَوْمِ
ٱلْفَٰسِقِينَ ﴿٢٦﴾ ﴾

26. (Allâh) said: "Therefore it (this holy land) is forbidden to them for forty years; in distraction they will wander through the land. So be not sorrowful over the people who are the Fâsiqûn (rebellious and disobedient to Allâh)."

Transliteration

20. Wa-ith qala moosa liqawmihi ya qawmi othkuroo niAAmata Allahi AAalaykum ith jaAAala feekum anbiyaa wajaAAalakum mulookan waatakum ma lam yu/ti ahadan mina alAAalameena 21. Ya qawmi odkhuloo al-arda almuqaddasata allatee kataba Allahu lakum wala tartaddoo AAala adbarikum fatanqaliboo khasireena 22. Qaloo ya moosa inna feeha qawman jabbareena wa-inna lan nadkhulaha hatta yakhrujoo minha fa-in yakhrujoo minha fa-inna dakhiloona 23. Qala rajulani mina allatheena yakhafoona anAAama Allahu AAalayhima odkhuloo AAalayhimu albaba fa-itha dakhaltumoohu fa-innakum ghaliboona waAAala Allahi fatawakkaloo in kuntum mu/mineena 24. Qaloo ya moosa inna lan nadkhulaha abadan ma damoo feeha fa-ithhab anta warabbuka faqatila inna hahuna qaAAidoona 25. Qala rabbi innee la amliku illa nafsee waakhee faofruq baynana wabayna alqawmi alfasiqeena 26. Qala fa-innaha muharramatun AAalayhim arbaAAeena sanatan yateehoona fee al-ardi fala ta/sa AAala alqawmi alfasiqeena

Tafsir Ibn Kathir

Musa Reminds His People of Allah's Favors on Them; The Jews Refuse to Enter the Holy Land

Allah states that His servant, Messenger, to whom He spoke directly, Musa, the son of `Imran, reminded his people that among the favors Allah granted them, is that He will give them all of the good of this life and the Hereafter, if they remain on the righteous and straight path. Allah said,

(And (remember) when Musa said to his people: "O my people! Remember the favor of Allah to you, when He made Prophets among you,) for whenever a Prophet died, another rose among them, from the time of their father Ibrahim and thereafter. There were many Prophets among the Children of Israel calling to Allah and warning against His torment, until `Isa was sent as the final Prophet from the Children of Israel. Allah then sent down the revelation to the Final Prophet and Messenger, Muhammad, the son of `Abdullah, from the offspring of Isma`il, the son of Ibrahim, peace be upon them. Muhammad is the most honorable Prophet of all times. Allah said next,

(made you kings) `Abdur-Razzaq recorded that Ibn `Abbas commented: "Having a servant, a wife and a house." In his Mustadrak, Al-Hakim recorded that Ibn `Abbas said, "A wife and a servant, and, a

(and gave you what He had not given to any other among the nations (`Alamin).) means, during their time." Al-Hakim said, "Sahih according to the criteria of the Two Sahihs, but they did not collect it." Qatadah said, "They were the first people to take servants." A Hadith states,

«مَنْ أَصْبَحَ مِنْكُمْ مُعَافًى فِي جَسَدِهِ، آمِنًا فِي سِرْبِهِ، عِنْدَهُ قُوتُ يَوْمِهِ، فَكَأَنَّمَا حِيزَتْ لَهُ الدُّنْيَا بِحَذَافِيرِهَا»

(He among you who wakes up while healthy in body, safe in his family and having the provision for that very day, is as if the world and all that was in it were collected for him.) Allah's statement,

(and gave you what He had not given to any other among the nations (Al-`Alamin).) means, during your time, as we stated. The Children of Israel were the most honorable among the people of their time, compared to the Greek, Copts and the rest of mankind. Allah said in another Ayah,

(And indeed We gave the Children of Israel the Scripture, and the understanding of the Scripture and its laws, and the Prophethood; and provided them with good things, and preferred them above the nations (Al-`Alamin).) Allah said,

(They said: "O Musa! Make for us a god as they have gods." He said: "Verily, you are an ignorant people." (Musa added:) "Verily, these people will be destroyed for that which they are engaged in (idol worship)." And all that they are doing is in vain. He said: "Shall I seek for you a god other than Allah, while He has given you superiority over the nations.") Therefore, they were the best among the people of their time. The Muslim Ummah is more respected and honored before Allah, and has a more perfect legislative code and system of life, it has the most honorable Prophet, the larger kingdom, more provisions, wealth and children, a larger domain and more lasting glory than the Children of Israel. Allah said,

(Thus We have made you, a just (the best) nation, that you be witnesses over mankind.) We mentioned the Mutawatir Hadiths about the honor of this Ummah and its status and honor with Allah, when we explained Allah's statement in Surah Al-`Imran (3),

(You are the best of peoples ever raised up for mankind...) Allah states next that Musa encouraged the Children of Israel to perform Jihad and enter Jerusalem, which was under their control during the time of their father Ya`qub. Ya`qub and his children later moved with his children and household to Egypt during the time of Prophet Yusuf. His offspring remained in Egypt until their exodus with Musa. They found a mighty, strong people in Jerusalem who had previously taken it over. Musa, Allah's Messenger, ordered the Children of Israel to enter Jerusalem and fight their enemy, and he promised them victory and triumph over the mighty people if they did so. They declined, rebelled and defied his order and were punished for forty years by being lost, wandering in the land uncertain of where they should go. This was their punishment for defying Allah's command. Allah said that Musa ordered them to enter the Holy Land,

(which Allah has assigned to you) meaning, which Allah has promised to you by the words of your father Isra'il, that it is the inheritance of those among you who believe.

(and turn not back) in flight from Jihad.

(". ..for then you will be returned as losers." They said, "O Musa! In it are a people of great strength, and we shall never enter it, till they leave it; when they leave, then we will enter.") Their excuse was this, in this very town you commanded us to enter and fight its people, there is a mighty, strong, vicious people who have tremendous physique and physical ability. We are unable to stand against these people or fight them. Therefore, they said, we are incapable of entering this city as long as they are still in it, but if they leave it, we will enter it. Otherwise, we cannot stand against them.

The Speeches of Yuwsha' (Joshua) and Kalib (Caleb)

Allah said,

(Two men of those who feared (Allah and) on whom Allah had bestowed His grace said...) When the Children of Israel declined to obey Allah and follow His Messenger Musa, two righteous men among them, on whom Allah had bestowed a great bounty and who were afraid of Allah and His punishment, encouraged them to go forward. It was also said that the Ayah reads in a way that means that these men were respected and honored by their people. These two men were Yuwsha`, the son of Nun, and Kalib, the son of Yufna, as Ibn `Abbas, Mujahid, `Ikrimah, `Atiyyah, As-Suddi, Ar-Rabi` bin Anas and several other Salaf and latter scholars stated. These two men said to their people,

("Assault them through the gate, for when you are in, victory will be yours. And put your trust in Allah if you are believers indeed.") Therefore, they said, if you rely on and trust in Allah, follow His command and obey His Messenger, then Allah will give you victory over your enemies and will give you triumph and dominance over them. Thus, you will conquer the city that Allah has promised you. This advice did not benefit them in the least,

(They said, "O Musa! We shall never enter it as long as they are there. So go, you and your Lord, and fight you two, we are sitting right here.") This is how they declined to join Jihad, defied their Messenger, and refused to fight their enemy.

The Righteous Response of the Companions During the Battle of Badr

Compare this to the better response the Companions gave to the Messenger of Allah during the battle of Badr, when he asked for their advice about fighting the Quraysh army that came to protect the caravan led by Abu Sufyan. When the Muslim army missed the caravan and the Quraysh army, between nine hundred and one thousand strong, helmeted and drawing closer,

Abu Bakr stood up and said something good. Several more Muhajirin also spoke, all the while the Messenger of Allah saying,

«أشيروا علي أيها المسلمون»

(Advise me, O Muslims!) inquiring of what the Ansar, the majority then, had to say. Sa`d bin Mu`adh said, "It looks like you mean us, O Messenger of Allah! By He Who has sent you with the Truth! If you seek to cross this sea and went in it, we will follow you and none among us will remain behind. We would not hate for you to lead us to meet our enemy tomorrow. We are patient in war, vicious in battle. May Allah allow you to witness from our efforts what comforts your eyes. Therefore, march forward with the blessing of Allah." The Messenger of Allah () was pleased with the words of Sa`d and was encouraged to march on. Abu Bakr bin Marduwyah recorded that Anas said that when the Messenger of Allah went to Badr, he asked the Muslims for their opinion, and `Umar gave his. The Prophet again asked the Muslims for their opinion and the Ansar said, "O Ansar! It is you whom the Prophet wants to hear." They said, "We will never say as the Children of Israel said to Musa,

(So go, you and your Lord, and fight you two, we are sitting right here.) By He Who has sent you with the Truth! If you took the camels to Bark Al-Ghimad (near Makkah) we shall follow you." Imam Ahmad, An-Nasa'i and Ibn Hibban also recorded this Hadith. In the Book of Al-Maghazi and At-Tafsir, Al-Bukhari recorded that `Abdullah bin Mas`ud said, "On the day of Badr, Al-Miqdad said, `O Messenger of Allah! We will never say to you what the Children of Israel said to Musa,

(So go, you and your Lord, and fight you two, we are sitting right here.) Rather, march on and we will be with you.' The Messenger of Allah was satisfied after hearing this statement."

Musa Supplicates to Allah Against the Jews

Musa said,

("O my Lord! I have power only over myself and my brother, so separate us from the rebellious people!") When the Children of Israel refused to fight, Musa became very angry with them and supplicated to Allah against them,

(O my Lord! I have power only over myself and my brother') meaning, only I and my brother Harun among them will obey, implement Allah's command and accept the call,

(So Ifruq us from the rebellious people!) Al-`Awfi reported that Ibn `Abbas said, "Meaning, judge between us and them." `Ali bin Abi Talhah reported similarly from him. Ad-Dahhak said that the Ayah means, "Judge and decide between us and them." Other scholars said that the Ayah means, "Separate between us and them."

Forbidding the Jews from Entering the Holy Land for Forty Years

Allah said,

(Therefore it is forbidden to them for forty years; in distraction they will wander through the land.) When Musa supplicated against the Jews for refusing to fight in Jihad, Allah forbade them from entering the land for forty years. They wandered about lost in the land of At-Tih, unable to find their way out. During this time, tremendous miracles occurred, such as the clouds that shaded them and the manna and quails Allah sent down for them. Allah brought forth water springs from solid rock, and the other miracles that He aided Musa bin `Imran with. During this time, the Tawrah was revealed and the Law was established for the Children of Israel and the Tabernacle of the Covenant was erected.

Conquering Jerusalem

Allah's statement,

(for forty years;) defines,

(in distraction they will wander through the land.) When these years ended, Yuwsha` bin Nun led those who remained among them and the second generation, and laid siege to Jerusalem, conquering it on a Friday afternoon. When the sun was about to set and Yuwsha` feared that the Sabbath would begin, he said (to the sun), "You are commanded and I am commanded, as well. O Allah! Make it stop setting for me." Allah made the sun stop setting until Yuwsha` bin Nun conquered Jerusalem. Next, Allah commanded Yuwsha` to order the Children of Israel to enter Jerusalem from its gate while bowing and saying Hittah, meaning, `remove our sins.' Yet, they changed what they were commanded and entered it while dragging themselves on their behinds and saying, `Habbah (a seed) in Sha`rah (a hair)." We mentioned all of this in the Tafsir of Surat Al-Baqarah. Ibn Abi Hatim recorded that Ibn `Abbas commented,

(Therefore it is forbidden to them for forty years; in distraction they will wander through the land.) "They wandered in the land for forty years, during which Musa and Harun died, as well as everyone above forty years of age. When the forty years ended, Yuwsha` son of Nun assumed their leadership and later conquered Jerusalem. When Yuwsha` was reminded that the day was Friday and the sun was about to set, while they were still attacking Jerusalem, he feared that the Sabbath might begin. Therefore, he said to the sun, `I am commanded and you are commanded.' Allah made the sun stop setting and the Jews conquered Jerusalem and found wealth unseen before. They wanted to let the fire consume the booty, but the fire would not do that. Yuwsha` said, `Some of you have committed theft from the booty.' So he summoned the twelve leaders of the twelve tribes and took the pledge from them. Then, the hand of one of them became stuck to the hand of Yuwsha` and Yuwsha` said, `You committed the theft, so bring it forth.' So, that man brought a cow's head made of gold with two eyes made of precious stones and a set of teeth made of pearls. When Yuwsha` added it to the booty, the fire consumed it, as they were prohibited to keep the booty." There is evidence supporting all of this in the Sahih.

Allah Comforts Musa

Conforting Musa, Allah said

(So do not greive for the rebellious people.) Allah said: Do not feel sorrow or sadness over My judgment against them, for they deserve such judgment. This story chastises the Jews, exposes their defiance of Allah and His Messenger, and their refusal to obey the order for Jihad. They were weak and could not bear the thought of fighting their enemy, being patient, and enduring this way. This occurred although they had the Messenger of Allah and the one whom He spoke to among them, the best of Allah's creation that time. Their Prophet promised them triumph and victory against their enemies. They also witnessed the torment and punishment of drowning with which Allah punished their enemy Fir`awn and his soldiers, so that their eyes were pleased and comforted. All this did not happen too long ago, yet they refused to perform Jihad against people who had less than a tenth of the power and strength than the people of Egypt had. Therefore, the evil works of the Jews were exposed to everyone, and the exposure was such an enormous one that the night, or the tail, can never cover its tracks. They were also blinded by their ignorance and transgression. Thus, they became hated by Allah, and they became His enemies. Yet, they claim that they are Allah's children and His loved ones! May Allah curse their faces that were transformed to the shape of swine and apes, and may Allah's curse accompany them to the raging Fire. May Allah make them abide in the Fire for eternity, and He did; all thanks are due to Him.

Surah: 5 Ayah: 27, Ayah: 28, Ayah: 29, Ayah: 30 & Ayah: 31

﴿ وَٱتۡلُ عَلَيۡهِمۡ نَبَأَ ٱبۡنَيۡ ءَادَمَ بِٱلۡحَقِّ إِذۡ قَرَّبَا قُرۡبَانٗا فَتُقُبِّلَ مِنۡ أَحَدِهِمَا وَلَمۡ يُتَقَبَّلۡ مِنَ
ٱلۡأٓخَرِ قَالَ لَأَقۡتُلَنَّكَۖ قَالَ إِنَّمَا يَتَقَبَّلُ ٱللَّهُ مِنَ ٱلۡمُتَّقِينَ ٢٧ ﴾

27. And (O Muhammad (peace be upon him)) recite to them (the Jews) the story of the two sons of Adam (Hâbil (Abel) and Qâbil (Cain)) in truth; when each offered a sacrifice (to Allâh), it was accepted from the one but not from the other. The latter said to the former: "I will surely kill you." The former said: "Verily, Allâh accepts only from those who are Al-Muttaqûn (the pious - see V.2:2)."

﴿ لَئِنۢ بَسَطتَ إِلَيَّ يَدَكَ لِتَقۡتُلَنِي مَآ أَنَا۠ بِبَاسِطٖ يَدِيَ إِلَيۡكَ لِأَقۡتُلَكَۖ إِنِّيٓ أَخَافُ ٱللَّهَ رَبَّ
ٱلۡعَٰلَمِينَ ٢٨ ﴾

28. "If you do stretch your hand against me to kill me, I shall never stretch my hand against you to kill you : for I fear Allâh, the Lord of the 'Alamîn (mankind, jinn, and all that exists)."

﴿ إِنِّيٓ أُرِيدُ أَن تَبُوٓأَ بِإِثۡمِي وَإِثۡمِكَ فَتَكُونَ مِنۡ أَصۡحَٰبِ ٱلنَّارِۚ وَذَٰلِكَ جَزَٰٓؤُاْ ٱلظَّٰلِمِينَ ٢٩ ﴾

29. "Verily, I intend to let you draw my sin on yourself as well as yours, then you will be one of the dwellers of the Fire; and that is the recompense of the Zâlimûn (polytheists and wrong-doers)."

﴿ فَطَوَّعَتۡ لَهُۥ نَفۡسُهُۥ قَتۡلَ أَخِيهِ فَقَتَلَهُۥ فَأَصۡبَحَ مِنَ ٱلۡخَٰسِرِينَ ٣٠ ﴾

30. So the Nafs (self) of the other (latter one) encouraged him and made fair-seeming to him the murder of his brother; he murdered him and became one of the losers.

﴿ فَبَعَثَ ٱللَّهُ غُرَابٗا يَبۡحَثُ فِي ٱلۡأَرۡضِ لِيُرِيَهُۥ كَيۡفَ يُوَٰرِي سَوۡءَةَ أَخِيهِۚ قَالَ يَٰوَيۡلَتَىٰٓ
أَعَجَزۡتُ أَنۡ أَكُونَ مِثۡلَ هَٰذَا ٱلۡغُرَابِ فَأُوَٰرِيَ سَوۡءَةَ أَخِيۖ فَأَصۡبَحَ مِنَ ٱلنَّٰدِمِينَ ٣١ ﴾

31. Then Allâh sent a crow who scratched the ground to show him to hide the dead body of his brother. He (the murderer) said: "Woe to me! Am I not even able to be as this crow and to hide the dead body of my brother?" Then he became one of those who regretted.

Transliteration

27. Waotlu AAalayhim nabaa ibnay adama bialhaqqi ith qarraba qurbanan fatuqubbila min ahadihima walam yutaqabbal mina al-akhari qala laaqtulannaka qala innama yataqabbalu Allahu mina almuttaqeena 28. La-in basatta ilayya yadaka litaqtulanee ma ana bibasitin yadiya ilayka li-aqtulaka innee akhafu Allaha rabba alAAalameena 29. Innee oreedu an taboo-a bi-ithmee wa-ithmika fatakoona min as-habi alnnari wathalika jazao alththalimeena 30. FatawwaAAat lahu nafsuhu qatla akheehi faqatalahu faasbaha mina alkhasireena 31. FabaAAatha Allahu ghuraban yabhathu fee al-ardi liyuriyahu kayfa yuwaree saw-ata akheehi qala ya waylata aAAajaztu an akoona mithla hatha alghurabi faowariya saw-ata akhee faasbaha mina alnnadimeena

Tafsir Ibn Kathir

The Story of Habil (Abel) and Qabil (Cain)

Allah describes the evil end and consequence of transgression, envy and injustice in the story of the two sons of Adam, Habil and Qabil. One of them fought against the other and killed him out of envy and transgression, because of the bounty that Allah gave his brother and because the sacrifice that he sincerely offered to Allah was accepted. The murdered brother earned forgiveness for his sins and was admitted into Paradise, while the murderer failed and earned a losing deal in both the lives. Allah said,

(And recite to them the story of the two sons of Adam in truth;) meaning, tell these envious, unjust people, the brothers of swine and apes from the Jews and their likes among mankind, the story of the two sons of Adam, Habil and Qabil, as many scholars among the Salaf and later generations said. Allah's statement,

(in truth;) means, clearly and without ambiguity, alteration, confusion, change, addition or deletion. Allah said in other Ayat,

(Verily, this is the true narrative (about the story of `Isa),)

(We narrate unto you their story with truth,) and,

(Such is `Isa, son of Maryam. (It is) a statement of truth.) Several scholars among the Salaf and the later generations said that Allah allowed Adam to marry his daughters to his sons because of the necessity of such action. They also said that in every pregnancy, Adam was given a twin, a male and a female, and he used to give the female of one twin, to the male of the other twin, in marriage. Habil's sister was not beautiful while Qabil's sister was beautiful, resulting in Qabil wanting her for himself, instead of his brother. Adam refused unless they both offer a sacrifice, and he whose sacrifice was accepted, would marry Qabil's sister. Habil's sacrifice was accepted, while Qabil's sacrifice was rejected, and thus what Allah told us about them occurred. Ibn Abi Hatim recorded that Ibn `Abbas said -- that during the time of Adam -- "The woman was not allowed in marriage for her male twin, but Adam was commanded to marry her to any of her other brothers. In each pregnancy, Adam was given a twin, a male and a female. A beautiful daughter was once born for Adam and another one that was not beautiful. So the twin brother of the ugly daughter said, `Marry your sister to me and I will marry my sister to you.' He said, `No, for I have more right to my sister.' So they both offered a sacrifice. The sacrifice of the one who offered the sheep was accepted while the sacrifice of the other (the twin brother of the beautiful daughter), which consisted of some produce, was not accepted. So the latter killed his brother." This story has a better than good chain of narration. The statement,

("Verily, Allah accepts only from those who have Taqwa.) who fear Allah in their actions. Ibn Abi Hatim recorded that Abu Ad-Darda' said, "If I become certain that Allah has accepted even one prayer from me, it will be better for me than this life and all that in it. This is because Allah says,

(Verily, Allah accepts only from the those who have Taqwa.) The statement,

("If you do stretch your hand against me to kill me, I shall never stretch my hand against you to kill you, for I fear Allah; the Lord of all that exists.") Qabil's brother, the pious man whose sacrifice was accepted because of his piety, said to his brother, who threatened to kill him without justification,

(If you do stretch your hand against me to kill me, I shall never stretch my hand against you to kill you,) I will not commit the same evil act that you threaten to commit, so that I will not earn the same sin as you,

(for I fear Allah; the Lord of the all that exists.) and, as a result, I will not commit the error that you threaten to commit. Rather, I will observe patience and endurance. `Abdullah bin `Amr said, "By Allah! Habil was the stronger of the two men. But, fear of Allah restricted his hand." The Prophet said in a Hadith recorded in the Two Sahihs,

«إِذَا تَوَاجَهَ الْمُسْلِمَانِ بِسَيْفَيهِمَا فَالْقَاتِلُ وَالْمَقْتُولُ فِي النَّارِ»

(When two Muslims fight (meet) each other with their swords, both the murderer as well as the murdered will go to the Hellfire.) They said, "O Allah's Messenger! It is all right for the murderer, but what about the victim" Allah's Messenger replied,

«إِنَّه كَانَ حَرِيصًا عَلى قَتْلِ صَاحِبِه»

(He surely had the intention to kill his comrade.) Imam Ahmad recorded that, at the beginning of the calamity that `Uthman suffered from, Sa`d bin Abi Waqqas said, "I bear witness that the Messenger of Allah said,

«إِنَّهَا سَتَكُونُ فِتْنَةٌ القَاعِدُ فِيهَا خَيْرٌ مِنَ الْقَائِمِ، وَالْقَائِمُ خَيْرٌ مِنَ الْمَاشِي، وَالْمَاشِي خَيْرٌ مِنَ السَّاعِي»

(There will be a Fitnah, and he who sits idle during it is better than he who stands up, and he who stands up in it is better than he who walks, and he who walks is better than he who is walking at a fast pace.) When he was asked, `What if someone enters my home and stretched his hand to kill me' He said,

«كُنْ كَابْنِ آدَم»

(Be just like (the pious) son of Adam.)" At-Tirmidhi also recorded it this way, and said, "This Hadith is Hasan, and similar is reported on this subject from Abu Hurayrah, Khabbab bin Al-Aratt, Abu Bakr, Ibn Mas\`ud, Abu Waqid and Abu Musa." The Qur'an continues,

("Verily, I intend to let you draw my sin on yourself as well as yours, then you will be one of the dwellers of the Fire, and that is the recompense of the wrongdoers.") Ibn \`Abbas, Mujahid, Ad-Dahhak, As-Suddi and Qatadah said that,

("Verily, I intend to let you draw my sin on yourself as well as yours...") means, the sin of murdering me, in addition to your previous sins. Ibn Jarir recorded this. Allah's statement,

(So the soul of the other encouraged him and made fair-seeming to him the murder of his brother; he murdered him and became one of the losers.) means, his conscience encouraged him to kill his brother by making it seem like a sensible thing to do, so he killed him, even after his brother admonished him. Ibn Jarir said, "When he wanted to kill his brother, he started to twist his neck. So Shaytan took an animal and placed its head on a rock, then he took another rock, and similar is reported on this subject from Abu Hurayrah, Khabbab bin Al-Aratt, Abu Bakr, Ibn Mas\`ud, Abu Waqid and Abu Musa." The Qur'an continues,

("Verily, I intend to let you draw my sin on yourself as well as yours, then you will be one of the dwellers of the Fire, and that is the recompense of the wrongdoers.") Ibn \`Abbas, Mujahid, Ad-Dahhak, As-Suddi and Qatadah said that,

("Verily, I intend to let you draw my sin on yourself as well as yours...") means, the sin of murdering me, in addition to your previous sins. Ibn Jarir recorded this. Allah's statement,

(So the soul of the other encouraged him and made fair-seeming to him the murder of his brother; he murdered him and became one of the losers.) means, his conscience encouraged him to kill his brother by making it seem like a sensible thing to do, so he killed him, even after his brother admonished him. Ibn Jarir said, "When he wanted to kill his brother, he started to twist his neck. So Shaytan took an animal and placed its head on a rock, then he took another rock, and smashed its head with it until he killed it while the son of Adam was looking. So he did the same thing to his brother." Ibn Abi Hatim also recorded this. \`Abdullah bin Wahb said that \`Abdur-Rahman bin Zayd bin Aslam said that his father said, "Qabil held Habil by the head to kill him, so Habil laid down for him and Qabil started twisting Habil's head, not knowing how to kill him. Shaytan came to Qabil and said, \`Do you want to kill him' He said, \`Yes.' Shaytan said, \`Take that stone and throw it on his head.' So Qabil took the stone and threw it at his brother's head and smashed his head. Shaytan then went to Hawwa' in a hurry and said to her, \`O Hawwa'! Qabil killed Habil.' She asked him, \`Woe to you! What does \`kill' mean' He said, \`He will no longer eat, drink or move.' She said, \`And that is death' He said, \`Yes it is.' So she started to weep until Adam came to her while she was weeping and said, \`What is the matter with you' She did not answer him. He asked her two more times, but she did not answer him. So he said, \`You and your daughters will inherit the practice of weeping, while I and my sons are free of it.'" Ibn Abi Hatim recorded it. Allah's statement,

(And became one of the losers.) in this life and the Hereafter, and which loss is worse than this Imam Ahmad recorded that \`Abdullah bin Mas\`ud said that the Messenger of Allah said,

«لَا تُقْتَلُ نَفْسٌ ظُلْمًا إِلَّا كَانَ عَلَى ابْنِ آدَمَ الْأَوَّلِ كِفْلٌ مِنْ دَمِهَا،لِأَنَّهُ كَانَ أَوَّلَ مَنْ سَنَّ الْقَتْلَ»

(Any soul that is unjustly killed, then the first son of Adam will carry a burden of its shedding, for he was the first to practice the crime of murder.) The Group, with the exception of Abu Dawud, also recorded this Hadith. Ibn Jarir recorded that `Abdullah bin `Amr used to say, "The son of Adam, who killed his brother, will be the most miserable among men. There is no blood shed on earth since he killed his brother, until the Day of Resurrection, but he will carry a burden from it, for he was the first person to establish murder." Allah said,

(Then Allah sent a crow who scratched the ground to show him how to hide the dead body of his brother. He (the murderer) said, "Woe to me! Am I not even able to be as this crow and to hide the dead body of my brother" Then he became one of those who regretted.) As-Suddi said that the Companions said, "When his brother died, Qabil left him on the bare ground and did not know how to bury him. Allah sent two crows, which fought with each other until one of them killed the other. So it dug a hole and threw sand over the dead corpse (which it placed in the hole). When Qabil saw that, he said,

("Woe to me! Am I not even able to be as this crow and to hide the dead body of my brother") `Ali bin Abi Talhah reported that Ibn `Abbas said, "A crow came to the dead corpse of another crow and threw sand over it, until it hid it in the ground. He who killed his brother said,

(Woe to me! Am I not even able to be as this crow and to hide the dead body of my brother)" Al-Hasan Al-Basri commented on the statement,

(Then he became one of those who regretted.) "Allah made him feel sorrow after the loss that he earned."

The Swift Punishment for Transgression and Cutting the Relations of the Womb

A Hadith states that the Prophet said,

«مَا مِنْ ذَنْبٍ أَجْدَرُ أَنْ يُعَجِّلَ اللهُ عُقُوبَتَهُ فِي الدُّنْيَا مَعَ مَا يَدَّخِرُ لِصَاحِبِهِ فِي الْآخِرَةِ مِنَ الْبَغْيِ وَقَطِيعَةِ الرَّحِمِ»

(There is no sin that is more worthy of Allah hastening its punishment in this life, in addition to what He has in store for its offender in the Hereafter, more than transgression and cutting the relations of the womb.) The act of Qabil included both of these. We are Allah's and to Him is our return.

Surah: 5 Ayah: 32, Ayah: 33 & Ayah: 34

﴿ مِنۡ أَجۡلِ ذَٰلِكَ كَتَبۡنَا عَلَىٰ بَنِيٓ إِسۡرَٰٓءِيلَ أَنَّهُۥ مَن قَتَلَ نَفۡسَۢا بِغَيۡرِ نَفۡسٍ أَوۡ فَسَادٖ فِي
ٱلۡأَرۡضِ فَكَأَنَّمَا قَتَلَ ٱلنَّاسَ جَمِيعٗا وَمَنۡ أَحۡيَاهَا فَكَأَنَّمَآ أَحۡيَا ٱلنَّاسَ جَمِيعٗاۚ وَلَقَدۡ
جَآءَتۡهُمۡ رُسُلُنَا بِٱلۡبَيِّنَٰتِ ثُمَّ إِنَّ كَثِيرٗا مِّنۡهُم بَعۡدَ ذَٰلِكَ فِي ٱلۡأَرۡضِ لَمُسۡرِفُونَ ٣٢ ﴾

32. Because of that We ordained for the Children of Israel that if anyone killed a person not in retaliation of murder, or (and) to spread mischief in the land - it would be as if he killed all mankind, and if anyone saved a life, it would be as if he saved the life of all mankind. And indeed, there came to them Our Messengers with clear proofs, evidences, and signs, even then after that many of them continued to exceed the limits (e.g. by doing oppression unjustly and exceeding beyond the limits set by Allâh by committing the major sins) in the land!.

﴿ إِنَّمَا جَزَٰٓؤُاْ ٱلَّذِينَ يُحَارِبُونَ ٱللَّهَ وَرَسُولَهُۥ وَيَسۡعَوۡنَ فِي ٱلۡأَرۡضِ فَسَادًا أَن يُقَتَّلُوٓاْ أَوۡ
يُصَلَّبُوٓاْ أَوۡ تُقَطَّعَ أَيۡدِيهِمۡ وَأَرۡجُلُهُم مِّنۡ خِلَٰفٍ أَوۡ يُنفَوۡاْ مِنَ ٱلۡأَرۡضِۚ ذَٰلِكَ لَهُمۡ
خِزۡيٞ فِي ٱلدُّنۡيَاۖ وَلَهُمۡ فِي ٱلۡأٓخِرَةِ عَذَابٌ عَظِيمٌ ٣٣ ﴾

33. The recompense of those who wage war against Allâh and His Messenger and do mischief in the land is only that they shall be killed or crucified or their hands and their feet be cut off from opposite sides, or be exiled from the land. That is their disgrace in this world, and a great torment is theirs in the Hereafter.

﴿ إِلَّا ٱلَّذِينَ تَابُواْ مِن قَبۡلِ أَن تَقۡدِرُواْ عَلَيۡهِمۡۖ فَٱعۡلَمُوٓاْ أَنَّ ٱللَّهَ غَفُورٞ رَّحِيمٞ ٣٤ ﴾

34. Except for those who (having fled away and then) came back (as Muslims) with repentance before they fall into your power; in that case, know that Allâh is Oft-Forgiving, Most Merciful.

Transliteration

32. Min ajli thalika katabna AAala banee isra-eela annahu man qatala nafsan bighayri nafsin aw fasadin fee al-ardi fakaannama qatala alnnasa jameeAAan waman ahyaha fakaannama ahya alnnasa jameeAAan walaqad jaat-hum rusuluna bialbayyinati thumma inna katheeran minhum baAAda thalika fee al-ardi lamusrifoona 33. Innama jazao allatheena yuhariboona Allaha warasoolahu wayasAAawna fee al-ardi fasadan an yuqattaloo aw yusallaboo aw tuqattaAAa aydeehim waarjuluhum min khilafin aw yunfaw mina al-ardi thalika lahum khizyun fee alddunya walahum fee al-akhirati AAathabun AAatheemun 34. Illa allatheena taboo min qabli an taqdiroo AAalayhim faiAAlamoo anna Allaha ghafoorun raheemun

Tafsir Ibn Kathir

Human Beings Should Respect the Sanctity of Other Human Beings

Allah says, because the son of Adam killed his brother in transgression and aggression,

(We ordained for the Children of Israel...) meaning, We legislated for them and informed them,

(that if anyone killed a person not in retaliation of murder, or (and) to spread mischief in the land - it would be as if he killed all mankind, and if anyone saved a life, it would be as if he saved the life of all mankind.) The Ayah states, whoever kills a soul without justification -- such as in retaliation for murder or for causing mischief on earth -- will be as if he has killed all mankind, because there is no difference between one life and another.

(and if anyone saved a life...) by preventing its blood from being shed and believing in its sanctity, then all people will have been saved from him, so,

(it would be as if he saved the life of all mankind.) Al-A`mash and others said that Abu Salih said that Abu Hurayrah said, "I entered on `Uthman when he was under siege in his house and said, `I came to give you my support. Now, it is good to fight (defending you) O Leader of the Faithful!' He said, `O Abu Hurayrah! Does it please you that you kill all people, including me' I said, `No.' He said, `If you kill one man, it is as if you killed all people. Therefore, go back with my permission for you to leave. May you receive your reward and be saved from burden.' So I went back and did not fight."' `Ali bin Abi Talhah reported that Ibn `Abbas said, "It is as Allah has stated,

(if anyone killed a person not in retaliation of murder, or (and) to spread mischief in the land - it would be as if he killed all mankind, and if anyone saved a life, it would be as if he saved the life of all mankind.) Saving life in this case occurs by not killing a soul that Allah has forbidden. So this is the meaning of saving the life of all mankind, for whoever forbids killing a soul without justification, the lives of all people will be saved from him." Similar was said by Mujahid;

(And if anyone saved a life...) means, he refrains from killing a soul. Al-`Awfi reported that Ibn `Abbas said that Allah's statement,

(it would be as if he killed all mankind. .) means, "Whoever kills one soul that Allah has forbidden killing, is just like he who kills all mankind." Sa`id bin Jubayr said, "He who allows himself to shed the blood of a Muslim, is like he who allows shedding the blood of all people. He who forbids shedding the blood of one Muslim, is like he who forbids shedding the blood of all people." In addition, Ibn Jurayj said that Al-A`raj said that Mujahid commented on the Ayah,

(it would be as if he killed all mankind,) "He who kills a believing soul intentionally, Allah makes the Fire of Hell his abode, He will become angry with him, and curse him, and has prepared a tremendous punishment for him, equal to if he had killed all people, his punishment will still be the same." Ibn Jurayj said that Mujahid said that the Ayah,

(and if anyone saved a life, it would be as if he saved the life of all mankind.) means, "He who does not kill anyone, then the lives of people are safe from him."

Warning Those who Commit Mischief

Allah said,

(And indeed, there came to them Our Messengers with Al-Bayyinat,) meaning, clear evidences, signs and proofs, (even then after that many of them continued to exceed the limits in the land!) This Ayah chastises and criticizes those who commit the prohibitions, after knowing that they are prohibited from indulging in them. The Jews of Al-Madinah, such as Banu Qurayzah, An-Nadir and Qaynuqa`, used to fight along with either Khazraj or Aws, when war would erupt between them during the time of Jahiliyyah. When these wars would end, the Jews would ransom those who were captured and pay the blood money for those who were killed. Allah criticized them for this practice in Surat Al-Baqarah,

(And (remember) when We took your covenant (saying): Shed not your (people's) blood, nor turn out your own people from their dwellings. Then, (this) you ratified and (to this) you bear witness. After this, it is you who kill one another and drive out a party of your own from their homes, assist (their enemies) against them, in sin and transgression. And if they come to you as captives, you ransom them, although their expulsion was forbidden to you. Then do you believe in a part of the Scripture and reject the rest Then what is the recompense of those who do so among you, except disgrace in the life of this world, and on the Day of Resurrection they shall be consigned to the most grievous torment. And Allah is not unaware of what you do.) (2:84-85)

The Punishment of those Who Cause Mischief in the Land

Allah said next,

(The recompense of those who wage war against Allah and His Messenger and do mischief in the land is only that they shall be killed or crucified or their hands and their feet be cut off on the opposite sides, or be exiled from the land.) `Wage war' mentioned here means, oppose and contradict, and it includes disbelief, blocking roads and spreading fear in the fairways. Mischief in the land refers to various types of evil. Ibn Jarir recorded that `Ikrimah and Al-Hasan Al-Basri said that the Ayat,

(The recompense of those who wage war against Allah and His Messenger) until,

(Allah is Of-Forgiving, Most Merciful,) "Were revealed about the idolators. Therefore, the Ayah decrees that, whoever among them repents before you apprehend them, then you have no right to punish them. This Ayah does not save a Muslim from punishment if he kills, causes mischief in the land or wages war against Allah and His Messenger and then joins rank with the disbelievers, before the Muslims are able to catch him. He will still be liable for punishment for the crimes he committed." Abu Dawud and An-Nasa'i recorded that `Ikrimah said that Ibn `Abbas said that the Ayah,

(The recompense of those who wage war against Allah and His Messenger and do mischief in the land...) "Was revealed concerning the idolators, those among them who repent before being apprehended, they will still be liable for punishment for the crimes they committed." The correct opinion is that this Ayah is general in meaning and includes the idolators and all others who commit the types of crimes the Ayah mentioned. Al-Bukhari and Muslim recorded that Abu Qilabah `Abdullah bin Zayd Al-Jarmi, said that Anas bin Malik said, "Eight people of the `Ukl tribe came to the Messenger of Allah and gave him their pledge to follow Islam. Al-Madinah's climate did not suit them and they became sick and complained to Allah's Messenger . So he said,

«أَلَا تَخْرُجُونَ مَعَ رَاعِينَا فِي إِبِلِهِ، فَتُصِيبُوا مِنْ أَبْوَالِهَا وَأَلْبَانِهَا»

(Go with our shephard to be treated by the milk and urine of his camels.) So they went as directed, and after they drank from the camels' milk and urine, they became healthy, and they killed the shepherd and drove away all the camels. The news reached the Prophet and he sent (men) in their pursuit and they were captured. He then ordered that their hands and feet be cut off (and it was done), and their eyes were branded with heated pieces of iron. Next, they were put in the sun until they died." This is the wording of Muslim. In another narration for this Hadith, it was mentioned that these people were from the tribes of `Ukl or `Uraynah. Another narration reported that these people were put in the Harrah area (of Al-Madinah), and when they asked for water, no water was given to them. Allah said,

(they shall be killed or crucified or their hands and their feet be cut off on the opposite sides, or be exiled from the land.) `Ali bin Abi Talhah said that Ibn `Abbas said about this Ayah, `He who takes up arms in Muslim land and spreads fear in the fairways and is captured, the Muslim Leader has the choice to either have him killed, crucified or cut off his hands and feet." Similar was said by Sa`id bin Al-Musayyib, Mujahid, `Ata', Al-Hasan Al-Basri, Ibrahim An-Nakha`i and Ad-Dahhak, as Abu Ja`far Ibn Jarir recorded. This view is supported by the fact that the word Aw (or), indicates a choice. As Allah said,

(The penalty is an offering, brought to the Ka`bah, of an eatable animal equivalent to the one he killed, as adjudged by two just men among you; or, for expiation, he should feed the poor, or its equivalent in fasting.)(5:95) Allah said,

(And whosoever of you is ill or has an ailment in his scalp (necessitating shaving), he must pay a ransom of either fasting or giving charity or offering a sacrifice.) and,

(...for its expiation feed ten of the poor, on a scale of the average of that with which you feed your own families, or clothe them, or free a slave.) All of these Ayat offer a choice, just as the Ayah above. As for Allah's statement,

(or be exiled from the land.) some said that it means, he is actively pursued until he is captured, and thus receives his prescribed punishment, or otherwise he escapes from the land of Islam, as Ibn Jarir recorded from Ibn `Abbas, Anas bin Malik, Sa`id bin Jubayr, Ad-Dahhak, Ar-Rabi` bin Anas, Az-Zuhri, Al-Layth bin Sa`d and Malik bin Anas. Some said that the Ayah means these people are expelled to another land, or to another state by the Muslims authorities. Sa`id bin Jubayr, Abu Ash-Sha`tha', Al-Hasan, Az-Zuhri, Ad-Dahhak and Muqatil bin Hayyan said that he is expelled, but not outside of the land of Islam, while others said that he is to be imprisoned. Allah's statement,

(That is their disgrace in this world, and a great torment is theirs in the Hereafter.) means, the punishment We prescribed, killing these aggressors, crucifying them, cutting off their hands and feet on opposite sides, or expelling them from the land is a disgrace for them among mankind in this life, along with the tremendous torment Allah has prepared for them in the Hereafter. This view supports the opinion that these Ayat were revealed about the idolators. As for Muslims, in his Sahih, Muslim recorded that `Ubadah bin As-Samit said, "The Messenger of Allah took the same pledge from us that he also took from women: That we do not associate anything with Allah in worship, we do not steal, commit adultery, or kill our children, and that we do not spread falsehood about each other. He said that he who keeps this pledge, then his reward will be with Allah. He who falls into shortcomings and was punished, then this will be his expiation. And those whose errors were covered by Allah, then their matter is for Allah: If He wills, He will punish them and If He wills, He will pardon them." `Ali narrated that the Messenger of Allah said,

«مَنْ أَذْنَبَ ذَنْبًا فِي الدُّنْيَا فَعُوقِبَ بِهِ، فَاللهُ أَعْدَلُ مِنْ أَنْ يُثَنِّيَ عُقُوبَتَهُ عَلى عَبْدِهِ، وَمَنْ أَذْنَبَ ذَنْبًا فِي الدُّنْيَا فَسَتَرَهُ اللهُ عَلَيْهِ وَعَفَا عَنْهُ، فَاللهُ أَكْرَمُ مِنْ أَنْ يَعُودَ عَلَيْهِ فِي شَيْءٍ قَدْ عَفَا عَنْه»

(He who sins in this life and was punished for it, then Allah is far more just than to combine two punishments on His servant. He who commits an error in this life and Allah hides this error and pardons him, then Allah is far more generous than to punish the servant for something that He has already pardoned.) iRecorded by Ahmad, Ibn Majah and At-Tirmidhi who said, "Hasan Gharib."Al-Hafiz Ad-Daraqutni was asked about this Hadith, and he said that it was related to the Prophet in some narrations, and it was related to the Companions in others, and that this narration from the Prophet is Sahih. Ibn Jarir commented on Allah's statement,

(That is their disgrace in this world,) "Meaning, shame, humiliation, punishment, contempt and torment in this life, before the Hereafter,

(and a great torment is theirs in the Hereafter.) if they do not repent from these errors until death overcomes them. In this case, they will be stricken by the punishment that We prescribed for them in this life and the torment that We prepared for them therein,

(a great torment) in the Fire of Jahannam."

The Punishment of those who Wage War Against Allah and His Messenger is Annulled if They Repent Before their Apprehension

Allah said,

(Except for those who (having fled away and then) came back (as Muslims) with repentance before they fall into your power; in that case, know that Allah is Oft-Forgiving, Most Merciful.) This Ayah is clear in its indication that it applies to the idolators. As for the Muslims who commit this crime and repent before they are apprehended, the punishment of killing, crucifixion and cutting the limbs will be waved. The practice of the Companions in this regard is that all of the punishments prescribed in this case will be waved, as is apparent from the wording of the Ayah. Ibn Abi Hatim recorded that Ash-Sha`bi said, "Harithah bin Badr At-Tamimi was living in Al-Basrah, and he committed the crime of mischief in the land. So he talked to some men from Quraysh, such as Al-Hasan bin `Ali, Ibn `Abbas and `Abdullah bin Ja`far, and they talked to `Ali about him so that he would grant him safety, but `Ali refused. So Harithah went to Sa`id bin Qays Al-Hamadani who kept him in his house and went to `Ali, saying, `O Leader of the Faithful! What about those who wage war against Allah and His Messenger and cause mischief in the land' So he recited the Ayah until he reached,

(Except for those who (having fled away and them) came back cas Muslims) with repentance before they fall into your power.) So `Ali wrote a document that granted safety, and Sa`id bin Qays said, `This is for Harithah bin Badr.'" Ibn Jarir recorded this Hadith. Ibn Jarir recorded that `Amir Ash-Sha`bi said, "A man from Murad came to Abu Musa, while he was the governor of Al-Kufah during the reign of `Uthman, and said to him after he offered the obligatory prayer, `O Abu Musa! I seek your help. I am so-and-so from Murad and I waged war against Allah and His Messenger and caused mischief in the land. I repented before you had any authority over me.' Abu Musa proclaimed, `This is so-and-so, who had waged war against Allah and His Messenger and caused mischief in the land, and he repented before we had authority over him. Therefore, anyone who meets him, should deal with him in a better way. If he is saying the truth, then this is the path of those who say the truth. If he is saying a lie, his sins will destroy him. So the man remained idle for as long as Allah willed, but he later rose against the leaders, and Allah punished him for his sins and he was killed." Ibn Jarir recorded that Musa bin Ishaq Al-Madani said that `Ali Al-Asadi waged war, blocked the roads, shed blood and plundered wealth. The leaders and the people alike, sought to capture him, but they could not do that until he came after he repented, after he heard a man reciting the Ayah,

(O My servants who have transgressed against themselves! Despair not of the mercy of Allah, verily, Allah forgives all sins. Truly, He is Oft-Forgiving, Most Merciful.) So he said to that man, "O servant of Allah! Recite it again." So he recited it again, and `Ali put down his sword and went to Al-Madinah in repentance, arriving during the night. He washed up and went to the Masjid of the Messenger of Allah and prayed the dawn prayer. He sat next to Abu Hurayrah amidst his companions. In the morning, the people recognized him and went after him. He said, "You have no way against me. I came in repentance before you had any authority over me." Abu Hurayrah said, "He has said the truth," and he held his hand and went to Marwan bin Al-Hakam, who was the governor of Al-Madinah during the reign of Mu`awiyah. Abu Hurayrah said, "This is `Ali and he came in repentance and you do not have a way against him, nor can you have him killed." So `Ali was absolved of punishment and remained on his repentance and went to the sea to perform Jihad in Allah's cause. The Muslims met the Romans in battle, and the Muslims brought the ship `Ali was in to one of the Roman ships, and `Ali crossed to that ship and the Romans escaped from him to the other side of the ship, and the ship capsized and they all drowned."

Surah: 5 Ayah: 35, Ayah: 36 & Ayah: 37

﴿ يَٰٓأَيُّهَا ٱلَّذِينَ ءَامَنُواْ ٱتَّقُواْ ٱللَّهَ وَٱبۡتَغُوٓاْ إِلَيۡهِ ٱلۡوَسِيلَةَ وَجَٰهِدُواْ فِي سَبِيلِهِۦ لَعَلَّكُمۡ
تُفۡلِحُونَ ٣٥ ﴾

35. O you who believe! Do your duty to Allâh and fear Him. And seek the means of approach to Him, and strive hard in His Cause as much as you can. So that you may be successful.

﴿ إِنَّ ٱلَّذِينَ كَفَرُواْ لَوۡ أَنَّ لَهُم مَّا فِي ٱلۡأَرۡضِ جَمِيعٗا وَمِثۡلَهُۥ مَعَهُۥ لِيَفۡتَدُواْ بِهِۦ مِنۡ
عَذَابِ يَوۡمِ ٱلۡقِيَٰمَةِ مَا تُقُبِّلَ مِنۡهُمۡۖ وَلَهُمۡ عَذَابٌ أَلِيمٞ ٣٦ ﴾

36. Verily, those who disbelieve, if they had all that is in the earth, and as much again therewith to ransom themselves thereby from the torment on the Day of Resurrection, it would never be accepted of them, and theirs would be a painful torment.

﴿ يُرِيدُونَ أَن يَخۡرُجُواْ مِنَ ٱلنَّارِ وَمَا هُم بِخَٰرِجِينَ مِنۡهَاۖ وَلَهُمۡ عَذَابٞ مُّقِيمٞ ٣٧ ﴾

37. They will long to get out of the Fire, but never will they get out therefrom; and theirs will be a lasting torment.

Transliteration

35. Ya ayyuha allatheena amanoo ittaqoo Allaha waibtaghoo ilayhi alwaseelata wajahidoo fee sabeelihi laAAallakum tuflihoona 36. Inna allatheena kafaroo law anna lahum ma fee al-ardi jameeAAan wamithlahu maAAahu liyaftadoo bihi min AAathabi yawmi alqiyamati ma tuqubbila minhum walahum AAathabun aleemun 37. Yureedoona an yakhrujoo mina alnnari wama hum bikharijeena minha walahum AAathabun muqeemun

Tafsir Ibn Kathir

Commanding Taqwa, Wasilah, and Jihad

Allah commands His faithful servants to fear Him in Taqwa, which if mentioned along with acts of obedience, it means to refrain from the prohibitions and the prohibited matters. Allah said next,

(seek the Wasilah to Him.) Sufyan Ath-Thawri said that Talhah said that `Ata' said that Ibn `Abbas said that Wasilah means `the means of approach'. Mujahid, Abu Wa'il, Al-Hasan, Qatadah, `Abdullah bin Kathir, As-Suddi, Ibn Zayd and others gave the same meaning for Wasilah. Qatadah said that the Ayah means, "Seek the means of approach to Him by obeying Him and performing the acts that please Him."

(Those whom they call upon seek a means of access to their Lord (Allah).) (17:57) Wasilah is a means of approach to achieve something, and it is also used to refer to the highest grade in Paradise, and it is the grade of the Messenger of Allah , his residence and the nearest grade in Paradise to Allah's Throne. Al-Bukhari recorded that Jabir bin `Abdullah said that the Messenger of Allah said,

«مَنْ قَالَ حِينَ يَسْمَعُ النِّدَاءَ: اللَّهُمَّ رَبَّ هذِهِ الدَّعْوَةِ التَّامَّةِ، وَالصَّلَاةِ الْقَائِمَةِ، آتِ مُحَمَّدًا الْوَسِيلَةَ وَالْفَضِيلَةَ، وَابْعَثْهُ مَقَامًا مَحْمُودًا الَّذِي وَعَدْتَهُ،إِلَّا حَلَّتْ لَهُ الشَّفَاعَةُ يَوْمَ الْقِيَامَةِ»

(Whoever, after hearing to the Adhan says, "O Allah! Lord of this perfect call and of the regular prayer which is going to be established! Grant Muhammad the Wasilah and superiority and send him (on the Day of Judgment) to the praiseworthy station which You have promised him," then intercession from me will be permitted for him on the Day of Resurrection.) Muslim recorded that `Abdullah bin `Amr bin Al-`As said that he heard the Prophet saying,

«إِذَا سَمِعْتُمُ الْمُؤَذِّنَ فَقُولُوا مِثْلَ مَا يَقُولُ، ثُمَّ صَلُّوا عَلَيَّ، فَإِنَّهُ مَنْ صَلَّى عَلَيَّ صَلَاةً صَلَّى اللهُ عَلَيْهِ عَشْرًا، ثُمَّ سَلُوا لِيَ الْوَسِيلَةَ، فَإِنَّهَا مَنْزِلَةٌ فِي الْجَنَّةِ لَا تَنْبَغِي إِلَّا لِعَبْدٍ مِنْ عِبَادِ اللهِ، وَأَرْجُو أَنْ أَكُونَ أَنَا هُوَ، فَمَنْ سَأَلَ لِيَ الْوَسِيلَةَ حَلَّتْ عَلَيْهِ الشَّفَاعَةُ»

(When you hear the Mu'adhdhin, repeat what he says, and then ask for Salah (blessing, mercy from Allah) for me. Verily, whoever asks for Salah for me, then Allah will grant ten Salah to him. Then, ask for the Wasilah for me, for it is a grade in Paradise that only one servant of Allah deserves, and I hope that I am that servant. Verily, whoever asks (Allah) for Wasilah for me, he will earn the right of my intercession.) Allah said,

(and strive hard in His cause as much as you can. So that you may be successful.) After Allah commanded Muslims to avoid the prohibitions and to work towards obedience, He commanded them to fight against their enemies, the disbelievers and idolators who have deviated from the straight path and abandoned the correct religion. Allah encouraged the believers by reminding them of the unending success and great happiness that He prepared for them for the Day of Resurrection, which will never change or decrease for those who join Jihad in His cause. They will remain in the lofty rooms of Paradise that are safe and beautiful. Those who live in these dwellings will always be comfortable and will never be miserable, living, never dying, and their clothes will never grow thin, nor will their youth ever end.

No Amount of Ransom Shall Be Accepted from the Disbelievers on the Day of the Judgment and They Will Remain in the Fire

Allah then describes the painful torment and punishment that He has prepared for His disbelieving enemies for the Day of Resurrection. Allah said,

(Verily, those who disbelieve, if they had all that is in the earth, and as much again therewith to ransom themselves thereby from the torment on the Day of Resurrection, it would never be accepted of them. And theirs would be a painful torment.) So if a disbeliever brought the earth's fill of gold, and twice as much as that amount on the Day of Judgment to ransom himself from Allah's torment that has surrounded him, and he is certain that he will suffer from it, it will not be accepted of him. Rather, there is no escaping the torment, and he will not be able to evade or save himself from it. Hence Allah's statement,

(And theirs would be a painful torment.) meaning, hurtful,

(They will long to get out of the Fire, but never will they get out therefrom, and theirs will be a lasting torment.) In another Ayah, Allah said,

(Every time they seek to get away therefrom, in anguish, they will be driven back therein.) Therefore, they will still long to leave the torment because of the severity and the pain it causes. They will have no way of escaping it. The more the flames lift them to the upper part of Hell, the more the angels of punishment will strike them with iron bars and they will fall down to its depths,

(And theirs will be a lasting torment.) meaning, eternal and everlasting, and they will never be able to depart from it or avoid it. Anas bin Malik said that the Messenger of Allah said,

«يُؤْتَى بِالرَّجُلِ مِنْ أَهْلِ النَّارِ فَيُقَالُ لَهُ: يَا ابْنَ آدَمَ كَيْفَ وَجَدْتَ مَضْجَعَكَ؟ فَيَقُولُ: شَرَّ مَضْجَعٍ، فَيُقَالُ: هَلْ تَفْتَدِي بِقُرَابِ الْأَرْضِ ذَهَبًا؟ قَالَ: فَيَقُولُ: نَعَمْ يَارَبِّ فَيَقُولُ اللهُ: كَذَبْتَ، قَدْ سَأَلْتُكَ أَقَلَّ مِنْ ذلِكَ فَلَمْ تَفْعَلْ، فَيُؤْمَرُ بِهِ إِلَى النَّارِ»

(A man from the people of the Fire will be brought forth and will be asked, `O son of Adam! How did you find your dwelling' He will say, `The worst dwelling.' He will be told, `Would you ransom yourself with the earth's fill of gold' He will say, `Yes, O Lord!' Allah will say to him, `You have lied. I asked you for what is less than that and you did not do it,' and he will be ordered to the Fire.) Muslim and An-Nasa'i recorded it.

Surah: 5 Ayah: 38, Ayah: 39 & Ayah: 40

﴿ وَٱلسَّارِقُ وَٱلسَّارِقَةُ فَٱقْطَعُوٓا۟ أَيْدِيَهُمَا جَزَآءًۢ بِمَا كَسَبَا نَكَـٰلًا مِّنَ ٱللَّهِ ۗ وَٱللَّهُ عَزِيزٌ
حَكِيمٌ ﴿٣٨﴾ ﴾

38. And (as for) the male thief and the female, cut off (from the wrist joint) their (right) hand as a recompense for that which they committed, a punishment by way of example from Allâh. And Allâh is All-Powerful, All-Wise.

﴿ فَمَن تَابَ مِنۢ بَعْدِ ظُلْمِهِۦ وَأَصْلَحَ فَإِنَّ ٱللَّهَ يَتُوبُ عَلَيْهِ ۗ إِنَّ ٱللَّهَ غَفُورٌ رَّحِيمٌ ﴿٣٩﴾ ﴾

39. But whosoever repents after his crime and does righteous good deeds (by obeying Allâh), then verily, Allâh will pardon him (accept his repentance). Verily, Allâh is Oft-Forgiving, Most Merciful.

﴿ أَلَمْ تَعْلَمْ أَنَّ ٱللَّهَ لَهُۥ مُلْكُ ٱلسَّمَـٰوَٰتِ وَٱلْأَرْضِ يُعَذِّبُ مَن يَشَآءُ وَيَغْفِرُ لِمَن يَشَآءُ ۗ
وَٱللَّهُ عَلَىٰ كُلِّ شَىْءٍ قَدِيرٌ ﴿٤٠﴾ ﴾

40. Know you not that to Allâh (Alone) belongs the dominion of the heavens and the earth! He punishes whom He wills and He forgives whom He wills. And Allâh is Able to do all things.

Transliteration

38. Waalssariqu waalssariqatu faiqtaAAoo aydiyahuma jazaan bima kasaba nakalan mina Allahi waAllahu AAazeezun hakeemun 39. Faman taba min baAAdi thulmihi waaslaha fa-inna Allaha yatoobu AAalayhi inna Allaha ghafoorun raheemun 40. Alam taAAlam anna Allaha lahu mulku alssamawati waal-ardi yuAAaththibu man yashao wayaghfiru liman yashao waAllahu AAala kulli shay-in qadeerun

Tafsir Ibn Kathir

The Necessity of Cutting off the Hand of the Thief

Allah commands and decrees that the hand of the thief, male or female be cut off. During the time of Jahiliyyah, this was also the punishment for the thief, and Islam upheld this punishment. In Islam, there are several conditions that must be met before this punishment is carried out, as we will come to know, Allah willing. There are other rulings that Islam upheld after modifying these rulings, such as that of blood money for example. When Does Cutting the Hand of the Thief Become Necessary In is recorded in the Two Sahihs that Abu Hurayrah said that the Messenger of Allah said,

«لَعَنَ اللهُ السَّارِقَ يَسْرِقُ الْبَيْضَةَ فَتُقْطَعُ يَدُهُ، وَيَسْرِقُ الْحَبْلَ فَتُقْطَعُ يَدُه»

(May Allah curse the thief who steals an egg and as a result his hand is cut off, and who steals rope and as a result his hand is cut off.) Al-Bukhari and Muslim recorded that `A'ishah said that the Messenger of Allah said,

«تُقْطَعُ يَدُ السَّارِقِ فِي رُبْعِ دِينَارٍ فَصَاعِدًا»

(The hand of the thief shall be cut off if he steals a quarter of a Dinar or more.) Muslim recorded that `A'ishah, may Allah be pleased with her, said that the Messenger of Allah said,

«لَا تُقْطَعُ يَدُ السَّارِقِ إِلَّا فِي رُبْعِ دِينَارٍ فَصَاعِدًا»

(The hand of the thief shall only be cut off if he steals a quarter of a Dinar or more.) This Hadith is the basis of the matter since it specifies (that the least amount of theft that deserves cutting the hand) is a quarter of a Dinar. So this Hadith fixes the value. And saying that it is three Dirhams is not a contradiction. This is because the Dinar in question was equal to twelve Dirhams, so three Dirhams equalled a fourth of a Dinar. So in this way it is possible to harmonize these two views. This opinion was reported from `Umar bin Al-Khattab, `Uthman bin `Affan,

When Does Cutting the Hand of the Thief Become Necessary

In is recorded in the Two Sahihs that Abu Hurayrah said that the Messenger of Allah said,

«لَعَنَ اللهُ السَّارِقَ يَسْرِقُ الْبَيْضَةَ فَتُقْطَعُ يَدُهُ، وَيَسْرِقُ الْحَبْلَ فَتُقْطَعُ يَدُه»

(May Allah curse the thief who steals an egg and as a result his hand is cut off, and who steals rope and as a result his hand is cut off.) Al-Bukhari and Muslim recorded that `A'ishah said that the Messenger of Allah said,

«تُقْطَعُ يَدُ السَّارِقِ فِي رُبْعِ دِينَارٍ فَصَاعِدًا»

(The hand of the thief shall be cut off if he steals a quarter of a Dinar or more.) Muslim recorded that `A'ishah, may Allah be pleased with her, said that the Messenger of Allah said,

«لَا تُقْطَعُ يَدُ السَّارِقِ إِلَّا فِي رُبْعِ دِينَارٍ فَصَاعِدًا»

(The hand of the thief shall only be cut off if he steals a quarter of a Dinar or more.) This Hadith is the basis of the matter since it specifies (that the least amount of theft that deserves cutting the hand) is a quarter of a Dinar. So this Hadith fixes the value. And saying that it is three Dirhams is not a contradiction. This is because the Dinar in question was equal to twelve Dirhams, so three Dirhams equalled a fourth of a Dinar. So in this way it is possible to harmonize these two views. This opinion was reported from `Umar bin Al-Khattab, `Uthman bin `Affan, `Ali bin Abi Talib - may Allah be pleased with them - and it is the view of `Umar bin `Abdul-`Aziz, Al-Layth bin Sa`d, Al-Awza`i, and Ash-Shafi`i and his companions. This is also the view of Imam Ahmad bin Hanbal and Ishaq bin Rahwayh in one of the narrations from him, as well as Abu Thawr, and Dawud bin `Ali Az-Zahari, may Allah have mercy upon them. As for Imam Abu Hanifah and his students Abu Yusuf, Muhammad and Zufar, along with Sufyan Ath-Thawri, they said that the least amount of theft that deserves cutting off the hand is ten Dirhams, whereas a Dinar was twelve Dirhams at that time. The first ruling is the correct one, that the least amount of theft is one forth of a Dinar or more. This meager amount was set as the limit for cutting the hand, so that the people would refrain from theft, and this is a wise decision to those who have sound comprehension. Hence Allah's statement,

(as a recompense for that which both committed, a punishment by way of example from Allah. And Allah is All-Powerful, All-Wise.) This is the prescribed punishment for the evil action they committed, by stealing the property of other people with their hands. Therefore, it is fitting that the tool they used to steal the people's wealth be cut off as punishment from Allah for their error.

(And Allah is All-Powerful,) in His torment,

(All-Wise.) in His commands, what he forbids, what He legislates and what He decrees.

Repentance of the Thief is Acceptable

Allah said next,

(But whosoever repents after his crime and does righteous good deeds, then verily, Allah will pardon him. Verily, Allah is Oft-Forgiving, Most Merciful.) Therefore, whoever repents and goes back to Allah after he commits theft, then Allah will forgive him. Imam Ahmad recorded that `Abdullah bin `Amr said that a woman committed theft during the time of the Messenger of Allah and those from whom she stole brought her and said, "O Allah's Messenger! This woman stole from us." Her people said, "We ransom her." The Messenger of Allah said,

«اقْطَعُوا يَدَهَا»

(Cut off her hand.) They said, "We ransom her with five hundred Dinars." The Prophet said,

«اقْطَعُوا يَدَهَا»

(Cut off her hand.) Her right hand was cut off and the woman asked, "O Messenger of Allah! Is there a chance for me to repent" He said,

«نَعَمْ أَنْتِ الْيَوْمَ مِنْ خَطِيئَتِكِ كَيَوْمَ وَلَدَتْكِ أُمُّكِ»

(Yes. This day, you are free from your sin just as the day your mother gave birth to you.) Allah sent down the verse in Surat Al-Ma'idah,

(But whosoever repents after his crime and does righteous good deeds (by obeying Allah), then verily, Allah will pardon him. Verily, Allah is Oft-Forgiving, Most Merciful.) This woman was from the tribe of Makhzum. Her story was narrated in the Two Sahihs from Az-Zuhri from `Urwah from `A'ishah, The incident caused concern for the Quraysh after she committed the theft during the time of the battle of the Conquest (of Makkah). They said, "Who can talk to Allah's Messenger about her matter" They then said, "Who dares speak to him about such matters other than Usamah bin Zayd, his loved one." When the woman was brought to the Messenger of Allah , Usamah bin Zayd talked to him about her and the face of the Messenger changed color (because of anger) and he said,

«أَتَشْفَعُ فِي حَدٍّ مِنْ حُدُودِ اللهِ عَزَّ وَجَلَّ؟»

(Do you intercede in a punishment prescribed by Allah) Usamah said to him, "Ask Allah to forgive me, O Allah's Messenger!" During that night, the Messenger of Allah stood up and gave a speech and praised Allah as He deserves to be praised. He then said,

«أَمَّا بَعْدُ فَإِنَّمَا أَهْلَكَ الَّذِينَ مِنْ قَبْلِكُمْ أَنَّهُمْ كَانُوا إِذَا سَرَقَ فِيهِمُ الشَّرِيفُ تَرَكُوهُ، وَإِذَا سَرَقَ فِيهِمُ الضَّعِيفُ أَقَامُوا عَلَيْهِ الْحَدَّ، وَإِنِّي وَالَّذِي نَفْسِي بِيَدِهِ لَوْ أَنَّ فَاطِمَةَ بِنْتَ مُحَمَّدٍ سَرَقَتْ لَقَطَعْتُ يَدَهَا»

(Those who were before you were destroyed because when an honorable person among them would steal, they would leave him. But, when a weak man among them stole, they implemented the prescribed punishment against him. By Him in Whose Hand is my soul! If Fatimah the daughter of Muhammad stole, I will have her hand cut off.) The Prophet commanded that the hand of the woman who stole be cut off, and it was cut off. `A'ishah said, `Her repentance was sincere afterwards, and she got married and she used to come to me so that I convey her needs to the Messenger of Allah." This is the wording that Muslim collected, and in another narration by Muslim, `A'ishah said, "She was a woman from Makhzum who used to borrow things and deny that she took them. So the Prophet ordered that her hand be cut off." Allah then said,

(Know you not that to Allah (Alone) belongs the dominion of the heavens and the earth!) He owns everything and decides what He wills for it and no one can resist His judgment,

(He forgives whom He wills and punishes whom He wills. And Allah is able to do all things.)

Surah: 5 Ayah: 41, Ayah: 42, Ayah: 43 & Ayah: 44

﴿ يَٰٓأَيُّهَا ٱلرَّسُولُ لَا يَحْزُنكَ ٱلَّذِينَ يُسَٰرِعُونَ فِي ٱلْكُفْرِ مِنَ ٱلَّذِينَ قَالُوٓا۟ ءَامَنَّا
بِأَفْوَٰهِهِمْ وَلَمْ تُؤْمِن قُلُوبُهُمْ ۛ وَمِنَ ٱلَّذِينَ هَادُوا۟ ۛ سَمَّٰعُونَ لِلْكَذِبِ سَمَّٰعُونَ
لِقَوْمٍ ءَاخَرِينَ لَمْ يَأْتُوكَ ۖ يُحَرِّفُونَ ٱلْكَلِمَ مِنۢ بَعْدِ مَوَاضِعِهِۦ ۖ يَقُولُونَ إِنْ أُوتِيتُمْ هَٰذَا
فَخُذُوهُ وَإِن لَّمْ تُؤْتَوْهُ فَٱحْذَرُوا۟ ۚ وَمَن يُرِدِ ٱللَّهُ فِتْنَتَهُۥ فَلَن تَمْلِكَ لَهُۥ مِنَ ٱللَّهِ شَيْـًٔا ۚ

أُوْلَٰٓئِكَ ٱلَّذِينَ لَمْ يُرِدِ ٱللَّهُ أَن يُطَهِّرَ قُلُوبَهُمْ ۚ لَهُمْ فِى ٱلدُّنْيَا خِزْىٌ ۖ وَلَهُمْ فِى ٱلْءَاخِرَةِ
عَذَابٌ عَظِيمٌ ﴿٤١﴾

41. O Messenger (Muhammad (peace be upon him))! Let not those who hurry to fall into disbelief grieve you, of such who say: "We believe" with their mouths but their hearts have no faith. And of the Jews are men who listen much and eagerly to lies - listen to others who have not come to you. They change the words from their places; they say, "If you are given this, take it, but if you are not given this, then beware!" And whomsoever Allâh wants to put in Al-Fitnah (error, because of his rejecting of Faith), you can do nothing for him against Allâh. Those are the ones whose hearts Allâh does not want to purify (from disbelief and hypocrisy); for them there is a disgrace in this world, and in the Hereafter a great torment.

﴿ سَمَّٰعُونَ لِلْكَذِبِ أَكَّٰلُونَ لِلسُّحْتِ ۚ فَإِن جَآءُوكَ فَٱحْكُم بَيْنَهُمْ أَوْ أَعْرِضْ عَنْهُمْ ۖ
وَإِن تُعْرِضْ عَنْهُمْ فَلَن يَضُرُّوكَ شَيْـًٔا ۖ وَإِنْ حَكَمْتَ فَٱحْكُم بَيْنَهُم بِٱلْقِسْطِ ۚ إِنَّ ٱللَّهَ يُحِبُّ
ٱلْمُقْسِطِينَ ﴿٤٢﴾

42. (They like to) listen to falsehood, to devour anything forbidden. So if they come to you (O Muhammad (peace be upon him)) either judge between them, or turn away from them. If you turn away from them, they cannot hurt you in the least. And if you judge, judge with justice between them. Verily, Allâh loves those who act justly.

﴿ وَكَيْفَ يُحَكِّمُونَكَ وَعِندَهُمُ ٱلتَّوْرَىٰةُ فِيهَا حُكْمُ ٱللَّهِ ثُمَّ يَتَوَلَّوْنَ مِنۢ بَعْدِ
ذَٰلِكَ ۚ وَمَآ أُوْلَٰٓئِكَ بِٱلْمُؤْمِنِينَ ﴿٤٣﴾

43. But how do they come to you for decision while they have the Taurât (Torah), in which is the (plain) Decision of Allâh; yet even after that, they turn away. For they are not (really) believers.

﴿ إِنَّآ أَنزَلْنَا ٱلتَّوْرَىٰةَ فِيهَا هُدًى وَنُورٌ ۚ يَحْكُمُ بِهَا ٱلنَّبِيُّونَ ٱلَّذِينَ أَسْلَمُوا۟ لِلَّذِينَ هَادُوا۟
وَٱلرَّبَّٰنِيُّونَ وَٱلْأَحْبَارُ بِمَا ٱسْتُحْفِظُوا۟ مِن كِتَٰبِ ٱللَّهِ وَكَانُوا۟ عَلَيْهِ شُهَدَآءَ ۚ فَلَا تَخْشَوُا۟
ٱلنَّاسَ وَٱخْشَوْنِ وَلَا تَشْتَرُوا۟ بِـَٔايَٰتِى ثَمَنًا قَلِيلًا ۚ وَمَن لَّمْ يَحْكُم بِمَآ أَنزَلَ ٱللَّهُ فَأُوْلَٰٓئِكَ هُمُ
ٱلْكَٰفِرُونَ ﴿٤٤﴾

44. Verily, We did send down the Taurât (Torah) (to Mûsâ (Moses)) therein was guidance and light, by which the Prophets, who submitted themselves to Allâh's Will, judged for the Jews. And the rabbis and the priests (too judged for the Jews by the Taurât (Torah) after those Prophets), for to them was entrusted the protection of Allâh's Book, and they were witnesses thereto. Therefore fear not men but fear Me (O Jews) and sell not My Verses for a miserable price. And whosoever does not judge by what Allâh has revealed, such are the Kâfirûn (i.e. disbelievers - of a lesser degree as they do not act on Allâh's Laws).

Transliteration

41. Ya ayyuha alrrasoolu la yahzunka allatheena yusariAAoona fee alkufri mina allatheena qaloo amanna bi-afwahihim walam tu/min quloobuhum wamina allatheena hadoo sammaAAoona lilkathibi sammaAAoona liqawmin akhareena lam ya/tooka yuharrifoona alkalima min baAAdi mawadiAAihi yaqooloona in ooteetum hatha fakhuthoohu wa-in lam tu/tawhu faihtharoo waman yuridi Allahu fitnatahu falan tamlika lahu mina Allahi shay-an ola-ika allatheena lam yuridi Allahu an yutahhira quloobahum lahum fee alddunya khizyun walahum fee al-akhirati AAathabun AAatheemun
42. SammaAAoona lilkathibi akkaloona lilssuhti fa-in jaooka faohkum baynahum aw aAArid AAanhum wa-in tuAArid AAanhum falan yadurrooka shay-an wa-in hakamta faohkum baynahum bialqisti inna Allaha yuhibbu almuqsiteena
43. Wakayfa yuhakkimoonaka waAAindahumu alttawratu feeha hukmu Allahi thumma yatawallawna min baAAdi thalika wama ola-ika bialmu/mineena
44. Inna anzalna alttawrata feeha hudan wanoorun yahkumu biha alnnabiyyoona allatheena aslamoo lillatheena hadoo waalrrabbaniyyoona waal-ahbaru bima istuhfithoo min kitabi Allahi wakanoo AAalayhi shuhadaa fala takhshawoo alnnasa waikhshawni wala tashtaroo bi-ayatee thamanan qaleelan waman lam yahkum bima anzala Allahu faola-ika humu alkafiroona

Tafsir Ibn Kathir

Do Not Feel Sad Because of the Behavior of the Jews and Hypocrites

These honorable Ayat were revealed about those who rush into disbelief, deviating from the obedience of Allah, His Messenger, prefering their opinions and lusts to what Allah has legislated,

(of such who say, "We believe" with their mouths but their hearts have no faith.) These people pretend to be faithful with their words, but their hearts are empty from faith, and they are the hypocrites.

(And of the Jews...) the enemies of Islam and its people, they and the hypocrites all,

(listen much and eagerly to lies...) and they accept and react to it positively,

(listening to others who have not come to you,) meaning, they listen to some people who do not attend your meetings, O Muhammad. Or, the Ayah might mean, they listen to what you say and convey it to your enemies who do not attend your audience.

The Jews Alter and Change the Law, Such As Stoning the Adulterer

(They change the words from their places:) by altering their meanings and knowingly distorting them after they comprehended them,

(they say, "If you are given this, take it, but if you are not given this, then beware!") It was reported that this part of the Ayah was revealed about some Jews who committed murder and who said to each other, "Let us ask Muhammad to judge between us, and if he decides that we pay the Diyah, accept his judgement. If he decides on capital punishment, do not accept his judgement." The correct opinion is that this Ayah was revealed about the two Jews who committed adultery. The Jews changed the law they had in their Book from Allah on the matter of punishment for adultery, from stoning to death, to a hundred flogs and making the offenders ride a donkey facing the back of the donkey. When this incident of adultery occurred after the Hijrah, they said to each other, "Let us go to Muhammad and seek his judgement. If he gives a ruling of flogging, then implement his decision and make it a proof for you with

Allah. This way, one of Allah's Prophets will have upheld this ruling amongst you. But if he decides that the punishment should be stoning to death, then do not accept his decision." There are several Hadiths mentioning this story. Malik reported that Nafi` said that `Abdullah bin `Umar said, "The Jews came to Allah's Messenger and mentioned that a man and a woman from them committed adultery. Allah's Messenger said to them,

«مَا تَجِدُونَ فِي التَّوْرَاةِ فِي شَأْنِ الرَّجْمِ؟»

(What do find of the ruling about stoning in the Tawrah) They said, `We only find that they should be exposed and flogged.' `Abdullah bin Salam said, `You lie. The Tawrah mentions stoning, so bring the Tawrah.' They brought the Tawrah and opened it but one of them hid the verse about stoning with his hand and recited what is before and after that verse. `Abdullah bin Salam said to him, `Remove your hand,' and he removed it, thus uncovering the verse about stoning. So they said, He (`Abdullah bin Salam) has said the truth, O Muhammad! It is the verse about stoning.' The Messenger of Allah decided that the adulterers be stoned to death and his command was carried out. I saw that man shading the woman from the stones with his body." Al-Bukhari and Muslim also collected this Hadith and this is the wording collected by Al-Bukhari. In another narration by Al-Bukhari, the Prophet said to the Jews,

«مَا تَصْنَعُون بِهِمَا؟»

(What would you do in this case) They said, "We would humiliate and expose them." The Prophet recited,

(Bring here the Tawrah and recite it, if you are truthful.) So they brought a man who was blind in one eye and who was respected among them and said to him, "Read (from the Tawrah)." So he read until he reached a certain verse and then covered it with his hand. He was told, "Remove your hand," and it was the verse about stoning. So that man said, "O Muhammad! This is the verse about stoning, and we had hid its knowledge among us." So the Messenger ordered that the two adulterers be stoned, and they were stoned. Muslim recorded that a Jewish man and a Jewish woman were brought before Allah's Messenger because they committed adultery. The Messenger of Allah went to the Jews and asked them,

«مَا تَجِدُونَ فِي التَّوْرَاةِ عَلى مَنْ زَنَى؟»

(What is the ruling that you find in the Tawrah for adultery) hThey said, "We expose them, carry them (on donkeys) backwards and parade them in public." The Prophet recited;

(Bring here the Tawrah and recite it, if you are truthful.) So they brought the Tawrah and read from it until the reader reached the verse about stoning. Then he placed his hand on that verse and read what was before and after it. `Abdullah bin Salam, who was with the Messenger of Allah , said, "Order him to remove his hand," and he removed his hand and under it was the verse about stoning. So the Messenger of Allah commanded that the adulterers be stoned, and they were stoned. `Abdullah bin `Umar said, "I was among those who stoned them and I saw the man shading the woman from the stones with his body." Abu Dawud recorded that Ibn `Umar said, "Some Jews came to the Messenger of Allah and invited him to go to the Quff area. So he went to the house of Al-Midras and they said, `O Abu Al-

Qasim! A man from us committed adultery with a woman, so decide on their matter.' They arranged a pillow for the Messenger of Allah and he sat on it and said,

«ائْتُونِي بِالتَّوْرَاة»

(Bring the Tawrah to me.) He was brought the Tawrah and he removed the pillow from under him and placed the Tawrah on it, saying,

«آمَنْتُ بِكِ وَبِمَنْ أَنْزَلَك»

(I trust you and He Who revealed it to you.) He then said,

«ائْتُونِي بِأَعْلَمِكُم»

(Bring me your most knowledgeable person.) So he was brought a young man... " and then he mentioned the rest of the story that Malik narrated from Nafi`. These Hadiths state that the Messenger of Allah issued a decision that conforms with the ruling in the Tawrah, not to honor the Jews in what they believe in, for the Jews were commanded to follow the Law of Muhammad only. Rather, the Prophet did this because Allah commanded him to do so. He asked them about the ruling of stoning in the Tawrah to make them admit to what the Tawrah contains and what they collaborated to hide, deny and exclude from implementing for all that time. They had to admit to what they did, although they did it while having knowledge of the correct ruling. What made them go to the Prophet for judgement in this matter was their lusts and desires, hoping that the Prophet would agree with their opinion, not that they believed in the correctness of his judgment. This is why they said,

(If you are given this,) referring to flogging, then take it,

(but if you are not given this, then beware!) and do not accept or implement it. Allah said next,

(And whomsoever Allah wants to put in Fitnah, you can do nothing for him against Allah. Those are the ones whose hearts Allah does not want to purify; for them there is a disgrace in this world, and in the Hereafter a great torment. They (like to) listen to falsehood, to devour Suht) `Suht' refers to bribes, as Ibn Mas`ud and others stated. The Ayah states that if one is like this, how can Allah cleanse his heart and accept his supplication Allah said to His Prophet ,

(So if they come to you...) so that you judge between them,

(either judge between them, or turn away from them. If you turn away from them, they cannot hurt you in the least.) meaning, there is no harm if you do not judge between them. This is because when they came to you to judge between them, they did not seek to follow the truth, but only what conformed to their lusts. We should mention here that Ibn `Abbas, Mujahid, `Ikrimah, Al-Hasan, Qatadah, As-Suddi, Zayd bin Aslam, `Ata' Al-Khurasani, and several others said that this part of the Ayah was abrogated by Allah's statement,

(And so judge among them by what Allah has revealed.)

(And if you judge, judge with justice between them.) and with fairness, even if the Jews were unjust and outcasts from the path of fairness,

(Verily, Allah loves those who act justly.)

Chastising the Jews for Their Evil Lusts and Desires, While Praising the Tawrah

Allah then chastises the Jews for their false ideas and deviant desires to abandon what they believe is true in their Book, and which they claim is their eternal Law that they are always commanded to adhere to. Yet, they do not adhere to the Tawrah, but they prefer other laws over it, although they believe that these other laws are not correct and do not apply to them. Allah said,

(But how do they come to you for decision while they have the Tawrah, in which is the decision of Allah; yet even after that they turn away. For they are not believers.) Allah next praises the Tawrah that He sent down to His servant and Messenger Musa, son of `Imran,

(Verily, We did send down the Tawrah (to Musa), therein was guidance and light, by which the Prophets who submitted themselves to Allah's will, judged the Jews.) and these Prophets did not deviate from the law of the Tawrah, change or alter it,

(And (also) the Rabbaniyyun and the Ahbar...) wherein Rabbaniyyun refers to the worshippers who are learned and religious, and Ahbar refers to the scholars,

(for to them was entrusted the protection of Allah's Book,) meaning, they were entrusted with the Book of Allah, and they were commanded to adhere to it and not hide any part of,

(and they were witnesses thereto. Therefore fear not men but fear Me and sell not My verses for a miserable price. And whosoever does not judge by what Allah has revealed, such are the disbelievers.) There are two ways to explain this Ayah and we will mention the later.

Another Reason Behind Revealing these Honorable Ayat

Imam Ahmad recorded that Ibn `Abbas said, "Allah sent down the Ayat,

(And whosoever does not judge by what Allah has revealed, such are the disbelievers,)

(Such are the unjust,) and,

(Such are the rebellious.) about two groups among the Jews. During the time of Jahiliyyah, one of them had defeated the other. As a result, they made a treaty that they would pay blood money totaling fifty Wasaq (of gold) (each Wasaq approx. 3 kg) for every dead person from the defeated group killed by the victors, and a hundred Wasaq for every dead person the defeated group killed from the victors. This treaty remained in effect until the Prophet came to Al-Madinah and both of these groups became subservient under the Prophet . Yet, when the mighty group once suffered a casualty at the hands of the weaker group, the mighty group sent a delegation demanding the hundred Wasaq. The weaker group said, `How can two groups who have the same religion, one ancestral lineage and a common land, have a Diyah that for some of them is half of that of the others We only agreed to this because you oppressed us and because we feared you. Now that Muhammad has come, we will not give you what you asked.' So war was almost rekindled between them, but they agreed to seek Muhammad's judgement in their dispute. The mighty group among them said (among themselves), `By Allah! Muhammad will never give you double the Diyah that you pay to them compared to what they pay to you. They have said the truth anyway, for they only gave us this amount because we oppressed and overpowered them. Therefore, send someone to Muhammad who will sense what his judgement will be. If he agrees to give you what you demand, accept his judgment, and if he does not give you what you seek, do not refer to him for judgement.' So they sent some hypocrites to the Messenger of Allah to try and find out the Messenger's judgement. When they came to the Messenger , Allah informed him of their matter and of their plot. Allah sent down,

(O Messenger! Let not those who hurry to fall into disbelief grieve you,) until,

(Such are the rebellious.) By Allah! It is because of their problem that Allah sent down these verses and it is they whom Allah meant." Abu Dawud collected a similar narration for this Hadith. Abu Ja`far Ibn Jarir recorded that Ibn `Abbas said that the Ayah in Surat Al-Ma'idah,

(either judge between them, or turn away from them...) until,

(Those who act justly.) was revealed concerning the problem of blood money between Bani An-Nadir and Bani Qurayzah. The dead of Bani An-Nadir were being honored more and they received the full amount of Diyah, while Qurayzah received half the Diyah for their dead. So they referred to the Messenger of Allah for judgement and Allah sent down these verses about them. The Messenger of Allah compelled them to adhere to the true judgement in this matter and made the Diyah the same for both groups and Allah knows best about that matter." Ahmad, Abu Dawud and An-Nasa'i also recorded this Hadith from Abu Ishaq. Al-`Awfi and `Ali bin Abi Talhah reported that Ibn `Abbas said that these Ayat were revealed about the two Jews who committed adultery, and we mentioned the Hadiths about this story before. It appears that both of these were the reasons behind revealing these Ayat, and Allah knows best. This is why Allah said afterwards,

(And We ordained therein for them: Life for life, eye for eye) until the end of the Ayah, which strengthens the opinion that the story of the Diyah was behind revealing the Ayat as we explained above. Allah knows best. Allah said,

(And whosoever does not judge by what Allah has revealed, such are the disbelievers.) Al-Bara' bin `Azib, Hudhayfah bin Al-Yaman, Ibn `Abbas, Abu Mijlaz, Abu Raja' Al-`Utaridi, `Ikrimah, `Ubaydullah bin `Abdullah, Al-Hasan Al-Basri and others said that this Ayah was revealed about the People of the Book. Al-Hasan Al-Basri added that this Ayah also applies to us. `Abdur-Razzaq said that Ath-Thawri said that Mansur said that Ibrahim said that these Ayat, "Were revealed about the Children of Israel, and Allah accepted them for this Ummah." Ibn Jarir recorded this statement. `Ali bin Abi Talhah also stated that Ibn `Abbas commented on Allah's statement,

(And whosoever does not judge by what Allah has revealed, such are the disbelievers,) "Whoever rejects what Allah has revealed, will have committed Kufr, and whoever accepts what Allah has revealed, but did not rule by it, is a Zalim (unjust) and a Fasiq (rebellious) and a sinner." Ibn Jarir recorded this statement. `Abdur-Razzaq said, "Ma`mar narrated to us that Tawus said that Ibn `Abbas was asked about Allah's statement,

(And whosoever does not judge...) He said, `It is an act of Kufr.' Ibn Tawus added, `It is not like those who disbelieve in Allah, His angels, His Books and His Messengers.' Ath-Thawri narrated that Ibn Jurayj said that `Ata' said, `There is Kufr and Kufr less than Kufr, Zulm and

Zulm less than Zulm, Fisq and Fisq less than Fisq."' Waki` said that Sa`id Al-Makki said that Tawus said that,

(And whosoever does not judge by what Allah has revealed, such are the disbelievers,) "This is not the Kufr that annuls one's religion."

Surah: 5 Ayah: 45

﴿ وَكَتَبْنَا عَلَيْهِمْ فِيهَآ أَنَّ ٱلنَّفْسَ بِٱلنَّفْسِ وَٱلْعَيْنَ بِٱلْعَيْنِ وَٱلْأَنفَ بِٱلْأَنفِ
وَٱلْأُذُنَ بِٱلْأُذُنِ وَٱلسِّنَّ بِٱلسِّنِّ وَٱلْجُرُوحَ قِصَاصٌ ۚ فَمَن تَصَدَّقَ بِهِۦ فَهُوَ
كَفَّارَةٌ لَّهُۥ ۚ وَمَن لَّمْ يَحْكُم بِمَآ أَنزَلَ ٱللَّهُ فَأُو۟لَـٰٓئِكَ هُمُ ٱلظَّـٰلِمُونَ ﴿٤٥﴾ ﴾

45. And We ordained therein for them: "Life for life, eye for eye, nose for nose, ear for ear, tooth for tooth, and wounds equal for equal." But if anyone remits the retaliation by way of charity, it shall be for him an expiation. And whosoever does not judge by that which Allâh has revealed, such are the Zâlimûn (polytheists and wrong-doers - of a lesser degree).

Transliteration

45. Wakatabna AAalayhim feeha anna alnnafsa bialnnafsi waalAAayna bialAAayni waal-anfa bial-anfi waalothuna bialothuni waalssinna bialssinni waaljurooha qisasun faman tasaddaqa bihi fahuwa kaffaratun lahu waman lam yahkum bima anzala Allahu faola-ika humu alththalimoona

Tafsir Ibn Kathir

This Ayah also chastises and criticizes the Jews because in the Tawrah, they have the law of a life for a life. Yet, they defied this ruling by transgression and rebellion. They used to apply this ruling when a person from Bani An-Nadir was killed by a Qurayzah person, but this was not the case when the opposite occurred. Rather, they would revert to Diyah in this case. They also defied the ruling in the Tawrah to stone the adulterer and instead came up with their own form of punishment, flogging, humiliation and parading them in public. This is why Allah said in the previous Ayah, t

(And whosoever does not judge by what Allah has revealed, such are the disbelievers.) because they rejected Allah's command with full intention and with transgression and rebellion. In this Ayah, Allah said,

(such are the unjust.) because they did not exact the oppressed his due rights from the oppressor in a matter which Allah ordered that all be treated equally and fairly. Instead, they defied that command, committed injustice and transgressed against each other.

A Man is Killed for a Woman Whom He Kills

Imam Abu Nasr bin As-Sabbagh stated in his book, Ash-Shamil, that the scholars agree that this Ayah (5:45) should be implemented, and the Imams agree that the man is killed for a woman whom he kills, according to the general indications of this Ayah. A Hadith that An-Nasa'i recorded states that the Messenger of Allah had this statement written in the book that he gave `Amr bin Hazm,

«أَنَّ الرَّجُلَ يُقْتَلُ بِالْمَرْأَةِ»

(The man is killed for the woman (whom he kills).) In another Hadith, the Messenger said,

«الْمُسْلِمُونَ تَتَكَافَأُ دِمَاؤُهُم»

(Muslims are equal regarding the sanctity of their blood.) This is also the opinion of the majority of the scholars. What further supports what Ibn As-Sabbagh said is the Hadith that Imam Ahmad recorded that Anas bin Malik said, "Ar-Rabi` (his aunt) broke the tooth of a girl, and the relatives of Ar-Rabi` requested the girl's relatives to forgive (the offender), but they refused. So, they went to the Prophet who ordered them to bring about retaliation. Anas bin An-Nadr, her brother, asked, `O Allah's Messenger! Will the tooth of Ar-Rabi` be broken' The Messenger of Allah said, `O Anas! The Book of Allah prescribes retaliation.' Anas said, `No, by Him Who has sent you with the Truth, her tooth will not be broken. ' Later the relatives of the girl agreed to forgive Ar-Rabi` and forfeit their right to retaliation. The Messenger of Allah said,

«إن من عباد الله من لو أقسم على الله لأبره»

(There are some of Allah's servants who, if they take an oath by Allah, Allah fullfils them.)" It was recorded in the Two Sahihs.

Retaliation for Wounds

Allah said,

(and wounds equal for equal.) `Ali bin Abi Talhah reported that Ibn `Abbas said, "Life for life, an eye for an eye, a nose, if cut off, for a nose, a tooth broken for a tooth and wounds equal for wound." The free Muslims, men and women, are equal in this matter. And their slaves, male and female, are equal in this matter. And this ruling is the same regarding intentional murder and lesser offenses, as Ibn Jarir and Ibn Abi Hatim recorded.

An Important Ruling

The retaliation for wounds should not be implemented until the wounds of the victim heal. If retaliation occurs before the wound heals, and then the wound becomes aggravated, the victim will have no additional rights in this case. The proof for this ruling is what Imam Ahmad narrated from `Amr bin Shu`ayb, from his father, from his grandfather that a man once stabbed another man in his leg using a horn. The victim came to the Prophet asking for retaliation, and the Prophet said,

«حَتَّى تَبْرَأ»

(Not until you heal.) The man again came to the Prophet and asked for equality in retaliation and the Prophet allowed him that. Later on, that man said, "O Messenger of Allah! I limp now." The Messenger said,

«قَدْ نَهَيْتُكَ فَعَصَيْتَنِي، فَأَبْعَدكَ اللهُ وَبَطَلَ عَرَجُكَ»

(I had asked you to wait, but you disobeyed me. Therefore, Allah cast you away and your limp has no compensation.) Afterwards, the Messenger of Allah forbade that the wound be retaliated for until the wound of the victim heals. If the victim is allowed to retaliate for his wound caused by the aggressor and the aggressor dies as a result, there is no compensation in this case, according to the majority of the Companions and their followers.

The Pardon is Expiation for Such Offenses

Allah said,

(But if anyone remits the retaliation by way of charity, it shall be for him an expiation.) `Ali bin Abi Talhah reported that Ibn `Abbas commented that

(But if anyone remits the retaliation by way of charity) means; "If one pardons by way of charity, it will result in expiation for the aggressor and reward for the victim." Sufyan Ath-Thawri said that `Ata' bin As-Sa'ib said that Sa`id bin Jubayr said that Ibn `Abbas said, `He who pardons the retaliation by way of charity, it will be an expiation for the aggressor and a reward for the victim with Allah." Ibn Abi Hatim recorded this statement. Jabir bin `Abdullah said that Allah's statement,

(But if anyone remits the retaliation by way of charity, it shall be for him an expiation,) "For the victim." This is also the opinion of Al-Hasan Al-Basri, Ibrahim An-Nakha`i and Abu Ishaq Al-Hamdani. Imam Ahmad recorded that `Ubadah bin As-Samit said, "I heard the Messenger of Allah saying,

«مَا مِنْ رَجُلٍ يُجْرَحُ مِنْ جَسَدِهِ جَرَاحَةً فَيَتَصَدَّقُ بِهَا، إِلَّا كَفَّرَ اللهُ عَنْهُ مِثْلَ مَا تَصَدَّقَ بِه»

(Any man who suffers a wound on his body and forfeits his right of retaliation as way of charity, then Allah will pardon him that which is similar to what he forfeited.) An-Nasa'i and Ibn Jarir recorded this Hadith. Allah's statement,

(And whosoever does not judge by that which Allah has revealed, such are the unjust.) Earlier we mentioned the statements of `Ata' and Tawus that there is Kufr and lesser Kufr, injustice and lesser injustice and Fisq and lesser Fisq.

Surah: 5 Ayah: 46 & Ayah: 47

﴿ وَقَفَّيْنَا عَلَىٰٓ ءَاثَـٰرِهِم بِعِيسَى ٱبْنِ مَرْيَمَ مُصَدِّقًا لِّمَا بَيْنَ يَدَيْهِ مِنَ ٱلتَّوْرَىٰةِ ۖ وَءَاتَيْنَـٰهُ ٱلْإِنجِيلَ فِيهِ هُدًى وَنُورٌ وَمُصَدِّقًا لِّمَا بَيْنَ يَدَيْهِ مِنَ ٱلتَّوْرَىٰةِ وَهُدًى وَمَوْعِظَةً لِّلْمُتَّقِينَ ﴿٤٦﴾ ﴾

46. And in their footsteps, We sent 'Isâ (Jesus), son of Maryam (Mary), confirming the Taurât (Torah) that had come before him, and We gave him the Injeel (Gospel), in which was guidance and light and confirmation of the Taurât (Torah) that had come before it, a guidance and an admonition for Al-Muttaqûn (the pious - see V.2:2).

﴿ وَلْيَحْكُمْ أَهْلُ ٱلْإِنجِيلِ بِمَآ أَنزَلَ ٱللَّهُ فِيهِ ۚ وَمَن لَّمْ يَحْكُم بِمَآ أَنزَلَ ٱللَّهُ فَأُو۟لَٰٓئِكَ هُمُ
ٱلْفَٰسِقُونَ ﴿٤٧﴾ ﴾

47. Let the people of the Injeel (Gospel) judge by what Allâh has revealed therein. And whosoever does not judge by what Allâh has revealed (then) such (people) are the Fâsiqûn (the rebellious i.e. disobedient (of a lesser degree)) to Allâh.

Transliteration

46. Waqaffayna AAala atharihim biAAeesa ibni maryama musaddiqan lima bayna yadayhi mina alttawrati waataynahu al-injeela feehi hudan wanoorun wamusaddiqan lima bayna yadayhi mina alttawrati wahudan wamawAAithatan lilmuttaqeena 47. Walyahkum ahlu al-injeeli bima anzala Allahu feehi waman lam yahkum bima anzala Allahu faola-ika humu alfasiqoona

Tafsir Ibn Kathir

Allah Mentions `Isa and Praises the Injil

Allah said,

(and We sent...) meaning, We sent

(in their footsteps) meaning the Prophets of the Children of Israel,

(`Isa, son of Maryam, confirming the Tawrah that had come before him,) meaning, he believed in it and ruled by it.

(and We gave him the Injil, in which was guidance and light) a guidance that directs to the truth and a light that removes the doubts and solves disputes,

(and confirmation of the Tawrah that had come before it,) meaning, he adhered to the Tawrah, except for the few instances that clarified the truth where the Children of Israel differed. Allah states in another Ayah that `Isa said to the Children of Israel,

(. ..and to make lawful to you part of what was forbidden to you.) So the scholars say that the Injil abrogated some of the rulings of the Tawrah. Allah's statement,

(a guidance and an admonition for those who have Taqwa.) means, We made the Injil guidance and an admonition that prohibits committing sins and errors, for those who have Taqwa of Allah and fear His warning and torment. Allah said next,

(Let the people of the Injil judge by what Allah has revealed therein.) meaning, so that He judges the people of the Injil by it in their time. Or, the Ayah means, so that they believe in all that is in it and adhere to all its commands, including the good news about the coming of Muhammad and the command to believe in and follow him when he is sent. Allah said in other Ayat,

(Say "O People of the Scripture! You have nothing (guidance) until you act according to the Tawrah, the Injil, and what has been sent down to you from your Lord.") and,

(Those who follow the Messenger, the Prophet who can neither read nor write whom they find written with them in the Tawrah...) until,

(...successful.) Here, Allah said,

(And whosoever does not judge by what Allah has revealed, such are the rebellious.) meaning, the rebellious and disobedient of Allah who prefer falsehood and abandon truth. We mentioned before that this Ayah was revealed about the Christians, and this is evident from the context of the Ayah.

Surah: 5 Ayah: 48, Ayah: 49 & Ayah: 50

﴿ وَأَنزَلْنَآ إِلَيْكَ ٱلْكِتَـٰبَ بِٱلْحَقِّ مُصَدِّقًا لِّمَا بَيْنَ يَدَيْهِ مِنَ ٱلْكِتَـٰبِ وَمُهَيْمِنًا عَلَيْهِ ۖ
فَٱحْكُم بَيْنَهُم بِمَآ أَنزَلَ ٱللَّهُ ۖ وَلَا تَتَّبِعْ أَهْوَآءَهُمْ عَمَّا جَآءَكَ مِنَ ٱلْحَقِّ ۚ لِكُلٍّ جَعَلْنَا
مِنكُمْ شِرْعَةً وَمِنْهَاجًا ۚ وَلَوْ شَآءَ ٱللَّهُ لَجَعَلَكُمْ أُمَّةً وَٰحِدَةً وَلَـٰكِن لِّيَبْلُوَكُمْ فِى مَآ ءَاتَىٰكُمْ ۖ
فَٱسْتَبِقُوا۟ ٱلْخَيْرَٰتِ ۚ إِلَى ٱللَّهِ مَرْجِعُكُمْ جَمِيعًا فَيُنَبِّئُكُم بِمَا كُنتُمْ فِيهِ تَخْتَلِفُونَ ﴿٤٨﴾ ﴾

48. And We have sent down to you (O Muhammad (peace be upon him)) the Book (this Qur'ân) in truth, confirming the Scripture that came before it and Muhaymin (trustworthy in highness and a witness) over it (old Scriptures). So judge among them by what Allâh has revealed, and follow not their vain desires, diverging away from the truth that has come to you. To each among you, We have prescribed a law and a clear way. If Allâh had willed, He would have made you one nation, but that (He) may test you in what He has given you; so compete in good deeds. The return of you (all) is to Allâh; then He will inform you about that in which you used to differ.

﴿ وَأَنِ ٱحْكُم بَيْنَهُم بِمَآ أَنزَلَ ٱللَّهُ وَلَا تَتَّبِعْ أَهْوَآءَهُمْ وَٱحْذَرْهُمْ أَن يَفْتِنُوكَ عَنۢ بَعْضِ
مَآ أَنزَلَ ٱللَّهُ إِلَيْكَ ۖ فَإِن تَوَلَّوْا۟ فَٱعْلَمْ أَنَّمَا يُرِيدُ ٱللَّهُ أَن يُصِيبَهُم بِبَعْضِ ذُنُوبِهِمْ ۗ وَإِنَّ كَثِيرًا
مِّنَ ٱلنَّاسِ لَفَـٰسِقُونَ ﴿٤٩﴾ ﴾

49. And so judge (you O Muhammad (peace be upon him)) among them by what Allâh has revealed and follow not their vain desires, but beware of them lest they turn you (O Muhammad (peace be upon him)) far away from some of that which Allâh has sent down to you. And if they turn away, then know that Allâh's Will is to punish them for some sins of theirs. And truly, most of men are Fâsiqûn (rebellious and disobedient to Allâh).

﴿ أَفَحُكْمَ ٱلْجَـٰهِلِيَّةِ يَبْغُونَ ۚ وَمَنْ أَحْسَنُ مِنَ ٱللَّهِ حُكْمًا لِّقَوْمٍ يُوقِنُونَ ﴿٥٠﴾ ﴾

50. Do they then seek the judgement of (the Days of) Ignorance? And who is better in judgement than Allâh for a people who have firm Faith.

Transliteration

48. Waanzalna ilayka alkitaba bialhaqqi musaddiqan lima bayna yadayhi mina alkitabi wamuhayminan AAalayhi faohkum baynahum bima anzala Allahu wala tattabiAA ahwaahum AAamma jaaka mina alhaqqi likullin jaAAalna minkum shirAAatan waminhajan walaw shaa Allahu lajaAAalakum ommatan wahidatan walakin liyabluwakum feema atakum faistabiqoo alkhayrati ila Allahi marjiAAukum jameeAAan fayunabbi-okum bima kuntum feehi takhtalifoona
49. Waani ohkum baynahum bima anzala Allahu wala tattabiAA ahwaahum waihtharhum an yaftinooka AAan baAAdi ma anzala Allahu ilayka fa-in tawallaw faiAAlam annama yureedu Allahu an yuseebahum bibaAAdi thunoobihim wa-inna katheeran mina alnnasi lafasiqoona 50.
Afahukma aljahiliyyati yabghoona waman ahsanu mina Allahu hukman liqawmin yooqinoona

Tafsir Ibn Kathir

Praising the Qur'an; the Command to Refer to the Qur'an for Judgment

Allah mentioned the Tawrah that He sent down to His Prophet Musa, the one whom He spoke directly to, praising it, commanding that it should be implemented, before it was abrogated. Allah then mentioned the Injil, praised it and commanded its people to adhere to it and follow it, as we stated. He next mentioned the Glorious Qur'an that He sent down to His honorable servant and Messenger. Allah said,

(And We have sent down to you the Book in truth...) meaning, with the truth that, no doubt, is coming from Allah,

(confirming the Scripture that came before it) meaning, the Divinely Revealed Books that praised the Qur'an and mentioned that it would be sent down from Allah to His servant and Messenger Muhammad . The Qur'an was revealed as was foretold in the previous Scriptures. This fact increased faith in the previous Scriptures for the sincere who have knowledge of these Scriptures, those who adhered to Allah's commands and Laws and believed in His Messengers. Allah said,

(Say: "Believe in it or do not believe (in it). Verily, those who were given knowledge before it, when it is recited to them, fall down on their faces in humble prostration." And they say: "Glory be to our Lord! Truly, the promise of our Lord must be fulfilled.") meaning that they say, the promise of our Lord, concerning the coming of Muhammad by the words of His previous Messengers, will certainly be fulfilled. Allah's statement,

(and Muhayminan over it) means entrusted over it, according to Sufyan Ath-Thawri who narrated it from Abu Ishaq from At-Tamimi from Ibn `Abbas. `Ali bin Abi Talhah reported that Ibn `Abbas said, "Muhaymin is, `the Trustworthy'. Allah says that the Qur'an is trustworthy over every Divine Book that preceded it." This was reported from `Ikrimah, Sa`id bin Jubayr, Mujahid, Muhammad bin Ka`b, `Atiyyah, Al-Hasan, Qatadah, `Ata' Al-Khurasani, As-Suddi and Ibn Zayd. Ibn Jarir said, "The Qur'an is trustworthy over the Books that preceded it. Therefore, whatever in these previous Books conforms to the Qur'an is true, and whatever disagrees with the Qur'an is false." Al-Walibi said that Ibn `Abbas said that Muhayminan means, `Witness'. Mujahid, Qatadah and As-Suddi said the same. Al-`Awfi said that Ibn `Abbas said that Muhayminan means, `dominant over the previous Scriptures'. These meanings are similar, as the word Muhaymin includes them all. Consequently, the Qur'an is trustworthy, a witness, and dominant over every Scripture that preceded it. This Glorious Book, which Allah revealed as the Last and Final Book, is the most encompassing, glorious and perfect Book of all times. The Qur'an includes all the good aspects of previous Scriptures and even more, which no previous Scripture ever contained. This is why Allah made it trustworthy, a witness and dominant over all Scriptures. Allah promised that He will protect the Qur'an and swore by His Most Honorable Self,

(Verily, We, it is We Who have sent down the Dhikr and surely, We will guard it (from corruption).) Allah said,

(So judge between them by what Allah has revealed.) The Ayah commands: O Muhammad! Rule between the people, Arabs and non-Arabs, lettered and unlettered, by what Allah has revealed to you in this Glorious Book and what it approves of for you from the Law of the previous Prophets, as Ibn Jarir said. Ibn Abi Hatim reported that Ibn `Abbas said, "The Prophet had the choice to judge between them or to turn away from them and refer them to their own Law. Then this Ayah was revealed,

(So judge between them by what Allah has revealed, and follow not their vain desires. ..) and he was commanded to judge between them by our Book.". Allah's statement

(and follow not their vain desires...) This means the ideas they promote, because of which they turned away from what Allah revealed to His Messengers. This is why Allah said,

(And follow not their vain desires, diverging away from the truth that has come to you.) The Ayah commands: Do not diverge from the truth that Allah has ordained for you, to the vain desires of these miserable, ignorant people. Allah's statement,

(To each among you, We have prescribed a law and a clear way.)

(To each among you, We have prescribed a law) Shir`at meaning, a clear path, as Ibn Abi Hatim recorded from Ibn `Abbas.

(If Allah willed, He would have made you one nation.) This is a general proclamation to all nations informing them of Allah's mighty ability. If Allah wills, He would make all mankind follow one religion and one Law, that would never be abrogated. Allah decided that every Prophet would have his own distinct law that is later abrogated partially or totally with the law of a latter Prophet. Later on, all previous laws were abrogated by the Law that Allah sent with Muhammad , His servant and Messenger, whom Allah sent to the people of earth as the Final Prophet. Allah said,

(If Allah willed, He would have made you one nation, but that (He) may test you in what He has given you.) This Ayah means, Allah has instituted different laws to test His servants' obedience to what He legislates for them, thus, He rewards or punishes them according to their actions and what they intend. `Abdullah bin Kathir said that the Ayah,

(In what He has given you.) means, of the Book. Next, Allah encouraged rushing to perform good deeds,

(so strive as in a race in good deeds.) which are obedience to Allah, following His Law that abrogated the laws that came before it, and believing in His Book, the Qur'an, which is the Final Book that He revealed. Allah said next,

(The return of you (all) is to Allah;) Therefore, O people, your return and final destination is to Allah on the Day of Resurrection, (then He will inform you about that in which you used to differ.) Allah will inform you about the truth in which you used to differ and will reward the sincere, as compensation for their sincerity, and will punish the disbelieving, rebellious people who rejected the truth and deviated from it to other paths, without proof or evidence to justify their actions. Rather, they have rejected the clear evidences, unequivocal proofs and established signs. Ad-Dahhak said that,

(So strive as in a race in good deeds.)is directed at the Ummah of Muhammad , but the first view is more apparent. Allah's statement,

(And so judge between them by what Allah has revealed and follow not their vain desires,) emphasizes this command and forbids ignoring it. Allah said next,

(but beware of them lest they turn you far away from some of that which Allah has sent down to you.) meaning; beware of the Jews, your enemies, lest they distort the truth for you in what they convey to you. Therefore, do not be deceived by them, for they are liars, treacherous and disbelievers.

(And if they turn away,) from the judgement that you pass in their disputes, and they defy Allah's Law,

(then know that Allah's will is to punish them for some sins of theirs.) meaning, know that this will occur according to the decree of Allah, and because out of His wisdom they have deviated from the truth, and because of their previous sins.

(And truly, most men are rebellious.) Therefore, the majority of humans are disobedient to their Lord, defiant of the truth and deviate away from it. Allah said in other Ayat,

(And most people will not believe even if you desire it eagerly,) and,

(And if you obey most of those on the earth they will mislead you far away from Allah's path.) Muhammad bin Ishaq reported that Ibn `Abbas said, "Ka`b bin Asad, Ibn Saluba, `Abdullah bin Surya and Shas bin Qays said to each other, `Let us go to Muhammad to try and misguide him from his religion.' So they went to the Prophet and said, `O Muhammad! You know that we are the scholars, noblemen and chiefs of the Jews. If we follow you, the Jews will follow suit and will not contradict us. But, there is enmity between us and some of our people, so we will refer to you for judgement in this matter, and you should rule in our favor against them and we will believe in you.' The Messenger of Allah refused the offer and Allah sent down these Ayat about them,

(And so judge between them by what Allah has revealed and follow not their vain desires, but beware of them lest they turn you far away from some of that which Allah has sent down to you.) until,

(for a people who have firm faith.)" Ibn Jarir and Ibn Abi Hatim recorded this Hadith. Allah continues,

(Do they then seek the judgement of (the days of) ignorance And who is better in judgement than Allah for a people who have firm faith) Allah criticizes those who ignore Allah's commandments, which include every type of righteous good thing and prohibit every type of evil, but they refer instead to opinions, desires and customs that people themselves invented, all of which have no basis in Allah's religion. During the time of Jahiliyyah, the people used to abide by the misguidance and ignorance that they invented by sheer opinion and lusts. The Tatar (Mongols) abided by the law that they inherited from their king Genghis Khan who wrote Al-Yasiq, for them. This book contains some rulings that were derived from various religions, such as Judaism, Christianity and Islam. Many of these rulings were derived from his own opinion and desires. Later on, these rulings became the followed law among his children, preferring them to the Law of the Book of Allah and the Sunnah of His Messenger . Therefore, whoever does this, he is a disbeliever who deserves to be fought against, until he reverts to Allah's and His Messenger's decisions, so that no law, minor or major, is referred to except by His Law. Allah said,

(Do they then seek the judgement of (the days of) ignorance) meaning, they desire and want this and ignore Allah's judgement,

(And who is better in judgement than Allah for a people who have firm faith) Who is more just in decision than Allah for those who comprehend Allah's Law, believe in Him, who are certain that Allah is the best among those who give decisions and that He is more merciful with His creation than the mother with her own child Allah has perfect knowledge of everything, is able to do all things, and He is just in all matters. Al-Hafiz Abu Al-Qasim At-Tabarani recorded that Ibn `Abbas said that the Messenger of Allah said,

«أَبْغَضُ النَّاسِ إِلَى اللهِ عَزَّ وَجَلَّ، مَنْ يَبْتَغِي فِي الْإِسْلَامِ سُنَّةَ الْجَاهِلِيَّةِ، وَطَالِبُ دَمِ امْرِىءٍ بِغَيْرِ حَقَ لِيُرِيقَ دَمَه»

(The most hated person to Allah is the Muslim who seeks the ways of the days of ignorance and he who seeks to shed the blood of a person without justification.) Al-Bukhari recorded Abu Al-Yaman narrating a similar Hadith, with some addition.

Surah: 5 Ayah: 51, Ayah: 52 & Ayah: 53

﴿ ۞ يَـٰٓأَيُّهَا ٱلَّذِينَ ءَامَنُوا۟ لَا تَتَّخِذُوا۟ ٱلْيَهُودَ وَٱلنَّصَـٰرَىٰٓ أَوْلِيَآءَ ۘ بَعْضُهُمْ أَوْلِيَآءُ بَعْضٍ ۚ وَمَن يَتَوَلَّهُم مِّنكُمْ فَإِنَّهُۥ مِنْهُمْ ۗ إِنَّ ٱللَّهَ لَا يَهْدِى ٱلْقَوْمَ ٱلظَّـٰلِمِينَ ﴿٥١﴾ ﴾

51. O you who believe! Take not the Jews and the Christians as Auliyâ' (friends, protectors, helpers), they are but Auliyâ' of one another. And if any amongst you takes them (as Auliyâ'), then surely he is one of them. Verily, Allâh guides not those people who are the Zâlimûn (polytheists and wrong-doers and unjust).

﴿ فَتَرَى ٱلَّذِينَ فِى قُلُوبِهِم مَّرَضٌ يُسَـٰرِعُونَ فِيهِمْ يَقُولُونَ نَخْشَىٰٓ أَن تُصِيبَنَا دَآئِرَةٌ ۚ فَعَسَى ٱللَّهُ أَن يَأْتِىَ بِٱلْفَتْحِ أَوْ أَمْرٍ مِّنْ عِندِهِۦ فَيُصْبِحُوا۟ عَلَىٰ مَآ أَسَرُّوا۟ فِىٓ أَنفُسِهِمْ نَـٰدِمِينَ ﴿٥٢﴾ ﴾

52. And you see those in whose hearts there is a disease (of hypocrisy), they hurry to their friendship, saying: "We fear lest some misfortune of a disaster may befall us." Perhaps

Allâh may bring a victory or a decision according to His Will. Then they will become regretful for what they have been keeping as a secret in themselves.

﴿ وَيَقُولُ ٱلَّذِينَ ءَامَنُوٓا۟ أَهَٰٓؤُلَآءِ ٱلَّذِينَ أَقْسَمُوا۟ بِٱللَّهِ جَهْدَ أَيْمَٰنِهِمْ ۙ إِنَّهُمْ لَمَعَكُمْ ۚ حَبِطَتْ أَعْمَٰلُهُمْ فَأَصْبَحُوا۟ خَٰسِرِينَ ﴿٥٣﴾ ﴾

53. And those who believe will say: "Are these the men (hypocrites) who swore their strongest oaths by Allâh that they were with you (Muslims)?" All that they did has been in vain (because of their hypocrisy), and they have become the losers.

Transliteration

51. Ya ayyuha allatheena amanoo la tattakhithoo alyahooda waalnnasara awliyaa baAAduhum awliyao baAAdin waman yatawallahum minkum fa-innahu minhum inna Allaha la yahdee alqawma alththalimeena 52. Fatara allatheena fee quloobihim maradun yusariAAoona feehim yaqooloona nakhsha an tuseebana da-iratun faAAasa Allahu an ya/tiya bialfathi aw amrin min AAindihi fayusbihoo AAala ma asarroo fee anfusihim nadimeena 53. Wayaqoolu allatheena amanoo ahaola-i allatheena aqsamoo biAllahi jahda aymanihim innahum lamaAAakum habitat aAAmaluhum faasbahoo khasireena

Tafsir Ibn Kathir

The Prohibition of Taking the Jews, Christians and Enemies of Islam as Friends

Allah forbids His believing servants from having Jews and Christians as friends, because they are the enemies of Islam and its people, may Allah curse them. Allah then states that they are friends of each other and He gives a warning threat to those who do this,

(And if any among you befriends them, then surely he is one of them.) Ibn Abi Hatim recorded that `Umar ordered Abu Musa Al-Ash`ari to send him on one sheet of balance the count of what he took in and what he spent. Abu Musa then had a Christian scribe, and he was able to comply with `Umar's demand. `Umar liked what he saw and exclaimed, "This scribe is proficient. Would you read in the Masjid a letter that came to us from Ash-Sham" Abu Musa said, `He cannot." `Umar said, "Is he not pure" Abu Musa said, "No, but he is Christian." Abu Musa said, "So `Umar admonished me and poked my thigh (with his finger), saying, `Drive him out (from Al-Madinah).' He then recited,

(O you who believe! Take not the Jews and the Christians as friends...)" Then he reported that `Abdullah bin `Utbah said, "Let one of you beware that he might be a Jew or a Christian, while unaware." The narrator of this statement said, "We thought that he was referring to the Ayah,

(O you who believe! Take not the Jews and the Christians as friends,)" Allah said,

(And you see those in whose hearts there is a disease...) A disease of doubt, hesitation and hypocrisy.

(they hurry to their friendship,) meaning, they rush to offer them their friendship and allegiances in secret and in public, (saying: "We fear lest some misfortune of a disaster may befall us.") They thus offer this excuse for their friendship and allegiances to the disbelievers, saying that they fear that the disbelievers might defeat the Muslims, so they want to be in favor with the Jews and Christians, to use this favor for their benefit in that eventuality! Allah replied,

(Perhaps Allah may bring a victory...) referring to the conquering of Makkah, according to As-Suddi.

(or a decision according to His will) requiring the Jews and Christians to pay the Jizyah, as As-Suddi stated,

(Then they will become) meaning, the hypocrites who gave their friendship to the Jews and Christians, will become,

(for what they have been keeping as a secret in themselves) of allegiances,

(regretful,) for their friendship with the Jews and Christians which did not benefit them or protect them from any harm. Rather, it was nothing but harm, as Allah exposed their true reality to His faithful servants in this life, although they tried to conceal it. When the signs that exposed their hypocrisy were compiled against them, their matter became clear to Allah's faithful servants. So the believers were amazed at these hypocrites who pretended to be believers, swearing to their faithfulness, yet their claims were all lies and deceit. This is why Allah said, s

(And those who believe will say, "Are these the men who swore their strongest oaths by Allah that they were with you" All that they did has been in vain, and they have become the losers.)

Surah: 5 Ayah: 54, Ayah: 55 & Ayah: 56

﴿ يَٰٓأَيُّهَا ٱلَّذِينَ ءَامَنُواْ مَن يَرْتَدَّ مِنكُمْ عَن دِينِهِۦ فَسَوْفَ يَأْتِى ٱللَّهُ بِقَوْمٍ يُحِبُّهُمْ وَيُحِبُّونَهُۥٓ
أَذِلَّةٍ عَلَى ٱلْمُؤْمِنِينَ أَعِزَّةٍ عَلَى ٱلْكَٰفِرِينَ يُجَٰهِدُونَ فِى سَبِيلِ ٱللَّهِ وَلَا يَخَافُونَ لَوْمَةَ لَآئِمٍ ۚ
ذَٰلِكَ فَضْلُ ٱللَّهِ يُؤْتِيهِ مَن يَشَآءُ ۚ وَٱللَّهُ وَٰسِعٌ عَلِيمٌ ﴿٥٤﴾ ﴾

54. O you who believe! Whoever from among you turns back from his religion (Islâm), Allâh will bring a people whom He will love and they will love Him; humble towards the believers, stern towards the disbelievers, fighting in the Way of Allâh, and never fear of the blame of the blamers. That is the Grace of Allâh which He bestows on whom He wills. And Allâh is All-Sufficient for His creatures' needs, All-Knower.

﴿ إِنَّمَا وَلِيُّكُمُ ٱللَّهُ وَرَسُولُهُۥ وَٱلَّذِينَ ءَامَنُواْ ٱلَّذِينَ يُقِيمُونَ ٱلصَّلَوٰةَ وَيُؤْتُونَ ٱلزَّكَوٰةَ وَهُمْ
رَٰكِعُونَ ﴿٥٥﴾ ﴾

55. Verily, your Walî (Protector or Helper) is none other than Allâh, His Messenger, and the believers, - those who perform As-Salât (Iqâmat-as-Salât), and give Zakât, and they are Râki'ûn (those who bow down or submit themselves with obedience to Allâh in prayer).

﴿ وَمَن يَتَوَلَّ ٱللَّهَ وَرَسُولَهُۥ وَٱلَّذِينَ ءَامَنُواْ فَإِنَّ حِزْبَ ٱللَّهِ هُمُ ٱلْغَٰلِبُونَ ﴿٥٦﴾ ﴾

56. And whosoever takes Allâh, His Messenger, and those who have believed, as Protectors, then the party of Allâh will be the victorious.

Transliteration

54. Ya ayyuha allatheena amanoo man yartadda minkum AAan deenihi fasawfa ya/tee Allahu biqawmin yuhibbuhum wayuhibboonahu athillatin AAala almu/mineena aAAizzatin AAala alkafireena yujahidoona fee sabeeli Allahi wala yakhafoona lawmata la-imin thalika fadlu Allahi yu/teehi man yashao waAllahu wasiAAun AAaleemun 55. Innama waliyyukumu Allahu warasooluhu waallatheena amanoo allatheena yuqeemoona alssalata wayu/toona alzzakata wahum rakiAAoona 56. Waman yatawalla Allaha warasoolahu waallatheena amanoo fa-inna hizba Allahi humu alghaliboona

Tafsir Ibn Kathir

Threatening to Replace the Believers With Another People if They Revert from Islam

Allah emphasizes His mighty ability and states that whoever reverts from supporting His religion and establishing His Law, then Allah will replace them with whomever is better, mightier and more righteous in Allah's religion and Law. Allah said in other Ayat,

(And if you turn away, He will exchange you for some other people and they will not be your likes.) and,

(Do you not see that Allah has created the heavens and the earth with truth If He will, He can remove you and bring (in your place) a new creation! And for Allah that is not hard or difficult.)(14:19-20). Verily this is not difficult or hard on Allah. Allah said here,

(O you who believe! Whoever from among you turns back from his religion...) and turns back from the truth to falsehood, from now until the commencement of the Last Hour. Allah said next,

(humble towards the believers, stern towards the disbelievers.) These are the qualities of perfect believers, as they are humble with their believing brothers and allies, stern with their enemies and adversaries. In another Ayah, Allah said,

(Muhammad is the Messenger of Allah. And those who are with him are severe against disbelievers, and merciful among themselves.) The Prophet is described as the smiling fighter, smiling to his allies and fighting his enemies. Allah's statement,

(Fighting in the way of Allah, and never fearing the blame of the blamers.) Nothing prevents them from obeying Allah, establishing His Law, fighting His enemies, enjoining righteousness and forbidding evil. Certainly, nothing prevents them from taking this path, neither someone who seeks to hinder them, nor one who blames or chastises them. Imam Ahmad recorded that Abu Dharr said, "My Khalil (intimate friend, the Messenger) has commanded me to do seven deeds. He commanded me to love the poor and to be close to them. He commanded me to look at those who are less than me and not those who are above me. He commanded me to keep the relations of the womb, even if they cut it. He commanded me not to ask anyone for anything, to say the truth even if it was bitter, and to not fear the blame of anyone for the sake of Allah. He commanded me to often repeat, `La hawla wa la quwwata illa billah (There is no strength or power except from Allah)', for these words are from a treasure under the Throne (of Allah)." It is confirmed in the Sahih;

«مَا يَنْبَغِي لِلْمُؤْمِنِ أَنْ يُذِلَّ نَفْسَه»

(The believer is not required to humiliate himself.) He was asked; "How does one humiliate himself, O Messenger of Allah" So he replied;

«يَتَحَمَّلُ مِنَ الْبَلَاءِ مَا لَا يُطِيق»

(He takes on tests that he cannot bear.)

(That is the grace of Allah which He bestows on whom He wills.) meaning, those who have these qualities, acquired it by Allah's bounty and favor and because He granted them these qualities.

(And Allah is All-Sufficient for His creatures' needs, All-Knower,) His favor is ever extending, and He has perfect knowledge of those who deserve or do not deserve His favor and bounty. Allah's statement,

(Verily, your Protector is Allah, His Messenger, and the believers...) means, the Jews are not your friends. Rather, your allegiance is to Allah, His Messenger and the faithful believers.

(those who perform the Salah, and give the Zakah...) referring to the believers who have these qualities and establish the prayer, which is one of the most important pillars of Islam, for it includes worshipping Allah alone without partners. They pay Zakah, which is the right of the creation and a type of help extended to the needy and the poor. As for Allah's statement,

(and they bow down,) some people thought that they give the Zakah while bowing down. If this were the case, then paying the Zakah while bowing would be the best form of giving Zakah. No scholar from whom religious rulings are taken says this, as much as we know. Therefore,

(and they bow down,) means, they attend the prayer in congregation in Allah's Masjids and spend by way of charity on the various needs of Muslims. Allah said;

(And whosoever takes Allah, His Messenger, and those who have believed, as protectors, then the party of Allah will be the victorious.) similarly Allah said;

(Allah has decreed: "Verily, it is I and My Messengers who shall be the victorious." Verily, Allah is All-Powerful, Almighty. You will not find any people who believe in Allah and the Last Day, making friendship with those who oppose Allah and His Messenger, even though they were their fathers or their sons or their brothers or their kindred (people). For such He has written faith in their hearts, and strengthened them with a Ruh (proof) from Himself. And He will admit them to Gardens (Paradise) under which rivers flow to dwell therein (forever). Allah is pleased with them, and they with Him. They are the party of Allah. Verily, it is the party of Allah that will be the successful.) Therefore, those who accept the allegiance of Allah - His Messenger and the faithful believers - will gain success in this life and the Hereafter. Hence Allah's statement here,

(And whosoever takes Allah, His Messenger, and those who have believed, as protectors, then the party of Allah will be the victorious.)

Surah: 5 Ayah: 57 & Ayah: 58

﴿ يَـٰٓأَيُّهَا ٱلَّذِينَ ءَامَنُوا۟ لَا تَتَّخِذُوا۟ ٱلَّذِينَ ٱتَّخَذُوا۟ دِينَكُمْ هُزُوًا وَلَعِبًا مِّنَ ٱلَّذِينَ أُوتُوا۟
ٱلْكِتَـٰبَ مِن قَبْلِكُمْ وَٱلْكُفَّارَ أَوْلِيَآءَ ۚ وَٱتَّقُوا۟ ٱللَّهَ إِن كُنتُم مُّؤْمِنِينَ ﴿٥٧﴾ ﴾

57. O you who believe! Take not as Auliyâ' (protectors and helpers) those who take your religion as a mockery and fun from among those who received the Scripture (Jews and Christians) before you, and nor from among the disbelievers; and fear Allâh if you indeed are true believers.

﴿ وَإِذَا نَادَيْتُمْ إِلَى ٱلصَّلَوٰةِ ٱتَّخَذُوهَا هُزُوًا وَلَعِبًا ۚ ذَٰلِكَ بِأَنَّهُمْ قَوْمٌ لَّا يَعْقِلُونَ ﴿٥٨﴾ ﴾

58. And when you proclaim the call for As-Salât (call for the prayer (Adhân)) they take it (but) as a mockery and fun; that is because they are a people who understand not.

Transliteration

57. Ya ayyuha allatheena amanoo la tattakhithoo allatheena ittakhathoo deenakum huzuwan walaAAiban mina allatheena ootoo alkitaba min qablikum waalkuffara awliyaa waittaqoo Allaha in kuntum mu/mineena 58. Wa-itha nadaytum ila alssalati ittakhathooha huzuwan walaAAiban thalika bi-annahum qawmun la yaAAqiloona

Tafsir Ibn Kathir

The Prohibition of Being Loyal Friends with Disbelievers

This Ayah discourages and forbids taking the enemies of Islam and its people, such as the People of the Book and the polytheists, as friends. These disbelievers mock the most important acts that any person could ever perform, the honorable, pure acts of Islam which include all types of good for this life and the Hereafter. They mock such acts and make them the subject of jest and play, because this is what these acts represent in their misguided minds and cold hearts. Allah said;

(from those who received the Scriptures before you and (nor) the disbelievers...) This is to clarify the particular category (of disbelievers). As Allah said,

(So shun the evil of the idols...) (22:30) So some recited it "Kuffari", making it an object of the preposition, and others recited it "Kuffara", making it a predicate noun;

(Take not as friends those who take your religion for a mockery and fun from those who received the Scriptures before you...) with the meaning of "nor",

(nor the disbelievers as friends) That is, do not take these people nor those people as friends. The meaning here of "Kuffar" (disbelievers) is idolators. Similarly, Ibn Jarir recorded that in the recitation of Ibn Mas`ud (in place of "Kuffar" he recited it: "and those who commit Shirk. Allah's statement,

(And have Taqwa of Allah if you indeed are true believers.) means, fear Allah and do not take the enemies of you and your religion as friends, if you believe in Allah's Law and religion that these people mocked and jested about. Allah said in another Ayah,

(Let not the believers take the disbelievers as friends instead of the believers, and whoever does that, will never be helped by Allah in any way, except if you indeed fear a danger from them. And Allah warns you against Himself, and to Allah is the final return.)

The Disbelievers Mock the Prayer and the Adhan

Allah said,

(And when you proclaim the call for the Salah, they take it (but) as a mockery and fun;) When you proclaim the Adhan for the prayer, which is the best action there is, for those who have sound minds and good comprehension,

(they take it...) also,

(as a mockery and fun; that is because they are a people who understand not.) the acts of worship and Allah's Law. These are the characteristics of the followers of Shaytan who,

«إِذَا سَمِعَ الْأَذَانَ أَدْبَرَ وَلَهُ حُصَاصٌ، أَيْ ضُرَاطٌ، حَتَّى لَا يَسْمَعَ التَّأْذِينَ فَإِذَا قُضِيَ التَّأْذِينُ، أَقْبَلَ فَإِذَا ثُوِّبَ لِلصَّلَاةِ أَدْبَرَ، فَإِذَا قُضِيَ التَّثْوِيبُ أَقْبَلَ حَتَّى يَخْطُرَ بَيْنَ الْمَرْءِ وَقَلْبِهِ، فَيَقُولُ: اذْكُرْ كَذَا اذْكُرْ كَذَا، لِمَا لَمْ يَكُنْ يَذْكُرُ حَتَّى يَظَلَّ الرَّجُلُ لَا يَدْرِي كَمْ صَلَّى، فَإِذَا وَجَدَ أَحَدُكُمْ ذلِكَ، فَلْيَسْجُدْ سَجْدَتَيْنِ قَبْلَ السَّلَامِ»

(When the call for prayer is made, Shaytan takes to his heels passing wind so that he may not hear the Adhan. When the call is finished he comes back, and when the Iqamah is pronounced, Shaytan again takes to his heels. When the Iqamah is finished he comes back again and tries to interfere with the person and his thoughts and to say, `Remember this and that,' which he has not thought of before the prayer, until the praying person forgets how much he has prayed. If anyone of you does not remember, then he should perform two prostrations before pronouncing the Salam.) This Hadith is agreed upon. Az-Zuhri said, "Allah mentioned the Adhan in His Book,

(And when you proclaim the call for the Salah, they take it (but) as a mockery and fun; that is because they are a people who understand not.)" Ibn Abi Hatim recorded this statement.

Surah: 5 Ayah: 59, Ayah: 60, Ayah: 61, Ayah: 62 & Ayah: 63

﴿قُلْ يَٰٓأَهْلَ ٱلْكِتَٰبِ هَلْ تَنقِمُونَ مِنَّآ إِلَّآ أَنْ ءَامَنَّا بِٱللَّهِ وَمَآ أُنزِلَ إِلَيْنَا وَمَآ أُنزِلَ مِن قَبْلُ
وَأَنَّ أَكْثَرَكُمْ فَٰسِقُونَ ٥٩﴾

59. Say: "O people of the Scripture (Jews and Christians)! Do you criticize us for no other reason than that we believe in Allâh, and in (the revelation) which has been sent down to

us and in that which has been sent down before (us), and that most of you are Fâsiqûn (rebellious and disobedient (to Allâh))"

﴿ قُلْ هَلْ أُنَبِّئُكُم بِشَرٍّ مِّن ذَٰلِكَ مَثُوبَةً عِندَ ٱللَّهِ ۚ مَن لَّعَنَهُ ٱللَّهُ وَغَضِبَ عَلَيْهِ
وَجَعَلَ مِنْهُمُ ٱلْقِرَدَةَ وَٱلْخَنَازِيرَ وَعَبَدَ ٱلطَّٰغُوتَ ۚ أُو۟لَٰٓئِكَ شَرٌّ مَّكَانًا وَأَضَلُّ عَن
سَوَآءِ ٱلسَّبِيلِ ﴿٦٠﴾ ﴾

60. Say (O Muhammad (peace be upon him) to the people of the Scripture): "Shall I inform you of something worse than that, regarding the recompense from Allâh: those (Jews) who incurred the Curse of Allâh and His Wrath, and those of whom (some) He transformed into monkeys and swines, and those who worshipped Tâghût (false deities); such are worse in rank (on the Day of Resurrection in the Hell-fire), and far more astray from the Right Path (in the life of this world)."

﴿ وَإِذَا جَآءُوكُمْ قَالُوٓا۟ ءَامَنَّا وَقَد دَّخَلُوا۟ بِٱلْكُفْرِ وَهُمْ قَدْ خَرَجُوا۟ بِهِۦ ۚ وَٱللَّهُ أَعْلَمُ بِمَا كَانُوا۟
يَكْتُمُونَ ﴿٦١﴾ ﴾

61. When they come to you, they say: "We believe." But in fact they enter with (an intention of) disbelief and they go out with the same. And Allâh knows all what they were hiding.

﴿ وَتَرَىٰ كَثِيرًا مِّنْهُمْ يُسَٰرِعُونَ فِى ٱلْإِثْمِ وَٱلْعُدْوَٰنِ وَأَكْلِهِمُ ٱلسُّحْتَ ۚ لَبِئْسَ مَا كَانُوا۟
يَعْمَلُونَ ﴿٦٢﴾ ﴾

62. And you see many of them (Jews) hurrying for sin and transgression, and eating illegal things

﴿ لَوْلَا يَنْهَىٰهُمُ ٱلرَّبَّٰنِيُّونَ وَٱلْأَحْبَارُ عَن قَوْلِهِمُ ٱلْإِثْمَ وَأَكْلِهِمُ ٱلسُّحْتَ ۚ لَبِئْسَ مَا
كَانُوا۟ يَصْنَعُونَ ﴿٦٣﴾ ﴾

63. Why do not the rabbis and the religious learned men forbid them from uttering sinful words and from eating illegal things. Evil indeed is that which they have been performing.

Transliteration

59. Qul ya ahla alkitabi hal tanqimoona minna illa an amanna biAllahi wama onzila ilayna wama onzila min qablu waanna aktharakum fasiqoona
60. Qul hal onabbi-okum bisharrin min thalika mathoobatan AAinda Allahi man laAAanahu Allahu waghadiba AAalayhi wajaAAala minhumu alqiradata waalkhanazeera waAAabada alttaghooti ola-ika sharrun makanan waadallu AAan sawa-i alssabeeli
61. Wa-itha jaookum qaloo amanna waqad dakhaloo bialkufri wahum qad kharajoo bihi waAllahu aAAlamu bima kanoo yaktumoona
62. Watara katheeran minhum yusariAAoona fee al-ithmi waalAAudwani waaklihimu alssuhta labi/sa ma kanoo yaAAmaloona
63. Lawla yanhahumu alrrabbaniyyoona waal-ahbaru AAan qawlihimu al-ithma waaklihimu alssuhta labi/sa ma kanoo yasnaAAoona

Tafsir Ibn Kathir

The People of the Book are Enraged at the Believers Because of their Faith in Allah

Allah commands: Say, O Muhammad, to those who mock and jest about your religion from among the People of the Scriptures,

(Do you criticize us for no other reason than that we believe in Allah, and in what has been sent down to us and in that which has been sent down before (us)) Do you have any criticism or cause of blame for us, other than this This, by no means, is cause of blame or criticism. Allah said in other Ayat,

(And they had no fault except that they believed in Allah, the Almighty, Worthy of all praise!) and,

(and they could not find any cause to do so except that Allah and His Messenger had enriched them of His bounty.)(9:74) In an agreed upon Hadith, the Prophet said,

«مَا يَنْقِمُ ابْنُ جَمِيلٍ إِلَّا أَنْ كَانَ فَقِيرًا فَأَغْنَاهُ اللهُ»

(What caused Ibn Jamil to Yanqim (refuse to give Zakah), although he was poor and Allah made him rich) Allah's statement,

(and that most of you are rebellious. ..) is connected to

(that we believe in Allah, and in that which has been sent down to us and in that which has been sent down before (us).) Therefore, the meaning of this part of the Ayah is: we also believe that most of you are rebellious and deviated from the straight path.

The People of the Scriptures Deserve the Worst Torment on the Day of Resurrection

Allah said next,

(Say: "Shall I inform you of something worse than that, regarding the recompense from Allah") The Ayah commands the Prophet to say: Shall I inform you about a worse people with Allah on the Day of Resurrection than what you think of us They are you, with these characteristics,

(those who incurred the curse of Allah) were expelled from His mercy,

(and who incurred His wrath) and anger, after which He will never be pleased with them,

(those of whom He transformed into monkeys and swine,) as we mentioned in Surat Al-Baqarah (2) and as we will mention in Surat Al-A`raf (7). Sufyan Ath-Thawri narrated that Ibn Mas`ud said, "Allah's Messenger was asked if the current monkeys and swine were those whom Allah transformed. He said,

«إِنَّ اللهَ لَمْ يُهْلِكْ قَوْمًا، أَوْ لَمْ يَمْسَخْ قَوْمًا فَيَجْعَلَ لَهُمْ نَسْلًا وَلَا عَقِبًا، وَإِنَّ الْقِرَدَةَ وَالْخَنَازِيرَ كَانَتْ قَبْلَ ذٰلِكَ»

(Allah never destroyed a people by transforming them and making offspring or descendants for them. The monkeys and swine existed before that.)" This was also recorded by Muslim. Allah said,

(Those who worshipped Taghut...) and served them, becoming their servants. The meaning of this Ayah is: you, O People of the Scriptures, who mock our religion, which consists of Allah's Tawhid, and singling Him out in worship without others, how can you mock us while these are your characteristics This is why Allah said,

(such are worse in rank...) than what you -- People of the Scriptures -- think of us Muslims,

(and far more astray from the straight path.) `More' in the Ayah does not mean that the other party is `less' astray, but it means that the People of the Scriptures are far astray. In another Ayah, Allah said,

(The dwellers of Paradise will, on that Day, have the best abode, and have the fairest of places for repose.)

The Hypocrites Pretend to be Believers but Hide their Kufr

Allah said,

(When they come to you, they say, "We believe." But in fact they enter with (an intention of) disbelief and they go out with the same.) This is the description of the hypocrites, for they pretend to be believers while their hearts hide Kufr. So Allah said;

(But in fact they enter) on you, O Muhammad,

(with disbelief) in their hearts and they depart with Kufr, and this is why they do not benefit from the knowledge they hear from you, nor does the advice and reminder move them. So,

(and they go out with the same) meaning, they alone,

(and Allah knows all that they were hiding.) Allah knows their secrets and what their hearts conceal, even if they pretend otherwise with His creatures, thus pretending to be what they are not. Allah, Who has perfect knowledge of the seen and unseen, has more knowledge about the hypocrites than any of His creatures do and He will recompense them accordingly. Allah's statement,

(And you see many of them (Jews) hurrying for sin and transgression, and eating illegal things.) They hurry to devour prohibited and illegal things, all the while transgressing against people, unjustly consuming their property through bribes and Riba,

(Evil indeed is that which they have been doing.) Indeed, horrible is that which they used to do and the transgression that they committed.

Criticizing Rabbis and Learned Religious Men for Giving up on Forbidding Evil

Allah said,

(Why do not the Rabbaniyyun and the Ahbar forbid them from uttering sinful words and from eating illegal things. Evil indeed is that which they have been performing.) meaning why don't the Rabbaniyyun and the Ahbar forbid them from this evil The Rabbaniyyun are the scholars who are in positions of authority, while the Ahbar are the regular scholars.

(Evil indeed is that which they have been performing.) referring to the Rabbaniyyun, as `Ali bin Abi Talhah reported from Ibn `Abbas, because they abandoned forbidding evil. Ibn Jarir recorded that Ibn `Abbas said, "There is no Ayah in the Qur'an that has more severe admonition than this Ayah, (Why do not the Rabbaniyyun and the Ahbar forbid them from uttering sinful words and from eating illegal things. Evil indeed is that which they have been performing.)" Ibn Abi Hatim recorded that Yahya bin Ya`mar said, " `Ali bin Abi Talib once gave a speech, which he started by praising Allah and thanking Him. He then said, `O people! Those who were before you were destroyed because they committed sins and the Rabbaniyyun and Ahbar did not forbid them from evil. When they persisted in sin, they were overcome by punishment. Therefore, enjoin righteousness and forbid evil before what they suffered also strikes you. Know that enjoining righteousness and forbidding evil does not reduce the provision or shorten the term of life." Imam Ahmad recorded that Jarir said that the Messenger of Allah said,

«مَا مِنْ قَوْمٍ يَكُونُ بَيْنَ أَظْهُرِهِمْ مَنْ يَعْمَلُ بِالْمَعَاصِي هُمْ أَعَزُّ مِنْهُ وَأَمْنَعُ، وَلَمْ يُغَيِّرُوا إِلَّا أَصَابَهُمُ اللهُ مِنْهُ بِعَذَاب»

(There is no people among whom there are those who commit sins, while the rest are more powerful and mightier than the sinners, yet they do not stop them, but Allah will send a punishment upon them.) Ahmad was alone with this wording. Abu Dawud recorded it, but in his narration Jarir said, "I heard the Messenger of Allah saying,

«مَا مِنْ رَجُلٍ يَكُونُ فِي قَوْمٍ يُعْمَلُ فِيهِمْ بِالْمَعَاصِي، يَقْدِرُونَ أَنْ يُغَيِّرُوا عَلَيْهِ، فَلَا يُغَيِّرُوا إِلَّا أَصَابَهُمُ اللهُ بِعِقَابٍ قَبْلَ أَنْ يَمُوتُوا»

(There is no one who resides among people commiting evil among them, and they do not stop him though they are able to do so, but Allah will punish them (all) before they die.)" Ibn Majah also recorded this Hadith.

Surah: 5 Ayah: 64, Ayah: 65 & Ayah: 66

﴿ وَقَالَتِ ٱلْيَهُودُ يَدُ ٱللَّهِ مَغْلُولَةٌ ۚ غُلَّتْ أَيْدِيهِمْ وَلُعِنُوا۟ بِمَا قَالُوا۟ ۘ بَلْ يَدَاهُ مَبْسُوطَتَانِ يُنفِقُ كَيْفَ يَشَآءُ ۚ وَلَيَزِيدَنَّ كَثِيرًا مِّنْهُم مَّآ أُنزِلَ إِلَيْكَ مِن رَّبِّكَ طُغْيَـٰنًا وَكُفْرًا ۚ وَأَلْقَيْنَا بَيْنَهُمُ

ٱلْعَدَٰوَةَ وَٱلْبَغْضَآءَ إِلَىٰ يَوْمِ ٱلْقِيَٰمَةِ ۚ كُلَّمَآ أَوْقَدُوا۟ نَارًا لِّلْحَرْبِ أَطْفَأَهَا ٱللَّهُ ۚ وَيَسْعَوْنَ فِى
ٱلْأَرْضِ فَسَادًا ۚ وَٱللَّهُ لَا يُحِبُّ ٱلْمُفْسِدِينَ ﴿٦٤﴾

64. The Jews say: "Allâh's Hand is tied up (i.e. He does not give and spend of His Bounty)." Be their hands tied up and be they accursed for what they uttered. Nay, both His Hands are widely outstretched. He spends (of His Bounty) as He wills. Verily, the Revelation that has come to you from your Lord (Allâh) increases in most of them (their) obstinate rebellion and disbelief. We have put enmity and hatred amongst them till the Day of Resurrection. Every time they kindled the fire of war, Allâh extinguished it; and they (ever) strive to make mischief on the earth. And Allâh does not like the Mufsidûn (mischief-makers).

﴿ وَلَوْ أَنَّ أَهْلَ ٱلْكِتَٰبِ ءَامَنُوا۟ وَٱتَّقَوْا۟ لَكَفَّرْنَا عَنْهُمْ سَيِّـَٔاتِهِمْ وَلَأَدْخَلْنَٰهُمْ جَنَّٰتِ
ٱلنَّعِيمِ ﴿٦٥﴾

65. And if only the people of the Scripture (Jews and Christians) had believed (in Muhammad (peace be upon him)) and warded off evil (sin, ascribing partners to Allâh) and had become Al-Muttaqûn (the pious - see V.2:2) We would indeed have expiated from them their sins and admitted them to Gardens of pleasure (in Paradise).

﴿ وَلَوْ أَنَّهُمْ أَقَامُوا۟ ٱلتَّوْرَىٰةَ وَٱلْإِنجِيلَ وَمَآ أُنزِلَ إِلَيْهِم مِّن رَّبِّهِمْ لَأَكَلُوا۟ مِن فَوْقِهِمْ وَمِن
تَحْتِ أَرْجُلِهِم ۚ مِّنْهُمْ أُمَّةٌ مُّقْتَصِدَةٌ ۖ وَكَثِيرٌ مِّنْهُمْ سَآءَ مَا يَعْمَلُونَ ﴿٦٦﴾

66. And if only they had acted according to the Taurât (Torah), the Injeel (Gospel), and what has (now) been sent down to them from their Lord (the Qur'ân), they would surely have gotten provision from above them and from underneath their feet. There are from among them people who are on the right course (i.e. they act on the revelation and believe in Prophet Muhammad (peace be upon him) like 'Abdullâh bin Salâm (may Allah be pleased with him)) but many of them do evil deeds.

Transliteration

64. Waqalati alyahoodu yadu Allahi maghloolatun ghullat aydeehim waluAAinoo bima qaloo bal yadahu mabsootatani yunfiqu kayfa yashao walayazeedanna katheeran minhum ma onzila ilayka min rabbika tughyanan wakufran waalqayna baynahumu alAAadawata waalbaghdaa ila yawmi alqiyamati kullama awqadoo naran lilharbi atfaaha Allahu wayasAAawna fee al-ardi fasadan waAllahu la yuhibbu almufsideena 65. Walaw anna ahla alkitabi amanoo waittaqaw lakaffarna AAanhum sayyi-atihim walaadkhalnahum jannati alnnaAAeemi 66. Walaw annahum aqamoo alttawrata waal-injeela wama onzila ilayhim min rabbihim laakaloo min fawqihim wamin tahti arjulihim minhum ommatun muqtasidatun wakatheerun minhum saa ma yaAAmaloona

Tafsir Ibn Kathir

The Jews Say That Allah's Hand is Tied up!

Allah states that the Jews, may Allah's continuous curses descend on them until the Day of Resurrection, describe Him as a miser. Allah is far holier than what they attribute to Him. The

Jews also claim that Allah is poor, while they are rich. `Ali bin Abi Talhah reported that Ibn `Abbas commented on Allah's statement,

(The Jews say, "Allah's Hand is tied up.") "They do not mean that Allah's Hand is literally tied up. Rather, they mean that He is a miser and does not spend from what He has. Allah is far holier than what they attribute to Him." Similar was reported from Mujahid, `Ikrimah, Qatadah, As-Suddi and Ad-Dahhak. Allah said in another Ayah,

(And let not your hand be tied (like a miser) to your neck, nor stretch it forth to its utmost reach (like a spendthrift), so that you become blameworthy and in severe poverty.) In this Ayah, Allah prohibits stinginess and extravagance, which includes unnecessary and improper expenditures. Allah describes stinginess by saying,

(And let not your hand be tied (like a miser) to your neck.) Therefore, this is the meaning that the Jews meant, may Allah's curses be on them. `Ikrimah said that this Ayah was revealed about Finhas, one of the Jews, may Allah curse him. We mentioned before that Finhas said,

("Truly, Allah is poor and we are rich!") and that Abu Bakr smacked him. Allah has refuted what the Jews attribute to Him and cursed them in retaliation for their lies and fabrications about Him. Allah said,

(Be their hands tied up and be they accursed for what they uttered.) What Allah said occurred, for the Jews are indeed miserly, envious, cowards and tremendously humiliated. Allah said in other Ayat,

(Or have they a share in the dominion Then in that case they would not give mankind even a Naqir. Or do they envy men for what Allah has given them of His bounty Then, We had already given the family of Ibrahim the Book and the Hikmah, and conferred upon them a great kingdom.) and, n

(Indignity is put over them.)

Allah's Hands are Widely Outstretched

Allah said next,

(Nay, both His Hands are widely outstretched. He spends (of His bounty) as He wills.) Allah's favors are ample, His bounty unlimited, as He owns the treasures of everything. Any good that reaches His servants is from Him alone, without partners. He has created everything that we need by night or by day, while traveling or at home and in all situations and conditions. Allah said,

(And He gave you of all that you asked for, and if you count the blessings of Allah, never will you be able to count them. Verily, man is indeed an extreme wrongdoer, an extreme ingrate.) There are many other Ayat on this subject. Imam Ahmad bin Hanbal said that `Abdur-Razzaq narrated to him that Ma`mar said that Hammam bin Munabbih said, "This is what Abu Hurayrah narrated to us that the Messenger of Allah said,

«إِنَّ يَمِينَ اللهِ مَلْأَى، لَا يَغِيضُهَا نَفَقَةٌ، سَحَّاءُ اللَّيْلَ وَالنَّهَارَ، أَرَأَيْتُمْ مَا أَنْفَقَ مُنْذُ خَلَقَ السَّموَاتِ وَالْأَرْضَ، فَإِنَّهُ لَمْ يَغِضْ مَا فِي يَمِينِهِ قال : وَعَرْشُهُ عَلَى الْمَاءِ، وَفِي يَدِهِ الْأُخْرَى الْقَبْضُ يَرْفَعُ وَيَخْفِضُ»

(Allah's Right Hand is perfectly full, and no amount of spending can decrease what He has, even though He spends by night and by day. Do you see how much Allah has spent since He created the heavens and earth Yet surely it has not decreased what He has in His Right Hand. His Throne is over the water and in His Other Hand is the hold by which He raises and lowers.) He also said,

«أَنْفِقْ، أُنْفِقْ عَلَيْكَ»

(Allah said, `Spend and I will spend on you.')" This Hadith was recorded in the Two Sahihs.

The Revelation to the Muslims only Adds to the Transgression and Disbelief of the Jews

Allah said,

(Verily, the revelation that has come to you from your Lord makes many of them increase in rebellion and disbelief.) meaning, the bounty that comes to you, O Muhammad, is a calamity for your enemies, the Jews and their kind. The more the revelation increases the believers in faith, good works, and beneficial knowledge, the more the disbelievers increase in envy for you and your Ummah, the more they increase in Tughyan -- which is to exceed the ordained limits for things -- and in disbelief -- meaning denial of you. Allah said in other Ayat,

(Say: "It is for those who believe, a guide and a healing. And as for those who disbelieve, there is heaviness (deafness) in their ears, and it is blindness for them. They are those who are called from a place far away.") and,

(And We send down of the Qur'an that which is a healing and a mercy to those who believe, and it increases wrongdoers in nothing but loss.) Allah said next,

(We have put enmity and hatred among them till the Day of Resurrection.) Therefore, their hearts are never united. Rather, their various groups and sects will always have enmity and hatred for each other, because they do not agree on the truth, and because they opposed you and denied you. Allah's statement,

(Every time they kindled the fire of war, Allah extinguished it;) means, every time they try to plot against you and kindled the fire of war, Allah extinguishes it and makes their plots turn against them. Therefore, their evil plots will return to harm them.

(and they (ever) strive to make mischief on earth. And Allah does not like the mischief-makers.) It is their habit to always strive to cause mischief on the earth, and Allah does not like those with such behavior.

Had the People of the Book Adhered to their Book, they Would Have Acquired the Good of this Life and the Hereafter

Allah said next,

(And if only the People of the Scripture had believed and had Taqwa...) Consequently, had the People of the Book believed in Allah and His Messenger and avoided the sins and prohibitions that they committed;

(We would indeed have expiated for them their sins and admitted them to Gardens of pleasure (in Paradise).) meaning We would have removed the dangers from them and granted them their objectives.

(And if only they had acted according to the Tawrah, the Injil, and what has (now) been sent down to them from their Lord,) meaning, the Qur'an, as Ibn `Abbas and others said.

(they would surely have gotten provision from above them and from underneath their feet.) Had they adhered to the Books that they have with them which they inherited from the Prophets, without altering or changing these Books, these would have directed them to follow the truth and implement the revelation that Allah sent Muhammad with. These Books testify to the Prophet's truth and command that he must be followed. Allah's statement,

(they would surely have gotten provision from above them and from underneath their feet.) refers to the tremendous provision that would have descended to them from the sky and grown for them on the earth. Allah said in another Ayah,

(And if the people of the towns had believed and had Taqwa, certainly, We should have opened for them blessings from the heaven and the earth.) Allah's statement,

(And among them is a Muqtasid Ummah, but for most of them; evil is their work.) is similar to Allah's statement,

(And of the people of Musa there is a community who lead (the men) with truth and establish justice therewith.)(7:159) and His statement about the followers of `Isa, peace be upon him,

(So We gave those among them who believed, their (due) reward.) Therefore, Allah gave them the highest grade of Iqtisad, which is the middle course, given to this Ummah. Above them there is the grade of Sabiqun, as Allah described in His statement;

(Then We gave the Book as inheritance to such of Our servants whom We chose. Then of them are some who wrong themselves, and of them are some who follow a middle course, and of them are some who, by Allah's permission, are Sabiq (foremost) in good deeds. That itself is indeed a great grace. `Adn (Eden) Paradise (everlasting Gardens) will they enter, therein will they be adorned with bracelets of gold and pearls, and their garments there will be of silk.)(35:32-33)

Surah: 5 Ayah: 67

﴿ ۞ يَـٰٓأَيُّهَا ٱلرَّسُولُ بَلِّغْ مَآ أُنزِلَ إِلَيْكَ مِن رَّبِّكَ ۖ وَإِن لَّمْ تَفْعَلْ فَمَا بَلَّغْتَ رِسَالَتَهُۥ ۚ وَٱللَّهُ
يَعْصِمُكَ مِنَ ٱلنَّاسِ ۗ إِنَّ ٱللَّهَ لَا يَهْدِى ٱلْقَوْمَ ٱلْكَـٰفِرِينَ ﴿٦٧﴾ ﴾

67. O Messenger (Muhammad (peace be upon him))! Proclaim (the Message) which has been sent down to you from your Lord. And if you do not, then you have not conveyed His Message. Allâh will protect you from mankind. Verily, Allâh guides not the people who disbelieve.

Transliteration

67. Ya ayyuha alrrasoolu balligh ma onzila ilayka min rabbika wa-in lam tafAAal fama ballaghta risalatahu waAllahu yaAAsimuka mina alnnasi inna Allaha la yahdee alqawma alkafireena

Tafsir Ibn Kathir

Commanding the Prophet to Convey the Message; Promising Him Immunity and Protection

Allah addresses His servant and Messenger Muhammad by the title `Messenger' and commands him to convey all that He has sent him, a command that the Prophet has fulfilled in the best manner. Al-Bukhari recorded that `A'ishah said, "Whoever says to you that Muhammad hid any part of what Allah revealed to him, then he is uttering a lie. Allah said,

(O Messenger! Convey what has been sent down to you from your Lord.)" Al-Bukhari collected the short form of this story here, but mentioned the full narration in another part of his book. Muslim in the Book of Iman, At-Tirmidhi, and An-Nasa'i in the Book of Tafsir of their Sunans also collected this Hadith. In is recorded in the Two Sahihs that `A'ishah said, "If Muhammad hid anything from the Qur'an, he would have hidden this Ayah,

(But you did hide in yourself that which Allah will make manifest, you did fear the people while Allah had a better right that you should fear Him.)" Al-Bukhari recorded that Az-Zuhri said, "From Allah comes the Message, for the Messenger is its deliverance and for us is submission to it." The Ummah of Muhammad has testified that he has delivered the Message and fulfilled the trust, when he asked them during the biggest gathering in his speech during the Farewell Hajj. At that time, there were over forty thousand of his Companions. Muslim recorded that Jabir bin `Abdullah said that the Messenger of Allah said in his speech on that day,

«أَيُّهَا النَّاسُ إِنَّكُمْ مَسْؤُولُونَ عَنِّي، فَمَا أَنْتُمْ قَائِلُونَ؟»

(O people! You shall be asked about me, so what are you going to reply) They said, "We bear witness that you have conveyed (the Message), fulfilled (the trust) and offered sincere advice." The Prophet kept raising his finger towards the sky and then pointing at them, saying,

«اللَّهُمَّ هَلْ بَلَّغْتُ؟ اللَّهُمَّ هَلْ بَلَّغْتُ؟»

(O Allah! Did I convey O Allah! Did I convey) Allah's statement,

(And if you do not, then you have not conveyed His Message.) meaning: If you do not convey to the people what I sent to you, then you have not conveyed My Message. Meaning, the Prophet knows the consequences of this failure. `Ali bin Abi Talhah reported that Ibn `Abbas commented on the Ayah,

(And if you do not, then you have not conveyed His Message.) "It means, if you hide only one Ayah that was revealed to you from your Lord, then you have not conveyed His Message." Allah's statement,

(Allah will protect you from mankind.) means, you convey My Message and I will protect, aid and support you over your enemies and will grant you victory over them. Therefore, do not have any fear or sadness, for none of them will be able to touch you with harm. Before this Ayah was revealed, the Prophet was being guarded, as Imam Ahmad recorded that `A'ishah said that the Prophet was vigilant one night when she was next to him; she asked him, "What is the matter, O Allah's Messenger" He said,

«لَيْتَ رَجُلًا صَالِحًا مِنْ أَصْحَابِي يَحْرُسُنِي اللَّيْلَة»

(Would that a pious man from my companions guard me tonight!) She said, "Suddenly we heard the clatter of arms. The Prophet said,

«مَنْ هَذَا؟»

(Who is that".) He (the new comer) replied, "I am Sa`d bin Malik (Sa`d bin Abi Waqqas)." The Prophet asked,

«مَا جَاءَ بِكَ؟»

(What brought you here) He said, "I have come to guard you, O Allah's Messenger." `A'ishah said, "So, the Prophet slept (that night) and I heard the noise of sleep coming from him.)" This Hadith is recorded in Two Sahihs. Another narration for this Hadith reads, "The Messenger of Allah was vigilant one night, after he came to Al-Madinah...", meaning, after the Hijrah and after the Prophet consummated his marriage to `A'ishah in the second year of Hijrah. Ibn Abi Hatim recorded that `A'ishah said, "The Prophet was being guarded until this Ayah,

(Allah will protect you from mankind) was revealed." She added; "The Prophet raised his head from the room and said;

«يَا أَيُّهَا النَّاسُ انْصَرِفُوا فَقَدْ عَصَمَنِي اللهُ عَزَّ وَجَل»

(O people! Go away, for Allah will protect me.)"' At-Tirmidhi recorded it and said,"This Hadith is Gharib." It was also recorded by Ibn Jarir, and Al-Hakim in his Mustadrak, where he said, "Its chain is Sahih, but they did not record it." Allah's statement,

(Verily, Allah guides not those who disbelieve.) means, O Muhammad, you convey, and Allah guides whom He wills, and misguides whom He wills. In other Ayat, Allah said,

(Not upon you is their guidance, but Allah guides whom He wills,) and,

(Your duty is only to convey and on Us is the reckoning.)

Surah: 5 Ayah: 68 & Ayah: 69

﴿ قُلْ يَـٰٓأَهْلَ ٱلْكِتَـٰبِ لَسْتُمْ عَلَىٰ شَىْءٍ حَتَّىٰ تُقِيمُوا۟ ٱلتَّوْرَىٰةَ وَٱلْإِنجِيلَ وَمَآ أُنزِلَ إِلَيْكُم مِّن
رَّبِّكُمْ ۗ وَلَيَزِيدَنَّ كَثِيرًا مِّنْهُم مَّآ أُنزِلَ إِلَيْكَ مِن رَّبِّكَ طُغْيَـٰنًا وَكُفْرًا ۖ فَلَا تَأْسَ عَلَى ٱلْقَوْمِ
ٱلْكَـٰفِرِينَ ﴿٦٨﴾ ﴾

68. Say (O Muhammad (peace be upon him)) "O people of the Scripture (Jews and Christians)! You have nothing (as regards guidance) till you act according to the Taurât (Torah), the Injeel (Gospel), and what has (now) been sent down to you from your Lord (the Qur'ân)." Verily, that which has been sent down to you (Muhammad (peace be upon him)) from your Lord increases in most of them (their) obstinate rebellion and disbelief. So be not sorrowful over the people who disbelieve.

﴿ إِنَّ ٱلَّذِينَ ءَامَنُوا۟ وَٱلَّذِينَ هَادُوا۟ وَٱلصَّـٰبِـُٔونَ وَٱلنَّصَـٰرَىٰ مَنْ ءَامَنَ بِٱللَّهِ وَٱلْيَوْمِ
ٱلْـَٔاخِرِ وَعَمِلَ صَـٰلِحًا فَلَا خَوْفٌ عَلَيْهِمْ وَلَا هُمْ يَحْزَنُونَ ﴿٦٩﴾ ﴾

69. Surely, those who believe (in the Oneness of Allâh, in His Messenger Muhammad (peace be upon him) and all that was revealed to him from Allâh), and those who are the Jews and the Sabians and the Christians, - whosoever believed in Allâh and the Last Day, and worked righteousness, on them shall be no fear, nor shall they grieve.

Transliteration

68. Qul ya ahla alkitabi lastum AAala shay-in hatta tuqeemoo alttawrata waal-injeela wama onzila ilaykum min rabbikum walayazeedanna katheeran minhum ma onzila ilayka min rabbika tughyanan wakufran fala ta/sa AAala alqawmi alkafireena 69. Inna allatheena amanoo waallatheena hadoo waalssabi-oona waalnnasara man amana biAllahi waalyawmi al-akhiri waAAamila salihan fala khawfun AAalayhim wala hum yahzanoona

Tafsir Ibn Kathir

There is no Salvation Except through Faith in the Qur'an

Allah says: O Muhammad, say,

(O People of the Scripture! You have nothing...) meaning no real religion until you adhere to and implement the Tawrah and the Injil. That is, until you believe in all the Books that you have that Allah revealed to the Prophets. These Books command following Muhammad and believing in his prophecy, all the while adhering to his Law. Before, we explained Allah's statement,

(Verily, the revelation that has come to you from your Lord makes many of them increase in rebellion and disbelief.)

(So do not grieve for the people who disbelieve), Do not be sad or taken aback by their disbelief. Allah said next,

(Surely, those who believe) referring to Muslims,

(those who are the Jews) who were entrusted with the Tawrah,

(and the Sabians. ..) a sect from the Christians and Magians who did not follow any particular religion, as Mujahid stated. As for the Christians, they are known and were entrusted with the Injil. The meaning here is that if each of these groups believed in Allah and the Hereafter, which is the Day of Judgement and Reckoning, and performed good actions, which to be so, must conform to Muhammad's Law, after Muhammad was sent to all mankind and the Jinns. If any of these groups held these beliefs, then they shall have no fear of what will come or sadness regarding what they lost, nor will grief ever affect them. We discussed a similar Ayah before in Surat Al-Baqarah (2:62).

Surah: 5 Ayah: 70 & Ayah: 71

﴿ لَقَدْ أَخَذْنَا مِيثَـٰقَ بَنِىٓ إِسْرَٰٓءِيلَ وَأَرْسَلْنَآ إِلَيْهِمْ رُسُلًا ۖ كُلَّمَا جَآءَهُمْ رَسُولٌۢ بِمَا لَا تَهْوَىٰٓ أَنفُسُهُمْ فَرِيقًا كَذَّبُوا۟ وَفَرِيقًا يَقْتُلُونَ ﴿٧٠﴾ ﴾

70. Verily, We took the covenant of the Children of Israel and sent Messengers to them. Whenever there came to them a Messenger with what they themselves desired not, - a group of them they called liars, and others among them they killed.

﴿ وَحَسِبُوٓا۟ أَلَّا تَكُونَ فِتْنَةٌ فَعَمُوا۟ وَصَمُّوا۟ ثُمَّ تَابَ ٱللَّهُ عَلَيْهِمْ ثُمَّ عَمُوا۟ وَصَمُّوا۟ كَثِيرٌ مِّنْهُمْ ۚ وَٱللَّهُ بَصِيرٌۢ بِمَا يَعْمَلُونَ ﴿٧١﴾ ﴾

71. They thought there will be no Fitnah (trial or punishment), so they became blind and deaf; after that Allâh turned to them (with Forgiveness); yet again many of them became blind and deaf. And Allâh is the All-Seer of what they do.

Transliteration

70. Laqad akhathna meethaqa banee isra-eela waarsalna ilayhim rusulan kullama jaahum rasoolun bima la tahwa anfusuhum fareeqan kaththaboo wafareeqan yaqtuloona 71. Wahasiboo alla takoona fitnatun faAAamoo wasammoo thumma taba Allahu AAalayhim thumma AAamoo wasammoo katheerun minhum waAllahu baseerun bima yaAAmaloona

Tafsir Ibn Kathir

Allah reminds that He took the covenant and pledges from the Children of Israel to hear and obey Him and His Messenger. They broke these pledges and covenants and followed their lusts and desires instead of the law, and whichever part of the law they agreed with, they took it. Otherwise, they abandoned it, if it did not conform to their desires. This is why Allah said,

(Whenever there came to them a Messenger with what they themselves desired not - a group of them they called liars, and others among them they killed. They thought there will be no Fitnah (trial or punishment) so they became blind and deaf.) thinking that they would suffer no repercussions for of the evil that they committed. Consequently, they were blinded from the truth and became deaf, incapable of hearing the truth. For these reasons they were unable to be guided by it. Allah forgave that, then, (yet they became blind and deaf) again, (many of them, and Allah is the All-Seer of what they do.) He has perfect knowledge of what they do and whomever among them deserves the guidance and whomever deserves misguidance.

Surah: 5 Ayah: 72, Ayah: 73, Ayah: 74 & Ayah: 75

﴿ لَقَدۡ كَفَرَ ٱلَّذِينَ قَالُوٓاْ إِنَّ ٱللَّهَ هُوَ ٱلۡمَسِيحُ ٱبۡنُ مَرۡيَمَۖ وَقَالَ ٱلۡمَسِيحُ يَٰبَنِيٓ
إِسۡرَٰٓءِيلَ ٱعۡبُدُواْ ٱللَّهَ رَبِّي وَرَبَّكُمۡۖ إِنَّهُۥ مَن يُشۡرِكۡ بِٱللَّهِ فَقَدۡ حَرَّمَ ٱللَّهُ عَلَيۡهِ ٱلۡجَنَّةَ وَمَأۡوَىٰهُ
ٱلنَّارُۖ وَمَا لِلظَّٰلِمِينَ مِنۡ أَنصَارٖ ٧٢ ﴾

72. Surely, they have disbelieved who say: "Allâh is the Messiah ('Isâ (Jesus)) son of Maryam (Mary)." But the Messiah ('Isâ (Jesus)) said: "O Children of Israel! Worship Allâh, my Lord and your Lord." Verily, whosoever sets up partners (in worship) with Allâh, then Allâh has forbidden Paradise to him, and the Fire will be his abode. And for the Zâlimûn (polytheists and wrong-doers) there are no helpers.

﴿ لَّقَدۡ كَفَرَ ٱلَّذِينَ قَالُوٓاْ إِنَّ ٱللَّهَ ثَالِثُ ثَلَٰثَةٖۘ وَمَا مِنۡ إِلَٰهٍ إِلَّآ إِلَٰهٞ وَٰحِدٞۚ وَإِن لَّمۡ
يَنتَهُواْ عَمَّا يَقُولُونَ لَيَمَسَّنَّ ٱلَّذِينَ كَفَرُواْ مِنۡهُمۡ عَذَابٌ أَلِيمٌ ٧٣ ﴾

73. Surely, disbelievers are those who said: "Allâh is the third of the three (in a Trinity)." But there is no Iilâh (god) (none who has the right to be worshipped) but One Ilâh (God - Allâh). And if they cease not from what they say, verily, a painful torment will befall on the disbelievers among them.

﴿ أَفَلَا يَتُوبُونَ إِلَى ٱللَّهِ وَيَسۡتَغۡفِرُونَهُۥۚ وَٱللَّهُ غَفُورٞ رَّحِيمٞ ٧٤ ﴾

74. Will they not turn with repentance to Allâh and ask His Forgiveness? For Allâh is Oft-Forgiving, Most Merciful.

﴿ مَّا ٱلۡمَسِيحُ ٱبۡنُ مَرۡيَمَ إِلَّا رَسُولٞ قَدۡ خَلَتۡ مِن قَبۡلِهِ ٱلرُّسُلُ وَأُمُّهُۥ صِدِّيقَةٞۖ
كَانَا يَأۡكُلَانِ ٱلطَّعَامَۗ ٱنظُرۡ كَيۡفَ نُبَيِّنُ لَهُمُ ٱلۡأٓيَٰتِ ثُمَّ ٱنظُرۡ أَنَّىٰ
يُؤۡفَكُونَ ٧٥ ﴾

75. The Messiah ('Isâ (Jesus)) son of Maryam (Mary), was no more than a Messenger; many were the Messengers that passed away before him. His mother (Maryam (Mary)) was a Siddiqah (i.e. she believed in the words of Allâh and His Books (see Verse 66:12)) They both used to eat food (as any other human being, while Allâh does not eat). Look how We make the Ayât (proofs, evidences, verses, lessons, signs, revelations, etc.) clear to them, yet look how they are deluded away (from the truth).

Transliteration

72. Laqad kafara allatheena qaloo inna Allaha huwa almaseehu ibnu maryama waqala almaseehu ya banee isra-eela oAAbudoo Allaha rabbee warabbakum innahu man yushrik

biAllahi faqad harrama Allahu AAalayhi aljannata wama/wahu alnnaru wama lilththalimeena min ansarin

73. Laqad kafara allatheena qaloo inna Allaha thalithu thalathatin wama min ilahin illa ilahun wahidun wa-in lam yantahoo AAamma yaqooloona layamassanna allatheena kafaroo minhum AAathabun aleemun 74. Afala yatooboona ila Allahi wayastaghfiroonahu waAllahu ghafoorun raheemun 75. Ma almaseehu ibnu maryama illa rasoolun qad khalat min qablihi alrrusulu waommuhu siddeeqatun kana ya/kulani alttaAAama onthur kayfa nubayyinu lahumu al-ayati thumma onthur anna yu/fakoona

Tafsir Ibn Kathir

The Disbelief of the Christians; `Isa Only called to Tawhid

Allah states that the Christians such sects as Monarchite, Jacobite and Nestorite are disbelievers, those among them who say that `Isa is Allah. Allah is far holier than what they attribute to Him. They made this claim in spite of the fact that `Isa made it known that he was the servant of Allah and His Messenger. The first words that `Isa uttered when he was still a baby in the cradle were, "I am `Abdullah (the servant of Allah)." He did not say, "I am Allah," or, "I am the son of Allah." Rather, he said,

(Verily, I am a servant of Allah, He has given me the Scripture and made me a Prophet.) until he said,

("And verily Allah is my Lord and your Lord. So worship Him (Alone). That is the straight path.") He also proclaimed to them when he was a man, after he was sent as a Prophet, commanding them to worship his Lord and their Lord, alone without partners,

(But the Messiah said, "O Children of Israel! worship Allah, my Lord and your Lord." Verily, whosoever sets up partners with Allah...) in worship;

(. ..then Allah has forbidden Paradise for him, and the Fire will be his abode.) as He will send him to the Fire and forbid Paradise for him. Allah also said;

(Verily, Allah forgives not that partners should be set up with Him (in worship), but He forgives except that (anything else) to whom He wills.) and,

(And the dwellers of the Fire will call to the dwellers of Paradise; "Pour on us some water or anything that Allah has provide you with." They will say: "Allah has forbidden both to the disbelievers.") It is recorded in the Sahih that the Prophet had someone proclaim to the people,

«إِنَّ الْجَنَّةَ لَا يَدْخُلُهَا إِلَّا نَفْسٌ مُسْلِمَةٌ»

(Only a Muslim soul shall enter Paradise.) In another narration,

«مُؤْمِنَةٌ»

(Only a believing soul...) This is why Allah said that `Isa said to the Children of Israel,

(Verily, whosoever sets up partners with Allah, then Allah has forbidden Paradise for him, and the Fire will be his abode. And there are no helpers for the wrongdoers.) There is no help from Allah, nor anyone who will support or protect them from the state they will be in. Allah's statement,

(Surely, they have disbelieved who say: "Allah is the third of three.") Mujahid and several others said that this Ayah was revealed about the Christians in particular. As-Suddi and others said that this Ayah was revealed about taking `Isa and his mother as gods besides Allah, thus making Allah the third in a trinity. As-Suddi said, "This is similar to Allah's statement towards the end of the Surah,

(And (remember) when Allah will say: "O `Isa, son of Maryam! Did you say unto men: `Worship me and my mother as two gods besides Allah' He will say, "Glory be to You!")(5:116). Allah replied,

(But there is no god but One God.) meaning there are not many worthy of worship but there is only One God without partners, and He is the Lord of all creation and all that exists. Allah said next, while threatening and admonishing them,

(And if they cease not from what they say,) their lies and false claims,

(verily, a painful torment will befall the disbelievers among them.) in the Hereafter, shackled and tormented. Allah said next,

(Will they not repent to Allah and ask His Forgiveness For Allah is Oft-Forgiving, Most Merciful.) This demonstrates Allah's generosity, kindness and mercy for His creatures, even though they committed this grave sin and invented such a lie and false allegation. Despite all of this, Allah calls them to repent so that He will forgive them, for Allah forgives those who sincerely repent to Him.

`Isa is Allah's Servant and His Mother is a Truthful Believer

Allah said,

(The Messiah, son of Maryam, was no more than a Messenger; many were the Messengers that passed away before him.) `Isa is just like the previous Prophets, and he is one of the servants of Allah and one of His honorable Messengers. Allah said in another Ayah,

(He (`Isa) was not more than a servant. We granted Our favor to him, and We made him an example for the Children of Israel.) Allah said next,

(His mother was a Siddiqah) for she believed in Allah with complete trust in Him. This is the highest rank she was given, which proves that she was not a Prophet. Allah said next,

(They both used to eat food) needing nourishment and to relieve the call of nature. Therefore, they are just servants like other servants, not gods as ignorant Christian sects claim, may Allah's continued curses cover them until the Day of Resurrection. Allah said next,

(Look how We make the Ayat clear to them.) making them unequivocal and plain,

(yet look how they are deluded away (from the truth).) look at the opinions, misguided ideas, and claims they cling to, even after Our clarification and plain, unequivocal explanation.

Surah: 5 Ayah: 76 & Ayah: 77

﴿ قُلْ أَتَعْبُدُونَ مِن دُونِ ٱللَّهِ مَا لَا يَمْلِكُ لَكُمْ ضَرًّا وَلَا نَفْعًا ۚ وَٱللَّهُ هُوَ ٱلسَّمِيعُ
ٱلْعَلِيمُ ﴿٧٦﴾ ﴾

76. Say (O Muhammad (peace be upon him) to mankind): "How do you worship besides Allâh something which has no power either to harm or to benefit you? But it is Allâh Who is the All-Hearer, All-Knower."

﴿ قُلْ يَٰٓأَهْلَ ٱلْكِتَٰبِ لَا تَغْلُوا۟ فِى دِينِكُمْ غَيْرَ ٱلْحَقِّ وَلَا تَتَّبِعُوٓا۟ أَهْوَآءَ قَوْمٍ قَدْ
ضَلُّوا۟ مِن قَبْلُ وَأَضَلُّوا۟ كَثِيرًا وَضَلُّوا۟ عَن سَوَآءِ ٱلسَّبِيلِ ﴿٧٧﴾ ﴾

77. Say (O Muhammad (peace be upon him)) "O people of the Scripture (Jews and Christians)! Exceed not the limits in your religion (by believing in something) other than the truth, and do not follow the vain desires of people who went astray in times gone by, and who misled many, and strayed (themselves) from the Right Path."

Transliteration

76. Qul ataAAbudoona min dooni Allahi ma la yamliku lakum darran wala nafAAan waAllahu huwa alssameeAAu alAAaleemu 77. Qul ya ahla alkitabi la taghloo fee deenikum ghayra alhaqqi wala tattabiAAoo ahwaa qawmin qad dalloo min qablu waadalloo katheeran wadalloo AAan sawa-i alssabeeli

Tafsir Ibn Kathir

The Prohibition of Shirk (Polytheism) and Exaggeration in the Religion

Allah admonishes those who take up rivals with Him and worship the idols, monuments and false deities. Allah states that such false deities do not deserve any degree of Divinity. Allah said,

(Say) O Muhammad, to those from among the Children of Adam, such as the Christians, who worship other than Allah,

(How do you worship besides Allah something which has no power either to harm or to benefit you) meaning, which cannot prevent harm for you nor bring about your benefit,

(But it is Allah Who is the All-Hearer, All-Knower.) He hears what His servants say and has knowledge of all things. Therefore, how did you worship inanimate objects that do not hear, see or know anything - having no power to bring harm or benefit to themselves let alone others - instead of worshipping Allah Allah then said,

(Say: "O People of the Scipture! Exceed not the limits in your religion beyond the truth,) Meaning: Do not exceed the limits concerning the truth and exaggeration in praising whom you were commanded to honor. You exaggerated in his case and elevated him from the rank of Prophet to the rank of a god. You did this with `Isa, who was a Prophet, yet you claimed that he is god besides Allah. This error occurred because you followed your teachers, the advocates of misguidance who came before your time and who,

(...and who misled many, and strayed (themselves) from the right path,) deviated from the straight path, to the path of misguidance and deviation.

Surah: 5 Ayah: 78, Ayah: 79, Ayah: 80 & Ayah: 81

﴿ لُعِنَ ٱلَّذِينَ كَفَرُوا۟ مِنۢ بَنِىٓ إِسْرَٰٓءِيلَ عَلَىٰ لِسَانِ دَاوُۥدَ وَعِيسَى ٱبْنِ مَرْيَمَ ۚ ذَٰلِكَ
بِمَا عَصَوا۟ وَّكَانُوا۟ يَعْتَدُونَ ﴿٧٨﴾ ﴾

78. Those among the Children of Israel who disbelieved were cursed by the tongue of Dâwûd (David) and 'Isâ (Jesus), son of Maryam (Mary). That was because they disobeyed (Allâh and the Messengers) and were ever transgressing beyond bounds.

﴿ كَانُوا۟ لَا يَتَنَاهَوْنَ عَن مُّنكَرٍ فَعَلُوهُ ۚ لَبِئْسَ مَا كَانُوا۟ يَفْعَلُونَ ﴿٧٩﴾ ﴾

79. They used not to forbid one another from Al-Munkar (wrong, evil-doing, sins, polytheism, disbelief) which they committed. Vile indeed was what they used to do.

﴿ تَرَىٰ كَثِيرًا مِّنْهُمْ يَتَوَلَّوْنَ ٱلَّذِينَ كَفَرُوا۟ ۚ لَبِئْسَ مَا قَدَّمَتْ لَهُمْ أَنفُسُهُمْ أَن
سَخِطَ ٱللَّهُ عَلَيْهِمْ وَفِى ٱلْعَذَابِ هُمْ خَٰلِدُونَ ﴿٨٠﴾ ﴾

80. You see many of them taking the disbelievers as their Auliyâ' (protectors and helpers). Evil indeed is that which their own selves have sent forward before them; for that (reason) Allâh's Wrath fell upon them, and in torment they will abide.

﴿ وَلَوْ كَانُوا۟ يُؤْمِنُونَ بِٱللَّهِ وَٱلنَّبِىِّ وَمَآ أُنزِلَ إِلَيْهِ مَا ٱتَّخَذُوهُمْ أَوْلِيَآءَ وَلَٰكِنَّ
كَثِيرًا مِّنْهُمْ فَٰسِقُونَ ﴿٨١﴾ ﴾

81. And had they believed in Allâh, and in the Prophet (Muhammad (peace be upon him)) and in what has been revealed to him, never would they have taken them (the disbelievers) as Auliyâ' (protectors and helpers); but many of them are the Fâsiqûn (rebellious, disobedient to Allâh).

Transliteration

78. LuAAina allatheena kafaroo min banee isra-eela AAala lisani dawooda waAAeesa ibni maryama thalika bima AAasaw wakanoo yaAAtadoona 79. Kanoo la yatanahawna AAan munkarin faAAaloohu labi/sa ma kanoo yafAAaloona 80. Tara katheeran minhum yatawallawna allatheena kafaroo labi/sa ma qaddamat lahum anfusuhum an sakhita Allahu AAalayhim wafee alAAathabi hum khalidoona 81. Walaw kanoo yu/minoona biAllahi waalnnabiyyi wama onzila ilayhi ma ittakhathoohum awliyaa walakinna katheeran minhum fasiqoona

Tafsir Ibn Kathir

Allah Cursed the Disbelievers Among the Children of Israel

Allah states that He has cursed the disbelievers among the Children of Israel long ago, and revealed this fact to His Prophets Dawud and `Isa, son of Maryam. He cursed them because they disobeyed Allah and transgressed against His creatures. Al-`Awfi reported that Ibn `Abbas said, "They were cursed in the Tawrah, the Injil, the Zabur (Psalms) and the Furqan (Qur'an)." Allah then states that during their time, their habit was that,

(They used not to forbid one another from the evil they committed.) They did not forbid each other from committing sins and the prohibitions. Allah chastised them for this behavior, so that their behavior would not be imitated. Allah said,

(Vile indeed was what they used to do.)

Hadiths that Order Enjoining Righteousness and Forbidding Evil

There are many Hadiths that order enjoining righteousness and forbidding evil. Imam Ahmad recorded that Hudhayfah bin Al-Yaman said that the Prophet said,

«وَالَّذِي نَفْسِي بِيَدِهِ، لَتَأْمُرُنَّ بِالْمَعْرُوفِ، وَلَتَنْهَوُنَّ عَنِ الْمُنْكَرِ، أَوْ لَيُوشِكَنَّ اللهُ أَنْ يَبْعَثَ عَلَيْكُمْ عِقَابًا مِنْ عِنْدِهِ، ثُمَّ لَتَدْعُنَّهُ فَلَا يَسْتَجِيبَ لَكُم»

(By He in Whose Hand is my soul! You will enjoin righteousness and forbid evil, or Allah will send a punishment on you from Him. Then, you will supplicate to Him, but He will not accept your supplication.) At-Tirmidhi also recorded it and said, "This Hadith is Hasan." Muslim recorded that Abu Sa`id Al-Khudri said that the Messenger of Allah said,

«مَنْ رَأَى مِنْكُمْ مُنْكَرًا فَلْيُغَيِّرْهُ بِيَدِهِ، فَإِنْ لَمْ يَسْتَطِعْ فَبِلِسَانِهِ، فَإِنْ لَمْ يَسْتَطِعْ فَبِقَلْبِهِ، وَذلِكَ أَضْعَفُ الْإِيمَان»

(He among you who witnesses an evil, let him change it with his hand, if he cannot do that, then by his tongue, if he cannot do even that, then with his heart, and this is the weakest faith.) Abu Dawud said that Al-`Urs, meaning Ibn `Amirah, said that the Prophet said,

«إِذَا عُمِلَتِ الْخَطِيئَةُ فِي الْأَرْضِ كَانَ مَنْ شَهِدَهَا فَكَرِهَهَا، وَقَالَ مَرَّةً فَأَنْكَرَهَا كَانَ كَمَنْ غَابَ عَنْهَا، وَمَنْ غَابَ عَنْهَا فَرَضِيَهَا كَانَ كَمَنْ شَهِدَهَا»

(When sin is committed on the earth, then whoever witnesses it and hates - (once he said): forbids it, will be like those who did not witness it. Whoever was absent from it, but agreed with it, will be like those who witness it.) Only Abu Dawud recorded this Hadith. Abu Dawud recorded that one of the Companions said that the Prophet said,

«لَنْ يَهْلِكَ النَّاسُ حَتَّى يَعْذِرُوا أَوْ يُعْذِرُوا مِنْ أَنْفُسِهِم»

(The people will not perish until they do not leave -or- have any excuse for themselves.) Ibn Majah recorded that Abu Sa`id Al-Khudri said that the Messenger of Allah gave a speech once and said,

«أَلَا لَا يَمْنَعَنَّ رَجُلًا هَيْبَةُ النَّاسِ أَنْ يَقُولَ الْحَقَّ إِذَا عَلِمَه»

(Behold! Fear from people should not prevent one from saying the truth if he knows it.) Abu Sa`id then cried and said, "By Allah! We have seen some errors, but we feared (the people)." Another Hadith that Abu Sa`id narrated states that the Messenger of Allah said,

«أَفْضَلُ الْجِهَادِ كَلِمَةُ حَقَ عِنْدَ سُلْطَانٍ جَائِر»

(The best Jihad is a word of truth proclaimed before an unjust ruler.) Recorded by Abu Dawud, At-Tirmidhi, and Ibn Majah. At-Tirmidhi said, "Hasan Gharib from this route of narration." Imam Ahmad recorded that Hudhayfah said that the Prophet said,

«لَا يَنْبَغِي لِمُسْلِمٍ أَنْ يُذِلَّ نَفْسَه»

(It is not required of the Muslim that he humiliate himself.) They said, `How does one humiliate himself" he said;

«يَتَعَرَّضُ مِنَ الْبَلَاءِ لِمَا لَا يُطِيق»

(He takes on trials that he is not capable of enduring.) This was recorded by At-Tirmidhi and Ibn Majah, and At-Tirmidhi said, "This Hadith is Hasan Sahih Gharib."

Censuring the Hypocrites

Allah said,

(You see many of them taking the disbelievers as their friends.) Mujahid said that this Ayah refers to the hypocrites. Allah's statement,

(Evil indeed is that which they have sent forward before themselves;) by giving their loyalty and support to the disbelievers, instead of the believers. This evil act caused them to have hypocrisy in their hearts and brought them the anger of Allah, that will remain with them until the Day of Return. Allah said;

(for that (reason) Allah is wrath with them) because of what they did. Allah next said that,

(in torment they will abide) on the Day of Resurrection. Allah's statement,

(And had they believed in Allah, and in the Prophet and in what has been revealed to him, never would they have taken them as friends.) meaning, had they sincerely believed in Allah, His Messenger and the Qur'an, they would not have committed the evil act of supporting the disbelievers in secret and being enemies with those who believe in Allah, the Prophet and what was revealed to him, (but many of them are rebellious). disobedient to Allah and His Messenger and defiant of the Ayat of His revelation that He sent down.

LaVergne, TN USA
02 November 2009

162846LV00003B/48/P

9 781861 796448